CAMBRIDGE GREE

GENER

P. E. L
Regius Professor Emeritus of Greek, University of Cambridge

PHILIP HARDIE
*Senior Research Fellow, Trinity College, and Honorary Professor of Latin,
University of Cambridge*

RICHARD HUNTER
Regius Professor of Greek, University of Cambridge

E. J. KENNEY
Kennedy Professor Emeritus of Latin, University of Cambridge

S. P. OAKLEY
Kennedy Professor of Latin, University of Cambridge

HERODOTUS
HISTORIES
BOOK V

EDITED BY
SIMON HORNBLOWER
Senior Research Fellow, All Souls College, Oxford

CAMBRIDGE
UNIVERSITY PRESS

CAMBRIDGE
UNIVERSITY PRESS

University Printing House, Cambridge CB2 8BS, United Kingdom

Cambridge University Press is part of the University of Cambridge.

It furthers the University's mission by disseminating knowledge in the pursuit of education, learning and research at the highest international levels of excellence.

www.cambridge.org
Information on this title: www.cambridge.org/9780521703406

© Cambridge University Press 2013

First published 2013

A catalogue record for this publication is available from the British Library

Library of Congress Cataloguing in Publication data
Herodotus.
[History. Book 5]
Histories, Book V / Herodotus ; edited by Simon Hornblower.
pages cm. – (Cambridge Greek and Latin classics)
Includes bibliographical references and index.
ISBN 978-0-521-87871-5 (hardback)
1. Greece – History – Ionian Revolt, 499–494 B.C. I. Hornblower, Simon. II. Title.
PA4002.A35 2013
938'.03 – dc23 2013016267

ISBN 978-0-521-87871-5 Hardback
ISBN 978-0-521-70340-6 Paperback

CONTENTS

MAPS

PREFACE

This single-authored volume is planned as one of a pair with an edition of and commentary on bk. 6 in the same series, by the present author and Christopher Pelling in collaboration. Some sections of the Introduction to the present volume concern bk. 5 only; some concern both books; and some topics common to both books (Hdt. and Homer; Hdt.'s handling of Kleomenes and of Aigina) will be covered in the Introduction to bk. 6. Chronology will be covered in both volumes; for the distribution, see the Introduction, 3. For what is known or can be plausibly inferred about Herodotus' life and travels, see S. West in Bowie 2007: 127–130.

The groundwork for the commentary on book 5 was done as part of graduate (MA) teaching at University College London (UCL). In 2008–9, I taught books 5 and 7 jointly with Professor C. Carey, and in 2009–10, my last academic year at UCL, I taught books 5 and 6 on my own. I am grateful to Chris Carey for many insights and much shared enjoyment, and to all the students for their stimulating contributions.

The text is an adapted version of Hude's OCT, taking account of the changes which will be made by Nigel Wilson in his forthcoming replacement OCT and in his companion volume *Herodotea*. Wilson and I went through the text of book 5 in July 2012 and discussed, to my great profit, problem passages flagged up by one or other or both of us. I have also exploited Paul Maas's marginal suggestions, as published in Wilson 2011. I warmly acknowledge all Nigel Wilson's help, and his willingness to make his material and conclusions available to me in advance of publication. My own apparatus is short and mostly confined to essentials.

Richard Catling, Stephen Colvin, Esther Eidinow, Maria Fragoulaki, Alan Griffiths, Patrick James, Anne Thompson, Martin West and Stephanie West helped over particular problems. Chris Pelling read and commented very valuably on an early draft of the commentary. The General Editors, Pat Easterling and Richard Hunter, commented in great detail and with great patience on more than one draft of the entire work, Introduction as well as commentary, and the book is much better as a result of their trenchant comments. Angus Bowie kindly gave permission to reprint his section on Hdt.'s language. Alan Griffiths helped with the proof-correction, and made valuable last-minute suggestions of substance, indicated by 'AHG'. Everyone told me how lucky I was to be given Muriel Hall as copy-editor, and they were quite right. I thank her too.

I am grateful to my college, All Souls, for electing me to the research fellowship which since October 2010 has enabled me to work simultaneously on this book and on a larger-scale commentary on the *Alexandra* of Lykophron.

Finally, I thank Oswyn Murray for undergraduate teaching at Balliol College Oxford more than forty years ago, as well as for his writings on Herodotus generally and on the Ionian revolt in particular.

Note: inscriptions are quoted, in full or in part, only when not available in easily accessible collections. Otherwise mere references are given, including, where possible, additional references (with '=') to English translations in sourcebooks or elsewhere.

ABBREVIATIONS

I ANCIENT AUTHORS AND WORKS

Abbreviations for Greek and Latin authors usually follow those in *OCD*[4], except that Th. is Thucydides, Diod. is Diodorus and Pol. is Polybius; and Greek not Latin spellings are generally used, thus Lykoph. (i.e. Lykophron), not Lycoph., but not when a Latin spelling is very familiar indeed (thus Aesch. not Aiskh. for Aeschylus).

II HERODOTUS TEXTS AND COMMENTARIES REFERRED TO (SOME RELATING TO INDIVIDUAL BOOKS OR PAIRS OF BOOKS ONLY)

Abicht	K. Abicht, *Herodotos für den Schulgebrauch erklärt* vol. III, books 5 and 6, Leipzig, 1883
Bowie	A. M. Bowie, *Herodotus Histories book VIII*, Cambridge, 2007
Flower and Marincola	M. Flower and J. Marincola, *Herodotus Histories book IX*, Cambridge, 2002
How and Wells	W. W. How and J. Wells, *Commentary on Herodotus*, 2 vols, Oxford, 1912
Hude	C. Hude, *Herodoti Historiae*, 2 vols., Oxford 1912 (OCT)
Legrand	P. Legrand, *Hérodote livre V. Terpsichore*[2], Paris
Macan	R. W. Macan, *Herodotus, the fourth, fifth and sixth books* (2 vols., London, 1895) or occasionally *Herodotus: the seventh, eighth and ninth books* (3 vols., London, 1908)
Nenci	(as appropriate) *either* G. Nenci, *Erodoto: le storie libro V, La rivolta della Ionia*, Florence, 1994 *or* G. Nenci, *Erodoto: le storie Libro VI, La battaglia di Maratona*, Florence, 1998
OCT	Oxford Classical Text. See under Hude, also Wilson
Rosén	H. B. Rosén, *Herodoti historiae* (Teubner edn of Hdt.), 2 vols., Leipzig, 1987–97
Scott	L. Scott, *Historical commentary on Herodotus book 6*, Leiden and Boston, 2005
Stein	H. Stein, *Herodotos*[6], Berlin, 1901

Wilson	N. G. Wilson, forthcoming new OCT of Hdt., or the accompanying *Herodotea*, where particular passages are discussed in greater detail

III   OTHER ABBREVIATIONS

AHG	Alan Griffiths, personal communication
AO	R. Develin, *Athenian officials 684–321 BC*, Cambridge, 1989
APF	J. K. Davies, *Athenian propertied families 600–300 BC*, Oxford
app. (crit.)	apparatus (criticus), i.e. the material printed at the foot of the text, giving textual variants and emendations
AR	*Archaeological Reports*, booklet issued annually with *JHS*
ATL	B. D. Meritt, H. T. Wade-Gery and M. F. McGregor, *The Athenian tribute lists*, 4 vols., Princeton, 1939–53
Barr.	R. Talbert (ed.), *Barrington atlas of the Greek and Roman world*, Princeton, 2000; the accompanying map-by-map Directory (also 2000, also ed. R. Talbert: 2 vols. with continuous pagination) is also sometimes cited
BE	*Bulletin Épigraphique* (in *Revue des Études grecques*)
Beloch	K. J. Beloch, *Griechische Geschichte*, 2nd edn, 4 vols. in 8, Strasburg, Berlin and Leipzig, 1912–27
BNJ	I. Worthington (general ed.), *Brill's new Jacoby*, Leiden, 2006–
Brill's companion	E. J. Bakker, I. de Jong and H. van Wees (eds.), *Brill's companion to Herodotus*, Leiden, Boston and Cologne, 2002
Busolt	G. Busolt, *Griechische Geschichte*, 3 vols., Gotha, 1893–1904 (vols. 1 and 2 in a 2nd edn)
CAH	*Cambridge Ancient History*, new edn. The vols. most cited are J. Boardman, I. E. S. Edwards, N. G. L. Hammond and E. Sollberger (eds.), vol. 3 part 1 (1982); J. Boardman and N. G. L. Hammond (eds.), vol. 3 part 3 (1982); D. M. Lewis, J. Boardman, J. K. Davies and M. Ostwald (eds.), vol. 5 (1992); D. M. Lewis, J. Boardman, S. Hornblower and M. Ostwald (eds.), vol. 6 (1994). Note also J. Boardman (ed.), *Plates Volume to Vols. 5 and 6* (1994)

Cambridge companion	C. Dewald and J. Marincola (eds.), *Cambridge companion to Herodotus*, 2006
CEG	P. Hansen, *Carmina epigraphica graeca*. Berlin and New York, 1983 and 1989 (2 vols., numbering of inscriptions continuous)
CHGRW I	P. Sabin, H. van Wees and M. Whitby (eds.), *The Cambridge history of Greek and Roman warfare* vol. I, *Greece, the Hellenistic world and the rise of Rome*, Cambridge, 2007
CT I, II, III	S. Hornblower, *A Commentary on Thucydides*, 3 vols., Oxford, 1991, 1996, 2008
Derow/Parker	P. Derow and R. Parker (eds.), *Herodotus and his world*, Oxford, 2003
DGE	E. Schwyzer, *Dialectorum Graecarum exempla potiora epigraphica*, Leipzig, 1923
DK	H. Diels and W. Kranz (eds.), *Die Fragmente der Vorsokratiker*^{6}, 3 vols., Berlin 1952
Ebert	J. Ebert, *Griechische Epigramme auf Sieger an gymnischen und hippischen Agonen, Abh. sächs. Ges. Wiss.* 63. 2, Berlin, 1972
EGM	R. L. Fowler, *Early Greek mythography*, vol. I: *Text and introduction*, vol. II: *Commentary*, Oxford, 2000–13
Eretria	P. Ducrey, S. Fachard, D. Knoepfler, T. Theurillat, D. Wagner and A. G. Zannis, *Eretria, a guide to the ancient city*, Fribourg, 2004
F	fragment (of historian in *FGrHist*)
FGE	D. L. Page, *Further Greek epigrams*, Cambridge, 1981
FGrHist	F. Jacoby, *Die Fragmente der griechischen Historiker*, 15 vols, Leiden 1923–58
Fornara	C. W. Fornara, *Translated documents, archaic times to the end of the Peloponnesian war*^{2}, Cambridge, 1983
Fowler	See *EGM*
GGM	C. Müller, *Geographi Graeci minores*, 2 vols., Paris, 1861
Greek world	S. Hornblower, *The Greek world 479–323 BC*^{4}, London, 2011
GSW	W. K. Pritchett, *The Greek state at war*, 5 vols., Berkeley and Los Angeles, 1969–91
HCP	F. W. Walbank, *Historical commentary on Polybius*, 3 vols., Oxford, 1957–79
HM I, II	N. G. L. Hammond, *History of Macedonia* vol. I, Oxford, 1972; N. G. L. Hammond and G. T. Griffith, *History of Macedonia* vol. II, Oxford, 1979
IACP	M. H. Hansen and T. H. Nielsen (eds.), *An inventory of Archaic and Classical poleis*, Oxford,

	2004. Usually refs. are to entry nos., occasionally to page numbers, prefaced by 'p.'
ICS	O. Masson, *Inscriptions chypriotes syllabiques*, Paris, 1961, reprinted with expansions as *Études Chypriotes*, Paris, 1983
IG	*Inscriptiones Graecae*, Berlin, 1873–
I. Labraunda	J. Crampa (ed.), *Labraunda, Swedish excavations and researches 3(1) and 3(2): The Greek inscriptions*, Lund, 1969 and Stockholm, 1972
Irwin/Greenwood	E. Irwin and E. Greenwood (eds.), *Reading Herodotus: a study of the* Logoi *in Book 5 of Herodotus'* Histories, Cambridge, 2007
LGPN	*A Lexicon of Greek personal names*, 6 vols. published to date, Oxford, 1987–2010
LIMC	*Lexicon iconographicum mythologiae classicae*, Zurich and New York, 1981–1997
LSAG²	L. H. Jeffery, revised A. W. Johnston, *Local scripts of Archaic Greece*, Oxford, 1990
LSJ	H. G. Liddell, R. Scott and H. Stuart Jones, *A Greek–English Lexicon*, Oxford, 1996
LSS	F. Sokolowski, *Lois sacrées des cités grecques*, suppl., Paris, 1962
Maas	*see* Wilson 2011 in Works cited (marginalia in Maas' personal copy of Hude's OCT; most of them not previously published)
Mausolus	S. Hornblower, *Mausolus*, Oxford, 1982
ML	R. Meiggs and D. Lewis, *A selection of Greek historical inscriptions to the end of the fifth century BC*, revised edn, Oxford, 1988
Moretti	*see* Moretti 1957 in Works cited
OCD⁴	S. Hornblower, A. J. S. Spawforth and E. Eidinow (eds.), *The Oxford Classical Dictionary*, 4th edn, Oxford, 2012
OGIS	W. Dittenberger, *Orientis graecae inscriptiones selectae*, 2 vols, Leipzig, 1903–5
Onomatologos	R. W. V. Catling and F. Marchand (eds.), *Onomatologos: Studies in Greek personal names presented to Elaine Matthews*, Oxford, 2010
PECS	R. Stillwell (ed.), *Princeton encyclopedia of classical sites*, Princeton, 1976
Pf.	R. Pfeiffer, *Callimachus*, 2 vols., Oxford, 1949–53
PMG	D. L. Page (ed.), *Poetae melici graeci*, Oxford, 1962

PMGF	M. Davies, *Poetarum melicorum graecorum fragmenta*, vol. 1, Oxford, 1991
P. Oxy.	*Oxyrhynchus papyri*
Powell	J. E. Powell, *Lexicon to Herodotus*, Cambridge, 1938
Powell tr.	J. E. Powell (translated), *Herodotus*, Oxford, 2 vols., 1949. Note esp. Critical [i.e. textual] Appendix at 2. 687–722
PT	G. G. Cameron, *Persepolis treasury tablets*, Chicago, 1948
RC	C. B. Welles, *Royal correspondence in the Hellenistic period*, New Haven, 1934
R.-E.	*Real-Encyclopädie der classischen Altertumswissenschaft*, ed. A. F. Pauly, G. Wissowa, W. Kroll, 66 vols and 15 supplements (Stuttgart, 1894–1980)
R/O	P. J. Rhodes and R. Osborne, *Greek historical inscriptions 404–323 BC*, Oxford, 2003 (revised paperback edn, 2007)
SEG	*Supplementum epigraphicum graecum*, 1923–
SGDI	H. Collitz and F. Bechtel, *Sammlung der griechischen Dialekt-Inschriften*, 4 vols., Göttingen, 1884–1915
SvT	H. H. Schmitt, *Die Staatsverträge des Altertums*, vol. 3², Munich, 1969
Syll³	W. Dittenberger, *Sylloge inscriptionum Graecarum*, 4 vols., 3rd edn, Leipzig, 1915–24
Th. and Pi.	S. Hornblower, *Thucydides and Pindar: historical narrative and the world of epinikian poetry*, Oxford, 2004
ThesCRA	*Thesaurus cultus et rituum antiquorum*, 7 vols., Los Angeles, 2004–11
Thucydides	S. Hornblower, *Thucydides*, London, 1994
Tod	M. N. Tod, *A selection of Greek historical inscriptions*, vol. I: *To the end of the fifth century BC*, Oxford, 1933; vol. II, *From 403 to 323 BC*, Oxford, 1948 (numbering of inscriptions is continuous)
Tozzi	P. Tozzi, *La rivolta ionica*, Pisa, 1978
TT	S. Hornblower, *Thucydidean themes*, Oxford, 2011
Voigt	E.-M. Voigt, *Sappho et Alcaeus: fragmenta*, Amsterdam, 1971
Waterfield	*Herodotus, the Histories*, tr. R. Waterfield, with introduction and notes by C. Dewald, Oxford, World's Classics 1998

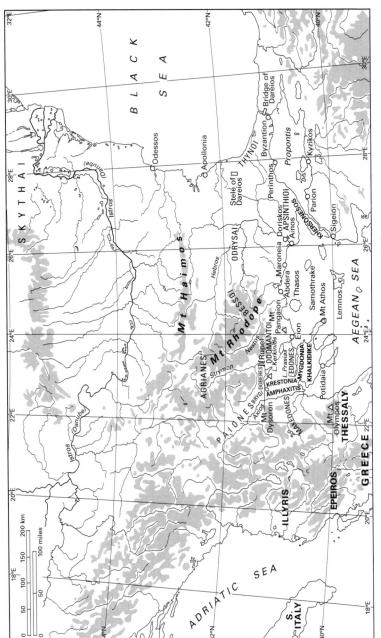

Map 1 Thrace, Macedonia and north Greece

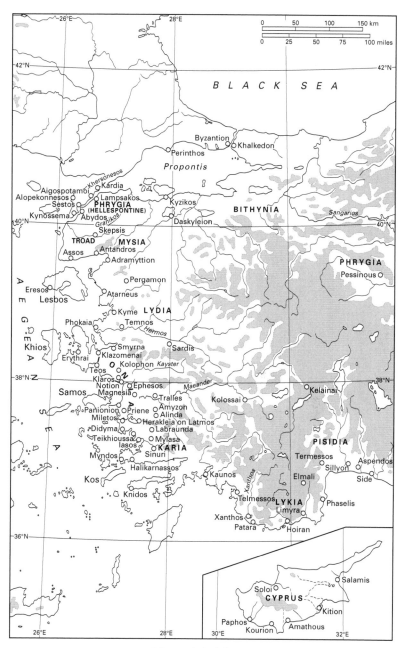

Map 2 Asia Minor

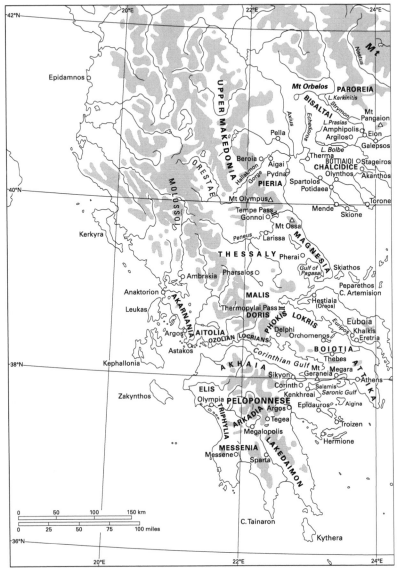

Map 3 Greece and the Aegean

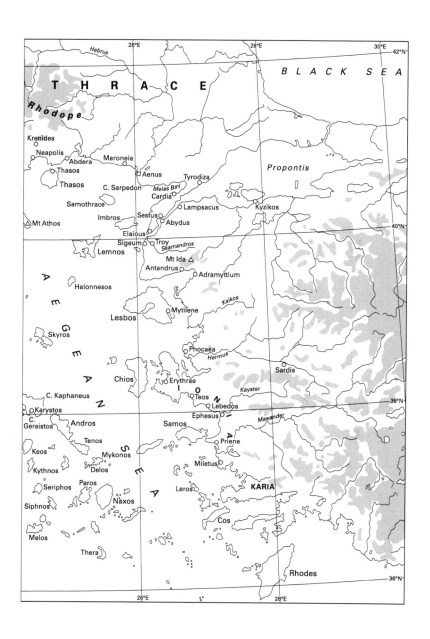

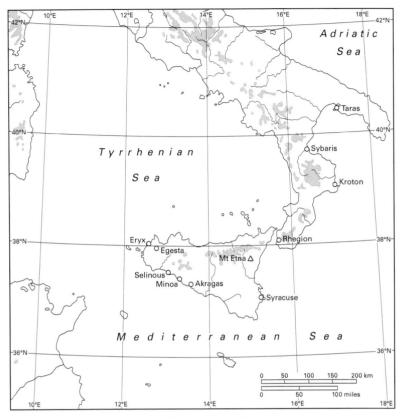

Map 4 Sicily and south Italy

Map 5 Western Achaemenid empire

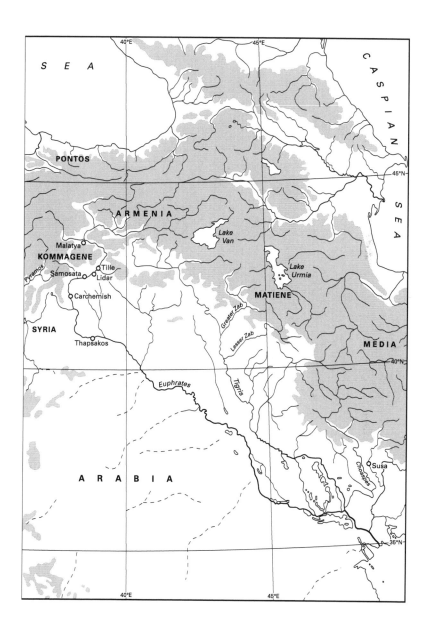

INTRODUCTION

1 STRUCTURAL QUESTIONS

(a) Book divisions

Bks. 5 and 6 of Hdt., which contain the narratives of the Ionian revolt and the Marathon campaign, are central to the *Histories*. The present section will, after some remarks about book divisions, discuss the structure of bks. 5 and 6, both internally and in relation to the *Histories* as a whole.

The first requirement is to think away the conventional book divisions altogether; such divisions seem generally to be a fourth-century innovation.[1] There is no good reason[2] to think that Herodotus divided his own work into nine books (unlike, say, Polybius, he does not use them himself to cross-refer or rather back-refer).[3] The Herodotean division is probably Alexandrian i.e. Hellenistic, perhaps third or fourth century BC. We must distinguish two questions: who first says that Hdt.'s work was in nine books, and who first cited him by book number.

The 'chronographic' source of Diodorus, which provided him with some good-quality historiographic and poetic dates, as well as king lists and dates of city-foundations and mergers (synoikisms), tells us that Hdt.'s work was in nine books.[4] Diodorus himself wrote in the time of Julius Caesar or the early years of Augustus' principate, but the chronographer worked in perhaps the second century BC, the time of Apollodoros the Chronicler (*FGrHist* 244). Apollodoros is, however, an unlikely candidate himself, as is Kastor of Rhodes (*FGrHist* 250), whose chronicle ended with Pompey's triumph in 61 BC. It is better to leave the Diodoran chronographer without a name.[5]

The first scholarly text to use Hdt.'s book-numbers as a means to cite him is the inscribed Lindian *anagraphe* from Rhodes (the so-called

---

[1] At any rate, Polybius (8.9.5) cites Theopompos by 'the beginning of his forty-ninth book'. See generally Higbie 2010.

[2] Irwin and Greenwood 2007: 14 n. 31 say there is 'room to challenge the orthodoxy' that the conventional book divisions are not the work of Hdt. himself, though they hesitate between the opposite claim that they really were his work, and the weaker and more plausible position that it is legitimate for modern scholarly purposes to treat Herodotean books as units. It is unlikely that book divisions were established as early as the fifth century, whether for Hdt. or Homer or anyone else.

[3] See e.g. Polyb. 3.1.1 'in my first book', 4.1.4 'in my second book', 7.13.2 'in my fifth book', 11.1 'in my first six books', 18.28.1 'as I promised in my sixth book'. It will be noticed that all these are retrospective.

[4] Schwartz 1959: 43. See Diod. 11.37.6, giving Hdt.'s terminal point as 479/8.

[5] Schwartz 1959: 39, and Jacoby's introd. to Kastor. But we shall see below that the nine-book division of Hdt. was established well before 61, at least as early as 99 BC.

1

'Lindian Chronicle') in 99 BC, by which time the book-numbers were presumably well established.[6] After that Plutarch, two hundred years later, around 100 AD, cites by it half-a-dozen times in his *On the malice of Herodotus*.[7] Lucian, a few decades later than Plutarch, was aware of the division of the *Histories* according to the nine Muses,[8] and a generation earlier than Lucian, a writer called Kephalio wrote a history in Ionic dialect and called it after the Muses, in obvious imitation of Hdt.[9] That Pausanias, writing later than Plutarch, cites Hdt. without book-numbers does not mean that he was unaware of the book divisions;[10] he does the same with every author, Thucydides and Homer included, and the reason is presumably stylistic, a desire for uncluttered elegance.

Once the nine-book division of Hdt. had been established, there was no rival division. Contrast Th., of whom there were nine-book and thirteen-book divisions in antiquity, as well as the usual and now canonical eight-book division.[11]

The chapter divisions have even less claim to respect. One cannot feel gratitude towards Jungermann,[12] who in 1608 divided Hdt.'s text into chapters and inflicted on posterity the monster ch. 92, with subdivisions involving letters of the Greek alphabet and further paragraphing by numerals. The reason for this awkwardness was evidently a bad decision that no speech should be allowed to run for more than one chapter; 6.86, 7.8–10 and 8.140 are also affected by this 'rule', though less absurdly (2.121, the main Rhampsinitos story, is also so affected, but that is at best indirect speech, a tale told by the priests). Imagine the seven OCT pages of Th.'s funeral speech as one long chapter! But it is too late to change the traditional chapter divisions of Hdt. now.

---

[6] See *FGrHist* 532 C 29 (Amasis) lines 38–9, Ἡρόδοτος [ὁ Θ]ούριος ἐν τᾶι Β /τᾶν ἱστοριᾶν; Higbie 2003: 35 and 117. The importance of this ref. (which is to 2.182.1) for the date of the book divisions was seen by Myres 1953: 65.

[7] Bauer 1878: 5 n. 1. See Plut. *On the malice of Hdt.* chs. 12 (bk. 2), 21 (bk. 3), 23 (bk. 5), 25 (bk. 6), 34 (bk. 8), 41 (bk. 9) = *Mor.* 857a, 859b, 860c, 861d, 867b, 871d. It will be noticed that these book-citations are in correct Herodotean order, but in fact the treatise jumps around a good deal.

[8] Lucian: *Hist. conscr.* ch. 41 is aware that Hdt.'s books were called after the (nine) Muses; this is repeated at *Her.* ch. 1, but here the number nine is explicitly mentioned.

[9] *FGrHist* 93 T1; cf. Jones 1986: 61 and n. 14.

[10] As is argued by Bauer 1878: 5 n. 1; 10 and nn. 2 and 3.

[11] Diodorus' chronographic source, for which see above, says at 12.37.2 (repeated at 13.42.5 about Th.'s closural point in 411) that Th. began his history in 432/2, and 'wrote up twenty-two years in eight books, or as some divide it, in nine'. See, again, Schwartz 1959: 43. For the thirteen-book division, see the Th. scholia on 3.116 and esp. 4.135. Dionysios of Halikarnassos, in the time of Augustus, cites Th. correctly but not systematically by book-numbers (on the eight-book scheme) in his treatise *On Thucydides*, from ch. 8 onwards.

[12] See Myres 1953: 19 and 64.

The main thread of narration in 5 and 6 runs through the ten years 500–490 BC, from the outbreak of the Ionian revolt to the Parian and Lemnian aftermath of Marathon. In particular, the Ionian revolt[13] narrative straddles the two books, with virtually no break in between; the death of Aristagores closes bk. 5, but the first ch. of 6 immediately addresses the question, focalised through Artaphrenes, of who was the more responsible for the revolt, Aristagores or Histiaios. The revolt is prepared for in various ways in the early chapters of bk. 5, most obviously by the biographical material about Histiaios of Miletos (**11** and **23–5**), but in subtler ways too, such as the forward-looking handling of the Paionians (**1**.1 and **15**.1nn.; cf. **98**). Indeed, the Ionian, Aiolian and Hellespontine tyrants whose deposition inaugurates the revolt (**37–8**) were introduced already in bk. 4 (mostly at 4.137–8, but see also 4.97 for Koes of Mytilene). But the Ionian revolt narrative proper begins at 5.**28**,[14] and after many excursuses (some of them snaking back a couple of centuries)[15] it ends when bk. 6 is well advanced. There is more than one candidate for the precise closural point. One of them is the final sentence of 6.32, 'so for the third time the Ionians were enslaved, Ἴωνες κατεδουλώθησαν, the first time by the Lydians, and then twice by the Persians'; cf. 1.92.1 and then 1.169.2, οὕτω δὴ τὸ δεύτερον Ἰωνίη ἐδεδούλωτο. But a good case could also be made for a later moment, the political settlement of Ionia by Mardonios, who in 493 'suppressed all Ionian tyrannies and established democracies in the cities' (6.43.3). This recalls, with verbal as well as thematic closeness, the abolition, κατάπαυσις, of tyrannies in the cities at the start of the revolt (5.**38**.2).

In some ways bk. 6 is a structural unit: for example, it begins and ends with a prominent man being wounded in the thigh (Histiaios at 6.5.2; Miltiades at 6.134.2). But more than perhaps any other two books of Hdt., 5 and 6 together form a unit or block. To be sure, bk. 5 resumes bk. 4 thematically, actually picking up the story from 4.144, so to that important extent it is true that 'Book V 1–27 are the sequel of the Scythian story in Book IV'.[16] But that was a long time ago in Hdt.'s text, and bk. 4 actually ends (ch. 205) with Pheretime's death, which forms the frightening

---

[13] This brief expression is used for convenience, although (see the detailed comm. below) it ignores the Karian, Hellespontine and Cypriot aspects of the revolt.

[14] Myres repeatedly used the 'remission, ἄνεσις, of troubles' at **28**.1 as evidence for a definite break (e.g. twice at Myres 1953: 100), but the text is not secure. See n.

[15] The Bacchiads (**92**β) and the Lelantine War (**99**.1) both take us back to c. 700 BC.

[16] Myres 1953: 65 and 100. For the motif of thigh-wounds, see Harder 2012: 1023.

closure of the very long section about Libya and Kyrene.[17] At the other
end of the block, the main Persian War narrative and the reign of Xerxes
begin very soon after bk. 7 begins, in fact at 7.4; three years are covered
in the very first ch. of the book, after the discursive slow-motion narrative
which began at 6.43 and culminated in the battle of Marathon.

(b) Books 5 and 6 in relation to the Histories as a whole

A striking feature of bk. 5 and the early part of bk. 6 is the frequent occurrence of more or less explicit back-references to bk. 1. A list of these is
provided as an Annex to the present section, in the hope of showing that
the density of parallels is unusual.[18] Only once (**36**.4, about the rich offerings at Branchidai near Miletos) does Hdt. actually use an explicit cross-
referring formula: ὡς δεδήλωταί μοι ἐν τῶι πρώτωι τῶν λόγων, where the reference is to 1.92.1. 'In the first λόγος' does not mean 'in bk. 1' (see §1 (a)
above), but it is nevertheless of great interest as showing that in Hdt.'s
mind the work was organised into units, and that 1.92 fell within the first
of those units.

Some of the other back-references are almost as explicit as this, but
they are differently achieved, by the Homeric technique of identity, or very
close similarity, of phrasing. Sometimes Hdt. is 'merely' repeating material
already given in bk. 1 (such repetitions should not be assumed to be the
result of mere absent-mindedness, but may well be there for a purpose).
Thus **101**.2 reminds us, in closely similar words to 1.93.1, of the gold dust
which comes down from Mt Tmolos in the waters of the River Paktolos.

In other verbally parallel pairs, a comparison may be effected between
two items whose subject matter is not identical in the 'Paktolos' manner
(so that we are not being reminded of anything we have been told already).
To take one example from early in bk. 5, the good-looking multi-tasking
sister of the Paionian brothers is described in exactly the same words as
Phye, whom Peisistratos passed off as Athena; and the same participle is
used for the way in which Peisistratos and the Paionian brothers dressed
up their respective women (**12**.1–2 and 1.60.4).

A common-sense or reductive explanation of these reminiscences will
insist that they are no more than a function of the similarity or identity

---

[17] But from the Persian angle there is no break here because the reign of Dareios
more than fills all three bks. 4–6.
[18] To prove the point properly, it needs to be accompanied by a list of places in
bk. 5–early bk. 6 which refer to, or resume themes from, bks. 2, 3 or 4. A list of
these is therefore provided in the Annex, underneath the list of parallels between
bk. 5–early bk. 6 and bk. 1. Naturally, there are also a few correspondences between
bk. 1 and bks. 7, 8, 9 and the latter part of 6, but these are not numerous enough
to be worth listing.

of subject matter. Hdt. has not had much to say about Asia Minor since bk. 1, so it is only natural that he should now remind us that Miletos was colonised by the Athenians (97.2 and 6.21.2 recall 1.170); and so on for several of the Asia Minor parallels. And – it can be argued – it is only now that the Athenians and Spartans begin to be important players again. Sometimes, a bk. 1 item helps the reader in a straightforward way to cope with the detail of the much later narrative. For instance, the unexplained mention of the small Ionian *polis* of Myous as the destination of Ietragores' mission (36.4 with 37.1) is more intelligible if we have long memories and can recall the information about its geographical position, and proximity to Miletos, supplied in bk. 1 (142.3).

But this will not quite do as an explanation. At least one of the parallels goes well beyond the requirements of factual reminder, and involves significant thematic repetition. It concerns Dionysios of Phokaia, who tried to train the Greek sailors in preparation for the battle of Lade (when we hear his ethnic at 6.11.1, we may recall 1.163.1, the Phokaians as naval pioneers). Hdt. closes the account of the Greek naval defeat in 494 by recounting briefly and proleptically what happened to Dionysios after it (6.17). He went to the western Mediterranean, because he knew that his home city would be enslaved along with the rest of Ionia. When he got there, he became a pirate and attacked Carthaginian and Etruscan ships only, sparing all Greeks. No explanation of this selective plundering policy is given (perhaps we merely reflect, 'well, he's a Greek so he would, wouldn't he?'). But a reading of the much longer and structurally very important Phokaian narrative of bk. 1 reveals several interesting correspondences (see 1.163–7, a famously sad passage, drawn on by Horace in *Epode* 16 lines 17ff.).[19] In 546, the Phokaians, or some of them, went west to avoid slavery: 1.164.2, with the strong word περιημεκτέοντες, they were 'incensed' at the prospect. Dionysios must in fact have been descended from one of the families who broke their oath (ψευδόρκιοι γενόμενοι) never to return to Phokaia, 1.165.3. Those Phokaians who did go west based themselves for a while on Corsica, and from there plundered their neighbours by sea (1.166.1). This got them into trouble with the Etruscans and Carthaginians, who attacked them and stoned some of their Phokaian prisoners to death. Now it is a curious detail that the combination 'Carthaginians and Etruscans' or *vice versa* is found nowhere in the *Histories* except in these two sections of narrative, namely the Phokaian section of bk. 1 and the short chapter about Dionysios of Phokaia in bk. 6. Surely we are meant to put the two widely-separated passages together and conclude that Dionysios' special piratical treatment of the Carthaginians and

---

[19] Myres 1953: 94 argued that the expulsion of the Phokaians and Teians to new homes stands at the centre of a large 'pedimental' composition.

Etruscans was in reprisal for the horrible deaths of his fellow-countrymen half a century before – deaths which were in turn reprisal for piratical activity by Phokaians.²⁰ These parallels are no mere coincidences generated by Hdt.'s need, not felt since bk. 1, to speak about Phokaia and Phokaians. Hdt. wishes us to think about a pattern of oppression, escape, and revenge, repeated with variations after fifty years.

That was an example of a passage in bk. 6 which might well seem inconsequential, though not actually unintelligible, without the benefit of the narrative in bk. 1. Something like the converse is true of the Kylonian curse which affected the Alkmaionids of Athens. Here the three-word statement in bk. 1 that the Alkmaionids were 'said to be under a curse', λεγομένων ἐναγέων εἶναι (1.61.1), is intriguing but completely baffling on its own: there is no mention of Kylon. Not until the middle of bk. 5 will it be explained, and Kylon's story given in full (71). Four books is a remarkably long time to wait for an explanation of a curse which affected the family down to the time of Perikles (Th. 1.126). It does not seem a satisfactory solution to say that Hdt. took for granted knowledge in his contemporaries and his audience (not all of whom were Athenians) of so well-known a taint of pollution.

Elsewhere in bk. 5 and the early part of bk. 6 we have simpler forms of resumption. The material about the Athenian Peisistratids and about Sparta almost continues where the bk. 1 narratives left off. Thus at 39.1 we are told that Anaxandrides of Sparta was 'no longer living and ruling but had died', οὐκέτι περιεὼν ἐβασίλευε ἀλλὰ ἐτετελευτήκεε. This is elaborate and emphatic, and οὐκέτι ('no longer') resumes a passage in bk. 1 (67.1), where Anaxandrides and Ariston were said to have been the kings of Sparta when in about 550 Kroisos sent his messengers with gifts to ask for an alliance (69.1). Actually, we could have inferred from 3.148.1 – the attempted bribe of 'Kleomenes son of Anaxandrides' by Maiandrios of Samos – that Anaxandrides had died by 520 BC. But Hdt. waits until bk. 5 before spelling out the fact. This might suggest that he wanted bk. 5 to function as the new start, and for that reason held back the explicit statement of Anaxandrides' death. To be sure, there is a further reason for this delay. Anaxandrides is, in narrative terms, not dead at all at 39.1, but is brought back to life (39–41, the story of his two wives) because Hdt. wants to explain in detail how Kleomenes, not Dorieus, came to be king. That story, which takes Dorieus across the Adriatic, fits very well in bk. 5 because of the way it tracks the Ionian revolt thematically, in particular by the parallel between Miletos and the Italian polis of Sybaris (see introd. n. to 39–48).

²⁰ Dionysios was evidently not impressed by the hero-cult accorded to the victims of the stoning, on the instructions of the Pythia (1.167.2).

Similarly the story of the Peisistratids and Alkmaionids is resumed from bk. 1, and here there are no intervening mentions of either family at all. Of particular importance is the brief early statement (i.e. in bk. 1) that the Alkmaionids went into exile together with other defeated survivors of the battle of Pallene in 546, by which Peisistratos finally established himself securely (1.64.3, οἱ δὲ αὐτῶν μετ' Ἀλκμεωνιδέων ἔφευγον ἐκ τῆς οἰκηίης). This exiling of the Alkmaionids will crucially recur (**62**.2, γένος ἐόντες Ἀθηναῖοι καὶ φεύγοντες Πεισιστρατίδας) as part of the narrative of the final phase of the tyranny. The resumptions and echoes of bk. 1 in bk. 5 and the early part of bk. 6 are there for a purpose which goes beyond factual reminder. We are starting again. The narrative which begins in 500 BC is both a new narrative beginning, and a near-repetition of a pattern of human behaviour and human response. We have already seen that the handling of Anaxandrides of Sparta and of Dionysios of Phokaia invite us to think of bks. 5 and 6 in this sort of way. We can go further and say that the opening of the second half of the *Histories* is to be thought of as, more generally, a second beginning. If so, there is an obvious comparison with Th., who seems in important ways to start again at the beginning of bk. 6 (out of eight books, but there would have been a good deal more text if Th. had taken the story down to 404, as he surely intended: perhaps the equivalent of ten books in all,[21] so that the start of 6 would be at an approximate half-way point).[22]

There are obvious limits to the analogy with Th. For instance, the *Histories* of Hdt. open with a series of mythical female abductions, which have no exact counterpart in his bk. 5. Contrast the structural balancing of Th.'s *Archaeology* by his *Sikelika*, above. And Th.'s work is incomplete in the sense that the narrative would have continued beyond its present terminal point in 411 BC (n. 22 below), whereas there is no reason to doubt that Hdt.'s is complete,[23] and ends where he meant it to end. This actually makes it easier, or at any rate more legitimate, to speculate about the architecture of Hdt.'s whole work than about Th.'s.

[21] But Liberman 2011: 627, suggests that Th.'s eight books should be thought of as nine (the Muses) minus one. The 'one' would have contained the unwritten history of the last phase of the war.
[22] The *Sikelika*, the account of early barbarian and Greek settlement on Sicily (6.2–5), corresponds to the *Archaeology* (1.1–19), and there is other, smaller-scale but important, thematic near-repetition. In particular, the celebrated and paradoxical phrase ἀληθεστάτη πρόφασις at 1.23.6 recurs at 6.6.1 but nowhere else in Th.; on both occasions it refers to the realities of Athenian ambition, as opposed to a pretext or what was said in public.
[23] Except perhaps for the 'Assyrian *logos*' promised at 1.184 but not extant, and perhaps lost after the 4th cent. BC (Aristotle apparently knew it, see *Hist. An.* 601b4 for a detailed citation of Hdt. on the 'siege of Nineveh', cf. Myres 1953: 18 and n. 1).

One feature shared between bk. 1 of Hdt. and bk. 1 of Th. is the
preparatory or introductory function performed by the material about
Athenians and Spartans; and this arguably happens in Hdt. bk. 5 as well.
(See further below, introd. n. to 39–97.1.) The essential narrative device in
bk. 5 is similar to that used in bk. 1: an inquiry or a visit by a man from the
east (Kroisos; Aristagores) is the peg from which is hung a pair of excursuses, one about Athens, the other about Sparta. But in bk. 1, the order of
treatment is Athens, then Sparta (1.59.1 and 65.1), whereas in bk. 5 it is
Sparta then Athens. In both bks., the excursuses enable the feeding in of
much explanatory and background information about the two great powers, Ionian and Dorian (and there is further Spartan material, of a quasi-
ethnographic sort, at 6.56–60). The device of the double introduction was
re-used by Th. in his bk. 1 (the Pausanias and Themistokles material), but
he dispenses with the 'man from the east', as does Xenophon, in whose
Hellenika the Arginousai trial (1.7) and the Kinadon affair (3.3) introduce
us in like manner to Athenian and Spartan ways as exhibited in times of
crisis.

We must also ask how bks. 5 and 6 relate to the Persian War narrative of
bks. 7–9. Climactically placed near the end of the entire main narrative,
after the battle of Mykale, is the obviously backward-looking statement 'so
for the second time Ionia revolted from the Persians', οὕτω δὴ τὸ δεύτερον
Ἰωνίη ἀπὸ Περσέων ἀπέστη (9.104), where the implied first revolt is that
in bks. 5-early 6; but the closural comment is also forward-looking ('false
closure') in that it invites us to contemplate the fifth-century future of
Ionia as well.

The three large-scale Ionian narratives can be seen as a kind of triptych separated by large quantities of intervening material: first, the conquest in 546 (actually a conquest, revolt and then reconquest); second, the
Ionian revolt; and third, the liberation of Ionia after the Persian Wars are
over.[24] One place seems to stand as a signifier for each of the three panels:
Mykale. In bk. 1, Mykale features as the location of the Panionion (1.148.1,
where geographical indicators are provided). After bk. 1 the Panionion
itself will not be mentioned again until shortly before Lade in 494, where
it is the location of the Ionian political gathering which debated resistance policy (6.7), and then after the battle, and a few chapters later,
the Chians flee to Mykale, which is now named (6.16.1). Then in bk. 9,
Mykale is the scene of the final battle between Greeks and Persians in 479
(9.96–104).

So far, we have looked at the structure of the *Histories* in purely Greek
terms, and this, as we saw, invites treatment of 5 and 6 as a unit. If,

---

[24] The general approach here owes a debt to Myres 1953, but his scheme is
different.

however, we look at the *Histories* as a series of Persian reigns (an approach encouraged by Hdt. himself at 6.98.2 where he speaks of the ills suffered by Greeks and barbarians in the three most recent Persian reigns), we find another sort of triptych.[25] We saw above that Xerxes' reign almost exactly fills bks. 7–9, which we may call the third panel of the triptych on this scheme, and that Hdt. gallops through the last four years of Dareios' reign in as many short chapters. Very crudely, we can assign the first triptych to Kyros and Kambyses, and the second and central triptych to Dareios. This works only very approximately in terms of book divisions (Kambyses dies at 3.66, and Babylon is captured by Dareios in a lengthy narrative, all of which is inside bk. 3), but we have seen that these divisions are not Herodotean anyway. In any case, bks. 4–6 certainly belong to Dareios alone, so that the break between 4 and 5, commented on above, is thus softened.

Let us now put aside consideration of large subdivisions and think instead of themes, in particular the requital and reciprocity which John Gould in 1989 identified as the governing and organising principle of the *Histories*. From this point of view, the most important sentence in the whole Ionian revolt narrative is a proleptic authorial comment positioned just after the accidental burning of Sardis and of the temple of Kybebe. The Persians, says Hdt., used this as an excuse for their counter-burning of the temples in Greece (**102**.1). The word for 'counter-burning' ('burn in revenge': Powell, 'set on fire in return': LSJ) is ἀντενεπίμπρασαν. Hdt. here adopts or reports a Persian line of explanation, one which presented the Ionian revolt as Greek aggression, to which the Persians then replied in kind. The 'orientalising' theme of Persian temple-burning in 480 was important long after Hdt.'s own time, because it was used (as Polybius noted, 3.6.13) as the pretext for Alexander the Great's invasion of Asia. Hdt.'s opposite point about Sardis was naturally forgotten, or at any rate not followed up, in later accounts and later propaganda. But that was outside Hdt.'s lifetime and knowledge. Within his *History*, the burning of Sardis explains the unsuccessful assault on Delphi and, above all, the burning of the Athenian acropolis (8.53.2, ἐνέπρησαν πᾶσαν τὴν ἀκρόπολιν). The historical cycle of revenge and reciprocity, Greek aggression alternating with Persian, does after all take us back to the opening chapters and the abductions and counter-abductions of women. And yet, there was no inevitability about this: the burning of Sardis was contingent, because the city would not have burnt except for the accident that the houses were made of a certain type of material (**101**.1).

---

[25] But though that passage arranges Persian history according to a sequence of three, the three are Dareios, Xerxes and (proleptically) Artaxerxes rather than the three regnal blocks here suggested, viz. Kyros+Kambyses, Dareios, Xerxes.

(c) The structure of books 5 and 6

Let us move on to internal structure, that is the architecture of bks. 5 and 6.

In the opening section (1–16) we have a tripartite arrangement: Paionian story – Thracian ethnography – Paionian story; then follows Macedonian material (**17–27**), the full point of which will not become clear until the last part of bk. 8, where Alexandros will play a lead part.

The long Ionian revolt section (5.**28** – 6.43.3) seems at first sprawling and confusing in the number and range of its excursuses and lesser insertions. In bk. 5 alone, we encounter important material about mainland and west Greek *poleis*, presented in a leisurely way, and on a scale not easy to parallel elsewhere in the *Histories*: Sybaris and Kroton in south Italy, Thebes (sometimes called 'the Boiotians'),[26] Sikyon, Aigina, Korinth, and the two main cities of Euboia (Chalkis and Eretria) – quite apart from the chief *poleis* Sparta, Athens, and Athens' daughter city Miletos. In addition, Thessalians (**63** and **94**, part of the Peisistratid story) and Epidaurians (**82–4**, part of the Aiginetan story) enjoy brief prominence.

We have seen already, when considering the parallels with bk. 1, that one main organisational principle is the help-raising itinerary of Aristagores. It is this which enables Hdt. to update us, in a balanced arrangement, about first Sparta at **39–54**, then Athens at **55–97**.[27] (For the possibility that he deliberately passed over a visit of Aristagores to Argos, see **55**n. At any rate, Hdt. has decided to postpone a full-on treatment of Argive history until bks. 6 and 7.)[28] He was evidently aware of the complexity of what he was doing, and felt the need for some signposting: the announcement at **65**.5 is unusually explicit and helpful. He there says that before returning to the Ionian revolt he will first relate, ταῦτα πρῶτα φράσω, everything that the Athenians did or experienced between getting rid of their tyrants and the revolt.[29] The west Greek material at **42–8** (Sicily, Sybaris, Kroton) is occasioned by the need to explain how Kleomenes came to be king. The excursus about Kleisthenes of Sikyon is attached to the story of his homonymous grandson of Athens, the political reformer (**67–8**). The first Theban section (**59–61**) is an antiquarian appendage to the account of the origins of the Gephyraioi, the *genos* to which the Athenian tyrannicides belonged, but the second is a contemporary clash between the Boiotians/Thebans and the Chalkidians on the one hand and the Athenians on the other. This leads neatly to the first (**80–9**)

[26] See **77**.1 and **79**.1n. for the way 'the Boiotians' imperceptibly morph into 'the Thebans'.
[27] Myres 1953: 63.
[28] The Argives do feature in a minor way in bk. 5, for instance as the objects of the hostility of Kleisthenes of Sikyon (**67–8**) and in connection with Aigina (**86–8**).
[29] For this interpretation, see the n. on the passage.

of the series of lengthy excursuses about Aigina, which will continue into bk. 6 and will find their justification later still, at the authorial 7.144.2: 'it was the [Athenian] war against Aigina which saved Greece by forcing the Athenians to become sailors'. The narrative link between Thebes and Aigina is constructed by means of 'kinship diplomacy':[30] Thebe (*sic*) and Aigina are twin sisters and daughters of Asopos in myth, and this is why the Thebans ask the Aiginetans for help against the Athenians (see **80.**1 for the correct interpretation of the oracular advice to the Thebans to 'seek help from your nearest', **79.**1). The myth conveys an important contemporary truth: the Thebans by land and the Aiginetans by sea were the enemies whose threats most strengthened the Athenians. Finally, the Korinthians at **90–4** bring the two chief strands together, the Athenian and Spartan, because they veto the Spartan attempt to put the tyrant Hippias back in power at Athens; cue the Kypselids of Korinth (**92,** Soklees' speech).

From that point the narrative, from the burning of Sardis, through the operations in Cyprus, Karia and the Hellespont (**100–22**), to the battle of Lade and its aftermath in early 6, is more like a straight line; biographical interest in Histiaios directs the flow of some of the narrative until his execution (6.30), and in this context Hdt. resumes the theme of Chian misfortunes which began in bk. 1 and will continue right up to the story of Panionios and Hermotimos in bk. 8 (104–6).[31] But in the early chapters of bk. 6 Hdt. also continues (as at 5.**42–8**) to remind us of the wider Mediterranean world, above all by means of the parallel between Miletos and Italian Sybaris (6.21), two great cities brought low in the way anticipated long before, at 1.5.4. He also insists that Greeks in the west were affected by the convulsions in the Aegean and Asia Minor because of westward migration by Ionian refugees. Two proleptic post-Lade insertions perform this function, the brief but rich chapter about Dionysios of Phokaia, already discussed above, and the narrative about the Samian exiles, culminating in their acquisition of the 'lovely city' of Zankle/Messina in Sicily (6.17 and 22–4).

After Lade the Persian territorial recovery continues. The subjugation of Karia to the south is covered in a mere couple of words (6.25.2), a surprise after the lengthy narrative at the end of bk. 5, which had actually ended with a Karian success (the ambush at **121**). The northward Persian penetration into the Hellespontine region allows Hdt. to expand on the tyranny of the family of Miltiades, a preparation for the younger Miltiades' role at Marathon (6.34–41). The family story is in fact distributed across three sections of bk. 6; the next is at 103–4, just before the battle, and then bk. 6 ends with Miltiades' activity on Paros and Lemnos.

---

[30] See C. P. Jones 1999 for this notion.   [31] See below, **98.**3n.

Next in the sequence of Persian successes comes the annexation of wealthy Thasos, from where we pass to another large and equally wealthy island, Aigina. These were the only two thirty-talent payers in the later Athenian empire. And now Kleomenes re-enters the stage, with his high-handed action against Aiginetan medisers (50). The quarrel between Kleomenes and Demaretos, already clearly alluded to in bk. 5 (**75**.1), now erupts. This is the cue not only for the story of Demaretos' birth but for an ethnographic-style excursus about Sparta (51–60). Kleomenes now dominates the narrative until 84 and beyond, and the Aiginetan theme which he helped to precipitate continues well after that. Aigina is the occasion for the story of Glaukos and the Milesian (told by Leutychides at the long ch. 86), which runs until ch. 93, with a closural sentence at the start of 94.

Datis the Mede now crosses the Aegean; the Marathon campaign has begun. The Spartans are an absent presence (they turn up after the battle to inspect the Persian dead, 120): we are reminded of them in two ways. First, Philippides experiences his epiphany of Pan (105) on his run from Athens to Sparta. Second, Kleomenes is influential on the narrative from beyond the grave, because of the important way he features in the excursus about Plataia (108). This looks back in time to something which occurred outside the narrative (it is an 'external analepsis'), but is at the same time a forward-looking gesture: the fluctuating fate of the Plataians – geographical Boiotians but spiritual Athenians – was a topic with a long future ahead of it in later Greek historiography and oratory.[32]

If the run-up to Marathon serves as a peg for more information about Miltiades' family, the battle's aftermath does the same for another great Athenian family, the Alkmaionidai, because of their alleged treachery in displaying a signal by means of a flashing shield. See 121–31, which additionally continues from bk. 5 (**67–8**) the story of Kleisthenes of Sikyon, whose daughter Agariste marries the Alkmaionid Megakles. Miltiades himself closes bk. 6, and so also the second main triptych of the *Histories*. His failure on Paros and miserable death and disgrace (132–6) are, however, not allowed to leave an ineradicably nasty taste. Hdt. uses an analepsis to tell us of a much earlier success on Lemnos (137–40), enabling him to end on a ringingly positive note: 'so Lemnos was possessed by the Athenians – and by Miltiades', in that order.

Much of the above account has been in terms of cities, islands and regions. There is another recognisable principle of organisation: by human individual. The hero of these books, it has been said, is Kleomenes I of Sparta,[33] (a topic which will be treated in the Introduction to bk. 6).

---

[32] *TT*: 309–10.
[33] Myres 1953: 77–8, who begins with the (debatable) claim 'Herodotus loves a hero', suggests that he was really writing a prose tragedy *Kleomenes mainomenos*, corresponding to *Mardonios hybristes* in bks. 7–9.

Certainly he dominates the central part of bk. 6, after featuring crucially in bk. 5 as well (see esp. **72**, his visit to the Athenian acropolis and his exchange with the unnamed priestess). But his rival Demaretos can also be seen as a structuring device, and he continues into the third main triptych as well (bks. 7 and 8); while on the Athenian side we have seen that Miltiades is also a dominant personality with a shaping effect on the narrative, and one whose career, like that of Kleomenes (and of Pausanias and Themistokles later) ends in controversy and disgrace after brilliant initial successes.

Annex: bk. 5 + early bk. 6 as resumption of bk. 1: parallel passages

Bk. 5	Bk. 1	Content
1.1	6.1	κατεστρέψατο
2.1	95.2 and 169.1	'fighting bravely for freedom/to avoid slavery'
11 (+23.1)	64.1	revenues from Strymon region (Myres 1953: 196)
12.1–2	60.4	(Paionian sister, Phye) tall, εὐειδής, σκευάσαντες
18–20	106.2	make foreign guests drunk at banquet, then kill them
19.1	32.6	ἀπαθὴς κακῶν (cf. below on 6.12.2)
25.1	153.3	admin. arrangements at Sardis
28	65.2	shift from *stasis* to good order, Miletos/Sparta
36.2	170	advice to Ionians by local sages (cf. 1.27–8 to Kroisos)
36.3	46, 158	Branchidai
36.4	92.2	Branchidai treasures, with explicit back-ref.: ὡς δεδήλωταί μοι ἐν τῶι πρώτωι τῶν λόγων (cf. 6.19.3 below)
36.4	142.3	Myous (cf. below on 6.8, Lade)
39.1	67.1	Anaxandrides son of Leon, Spartan king
45.1	145	river Krathis (name explained)
49.2	69.2	an Easterner flatters the Spartans as 'leaders of Greece'
49.7	188–9	Susa, the river Choaspes
49.8	82.4	ἰσοπαλής (found nowhere else in Hdt.)
52.5	189	River Gyndes
55; 97.1	56.2, 59.1, 65.1	Sparta/Athens introduced via man from east
55–65	59–64	fall/rise of Peisistratids

(cont.)

Bk. 5	Bk. 1	Content
56.2	107–8, 128.2	ὀνειροπόλοι (found nowhere else in Hdt.)
59	52, 92.1	offerings to Apollo Ismenios at Thebes
62.2	64.3	Alkmaionids in exile under the tyranny
65.3	147.1	Kodros and Melanthos
66.1	171.6	Karian Zeus
69.1	170.3	Kleisthenes/Thales' federal plan (Myres 1953: 180)
70–71	61.1	Alkmaionids accursed, ἐναγής nowhere else in Hdt.
72.3	67	Spartans pose as Achaians not Dorians
77.1	proem	ἀκλεής (found nowhere else in Hdt.)
88.2	82.7–8	symmetrical aitiological reversals
90.2; 93.2	62–4	Peisistratids specially keen on divination
91.2	66.3 and 75.2	κίβδηλος (of oracles); only in these passages
92.2 ἰθέως	65.2 ἰθύς	of oracles given to Eetion and Lykourgos
92. ζ–η	20	Periandros' relations with Thrasyboulos
94.1	61.4	Peisistratid links with Argives
97.2	146	Miletos colonised from Athens (cf. on 6.21.2)
100	84.3	Mt Tmolos
101.2	86.5	fires at Sardis consume the edges, περιέσχατα, of something (the word found nowhere else in Hdt.)
101.2	93.1	gold dust from River Paktolos
103.2	171–172	Kaunos
106.6	170.2	Sardinia νήσων ἀπασέων μεγίστην / νῆσον τὴν μεγίστην
113.2	29 etc.	Solon
119.2	171.6	Labraunda/Mylasa and their temples
123	16	Klazomenai
Bk. 6	**Bk. 1**	
8	passim	various Ionian cities which provided ships at Lade
12.2	32.6	ἀπαθὴς κακῶν (cf. above on 5.19.1)
16.1	148.1	Mykale
17	163–7	Phokaians go west to avoid slavery
19.3	92.2 and 5.36.4 (see above on that passage)	treasures at Didyma/Branchidai, τῶν δ' ἐν τῶι ἱρῶι τούτωι χρημάτων πολλάκις μνήμην ἑτέρωθι τοῦ λόγου ἐποιησάμην

(*cont.*)

Bk. 6	Bk. 1	Content
21.2	146	Miletos colonised from Athens (cf. on 5.97.2)
28.2	160.3–5	Atarneus polluted/sinister
32	169	'enslavements' of Ionia
37.2	passim (Kroisos)	Kroisos saves Miltiades
38.1	167.2	hero-cults (the Chersonesites for Miltiades, the Agyllaioi for the Phokaians): ἀγῶνα ἱππικόν τε καὶ γυμνικὸν ἐπιστᾶσι both times. The verb is used in this sense in these passages only.

Passages in bk. 5+ early bk. 6 which pick up bks. 2, 3 or 4
There are not many, after the opening chs. (which naturally pick up Thracian items from bk. 4; see esp. 5.4.1, on the Getai, where εἴρηταί μοι explicitly back-refers to 4.93–4).

- with ἰσονομία at 5.37.2, cf. 3.80.6, 83.1, 142.3.
- Kinyps and the Makai at 5.42–3 (Dorieus in Libya) recall 4.175 and 198
- parasangs as thirty stades at 5.53 emphatically repeats 2.6.3.
- with the death of Periandros' wife Melissa at 3.50, cf. 5.92η. But note that bk. 5 does not repeat the bk. 3 allegation that Periandros caused her death.
- 3.148: Anaxandrides of Sparta mentioned, but as a patronym, without saying he was dead; cf. 5.39.1.
- 'sailing ἐκπλώσαντες out of your mind' = mad: with 6.12.3 cf. 3.155.2
- Kleomenes' behaviour recalls that of Kambyses in bk. 3 (see Griffiths 1989).
- Persians promoting democracy: 6.43.3 emphatically replies to sceptics about 3.80.

2 THE CAUSES OF THE IONIAN REVOLT

To ask 'why did the Ionian revolt[34] happen?' may be the wrong approach.[35] We should ask instead why the revolt happened as late as it

[34] The revolt was not confined to Ionia, but included Karia and Cyprus to the south and the Hellespont to the north. But Hdt. himself often speaks of Ionia only, without specifying the whole rebel area (e.g. 28.1; 9.105), and it is convenient short-hand.

[35] Hdt.'s attitude to historical explanation and causation will be treated in the Introduction to bk. 6. On the difficulty that Hdt. at 5.28 presents the Ionian revolt as a '*beginning* of troubles', whereas the logic of the *Histories* so far (bks. 1–4, a theme resumed early in bk. 7) has been to suggest inevitable Persian imperial expansion, see 5.28n.

did, rather than at any time in the nearly half-century period since the original Persian subjugation of Ionia (546).[36] Part of the answer to both questions is to be found in an event which happened on the other side of the Aegean in 508/7, a very few years before the outbreak of the revolt: the democratic or 'isonomic' (equalising) reforms of Kleisthenes at Athens, the mother-city of Ionia and the Milesians in particular.[37] This radical change surely made a profound political impact on the daughter-region. Before that, the usual regime in Greek states was some form of tyranny.[38] Hdt. does not spell out this causal connection between the revolt and Athens, but the word *isonomie* at **37**.2 is a clue – not so much the Milesian Aristagores' proclamation of it, but the implication of his expressly stated belief that this state of affairs will be welcome to the Milesians generally. If the Athenian political convulsions, which began with the assassination of Hipparchos in 514 and ended with Kleisthenes, had taken place many years earlier, perhaps Ionia would have risen earlier too. Actually, there are hints in bk. 4 of Hdt. that a desire for freedom and democracy was general in Ionia as early as the teens of the sixth century. Miltiades, in the context of Dareios' Skythian expedition, speaks in favour of the Skythian proposal to 'liberate Ionia', and says that each of the cities there would prefer to be democratically ruled than to be under tyrants (4.137). The claim has been suspected of anachronism, and it is certainly ironic, since the chapter in question begins by explaining that Miltiades was himself a tyrant (of the Chersonese). But the idea of *isonomie* was in the air even earlier, in fact as early as the 520s, if we can believe the story of the abortive proclamation of *isonomie* and freedom (including the establishment of a cult-place of Zeus the liberator) by Maiandrios on the Ionian island of Samos, so close geographically to mainland Ionia (3.142–3).[39] There is even an amazing suggestion that a Persian, Otanes, could advocate *isonomie* for the Persians themselves in 524 (3.80). So although the Athenian lead was surely important, there may already have been a growing awareness in Ionia that

---

[36] Murray 1988: 480 acutely observes 'the surprising fact is that the Greeks [of the Ionian cities] did not seize the far more favourable occasion of the accession of Darius, when so many other areas of the empire broke free' (referring to the late 520s). Murray himself (477, followed by Green 1996: xv) sees the western expansion of Persian power as disastrous for the merchant cities of Ionia, who had traded in the Aegean and Black Sea.

[37] Hdt. calls Kleisthenes 'the man who introduced the tribes and the democracy' (6.131). The evidence for the association of the Athenian changes with *isonomie* is indirect but real; see **37**.2n., also discussing the meaning of the word.

[38] In southern mainland Greece, the other main alternative was Spartan-supported oligarchy (cf. Th. 1.19), but that is not relevant in western Asia Minor.

[39] But Hdt. remarks that these Ionians 'did not, it seems, want to be free' (3.143.2), in other words, *isonomie* was an idea whose time had not yet come. See Robinson 1997: 119.

democratic self-determination was a possibility, and that submission to Persian rule, or the rule of Persian-supported tyrants, was not an inevitable part of life.

Good evidence for the causes of the revolt may be found in the Persian settlement after it. Mardonios' abolition of tyrannies and establishment of democracies (6.43.3) surely implies awareness of earlier grievances (see **36**nn. for the difficulty that this abolition had already been effected by Aristagores).

Economic disruption in the east Mediterranean, the result of Persian expansion into Europe, has been blamed for the revolt (n. 36). But the mainland Asiatic city which took the lead in the revolt was Miletos, described by Hdt. as in a 'flourishing condition' at that time (κατὰ τὸν αὐτὸν χρόνον...μάλιστα δὴ ἀκμάσασα, **28**), after the cure of an *earlier* bout of political instability, which had led to widespread economic ruin (**29**.1, δεινῶς οἰκοφθορημένους). This suggests that the simple economic argument is incorrect to the extent that, if Miletos was flourishing, a commercial explanation for the revolt will not do.[40] In any case, recent work on Miletos emphasises its agricultural riches and the extent of its *chora* or territory.[41] And the Milesian list of *stephanephoroi* (see §4) has an unbroken run of human names in this period, the late sixth and early fifth centuries: there is as yet no need to shift the financial burden onto 'Apollo son of Zeus', so perhaps the upper class was not in financial trouble. For all this see **30**.2n. on Ἀρισταγόρης ὁ Μολπαγόρεω...There was one extremely wealthy but anonymous early Milesian 'three generations' before the time of the early fifth-century Spartan king Leutychides: 6.86 α2 (but perhaps this time-indicator is added merely for the sake of 'verisimilitude': Myres 1953: 74).

Economic factors may after all have played a part in the revolt. There was surely a growing resentment in the coastal Greek cities of Asia Minor at Persian grants of desirable land, grants which must have been made at the expense of those cities. The process had begun as early as Kyros the Great, the Persian king who controlled western Asia Minor after 546.[42]

Hdt., however, presents the revolt largely as a matter of short-term and highly personal considerations to do with the motives of the Milesian Histiaios and his kinsman and deputy as ruler of Miletos, Aristagores. Hdt.

---

[40] So rightly Hignett 1963: 253 n. 2.   [41] Greaves 2002: 97.

[42] Kyros made a grant of local cities to one Pytharchos of Kyzikos: *FGrHist* 472 Agathokles F 6 (for an attestation of Pytharchos himself in a Greek inscription found at Persepolis in the 1960s, see Fornara: no. 46). For this kind of territorial rewarding of favourites as a likely grievance in Ionian Greek cities, see Murray 1988: 480 and *CAH* 6² : 211 and 213 (Hornblower), giving other, later, examples. See also Cawkwell 2005: 74.

would have approved of W. G. Runciman's analysis of human social activity as permanently at risk from cheats, free-riders and self-aggrandisers.[43] Hdt.'s Histiaios and Aristagores are a couple of plausible chancers. In particular, he brings out admirably the element of contingency, by the threefold statement of converging causes at **36**.1: Aristagores was unable to keep his promises to the Persian Artaphrenes; he had quarrelled with Megabates over the humiliating ship-board punishment of Aristagores' guest-friend Skylax of Myndos; and the slave with the tattooed head arrived from Histiaios, detained at Sousa, urging Aristagores to revolt.

Once the revolt had begun at Miletos and in Ionia, kinship ties began to be relevant to its spread northwards. We shall see in §4 that many Milesian colonies joined in (Miletos was daughter-city of Athens and was herself a fertile 'mother' or metropolis of cities. Here, for once, the modern habit of referring to cities as 'she' makes good sense). Hdt. does not stress this factor: he did not need to. Colonial ties of this sort were well known to his readers and hearers.

The most recent good full-length treatments of the revolt and its causes are Tozzi 1978 and Murray 1988. See also Walter 1993, who sees the revolt as the product of aristocratic rivalries.

3 CHRONOLOGY OF BOOK 5 (THE IONIAN REVOLT NARRATIVE)

The principal narrative thread of bk. 5 is the Ionian revolt, and this section will confine itself to the chronology of that episode, up to approximately 494 BC.[44] (The period from 494 to the early 480s will be covered in the Introduction to bk. 6 as will the sixth-century careers of Miltiades the oikist and his nephew Miltiades the hero of Marathon). But bk. 5 contains numerous inserted non-revolt narratives, and these too present chronological problems. These problems are, however, dealt with in the commentary, and will not be discussed further here. See esp. **22**.2n. (the Olympic victory of Alexandros I of Macedon); **48**n. (length of Kleomenes' reign); **71**.1n. (Kylon's coup at Athens); **81**.2 (Athenian-Aiginetan hostilities); introd. n. to **92** (the Kypselids of Korinth); **94**.2n. (Athenian acquisition of Sigeion).

The revolt narrative is like an hourglass: two detailed sections of narrative are separated by a much thinner section, which comes roughly at the end of bk. 5.[45] The 'waist' of the hourglass is the most problematic

---

[43] Runciman 2005: 131.

[44] In this section, Hdt. references are to bk. 5 except where specified.

[45] On the two 'blocks' of narrative (outbreak of revolt to flight of Aristagores; preparations for Lade to Marathon) see Murray 1988: 472f. Macan 1895: app. V

feature: two or three years are not accounted for in Hdt.'s narrative, and he may even have omitted at least one campaigning season.

Non-Greek sources do not help at this level of detail, although the Persepolis Fortification Tablets show several 'Herodotean' Persians active in 510–493. The starting point for the chronology of the Ionian revolt is a passage near the end of the relevant narrative unit of Hdt. (i.e. 5.28–6.43). At 6.18, he says that the Persians captured Miletos 'in the sixth year from Aristagores' revolt', ἕκτωι ἔτεϊ ἀπὸ τῆς ἀποστάσιος τῆς Ἀρισταγόρεω. Those years are the period with which we are concerned in this section. They run roughly from 499 to 494 and it is not possible to arrange the events in between with total precision. The other fixed point is the date for the battle of Marathon in the archonship of Phainippos, 490/89: *Ath. Pol.* 22.3.[46] The four campaigning years between the fall of Miletos and Marathon are told off in turn by Hdt. with sufficient precision as to fix the former event to 494, although the distribution of particular events within those years 494–490 is problematic, and the Persian preparations for the Marathon campaign should perhaps be back-dated. The revolt thus began in 499, soon after the Persian capture of Lemnos.[47] Presumably Hdt. thought of the first act of 'apostasy' by Aristagores as the arrest of tyrants at Myous and the proclamation of *isonomie* (37). This must have been in late summer, because Aristagores had sailed to Naxos in the spring of that year (31.4, Artaphrenes says the ships will be ready ἅμα τῶι ἔαρι) and the siege of Naxos lasted four months (34.2). Aristagores set off for Sparta and Athens (38.2); there is no time indicator, but he is there said to be in need of some great alliance, so he presumably lost no time before leaving. Kleomenes did not detain Aristagores long (though we may have to allow for a visit to Argos, cf. 55.1n., and he certainly visited Eretria, 99). Athenian help was instantly granted (97.3), and though Hdt. may have telescoped procedures at Athens by omitting deliberations in the Council of Five Hundred, thus increasing the impression of popular impetuosity, this will not have

---

(vol. 2: 62–70) is still useful, as is Busolt 2²: 537 n. 3 and 553 n. 3. Beloch 2.2: 57–60 is, as always, clear and succinct. See also Tozzi 1978: 100–13. Detailed refs. to these works are not given below.

[46] Beloch 2.2: 55. Hdt. gives no archon-date for this battle, as he does (uniquely) for that at Salamis: 8.51.1, archonship of Kalliades, 480/79.

[47] The Ionian revolt narrative begins after the Persian Otanes' capture of Lemnos in 26–7. At 28, there is a textual crux which might bear on chronology. If the right reading were μετὰ δὲ οὐ πολλὸν χρόνον ἄνεσις κακῶν ἦν, Hdt. would be saying 'after a short time there was remission of ills' for an unspecified period, and we would have to allow considerable time for this remission, perhaps even years. But the better solution is to read e.g. ἀνανέωσις κακῶν, so the meaning is 'after a short time there was a resumption of ills', and the passage loses the above chronological implication.

affected chronology much. The attack on Sardis can therefore be put in the spring of 498. The Cypriots joined the revolt at that point (**104**.1) and their revolt lasted a year, i.e. to 497 (**116**).

The Persian backlash caused Aristagores to abandon Miletos and go to Thrace, where he was killed (**126**). Here Thucydides helps us (4.102.1–3). He dates Aristagores' death thirty-two years before the disaster at Drabeskos, itself dated to 465, in the twenty-ninth year before Amphipolis was founded by the Athenians under Hagnon in 437 (scholiast to Aeschines 3.31);[48] so Aristagores died in 497. The data thus converge on 497 as the point reached at the end of the main bk. 5 narrative of Hdt. But it is possible that the Karian operations, which in Hdt.'s text precede the final ch. of bk. 5, actually postdated them by a year or two (496, 495). This possibility we must now consider.

The problem presented by the final stages of bk. 5 is that Hdt. gives the impression that military operations were carried out with no long gap in time between the burning of Sardis (**102**.1), the Persian mobilisation, and the Persian assault on Miletos early in bk. 6. It is hard, but not impossible (below), to stretch those military operations so as to fill enough of the period 497–494. And yet we do seem to have moved on a long way by the beginning of bk. 6 (1.1), because Aristagores then arrives at Sardis as if the city were functioning normally i.e. completely intact; and yet Dareios had spoken of himself as 'deprived of Sardis' (**106**.1), as if the city no longer existed. We should probably assume that Dareios is represented as exaggerating (see **106**.1n.) and that the destruction of Sardis was not total. But this difficulty (which does not seem to have been noticed in earlier discussions) is eased, and more time provided for the rebuilding of Sardis, if with Macan we spread the Persian operations in Karia over two campaigning seasons: battle of the Marsyas (**119**) in 496, battle of Labraunda (**120**) in 495.[49] This solution, though not ideal, is probably best. But if so, Hdt. has given a badly misleading impression, because the narrative of those two chapters is brisk, and does not encourage the reader to drive much of a chronological wedge between them; nor does he obviously jump back in time to record Aristagores' death at the end of the bk. (**126**), and yet this is fixed to 497. The gap from 497 to 494, and alternative but less attractive 'filling solutions' which have been proposed (the elongation either of the siege of Miletos,[50] or of Histiaios' adventures) will be discussed in the Introduction to bk. 6.

---

[48] See *CT* II: 323.   [49] Macan 1895: 2.68–9.
[50] Busolt 2²: 553 and n. 3 makes the siege begin, improbably, in 497 and end in 494.

4 KINSHIP TIES IN BOOKS 5 AND 6

All Greeks could, for some rhetorical purposes, be regarded as kin. Aristagores, an Ionian Greek, appeals to the king of Dorian Sparta to help free the Ionians from slavery, calling them the Spartans' kinsmen, ἄνδρας ὁμαίμονας.[51] More specific ties of kinship, συγγένεια, between Greek cities mitigated the particularism of Greek inter-polis life, not only in the Hellenistic period, when we have relevant inscriptions in profusion, but already in classical times.[52] The family metaphor was taken seriously: because the nymphs Thebe and Aigina are twin sisters and daughters of the river-god Asopos in myth, the Thebans in Hdt. feel able to call on the Aiginetans for aid.[53] More surprisingly, Hdt. represents the Persians as claiming kinship with the Argives through Persian descent from Perseus son of Danae.[54] On the other hand, Hdt. can express closeness between distant cities in language which does not derive from blood relationships. For the unusual degree of friendliness between the Milesians in Asia Minor and the Sybaritai in south Italy, Hdt. uses the unique verb ξεινοῦμαι, which is suggestive of ritualised guest-friendship, hospitality or entertainment: πόλιες γὰρ αὗται μάλιστα δὴ τῶν ἡμεῖς ἴδμεν ἀλλήλοισι ἐξεινώθησαν.[55] But even here the family idea is not far away, because this friendship led the Milesians to shave their heads and put on mourning when Sybaris was captured by the men of Kroton, just as if a close relative had died.

The commonest manifestation of metaphorical kinship was that between colony and mother-city, *apoikia* and *metropolis*, although this does not explain the frankly mysterious relationship between Thebes and Aigina (shared fear and dislike of the Athenians may be enough to explain it),[56] or that between Miletos and Sybaris; 'doubtless commercial', say How and Wells of the latter.[57] Again, past benefactions, in the form of military help, could result in non-colonial closeness; thus the Eretrians sent a contribution of five triremes to the Ionian revolt 'not as a favour to the

---

[51] **49**.3. The passage is puzzling, and one might consider an alternative way of taking it, as an indistinct allusion to the tradition that Miletos in particular was founded from Dorian Krete; but see n.

[52] The essential work on 'kinship diplomacy', the political exploitation of such ties, is now C. P. Jones 1999. The phenomenon was classical, not just Hellenistic: *CT* II: 61–80 and esp. M. Fragoulaki, forthcoming.

[53] **79–81**. The Theban Pindar, who wrote many victory odes for Aiginetans, naturally emphasises this connection, most vividly in *Isthm.* 8.

[54] 7. 150.2.   [55] 6. 21.1. For ritualised friendship, see Herman 1987.

[56] As AHG suggests.

[57] There is (slight) ancient evidence for this. In *c.* 300 BC, the Sicilian historian Timaios (*FGrHist* 566 F 50) explained the friendship as due to the wearing by Sybarites of Milesian wool. See 6.21.1n.

Athenians but to repay a favour' when the Milesians had helped them in
the Lelantine War against the Eretrians' Euboian neighbours the Chalkidians, perhaps as much as two centuries earlier.⁵⁸ The Samians, at odds with
the Milesians as so often throughout their history, helped the Chalkidians
in that earlier war.

But from now on we shall be concerned only with kinship ties between
colony and mother-city. It was not necessary that the two sides of a colonial
relationship should be *poleis*: the kings of Macedon, not the Macedonian
poleis, claimed descent from the Peloponnesian *polis* of Argos as the result
of – in effect – a mythically and picturesquely presented act of colonisa-
tion.⁵⁹

Colonial kinship ties are not always spelt out by Hdt. For instance, he
tells us in bk. 3 (the narrative about Demokedes the doctor from Kroton)
that the people of Taras in south Italy were specially friendly, φίλοι μάλιστα,
with the Knidians in Karia. In fact, we can go further: the two cities were
colonial 'sisters', because both places ranked as Spartan colonies.⁶⁰ Hdt.
took this knowledge for granted.⁶¹ This example shows that we must not
always demand that Hdt. should tell us explicitly of a colonial connection.
Such kinship ties are, however, likely to have been important factors in the
outbreak and spread of the Ionian revolt, although the only one he admits
is that between Miletos and Athens. We have seen above (p. 16) that one
powerful catalyst for the revolt is likely to have been the example of the
Kleisthenic reforms in 508/7 at Athens, which saw itself and was seen as
the mother-city of the Ionians. Once the revolt had started, Aristagores
the Milesian was able, at Athens, to appeal to considerations of kinship in
a more precise and compelling way than he had done at Sparta: Hdt. tells
us, in indirect speech, that he said the same as at Sparta but *added that the
Milesians are colonists of the Athenians*, ταῦτά τε δὴ ἔλεγε καὶ πρὸς τοῖσι τάδε,
ὡς οἱ Μιλήσιοι τῶν Ἀθηναίων εἰσι ἄποικοι... Hdt. introduced this notion long

⁵⁸ **99**.1.   ⁵⁹ **22**; 8.138–9.
⁶⁰ 3.138.2, where the unstated reason for the friendship was already seen by
Stein. For Knidos as Spartan colony, see 1.174.2 with Lewis 1977: 97 and Malkin
1994: 81, cf. *CT* III: 137. For Taras see Malkin ch. 4 and the testimonia at 128 n.
67. The fact was well known – Taras is Sparta's best attested and most important
historical colony – but Hdt. does not happen to mention it. The earliest literary
source is *FGrHist* 555 Antiochos F 13 (5th cent.).
⁶¹ For a much more speculative example, from bk. 5, see **1**.1n. on πρώτους μὲν
Περινθίους (Samian colonisation of Perinthos, never mentioned by Hdt., may help
to explain his good knowledge of Perinthian history and his manner of handling
it). It is a curious fact that Hdt. represents Thasos as a purely Phoenician settlement
(6.47.1). The usual story had Thasos colonised from Greek Paros. See Th. 4.104.4,
Thasos a Παρίων ἀποικία, quietly correcting Hdt.'s omission; Strabo 10.5.7; and esp.
Archilochos fr. 21 West (from Plut. *Mor.* 604c) 'slandering Thasos' by calling it a
hog's back, ὄνου ῥάχις and 22 West (from Ath. 523d).

ago, in bk. 1.[62] To be sure, we cannot be certain that Aristagores spoke exactly as Hdt. reports, or that the appeal was viewed by all Athenians as more than clever rhetoric. But they did send a fleet of twenty ships, and the name of the Athenian commander Melanthios, which recalls that of Melanthos, one of the mythical Ionian kings of Athens, is a small indication that Ionian solidarity was indeed a factor.[63]

Miletos was itself a great colonising polis in the archaic period, particularly in the Hellespontine, Propontic and Black Sea regions. This surely has a bearing on the northward spread of the revolt, though we must not exaggerate: the Black Sea region was not affected, and the secession of Megarian colonies like Byzantion cannot be explained in this way (though see 103 and 117nn. for a possible Milesian element at Byzantion). When Aristagores wins over cities in this area, Hdt. reports his success vaguely ('he sailed to the Hellespont and won over Byzantion and the other cities there'), but he enumerates them later, when they are reconquered by the Persian Daurises:[64] Dardanos, Abydos, Perkote, Lampsakos, Paisos, Parion; a later ch. adds Kios, and from bk. 6 we can add to the list of rebel states Prokonnesos, Artake and apparently Kyzikos. Several of these were Milesian colonies: Abydos, Paisos, Prokonnesos, Artake and Kyzikos were so for sure, and the Milesians laid a claim to Parion. Dardanos and Perkote are of unknown origin, i.e. are not known to be non-Milesian. Lampsakos may have contained a Milesian element, and Kios was certainly a Milesian foundation.[65] Surely these cities were consciously following the lead of the mother-city, and colonial loyalty should be added to the causes of the Ionian revolt in its wider extension.

5 PERSONAL NAMES IN BOOKS 5 AND 6

(a) General considerations

Personal names provide a check on a historian's accuracy.[66] One category of names is particularly helpful: those which are generally rare, but

---

[62] **97**.2; 1.146.　　[63] **97**.3, cf. **65**.3.　　[64] **103**.2; **117**.

[65] See **117** with *IACP* nos. 774 (Dardanos), 765 (Abydos), 788 (Perkote), 748 (Lampsakos), 755 (Paisos), 756 (Parion). For Prokonnesos (759), Artake (736), and Kyzikos (747) see 6.33.2–3 and nn. Lampsakos, though Phokaian, is said to be Milesian by Strabo (13.1.9) and though *IACP* p. 987 (Avram) dismisses this as erroneous, it may indicate a Milesian element in the population. For Kios (also a Milesian foundation, *IACP* no. 745), see **122**.1.

[66] The present discussion is not concerned with 'speaking names' in Hdt., or with his marked interest in names generally. (Two crude indicators: (1) οὔνομα alone occurs 277 times in the *Histories* as a whole, as against Th.'s 32 uses of ὄνομα; (2) there are 473 named persons in Th., but 940 in Hdt., cf. *TT*: 105). For these topics in bk. 5, see Irwin 2007: 46–7 and 58. In bk. 6, good exx. of speaking names are

common in, and even characteristic of, a particular *polis* or region.[67] Good examples are the purely Cypriot name Stesenor or Stasanor also borne by one of Alexander the Great's satraps, from Cypriot Soloi (**113**.1 n.), and Onesilos, who has a characteristically Cypriot name in Ones- (**104**.1 n.). Another is the Thessalian name Kineas (**63**.3 and n.).[68] In Hdt., a Thessalian name found out of its natural context is that of Echekrates, the father of Eetion and grandfather of Kypselos of Korinth (**92β** 1), and so one of the earliest historical individuals in all the *Histories*, given that Kypselos himself came to power *c.* 650 BC. Some kind of marriage or other connection with Thessaly has been conjectured for Echekrates, just as the patronym of the Athenian Miltiades son of Kypselos (6.34.1) indicates a similar sort of connection: between the same Korinthian family, and an Athenian aristocratic one. (The Athenian Kypselos is also attested epigraphically, as an archon at Athens in 597/6, but the name did not thereafter establish itself at Athens.)[69]

By contrast, unique names (like that of the Mytilenaian tyrant Koes, **37**.1) are of little use, though they may be interestingly formed, and a name which has no resemblance whatever to any attested name is unusual indeed. Thus the Spartan name Anchimolios or -olos (**63**.4 and n.) cannot be paralleled exactly anywhere in the Greek world, except by hypothetical restorations which are based on the secure Herodotean individual (so that to generalise about distribution is to risk circularity). The meaning must be something like 'coming near', ἀγχοῦ; compare Anchises, to whom the goddess Aphrodite was so 'near' that a son, Aineias, was the result. Philokypros (**113**.2) is, as we might have expected, confined to Cyprus, where there are half a dozen examples, most of them early; like other names formed in -kypros it displays pride in whole-island status, despite the political

---

Krios the Aiginetan 'Mr Ram', subject of a grim joke by Kleomenes (6.50.3) and the Spartan king Demaretos, 'prayed for by the people' (6.63.3). For concealed name-play see 6.37.2, where part of the point of the simile about the Lampsakenes being chopped down like a pine-tree, πίτυος τρόπον, resides in the old name for Lampsakos, Pityousa; but Hdt. does not say so. Hdt.'s general interest in names: see e.g. 6.80 (two places called Argos) and 131.1–2, the inherited names Kleisthenes and Agariste.

[67] *TT* 102. The whole of *TT* ch. 4 discusses the value of personal names for the study of the ancient Greek historians.

[68] In what follows, it may be assumed for passages from bks. 5 and 6 that the relevant n. in the comm. discusses onomastic aspects and gives the distribution and detailed references; so from here on 'and n.' will be omitted.

[69] Generalisations and prosopographical assertions such as have been made or implied above about the names Kineas, Echekrates and Kypselos are possible only now, thanks to the near-completion in 2011 of the regionally organised *Lexicon of Greek Personal Names* (*LGPN*). Six physical volumes have appeared between 1987 and 2010, with different editors, but mostly P. M. Fraser and E. Matthews.

fragmentation of Cyprus into many city-states with separate ethnics.[70] A possible alternative or simultaneous explanation is that they are theophoric names formed from Κύπρις i.e. Cyprus-born Aphrodite (see already Hom. *Il.* 5.330); but the difference is not great, because that *epiklesis* or cult epithet is itself patriotically Cypriot.

At the other extreme, nothing can be done with names which are very frequently found everywhere, like that of the Phokaian Dionysios who is briefly prominent in the narrative of the battle of Lade (6.11–17). The theophoric names Dionysios and Apollonios are the two commonest at all periods of Greek history and in all regions.

The category of *polis*-specific names is, then, the most promising for the historian, and it must be extended so as to include colonial daughter-cities of the *polis* or region in question.[71] So, to return to Koes of Aiolian Mytilene (above), his own name may be unique, and his patronym Erxandros is not attested on Lesbos itself; but there are two attestations of Erxandros at Aiolian places on the Asiatic mainland opposite Lesbos.

(b) Milesian names in book 5

Miletos was the heart of the Ionian revolt, and this Milesian dominance is reflected onomastically in bk. 5: ten Milesian names in all. The revolt's two main instigators, Histiaios and Aristagores, were both Milesians, and the only individual in the revolt narrative who is famous for other reasons is also a Milesian: Hekataios the 'logographer' (*FGrHist* 1). These three, and their patronyms, account for six of the ten Milesian names. The other four are bit-part Milesian actors in the drama, mentioned without patronymic. All ten names are rewarding in different ways, and almost in inverse proportion to the political importance of their bearers.[72]

We may start with the most famous of all, the geographer and logographer Hekataios (see **36**.2n.). The name is theophoric, from the originally Karian goddess Hekate. It has been said that 'the East Greek bias in theophoric names formed from Hekate is quite unusually marked'.[73]

---

[70] Cf. **113**.2n. for Stasikypros.

[71] For example, if we are interested in an Aiolian name, we need to look at three separate vols. of *LGPN* IIIB (2005) for the Boiotian and Thessalian homelands, I (1987) for the islands Lesbos and Tenedos, and VA (2010) for the Aiolid, the area of Greek colonial settlement in NW Asia Minor, including the *peraia* (mainland possessions) of Lesbos. In other words, the publication of the entire Aiolian name-pool was begun in 1987 and completed only in 2010.

[72] Because Miletos is regarded by *LGPN* as Karian, it is not included in *LGPN* VA, which includes coastal Ionia but runs no further south. The information drawn on below and in the comm. was provided in summer 2011 by Richard Catling from unpublished but virtually complete *LGPN* files.

[73] Parker 2000: 69–70.

The earliest evidence for the cult of Hekate comes from, precisely, Mile-tos. In the important 'Molpoi decree' from the mid fifth century, an offer-ing is to be placed at the sanctuary of Hekate, and a paian is to be sung there.[74] Hekataios is not a rare name and is widely dispersed; but the files of *LGPN* show the name to be particularly favoured in Karia. Hekataios' patronym Hegesandros is delayed until almost the end of bk. 5 (**125**). The name is common, but is particularly so in the Dodecanese and above all on Rhodes.

But the first Milesian we encounter is not Hekataios but Histiaios, who will also be the last Milesian to be named in the unit composed of bk. 5 and early bk. 6 (**11**.1 and 6.46.2);[75] the Milesian who, in the story told by Leutychides, leaves a deposit with the Spartan Glaukos (6.86) is not named. Histiaios has in fact featured even earlier than bk. 5 (see 4.137–9 and 141 for his role at the Hellespont), but we will not find out his patronym Lysagores until **30**.2. The name Histiaios is specially common at Miletos and Milesian colonies, and the cult of Hestia was prominent at Miletos.

Alongside Histiaios, the most prominent Milesian in Herodotus bk. 5 is Aristagores, whose own name is common everywhere in the Greek world. By contrast his unusual but epigraphically attested patronym Molpagores (derived from *molpos*, 'singer') is of great interest. The name appears sev-eral times in the fifth century, sometimes as patronym, in the series of inscriptions from the Delphinion (temple of Apollo at Miletos) listing the eponymous magistrates of the city, who are variously and at different peri-ods called *stephanephoroi, aisymnetai,* or Molpoi.[76]

Names in –agores (from ἀγορεύω, I speak) are common everywhere, but seem specially so at Miletos; another Herodotean example is Lysagores the father of Histiaios (**30**.2. Hdt. delays the patronymic until he can give it together with the name and patronym of his kinsman Aristagores son of Molpagores). In addition to the present two, and Lysagores just below, see **37**.1 (Ietragores) and **126**.1 (Pythagores). As we shall see, Ietragores and Pythagores both have Apolline flavours, as does Molpagores.

The name Molpagores is much rarer, and therefore more interesting, than Aristagores. The name Molpagores/oras is virtually unattested in the Greek world except at Miletos itself and its colonies: printouts of unpub-lished material show there were eleven bearers of the name at Miletos. We can trace it at Milesian colonies in the Black Sea and pro-Pontic regions (Sinope, Kyzikos, Pantikapaion and neighbours, Olbia, and the Kian at Polyb. 15.20.1), and at Hellenistic Amorgos, where we know Milesians

---

[74] Herda 2006. The root *molp-* means singing.
[75] His absolutely final mention is in the speech of Artabanos at 7.10 γ 2.
[76] Rehm 1914: nos. 122–8. See **30**.2n.

settled. This is a very remarkable example of *polis*-specific name-diffusion. Otherwise there are just two Abderans and two Ephesians.[77]

Onomastically, the prize for interest goes to Ietragores, who is sent by Aristagores on a James Bond-like mission to seize by trickery a group of Asia Minor tyrants (**37**.1). Herodotus does not actually say that he was a Milesian, but his narrative in **36** implies it, and the name, though exceptionally rare elsewhere, is in fact attested at Miletos: a Diomedon son of Ietragores was *stephanephoros* in 417/16. (Otherwise, there is just one other attested anywhere, and he too is from not far away in Karia, from Hydis(s)os south of Mylasa.) Diomedon is perhaps a little too young to be the son of Hdt.'s Ietragores, but he could be another close relative. Such 'floating kindreds' can be as useful to the social historian as is exact identity. For the prefix Ietr- (Attic Iatr-) it is relevant that Apollo was the healer god and is sometimes actually referred to by the title ἰατρός.[78]

Similarly Pythagores, whom Aristagores appoints as his deputy at Miletos (**126**.1), has a theophoric name formed from Pythian Apollo. He is not identical with Pythagores son of Mnesarchos at 4.95.1-2 (more familiar as the Samian philosopher Pythagoras). The name is fairly common everywhere. There are, however, no occurrences in the earliest two of the Milesian *stephanephoroi* lists. There is another possible Milesian, at Delos; and there are several at Karian Tralles.

The two remaining Milesian names, Charopinos (brother of Aristagores) and Hermophantos, form a pair. They were appointed by Aristagores to command the allied expedition against Sardis while he himself stayed at Miletos (**99**.2). That Aristagores had a brother is news to us at this point, although we were told earlier (**30**.2) that Histiaios and Aristagores were related in more than one way, and so we saw that these people liked to keep things in the family. Charopinos is not a specially rare name, but the greatest concentrations are at Ephesos (five bearers of the name) and at Miletos, where there are six bearers, all earlier than 200 BC, of whom Hdt.'s man is no. (1); three of the others are in the list of *stephanephoroi*. The most interesting of these is Charopinos son of Mandronaktides (and therefore not identical with Hdt.'s Charopinos, who is son of Molpagores because brother of Aristagores), *stephanephoros* in 476/5 BC. It is a 'herophoric' name, formed from the heroic name Χάροψ or Χάροπος (which was e.g. the patronym of Nireus at *Il.* 2.672). The patronym Mandronaktides is a river-name, formed from the Maeander (Thonemann 2006).

The name Hermophantos can be either theophoric from Hermes, or else another river-name, derived from the Hermos. The suffix – phantos,

---

[77] See also Jones 1988: 194 (discussing an inscription from Sinope).
[78] See e.g. Lykoph. *Alex.* 1207 and 1377.

'revealed by', is consistent with either. The name is specially common in Chios and in Karia: there are seven attested bearers of the name at Miletos alone.

(c) Milesian conclusions

At the most basic level, onomastic evidence has allowed us to identify as Milesian a man given no patronym or ethnic by Hdt.: Ietragores. But 'confirm' might be a better word, because the historical context of his mission makes that identification attractive on other grounds.

Ietragores resembles other of our ten Milesians, and very many Milesians known from epigraphy, in having a theophoric name derived from an aspect or *epiklesis* (cult epithet) of Apollo, the patron god of Didyma.[79] After all, that great treasure-store of onomastic evidence, the series of lists of the Milesian *stephanephoroi*, was found at the Delphinion, Apollo's temple. Of the names considered above, Ietragores, Molpagores and Pythagores are all Apolline.

For the student of Hdt., the main importance of these names is prosopographic: the '*molpoi* mafia' is behind the Ionian revolt in its Milesian aspect. Not only are Aristagores and Histiaios closely related to each other, and in more than one way; they also belong to a cluster of families which onomastic evidence suggests was a wealthy elite, because it was well represented among the *stephanephoroi* of the fifth century. It therefore survived the failure of the Ionian revolt, the capture of Miletos, and the consequent redistribution of territory. When the assault on Sardis is launched, we learn that Aristagores has another kinsman, his brother Charopinos, whom he appoints as co-commander of the army. Hdt. does not tell us, and we should not assume, that the distinguished Milesian Pythagores, whom Aristagores leaves to govern Miletos at the end of bk. 5, was yet another relative; Hdt.'s silence on the point should be respected, since he is so well informed about Aristagores' family and its ramifications.

(d) Non-Greek names in books 5 and 6

Miletos was a part-Karian city, so that some of those already considered may well have had Karian blood. Histiaios son of Tymnes of Karian Termera (one of Ietragores' victims at the start of the revolt, **37**.1) has a Greek theophoric name but a Karian patronym. Pure Karians are also onomastically well attested in bk. 5, beginning with the name and patronym of another of Ietragores' victims, Oliatos son of Ibanollis of Mylasa. Such names can be paralleled from Greco-Karian epigraphy, above all a long

---

[79] Though Ietros/Iatros may have been a separate healer hero.

mid fifth-century list of names from Hdt.'s home city, half-Karian Halikarnassos.[80] But naturally the Karian phase of the developed 'Ionian' revolt is also onomastically productive: Herakleides son of Ibanollis (and so a brother of the probable tyrant of Mylasa, Oliatos?) was the hero of the ambush at Karian Pidasa (**121**), and was the subject of the first biography, by Skylax of Karyanda. Herakleides, like Histiaios son of Tymnes, has a Greek name; but his father and perhaps his brother have Karian ones.

The most prosopographically suggestive individual in this Karian section of bk. 5 is Pixodaros son of Mausolos of Kindye (**118.2**). Those two names are Karian not Greek, and were borne in the fourth century by a pair of brothers, both of them satraps of Karia and sons of Hekatomnos, who gave his name to the Hekatomnid dynasty whose last member was the female satrap Ada. Some family connection is likely, perhaps even direct ancestry, in which case Pixodaros is a top man in his region. It is surely relevant that Hdt. tells us that he is married to a Kilikian princess, daughter of Syennesis (for the anonymity see (*d*) below); this may be a way of indicating Pixodaros' high social standing. Syennesis' family ruled Kilikia as a pocket principality inside the Achaemenid Persian empire from the sixth century to the fourth; it invites comparison with the Karian Hekatomnid dynasty.[81] The evidence for the Kilikian family comes from Aeschylus, Xenophon and now an inscription from Karian Iasos, as well as from Hdt.

Lydian names are in short supply in bk. 5: there is no named Lydian individual in the Sardis narrative (**100–2**). But in the Karian sequel we hear of one Lydian, Myrsos son of Gyges. He died fighting on the Persian side against the Karians at the ambush led by Herakleides of Mylasa (**121**). So at least one elite Lydian was not tempted to throw in his lot with the anti-Persian rebels. A 'Myrsos son of Gyges, a Lydian man' has already featured in the Samian narrative (3.122.1). Identity cannot be proved, but is likely. Myrsos is also the patronym of the Lydian king Kandaules (1.7.4).

Persian names in bks. 5 and 6 are given with reasonable accuracy, subject to the usual shifts by which, for instance, theophoric names in Baga- become Mega-.[82] The activity of some, like Datis the Mede, has been further illuminated by the publication from the late 1960s of the Persepolis Fortification Tablets. The cluster of named royal generals sent to deal with the trouble in the westernmost satrapies (**116**) is an index of the seriousness with which the king takes it.

---

[80] *Syll.*[3] : no. 46.

[81] Hornblower 2011, and for a suggested family tree of the Kilikian rulers, see below: p. 302.

[82] See on **1**.1 for Megabyzos (Bagabadus).

(e) Non-naming

Anonymity can be as effective a strategy as naming. But sometimes a historian may not give a personal name for the banal reason that he does not know it and could not find it out. The same reason may explain why a name is supplied but not a patronym; occasionally (as with the casual sole mention of Ietragores at **37**.1) it may be that Hdt. has forgotten that a character has not yet been introduced. A woman may be left respectfully unnamed for cultural reasons,[83] but these were less obviously operative on the east Greek Hdt. than on Th. and the Attic orators. The Spartan princess Gorgo is named (**48**); the Kilikian princess married to Pixodaros (above) is not. The former, unlike the latter, will have a part to play later in the narrative, both inside bk. 5 and beyond it. Again, two tall and beautiful women are dressed up by men as a ruse, one in bk. 1 and the other in bk. 5, but one is named while the other is not, although the women are described in very similar language.[84] The men (Peisistratos of Athens, the Paionian brothers Pigres and Mastyes) are named. Here the reason for the difference in naming is not so easy to see. Perhaps the Phye story was better known.

Some non-namings present even greater challenges. The cautionary story of Glaukos the Spartan, told by Leutychides (6.86), involves a Milesian who leaves a deposit of money with Glaukos. But the Milesian is not named, even when he introduces himself (86 α 3): εἰμὶ μὲν Μιλήσιος, ἥκω δέ... and so on. In real life, he could hardly not have given his name at this point.[85] Nor are we told the names of any of the Milesian's children, who come to Sparta at a much later date to collect their father's money (86 β 1). Hdt. evidently wishes to direct our attention exclusively to Glaukos himself. He will leave no descendants (unlike the Milesian) and no 'hearth' (86 δ). The utter horror of the complete elimination of his line is paradoxically enhanced by the narrative technique which makes him the one named individual in the story. He will otherwise leave no name behind him.[86]

---

[83] Schaps 1977. For a dynastically important but unnamed royal Spartan woman, see the tree below, p. 152.

[84] 1. 60.4 (Phye), contrast **12**.2 (the anonymous sister).

[85] An important theme here is the reminiscence of Kleomenes and Aristagores (**49–51**): two elite Spartans are tempted by money brought by rich Milesians. This helps to explain the anonymity of the Milesian ξεῖνος; cf. Kleomenes' address at **49**.9, ὦ ξεῖνε Μιλήσιε, and note that 6.86. β 2, ἀναβάλλομαι κυρώσειν ἐς τέταρτον μῆνα, is a palpable echo of the same bk. 5 passage (ἀναβάλλομαί τοι ἐς τρίτην ἡμέρην).

[86] Glaukos, whose name occurs ten times in 6.86, will leave nothing and nobody behind him. It is a curious fact that although the name Glaukos ('sparkling eyed') is not at all uncommon anywhere and at any period (fifty bearers of the name at Athens, thirty-one in the Peloponnese as a whole, see *LGPN* II and IIIA), the only Spartan Glaukos in a thousand onomastically covered years is precisely Hdt.'s man.

In a comparable way, the extended Cypriot narrative of Artybios the Persian and his clever Karian squire (**111–12**) needs the squire to be anonymous in a way that Oibares, Dareios' clever and otherwise comparable groom, is not (3.85–8): the Karian squire insists on his own insignificance compared to his master (**111**.4). The priestess on the Athenian acropolis who challenges Kleomenes (**72**.3) is arguably anonymous because she speaks for Athena and Athena's city.[87]

One category of person is anonymous because the story-type virtually requires it: the pattern of the one smart person (τις) who realises what others do not. In bk. 5 there is the Theban who eventually sees that the city's 'nearest' are not physical neighbours but the Aiginetans (because the nymphs Thebe and Aigina are twin sisters in myth), and in bk. 6, the elderly Lampsakene who is eventually able to explain to his baffled fellow-citizens the true and terrible meaning of 'cutting down like a pine-tree': **80**.1 and 6.37.2, both times with the formula κοτὲ μαθών τις. But Gorgo breaks the rules here too, because only she will work out that the blank tablet will reveal a message if the wax is scraped off (7.239.4), and she is named.

(f) General conclusions

The claim that names are a control on a historian's accuracy does not imply a claim as to the truth of everything else he says. To take only the most satisfying single example from bk. 5, onomastic evidence, derived from an inscribed list of Milesian names, makes it very likely that Hdt. has recorded accurately the close-to-unique name Ietragores. More generally, the same sort of epigraphic evidence shows that Aristagores and Histiaios belonged to a close-knit Milesian elite. But that does not carry with it a guarantee of, say, the truth of the story of the slave with the tattooed head sent by Histiaios (**35**). It does, however, show that careful detailed research went into Hdt.'s narrative of the Ionian revolt. Many of the non-Greek names and patronyms in his text can also be checked against epigraphic evidence, and with the same impressive results for his accuracy.

In book 6, the list of Agariste's suitors can also be checked onomastically.[88] The story has been radically doubted, partly because of its similarity to folk-tales in other cultures and to Greek epic precedents, partly because, on an ultra-sceptical view, the suitors are thrown together, in splendid defiance of chronology, as a mere elaboration of the initial proposition (126.1) that Kleisthenes of Sikyon wanted 'the best of the Greeks' for his

---

[87] For the anonymity of the seven Persians at **17**.1, see n. there.

[88] 6. 127. For example, Laphanes son of Euphorion from Arkadian Paion has a good Arkadian name, attested in R/O no. 32 (inscription from c. 369 honouring the Athenian Phylarchos). He is from Kynouria.

daughter.[89] A name-check does, however, suggest that at very least, Hdt. took the trouble to invent plausible names. But we can go further if we look at the suitors' ethnics (indicators of local origin) as well as their names, and ethnics are part of full nomenclature. If we start from Kleisthenes' proclamation at the Olympia festival (126.2), the suitors' places of origin make good sense. The local nature of the early Olympic victor lists is a guarantee of believability (thus there is a good showing of Messenians until their loss of independence to Sparta at the end of the eighth century). Hdt.'s own emphasis on the Peloponnese (127.3 and 4) corresponds to the reality as evidenced in the Olympic victor lists.[90] The general areas indicated by Hdt. can, with the sole exception of Aitolia – and even here there is a mythical tradition of wrestling and foot-races – be satisfyingly paralleled from the historical victor lists in the early stretches. The conspicuous and often-remarked absences of important cities and areas can also be explained along these lines.[91]

Again, as with the convincing-looking Milesians in bk. 5, these plausible names and ethnics at the end of bk. 6 do not prove the truth of the story of Agariste's suitors. For one thing we should allow for what Roland Barthes called the 'reality effect':[92] the best fiction is improved by a degree of circumstantiality. But these historically plausible details and patterns need to be set against the folkloric features: historical considerations must, as always with Hdt., be balanced with literary.

Naming and non-naming are also narrative techniques – as is the use of name-replacing patronyms, and other forms of denomination.[93] When Hdt. makes Kleisthenes of Sikyon, at a climactic moment, address Hippokleides of Athens as 'son of Teisandros' (6.129.4), he is both adding to the existing Homeric decor of the story and also avoiding over-use of the man's own name, which will be needed for the punch-line 'Hippokleides doesn't care'. It is also possible that the patronym here implies ironic imitation of politeness.[94] When reading Hdt., it is always worth asking 'why this name or designation, in this form, here?' or 'why is this person not named?'

6 RELIGION: GODS, HEROES AND EPIPHANIES

'It is all on a human level', Chris Pelling has observed about the Ionian revolt, and he continues 'This is perhaps part of the general absence of

---

[89] Müller 2006: 230, 232.   [90] For which see Moretti 1957.

[91] For all this, see Hornblower, 'Agariste's suitors: an Olympic note', forthcoming. Note that some of the descriptors in 6.127 take the form ἀπό or ἐκ followed by city or area. Such descriptors usually form part of 'expanded ethnics' (indicating region+city), for which see Fraser 2009: 119–45.

[92] See *TT*: 112.   [93] For this notion, see esp. de Jong 1993.

[94] Dickey 1996: 55, though she nowhere discusses this particular passage.

the gods and the divine from the surface of Book 5'.[95] The formulation
is careful, and the qualification ('from the *surface*') is important.[96] This
section will ask how the 'divine' (τὸ θεῖον)[97] makes itself felt in bks.
5 and 6, whether on or beneath the surface. It is not intended as a general treatment of Hdt. and religion, whether that is taken to mean his own attitude to religion,[98] or the plentiful evidence he provides for Greek religion, which he often does not directly but through comparative remarks
about non-Greeks.[99]

(a) Gods and epiphanies

The manifested presence of a god is an epiphany.[100] It is not necessarily
a visual experience: Philippides heard the voice of Pan, he did not see a
little goat-like figure with horns and a tail. An epiphany denied is still an
epiphany narrated, and Hdt. has it both ways when in bk. 5 he reports,
with a formula for personal religious disbelief found elsewhere, that the
statues of Damie and Auxesie fell to their knees.[101] On the other hand,
bk. 6 contains, in the alleged epiphany of Pan to Philippides before the
battle of Marathon,[102] the closest Hdt. gets to an epiphany narrative of an
'epic' sort, that is, a fully 'characterful narration of divine action';[103] and
here his disbelief is much less palpable. But that passage is exceptional.[104]
Hdt. is not normally comfortable with the physical collision of human and

95 Pelling 2007: 197f., and n. 68, where Rood is cited for his remark that bk. 5
is 'Herodotus' most Thucydidean book'.
96 Pelling himself – also n. 68 – cites another colleague, Thomas Harrison, for
the observation that 'there may be more divine suggestions below that surface'.
97 For this term for divinity, see Harrison 2000: 177–81 and Scullion 2006: 195.
98 On this contentious subject see Gould 1994, Harrison 2000, both criticised
by Scullion 2006: esp. 204, for whom Hdt. is a 'pious sceptic' not a 'pious believer'.
See also Roettig 2010, though her main focus is on bk. 7 and Xerxes.
99 For an interesting suggestion as to why this is so, see Scullion 2006: 201. (Hdt.
uses this 'indirect or diplomatic' approach as a way of criticising Greek religion.)
100 There are grey areas here. In a world full of gods, even a change of wind
direction could be regarded as an 'epiphany' (Hellenistic philosophers had fun
with this, see Parker 2011: 97 and n. 84). Consider 6.44.2, the storm which wrecked
Mardonios' fleet, βορῆς ἄνεμος μέγας. Powell distinguishes between βορέης, the N.
wind, and ὁ Βορῆς (contracted), 'the deity', as at 7.189. But Greeks would not have
made the theological distinction thus sharply. The Mardonios storm was indeed a
kind of epiphany. (Note the similarity of language at 7.189.)
101 **86**.3; cf. 1.182.1 and 4.5.1. See Scullion 2006: 207 n. 36.
102 6.105. See Hornblower 2003.
103 See Feeney 1991: 261 for such 'characterful' divine narration as the criterion
for distinguishing epic from history. Feeney 2007 offers a different criterion, in
terms of the difference between mythical and historical time.
104 It is balanced, at the end of the narrative of the greater miracle which is the
Marathon victory, by the strange apparition experienced by Epizelos (6.117.2–3).
This is unusual in that the huge figure is fighting on the Persian side. Hdt. does not
know, or at any rate does not report, the story that Theseus appeared in the battle

divine.[105] One pair of gods are, however, famously prone to epiphany, namely the Dioskouroi (or Tyndaridai),[106] and these two are reported in Hdt.'s text, just as they are in the poem which has become known as the 'New Simonides',[107] as having accompanied the Spartan army out to war.[108]

Hdt. is, however, happy to report, with no suggestion of disbelief or even doubt, that 'the god' sends warnings. We have to supply for ourselves the subject of the curiously truncated authorial comment that '[...] likes, it seems, to send warnings, φιλέει δέ κως προσημαίνειν, of impending disaster to a polis or ethnos'; this introduces the story of the double misfortune which befell the Chians after the battle of Lade.[109] A few lines later (para. 3), Hdt. says resumptively 'those were the signs which 'the god' sent. The otherwise similar comment which introduces the Delos earthquake attributes the warning explicitly to 'the god', ὁ θεός.[110] By contrast, no theological comment accompanies the two mentions of the priestess at Karian Pedasa who grew a beard when something bad was going to happen.[111]

Oracular utterances and other types of divinatory signs, including dreams, must be treated in this general context.[112] There are plenty in bks. 5 and 6, starting with the first ch. of bk. 5 and ending with the last ch. of bk. 6;[113] in between, the Peisistratids are specially singled out for their fondness for divination.[114] But the central and straddling theme of the two books is the Ionian revolt, and it is remarkable that, although the temple complex at Branchidai is mentioned for its financial resources in the

on the Greek/Athenian side (Plut. Thes. 35; maybe derived from the stoa poikile painting, Paus. 1.15).

[105] Scullion 2006: 202 on Hdt.'s 'resistance to association of corporeality with the divine', and similarly Harrison 2000: 88–9. For the possible epiphany of Helen at 6.61.4, see below, n. 140. For the phantom (Astrabakos?) which appeared to the wife of Ariston king of Sparta, see 6.69.1.

[106] R. C. T. P[arker], OCD⁴ 'Dioscuri': 'their characteristic mode of action is epiphany at a moment of crisis'.

[107] P. Oxy. 3965.

[108] 75.2 (both of them originally, then only one after the passing of the rule prohibiting both Spartan kings from campaigning together).

[109] 6. 27.1. For the problem about the ellipse here, see Harrison 2000: 172f. and n. 61, who offers the alternative tr. 'there tend to be signs in advance'. He notes that Macan suggested that 'the god' here is Zeus. The text may not be sound.

[110] 6. 98.1.

[111] 1. 175; also 8.104, which should not be deleted as interpolation.

[112] There is an overlap here with epiphanies. The 'tall, good-looking man' who stands over Hipparchos in his sleep at 56.1 is an epiphany ('standing over' is a regular formula for divine epiphanies, as shown by the Lindian anagraphe, see n. on the passage). But dreams are also one source of divination; see R. C. T. P[arker], OCD⁴, 'divination, Greek'. See n. 114 below, and esp. 56.2n. on ὀνειροπόλοισι.

[113] 1.2, 'the god' gives an oracle to the Paionians; 6.140.1, Delphic oracle about Athens and Lemnos.

[114] 93.2 and n. Note the dreams of both Hipparchos and Hippias (56; 6.107).

context of a discussion about revolt, Hdt. gives no hint that the local oracle was consulted by the Ionians on the advisability of revolt (**36**). There are three possibilities: there was in fact no consultation; there was one but Hdt. did not know about it; there was one but he chose not to report it. The last possibility seems the likeliest, especially given that another literary source, the Atthidographer (local historian of Attica) Demon, may attest a consultation by the Karians.[115] If this approach is right, it certainly bears out Pelling's remark about the revolt that it is 'all on a human level'. The secular implications of this passage (**36**) need, however, to be qualified in view of the double oracle supposedly given in about 499 to the Milesians (in their absence) and the Argives by another mantic Apollo: the god at Delphi.[116] It is not certain that this oracle was an invention after the fact. However that may be, it is notable that Hdt. does not mention this or any other oracle in his narrative of the opening phase of the revolt, just as Th. waits until after the Sicilian expedition was over and had failed before telling us (8.1.1) about the oracles and soothsayers by which the Athenians were fatally encouraged to sail in the first place. The difference is that the oracle given to the Milesians at Delphi was pessimistic.

There are other ways in which the divine can make itself felt, but they involve a subjective act of categorisation which (as Hdt. makes clear) might or might not command agreement. It may well be that when Hdt. says that *tisis*, requital, overtook somebody, he means that this was divinely sent, even though specifically divine vocabulary is absent. Both Leutychides and Kleomenes are said, just twelve chapters apart in bk. 6, to have 'requited requital' to Demaretos, and this has been seen as the hidden hand of the god who checks excess.[117] On the second occasion, but not the first, Hdt. adds that this is his own opinion. Elsewhere he can deny that a bad outcome was punishment for a bad action, again making clear that this is his

---

[115] See **36**.3n., *The sanctuary of Branchidai.*   [116] 6.19 and 77.2.

[117] 6. 72.1 and 84.3, both passages treated by Scullion 2006: 203 with 208 n. 43 as divine checking of excess, along with 4.202 and 205 (Pheretime punished for her impaling and mutilation of the Barkaians). Kleomenes and Pheretime fit the 'excess' category better than does Leutychides, and Nock 1972: 545 n. 48 observed that at 6.84.3, Hdt. 'speaks simply of C. as paying the penalty due to Demaratus, i.e. atoning for the human injustice and not the sacrilege'. See also 8.106.4 '*tisis* and Hermotimos overtook Panionios'. At 106.3, Hermotimos has said that 'the gods' have delivered Panionios into his hands. It is noticeable that in the matter of τίσις, Hdt. is not quite even-handed as between men and women. The appalling requital exacted by Pheretime is said to have drawn down the disapproval of the gods; the equally horrific requital which Hermotimos exacts (another dreadful mutilation) is merely said to be the greatest we know of, i.e. strictly greater than Pheretime's: 8.105.1, with no disapproving authorial comment. It seems that, in the view of our male author and his expected readers, horrific acts are worse when a woman does them. On Hdt.'s inconsistent attitude to these two horrors see Nilsson 1967: 761.

own view (the destruction of Attica was *not* the result of Athenian maltreatment of Xerxes' heralds).[118] This sort of subjectivity is less often available where divination is concerned (either a consultation took place or it did not), although Hdt. can make a speaker deny that dreams are divinely sent.[119] Sometimes Hdt. leaves us to draw our own conclusions. Leutychides, who wants to frighten the Athenians into returning some Aiginetan hostages, tells the Athenians an irrelevant story about Glaukos the oath-breaking Spartan, and he threatens the Athenians with the equivalent of Glaukos' fate, which was the annihilation of his family.[120] This annihilation does not happen to the Athenians, and we are surely meant to reflect that there is something wrong with the original analogy. The Athenians have not, in fact, sworn to anything at all, unlike the man in the story, nor does anything bad happen to them: if anything, it happens to Leutychides himself.[121] The conclusion that the Athenians suffer no annihilation can (it has been suggested) be avoided if we take the infinitely extendable long view: the Athenians do eventually suffer harm.[122] But this is not satisfactory. The kind of total extinction which Leutychides has in mind for the Athenians is more like what will actually happen to the Aiginetans after 431; even after their total defeat in 404 – surely far too late for Hdt. to have known about – the Athenians were not wiped out, though some of the Spartans' allies wanted this to happen.

But it is true that divine vengeance can be postponed, or may operate gradually, even across the entire *Histories*. The double Chian misfortune in bk. 6, already mentioned above (p. 34), is an episode in the working out of a kind of curse which began in bk. 1 with the Chians' sacrilegious and mercenary surrender of a suppliant in return for the mainland possession, Atarneus. Polluted Atarneus recurs thereafter as a signifier for Chian troubles, right up to the story of Panionios of Chios near the end of bk. 8.[123]

For the complicated dispute, involving Athenians, Epidaurians and Aiginetans, over the statues of the mysterious minor gods Damie and Auxesie, see §6(*b*). They are hard to categorise; Hdt. calls them δαίμονες, a slippery term.[124]

---

[118] 7.133.2 with Scullion 2006: 196 and 203.

[119] 7.16 β 2: Artabanos, a sophisticated argument. That Artabanos later changes his mind does not affect this point.

[120] 6.86 with *TT*: 157–9.   [121] Harrison 2000: 118.   [122] Munson 2001b.

[123] 1.160; 8.106.1–2 with Hornblower 2003; see **98**.3n. Contra, Harrison 2000: 115, who is confident that 'there is no suggestion that these disasters should be construed as instances of retribution'.

[124] **83**.3. For *daimones* see Harrison 2000: 164–9, esp. 165 on Damie and Auxesie.

(b) Heroes, heroines and hero-cults

It is to Hdt. that we owe what is perhaps the most important single piece of literary evidence[125] for the distinction between the cult of the gods and the cult of heroes.[126] In an excursus within his long Egyptian section, he says that the Greeks are right to honour Herakles in two ways or forms: to the one they sacrifice as to an immortal god and call him 'Olympian', and to the other they make special offerings (the word is ἐναγίσματα) as to a hero.[127] A Greek hero or heroine in the religious sense is thought of as a dead mortal, is often linked to a particular locality,[128] and is often honoured with a special type of 'chthonian' cult, i.e. with gloomy rituals suggestive of the underworld.[129] Heroes are potentially malign, and may need to be appeased. They are often said to be beautiful and tall, although the categories 'beautiful' and 'heroic' are certainly not isomorphic because Hdt., at any rate, describes in that way individuals who have no heroic status.[130] Some heroes (Herakles is the most obvious case) approximate to fully divine status and are part of general Greek mythology. But new heroes can be created[131] from fully historical and recently dead figures belonging to such overlapping categories as city-founders (oikists), athletes, and military enemies. Hdt. in bks. 5 and 6 provides examples of these various 'new' sorts. Miltiades the Elder received sacrifice in the Chersonese 'as

[125] As opposed to epigraphic evidence. The 5th-cent. sacred law from Selinous in W. Sicily also distinguishes clearly between sacrifice 'as to the gods' and 'as to the heroes': Jameson, Jordan and Kotansky 1993.

[126] The sharpness of the distinction has (see Ekroth 2007 with refs.) been queried, as part of a challenge to the related distinction between chthonian versus Olympian worship. That distinction is itself controversial. See R. C. T. P[arker], 'chthonian gods' in *OCD*[4]. The matter cannot be argued here. The validity of the notion of hero-cult is here assumed.

[127] 2. 44.5.   [128] But for mobility of heroes and/or their relics, see below.

[129] See above, n. 126.

[130] Harrison 2000: 162–3 argues that height and beauty are divine (and heroic) characteristics. This accounts interestingly and convincingly for some of Hdt.'s favourable refs. to physical appearance, but there is no automatic or necessary connection. Phye is beautiful and tall, and is made to impersonate Athena (1.60.4, cf. 4.180.3); but the Paionian sister who is dressed up by her brothers (**12.1**) is described in exactly similar language, and there is no suggestion that she is being passed off as a goddess or heroine. Nor is there anything heroic about the good-looking Hippokleides of Athens (6.127.4). The Persian Artachaies is very tall and is heroised by the Akanthians (7.117), but we are not told that the tall and good-looking Persian commander Tigranes (9.96.2) is heroised by anyone. Tallness and beauty make you fit for command or rule, like Xerxes (7.187), where Macan aptly compares 1 Sam. 9.2 on Saul, 'goodly... and from his shoulders and upward higher than any of the people'; cf. also Homer *Il.* 3.166–70 (the *teichoskopia*) on Agamemnon. Xerxes is neither god nor hero, despite the anonymous Hellespontine man at 7.56.2, who extravagantly compares Xerxes to Zeus, and Gorgias, who is supposed to have said that Xerxes was the Persians' Zeus ([Longinus] *Subl.* 3.2).

[131] Jones 2010.

was customary for an oikist', ὡς νόμος οἰκιστῆι, with horse-races and athletic contests – but he was also an Olympic victor in the four-horse-chariot race. Philippos of Kroton was another Olympic victor, honoured by the Egestaians of Sicily with hero-cult for his beauty – but he was also a dead enemy in need of appeasement, as was Onesilos of Cypriot Salamis, to whom the people of Amathous sacrificed as to a hero.[132]

Hdt. uses the Greek word ἥρως in the two senses recognised by many modern scholars, 'epic' and 'cultic' heroes.[133] Examples will make the point best. The first or Homeric sense[134] is unequivocally illustrated by his reference to 'the heroes who sailed in the Argo' i.e. the Argonauts (4.145.3);[135] the second and more frequent Herodotean usage is illustrated by the passage about Herakles just considered, and by the ἡρώιον awarded at Sicilian Egesta to Philippos of Kroton.[136] When Hdt. says that the Egyptians 'make no use at all of heroes', νομίζουσι δ' ὧν Αἰγύπτιοι οὐδ' ἥρωσι οὐδέν (2.50.3), he is talking about heroes of the cultic sort.[137] That remark about Egypt is valuable for its implication that hero-cult was felt

[132] Miltiades: 6.38.1 (cf. 36.1 for his Olympic victory); Philippos: **47**.2 (cf. **46**.1 for the battle between Egestaians and the invading Greeks including Philippos); Onesilos: **114**.2.

[133] Whitley 1994: 218f., citing West 1978: 370. By contrast, Harrison 2000: 159–64, who argues for confusion and contradiction in Hdt. on the topic of heroes, denies that Hdt. 'drew any of the distinctions customarily made between heroes in modern scholarship' (159). This goes too far. To be sure, Hdt. 'drew no distinctions', but that is because he was not Aristotle and did not offer that sort of analytical and taxonomic treatment (but 2.44.5 comes close to an explicit statement of the dichotomy). The question is, whether he operates with more than one sense of the same word. He surely did. His reference to the Argonauts as heroes is Homeric – see next n. – and is without religious implications. A scholarly debate in the 1970s–90s, about presence or absence of hero-cult in Homer, is relevant to Hdt.'s usage and conceptions. See Hadzisteliou-Price 1973 and Coldstream 1976. Whitley 1994 and Antonaccio 1994 give earlier bibliography.

[134] This sense is found in the very first sentence of the *Iliad* (1.4); Achilles sent down to Hades many powerful souls of heroes. The word never means 'cultic hero' in Homer, though hero-cult *sans la parole* may not be absent from the poems: for Athenian cult of Erechtheus see *Il.* 2.551–2 and perhaps *Od.* 7.81. Indeed, on one modern view, the origins of hero-cult lie in the worship paid to Homeric heroes, but this is not agreed; see previous n.

[135] Powell cites as another example 7.43.2 (Xerxes' magi at Troy make offerings to 'the [Homeric] heroes'), but this is less clear because it appears to combine both senses.

[136] Powell calls the first sort of hero 'denizen of the heroic age' and the second 'a mortal worshipped after death'.

[137] Cf. the gloss at LSJ νομίζω (3): 'they practise no such worship'. Perhaps forgetfully, but perhaps just by way of emphasis, Hdt. says that the priests of Zeus at Egyptian Thebes did not connect their ancestors with either gods *or heroes* (2.143.4 with Harrison 2000: 160). The remark at 2.50 helps to explain the oddity that at the very full 6.58, on the funerals of Spartan kings, Hdt. does not mention their heroisation, well attested by Xen. (Hdt. wishes, in that context, to play up, not play down, Spartan similarities with Egypt).

to be distinctively Greek, although Egesta does not provide unequivocal support for the implied generalisation, because it was not a purely Greek city.[138]

But Hdt. also provides evidence for occasional overlap between the 'epic' and 'cultic' type of hero,[139] and in one particularly important case, that of Helen, this evidence is now strengthened by epigraphy. The ἱρόν or shrine to Helen at Spartan Therapne features in the uncanny story of the birth of Demaretos.[140] This shrine is what modern scholars and excavators call the Menelaion (a name not actually attested before Pausanias); but as often[141] the female or heroine cult is the original one.[142] The publication in 1976 of inscribed dedications at the 'Menelaion' to Helen and Menelaos, some dating from as early as the 7th cent. BC, confirms that these two Homeric figures were recipients of cult in the full sense – at least at their own city of Sparta.[143] One criterion for cultic hero is strong attachment to a particular locality, and this is certainly true of Helen and Menelaos.

Hdt.'s *Histories* in general, and bk. 5 in particular, are full of stories of heroes being borrowed or otherwise transferred. For that rare event, the expulsion of a hero rather than his introduction, Hdt. also provides evidence: Kleisthenes of Sikyon's treatment of Adrastos, **67**.1.[144] There is also a long section of bk. 5 describing the contentious traffic in the statues of a pair of minor deities of agricultural increase, Damie and Auxesie, who appear not to be actual heroes or heroines.[145] Nevertheless, their treatment resembles in important ways the traffic in heroes and their relics.

---

[138] Egesta was a hellenised rather than a strictly Greek community. It was, however, unlucky not to get an entry in *IACP*, given that Th. called it a *polis* (6.2.3) and its culture (not only the hero-cult) and architecture had so many features normally found in Greek *poleis*.

[139] See above, n. 135 for 7.43.2.

[140] 6. 61.3, where the nurse prays to Helen's statue and is then addressed by a mysterious female stranger. Note that Helen is here called a goddess; cf. Harrison 2000: 161. But this hardly collapses the distinction between hero(ine)- and divine cult, any more than does the occasional use of θύειν (not ἐναγίζειν) for heroes, in sources of various kinds. The 'woman' who manifests herself at 6.61.4 is described in the language of epiphany, i.e. this is probably meant to be Helen (see Aston 2011: 317, the statue a 'proxy for the heroine's presence') but the story gains in effectiveness by leaving the identity of the mysterious stranger open. It is in any case set far in the past.

[141] Whitley 1994: 221 and n. 37, citing de Polignac 1984: 130–1 n. 12 (original French version of de Polignac 1995).

[142] This is relevant to the female cults in Lykoph. *Alex*, esp. those of Kassandra herself and of Agamemnon. Archaeological evidence from Lakonia suggests that the dominant cult is Kassandra's.

[143] *SEG* 26: nos. 457–9.

[144] **67**.1–2 with Ekroth 2007: 112 and Parker 2011: 118.

[145] **82–9**. See above n. 101 (they are *daimones*).

The frequency in bk. 5 of this motif – possession of heroes or their relics – calls for a special explanation. It must have something to do with the unusual quantity of retrospective archaic Greek narrative, but it would be a mistake to think that this feature of Greek religious politics had withered away by the fifth century. Thus the Aiakidai were summoned from Aigina before the battle of Salamis in 480, not to mention (from outside Hdt.'s narrative) Kimon's transportation from Skyros of the bones of Theseus, and his reburial of them in a central site in Athens (470s). Later still (437), the bones of the local hero Rhesos were deployed as part of the foundation of Amphipolis by the Athenian commander and oikist Hagnon.[146]

The apparent mobility of such heroes, who seem to function as a kind of negotiable propaganda currency, raises the question whether a hero or heroine could exist in two places simultaneously. When the Aiakids were 'sent for' from Aigina, we may wonder whether they also stayed put, and similarly it may be asked, in what sense the Thebans 'gave' Melanippos to the Sikyonians.[147] It is tempting to assume a physical transfer of bones, but this is not necessarily correct, because when Hdt. wants to say this he knows how to do so (see 1.68.6 where Liches gathers up the bones, τὰ ὀστέα, of Orestes). It is not clear whether the 'fetching' of Melanippos to Sikyon was thought of as involving his permanent departure from Thebes, or whether he could thereafter be in two places at once. Heroes (Adrastos is an example) could have cult in several places; but such rival cults were a form of inter-state competition, so that does not solve the matter.[148] On the general point, it is hardly plausible that the Thebans would say goodbye to Melanippos as casually as this. They could surely have allowed the Sikyonians to have a cult-image. It would seem that, as Kearns put it, 'a hero's physical remains are not indispensable to his presence'.[149]

---

[146] Aiakidai: Hdt. 8.64.2. Theseus: Plut. *Kim.* 8 and *Thes.* 36, an episode characteristically omitted by Th., see *CT* I: 150. Rhesos (also absent from Th.): Polyainos 6.53 with *CT* II: 323–3. Cf. *OCD*⁴, 'relics', and for exploitation of 'talismanic' statues, Faraone 1992.

[147] **67**.2.

[148] For the 'multilocality' of heroes in this competitive sense, see Ekroth 2007: 111. Schachter 1981–94: 2.125 says that Paus. and his informants 'were ignorant' of Hdt.'s account of the transfer of Melanippos; this implies a strong denial of bilocality. But Paus. could be regarded as evidence for bilocality of Melanippos in some sense.

[149] Kearns 1989: 47 discussing Aiakos at Hdt. 5.**89**. At 46 she says of the summoning of Aiakos in 480 (see 8.64), 'it is not clear in what form he was supposed to be brought'. Farnell 1921: 335 wrote of Kleisthenes inviting from Thebes the 'spirit' of Adrastos' enemy Melanippos.

(c) Conclusion

In some ways it is true that the divine plays little direct part in the Ionian revolt story. Milesian or Ionian consultation of the oracle at Branchidai is conspicuously lacking in the opening narrative of the revolt, although Branchidai itself does feature in Hdt.'s bk. 5 narrative for its treasures, and although there is possible non-Herodotean literary evidence that a consultation took place (but by Karians not Ionians). A Delphic warning to the Milesians is not related until well into bk. 6, after the revolt is over.

For a spectacular epiphany in the full sense we have to wait for Pan in the pre-Marathon narrative; but Hipparchos' dream-apparition is a kind of epiphany, and is recorded without scepticism. An epiphany by Helen is possible but not insisted on. Divinely orchestrated requital or *tisis* is a marked feature of the bk. 6 Kleomenes narrative in particular. But Hdt. makes clear, here and elsewhere, that the assessment of the degree of divine intervention is a subjective matter.

The most persistent way in which religion plays a role in bks. 5 and 6, and especially bk. 5, is by inter-state transactions involving heroes and their relics or statues; in this category we should include the statues of the *daimones* Damie and Auxesie. Some of this narration covers events much earlier than the time of the Ionian revolt; but the Aiakidai were summoned from Aigina as late as bk. 8 and the battle of Salamis, and the strange story of Damie and Auxesie is there to explain the origins of the bad blood between Athenians and Aiginetans which persisted until the Persian wars.[150]

Finally, kinship ties between cities and groups are very important in the two books, especially the Ionian revolt narrative. Such ties are mythically and religiously grounded, and might be expressed by ritual acts of deference from colony to mother-city.[151]

7 LANGUAGE AND DIALECT[152] (BY A. M. BOWIE)

Our MSS are descended from an 'archetype' written probably in the first century AD.[153] These MSS and the few surviving papyri do not suggest there is a wide divergence between our text and Herodotus' original in terms of expression, word order, order of incidents, etc. However,

[150] For a subtle analysis of the tension between secular and religious explanation in this whole section, see Haubold 2007.

[151] Th. 1.25.4 (report of Korinthian complaints about Kerkyraian refusal to pay the normal deference owed by colonies to mother-cities) is the classic literary text, even allowing for the tendentious rhetorical context – it is a kind of indirect speech.

[152] There is appended to this section a brief guide to the language of Herodotus, for those who wish speedily to see the differences from Attic.

[153] See S. West, cited at §8 below.

in matters of dialect, morphology, spelling, etc., considerable confusion reigns.[154] In the representation of particular forms, the MSS disagree with each other, are inconsistent with themselves, and contain some very peculiar spellings. It is clear that Herodotus' text has been heavily corrupted by the introduction of Attic and false Ionic forms by scribes and scholars who were more used to Attic or had their own theories about how his Ionic dialect should look. Furthermore, we have too little contemporary Ionic from inscriptions against which to check the MSS' readings, and the texts of other Ionic writers close in time to Herodotus, such as the early historians and Hippokrates, are themselves heavily Atticised (and in the former case, very fragmentary).

Faced with the plethora of competing variants in the MSS, editors have hard choices to make: when the MSS write ποιέει and ποιέειν more often than ποιεῖ and ποιεῖν, but by contrast prefer νοεῖ and νοεῖν to the corresponding uncontracted forms, do editors go with the majority verdict in the case of each individual verb or form, do they standardise either the contracted or uncontracted form, or do they have a mixture of the two, and if so, how do they decide what the mixture will be? When standardisation and consistency of spelling is a relatively late feature of English, how much should we demand of fifth-century BC Ionia?

Again, it is difficult when we come across unusual forms to know how they should be accounted for. There are a number of possibilities. (1) They might be 'false' Ionicisms, that is, forms created as a result of insufficient knowledge of how that dialect works. A good instance of this problem concerns the genitive plural of the pronoun αὐτός in which Ionic distinguishes between the feminine in -εων (< -ηων < -αων) and the masculine/neuter in -ων (< *-ōm). However, in the MSS we find the feminine αὐτέων used as a masculine or neuter. This might have been introduced by a scribe who saw -εων frequently in his text and extended its use falsely, but we have ἑκαστέων (neut.) on a Milesian inscription. The document itself dates from the mid-fifth century, which is promising, but the actual version we have was carved only c. 100: is ἑκαστέων an original form or a later one, based on what the writer thought it should be in Ionic?[155] (2) They might be Atticisms, wrongly substituted for Ionic forms: πόλει (beside usual πόλι) is also found in Homer, but is likely to be an Attic form both there and in Herodotus. However, not all Atticisms need be copyists' errors: Herodotus seems to have spent time in Athens, and his lexicon (especially in later books) shows words that seem to have been specifically Attic (e.g. καραδοκέω, δωροδοκέω, ἐπ' αὐτοφώρωι): why not Attic spellings as well? (3) They might be

---

[154] Most useful on Herodotus' dialect are Smyth 1894; Untersteiner 1949; Legrand 1955: 179–223; Rosén 1962; for later literary Ionic, Lightfoot 2003: 97–142.

[155] Κροισέω etc. found in some MSS, with the first declension genitive ending transferred to the second declension, is a better candidate for falsehood.

poeticisms borrowed by Herodotus perhaps from epic and used as part of an attempt to create a language suitably elevated for his great subject. (4) It has been argued that such doublets as μοῦνος / μόνος found in the MSS might be variant spellings of the same sound,[156] introduced by copyists if not Herodotus himself. (5) They might simply be mistakes. In the list that follows, therefore, there are many uncertainties.

Because Attic is the dialect that most people learn first, Herodotus' dialect will be discussed below largely in terms of the differences between Attic and his Ionic. Herodotus came from Halikarnassos (modern-day Bodrum) in Karia. This was a Dorian colony, but inscriptions from that area are in a form of 'East Ionic', a dialect spoken in the Ionic areas of the Asia Minor coast and some of the adjacent islands, as well as in their colonies around the Hellespont and Black Sea. Historically, Attic and Ionic are two branches of an earlier 'Attic-Ionic' dialect, one of the five main groupings into which the historical Greek dialects are divided.[157] This Attic-Ionic group separated from other dialects after the Mycenaean period, and subsequently divided into its two branches during the migrations that marked that period. This is important for understanding the material that follows. '*x* for *y*' below is merely a short-hand way of saying 'where in Attic we find form *y*, in Ionic we find form *x*'. It does *not* mean that 'Ionic replaced Attic *y* with its own *x*'. The differences between the two dialects are sometimes the result of *Attic* introducing innovations after it split from 'Attic-Ionic' (e.g. the contraction of ε + ο > ου: Ion. γένεος, Att. γένους < *γένε(σ)ος), sometimes the result of Ionic and Attic independently treating an inherited form in different ways after the split (e.g. Ion. μοῦνος, Att. μόνος < *μόνϝος). Here is a general account of the differences between Herodotus' language and Attic, with some historical explanations. It is followed by a much briefer survey for those who wish to see quickly what the differences are.

General. (a) *Psilosis*, the loss of the 'rough breathing', was a feature of East Ionic, but modern texts keep the initial aspirate as 'a venerable absurdity' (Powell):[158] e.g. Ἕλληνες should strictly be printed Ἔλληνες. In some compounds, which were no longer felt as compounds, the aspirate was preserved (e.g. καθεύδουσι), as it was in some non-Ionic names and words (Ἀφεταί (< ἀπό+ ἵημι), ἔφορος (< ἐπί + ὁράω)).[159] **(b)** *Etacism* involved the wholesale replacement in Ionic of original ᾱ by η, where Attic keeps ᾱ after ρ, ε, ι (πρῆγμα, Πυθέης, προθυμίη). Forms like πᾶσα (< *πάνσα <*πάντ-γα), which developed a secondary long α, were created after the shift ᾱ > η had

---

[156] ο is written in many forms for which the usual later spelling is ου.

[157] The others are Doric, North-West Greek, Aiolic and Arkado-Cyprian. For a clear account of the Greek dialects, cf. Chadwick 1956.

[158] Papyri of Herodotus display *psilosis* more often than not.

[159] Such non-Ionic words and names often keep their own dialectal forms.

ceased to operate.[160] **(c)** *Hiatus* (conjunction of two vowels, often caused by loss of intervocalic -ɉ-, -s-, -w-) is regularly found, especially between *e* and another vowel: Attic employs contraction more. Many examples of hiatus (e.g. νόος, πλήρεες, κυνέη, the many verbal forms in -εει, -εεις, -εειν etc.) are also alien to spoken Ionic but are found in Homer: it is not absolutely certain whether they were written by Herodotus, but most editors keep them. Others we know to be Ionic (e.g. genitives Ξέρξεω, μοιρέων, γένεος, ἔσεαι 'you will be', δοκέοι opt.).

Vowels. These are the most important differences in the treatment of vowels (note that in many cases here we are talking about a small number of particular words, not general rules).

α for ε	τάμνω, μέγαθος (Att. μέγεθος innovates by assimilation of α to the earlier ε).
α for η	μεσαμβρίη.
ε for α	τέσσερες, ἔρσην ('male').
ε for ει	κρέσσων (<κρέτ-γων: Att. κρείττων on analogy with χείρων etc.), μέζων; ἡμίσεαι (fem. pl. of adj. in -υς); ἀποδέξω etc. (but uncompounded δείξω); ἔργω 'restrain' < root * ϝεργ-; Att. εἴργω < *ἐ-(ϝ)εργω with a prothetic vowel); τέλεος (adj., Att. -ειος).
ει for ε	κεινός ('empty'), ξεῖνος, εἵνεκα/-εν (< κενϝός etc.; East Ionic is unusual in lengthening the vowel thus); εἰρωτῶ, εἰρόμην, εἰρύω, ἠνείχθην.
ε for η	ἐσσοῦμαι (but ἥσσων).
ε for ο	πεντηκόντερος.
ευ for ου	regularly in ποιεῖν (ποιεῦσι, ποιεῦντες), and when -εο, -εου is preceded by a vowel (θηεύμενος): the original sequence is εο, which contracts to ου in Attic, and either remains εο in Ionic or becomes ευ. These sounds were very close, so the variants are probably orthographic, i.e. two ways of representing basically the same sound.
η for ε	μαχήσομαι, ἠώς 'dawn'.
ηι for ει	nouns in -ηιον, -ηιη (ἀριστήιον); adjs. in -ηιος (οἰκήιος).
ι for ε	ἱστίη 'hearth' (by assimilation from ἑστία (cf. μέγαθος above); Att. is unusual in keeping the original form; cf. also Ἱστιαιεύς).
ι for ει	ἴκελος (but εἰκ- in compounds, which is a secondary form).
ι for ευ	ἰθύς, ἰθέως (Att. εὐθύς is unclear).
ο for ω	χρέον (< χρεὼ ὄν 'it being necessary').
ου for ο	οὖρος, μοῦνος, νοῦσος (but νοσέω etc.) from *ὄρϝος, *μόνϝος etc. (cf. κεινός above); οὔνομα is a borrowing of a metrically lengthened form from Homer (contrast ὀνομάζω).

---

[160] I.e. the change from short vowel + -νσ- to long vowel + -σ- started after the ᾱ > η shift stopped.

ω for αυ   θῶμα, τρῶμα.
ω for ευ   ἔπλωσα (from πλώω 'sail' rather than πλέω).
ω for ου   ὦν (= οὖν; unexplained), τοιγαρῶν etc.

Consonants. (a) κῶς, κως, ὁκότε, κότερος etc., i.e. interrogative and indefinite pronouns and enclitics derived from the root *k^wo- have forms with -κ-, where Attic and other dialects have -π-.[161] (b) δέκομαι in Herodotus, literary Ionic and other dialects: Attic δέχομαι, with -χ- from δέχαται. (c) οὐκί (< οὐ + k^wi) for οὐχί. (d) γίνομαι, γινώσκω for γίγνομαι, γιγνώσκω, probably with a weakening of the articulation of the second γ, by dissimilation (perhaps helped by forms in γεν- in the case of γίνομαι). (e) ἐνθαῦτα, ἐνθεῦτεν were turned by Attic through metathesis into ἐνταῦθα, ἐντεῦθεν.

Nouns and adjectives. (a) *a-stems.* (i) Gen. sg. masc. -εω (Ξέρξεω < -ηο < -αο). (ii) Gen. pl. -εων (μοιρέων, ἐουσέων < -ηων < -άων). (iii) Dat. pl. -ῃσι, which is descended from the locative in -āsu/i, and developed the iota on analogy with -οισι, locative of the o-stems: when Greek dispensed with the locative, some dialects used it to represent the dative; Attic -αις was created on analogy with -οις, an old instrumental. (b) *o-stems.* Dat. pl. -οισι, another locative; Attic again uses the instrumental -ōis. Note however τοῖσδε, also found in Homer. (c) *Consonant stems.* (i) Nouns and adjectives in -ος and -ης are uncontracted: γένος, γένεος, γένεϊ, γένεα, γενέων, γένεσι; Ἀστυάγης, Ἀστυάγεα etc.; ἀληθής, ἀληθέα, ἀληθέος etc. (ii) So nouns in -εύς: βασιλέα, βασιλέος etc. (iii) πόλις, ὕβρις, φύσις etc. retain the stem in -ι- throughout the paradigm (πόλιος, πόλι, πόλιες, πόλῑς, πολίων, πόλισι).

Pronouns. (a) ἐμέο, σέο, τέο for ἐμοῦ, σοῦ, and also with more closed pronunciation ἐμεῦ etc. (b) ὅστις gives ὅτευ, ὅτεωι, ὅτεων, ὁτέοισι. (c) ὅς, ἥ, τό, τόν, τήν, τό etc. is the relative; note also Herodotus' rare use of καὶ ὅς 'and he'; cf. ἦ δὲ ὅς 'he said'. They tend to be used where there is no preposition or a preposition that cannot be elided. Herodotus also uses ὅς, ἥ, ὅ; ὅν, ἥν, ὅ etc., especially in phrases such as ἐν ὧι = 'while', ἐς ὅ = 'until'. (d) σφεας, σφεων, σφι and σφισι are used like αὐτούς etc., not just to refer to the subject of the main clause as in Attic. (e) ἑωυτόν stands for ἑαυτόν (ἑω- generalised from crasis of ἕο αὐτοῦ). (f) Note also accusative sg. μιν = αὐτόν, αὐτήν.

Verbs. (a) *Syllabic augment* is omitted in pluperfects (παρατετάχατο) and iteratives in -σκον (ἔχεσκον). (b) *Temporal augment* is sometimes absent, especially in verbs beginning with the diphthongs αι, αυ, ει, ευ, οι (e.g. αἴνεσα); in some cases, imitation of Homer may be involved. (c) *Uncontracted terminations:* 2nd p. sg. mid. -εαι for Att. -ει or -ηι (ἔσεαι 'you will be'); -εο for ου (πείθεο pres. mid. imper.); -εε for -η (ἐγεγόνεε (ppf.), ἐτίθεε (impf.)). (d) δείκνυμι etc. have forms from the -ω conjugation in 2nd

---

[161] A problematic feature: the inscriptions usually give forms in π, but these are inscriptions where Koine influence is notable, so the π-forms may not be original. Forms in κ appear very rarely in the Ionic of the Asia Minor cities and their colonies. Cf. Lillo 1991, Stüber 1996.

and 3rd p. sg. and 3rd p. pl. pres. indic. and 3rd p. sg. impf.: προσαπολ-λύεις (for -υς), προδεικνύει (for -υσι), δεικνύουσι (for -ύασι), ἐδείκνυε (for -υ). **(e) -αται, -ατο** appear in the 3rd p. pl. of optatives, perfects and plu-perfects (ἀνελοίατο, ἀπίκαται, δειφθάρατο), and in the present and imper-fects of some verbs in -μι: regularly in δύναμαι, ἐπίσταμαι, ἵσταμαι (δυνέαται, ἠπιστέατο); less certainly also τιθέαται, ἐτιθέατο.[162] -αται etc. arose as a treat-ment of -νται after a consonant, and was then extended to other contexts. **(f) *Contract verbs.*** (i) Verbs in -εω are usually uncontracted, but note δεῖ, ἔδει. (ii) -ε- sometimes replaces -α- in -αω verbs: τολμέω, -ὁρέων (part.), -ὁρέωσι (subj.), beside expected 2nd and 3rd p. sg. ὁρᾶις and ὁρᾶι (con-tracted forms are also frequent: ὁρῶ etc.). **(g) -μι *verbs*,** in the 2nd and 3rd p. sg. and 3rd p. pl. of the present, have forms which show the influence of contract verbs: thus τίθημι, but τιθεῖς (Att. τίθης), τιθεῖ (Att. τίθησι), τιθεῖσι (as -εω verbs); δίδωμι, διδοῖς, διδοῖ, διδοῦσι (as -οω verbs); ἵστημι, ἱστᾶις, ἱστᾶι, ἱστᾶσι (as -αω verbs). **(h) *Other forms.*** (i) οἴδαμεν and οἴδασι beside ἴδμεν, ἴσασι. (ii) εἶπα, εἶπας (part.) beside εἶπον, εἰπών. (iii) λάμψομαι, ἐλάμφθην etc. from λαμβάνω. (iv) εἷς, εἰμέν are used for εἷ, ἐσμέν (cf. εἰμί < *ἐσμί); ἔωσι, ἐών, ἐοῦσα for ὦσι etc.; opt. εἴησαν is used beside εἶεν. (v) The frequentative suffix -σκον with the present or aorist stem: ἄγεσκον, λάβεσκον.

Brief guide to the language of Herodotus

(In this brief guide, Attic equivalents are given in brackets.)

Vowels and consonants

η for ᾱ : προθυμίη (προθυμία).

Uncontracted forms: νόος (νοῦς), γένεος (γένους), γένεϊ (γένει), πλήρεες (πλήρεις), προσπλέειν (προσπλεῖν), ἐπεβοήθεον (ἐπεβοήθουν), ἐτίθεε (ἐτίθει).

ει for ε: κεινός (κενός, 'empty'), ξεῖνος (ξένος), εἵνεκα/-εν (ἕνεκα).

ευ for ου: ποιεῦσι (ποιοῦσι), ποιεῦντες (ποιοῦντες).

ου for ο: οὖρος (ὄρος), μοῦνος (μόνος), νοῦσος (νόσος), οὔνομα (ὄνομα).

κ for π: κῶς (πῶς), ὀκότε (ὁπότε), κότερος (πότερος).

γίνομαι (γίγνομαι), γινώσκω (γιγνώσκω).

Nouns, adjectives and pronouns

Gen. sg. masc. -εω (ου): Ξέρξεω (Ξέρξου).
Gen. pl. -εων (-ων): μοιρέων (μοιρῶν).
Dat. pl. -ῃσι (-αις), -οισι (-οις): ἡμέρῃσι (ἡμέραις), λόγοισι (λόγοις).
Words like πόλις keep their iota: πόλιος (πόλεως), πόλι (πόλει).

---

[162] Where the verb stem has a long vowel, that is shortened: ὁρμέ-αται 'they have set out' (cf. ὥρμη-σα etc.).

ἐμέο (ἐμοῦ), σέο (σοῦ).

ὅστις: ὅτευ (οὗτινος, ὅτου), ὅτεωι (ὧιτινι, ὅτωι), ὅτεων (ὧντινων, ὅτων), ὁτέοισι (οἷστισι, ὅτοις).

Verbs

Augments are sometimes missing: ἀμειβόμην (ἠμειβόμην), αἴνεσα (ἤινεσα). -μι verbs sometimes conjugate like contract verbs: τίθημι but τιθεῖς (τίθης), τιθεῖ (τίθησι), τιθεῖσι (τιθέασι); δίδωμι but διδοῖς (δίδως), διδοῖ (δίδωσι), διδοῦσι (διδόασι).

In εἰμί an initial epsilon is often preserved: ἔωσι (ὦσι), ἐών (ὤν), ἐοῦσα (οὖσα).

Note also εἷς (εἶ), εἰμέν (ἐσμέν).

-αται, -ατο for -νται, -ντο: ἀπίκαται (ἀφίκονται), ἀνέλοιατο (ἀνέλοιντο).

Various

ὧν (οὖν); ἴθεως (εὐθύς); ἐνθαῦτα (ἐνταῦθα); ἑωυτόν (ἑαυτόν); μιν = αὐτόν, αὐτήν; σφεας often = αὐτούς; δέκομαι (δέχομαι); οἴδαμεν (ἴδμεν), οἴδασι (ἴσασι); εἶπα (εἶπον), εἴπας (εἰπών).

8 TEXT

The text printed in this edition is essentially Hude's OCT, but changed at many points, chiefly so as to take account of Nigel Wilson's new OCT, forthcoming (see Preface). In the app. crit., 'et Maas' indicates a suggestion which Maas made independently of the scholar whose name appears before that of Maas. For detailed discussion of the Herodotean textual tradition, see S. West in Bowie 2007: 30–2. The MSS used in this edition are denoted by the following sigla.

A   cod. Laur. 70, 3
B   cod. Romanus Angel. August. gr. 83
C   cod. Laur. conv. suppr. 207
D   cod. Vaticanus 2369
P   cod. Parisinus 1633
R   cod. Vaticanus 123
S   cod. Sancroftianus (Cantabr. Emm. 30)
V   cod. Vindobonensis hist. gr. 85
U   cod. Urbinas 88

ΗΡΟΔΟΤΟΥ ΙΣΤΟΡΙΩΝ Ε
ΤΕΡΨΙΧΟΡΗ

ΗΡΟΔΟΤΟΥ ΙΣΤΟΡΙΩΝ Ε ΤΕΡΨΙΧΟΡΗ

Οἱ δὲ ἐν τῆι Εὐρώπηι τῶν Περσέων καταλειφθέντες ὑπὸ Δαρείου, τῶν 1
ὁ Μεγάβαζος ἦρχε, πρώτους μὲν Περινθίους Ἑλλησποντίων οὐ βουλομένους ὑπηκόους εἶναι Δαρείου κατεστρέψαντο, περιεφθέντας πρότερον
καὶ ὑπὸ Παιόνων τρηχέως. οἱ γὰρ ὢν ἀπὸ Στρύμονος Παίονες χρήσαν- 2
τος τοῦ θεοῦ στρατεύεσθαι ἐπὶ Περινθίους, καὶ ἦν μὲν ἀντικατιζόμενοι
ἐπικαλέσωνταί σφεας οἱ Περίνθιοι ὀνομαστὶ βώσαντες, τοὺς δὲ ἐπιχειρέειν,
ἦν δὲ μὴ ἐπιβώσονται, μὴ ἐπιχειρέειν, ἐποίεον οἱ Παίονες ταῦτα. ἀντικατιζομένων δὲ τῶν Περινθίων ἐν τῶι προαστίωι, ἐνθαῦτα μουνομαχίη τριφασίη ἐκ προκλήσιός σφι ἐγένετο· καὶ γὰρ ἄνδρα ἀνδρὶ καὶ ἵππον ἵππωι
συνέβαλον καὶ κύνα κυνί. νικώντων δὲ τὰ δύο τῶν Περινθίων, ὡς ἐπαιώνι- 3
ζον κεχαρηκότες, συνεβάλοντο οἱ Παίονες τὸ χρηστήριον αὐτὸ τοῦτο
εἶναι καὶ εἶπάν κου παρὰ σφίσι αὐτοῖσι· "νῦν ἂν εἴη ὁ χρησμὸς ἐπιτελεό-
μενος ἡμῖν, νῦν ἡμέτερον τὸ ἔργον". οὕτω τοῖσι Περινθίοισι παιωνίσασι
ἐπιχειρέουσι οἱ Παίονες καὶ πολλόν τε ἐκράτησαν καὶ ἔλιπόν σφεων
ὀλίγους.

Τὰ μὲν δὴ ἀπὸ Παιόνων πρότερον γενόμενα ὧδε ἐγένετο· τότε δὲ 2
ἀνδρῶν ἀγαθῶν περὶ τῆς ἐλευθερίης γινομένων τῶν Περινθίων οἱ Πέρ- 2
σαι τε καὶ ὁ Μεγάβαζος ἐπεκράτησαν πλήθεϊ. ὡς δὲ ἐχειρώθη ἡ Πέριν- 2
θος, ἤλαυνε τὸν στρατὸν ὁ Μεγάβαζος διὰ τῆς Θρηίκης, πᾶσαν πόλιν καὶ
πᾶν ἔθνος τῶν ταύτηι οἰκημένων ἡμερούμενος βασιλέϊ· ταῦτα γάρ οἱ ἐνετέ-
ταλτο ἐκ Δαρείου, Θρηίκην καταστρέφεσθαι.

Θρηίκων δὲ ἔθνος μέγιστόν ἐστι μετά γε Ἰνδοὺς πάντων ἀνθρώπων. 3
εἰ δὲ ὑπ᾽ ἑνὸς ἄρχοιτο ἢ φρονέοι κατὰ τὠυτό, ἄμαχόν τ᾽ ἂν εἴη καὶ πολλῶι κράτιστον πάντων ἐθνέων κατὰ γνώμην τὴν ἐμήν. ἀλλὰ γὰρ τοῦτο
ἄπορόν σφι καὶ ἀμήχανον μή κοτε ἐγγένηται· εἰσὶ δὴ κατὰ τοῦτο ἀσθενέες.
οὐνόματα δ᾽ ἔχουσι πολλὰ κατὰ χώρας ἕκαστων, νόμοισι δὲ οὗτοι παρα- 2
πλησίοισι πάντες χρέωνται κατὰ πάντα, πλὴν Γετέων καὶ Τραυσῶν καὶ
τῶν κατύπερθε Κρηστωναίων οἰκεόντων.

Τούτων δὲ τὰ μὲν Γέται οἱ ἀθανατίζοντες ποιεῦσι, εἴρηταί μοι· Τραυ- 4
σοὶ δὲ τὰ μὲν ἄλλα πάντα κατὰ ταὐτὰ τοῖσι ἄλλοισι Θρήιξι ἐπιτελέουσι,
κατὰ δὲ τὸν γινόμενον σφίσι καὶ ἀπογινόμενον ποιεῦσι τοιάδε· τὸν μὲν 2
γενόμενον περιιζόμενοι οἱ προσήκοντες ὀλοφύρονται, ὅσα μιν δεῖ ἐπείτε
ἐγένετο ἀναπλῆσαι κακά, ἀπηγεόμενοι τὰ ἀνθρωπήια πάντα πάθεα, τὸν

3.2 ἑκάστων Wilson: ἕκαστοι codd.: ἑκάστου Nenci   4.2 ἀπηγεόμενοι Bekker:
ἀνηγεόμενοι codd.

δ' ἀπογενόμενον παίζοντές τε καὶ ἡδόμενοι γῆι κρύπτουσι, ἐπιλέγοντες ὅσων κακῶν ἐξαπαλλαχθείς ἐστι ἐν πάσηι εὐδαιμονίηι.

5 Οἱ δὲ κατύπερθε Κρηστωναίων ποιεῦσι τοιάδε· ἔχει γυναῖκας ἕκαστος πολλάς· ἐπεὰν ὦν τις αὐτῶν ἀποθάνηι, κρίσις γίνεται μεγάλη τῶν γυναικῶν καὶ φίλων σπουδαὶ ἰσχυραὶ περὶ τοῦδε, ἥτις αὐτέων ἐφιλέετο μάλιστα ὑπὸ τοῦ ἀνδρός· ἣ δ' ἂν κριθῆι καὶ τιμηθῆι, ἐγκωμιασθεῖσα ὑπό τε ἀνδρῶν καὶ γυναικῶν σφάζεται ἐς τὸν τάφον ὑπὸ τοῦ οἰκηιοτάτου ἑωυτῆς, σφαχθεῖσα δὲ συνθάπτεται τῶι ἀνδρί· αἱ δὲ ἄλλαι συμφορὴν μεγάλην ποιεῦνται· ὄνειδος γάρ σφι τοῦτο μέγιστον γίνεται.

6 Τῶν δὲ δὴ ἄλλων Θρηίκων ἐστὶ ὅδε νόμος· πωλεῦσι τὰ τέκνα ἐπ' ἐξαγωγῆι. τὰς δὲ παρθένους οὐ φυλάσσουσι, ἀλλ' ἐῶσι τοῖσι αὐταὶ βούλονται ἀνδράσι μίσγεσθαι. τὰς δὲ γυναῖκας ἰσχυρῶς φυλάσσουσι· καὶ ὠνέονται

2 τὰς γυναῖκας παρὰ τῶν γονέων χρημάτων μεγάλων. καὶ τὸ μὲν ἐστίχθαι εὐγενὲς κέκριται, τὸ δὲ ἄστικτον ἀγεννές. ἀργὸν εἶναι κάλλιστον, γῆς δὲ ἐργάτην ἀτιμότατον. τὸ ζῆν ἀπὸ πολέμου καὶ ληιστύος κάλλιστον. οὗτοι μέν σφεων οἱ ἐπιφανέστατοι νόμοι εἰσί.

7 Θεοὺς δὲ σέβονται μούνους τούσδε, Ἄρεα καὶ Διόνυσον καὶ Ἄρτεμιν· οἱ δὲ βασιλέες αὐτῶν, πάρεξ τῶν ἄλλων πολιητέων, σέβονται Ἑρμέην μάλιστα θεῶν καὶ ὀμνύουσι μοῦνον τοῦτον καὶ λέγουσι γεγονέναι ἀπὸ Ἑρμέω ἑωυτούς.

8 Ταφαὶ δὲ τοῖσι εὐδαίμοσι αὐτῶν εἰσὶ αἵδε· τρεῖς μὲν ἡμέρας προτιθεῖσι τὸν νεκρὸν καὶ παντοῖα σφάξαντες ἱρήια εὐωχέονται, προκλαύσαντες πρῶτον· ἔπειτα δὲ θάπτουσι κατακαύσαντες ἢ ἄλλως γῆι κρύψαντες, χῶμα δὲ χέαντες ἀγῶνα τιθεῖσι παντοῖον, ἐν τῶι τὰ μέγιστα ἄεθλα τίθεται κατὰ λόγον <εὐδαιμονίης διὰ> μουνομαχίης. ταφαὶ μὲν δὴ Θρηίκων εἰσὶ αὗται.

9 Τὸ δὲ πρὸς βορέω ἔτι τῆς χώρης ταύτης οὐδεὶς ἔχει φράσαι τὸ ἀτρεκές, οἵτινές εἰσι ἄνθρωποι οἰκέοντες αὐτήν, ἀλλὰ τὰ πέρην ἤδη τοῦ Ἴστρου ἔρημος χώρη φαίνεται ἐοῦσα καὶ ἄπειρος. μούνους δὲ δύναμαι πυθέσθαι οἰκέοντας πέρην τοῦ Ἴστρου ἀνθρώπους τοῖσι οὔνομα εἶναι Σιγύννας,

2 ἐσθῆτι δὲ χρεωμένους Μηδικῆι. τοὺς δὲ ἵππους αὐτῶν εἶναι λασίους ἅπαν τὸ σῶμα, καὶ ἐπὶ πέντε δακτύλους τὸ βάθος τῶν τριχῶν, σμικροὺς δὲ καὶ σιμοὺς καὶ ἀδυνάτους ἄνδρας φέρειν, ζευγνυμένους δὲ ὑπ' ἄρματα εἶναι ὀξυτάτους· ἁρματηλατέειν δὲ πρὸς ταῦτα τοὺς ἐπιχωρίους. κατήκειν δὲ

3 τούτων τοὺς οὔρους ἀγχοῦ Ἐνετῶν τῶν ἐν τῶι Ἀδρίηι. εἶναι δὲ Μήδων σφέας ἀποίκους λέγουσι· ὅκως δὲ οὗτοι Μήδων ἄποικοι γεγόνασι, ἐγὼ μὲν οὐκ ἔχω ἐπιφράσασθαι, γένοιτο δ' ἂν πᾶν ἐν τῶι μακρῶι χρόνωι. σιγύννας

---

8 <εὐδαιμονίης διὰ> add. Wilson: κατά λόγον del. Powell   9.3 σιγύννας ... δόρατα del. Reiske et Powell

δ' ὧν καλέουσι Λίγυες οἱ ἄνω ὑπὲρ Μασσαλίης οἰκέοντες τοὺς καπήλους,
Κύπριοι δὲ τὰ δόρατα.

Ὡς δὲ Θρήικες λέγουσι, μέλισσαι κατέχουσι τὰ πέρην τοῦ Ἴστρου,   10
καὶ ὑπὸ τουτέων οὐκ εἶναι διελθεῖν τὸ προσωτέρω. ἐμοὶ μέν νυν ταῦτα
λέγοντες δοκέουσι λέγειν οὐκ οἰκότα· τὰ γὰρ ζῶια ταῦτα φαίνεται εἶναι
δύσριγα· ἀλλά μοι τὰ ὑπὸ τὴν ἄρκτον ἀοίκητα δοκέει εἶναι διὰ τὰ ψύχεα.
ταῦτα μέν νυν τῆς χώρης ταύτης πέρι λέγεται, τὰ παραθαλάσσια δ' ὧν
αὐτῆς Μεγάβαζος Περσέων κατήκοα ἐποίεε.

Δαρεῖος δὲ ὡς διαβὰς τάχιστα τὸν Ἑλλήσποντον ἀπίκετο ἐς Σάρδις,   11
ἐμνήσθη τῆς ἐξ Ἱστιαίου τε τοῦ Μιλησίου εὐεργεσίης καὶ τῆς παραινέσιος
τοῦ Μυτιληναίου Κώεω, μεταπεμψάμενος δέ σφεας ἐς Σάρδις ἐδίδου
αὐτοῖσι αἵρεσιν. ὁ μὲν δὴ Ἱστιαῖος, ἅτε τυραννεύων τῆς Μιλήτου,   2
τυραννίδος μὲν οὐδεμιῆς προσεχρήιζε, αἰτέει δὲ Μύρκινον τὴν Ἠδώνων,
βουλόμενος ἐν αὐτῆι πόλιν κτίσαι. οὗτος μὲν δὴ ταύτην αἱρέεται, ὁ δὲ
Κώης, οἷά τε οὐ τύραννος δημότης δὲ ἐών, αἰτέει Μυτιλήνης τυραννεῦσαι.

τελεωθέντων δὲ ἀμφοτέροισι οὗτοι μὲν κατὰ τὰ εἵλοντο ἐτράποντο,
Δαρεῖον δὲ συνήνεικε πρῆγμα τοιόνδε ἰδόμενον ἐπιθυμῆσαι ἐντείλασθαι   12
Μεγαβάζωι Παίονας ἑλόντα ἀνασπάστους ποιῆσαι ἐκ τῆς Εὐρώπης ἐς
τὴν Ἀσίην· ἦν Πίγρης καὶ Μαστύης ἄνδρες Παίονες, οἳ ἐπείτε Δαρεῖος
διέβη ἐς τὴν Ἀσίην, αὐτοὶ ἐθέλοντες Παιόνων τυραννεύειν ἀπικνέονται
ἐς Σάρδις, ἅμα ἀγόμενοι ἀδελφεὴν μεγάλην τε καὶ εὐειδέα. φυλάξαντες
δὲ Δαρεῖον προκατιζόμενον ἐς τὸ προάστιον τὸ τῶν Λυδῶν ἐποίησαν   2
τοιόνδε· σκευάσαντες τὴν ἀδελφεὴν ὡς εἶχον ἄριστα ἐπ' ὕδωρ ἔπεμπον
ἄγγος ἐπὶ τῆι κεφαλῆι ἔχουσαν καὶ ἐκ τοῦ βραχίονος ἵππον ἐπέλκουσαν
καὶ κλώθουσαν λίνον. ὡς δὲ παρεξήιε ἡ γυνή, ἐπιμελὲς τῶι Δαρείωι   3
ἐγένετο· οὔτε γὰρ Περσικὰ ἦν οὔτε Λύδια τὰ ποιεύμενα ἐκ τῆς γυναικός,
οὔτε πρὸς τῶν ἐκ τῆς Ἀσίης οὐδαμῶν. ἐπιμελὲς δὲ ὥς οἱ ἐγένετο, τῶν
δορυφόρων τινὰς πέμπει κελεύων φυλάξαι ὅ τι χρήσεται τῶι ἵππωι ἡ
γυνή. οἱ μὲν δὴ ὄπισθε εἵποντο, ἡ δὲ ἐπείτε ἀπίκετο ἐπὶ τὸν ποταμόν,   4
ἦρσε τὸν ἵππον, ἄρσασα δὲ καὶ τὸ ἄγγος τοῦ ὕδατος ἐμπλησμένη τὴν
αὐτὴν ὁδὸν παρεξήιε, φέρουσα τὸ ὕδωρ ἐπὶ τῆς κεφαλῆς καὶ ἐπέλκουσα
ἐκ τοῦ βραχίονος τὸν ἵππον καὶ στρέφουσα τὸν ἄτρακτον.

Θωμάζων δὲ ὁ Δαρεῖος τά τε ἤκουσε ἐκ τῶν κατασκόπων καὶ τὰ αὐτὸς   13
ὥρα, ἄγειν αὐτὴν ἐκέλευε ἑαυτῶι ἐς ὄψιν. ὡς δὲ ἄχθη, παρῆσαν καὶ οἱ
ἀδελφεοὶ αὐτῆς οὔ κηι πρόσω σκοπίην ἔχοντες τούτων. εἰρωτῶντος δὲ
τοῦ Δαρείου ὁποδαπὴ εἴη, ἔφασαν οἱ νεηνίσκοι εἶναι Παίονες καὶ ἐκείνην
εἶναι σφέων ἀδελφεήν. ὁ δ' ἀμείβετο, τίνες δὲ οἱ Παίονες ἄνθρωποί εἰσι   2
καὶ κοῦ γῆς οἰκημένοι, καὶ τί κεῖνοι ἐθέλοντες ἔλθοιεν ἐς Σάρδις. οἱ δέ οἱ

12.1 ἦν del. Rosén

ἔφραζον ὡς ἔλθοιεν μὲν ἐκείνωι δώσοντες σφέας αὐτούς, εἴη δὲ ἡ Παιονίη
ἐπὶ τῶι Στρυμόνι ποταμῶι πεπολισμένη, ὁ δὲ Στρυμὼν οὐ πρόσω τοῦ
3 Ἑλλησπόντου, εἴησαν δὲ Τευκρῶν τῶν ἐκ Τροίης ἄποικοι. οἱ μὲν δὴ ταῦτα
ἕκαστα ἔλεγον, ὁ δὲ εἰρώτα εἰ καὶ πᾶσαι αὐτόθι αἱ γυναῖκες εἴησαν οὕτω
ἐργάτιδες. οἱ δὲ καὶ τοῦτο ἔφασαν προθύμως οὕτω ἔχειν· πάντα γὰρ ὧν
τούτου εἵνεκα καὶ ἐποιέετο.

14 Ἐνθαῦτα Δαρεῖος γράφει γράμματα Μεγαβάζωι, τὸν ἔλιπε ἐν τῆι
Θρηίκηι στρατηγόν, ἐντελλόμενος ἐξαναστῆσαι ἐξ ἠθέων Παίονας καὶ παρ᾽
2 ἑωυτὸν ἀγαγεῖν καὶ αὐτούς καὶ τέκνα τε καὶ γυναῖκας αὐτῶν. αὐτίκα δὲ
ἱππεὺς ἔθεε φέρων τὴν ἀγγελίην ἐπὶ τὸν Ἑλλήσποντον, περαιωθεὶς δὲ
διδοῖ τὸ βυβλίον τῶι Μεγαβάζωι. ὁ δὲ ἐπιλεξάμενος καὶ λαβὼν ἡγεμόνας
ἐκ τῆς Θρηίκης ἐστρατεύετο ἐπὶ τὴν Παιονίην.

15 Πυθόμενοι δὲ οἱ Παίονες τοὺς Πέρσας ἐπὶ σφέας ἰέναι, ἁλισθέντες ἐξεσ-
τρατεύσαντο πρὸς θαλάσσης, δοκέοντες ταύτηι ἐπιχειρήσειν τοὺς Πέρσας
2 ἐσβάλλοντας. οἱ μὲν δὴ Παίονες ἦσαν ἕτοιμοι τὸν Μεγαβάζου στρατὸν
ἐπιόντα ἐρύκειν, οἱ δὲ Πέρσαι πυθόμενοι συναλίσθαι τοὺς Παίονας καὶ τὴν
πρὸς θαλάσσης ἐσβολὴν φυλάσσοντας, ἔχοντες ἡγεμόνας τὴν ἄνω ὁδὸν
τράπονται, λαθόντες δὲ τοὺς Παίονας ἐσπίπτουσι ἐς τὰς πόλιας αὐτῶν,
ἐούσας ἀνδρῶν ἐρήμους. οἷα δὲ κεινῆισι ἐπιπεσόντες εὐπετέως κατέσχον.
3 οἱ δὲ Παίονες ὡς ἐπύθοντο ἐχομένας τὰς πόλιας, αὐτίκα διασκεδασθέντες
κατ᾽ ἑωυτοὺς ἕκαστοι ἐτράποντο καὶ παρεδίδοσαν σφέας αὐτοὺς τοῖσι
Πέρσηισι. οὕτω δὴ Παιόνων Σιριοπαιονές τε καὶ Παιόπλαι καὶ οἱ μέχρι τῆς
Πρασιάδος λίμνης ἐξ ἠθέων ἐξαναστάντες ἤγοντο ἐς τὴν Ἀσίην.

16 Οἱ δὲ περὶ τὸ Πάγγαιον ὄρος καὶ αὐτὴν τὴν λίμνην τὴν Πρασιάδα
οὐκ ἐχειρώθησαν ἀρχὴν ὑπὸ Μεγαβάζου. ἐπειρήθη δὲ καὶ Δόβηρας καὶ
Ἀγριᾶνας καὶ Ὀδομάντους καὶ τοὺς ἐν τῆι λίμνηι κατοικημένους ἐξαιρέειν
ὧδε· ἴκρια ἐπὶ σταυρῶν ὑψηλῶν ἐζευγμένα ἐν μέσηι ἕστηκε τῆι λίμνηι,
2 ἔσοδον ἐκ τῆς ἠπείρου στεινὴν ἔχοντα μιῆι γεφύρηι. τοὺς δὲ σταυροὺς
τοὺς ὑπεστεῶτας τοῖσι ἰκρίοισι τὸ μέν κου ἀρχαῖον ἔστησαν κοινῆι πάντες
οἱ πολιῆται, μετὰ δὲ νόμωι χρεώμενοι ἱστᾶσι τοιῶιδε· κομίζοντες ἐξ ὄρεος
τῶι οὔνομά ἐστι Ὄρβηλος κατὰ γυναῖκα ἑκάστην ὁ γαμέων τρεῖς σταυ-
3 ροὺς ὑπίστησι· ἄγεται δὲ ἕκαστος συχνὰς γυναῖκας. οἰκέουσι δὲ τοιοῦτον
τρόπον, κρατέων ἕκαστος ἐπὶ τῶν ἰκρίων καλύβης τε ἐν τῆι διαιτᾶται καὶ
θύρης καταρρακτῆς διὰ τῶν ἰκρίων κάτω φερούσης ἐς τὴν λίμνην. τὰ δὲ
νήπια παιδία δέουσι τοῦ ποδὸς σπάρτωι, μὴ κατακλυσθῆι δειμαίνοντες.
4 τοῖσι δὲ ἵπποισι καὶ τοῖσι ὑποζυγίοισι παρέχουσι χόρτον ἰχθῦς· τῶν δὲ
πλῆθός ἐστι τοσοῦτον ὥστε, ὅταν τὴν θύρην τὴν καταρρακτὴν ἀνακλίνηι,

13.3 πάντα Richards: αὐτοῦ codd.   16.1 καὶ Δόβηρας . . . Ὀδομάντους post ἐπειρήθη
δὲ transp. Weber 1937: περὶ τὸ Πάγγαιον ὄρος καὶ Δόβηρας (κτλ) codd.

κατίει σχοινίωι σπυρίδα κεινὴν ἐς τὴν λίμνην καὶ οὐ πολλόν τινα χρόνον
ἐπισχὼν ἀνασπᾶι πλήρεα ἰχθύων. τῶν δὲ ἰχθύων ἐστὶ γένεα δύο, τοὺς
καλέουσι πάπρακάς τε καὶ τίλωνας.

Παιόνων μὲν δὴ οἱ χειρωθέντες ἤγοντο ἐς τὴν Ἀσίην, Μεγάβαζος δὲ ὡς **17**
ἐχειρώσατο τοὺς Παίονας, πέμπει ἀγγέλους ἐς Μακεδονίην ἄνδρας ἑπτὰ
Πέρσας, οἳ μετ᾿ αὐτὸν ἐκεῖνον ἦσαν δοκιμώτατοι ἐν τῶι στρατοπέδωι.
ἐπέμποντο δὲ οὗτοι παρὰ Ἀμύντην αἰτήσοντες γῆν τε καὶ ὕδωρ Δαρείωι
βασιλέϊ. ἔστι δὲ ἐκ τῆς Πρασιάδος λίμνης σύντομος κάρτα ἐς τὴν Μακε- 2
δονίην· πρῶτον μὲν γὰρ ἔχεται τῆς λίμνης τὸ μέταλλον ἐξ οὗ ὕστερον
τούτων τάλαντον ἀργυρίου Ἀλεξάνδρωι ἡμέρης ἑκάστης ἐφοίτα, μετὰ
δὲ τὸ μέταλλον Δύσωρον καλεόμενον ὄρος ὑπερβάντι <ἔξεστι> εἶναι ἐν
Μακεδονίηι.

Οἱ ὦν Πέρσαι οἱ πεμφθέντες οὗτοι παρὰ τὸν Ἀμύντην ὡς ἀπίκοντο, **18**
αἴτεον ἐλθόντες ἐς ὄψιν τὴν Ἀμύντεω Δαρείωι βασιλέϊ γῆν τε καὶ ὕδωρ.
ὁ δὲ ταῦτά τε ἐδίδου καί σφεας ἐπὶ ξείνια καλέει, παρασκευασάμενος δὲ
δεῖπνον μεγαλοπρεπὲς ἐδέκετο τοὺς Πέρσας φιλοφρόνως. ὡς δὲ ἀπὸ δείπ- 2
νου ἐγίνοντο, διαπίνοντες εἶπαν οἱ Πέρσαι τάδε· "ξεῖνε Μακεδών, ἡμῖν
νόμος ἐστὶ τοῖσι Πέρσηισι, ἐπεὰν δεῖπνον προτιθώμεθα μέγα, τότε καὶ
τὰς παλλακὰς καὶ τὰς κουριδίας γυναῖκας ἐσάγεσθαι παρέδρους. σύ νυν,
ἐπεί περ προθύμως μὲν ἐδέξαο, μεγάλως δὲ ξεινίζεις, διδοῖς τε βασιλέϊ
Δαρείωι γῆν τε καὶ ὕδωρ, ἕπεο νόμωι τῶι ἡμετέρωι." εἶπε πρὸς ταῦτα 3
Ἀμύντης· "ὦ Πέρσαι, νόμος μὲν ἡμῖν γέ ἐστι οὐκ οὗτος, ἀλλὰ κεχωρίσθαι
ἄνδρας γυναικῶν· ἐπείτε δὲ ὑμεῖς ἐόντες δεσπόται προσχρηίζετε τούτων,
παρέσται ὑμῖν καὶ ταῦτα." εἴπας τοσαῦτα ὁ Ἀμύντης μετεπέμπετο τὰς
γυναῖκας, αἱ δ᾿ ἐπείτε καλεόμεναι ἦλθον, ἐπεξῆς ἀντίαι ἵζοντο τοῖσι Πέρ- 4
σηισι. ἐνθαῦτα οἱ Πέρσαι ἰδόμενοι γυναῖκας εὐμόρφους ἔλεγον πρὸς Ἀμύντην φάμενοι τὸ ποιηθὲν τοῦτο οὐδὲν εἶναι σοφόν· κρέσσον γὰρ εἶναι ἀρχῆ-
θεν μὴ ἐλθεῖν τὰς γυναῖκας ἢ ἐλθούσας καὶ μὴ παριζομένας ἀντίας ἵζεσθαι ἀλγηδόνας σφίσι ὀφθαλμῶν. ἀναγκαζόμενος δὲ ὁ Ἀμύντης ἐκέλευε 5
παρίζειν· πειθομένων δὲ τῶν γυναικῶν αὐτίκα οἱ Πέρσαι μαστῶν τε
ἅπτοντο οἷα πλεόνως οἰνωμένοι καί κού τις καὶ φιλέειν ἐπειρᾶτο.

Ἀμύντης μὲν δὴ ταῦτα ὁρέων ἀτρέμας εἶχε, καίπερ δυσφορέων, οἷα **19**
ὑπερδειμαίνων τοὺς Πέρσας. Ἀλέξανδρος δὲ ὁ Ἀμύντεω παρεών τε καὶ
ὁρέων ταῦτα, ἅτε νέος τε ἐὼν καὶ κακῶν ἀπαθής, οὐδαμῶς ἔτι κατέχειν
οἷός τε ἦν, ὥστε δὲ βαρέως φέρων εἶπε πρὸς Ἀμύντην τάδε· "σὺ μέν, ὦ
πάτερ, εἶκε τῆι ἡλικίηι ἀπιών τε ἀναπαύεο μηδὲ λιπάρεε τῆι πόσι· ἐγὼ δὲ
προσμένων αὐτοῦ τῆιδε πάντα τὰ ἐπιτήδεα παρέξω τοῖσι ξείνοισι." πρὸς 2

17.2 ὑπερβάντι Abicht: ὑπερβάντα codd.   ἔξεστι add. Wilson

ταῦτα συνιεὶς Ἀμύντης ὅτι νεώτερα πρήγματα πρήξειν μέλλοι Ἀλέξανδρος,
λέγει· "ὦ παῖ, σχεδὸν γάρ σεο ἀνακαιομένου συνίημι τοὺς λόγους, ὅτι
ἐθέλεις ἐμὲ ἐκπέμψας ποιέειν τι νεώτερον· ἐγὼ ὦν σεο χρηίζω μηδὲν νεοχμῶσαι κατ' ἄνδρας τούτους, ἵνα μὴ ἐξεργάσηι ἡμέας, ἀλλὰ ἀνέχεο ὁρέων
τὰ ποιεύμενα. ἀμφὶ δὲ ἀπόδωι τῆι ἐμῆι πείσομαί τοι."
20   Ὡς δὲ ὁ Ἀμύντης χρηίσας τούτων οἰχώκεε, λέγει ὁ Ἀλέξανδρος πρὸς
τοὺς Πέρσας· "γυναικῶν τουτέων, ὦ ξεῖνοι, ἐστι ὑμῖν πολλὴ εὐπετείη, καὶ
εἰ πάσηισι βούλεσθε μίσγεσθαι καὶ ὁκόσηισι ὦν αὐτέων. τούτου μὲν πέρι
2   αὐτοὶ ἀποσημανέετε. νῦν δέ, σχεδὸν γὰρ ἤδη τῆς κοίτης ὤρη προσέρχεται
ὑμῖν καὶ καλῶς ἔχοντας ὑμέας ὁρέω μέθης, γυναῖκας ταύτας, εἰ ὑμῖν φίλον
3   ἐστί, ἄφετε λούσασθαι, λουσαμένας δὲ ὀπίσω προσδέκεσθε." εἴπας ταῦτα,
συνέπαινοι γὰρ ἦσαν οἱ Πέρσαι, γυναῖκας μὲν ἐξελθούσας ἀπέπεμπε
ἐς τὴν γυναικηίην, αὐτὸς δὲ ὁ Ἀλέξανδρος ἴσους ἀριθμὸν τῆισι γυναιξὶ
ἄνδρας λειογενείους τῆι τῶν γυναικῶν ἐσθῆτι σκευάσας καὶ ἐγχειρίδια
4   δοὺς παρῆγε ἔσω, παράγων δὲ τούτους ἔλεγε τοῖσι Πέρσηισι τάδε· "ὦ
Πέρσαι, οἴκατε πανδαισίηι τελείηι ἱστιῆσθαι· τά τε γὰρ ἄλλα ὅσα εἴχομεν,
καὶ πρὸς τὰ οἷά τε ἦν ἐξευρόντας παρέχειν, πάντα ὑμῖν πάρεστι, καὶ δὴ
καὶ τόδε τὸ πάντων μέγιστον, τάς τε ἑωυτῶν μητέρας καὶ τὰς ἀδελφεὰς
ἐπιδαψιλευόμεθα ὑμῖν, ὡς παντελέως μάθητε τιμώμενοι πρὸς ἡμέων τῶν
πέρ ἐστε ἄξιοι, πρὸς δὲ καὶ βασιλέϊ τῶι πέμψαντι ἀπαγγείλητε ὡς ἀνὴρ
Ἕλλην, Μακεδόνων ὕπαρχος, εὖ ὑμέας ἐδέξατο καὶ τραπέζηι καὶ κοίτηι."
5   ταῦτα εἴπας ὁ Ἀλέξανδρος παρίζει Πέρσηι ἀνδρὶ ἄνδρα Μακεδόνα ὡς
γυναῖκα τῶι λόγωι· οἱ δέ, ἐπείτε σφέων οἱ Πέρσαι ψαύειν ἐπειρῶντο,
διεργάζοντο αὐτούς.
21   Καὶ οὗτοι μὲν τούτωι τῶι μόρωι διεφθάρησαν, καὶ αὐτοὶ καὶ ἡ θερ-
απηίη αὐτῶν· εἵπετο γὰρ δή σφι καὶ ὀχήματα καὶ θεράποντες καὶ ἡ πᾶσα
2   πολλὴ παρασκευή· πάντα δὴ ταῦτα ἅμα πᾶσι ἐκείνοισι ἠφάνιστο. μετὰ
δὲ χρόνωι οὐ πολλῶι ὕστερον ζήτησις τῶν ἀνδρῶν τούτων μεγάλη ἐκ
τῶν Περσέων ἐγίνετο, καί σφεας Ἀλέξανδρος κατέλαβε σοφίηι, χρήματά
τε δοὺς πολλὰ καὶ τὴν ἑωυτοῦ ἀδελφεὴν τῆι οὔνομα ἦν Γυγαίη· δοὺς δὲ
ταῦτα κατέλαβε ὁ Ἀλέξανδρος Βουβάρηι ἀνδρὶ Πέρσηι, τῶν διζημένων
τοὺς ἀπολομένους τῶι στρατηγῶι. ὁ μέν νυν τῶν Περσέων τούτων θάνατος οὕτω καταλαμφθεὶς ἐσιγήθη.
22   Ἕλληνας δὲ εἶναι τούτους τοὺς ἀπὸ Περδίκκεω γεγονότας, κατά περ
αὐτοὶ λέγουσι, αὐτός τε οὕτω τυγχάνω ἐπιστάμενος καὶ δὴ καὶ ἐν
τοῖσι ὄπισθε λόγοισι ἀποδέξω ὡς εἰσὶ Ἕλληνες, πρὸς δὲ καὶ οἱ τὸν ἐν
2   Ὀλυμπίηι διέποντες ἀγῶνα Ἑλλήνων οὕτω ἔγνωσαν εἶναι. βουλομένου

20.4 Μακεδών DPVU   22.1 Ἑλλήνων S: Ἑλλήνων καὶ DV: Ἑλληνοδίκαι ABCP
22.2 βουλομένου γὰρ Ἀλεξάνδρου ἀεθλεύειν ABC: Ἀλεξάνδρου γὰρ ἀεθλεύειν ἑλομένου
cett.

γὰρ Ἀλεξάνδρου ἀεθλεύειν καὶ καταβάντος ἐπ᾽ αὐτὸ τοῦτο οἱ ἀντιθευσόμενοι Ἑλλήνων ἐξεῖργόν μιν, φάμενοι οὐ βαρβάρων ἀγωνιστέων εἶναι τὸν
ἀγῶνα ἀλλὰ Ἑλλήνων. Ἀλέξανδρος δὲ ἐπειδὴ ἀπέδεξε ὡς εἴη Ἀργεῖος,
ἐκρίθη τε εἶναι Ἕλλην καὶ ἀγωνιζόμενος στάδιον συνεξέπιπτε τῶι πρώτωι.
ταῦτα μέν νυν οὕτω κηι ἐγένετο.

Μεγάβαζος δὲ ἄγων τοὺς Παίονας ἀπίκετο ἐπὶ τὸν Ἑλλήσποντον, **23**
ἐνθεῦτεν δὲ διαπεραιωθεὶς ἀπίκετο ἐς τὰς Σάρδις. ἅτε δὲ τειχέοντος
ἤδη Ἱστιαίου τοῦ Μιλησίου τὴν παρὰ Δαρείου αἰτήσας ἔτυχε δωρεὴν
<ἅτε> μισθὸν φυλακῆς τῆς σχεδίης, ἐόντος δὲ τοῦ χώρου τούτου παρὰ
Στρυμόνα ποταμόν, τῶι οὔνομά ἐστι Μύρκινος, μαθὼν ὁ Μεγάβαζος τὸ
ποιεύμενον ἐκ τοῦ Ἱστιαίου, ὡς ἦλθε τάχιστα ἐς τὰς Σάρδις ἄγων τοὺς
Παίονας, ἔλεγε Δαρείωι τάδε· "ὦ βασιλεῦ, κοῖόν τι χρῆμα ἐποίησας, **2**
ἀνδρὶ Ἕλληνι δεινῶι τε καὶ σοφῶι δοὺς ἐγκτίσασθαι πόλιν ἐν Θρηίκηι,
ἵνα ἴδη τε ναυπηγήσιμός ἐστι ἄφθονος καὶ πολλοὶ κωπέες καὶ μέταλλα
ἀργύρεα, ὅμιλός τε πολλὸς μὲν Ἕλλην περιοικέει, πολλὸς δὲ βάρβαρος,
οἳ προστάτεω ἐπιλαβόμενοι ποιήσουσι τοῦτο τὸ ἂν κεῖνος ἐξηγέηται καὶ
ἡμέρης καὶ νυκτός. σύ νυν τοῦτον τὸν ἄνδρα παῦσον ταῦτα ποιεῦντα, **3**
ἵνα μὴ οἰκηίωι πολέμωι συνέχηι. τρόπωι δὲ ἠπίωι μεταπεμψάμενος παῦ-
σον· ἐπεὰν δὲ αὐτὸν περιλάβηις, ποιέειν ὅκως μηκέτι κεῖνος ἐς Ἕλληνας
ἀπίξεται."

Ταῦτα λέγων ὁ Μεγάβαζος εὐπετέως ἔπειθε Δαρεῖον ὡς εὖ προορῶν **24**
τὸ μέλλον γίνεσθαι. μετὰ δὲ πέμψας ἄγγελον ἐς τὴν Μύρκινον ὁ Δαρεῖος
ἔλεγε τάδε· "Ἱστιαῖε, βασιλεὺς Δαρεῖος τάδε λέγει. ἐγὼ φροντίζων εὑρίσκω
ἐμοί τε καὶ τοῖσι ἐμοῖσι πρήγμασι εἶναι οὐδένα σέο ἄνδρα εὐνοέστερον,
τοῦτο δὲ οὐ λόγοισι ἀλλ᾽ ἔργοισι οἶδα μαθών. νῦν ὦν, ἐπινοέω γὰρ πρήγ- **2**
ματα μεγάλα κατεργάσασθαι, ἀπίκεό μοι πάντως, ἵνα τοι αὐτὰ ὑπερθέωμαι." τούτοισι τοῖσι ἔπεσι πιστεύσας ὁ Ἱστιαῖος καὶ ἅμα μέγα ποιεύμενος
βασιλέος σύμβουλος γενέσθαι ἀπίκετο ἐς τὰς Σάρδις. ἀπικομένωι δέ οἱ **3**
ἔλεγε Δαρεῖος τάδε· "Ἱστιαῖε, ἐγώ σε μετεπεμψάμην τῶνδε εἵνεκεν. ἐπείτε
τάχιστα ἐνόστησα ἀπὸ Σκυθέων καὶ σύ μοι ἐγένεο ἐξ ὀφθαλμῶν, οὐδέν
κω ἄλλο χρῆμα οὕτω ἐν βραχέϊ ἐπεζήτησα ὡς σὲ ἰδεῖν τε καὶ ἐς λόγους μοι
ἀπικέσθαι, ἐγνωκὼς ὅτι κτημάτων πάντων ἐστὶ τιμιώτατον ἀνὴρ φίλος
συνετός τε καὶ εὔνοος, τά τοι ἐγὼ καὶ ἀμφότερα συνειδὼς ἔχω μαρτυρέειν
ἐς πρήγματα τὰ ἐμά. νῦν ὦν, εὖ γὰρ ἐποίησας ἀπικόμενος, τάδε τοι ἐγὼ **4**
προτείνομαι· Μίλητον μὲν ἔα καὶ τὴν νεόκτιστον ἐν Θρηίκηι πόλιν, σὺ δέ
μοι ἑπόμενος ἐς Σοῦσα ἔχε τά περ ἂν ἐγὼ ἔχω, ἐμός τε σύσσιτος ἐὼν καὶ
σύμβουλος."

Ταῦτα Δαρεῖος εἴπας καὶ καταστήσας Ἀρταφρένεα ἀδελφεὸν ἑωυτοῦ **25**
ὁμοπάτριον ὕπαρχον εἶναι Σαρδίων, ἀπήλαυνε ἐς Σοῦσα ἅμα ἀγόμενος

23.1 μισθὸν post δωρεὰν transp. Abicht: <ἅτε> add. Wilson: ἔτυχε μισθὸν δωρεὴν
codd.: μισθὸν del. Schaefer: δωρεὴν del. Dobree

Ἱστιαῖον, Ὀτάνην δὲ ἀποδέξας στρατηγὸν εἶναι τῶν παραθαλασσίων
ἀνδρῶν, τοῦ τὸν πατέρα Σισάμνην βασιλεὺς Καμβύσης γενόμενον τῶν
βασιληίων δικαστέων, ὅτι ἐπὶ χρήμασι δίκην ἄδικον ἐδίκασε, σφάξας
ἀπέδειρε πᾶσαν τὴν ἀνθρωπηίην, σπαδίξας δὲ αὐτοῦ τὸ δέρμα ἱμάντας
2   ἐξ αὐτοῦ ἔταμε καὶ ἐνέτεινε τὸν θρόνον ἐς τὸν ἵζων ἐδίκαζε· ἐντανύσας
δὲ ὁ Καμβύσης ἀπέδεξε δικαστὴν εἶναι ἀντὶ τοῦ Σισάμνεω, τὸν ἀποκ-
τείνας ἀπέδειρε, τὸν παῖδα τοῦ Σισάμνεω, ἐντειλάμενός οἱ μεμνῆσθαι ἐν
τῶι κατίζων θρόνωι δικάζει.

26 Οὗτος ὢν ὁ Ὀτάνης, ὁ ἐγκατιζόμενος ἐς τοῦτον τὸν θρόνον, τότε διάδοχος γενόμενος Μεγαβάζωι τῆς στρατηγίης Βυζαντίους τε εἷλε καὶ Καλχηδονίους, εἷλε δὲ Ἄντανδρον τὴν ἐν τῆι Τρωιάδι γῆι, εἷλε δὲ Λαμπώνιον,
λαβὼν δὲ παρὰ Λεσβίων νέας εἷλε Λῆμνόν τε καὶ Ἴμβρον, ἀμφοτέρας ἔτι
τότε ὑπὸ Πελασγῶν οἰκεομένας.

27 Οἱ μὲν δὴ Λήμνιοι καὶ <Ἴμβριοι> ἐμαχέσαντο εὖ [καὶ] ἀμυνόμενοι
<δ'>ἀνὰ χρόνον ἐκακώθησαν· τοῖσι δὲ περιεοῦσι αὐτῶν οἱ Πέρσαι
ὕπαρχον ἐπιστᾶσι Λυκάρητον τὸν Μαιανδρίου τοῦ βασιλεύσαντος Σάμου
2   ἀδελφεόν. οὗτος ὁ Λυκάρητος ἄρχων ἐν Λήμνωι τελευτᾶι ... αἰτίη δὲ τούτου ἥδε· πάντας ἠνδραποδίζετο καὶ κατεστρέφετο, τοὺς μὲν λιποστρατίης
ἐπὶ Σκύθας αἰτιώμενος, τοὺς δὲ σίνεσθαι τὸν Δαρείου στρατὸν ἀπὸ Σκυθέων ὀπίσω ἀνακομιζόμενον.

28 Οὗτος μέν νυν τοσαῦτα ἐξεργάσατο στρατηγήσας, μετὰ δὲ οὐ πολλὸν χρόνον ἀνανέωσις κακῶν ἦν, καὶ ἤρχετο τὸ δεύτερον ἐκ Νάξου τε καὶ
Μιλήτου Ἴωσι γίνεσθαι κακά. τοῦτο μὲν γὰρ ἡ Νάξος εὐδαιμονίηι τῶν
νήσων προέφερε, τοῦτο δὲ κατὰ τὸν αὐτὸν χρόνον ἡ Μίλητος αὐτή τε
ἑωυτῆς μάλιστα δὴ τότε ἀκμάσασα καὶ δὴ καὶ τῆς Ἰωνίης ἦν πρόσχημα,
κατύπερθε δὲ τούτων ἐπὶ δύο γενεὰς ἀνδρῶν νοσήσασα ἐς τὰ μάλιστα
στάσι, μέχρι οὗ μιν Πάριοι κατήρτισαν. τούτους γὰρ καταρτιστῆρας ἐκ
πάντων Ἑλλήνων εἵλοντο οἱ Μιλήσιοι.

29 Κατήλλαξαν δέ σφεας ὧδε οἱ Πάριοι· ὡς ἀπίκοντο αὐτῶν ἄνδρες οἱ
ἄριστοι ἐς τὴν Μίλητον, ὥρων γὰρ δή σφεας δεινῶς οἰκοφθορημένους,
ἔφασαν αὐτῶν βούλεσθαι διεξελθεῖν τὴν χώρην. ποιεῦντες δὲ ταῦτα καὶ
διεξιόντες πᾶσαν τὴν Μιλησίην, ὅκως τινὰ ἴδοιεν <ἐν> ἀνεστηκυίηι τῆι
χώρηι ἀγρὸν εὖ ἐξεργασμένον, ἀπεγράφοντο τὸ οὔνομα τοῦ δεσπότεω
2   τοῦ ἀγροῦ. διεξελάσαντες δὲ πᾶσαν τὴν χώρην καὶ σπανίους εὑρόντες
τούτους, ὡς τάχιστα κατέβησαν ἐς τὸ ἄστυ, ἁλίην ποιησάμενοι ἀπέδεξαν
τούτους μὲν τὴν πόλιν νέμειν τῶν εὗρον τοὺς ἀγροὺς εὖ ἐξεργασμένους·

27.1 Ἴμβριοι et δ' add. Powell καὶ del. Powell   27.2 lacunam statuit Valckenaer
28 ἀνανέωσις κακῶν ἦν Gebhardt: ἄνεος vel ἄνεως codd.: ἀνέσις κακῶν ἦν Scaliger etc.:
νέα Ἴωσι κακὰ ἦν Griffiths

δοκέειν γὰρ ἔφασαν καὶ τῶν δημοσίων οὕτω δή σφεας ἐπιμελήσεσθαι
ὥσπερ τῶν σφετέρων· τοὺς δὲ ἄλλους Μιλησίους τοὺς πρὶν στασιάζον-
τας τούτων ἔταξαν πείθεσθαι.

Πάριοι μέν νυν Μιλησίους οὕτω κατήρτισαν· τότε δὲ ἐκ τουτέων τῶν 30
πολίων ὧδε ἤρχετο κακὰ γίνεσθαι τῆι Ἰωνίηι. ἐκ Νάξου ἔφυγον ἄνδρες
τῶν παχέων ὑπὸ τοῦ δήμου, φυγόντες δὲ ἀπίκοντο ἐς Μίλητον. τῆς δὲ 2
Μιλήτου ἐτύγχανε ἐπίτροπος ἐὼν Ἀρισταγόρης ὁ Μολπαγόρεω, γαμβρός τε ἐὼν καὶ ἀνεψιὸς Ἱστιαίου τοῦ Λυσαγόρεω, τὸν ὁ Δαρεῖος ἐν
Σούσοισι κατεῖχε. ὁ γὰρ Ἱστιαῖος τύραννος ἦν Μιλήτου καὶ ἐτύγχανε
τοῦτον τὸν χρόνον ἐὼν ἐν Σούσοισι, ὅτε οἱ Νάξιοι ἦλθον, ξεῖνοι πρὶν
ἐόντες τῶι Ἱστιαίωι. ἀπικόμενοι δὲ οἱ Νάξιοι ἐς τὴν Μίλητον ἐδέοντο τοῦ 3
Ἀρισταγόρεω, εἴ κως αὐτοῖσι παράσχοι δύναμίν τινα καὶ κατέλθοιεν ἐς
τὴν ἑωυτῶν. ὁ δὲ ἐπιλεξάμενος ὡς, ἢν δι᾽ αὐτοῦ κατέλθωσι ἐς τὴν πόλιν,
ἄρξει τῆς Νάξου, σκῆψιν δὲ ποιεύμενος τὴν ξεινίην τὴν Ἱστιαίου, τόνδε σφι
λόγον προσέφερε· "αὐτὸς μὲν ὑμῖν οὐ φερέγγυός εἰμι δύναμιν παρασχεῖν 4
τοσαύτην ὥστε κατάγειν ἀεκόντων τῶν τὴν πόλιν ἐχόντων Ναξίων·
πυνθάνομαι γὰρ ὀκτακισχιλίην ἀσπίδα Ναξίοισι εἶναι καὶ πλοῖα μακρὰ
πολλά· μηχανήσομαι δὲ πᾶσαν σπουδὴν ποιεύμενος. ἐπινοέω δὲ τῆιδε. 5
Ἀρταφρένης μοι τυγχάνει ἐὼν φίλος· ὁ δὲ Ἀρταφρένης ὑμῖν Ὑστάσπεος μέν
ἐστι παῖς, Δαρείου δὲ τοῦ βασιλέος ἀδελφεός, τῶν δ᾽ ἐπιθαλασσίων τῶν ἐν
τῆι Ἀσίηι ἄρχει πάντων, ἔχων στρατιήν τε πολλὴν καὶ πολλὰς νέας. τοῦτον ὦν δοκέω τὸν ἄνδρα ποιήσειν τῶν ἂν χρηίζωμεν." ταῦτα ἀκούσαντες 6
οἱ Νάξιοι προσέθεσαν τῶι Ἀρισταγόρηι πρήσσειν τῆι δύναιτο ἄριστα καὶ
ὑπίσχεσθαι δῶρα ἐκέλευον καὶ δαπάνην τῆι στρατιῆι ὡς αὐτοὶ διαλύσοντες, ἐλπίδας πολλὰς ἔχοντες, ὅταν ἐπιφανέωσι ἐς τὴν Νάξον, πάντα ποιήσειν τοὺς Ναξίους τὰ ἂν αὐτοὶ κελεύσωσι, ὣς δὲ καὶ τοὺς ἄλλους νησιώτας·
τῶν γὰρ νήσων τουτέων [τῶν Κυκλάδων] οὐδεμία κω ἦν ὑπὸ Δαρείωι.

Ἀπικόμενος δὲ ὁ Ἀρισταγόρης ἐς τὰς Σάρδις λέγει πρὸς τὸν Ἀρταφρένεα 31
ὡς Νάξος εἴη νῆσος μεγάθεϊ μὲν οὐ μεγάλη, ἄλλως δὲ καλή τε καὶ ἀγαθὴ καὶ
ἀγχοῦ Ἰωνίης, χρήματα δὲ ἔνι πολλὰ καὶ ἀνδράποδα. "σὺ ὦν ἐπὶ ταύτην
τὴν χώρην στρατηλάτεε, κατάγων ἐς αὐτὴν τοὺς φυγάδας ἐξ αὐτῆς. καί 2
τοι ταῦτα ποιήσαντι τοῦτο μέν ἐστι ἕτοιμα παρ᾽ ἐμοὶ χρήματα μεγάλα
πάρεξ τῶν ἀναισιμωμάτων τῆι στρατιῆι (ταῦτα μὲν γὰρ δίκαιον ἡμέας
τοὺς ἄγοντας παρέχειν), τοῦτο δὲ νήσους βασιλέϊ προσκτήσεαι αὐτήν τε
Νάξον καὶ τὰς ἐκ ταύτης ἠρτημένας, Πάρον καὶ Ἄνδρον καὶ ἄλλας τὰς Κυκ-
λάδας καλεομένας. ἐνθεῦτεν δὲ ὁρμώμενος εὐπετέως ἐπιθήσεαι Εὐβοίηι, 3
νήσωι μεγάληι τε καὶ εὐδαίμονι, οὐκ ἐλάσσονι Κύπρου καὶ κάρτα εὐπετέϊ

30.6 τῶν Κυκλάδων seclusit Hude

αἱρεθῆναι. ἀποχρῶσι δὲ ἑκατὸν νέες ταύτας πάσας χειρώσασθαι." ὁ δὲ
4 ἀμείβετο αὐτὸν τοισίδε· "σὺ ἐς οἶκον τὸν βασιλέος ἐσηγητὴς γίνεαι πρηγ-
μάτων ἀγαθῶν καὶ ταῦτα εὖ παραινέεις πάντα, πλὴν τῶν νεῶν τοῦ ἀρι-
θμοῦ. ἀντὶ δὲ ἑκατὸν νεῶν διηκόσιαί τοι ἕτοιμοι ἔσονται ἅμα τῶι ἔαρι. δεῖ
δὲ τούτοισι καὶ αὐτὸν βασιλέα συνέπαινον γίνεσθαι."
32 Ὁ μὲν δὴ Ἀρισταγόρης ὡς ταῦτα ἤκουσε, περιχαρὴς ἐὼν ἀπήιε ἐς
Μίλητον. ὁ δὲ Ἀρταφρένης, ὥς οἱ πέμψαντι ἐς Σοῦσα καὶ ὑπερθέντι τὰ
ἐκ τοῦ Ἀρισταγόρεω λεγόμενα συνέπαινος καὶ αὐτὸς Δαρεῖος ἐγένετο,
παρεσκευάσατο μὲν διηκοσίας τριήρεας, πολλὸν δὲ κάρτα ὅμιλον Περσέων
τε καὶ τῶν ἄλλων συμμάχων, στρατηγὸν δὲ τούτων ἀπέδεξε Μεγαβάτην
ἄνδρα Πέρσην τῶν Ἀχαιμενιδέων, ἑωυτοῦ τε καὶ Δαρείου ἀνεψιόν, τοῦ
Παυσανίης ὁ Κλεομβρότου Λακεδαιμόνιος, εἰ δὴ ἀληθής γέ ἐστι ὁ λόγος,
ὑστέρωι χρόνωι τούτων ἡρμόσατο θυγατέρα, ἔρωτα σχὼν τῆς Ἑλλάδος τύραννος γενέσθαι. ἀποδέξας δὲ Μεγαβάτην στρατηγὸν Ἀρταφρένης
ἀπέστειλε τὸν στρατὸν παρὰ τὸν Ἀρισταγόρεα.
33 Παραλαβὼν δὲ ὁ Μεγαβάτης ἐκ τῆς Μιλήτου τόν τε Ἀρισταγόρεα καὶ
τὴν Ἰάδα στρατιὴν καὶ τοὺς Ναξίους ἔπλεε πρόφασιν ἐπ' Ἑλλησπόντου,
ἐπείτε δὲ ἐγένετο ἐν Χίωι, ἔσχε τὰς νέας ἐς Καύκασα, ὡς ἐνθεῦτεν βορέηι
2 ἀνέμωι ἐς τὴν Νάξον διαβάλοι. καὶ οὐ γὰρ ἔδεε τούτωι τῶι στόλωι Ναξίους
ἀπολέσθαι, πρῆγμα τοιόνδε συνηνείχθη γενέσθαι· περιιόντος Μεγαβάτεω
τὰς ἐπὶ τῶν νεῶν φυλακὰς ἐπὶ νεὸς Μυνδίης ἔτυχε οὐδεὶς φυλάσσων·
ὁ δὲ δεινόν τι ποιησάμενος ἐκέλευσε τοὺς δορυφόρους ἐξευρόντας τὸν
ἄρχοντα ταύτης τῆς νεός, τῶι οὔνομα ἦν Σκύλαξ, τοῦτον δῆσαι διὰ
θαλαμίης διελκόντας τῆς νεὸς κατὰ τοῦτο, ἔξω μὲν κεφαλὴν ποιεῦντας, ἔσω
3 δὲ τὸ σῶμα. δεθέντος δὲ τοῦ Σκύλακος ἐξαγγέλλει τις τῶι Ἀρισταγόρηι
ὅτι τὸν ξεῖνόν οἱ τὸν Μύνδιον Μεγαβάτης δήσας λυμαίνοιτο. ὁ δ' ἐλθὼν
παραιτέετο τὸν Πέρσην, τυγχάνων δὲ οὐδενὸς τῶν ἐδέετο αὐτὸς ἐλθὼν
ἔλυσε. πυθόμενος δὲ κάρτα δεινὸν ἐποιήσατο ὁ Μεγαβάτης καὶ ἐσπέρχετο
4 τῶι Ἀρισταγόρηι. ὁ δὲ εἶπε· "σοὶ δὲ καὶ τούτοισι τοῖσι πρήγμασι τί ἐστι;
οὔ σε ἀπέστειλε Ἀρταφρένης ἐμέο πείθεσθαι καὶ πλέειν τῆι ἂν ἐγὼ κελεύω;
τί πολλὰ πρήσσεις;" ταῦτα εἶπε ὁ Ἀρισταγόρης. ὁ δὲ θυμωθεὶς τούτοισι,
ὡς νὺξ ἐγένετο, ἔπεμπε ἐς Νάξον πλοίωι ἄνδρας φράσοντας τοῖσι Ναξίοισι
πάντα τὰ παρεόντα σφι πρήγματα.
34 Οἱ γὰρ ὦν Νάξιοι οὐδὲν πάντως προσεδέκοντο ἐπὶ σφέας τὸν στόλον
τοῦτον ὁρμήσεσθαι. ἐπεὶ μέντοι ἐπύθοντο, αὐτίκα μὲν ἐσηνείκαντο τὰ ἐκ
τῶν ἀγρῶν ἐς τὸ τεῖχος, παρεσκευάσαντο δὲ ὡς πολιορκησόμενοι καὶ
2 σῖτα καὶ ποτά, καὶ τὸ τεῖχος ἐσάξαντο. καὶ οὗτοι μὲν παρεσκευάζοντο
ὡς παρεσομένου σφι πολέμου, οἱ δ' ἐπείτε διέβαλον ἐκ τῆς Χίου τὰς νέας

33.2 διέλκοντας Stein: διελόντας codd.: διέχοντας Powell

ἐς τὴν Νάξον, πρὸς πεφραγμένους προσεφέροντο καὶ ἐπολιόρκεον μῆνας
τέσσερας. ὡς δὲ τά τε ἔχοντες ἦλθον χρήματα οἱ Πέρσαι ταῦτα κατ- 3
εδεδαπάνητό σφι, καὶ αὐτῶι τῶι Ἀρισταγόρηι προσαναισίμωτο πολλά,
τοῦ πλεῦνός τε ἐδέετο ἡ πολιορκίη, ἐνθαῦτα τείχεα τοῖσι φυγάσι τῶν
Ναξίων οἰκοδομήσαντες ἀπαλλάσσοντο ἐς τὴν ἤπειρον, κακῶς πρήσσοντες.

Ἀρισταγόρης δὲ οὐκ εἶχε τὴν ὑπόσχεσιν τῶι Ἀρταφρένεϊ ἐκτελέσαι· 35
ἅμα δὲ ἐπίεζέ μιν ἡ δαπάνη τῆς στρατιῆς ἀπαιτεομένη, ἀρρώδεέ τε
τοῦ στρατοῦ πρήξαντος κακῶς καὶ Μεγαβάτηι διαβεβλημένος, ἐδόκεέ
τε τὴν βασιληίην τῆς Μιλήτου ἀπαιρεθήσεσθαι. ἀρρωδέων δὲ τούτων 2
ἕκαστα ἐβουλεύετο ἀπόστασιν· συνέπιπτε γὰρ καὶ τὸν ἐστιγμένον τὴν
κεφαλὴν ἀπῖχθαι ἐκ Σούσων παρὰ Ἱστιαίου, σημαίνοντα ἀπίστασθαι
Ἀρισταγόρην ἀπὸ βασιλέος. ὁ γὰρ Ἱστιαῖος βουλόμενος τῶι Ἀρισταγόρηι 3
σημῆναι ἀποστῆναι ἄλλως μὲν οὐδαμῶς εἶχε ἀσφαλέως σημῆναι ὥστε
φυλασσομένων τῶν ὁδῶν, ὁ δὲ τῶν δούλων τὸν πιστότατον ἀπο-
ξυρήσας τὴν κεφαλὴν ἔστιξε καὶ ἀνέμεινε ἀναφῦναι τὰς τρίχας, ὡς δὲ
ἀνέφυσαν τάχιστα, ἀπέπεμπε ἐς Μίλητον ἐντειλάμενος αὐτῶι ἄλλο μὲν
οὐδέν, ἐπεὰν δὲ ἀπίκηται ἐς Μίλητον, κελεύειν Ἀρισταγόρην ξυρήσαντά
μιν τὰς τρίχας κατιδέσθαι ἐς τὴν κεφαλήν· τὰ δὲ στίγματα ἐσήμαινε,
ὡς καὶ πρότερόν μοι εἴρηται, ἀπόστασιν. ταῦτα δὲ ὁ Ἱστιαῖος ἐποίεε 4
συμφορὴν ποιεύμενος μεγάλην τὴν ἑωυτοῦ κατοχὴν τὴν ἐν Σούσοισι·
ἀποστάσιος ὢν γινομένης πολλὰς εἶχε ἐλπίδας μετήσεσθαι ἐπὶ θάλασσαν, μὴ δὲ νεώτερόν τι ποιεύσης τῆς Μιλήτου οὐδαμὰ ἐς αὐτὴν ἥξειν ἔτι
ἐλογίζετο.

Ἱστιαῖος μέν νυν ταῦτα διανοεύμενος ἀπέπεμπε τὸν ἄγγελον, 36
Ἀρισταγόρηι δὲ συνέπιπτε τοῦ αὐτοῦ χρόνου πάντα ταῦτα συνελθόντα.
ἐβουλεύετο ὦν μετὰ τῶν στασιωτέων, ἐκφήνας τήν τε ἑωυτοῦ γνώμην
καὶ τὰ παρὰ τοῦ Ἱστιαίου ἀπιγμένα. οἱ μὲν δὴ ἄλλοι πάντες γνώμηι 2
κατὰ τώυτὸ ἐξεφέροντο, κελεύοντες ἀπίστασθαι, Ἑκαταῖος δ᾽ ὁ λογοποιὸς
πρῶτα μὲν οὐκ ἔα πόλεμον βασιλέϊ τῶν Περσέων ἀναιρέεσθαι, καταλέγων
τά τε ἔθνεα πάντα τῶν ἦρχε Δαρεῖος καὶ τὴν δύναμιν αὐτοῦ· ἐπείτε δὲ
οὐκ ἔπειθε, δεύτερα συνεβούλευε ποιέειν ὅκως ναυκρατέες τῆς θαλάσσης
ἔσονται. ἄλλως μέν νυν οὐδαμῶς ἔφη λέγων ἐνορᾶν ἐσόμενον τοῦτο (ἐπίσ- 3
τασθαι γὰρ τὴν δύναμιν τὴν Μιλησίων ἐοῦσαν ἀσθενέα), εἰ δὲ τὰ χρήματα καταιρεθείη τὰ ἐκ τοῦ ἱροῦ τοῦ ἐν Βραγχίδηισι, τὰ Κροῖσος ὁ
Λυδὸς ἀνέθηκε, πολλὰς εἶχε ἐλπίδας ἐπικρατήσειν τῆς θαλάσσης, καὶ οὕτω
αὐτούς τε ἕξειν <τοῖσι> χρήμασι χρᾶσθαι καὶ τοὺς πολεμίους οὐ συλήσειν
αὐτά. τὰ δὲ χρήματα ἦν ταῦτα μεγάλα, ὡς δεδήλωταί μοι ἐν τῶι πρώτωι 4
τῶν λόγων. αὕτη μὲν δὴ οὐκ ἐνίκα ἡ γνώμη, ἐδόκεε δὲ ὅμως ἀπίστασθαι, ἕνα τε αὐτῶν πλώσαντα ἐς Μυοῦντα ἐς τὸ στρατόπεδον τὸ ἀπὸ τῆς

Νάξου ἀπελθόν, ἐὸν ἐνθαῦτα, συλλαμβάνειν πειρᾶσθαι τοὺς ἐπὶ τῶν νεῶν ἐπιπλέοντας στρατηγούς.

37 Ἀποπεμφθέντος δὲ Ἰητραγόρεω κατ' αὐτὸ τοῦτο καὶ συλλαβόντος δόλωι Ὀλίατον Ἰβανώλλιος Μυλασέα καὶ Ἱστιαῖον Τύμνεω Τερμερέα καὶ Κώην Ἐρξάνδρου, τῶι Δαρεῖος Μυτιλήνην ἐδωρήσατο, καὶ Ἀρισταγόρην Ἡρακλείδεω Κυμαῖον καὶ ἄλλους συχνούς, οὕτω δὴ ἐκ τοῦ ἐμφανέος ὁ
2 Ἀρισταγόρης ἀπεστήκεε, πᾶν ἐπὶ Δαρείωι μηχανώμενος. καὶ πρῶτα μὲν λόγωι μετεὶς τὴν τυραννίδα ἰσονομίην ἐποίεε τῆι Μιλήτωι, ὡς ἂν ἑκόντες αὐτῶι οἱ Μιλήσιοι συναπισταίατο, μετὰ δὲ καὶ ἐν τῆι ἄλληι Ἰωνίηι τὠυτὸ τοῦτο ἐποίεε, τοὺς μὲν ἐξελαύνων τῶν τυράννων, τοὺς δ' ἔλαβε τυράννους ἀπὸ τῶν νεῶν τῶν συμπλευσασέων ἐπὶ Νάξον, τούτους δὲ φίλα βουλόμενος ποιέεσθαι τῆισι πόλισι ἐξεδίδου, ἄλλον ἐς ἄλλην πόλιν παραδιδούς, ὅθεν εἴη ἕκαστος.

38 Κώην μέν νυν Μυτιληναῖοι ἐπείτε τάχιστα παρέλαβον, ἐξαγαγόντες κατέλευσαν, Κυμαῖοι δὲ τὸν σφέτερον αὐτῶν ἀπῆκαν· ὡς δὲ καὶ ἄλλοι οἱ
2 πλέονες ἀπίεσαν. τυράννων μέν νυν κατάπαυσις ἐγίνετο ἀνὰ τὰς πόλιας, Ἀρισταγόρης δὲ ὁ Μιλήσιος ὡς τοὺς τυράννους κατέπαυσε, στρατηγοὺς ἐν ἑκάστηι τῶν πολίων κελεύσας ἑκάστους καταστῆσαι, δεύτερα αὐτὸς ἐς Λακεδαίμονα τριήρεϊ ἀπόστολος ἐγίνετο· ἔδεε γὰρ δὴ συμμαχίης τινός οἱ μεγάλης ἐξευρεθῆναι.

39 Τῆς δὲ Σπάρτης Ἀναξανδρίδης μὲν ὁ Λέοντος οὐκέτι περιεὼν ἐβασίλευε ἀλλὰ ἐτετελευτήκεε, Κλεομένης δὲ ὁ Ἀναξανδρίδεω εἶχε τὴν βασιληίην, οὐ κατ' ἀνδραγαθίην σχὼν ἀλλὰ κατὰ γένος. Ἀναξανδρίδηι γὰρ ἔχοντι γυναῖκα ἀδελφεῆς ἑωυτοῦ θυγατέρα καὶ ἐούσης ταύτης οἱ κατα-
2 θυμίης παῖδες οὐκ ἐγίνοντο. τούτου δὲ τοιούτου ἐόντος οἱ ἔφοροι εἶπαν ἐπικαλεσάμενοι αὐτόν· "εἴ τοι σὺ σεωυτοῦ μὴ προορᾶις, ἀλλ' ἡμῖν τοῦτό ἐστι οὐ περιοπτέον, γένος τὸ Εὐρυσθένεος γενέσθαι ἐξίτηλον. σύ νυν τὴν μὲν ἔχεις γυναῖκα, ἐπείτε τοι οὐ τίκτει, ἔξεο, ἄλλην δὲ γῆμον· καὶ ποιέων ταῦτα Σπαρτιήτηισι ἀδήσεις." ὁ δ' ἀμείβετο φὰς τούτων οὐδέτερα ποιή-σειν, ἐκείνους τε οὐ καλῶς συμβουλεύειν παραινέοντας, τὴν ἔχει γυναῖκα, ἐοῦσαν ἀναμάρτητον ἑωυτῶι, ταύτην ἀπέντα ἄλλην ἐσαγαγέσθαι· οὐδέ σφι πείσεσθαι.

40 Πρὸς ταῦτα οἱ ἔφοροι καὶ οἱ γέροντες βουλευσάμενοι προσέφερον Ἀναξανδρίδηι τάδε· "ἐπεὶ τοίνυν περιεχόμενόν σε ὁρῶμεν τῆς ἔχεις γυναικός, σὺ δὲ ταῦτα ποίεε καὶ μὴ ἀντίβαινε τούτοισι, ἵνα μή τι ἀλλοῖον
2 περὶ σεῦ Σπαρτιῆται βουλεύσωνται. γυναικὸς μὲν τῆς ἔχεις οὐ προσ-δεόμεθά σευ τῆς ἐξέσιος, σὺ δὲ ταύτηι τε πάντα ὅσα νῦν παρέχεις πάρεχε

37.2 λόγωι codd.: <τῶι> λεῶι Griffiths: <ἐν συλ>λόγωι Wilson

καὶ ἄλλην πρὸς ταύτηι ἐσάγαγε γυναῖκα τεκνοποιόν." ταῦτά κηι λεγόντων συνεχώρησε ὁ Ἀναξανδρίδης, μετὰ δὲ γυναῖκας ἔχων δύο διξὰς ἱστίας
οἴκεε, ποιέων οὐδαμῶς Σπαρτιητικά.

Χρόνου δὲ οὐ πολλοῦ διελθόντος ἡ ἐσύστερον ἐπελθοῦσα γυνή, **41**
<ἐοῦσα θυγάτηρ Πρινητάδεω τοῦ Δημαρμένου>, τίκτει τὸν δὴ Κλεομένεα
τοῦτον. καὶ αὕτη τε ἔφεδρον βασιλέα Σπαρτιήτηισι ἀπέφαινε καὶ ἡ
προτέρη γυνὴ τὸν πρότερον χρόνον ἄτοκος ἐοῦσα τότε κως ἐκύησε,
συντυχίηι ταύτηι χρησαμένη. ἔχουσαν δὲ αὐτὴν ἀληθέϊ λόγωι οἱ τῆς **2**
ἐπελθούσης γυναικὸς οἰκήιοι πυθόμενοι ὤχλεον, φάμενοι αὐτὴν κομπέειν
ἄλλως βουλομένην ὑποβαλέσθαι. δεινὰ δὲ ποιεύντων αὐτῶν, τοῦ χρόνου
συντάμνοντος, ὑπ᾿ ἀπιστίης οἱ ἔφοροι τίκτουσαν τὴν γυναῖκα περιιζόμενοι
ἐφύλαξαν. ἡ δὲ ὡς ἔτεκε Δωριέα, ἰθέως ἴσχει Λεωνίδην καὶ μετὰ τοῦτον **3**
ἰθέως ἴσχει Κλεόμβροτον· οἱ δὲ καὶ διδύμους λέγουσι Κλεόμβροτόν τε καὶ
Λεωνίδην γενέσθαι. ἡ δὲ Κλεομένεα τεκοῦσα [καὶ τὸ δεύτερον ἐπελθοῦσα
γυνή, ἐοῦσα θυγάτηρ Πρινητάδεω τοῦ Δημαρμένου,] οὐκέτι ἔτικτε τὸ
δεύτερον.

Ὁ μὲν δὴ Κλεομένης, ὡς λέγεται, ἦν τε οὐ φρενήρης ἀκρομανής τε, ὁ δὲ **42**
Δωριεὺς ἦν τῶν ἡλίκων πάντων πρῶτος, εὖ τε ἠπίστατο κατ᾿ ἀνδραγαθίην αὐτὸς σχήσων τὴν βασιληίην. ὥστε ὢν οὕτω φρονέων, ἐπειδὴ **2**
ὅ τε Ἀναξανδρίδης ἀπέθανε καὶ οἱ Λακεδαιμόνιοι χρεώμενοι τῶι νόμωι
ἐστήσαντο βασιλέα τὸν πρεσβύτατον Κλεομένεα, ὁ Δωριεὺς δεινόν τε
ποιεύμενος καὶ οὐκ ἀξιῶν ὑπὸ Κλεομένεος βασιλεύεσθαι, αἰτήσας λεῶν
Σπαρτιήτας ἦγε ἐς ἀποικίην, οὔτε τῶι ἐν Δελφοῖσι χρηστηρίωι χρησάμενος ἐς ἥντινα γῆν κτίσων ἴηι, οὔτε ποιήσας οὐδὲν τῶν νομιζομένων·
οἷα δὲ βαρέως φέρων, ἀπίει ἐς τὴν Λιβύην τὰ πλοῖα· κατηγέοντο δέ οἱ
ἄνδρες Θηραῖοι. ἀπικόμενος δὲ ἐς τὴν Κίνυπα οἴκισε χῶρον κάλλιστον **3**
τῶν Λιβύων παρὰ ποταμόν. ἐξελασθεὶς δὲ ἐνθεῦτεν τῶι τρίτωι ἔτεϊ ὑπὸ
Μακέων τε [καὶ] Λιβύων καὶ Καρχηδονίων ἀπίκετο ἐς Πελοπόννησον.

Ἐνθαῦτα δέ οἱ Ἀντιχάρης ἀνὴρ Ἐλεώνιος συνεβούλευσε ἐκ τῶν Λαΐου **43**
χρησμῶν Ἡρακλείην τὴν ἐν Σικελίηι κτίζειν, φὰς τὴν Ἔρυκος χώρην πᾶσαν
εἶναι Ἡρακλειδέων αὐτοῦ Ἡρακλέος κτησαμένου. ὁ δὲ ἀκούσας ταῦτα ἐς
Δελφοὺς οἴχετο χρησόμενος τῶι χρηστηρίωι, εἰ αἱρέει ἐπ᾿ ἣν στέλλεται
χώρην· ἡ δὲ Πυθίη οἱ χρᾶι αἱρήσειν. παραλαβὼν δὲ Δωριεὺς τὸν στόλον
τὸν καὶ ἐς Λιβύην ἦγε ἐκομίζετο παρὰ τὴν Ἰταλίην.

Τὸν χρόνον δὲ τοῦτον, ὡς λέγουσι Συβαρῖται, σφέας τε αὐτοὺς καὶ **44**
Τῆλυν τὸν ἑωυτῶν βασιλέα ἐπὶ Κρότωνα μέλλειν στρατεύεσθαι, τοὺς δὲ

41.1, 3 ἐοῦσα...Δημαρμένου transp. Maas   41.1 συντυχίηι θείηι Powell   41.3
καὶ...ἐπελθοῦσα del. Maas   43 Λάσου Schneidewin: Ἰάμου Valckenaer   Ἡρακλείην γῆν τὴν Stein

Κροτωνιήτας περιδεέας γενομένους δεηθῆναι Δωριέος σφίσι τιμωρῆσαι
καὶ τυχεῖν δεηθέντας· συστρατεύεσθαί τε δὴ ἐπὶ Σύβαριν Δωριέα καὶ
2 συνελεῖν τὴν Σύβαριν. ταῦτα μέν νυν Συβαρῖται λέγουσι ποιῆσαι Δωριέα
τε καὶ τοὺς μετ᾽ αὐτοῦ, Κροτωνιῆται δὲ οὐδένα σφίσι φασὶ ξεῖνον προσεπι-
λαβέσθαι τοῦ πρὸς Συβαρίτας πολέμου εἰ μὴ Καλλίην τῶν Ἰαμιδέων μάντιν
Ἠλεῖον μοῦνον, καὶ τοῦτον τρόπωι τοιῶιδε· παρὰ Τήλυος τοῦ Συβαριτέων
τυράννου ἀποδράντα ἀπικέσθαι παρὰ σφέας, ἐπείτε οἱ τὰ ἱρὰ οὐ προεχώρεε χρηστὰ θυομένωι ἐπὶ Κρότωνα.
45 Ταῦτα δ᾽ ὦν οὗτοι λέγουσι. μαρτύρια δὲ τούτων ἑκάτεροι
ἀποδεικνύουσι τάδε· Συβαρῖται μὲν τέμενός τε καὶ νηὸν ἐόντα παρὰ τὸν
ξηρὸν Κρᾶθιν, τὸν ἱδρύσασθαι συνελόντα τὴν πόλιν Δωριέα λέγουσι
Ἀθηναίηι ἐπωνύμωι Κραθίηι, τοῦτο δὲ αὐτοῦ Δωριέος τὸν θάνατον
μαρτύριον μέγιστον ποιεῦνται, ὅτι παρὰ τὰ μεμαντευμένα ποιέων
διεφθάρη· εἰ γὰρ δὴ μὴ παρέπρηξε μηδέν, ἐπ᾽ ὃ δὲ ἐστάλη ἐποίεε, εἷλε ἂν
τὴν Ἐρυκίνην χώρην καὶ ἑλὼν κατέσχε, οὐδ᾽ ἂν αὐτός τε καὶ ἡ στρατιὴ
2 διεφθάρη. οἱ δ᾽ αὖ Κροτωνιῆται ἀποδεικνύουσι Καλλίηι μὲν τῶι Ἠλείωι
ἐξαίρετα ἐν γῆι τῆι Κροτωνιήτιδι πολλὰ δοθέντα, τὰ καὶ ἐς ἐμὲ ἔτι
ἐνέμοντο οἱ Καλλίεω ἀπόγονοι, Δωριέϊ δὲ καὶ τοῖσι Δωριέος ἀπογόνοισι
οὐδέν. καίτοι, εἰ συνεπελάβετό γε τοῦ Συβαριτικοῦ πολέμου Δωριεύς,
δοθῆναι ἄν οἱ πολλαπλήσια ἢ Καλλίηι. ταῦτα μέν νυν ἑκάτεροι αὐτῶν
μαρτύρια ἀποφαίνονται· καὶ πάρεστι, ὁκοτέροισί τις πείθεται αὐτῶν,
τούτοισι προσχωρέειν.
46 Συνέπλεον δὲ Δωριέϊ καὶ ἄλλοι συγκτίσται Σπαρτιητέων, Θεσσαλὸς
καὶ Παραιβάτης καὶ Κελέης καὶ Εὐρυλέων, οἳ ἐπείτε ἀπίκοντο παντὶ
στόλωι ἐς τὴν Σικελίην, ἀπέθανον μάχηι ἑσσωθέντες ὑπό τε Φοινίκων
καὶ Ἐγεσταίων· μοῦνος δὲ Εὐρυλέων τῶν συγκτιστέων περιεγένετο τού-
2 του τοῦ πάθεος. συλλαβὼν δὲ οὗτος τῆς στρατιῆς τοὺς περιγενομένους
ἔσχε Μινώην τὴν Σελινουσίων ἀποικίην καὶ συνελευθέρου Σελινουσίους
τοῦ μουνάρχου Πειθαγόρεω. μετὰ δέ, ὡς τοῦτον κατεῖλε, αὐτὸς τυραννίδι
ἐπεχείρησε Σελινοῦντος καὶ ἐμουνάρχησε χρόνον ἐπ᾽ ὀλίγον· οἱ γάρ μιν
Σελινούσιοι ἐπαναστάντες ἀπέκτειναν καταφυγόντα ἐπὶ Διὸς Ἀγοραίου
βωμόν.
47 Συνέσπετο δὲ Δωριέϊ καὶ συναπέθανε Φίλιππος ὁ Βουτακίδεω
Κροτωνιήτης ἀνήρ, ὃς ἁρμοσάμενος Τήλυος τοῦ Συβαρίτεω θυγατέρα
ἔφυγε ἐκ Κρότωνος, ψευσθεὶς δὲ τοῦ γάμου οἴχετο πλέων ἐς Κυρήνην,
ἐκ ταύτης δὲ ὁρμώμενος συνέσπετο οἰκηίηι τε τριήρεϊ καὶ οἰκηίηι ἀνδρῶν
δυνάμι, ἐών τε Ὀλυμπιονίκης καὶ κάλλιστος Ἑλλήνων τῶν κατ᾽ ἑωυτόν.

45.1 ὦν de la Barre et Wilson: οὐχ ABSVU: οὐκ CP αὖ Bekker: δὴ Legrand
47.1 δυνάμι Powell: δαπάνηι codd.

διὰ δὲ τὸ ἑωυτοῦ κάλλος ἠνείκατο παρὰ Ἐγεσταίων τὰ οὐδεὶς ἄλλος· ἐπὶ   2
γὰρ τοῦ τάφου αὐτοῦ ἡρώιον ἱδρυσάμενοι θυσίηισι αὐτὸν ἱλάσκονται.

Δωριεὺς μέν νυν τρόπωι τοιούτωι ἐτελεύτησε· εἰ δὲ ἠνέσχετο βασιλευό-   48
μενος ὑπὸ Κλεομένεος καὶ κατέμενε ἐν Σπάρτηι, ἐβασίλευσε ἂν Λακεδαί-
μονος· οὐ γάρ τινα πολλὸν χρόνον ἦρξε ὁ Κλεομένης, ἀλλ᾽ ἀπέθανε ἄπαις,
θυγατέρα μούνην λιπών, τῆι οὔνομα ἦν Γοργώ.

Ἀπικνέεται δ᾽ ὧν ὁ Ἀρισταγόρης ὁ Μιλήτου τύραννος ἐς τὴν Σπάρτην   49
Κλεομένεος ἔχοντος τὴν ἀρχήν· τῶι δὴ ἐς λόγους ἤιε, ὡς Λακεδαιμόνιοι
λέγουσι, ἔχων χάλκεον πίνακα ἐν τῶι γῆς ἁπάσης περίοδος ἐνετέτμητο
καὶ θάλασσά τε πᾶσα καὶ ποταμοὶ πάντες. ἀπικνεόμενος δὲ ἐς λόγους   2
ὁ Ἀρισταγόρης ἔλεγε πρὸς αὐτὸν τάδε· "Κλεόμενες, σπουδὴν μὲν τὴν
ἐμὴν μὴ θωμάσηις τῆς ἐνθαῦτα ἀπίξιος· τὰ γὰρ κατήκοντά ἐστι τοιαῦτα.
Ἰώνων παῖδας δούλους εἶναι ἀντ᾽ ἐλευθέρων ὄνειδος καὶ ἄλγος μέγιστον
μὲν αὐτοῖσι ἡμῖν, ἔτι δὲ τῶν λοιπῶν ὑμῖν, ὅσωι προέστατε τῆς Ἑλλάδος.   3
νῦν ὦν πρὸς θεῶν τῶν Ἑλληνίων ῥύσασθε Ἴωνας ἐκ δουλοσύνης, ἄνδρας
ὁμαίμονας. εὐπετέως δὲ ὑμῖν ταῦτα οἷά τε χωρέειν ἐστί. οὔτε γὰρ οἱ βάρ-
βαροι ἄλκιμοί εἰσι, ὑμεῖς τε τὰ ἐς τὸν πόλεμον ἐς τὰ μέγιστα ἀνήκετε ἀρετῆς
πέρι. ἥ τε μάχη αὐτῶν ἐστι τοιήδε, τόξα καὶ αἰχμὴ βραχέα· ἀναξυρίδας δὲ
ἔχοντες ἔρχονται ἐς τὰς μάχας καὶ κυρβασίας ἐπὶ τῆισι κεφαλῆισι. οὕτω
εὐπετέες χειρωθῆναί εἰσι. ἔστι δὲ καὶ ἀγαθὰ τοῖσι τὴν ἤπειρον ἐκείνην   4
νεμομένοισι ὅσα οὐδὲ τοῖσι συνάπασι ἄλλοισι, ἀπὸ χρυσοῦ ἀρξαμένοισι,
ἄργυρος καὶ χαλκὸς καὶ ἐσθὴς ποικίλη καὶ ὑποζύγιά τε καὶ ἀνδράποδα·
τὰ θυμῶι βουλόμενοι αὐτοὶ ἂν ἔχοιτε. κατοίκηνται δὲ ἀλλήλων ἐχόμενοι   5
ὡς ἐγὼ φράσω. Ἰώνων μὲν τῶνδε οἵδε Λυδοί, οἰκέοντές τε χώρην ἀγα-
θὴν καὶ πολυαργυρώτατοι ἐόντες." δεικνὺς δὲ ἔλεγε ταῦτα ἐς τῆς γῆς τὴν
περίοδον τὴν ἐφέρετο ἐν τῶι πίνακι ἐντετμημένην. "Λυδῶν δέ", ἔφη λέγων
ὁ Ἀρισταγόρης, "οἵδε ἔχονται Φρύγες οἱ πρὸς τὴν ἠῶ, πολυπροβατώ-
τατοί τε ἐόντες πάντων τῶν ἐγὼ οἶδα καὶ πολυκαρπότατοι. Φρυγῶν δὲ   6
ἔχονται Καππαδόκαι, τοὺς ἡμεῖς Συρίους καλέομεν· τούτοισι δὲ πρόσουροι
Κίλικες, κατήκοντες ἐπὶ θάλασσαν τήνδε, ἐν τῆι ἥδε Κύπρος νῆσος κεῖται·
οἳ πεντακόσια τάλαντα βασιλέϊ τὸν ἐπέτειον φόρον ἐπιτελέουσι. Κιλίκων
δὲ τῶνδε ἔχονται Ἀρμένιοι οἵδε, καὶ οὗτοι ἐόντες πολυπρόβατοι, Ἀρμενίων
δὲ Ματιηνοὶ χώρην τήνδε ἔχοντες. ἔχεται δὲ τούτων γῆ ἥδε Κισσίη, ἐν   7
τῆι δὴ παρὰ ποταμὸν τόνδε Χοάσπην κείμενά ἐστι τὰ Σοῦσα ταῦτα,
ἔνθα βασιλεύς τε μέγας δίαιταν ποιέεται, καὶ τῶν χρημάτων οἱ θησαυροὶ
ἐνθαῦτά εἰσι· ἑλόντες δὲ ταύτην τὴν πόλιν θαρσέοντες ἤδη τῶι Διὶ πλούτου πέρι ἐρίζετε. ἀλλὰ περὶ μὲν χώρης ἄρα οὐ πολλῆς οὐδὲ οὕτω χρηστῆς   8

48 εἰ γάρ τινα πολλὸν Griffiths: οὐ γὰρ ἔτι πολλὸν Wilson

καὶ οὔρων σμικρῶν χρεόν ἐστι ὑμέας μάχας ἀναβάλλεσθαι πρός τε Μεσσηνίους ἐόντας ἰσοπαλέας καὶ Ἀρκάδας τε καὶ Ἀργείους, τοῖσι οὔτε χρυσοῦ
ἐχόμενόν ἐστι οὐδὲν οὔτε ἀργύρου, τῶν πέρι καί τινα ἐνάγει προθυμίη
μαχόμενον ἀποθνήισκειν, παρέχον δὲ τῆς Ἀσίης πάσης ἄρχειν εὐπετέως,
9 ἄλλο τι αἱρήσεσθε;" Ἀρισταγόρης μὲν ταῦτα ἔλεξε, Κλεομένης δὲ ἀμείβετο
τοισίδε· "ὦ ξεῖνε Μιλήσιε, ἀναβάλλομαί τοι ἐς τρίτην ἡμέρην ὑποκρινέεσ-
θαι."
50 Τότε μὲν ἐς τοσοῦτον ἤλασαν. ἐπείτε δὲ ἡ κυρίη ἡμέρη ἐγένετο
τῆς ὑποκρίσιος καὶ ἦλθον ἐς τὸ συγκείμενον, εἴρετο ὁ Κλεομένης τὸν
Ἀρισταγόρην ὁκοσέων ἡμερέων ἀπὸ θαλάσσης τῆς Ἰώνων ὁδὸς εἴη παρὰ
2 βασιλέα. ὁ δὲ Ἀρισταγόρης, τἆλλα ἐὼν σοφὸς καὶ διαβάλλων ἐκεῖνον εὖ, ἐν
τούτωι ἐσφάλη· χρεὸν γάρ μιν μὴ λέγειν τὸ ἐόν, βουλόμενόν γε Σπαρτιήτας ἐξαγαγεῖν ἐς τὴν Ἀσίην, λέγει δ᾽ ὦν τριῶν μηνῶν φὰς εἶναι τὴν ἄνοδον.
3 ὁ δὲ ὑπαρπάσας τὸν ἐπίλοιπον λόγον τὸν ὁ Ἀρισταγόρης ὥρμητο λέγειν
περὶ τῆς ὁδοῦ, εἶπε· "ὦ ξεῖνε Μιλήσιε, ἀπαλλάσσεο ἐκ Σπάρτης πρὸ δύντος ἡλίου· οὐδένα γὰρ λόγον εὐπρεπέα λέγεις Λακεδαιμονίοισι, ἐθέλων
σφέας ἀπὸ θαλάσσης τριῶν μηνῶν ὁδὸν ἀγαγεῖν."
51 Ὁ μὲν δὴ Κλεομένης ταῦτα εἴπας ἤιε ἐς τὰ οἰκία, ὁ δὲ Ἀρισταγόρης
λαβὼν ἱκετηρίην ἤιε ἐς τοῦ Κλεομένεος, ἐσελθὼν δὲ ἔσω ἅτε ἱκετεύων
ἐπακοῦσαι ἐκέλευε τὸν Κλεομένεα, ἀποπέμψαντα τὸ παιδίον· προσεστή-
κεε γὰρ δὴ τῶι Κλεομένεϊ ἡ θυγάτηρ, τῆι οὔνομα ἦν Γοργώ· τοῦτο δέ οἱ
καὶ μοῦνον τέκνον ἐτύγχανε ἐὸν ἐτέων ὀκτὼ ἢ ἐννέα ἡλικίην. Κλεομένης
δὲ λέγειν μιν ἐκέλευε τὰ βούλεται μηδὲ ἐπισχεῖν τοῦ παιδίου εἵνεκα.
2 ἐνθαῦτα δὴ ὁ Ἀρισταγόρης ἄρχετο ἐκ δέκα ταλάντων ὑπισχνεόμενος,
ἤν οἱ ἐπιτελέσηι τῶν ἐδέετο. ἀνανεύοντος δὲ τοῦ Κλεομένεος προέβαινε
τοῖσι χρήμασι ὑπερβάλλων ὁ Ἀρισταγόρης, ἐς οὗ πεντήκοντά τε τάλαντα
ὑπεδέδεκτο καὶ τὸ παιδίον ηὐδάξατο· "πάτερ, διαφθερέει σε ὁ ξεῖνος, ἢν
3 μὴ ἀποστὰς ἴηις." ὅ τε δὴ Κλεομένης ἡσθεὶς τοῦ παιδίου τῆι παραινέσι ἤιε
ἐς ἕτερον οἴκημα καὶ ὁ Ἀρισταγόρης ἀπαλλάσσετο τὸ παράπαν ἐκ τῆς
Σπάρτης, οὐδέ οἱ ἐξεγένετο ἐπὶ πλέον ἔτι σημῆναι περὶ τῆς ἀνόδου τῆς
παρὰ βασιλέα.
52 Ἔχει γὰρ ἀμφὶ τῆι ὁδῶι ταύτηι ὧδε. σταθμοί τε πανταχῆι εἰσι
βασιλήιοι καὶ καταλύσιες κάλλισται, διὰ οἰκεομένης τε ἡ ὁδὸς ἅπασα καὶ
ἀσφαλέος. διὰ μέν γε Λυδίης καὶ Φρυγίης σταθμοὶ τείνοντες εἴκοσί εἰσι,
2 παρασάγγαι δὲ τέσσερες καὶ ἐνενήκοντα καὶ ἥμισυ. ἐκδέκεται δὲ ἐκ τῆς
Φρυγίης ὁ Ἅλυς ποταμός, ἐπ᾽ ὧι πύλαι τε ἔπεισι, τὰς διεξελάσαι πᾶσα
ἀνάγκη καὶ οὕτω διεκπερᾶν τὸν ποταμόν, καὶ φυλακτήριον μέγα ἐπ᾽

50.3 εὐπρεπέα Richards et Maas: εὐπεέα codd.   52.1 Φρυγίης ἰόντι σταθμοὶ εἴκοσί
εἰσι Powell

αὐτῶι. διαβάντι δὲ ἐς τὴν Καππαδοκίην καὶ ταύτηι πορευομένωι μέχρι
οὔρων τῶν Κιλικίων σταθμοὶ δυῶν δέοντές εἰσι τριήκοντα, παρασάγγαι
δὲ τέσσερες καὶ ἑκατόν· ἐπὶ δὲ τοῖσι τούτων οὔροισι διξάς τε πύλας διεξ-
ελᾶις καὶ διξὰ φυλακτήρια παραμείψεαι. ταῦτα δὲ διεξελάσαντι καὶ διὰ 3
τῆς Κιλικίης ὁδὸν ποιευμένωι τρεῖς εἰσι σταθμοί, παρασάγγαι δὲ πεντεκαίδεκα καὶ ἥμισυ. οὖρος δὲ Κιλικίης καὶ τῆς Ἀρμενίης ἐστὶ ποταμὸς
νηυσιπέρητος, τῶι οὔνομα Εὐφρήτης. ἐν δὲ τῆι Ἀρμενίηι σταθμοὶ μέν
εἰσι [καταγωγέων] πεντεκαίδεκα, παρασάγγαι δὲ ἓξ καὶ πεντήκοντα καὶ
ἥμισυ, καὶ φυλακτήριον ἐν αὐτοῖσι. ποταμοὶ δὲ νηυσιπέρητοι τέσσερες 4
διὰ ταύτης ῥέουσι, τοὺς πᾶσα ἀνάγκη διαπορθμεῦσαί ἐστι, πρῶτος
μὲν Τίγρης, μετὰ δὲ δεύτερός τε καὶ τρίτος Ζάβατος ὀνομαζόμενος, οὐκ
ωὑτὸς ἐὼν ποταμὸς οὐδὲ ἐκ τοῦ αὐτοῦ ῥέων· ὁ μὲν γὰρ πρότερος αὐτῶν
καταλεχθεὶς ἐξ Ἀρμενίων ῥέει, ὁ δ᾽ ὕστερον ἐκ Ματιηνῶν· ὁ δὲ τέταρτος 5
τῶν ποταμῶν οὔνομα ἔχει Γύνδης, τὸν Κῦρος διέλαβέ κοτε ἐς διώρυχας
ἑξήκοντα καὶ τριηκοσίας. ἐκ δὲ ταύτης τῆς Ἀρμενίης ἐσβάλλοντι ἐς τὴν
Ματιηνὴν γῆν σταθμοί εἰσι τέσσερες <καὶ τριήκοντα, παρασάγγαι δὲ
ἑπτὰ καὶ τριήκοντα καὶ ἑκατόν>. ἐκ δὲ ταύτης ἐς τὴν Κισσίην χώρην 6
μεταβαίνοντι ἕνδεκα σταθμοί, παρασάγγαι δὲ δύο καὶ τεσσεράκοντα καὶ
ἥμισύ ἐστι ἐπὶ ποταμὸν Χοάσπην, ἐόντα καὶ τοῦτον νηυσιπέρητον, ἐπ᾽
ὧι Σοῦσα πόλις πεπόλισται. οὗτοι οἱ πάντες σταθμοί εἰσι ἕνδεκα καὶ
ἑκατόν. καταγωγαὶ μέν νυν σταθμῶν τοσαῦταί εἰσι ἐκ Σαρδίων ἐς Σοῦσα
ἀναβαίνοντι·

Εἰ δὲ ὀρθῶς μεμέτρηται ἡ ὁδὸς ἡ βασιληίη τοῖσι παρασάγγηισι καὶ ὁ 53
παρασάγγης δύναται τριήκοντα στάδια, ὥσπερ οὗτός γε δύναται ταῦτα,
ἐκ Σαρδίων στάδιά ἐστι ἐς τὰ βασιλήια τὰ Μεμνόνεια καλεόμενα· πεντακόσια καὶ τρισχίλια καὶ μύρια παρασαγγέων ἐόντων πεντήκοντα καὶ
τετρακοσίων. πεντήκοντα δὲ καὶ ἑκατὸν στάδια ἐπ᾽ ἡμέρηι ἑκάστηι διεξ-
ιοῦσι ἀναισιμοῦνται ἡμέραι ἀπαρτὶ ἐνενήκοντα.

Οὕτω τῶι Μιλησίωι Ἀρισταγόρηι εἴπαντι πρὸς Κλεομένεα τὸν 54
Λακεδαιμόνιον εἶναι τριῶν μηνῶν τὴν ἄνοδον τὴν παρὰ βασιλέα ὀρθῶς
εἴρητο. εἰ δέ τις τὸ ἀτρεκέστερον τούτων ἔτι δίζηται, ἐγὼ καὶ τοῦτο
σημανέω· τὴν γὰρ ἐξ Ἐφέσου ἐς Σάρδις ὁδὸν δεῖ προσλογίσασθαι ταύτηι.
καὶ δὴ λέγω σταδίους εἶναι τοὺς πάντας ἀπὸ θαλάσσης τῆς Ἑλληνικῆς 2
μέχρι Σούσων (τοῦτο γὰρ Μεμνόνιον ἄστυ καλέεται) τεσσεράκοντα
καὶ τετρακισχιλίους καὶ μυρίους· οἱ γὰρ ἐξ Ἐφέσου ἐς Σάρδις εἰσὶ
τεσσεράκοντα καὶ πεντακόσιοι στάδιοι· καὶ οὕτω τρισὶ ἡμέρηισι μηκύνε-
ται ἡ τρίμηνος ὁδός.

52.3 καταγωγέων del. Powell et Maas   52.6 καὶ τριάκοντα... ἑκατόν suppl. de la
Barre

68   ΗΡΟΔΟΤΟΥ

55   Ἀπελαυνόμενος δὲ ὁ Ἀρισταγόρης ἐκ τῆς Σπάρτης ἤιε ἐς τὰς Ἀθήνας
γενομένας τυράννων ὧδε ἐλευθέρας. ἐπεὶ Ἵππαρχον τὸν Πεισιστράτου,
Ἱππίεω δὲ τοῦ τυράννου ἀδελφεόν, ἰδόντα ὄψιν ἐνυπνίου τῶι ἑωυτοῦ
πάθεϊ ἐμφερεστάτην κτείνουσι Ἀριστογείτων καὶ Ἁρμόδιος, γένος ἐόντες τὰ ἀνέκαθεν Γεφυραῖοι, μετὰ ταῦτα ἐτυραννεύοντο Ἀθηναῖοι ἐπ' ἔτεα
τέσσερα οὐδὲν ἧσσον ἀλλὰ καὶ μᾶλλον ἢ πρὸ τοῦ. ἡ μέν νυν ὄψις τοῦ
Ἱππάρχου ἐνυπνίου ἦν ἥδε.

56   Ἐν τῆι προτέρηι νυκτὶ τῶν Παναθηναίων ἐδόκεε ὁ Ἵππαρχος ἄνδρα οἱ
ἐπιστάντα μέγαν καὶ εὐειδέα αἰνίσσεσθαι τάδε τὰ ἔπεα·
    τλῆθι λέων, ἄτλητα παθὼν τετληότι θυμῶι·
    οὐδεὶς ἀνθρώπων ἀδικῶν τίσιν οὐκ ἀποτίσει.
2 ταῦτα δέ, ὡς ἡμέρη ἐγένετο τάχιστα, φανερὸς ἦν ὑπερτιθέμενος
ὀνειροπόλοισι· μετὰ δὲ ἀπειπάμενος τὴν ὄψιν ἔπεμπε τὴν πομπήν, ἐν τῆι
δὴ τελευτᾶι.

57   Οἱ δὲ Γεφυραῖοι, τῶν ἦσαν οἱ φονέες οἱ Ἱππάρχου, ὡς μὲν αὐτοὶ
λέγουσι, ἐγεγόνεσαν ἐξ Ἐρετρίης τὴν ἀρχήν, ὡς δὲ ἐγὼ ἀναπυνθανό-
μενος εὑρίσκω, ἦσαν Φοίνικες τῶν σὺν Κάδμωι ἀπικομένων Φοινίκων ἐς
γῆν τὴν νῦν Βοιωτίην καλεομένην, οἴκεον δὲ τῆς χώρης ταύτης ἀπολαχόν-
2 τες τὴν Ταναγρικὴν μοῖραν. ἐνθεῦτεν δέ, Καδμείων πρότερον ἐξαναστάν-
των ὑπ' Ἀργείων, οἱ Γεφυραῖοι οὗτοι δεύτερα ὑπὸ Βοιωτῶν ἐξαναστάντες
ἐτράποντο ἐπ' Ἀθηνέων. Ἀθηναῖοι δέ σφεας ἐπὶ ῥητοῖσι ἐδέξαντο σφέων
αὐτῶν εἶναι πολιήτας, ὀλίγων τεων καὶ οὐκ ἀξιαπηγήτων ἐπιτάξαντες
ἔργεσθαι.

58   Οἱ δὲ Φοίνικες οὗτοι οἱ σὺν Κάδμωι ἀπικόμενοι, τῶν ἦσαν οἱ Γεφυραῖοι, ἄλλα τε πολλὰ οἰκήσαντες ταύτην τὴν χώρην ἐσήγαγον διδασκάλια
ἐς τοὺς Ἕλληνας καὶ δὴ καὶ γράμματα, οὐκ ἐόντα πρὶν Ἕλλησι ὡς ἐμοὶ
δοκέειν, πρῶτα μὲν τοῖσι καὶ ἅπαντες χρέωνται Φοίνικες· μετὰ δὲ χρόνου προβαίνοντος ἅμα τῆι φωνῆι μετέβαλον καὶ τὸν ῥυθμὸν τῶν γραμ-
2 μάτων. περιοίκεον δέ σφεας τὰ πολλὰ τῶν χώρων τοῦτον τὸν χρόνον
Ἑλλήνων Ἴωνες· οἳ παραλαβόντες διδαχῆι παρὰ τῶν Φοινίκων τὰ γράμματα, μεταρρυθμίσαντές σφεων ὀλίγα ἐχρέωντο, χρεώμενοι δὲ ἐφάτι-
σαν, ὥσπερ καὶ τὸ δίκαιον ἔφερε ἐσαγαγόντων Φοινίκων ἐς τὴν Ἑλλάδα,
3 Φοινικήια κεκλῆσθαι. καὶ τὰς βύβλους διφθέρας καλέουσι ἀπὸ τοῦ παλαιοῦ
οἱ Ἴωνες, ὅτι κοτὲ ἐν σπάνι βύβλων ἐχρέωντο διφθέρηισι αἰγέηισί τε καὶ
οἰέηισι· ἔτι δὲ καὶ τὸ κατ' ἐμὲ πολλοὶ τῶν βαρβάρων ἐς τοιαύτας διφθέρας
γράφουσι.

55 ἐμφερεστάτην Wyttenbach et Maas: ἐναργεστάτην codd.   56.1 λεώς Vollgraff
57.2 ὀλίγων Scheibe et Wilson: πολλῶν codd.: οὐ πολλῶν Madvig

Εἶδον δὲ καὶ αὐτὸς Καδμήια γράμματα ἐν τῶι ἱρῶι τοῦ Ἀπόλλωνος τοῦ **59**
Ἰσμηνίου ἐν Θήβῃσι τῇσι Βοιωτῶν ἐπὶ τρίποσι τρισὶ ἐγκεκολαμμένα, τὰ
πολλὰ ὅμοια ἐόντα τοῖσι Ἰωνικοῖσι. ὁ μὲν δὴ εἷς τῶν τριπόδων ἐπίγραμμα
ἔχει·

Ἀμφιτρύων μ’ ἀνέθηκεν †ἐὼν† ἀπὸ Τηλεβοάων.

ταῦτα ἡλικίην εἴη ἂν κατὰ Λάιον τὸν Λαβδάκου τοῦ Πολυδώρου τοῦ Κάδ-
μου.
Ἕτερος δὲ τρίπους ἐν ἑξαμέτρωι τόνωι λέγει· **60**

Σκαῖος πυγμαχέων με ἐκηβόλωι Ἀπόλλωνι
νικήσας ἀνέθηκε τεῒν περικαλλὲς ἄγαλμα.

Σκαῖος δ’ ἂν εἴη ὁ Ἱπποκόωντος, εἰ δὴ οὗτός γε ἐστὶ ὁ ἀναθεὶς καὶ μὴ ἄλλος
τὠυτὸ οὔνομα ἔχων τῶι Ἱπποκόωντος, ἡλικίην κατὰ Οἰδίπουν τὸν Λαΐου.
Τρίτος δὲ τρίπους λέγει καὶ οὗτος ἐν ἑξαμέτρωι· **61**

Λαοδάμας τρίποδ’ αὐτὸς ἐϋσκόπωι Ἀπόλλωνι
μουναρχέων ἀνέθηκε τεῒν περικαλλὲς ἄγαλμα.

ἐπὶ τούτου δὴ τοῦ Λαοδάμαντος τοῦ Ἐτεοκλέος μουναρχέοντος **2**
ἐξανιστέαται Καδμεῖοι ὑπ’ Ἀργείων καὶ τρέπονται ἐς τοὺς Ἐγχελέας, οἱ δὲ
Γεφυραῖοι ὑπολειφθέντες ὕστερον ὑπὸ Βοιωτῶν ἀναχωρέουσι ἐς Ἀθήνας·
καί σφι ἱρά ἐστι ἐν Ἀθήνῃσι ἱδρυμένα, τῶν οὐδὲν μέτα τοῖσι λοιποῖσι
Ἀθηναίοισι, ἄλλα τε κεχωρισμένα τῶν ἄλλων ἱρῶν καὶ δὴ καὶ Ἀχαιίης
Δήμητρος ἱρόν τε καὶ ὄργια.
Ἡ μὲν δὴ ὄψις τοῦ Ἱππάρχου ἐνυπνίου καὶ οἱ Γεφυραῖοι ὅθεν ἐγεγό- **62**
νεσαν, τῶν ἦσαν οἱ Ἱππάρχου φονέες, ἀπήγηταί μοι· δεῖ δὲ πρὸς τούτοισι ἔτι ἀναλαβεῖν τὸν κατ’ ἀρχὰς ἦια λέξων λόγον, ὡς τυράννων ἐλευ-
θερώθησαν Ἀθηναῖοι. Ἱππίεω τυραννεύοντος καὶ ἐμπικραινομένου Ἀθη- **2**
ναίοισι διὰ τὸν Ἱππάρχου θάνατον Ἀλκμεωνίδαι, γένος ἐόντες Ἀθηναῖοι καὶ
φεύγοντες Πεισιστρατίδας, ἐπείτε σφι ἅμα τοῖσι ἄλλοισι Ἀθηναίων φυγάσι
πειρωμένοισι κατὰ τὸ ἰσχυρὸν οὐ προεχώρεε κάτοδος, ἀλλὰ προσέπταιον
μεγάλως πειρώμενοι κατιέναι τε καὶ ἐλευθεροῦν τὰς Ἀθήνας, Λειψύδριον
τὸ ὑπὲρ Παιονίης τειχίσαντες, ἐνθαῦτα οἱ Ἀλκμεωνίδαι πᾶν ἐπὶ τοῖσι Πει-
σιστρατίδῃσι μηχανώμενοι παρ’ Ἀμφικτυόνων τὸν νηὸν μισθοῦνται τὸν
ἐν Δελφοῖσι, τὸν νῦν ἐόντα, τότε δὲ οὔκω, τοῦτον ἐξοικοδομῆσαι. οἷα δὲ **3**
χρημάτων εὖ ἥκοντες καὶ ἐόντες ἄνδρες δόκιμοι ἀνέκαθεν ἔτι, τόν τε νηὸν
ἐξεργάσαντο τοῦ παραδείγματος κάλλιον τά τε ἄλλα καὶ συγκειμένου σφι
πωρίνου λίθου ποιέειν τὸν νηόν, Παρίου τὰ ἔμπροσθε αὐτοῦ ἐξεποίησαν.

59 ἰὼν Bergler: ἐόντ’ Valckenaer: ἐλὼν Meineke: θεῶι Stein: νέων Bentley: νεῶν
Wilson

63 Ὡς ὦν δὴ οἱ Ἀθηναῖοι λέγουσι, οὗτοι οἱ ἄνδρες ἐν Δελφοῖσι κατή-
μενοι ἀνέπειθον τὴν Πυθίην χρήμασι, ὅκως ἔλθοιεν Σπαρτιητέων ἄνδρες
εἴτε ἰδίωι στόλωι εἴτε δημοσίωι χρησόμενοι, προφέρειν σφι τὰς Ἀθήνας
2 ἐλευθεροῦν. Λακεδαιμόνιοι δέ, ὥς σφι αἰεὶ τὠυτὸ πρόφαντον ἐγίνετο,
πέμπουσι Ἀγχιμόλιον τὸν Ἀστέρος, ἐόντα τῶν ἀστῶν ἄνδρα δόκιμον, σὺν
στρατῶι ἐξελῶντα Πεισιστρατίδας ἐξ Ἀθηνέων, ὅμως καὶ ξείνους σφι ἐόντας τὰ μάλιστα· τὰ γὰρ τοῦ θεοῦ πρεσβύτερα ἐποιεῦντο ἢ τὰ τῶν ἀνδρῶν.
3 πέμπουσι δὲ τούτους κατὰ θάλασσαν πλοίοισι. ὁ μὲν δὴ προσσχὼν ἐς
Φάληρον τὴν στρατιὴν ἀπέβησε. οἱ δὲ Πεισιστρατίδαι προπυνθανόμενοι
ταῦτα ἐπεκαλέοντο ἐκ Θεσσαλίης ἐπικουρίην· ἐπεποίητο γάρ σφι συμμαχίη πρὸς αὐτούς. Θεσσαλοὶ δέ σφι δεομένοισι ἀπέπεμψαν κοινῆι γνώμηι
χρεώμενοι χιλίην τε ἵππον καὶ τὸν βασιλέα τὸν σφέτερον Κινέην ἄνδρα
Κονδαῖον· τοὺς ἐπείτε ἔσχον συμμάχους οἱ Πεισιστρατίδαι, ἐμηχανῶντο
4 τοιάδε· κείραντες τῶν Φαληρέων τὸ πεδίον καὶ ἱππάσιμον ποιήσαντες
τοῦτον τὸν χῶρον ἐπῆκαν τῶι στρατοπέδωι τὴν ἵππον· ἐμπεσοῦσα
δὲ διέφθειρε ἄλλους τε πολλοὺς τῶν Λακεδαιμονίων καὶ δὴ καὶ τὸν
Ἀγχιμόλιον, τοὺς δὲ περιγενομένους αὐτῶν ἐς τὰς νέας κατεῖρξαν. ὁ μὲν
δὴ πρῶτος στόλος ἐκ Λακεδαίμονος οὕτω ἀπήλλαξε, καὶ Ἀγχιμολίου εἰσὶ
ταφαὶ τῆς Ἀττικῆς Ἀλωπεκῆσι, ἀγχοῦ τοῦ Ἡρακλείου τοῦ ἐν Κυνοσάργεϊ.
64 Μετὰ δὲ Λακεδαιμόνιοι μέζω στόλον στείλαντες ἀπέπεμψαν ἐπὶ τὰς
Ἀθήνας, στρατηγὸν τῆς στρατιῆς ἀποδέξαντες βασιλέα Κλεομένεα τὸν
Ἀναξανδρίδεω, οὐκέτι κατὰ θάλασσαν στείλαντες ἀλλὰ κατ' ἤπειρον.
2 τοῖσι ἐσβαλοῦσι ἐς τὴν Ἀττικὴν χώρην ἡ τῶν Θεσσαλῶν ἵππος πρώτη
προσέμειξε καὶ οὐ μετὰ πολλὸν ἐτράπετο, καὶ σφεων ἔπεσον ὑπὲρ
τεσσεράκοντα ἄνδρες· οἱ δὲ περιγενόμενοι ἀπαλλάσσοντο ὡς εἶχον ἰθὺς
ἐπὶ Θεσσαλίης. Κλεομένης δὲ ἀπικόμενος ἐς τὸ ἄστυ ἅμα Ἀθηναίων τοῖσι
βουλομένοισι εἶναι ἐλευθέροισι ἐπολιόρκεε τοὺς τυράννους ἀπεργμένους
ἐν τῶι Πελαργικῶι τείχεϊ.
65 Καὶ οὐδέν τι πάντως ἂν ἐξεῖλον τοὺς Πεισιστρατίδας οἱ Λακεδαιμόνιοι
(οὔτε γὰρ ἐπέδρην ἐπενόεον ποιήσασθαι, οἵ τε Πεισιστρατίδαι σίτοισι καὶ
ποτοῖσι εὖ παρεσκευάδατο) πολιορκήσαντές τε ἂν ἡμέρας ὀλίγας ἀπαλλάσσοντο ἐς τὴν Σπάρτην· νῦν δὲ συντυχίη τοῖσι μὲν κακὴ ἐπεγένετο,
τοῖσι δὲ ἡ αὐτὴ αὕτη σύμμαχος· ὑπεκτιθέμενοι γὰρ ἔξω τῆς χώρης οἱ
2 παῖδες τῶν Πεισιστρατιδέων ἥλωσαν. τοῦτο δὲ ὡς ἐγένετο, πάντα αὐτῶν
τὰ πρήγματα συνετετάρακτο, παρέστησαν δὲ ἐπὶ μισθῶι τοῖσι τέκνοισι
ἐπ' οἷσι ἐβούλοντο οἱ Ἀθηναῖοι, ὥστε ἐν πέντε ἡμέρησι ἐκχωρῆσαι ἐκ τῆς
3 Ἀττικῆς. μετὰ δὲ ἐξεχώρησαν ἐς Σίγειον τὸ ἐπὶ τῶι Σκαμάνδρωι, ἄρξαντες

63.1 Λακεδαιμόνιοι Valckenaer   63.3 Κονδαῖον Kip: Κονιαῖον codd.: Γόνναιον
Wachsmuth   64.2 Πελαργικῶι V: Πελασγικῶι rell.

μὲν Ἀθηναίων ἐπ' ἔτεα ἕξ τε καὶ τριήκοντα, ἐόντες δὲ καὶ οὗτοι ἀνέκαθεν
Πύλιοί τε καὶ Νηλεῖδαι, ἐκ τῶν αὐτῶν γεγονότες καὶ οἱ ἀμφὶ Κόδρον τε
καὶ Μέλανθον, οἳ πρότερον ἐπήλυδες ἐόντες ἐγένοντο Ἀθηναίων βασιλέες.
ἐπὶ τούτου δὲ καὶ τὠυτὸ οὔνομα ἀπεμνημόνευσε Ἱπποκράτης τῶι παιδὶ   4
θέσθαι τὸν Πεισίστρατον, ἐπὶ τοῦ Νέστορος Πεισιστράτου ποιεύμενος τὴν
ἐπωνυμίην. οὕτω μὲν Ἀθηναῖοι τυράννων ἀπαλλάχθησαν. ὅσα δὲ ἐλευθερ- 5
ωθέντες ἔρξαν ἢ ἔπαθον ἀξιόχρεα ἀπηγήσιος πρὶν ἢ Ἰωνίην τε ἀποστῆναι
ἀπὸ Δαρείου καὶ Ἀρισταγόρεα τὸν Μιλήσιον ἀπικόμενον ἐς Ἀθήνας χρηῖ-
σαι σφέων βοηθέειν, ταῦτα πρῶτα φράσω.

Ἀθῆναι, ἐοῦσαι καὶ πρὶν μεγάλαι, τότε ἀπαλλαχθεῖσαι τυράννων   **66**
ἐγένοντο μέζονες. Ἐν δὲ αὐτῆισι δύο ἄνδρες ἐδυνάστευον, Κλεισθένης
τε ἀνὴρ Ἀλκμεωνίδης, ὅς περ δὴ λόγον ἔχει τὴν Πυθίην ἀναπεῖσαι, καὶ
Ἰσαγόρης Τεισάνδρου οἰκίης μὲν ἐὼν δοκίμου, ἀτὰρ τὰ ἀνέκαθεν οὐκ
ἔχω φράσαι· θύουσι δὲ οἱ συγγενέες αὐτοῦ Διὶ Καρίωι. οὗτοι οἱ ἄνδρες   2
ἐστασίασαν περὶ δυνάμιος, ἑσσούμενος δὲ ὁ Κλεισθένης τὸν δῆμον προσεταιρίζεται. μετὰ δὲ τετραφύλους ἐόντας Ἀθηναίους δεκαφύλους ἐποίησε,
τῶν Ἴωνος παίδων Γελέοντος καὶ Αἰγικόρεος καὶ Ἀργάδεω καὶ Ὅπλ-
ητος ἀπαλλάξας τὰς ἐπωνυμίας, ἐξευρὼν δὲ ἑτέρων ἡρώων ἐπωνυμίας
ἐπιχωρίων, πάρεξ Αἴαντος· τοῦτον δέ, ἅτε ἀστυγείτονα καὶ σύμμαχον,
ξεῖνον ἐόντα προσέθετο.

Ταῦτα δέ, δοκέειν ἐμοί, ἐμιμέετο ὁ Κλεισθένης οὗτος τὸν ἑωυ-   **67**
τοῦ μητροπάτορα Κλεισθένεα τὸν Σικυῶνος τύραννον. Κλεισθένης γὰρ
Ἀργείοισι πολεμήσας τοῦτο μὲν ῥαψωιδοὺς ἔπαυσε ἐν Σικυῶνι ἀγωνίζεσθαι τῶν Ὁμηρείων ἐπέων εἵνεκα, ὅτι Ἀργεῖοί τε καὶ Ἄργος τὰ πολλὰ
πάντα ὑμνέαται· τοῦτο δέ, ἡρώιον γὰρ ἦν καὶ ἔστι ἐν αὐτῆι τῆι
ἀγορῆι τῶν Σικυωνίων Ἀδρήστου τοῦ Ταλαοῦ, τοῦτον ἐπεθύμησε ὁ
Κλεισθένης ἐόντα Ἀργεῖον ἐκβαλεῖν ἐκ τῆς χώρης. ἐλθὼν δὲ ἐς Δελφοὺς   2
ἐχρηστηριάζετο εἰ ἐκβάλοι τὸν Ἄδρηστον· ἡ δὲ Πυθίη οἱ χρᾶι φᾶσα
Ἄδρηστον μὲν εἶναι Σικυωνίων βασιλέα, ἐκεῖνον δὲ λευστῆρα. ἐπεὶ δὲ
ὁ θεὸς τοῦτό γε οὐ παρεδίδου, ἀπελθὼν ὀπίσω ἐφρόντιζε μηχανὴν τῆι
αὐτὸς ὁ Ἄδρηστος ἀπαλλάξεται. ὡς δέ οἱ ἐξευρῆσθαι ἐδόκεε, πέμψας ἐς
Θήβας τὰς Βοιωτίας ἔφη θέλειν ἐπαγαγέσθαι Μελάνιππον τὸν Ἀστακοῦ·
οἱ δὲ Θηβαῖοι ἔδοσαν. ἐπαγαγόμενος δὲ ὁ Κλεισθένης τὸν Μελάνιππον   3
τέμενός οἱ ἀπέδεξε ἐν αὐτῶι τῶι πρυτανηίωι καί μιν ἵδρυσε ἐνθαῦτα
ἐν τῶι ἰσχυροτάτωι. ἐπηγάγετο δὲ τὸν Μελάνιππον ὁ Κλεισθένης (καὶ
γὰρ τοῦτο δεῖ ἀπηγήσασθαι) ὡς ἔχθιστον ἐόντα Ἀδρήστωι, ὅς τόν τε
ἀδελφεόν οἱ Μηκιστέα ἀπεκτόνεε καὶ τὸν γαμβρὸν Τυδέα. ἐπείτε δέ οἱ   4

65.4 ἀπομνημονεύ<ων ἤθελη>σε Wilson

τὸ τέμενος ἀπέδεξε, θυσίας τε καὶ ὁρτὰς Ἀδρήστου ἀπελόμενος ἔδωκε
τῶι Μελανίππωι. οἱ δὲ Σικυώνιοι ἐώθεσαν μεγαλωστὶ κάρτα τιμᾶν τὸν
Ἄδρηστον· ἡ γὰρ χώρη ἦν αὕτη Πολύβου, ὁ δὲ Ἄδρηστος ἦν Πολύβου
5 θυγατριδέος, ἄπαις δὲ Πόλυβος τελευτῶν διδοῖ Ἀδρήστωι τὴν ἀρχήν· τά
τε δὴ ἄλλα οἱ Σικυώνιοι ἐτίμων τὸν Ἄδρηστον καὶ δὴ πρὸς τὰ πάθεα
αὐτοῦ τραγικοῖσι χοροῖσι ἐγέραιρον, τὸν μὲν Διόνυσον οὐ τιμῶντες, τὸν
δὲ Ἄδρηστον. Κλεισθένης δὲ χοροὺς μὲν τῶι Διονύσωι ἀπέδωκε, τὴν δὲ
ἄλλην θυσίην Μελανίππωι.

68 Ταῦτα μὲν ἐς Ἄδρηστόν οἱ ἐπεποίητο, φυλὰς δὲ τὰς Δωριέων, ἵνα δὴ
μὴ αἱ αὐταὶ ἔωσι τοῖσι Σικυωνίοισι καὶ τοῖσι Ἀργείοισι, μετέβαλε ἐς ἄλλα
οὐνόματα. ἔνθα καὶ πλεῖστον κατεγέλασε τῶν Σικυωνίων· ἐπὶ γὰρ ὑός
τε καὶ ὄνου <καὶ χοίρου> τὰς ἐπωνυμίας μετατιθεὶς αὐτὰ τὰ τελευταῖα
ἐπέθηκε, πλὴν τῆς ἑωυτοῦ φυλῆς· ταύτηι δὲ τὸ οὔνομα ἀπὸ τῆς ἑωυτοῦ
ἀρχῆς ἔθετο. οὗτοι μὲν δὴ Ἀρχέλαοι ἐκαλέοντο, ἕτεροι δὲ Ὑᾶται, ἄλλοι
2 δὲ Ὀνεᾶται, ἕτεροι δὲ Χοιρεᾶται. τούτοισι τοῖσι οὐνόμασι τῶν φυλέων
ἐχρέωντο οἱ Σικυώνιοι καὶ ἐπὶ Κλεισθένεος ἄρχοντος καὶ ἐκείνου τεθνεῶτος
ἔτι ἐπ᾽ ἔτεα ἑξήκοντα· μετέπειτα μέντοι λόγον σφίσι δόντες μετέβαλον ἐς
τοὺς Ὑλλέας καὶ Παμφύλους καὶ Δυμανάτας, τετάρτους δὲ αὐτοῖσι προσέθεντο ἐπὶ τοῦ Ἀδρήστου παιδὸς Αἰγιαλέος τὴν ἐπωνυμίην ποιεύμενοι κεκλῆσθαι Αἰγιαλέας. —

69 Ταῦτα μέν νυν ὁ Σικυώνιος Κλεισθένης ἐπεποιήκεε, ὁ δὲ δὴ Ἀθηναῖος
Κλεισθένης, ἐὼν τοῦ Σικυωνίου τούτου θυγατριδέος καὶ τὸ οὔνομα ἐπὶ
τούτου ἔχων, δοκέειν ἐμοὶ καὶ οὗτος ὑπεριδὼν Ἴωνας, ἵνα μὴ σφίσι αἱ
2 αὐταὶ ἔωσι φυλαὶ καὶ Ἴωσι, τὸν ὁμώνυμον Κλεισθένεα ἐμιμήσατο. ὡς γὰρ
δὴ τὸν Ἀθηναίων δῆμον πρότερον ἀπωσμένον τότε πάντως πρὸς τὴν ἑωυτοῦ μοῖραν προσεθήκατο, τὰς φυλὰς μετωνόμασε καὶ ἐποίησε πλέονας ἐξ
ἐλασσόνων· δέκα τε δὴ φυλάρχους ἀντὶ τεσσέρων ἐποίησε, δέκαχα δὲ καὶ
τοὺς δήμους κατένειμε ἐς τὰς φυλάς· ἦν τε τὸν δῆμον προσθέμενος πολλῶι
κατύπερθε τῶν ἀντιστασιωτέων.

70 Ἐν τῶι μέρει δὲ ἐσσούμενος ὁ Ἰσαγόρης ἀντιτεχνᾶται τάδε· ἐπικαλέεται Κλεομένεα τὸν Λακεδαιμόνιον, γενόμενον ἑωυτῶι ξεῖνον ἀπὸ τῆς Πεισιστρατιδέων πολιορκίης· τὸν δὲ Κλεομένεα εἶχε αἰτίη φοιτᾶν παρὰ τοῦ
2 Ἰσαγόρεω τὴν γυναῖκα. τὰ μὲν δὴ πρῶτα πέμπων ὁ Κλεομένης ἐς τὰς
Ἀθήνας κήρυκα ἐξέβαλλε Κλεισθένεα καὶ μετ᾽ αὐτοῦ ἄλλους πολλοὺς Ἀθηναίων, τοὺς ἐναγέας ἐπιλέγων· ταῦτα δὲ πέμπων ἔλεγε ἐκ διδαχῆς τοῦ
Ἰσαγόρεω· οἱ μὲν γὰρ Ἀλκμεωνίδαι καὶ οἱ συστασιῶται αὐτῶν εἶχον αἰτίην
τοῦ φόνου τούτου, αὐτὸς δὲ οὐ μετεῖχε οὐδ᾽ οἱ φίλοι αὐτοῦ.

68.1 καὶ χοίρου add. Sauppe   ἕτεροι δὲ Χοιρεᾶται del. Bicknell   69.2 τότε πάντως Bekker, Hude: τότε πάντων codd. pl.: τότε <μεταδιδοὺς τῶν> πάντων Stein, Forrest   δέκαχα Lolling: δέκα codd.

Οἱ δ᾽ ἐναγέες Ἀθηναίων ὧδε ὠνομάσθησαν· ἦν Κύλων τῶν Ἀθηναίων **71**
ἀνὴρ Ὀλυμπιονίκης· οὗτος ἐπὶ τυραννίδι ἐκόμησε, προσποιησάμενος δὲ
ἑταιρηίην τῶν ἡλικιωτέων καταλαβεῖν τὴν ἀκρόπολιν ἐπειρήθη· οὐ δυνάμενος δὲ ἐπικρατῆσαι, ἱκέτης ἵζετο πρὸς τὸ ἄγαλμα. τούτους ἀνιστᾶσι μὲν 2
οἱ πρυτάνιες τῶν ναυκράρων, οἵ περ ἔνεμον τότε τὰς Ἀθήνας, ὑπεγγύους
πλὴν θανάτου· φονεῦσαι δὲ αὐτοὺς αἰτίη ἔχει Ἀλκμεωνίδας. ταῦτα πρὸ
τῆς Πεισιστράτου ἡλικίης ἐγένετο.

Κλεομένης δὲ ὡς πέμπων ἐξέβαλλε Κλεισθένεα καὶ τοὺς ἐναγέας, **72**
Κλεισθένης μὲν αὐτὸς ὑπεξέσχε· μετὰ δὲ οὐδὲν ἧσσον παρῆν ἐς τὰς
Ἀθήνας ὁ Κλεομένης οὐ σὺν μεγάληι χειρί, ἀπικόμενος δὲ ἀγηλατέει
ἑπτακόσια ἐπίστια Ἀθηναίων, τά οἱ ὑπέθετο ὁ Ἰσαγόρης. ταῦτα δὲ
ποιήσας δεύτερα τὴν βουλὴν καταλύειν ἐπειρᾶτο, τριηκοσίοισι δὲ τοῖσι
Ἰσαγόρεω στασιώτηισι τὰς ἀρχὰς ἐνεχείριζε. ἀντιστατθείσης δὲ τῆς βουλῆς 2
καὶ οὐ βουλομένης πείθεσθαι ὅ τε Κλεομένης καὶ ὁ Ἰσαγόρης καὶ οἱ στασιῶται αὐτοῦ καταλαμβάνουσι τὴν ἀκρόπολιν. Ἀθηναίων δὲ οἱ λοιποὶ τὰ αὐτὰ
φρονήσαντες ἐπολιόρκεον αὐτοὺς ἡμέρας δύο· τῆι δὲ τρίτηι ὑπόσπον-
δοι ἐξέρχονται ἐκ τῆς χώρης ὅσοι ἦσαν αὐτῶν Λακεδαιμόνιοι. ἐπετελέετο 3
δὲ τῶι Κλεομένεϊ ἡ φήμη· ὡς γὰρ ἀνέβη ἐς τὴν ἀκρόπολιν μέλλων δὴ
αὐτὴν κατασχήσειν, ἤιε ἐς τὸ ἄδυτον τῆς θεοῦ ὡς προσερέων· ἡ δὲ
ἱερέη ἐξαναστᾶσα ἐκ τοῦ θρόνου πρίν ἢ τὰς θύρας αὐτὸν ἀμείψαι
εἶπε· "ὦ ξεῖνε Λακεδαιμόνιε, πάλιν χώρει μηδὲ ἔσιθι ἐς τὸ ἱρόν· οὐ γὰρ
θεμιτὸν Δωριεῦσι παριέναι ἐνθαῦτα." ὁ δὲ εἶπε· "ὦ γύναι, ἀλλ᾽ οὐ 4
Δωριεύς εἰμι ἀλλ᾽ Ἀχαιός." ὁ μὲν δὴ τῆι κληδόνι οὐδὲν χρεώμενος ἐπεχείρησέ τε καὶ τότε πάλιν ἐξέπιπτε μετὰ τῶν Λακεδαιμονίων· τοὺς δὲ
ἄλλους Ἀθηναῖοι κατέδησαν τὴν ἐπὶ θανάτωι, ἐν δὲ αὐτοῖσι καὶ Τιμησίθεον τὸν Δελφόν, τοῦ ἔργα χειρῶν τε καὶ λήματος ἔχοιμ᾽ ἂν μέγιστα
καταλέξαι.

Οὗτοι μὲν νῦν δεδεμένοι ἐτελεύτησαν, Ἀθηναῖοι δὲ μετὰ ταῦτα **73**
Κλεισθένεα καὶ τὰ ἑπτακόσια ἐπίστια τὰ διωχθέντα ὑπὸ Κλεομένεος
μεταπεμψάμενοι πέμπουσι ἀγγέλους ἐς Σάρδις, συμμαχίην βουλόμενοι
ποιήσασθαι πρὸς Πέρσας· ἠπιστέατο γὰρ σφίσι Λακεδαιμονίους τε καὶ
Κλεομένεα ἐκπεπολεμῶσθαι. ἀπικομένων δὲ τῶν ἀγγέλων ἐς τὰς Σάρδις 2
καὶ λεγόντων τὰ ἐντεταλμένα Ἀρταφρένης ὁ Ὑστάσπεος Σαρδίων ὕπαρχος ἐπειρώτα τίνες ἐόντες ἄνθρωποι καὶ κῆι γῆς οἰκημένοι δεοίατο Περσέων σύμμαχοι γενέσθαι, πυθόμενος δὲ πρὸς τῶν ἀγγέλων ἀπεκορύφου
σφι τάδε· εἰ μὲν διδοῦσι βασιλέϊ Δαρείωι Ἀθηναῖοι γῆν τε καὶ ὕδωρ, ὁ
δὲ συμμαχίην σφι συνετίθετο, εἰ δὲ μὴ διδοῦσι, ἀπαλλάσσεσθαι αὐτοὺς
ἐκέλευε. οἱ δὲ ἄγγελοι ἐπὶ σφέων αὐτῶν βαλόμενοι διδόναι ἔφασαν, 3

72.4 Δελφόν Palmerius: ἀδελφεόν codd.

βουλόμενοι τὴν συμμαχίην ποιήσασθαι. οὗτοι μὲν δὴ ἀπελθόντες ἐς τὴν ἑωυτῶν αἰτίας μεγάλας εἶχον.

74 Κλεομένης δὲ ἐπιστάμενος περιυβρίσθαι ἔπεσι καὶ ἔργοισι ὑπ᾽ Ἀθηναίων συνέλεγε ἐκ πάσης Πελοποννήσου στρατόν, οὐ φράζων ἐς τὸ συλλέγει, τείσασθαί τε ἐθέλων τὸν δῆμον τὸν Ἀθηναίων καὶ Ἰσαγόρην βουλόμενος τύραννον καταστῆσαι· συνεξῆλθε γὰρ οἱ οὗτος ἐκ τῆς ἀκροπόλιος.

2 Κλεομένης τε δὴ στόλωι μεγάλωι ἐσέβαλε ἐς Ἐλευσῖνα καὶ οἱ Βοιωτοὶ ἀπὸ συνθήματος Οἰνόην αἱρέουσι καὶ Ὑσιάς, δήμους τοὺς ἐσχάτους τῆς Ἀττικῆς, Χαλκιδέες τε ἐπὶ τὰ ἕτερα ἐσίνοντο ἐπιόντες χώρους τῆς Ἀττικῆς. Ἀθηναῖοι δέ, καίπερ ἀμφιβολίηι ἐχόμενοι, Βοιωτῶν μὲν καὶ Χαλκιδέων ἐσύστερον ἔμελλον μνήμην ποιήσεσθαι, Πελοποννησίοισι δὲ ἐοῦσι ἐν Ἐλευσῖνι ἀντία ἔθεντο τὰ ὅπλα.

75 Μελλόντων δὲ συνάψειν τὰ στρατόπεδα ἐς μάχην, Κορίνθιοι μὲν πρῶτοι σφίσι αὐτοῖσι δόντες λόγον ὡς οὐ ποιοῖεν τὰ δίκαια μετεβάλλοντό τε καὶ ἀπαλλάσσοντο, μετὰ δὲ Δημάρητος ὁ Ἀρίστωνος, ἐὼν καὶ οὗτος βασιλεὺς Σπαρτιητέων, καὶ συνεξαγαγών τε τὴν στρατιὴν ἐκ 2 Λακεδαίμονος καὶ οὐκ ἐὼν διάφορος ἐν τῶι πρόσθε χρόνωι Κλεομένεϊ. ἀπὸ δὲ ταύτης τῆς διχοστασίης ἐτέθη νόμος ἐν Σπάρτηι μὴ ἐξεῖναι ἕπεσθαι ἀμφοτέρους τοὺς βασιλέας ἐξιούσης στρατιῆς· τέως γὰρ ἀμφότεροι εἵποντο· παραλυομένου δὲ τούτων τοῦ ἑτέρου καταλείπεσθαι καὶ τῶν Τυνδαριδέων τὸν ἕτερον· πρὸ τοῦ γὰρ δὴ καὶ οὗτοι ἀμφότεροι ἐπίκλητοί 3 σφι ἐόντες εἵποντο. τότε δὴ ἐν τῆι Ἐλευσῖνι ὁρῶντες οἱ λοιποὶ τῶν συμμάχων τούς τε βασιλέας τῶν Λακεδαιμονίων οὐκ ὁμολογέοντας καὶ Κοριν- **76** θίους ἐκλιπόντας τὴν τάξιν οἴχοντο καὶ αὐτοὶ ἀπαλλασσόμενοι, τέταρτον δὴ τοῦτο ἐπὶ τὴν Ἀττικὴν ἀπικόμενοι Δωριέες, δίς τε ἐπὶ πολέμωι ἐσβαλόντες καὶ δὶς ἐπ᾽ ἀγαθῶι τοῦ πλήθεος τοῦ Ἀθηναίων, πρῶτον μὲν ὅτε καὶ Μέγαρα κατοίκισαν (οὗτος ὁ στόλος ἐπὶ Κόδρου βασιλεύοντος Ἀθηναίων ὀρθῶς ἂν καλέοιτο), δεύτερον δὲ καὶ τρίτον ὅτε ἐπὶ Πεισιστρατιδέων ἐξέλασιν ὁρμηθέντες ἐκ Σπάρτης ἀπίκοντο, τέταρτον δὲ τότε ὅτε ἐς Ἐλευσῖνα Κλεομένης ἄγων Πελοποννησίους ἐσέβαλε· οὕτω τέταρτον τότε Δωριέες ἐσέβαλον ἐς Ἀθήνας.

77 Διαλυθέντος ὦν τοῦ στόλου τούτου ἀκλεῶς, ἐνθαῦτα Ἀθηναῖοι τίνυσθαι βουλόμενοι πρῶτα στρατιὴν ποιεῦνται ἐπὶ Χαλκιδέας. Βοιωτοὶ δὲ τοῖσι Χαλκιδεῦσι βοηθέουσι ἐπὶ τὸν Εὔριπον. Ἀθηναίοισι δὲ ἰδοῦσι τοὺς βοηθοὺς ἔδοξε πρότερον τοῖσι Βοιωτοῖσι ἢ τοῖσι Χαλκιδεῦσι ἐπιχειρέειν· 2 συμβάλλουσί τε δὴ τοῖσι Βοιωτοῖσι οἱ Ἀθηναῖοι καὶ πολλῶι ἐκράτησαν, κάρτα δὲ πολλοὺς φονεύσαντες ἑπτακοσίους αὐτῶν ἐζώγρησαν. τῆς δὲ αὐτῆς ταύτης ἡμέρης οἱ Ἀθηναῖοι διαβάντες ἐς τὴν Εὔβοιαν συμβάλλουσι καὶ τοῖσι Χαλκιδεῦσι, νικήσαντες δὲ καὶ τούτους τετρακισχιλίους

κληρούχους ἐπὶ τῶν ἱπποβοτέων τῆι χώρηι λείπουσι· οἱ δὲ ἱπποβόται
ἐκαλέοντο οἱ παχέες τῶν Χαλκιδέων. ὅσους δὲ καὶ τούτων ἐζώγρησαν, 3
ἅμα τοῖσι Βοιωτῶν ἐζωγρημένοισι εἶχον ἐν φυλακῆι ἐν πέδαις δήσαντες·
χρόνωι δὲ ἔλυσάν σφεας δίμνεως ἀποτιμησάμενοι. τὰς δὲ πέδας αὐτῶν,
ἐν τῆισι ἐδεδέατο, ἀνεκρέμασαν ἐς τὴν ἀκρόπολιν, αἵ περ ἔτι καὶ ἐς ἐμὲ
ἦσαν περιεοῦσαι, κρεμάμεναι ἐκ τειχέων περιπεφλευσμένων πυρὶ ὑπὸ
τοῦ Μήδου, ἀντίον δὲ τοῦ μεγάρου τοῦ πρὸς ἑσπέρην τετραμμένου. καὶ 4
τῶν λύτρων τὴν δεκάτην ἀνέθηκαν ποιησάμενοι τέθριππον χάλκεον· τὸ
δὲ ἀριστερῆς χειρὸς ἕστηκε πρῶτον ἐσιόντι ἐς τὰ προπύλαια τὰ ἐν τῆι
ἀκροπόλι· ἐπιγέγραπται δέ οἱ τάδε·

> ἔθνεα Βοιωτῶν καὶ Χαλκιδέων δαμάσαντες
> παῖδες Ἀθηναίων ἔργμασιν ἐν πολέμου
> δεσμῶι ἐν ἀχνυόεντι σιδηρέωι ἔσβεσαν ὕβριν·
> τῶν ἵππους δεκάτην Παλλάδι τάσδ᾽ ἔθεσαν.

Ἀθηναῖοι μέν νυν ηὔξηντο. δηλοῖ δὲ οὐ κατ᾽ ἓν μοῦνον ἀλλὰ πανταχῆι ἡ 78
ἰσηγορίη ὡς ἐστὶ χρῆμα σπουδαῖον, εἰ καὶ Ἀθηναῖοι τυραννευόμενοι μὲν
οὐδαμῶν τῶν σφέας περιοικεόντων ἦσαν τὰ πολέμια ἀμείνονες, ἀπαλλαχθέντες δὲ τυράννων μακρῶι πρῶτοι ἐγένοντο. δηλοῖ ὦν ταῦτα ὅτι
κατεχόμενοι μὲν ἐθελοκάκεον ὡς δεσπότηι ἐργαζόμενοι, ἐλευθερωθέντων
δὲ αὐτὸς ἕκαστος ἑωυτῶι προεθυμέετο <τι> κατεργάζεσθαι.

Οὗτοι μέν νυν ταῦτα ἔπρησσον. Θηβαῖοι δὲ μετὰ ταῦτα ἐς θεὸν 79
ἔπεμπον, βουλόμενοι τείσασθαι Ἀθηναίους. ἡ δὲ Πυθίη ἀπὸ σφέων μὲν
αὐτῶν οὐκ ἔφη αὐτοῖσι εἶναι τίσιν, ἐς πολύφημον δὲ ἐξενείκαντας ἐκέλευε
τῶν ἄγχιστα δέεσθαι. ἀπελθόντων ὦν τῶν θεοπρόπων ἐξέφερον τὸ 2
χρηστήριον ἁλίην ποιησάμενοι· ὡς ἐπυνθάνοντο δὲ λεγόντων αὐτῶν τῶν
ἄγχιστα δέεσθαι, εἶπαν οἱ Θηβαῖοι ἀκούσαντες τούτων· "οὐκ ὦν ἄγχιστα
ἡμέων οἰκέουσι Ταναγραῖοί τε καὶ Κορωναῖοι καὶ Θεσπιέες; καὶ οὗτοί γε
ἅμα ἡμῖν αἰεὶ μαχόμενοι προθύμως συνδιαφέρουσι τὸν πόλεμον. τί δεῖ
τούτων γε δέεσθαι; ἀλλὰ μᾶλλον μὴ οὐ τοῦτο ἦι τὸ χρηστήριον."

Τοιαῦτα ἐπιλεγομένων εἶπε δή κοτε μαθών τις· "ἐγώ μοι δοκέω συνιέναι 80
τὸ θέλει λέγειν ἡμῖν τὸ μαντήιον. Ἀσωποῦ λέγονται γενέσθαι θυγατέρες
Θήβη τε καὶ Αἴγινα· τουτέων ἀδελφεῶν ἐουσέων δοκέω ἡμῖν Αἰγινητέων
δέεσθαι τὸν θεὸν χρῆσαι τιμωρητήρων γενέσθαι." καὶ οὐ γάρ τις ταύτης 2
ἀμείνων γνώμη ἐδόκεε φαίνεσθαι, αὐτίκα πέμψαντες ἐδέοντο Αἰγινητέων,
ἐπικαλεόμενοι κατὰ τὸ χρηστήριόν σφι βοηθέειν, ὡς ἐόντων ἀγχιστέων·

77.4 ἐς τὰ προπύλαια τὰ del. Powell: τὰ ἐν τῆι ἀκροπόλει del. Wilson   ἀχνυόεντι
Hecker: ἀχνυνθέντι AB Anth.Pal.6.343: ἀχνυθέντι C: ἀχλυόεντι PDUSV Diod. 10.24.3
78 <τι> add. Powell   79.1 <ἀγορήν> πολύφημον Wilson

οἱ δέ σφι αἰτέουσι ἐπικουρίην τοὺς Αἰακίδας συμ<πεισθέντας> πέμπειν
ἔφασαν.

81 Πειρησαμένων δὲ τῶν Θηβαίων κατὰ τὴν συμμαχίην τῶν Αἰακιδέων
καὶ τρηχέως περιεφθέντων ὑπὸ τῶν Ἀθηναίων, αὖτις οἱ Θηβαῖοι πέμψαν-
2 τες τοὺς μὲν Αἰακίδας σφι ἀπεδίδοσαν, τῶν δὲ ἀνδρῶν ἐδέοντο. Αἰγινῆται
δὲ εὐδαιμονίηι τε μεγάληι ἐπαρθέντες καὶ ἔχθρης παλαιῆς ἀναμνησθέντες ἐχούσης ἐς Ἀθηναίους, τότε Θηβαίων δεηθέντων πόλεμον ἀκήρυκτον
3 Ἀθηναίοισι ἐπέφερον. ἐπικειμένων γὰρ αὐτῶν Βοιωτοῖσι ἐπιπλώσαντες
μακρῆισι νηυσὶ ἐς τὴν Ἀττικὴν κατὰ μὲν ἔσυραν Φάληρον, κατὰ δὲ τῆς
ἄλλης παραλίης πολλοὺς δήμους, ποιεῦντες δὲ ταῦτα μεγάλως Ἀθηναίους
ἐσίνοντο.

82 Ἡ δὲ ἔχθρη ἡ προοφειλομένη ἐς Ἀθηναίους ἐκ τῶν Αἰγινητέων ἐγένετο
ἐξ ἀρχῆς τοιῆσδε. Ἐπιδαυρίοισι ἡ γῆ καρπὸν οὐδένα ἀνεδίδου. περὶ
ταύτης ὦν τῆς συμφορῆς οἱ Ἐπιδαύριοι ἐχρέωντο ἐν Δελφοῖσι· ἡ δὲ Πυθίη
σφέας ἐκέλευε Δαμίης τε καὶ Αὐξησίης ἀγάλματα ἱδρύσασθαι καί σφι
2 ἱδρυσαμένοισι ἄμεινον συνοίσεσθαι. ἐπειρώτεον ὦν οἱ Ἐπιδαύριοι κότερα
χαλκοῦ ποιέωνται τὰ ἀγάλματα ἢ λίθου· ἡ δὲ Πυθίη οὐδέτερα τούτων
ἔα, ἀλλὰ ξύλου ἡμέρης ἐλαίης. ἐδέοντο ὦν οἱ Ἐπιδαύριοι Ἀθηναίων ἐλαίην
σφι δοῦναι ταμέσθαι, ἱρωτάτας δὴ κείνας νομίζοντες εἶναι· λέγεται δὲ καὶ
3 ὡς ἐλαῖαι ἦσαν ἄλλοθι γῆς οὐδαμοῦ κατὰ χρόνον κεῖνον ἢ Ἀθήνηισι. οἱ δὲ
ἐπὶ τοῖσδε δώσειν ἔφασαν ἐπ᾽ ὧι ἀπάξουσι ἔτεος ἑκάστου τῆι τε Ἀθηναίηι
τῆι Πολιάδι ἱρὰ καὶ τῶι Ἐρεχθέϊ. καταινέσαντες δὲ ἐπὶ τούτοισι οἱ Ἐπιδαύριοι τῶν τε ἐδέοντο ἔτυχον καὶ ἀγάλματα ἐκ τῶν ἐλαιέων τουτέων
ποιησάμενοι ἱδρύσαντο· καὶ ἥ τε γῆ σφι ἔφερε [καρπὸν] καὶ Ἀθηναίοισι
ἐπετέλεον τὰ συνέθεντο.

83 Τοῦτον δ᾽ ἔτι τὸν χρόνον καὶ πρὸ τοῦ Αἰγινῆται Ἐπιδαυρίων ἤκουον
τά τε ἄλλα καὶ δίκας διαβαίνοντες ἐς Ἐπίδαυρον ἐδίδοσάν τε καὶ ἐλάμβανον παρ᾽ ἀλλήλων οἱ Αἰγινῆται· τὸ δὲ ἀπὸ τοῦδε νέας τε πηξάμενοι
2 καὶ ἀγνωμοσύνηι χρησάμενοι ἀπέστησαν ἀπὸ τῶν Ἐπιδαυρίων. ἅτε δὲ
ἐόντες διάφοροι ἐδηλέοντο αὐτούς, ὥστε δὴ θαλασσοκράτορες ἐόντες, καὶ
δὴ καὶ τὰ ἀγάλματα ταῦτα τῆς τε Δαμίης καὶ τῆς Αὐξησίης ὑπαιρέονται
αὐτῶν, καί σφεα ἐκόμισάν τε καὶ ἱδρύσαντο τῆς σφετέρης χώρης ἐς τὴν
μεσόγαιαν, τῆι Οἴη μέν ἐστι οὔνομα, στάδια δὲ μάλιστά κηι ἀπὸ τῆς πόλιος
3 ὡς εἴκοσι ἀπέχει. ἱδρυσάμενοι δὲ ἐν τούτωι τῶι χώρωι θυσίηισί τέ σφεα
καὶ χοροῖσι γυναικηίοισι κερτόμοισι ἱλάσκοντο, χορηγῶν ἀποδεικνυμένων
ἑκατέρηι τῶν δαιμόνων δέκα ἀνδρῶν· κακῶς δὲ ἠγόρευον οἱ χοροὶ ἄνδρα

80.2 συμ<πεισθέντας> πέμπειν Wilson: συμπείθειν ABC: συμπέμπειν cett.   82.2
ἡμέρης codd.: ἱρῆς Griffiths   82.3 καρπὸν del. Hude

μὲν οὐδένα, τὰς δὲ ἐπιχωρίας γυναῖκας. ἦσαν δὲ καὶ τοῖσι Ἐπιδαυρίοισι αἱ αὐταὶ ἱρουργίαι· εἰσὶ δέ σφι καὶ ἄρρητοι ἱρουργίαι.

Κλεφθέντων δὲ τῶνδε τῶν ἀγαλμάτων οἱ Ἐπιδαύριοι τοῖσι Ἀθηναίοισι **84** τὰ συνέθεντο οὐκέτι ἐπετέλεον. πέμψαντες δὲ οἱ Ἀθηναῖοι ἐμήνιον τοῖσι Ἐπιδαυρίοισι· οἱ δὲ ἀπέφαινον λόγωι ὡς οὐκ ἀδικέοιεν· ὅσον μὲν γὰρ χρόνον εἶχον τὰ ἀγάλματα ἐν τῆι χώρηι, ἐπιτελέειν τὰ συνέθεντο, ἐπεὶ δὲ ἐστερῆσθαι αὐτῶν, οὐ δίκαιοι εἶναι ἀποφέρειν ἔτι, ἀλλὰ τοὺς ἔχοντας αὐτὰ Αἰγινήτας πρήσσεσθαι ἐκέλευον. πρὸς ταῦτα οἱ Ἀθηναῖοι ἐς Αἴγιναν 2 πέμψαντες ἀπαίτεον τὰ ἀγάλματα· οἱ δὲ Αἰγινῆται ἔφασαν σφίσι τε καὶ Ἀθηναίοισι εἶναι οὐδὲν πρῆγμα.

Ἀθηναῖοι μέν νυν λέγουσι μετὰ τὴν ἀπαίτησιν ἀποσταλῆναι τριήρεϊ **85** μιῆι τῶν ἀστῶν †τούτους† οἳ πεμφθέντες ἀπὸ τοῦ κοινοῦ καὶ ἀπικόμενοι ἐς Αἴγιναν τὰ ἀγάλματα ταῦτα ὡς σφετέρων ξύλων ἐόντα ἐπειρῶντο ἐκ τῶν βάθρων ἐξανασπᾶν, ἵνα σφέα ἀνακομίσωνται. οὐ δυναμένους δὲ τούτωι 2 τῶι τρόπωι αὐτῶν κρατῆσαι, περιβαλόντας σχοινία ἕλκειν τὰ ἀγάλματα, καί σφι ἕλκουσι βροντήν τε καὶ ἅμα τῆι βροντῆι σεισμὸν ἐπιγενέσθαι· τοὺς δὲ τριηρίτας τοὺς ἕλκοντας ὑπὸ τούτων ἀλλοφρονῆσαι, παθόντας δὲ τοῦτο κτείνειν ἀλλήλους ἅτε πολεμίους, ἐς ὃ ἐκ πάντων ἕνα λειφθέντα ἀνακομισθῆναι αὐτόθεν ἐς Φάληρον.

Ἀθηναῖοι μέν νυν οὕτω λέγουσι γενέσθαι. Αἰγινῆται δὲ οὐ μιῆι νηὶ **86** ἀπικέσθαι Ἀθηναίους (μίαν μὲν γὰρ καὶ ὀλίγωι πλέονας μιῆς, καὶ εἰ σφίσι μὴ ἔτυχον ἐοῦσαι νέες, ἀπαμύνασθαι ἂν εὐπετέως) ἀλλὰ πολλῆισι νηυσὶ ἐπιπλέειν σφίσι ἐπὶ τὴν χώρην, αὐτοὶ δέ σφι εἶξαι καὶ οὐ ναυμαχῆσαι. οὐκ 2 ἔχουσι δὲ τοῦτο διασημῆναι ἀτρεκέως, οὔτε εἰ ἥσσονες συγγινωσκόμενοι εἶναι τῆι ναυμαχίηι κατὰ τοῦτο εἶξαν, οὔτε εἰ βουλόμενοι ποιῆσαι οἷόν τι καὶ ἐποίησαν. Ἀθηναίους μέν νυν, ἐπείτε σφι οὐδεὶς ἐς μάχην κατίστατο, 3 ἀποβάντας ἀπὸ τῶν νεῶν τρέπεσθαι πρὸς τὰ ἀγάλματα, οὐ δυναμένους δὲ ἀνασπάσαι ἐκ τῶν βάθρων αὐτὰ οὕτω δὴ περιβαλομένους σχοινία ἕλκειν, ἐς οὗ ἑλκόμενα τὰ ἀγάλματα ἀμφότερα τὠυτὸ ποιῆσαι, ἐμοὶ μὲν οὐ πιστὰ λέγοντες, ἄλλωι δέ τεωι· ἐς γούνατα γάρ σφι αὐτὰ πεσεῖν, καὶ τὸν ἀπὸ τούτου χρόνον διατελέειν οὕτως ἔχοντα. Ἀθηναίους μὲν δὴ ταῦτα 4 ποιέειν, σφέας δὲ Αἰγινῆται λέγουσι, πυθομένους τοὺς Ἀθηναίους ὡς μέλλοιεν ἐπὶ σφέας στρατεύεσθαι, ἑτοίμους Ἀργείους ποιέεσθαι· τούς τε δὴ Ἀθηναίους ἀποβεβάναι ἐς τὴν Αἰγιναίην καὶ παρεῖναι βοηθέοντας σφίσι τοὺς Ἀργείους καὶ λαθεῖν τε ἐξ Ἐπιδαύρου διαβάντας ἐς τὴν νῆσον καὶ οὐ

85.1 τούτους A: τουτέων DRSV: ὀλίγους Legrand: διηκοσίους Stein: τριηκοσίους Vollgraff: τινας vel ἄνδρας ἐπιλεκτοὺς Wilson: λογάδας vel αἱρετούς vel λ' αἱρετούς Griffiths
85.2 αὐτόθεν Wilson: αὐτὸν codd.

προακηκοόσι τοῖσι Ἀθηναίοισι ἐπιπεσεῖν ὑποταμομένους [τὸ] ἀπὸ τῶν νεῶν, ἅμα τε ἐν τούτωι τὴν βροντήν τε γενέσθαι καὶ τὸν σεισμὸν αὐτοῖσι.

87 Λέγεται μέν νυν ὑπ᾽ Ἀργείων τε καὶ Αἰγινητέων τάδε, ὁμολογέεται δὲ καὶ ὑπ᾽ Ἀθηναίων, ἕνα μοῦνον τὸν ἀποσωθέντα αὐτῶν ἐς τὴν
2 Ἀττικὴν γενέσθαι· πλὴν Ἀργεῖοι μὲν λέγουσι αὐτῶν τὸ Ἀττικὸν στρατόπεδον διαφθειράντων τὸν ἕνα τοῦτον περιγενέσθαι, Ἀθηναῖοι δὲ τοῦ δαιμονίου· περιγενέσθαι μέντοι οὐδὲ τοῦτον τὸν ἕνα, ἀλλ᾽ ἀπολέσθαι τρόπωι τοιῶιδε. κομισθεὶς ἄρα ἐς τὰς Ἀθήνας ἀπήγγελλε τὸ πάθος· πυθομένας δὲ τὰς γυναῖκας τῶν ἐπ᾽ Αἴγιναν στρατευσαμένων ἀνδρῶν, δεινόν τι ποιησαμένας κεῖνον μοῦνον ἐξ ἁπάντων σωθῆναι, πέριξ τὸν ἄνθρωπον τοῦτον λαβούσας καὶ κεντεούσας τῆισι περόνηισι τῶν ἱματίων εἰρωτᾶν ἑκάστην
3 αὐτέων ὅκου εἴη ὁ ἑωυτῆς ἀνήρ. καὶ τοῦτον μὲν οὕτω διαφθαρῆναι, Ἀθηναίοισι δὲ ἔτι τοῦ πάθεος δεινότερόν τι δόξαι εἶναι τὸ τῶν γυναικῶν ἔργον. ἄλλωι μὲν δὴ οὐκ ἔχειν ὅτεωι ζημιώσωσι τὰς γυναῖκας, τὴν δὲ ἐσθῆτα μετέβαλον αὐτέων ἐς τὴν Ἰάδα· ἐφόρεον γὰρ δὴ πρὸ τοῦ αἱ τῶν Ἀθηναίων γυναῖκες ἐσθῆτα Δωρίδα, τῆι Κορινθίηι παραπλησιωτάτην· μετέβαλον ὦν ἐς τὸν λίνεον κιθῶνα, ἵνα δὴ περόνηισι μὴ χρέωνται.

88 Ἔστι δὲ ἀληθέϊ λόγωι χρεωμένοισι οὐκ Ἰὰς αὕτη ἡ ἐσθὴς τὸ παλαιὸν ἀλλὰ Κάειρα, ἐπεὶ ἥ γε Ἑλληνικὴ ἐσθὴς πᾶσα ἡ ἀρχαίη τῶν γυναικῶν
2 ἡ αὐτὴ ἦν τὴν νῦν Δωρίδα καλέομεν. τοὺς δὲ Ἀργείους καὶ τοὺς Αἰγινήτας πρὸς ταῦτα ἔτι τόδε ποιῆσαι νόμον εἶναι, παρὰ σφίσι ἑκατέροισι τὰς περόνας ἡμιολίας ποιέεσθαι τοῦ τότε κατεστεῶτος μέτρου, καὶ ἐς τὸ ἱρὸν τῶν θεῶν τουτέων περόνας μάλιστα ἀνατιθέναι τὰς γυναῖκας, Ἀττικὸν δὲ μήτε τι ἄλλο προσφέρειν πρὸς τὸ ἱρὸν μήτε κέραμον, ἀλλ᾽ ἐκ χυτρίδων
3 ἐπιχωριέων νόμον τὸ λοιπὸν αὐτόθι εἶναι πίνειν. Ἀργείων μέν νυν καὶ Αἰγινητέων αἱ γυναῖκες ἐκ [τε] τόσου κατ᾽ ἔριν τὴν Ἀθηναίων περόνας ἔτι καὶ ἐς ἐμὲ ἐφόρεον μέζονας ἢ πρὸ τοῦ.

89 Τῆς δὲ ἔχθρης τῆς πρὸς Αἰγινητέων Ἀθηναίοισι γενομένης ἀρχὴ κατὰ τὰ εἴρηται ἐγένετο. τότε δὴ Θηβαίων ἐπικαλεομένων προθύμως τῶν περὶ τὰ ἀγάλματα γενομένων ἀναμιμνησκόμενοι οἱ Αἰγινῆται ἐβοήθεον τοῖσι
2 Βοιωτοῖσι. Αἰγινῆταί τε δὴ ἐδηίουν τῆς Ἀττικῆς τὰ παραθαλάσσια, καὶ Ἀθηναίοισι ὁρμημένοισι ἐπ᾽ Αἰγινήτας στρατεύεσθαι ἦλθε μαντήιον ἐκ Δελφῶν ἐπισχόντας ἀπὸ τοῦ Αἰγινητέων ἀδικίου τριήκοντα ἔτεα τῶι ἑνὶ

86.4 τὸ del. Wilson   88.2 τοὺς δὲ Ἀργείους καὶ τοὺς Αἰγινήτας... εἶναι Hude: τοῖσι δὲ Ἀργείοισι καὶ τοῖσι Αἰγινήτηισι καὶ πρὸς ταῦτα ἔτι τόδε ποιῆσαι νόμον εἶναι codd.: τοῖσι δὲ Ἀργείοισι καὶ τοῖσι Αἰγινήτηισι δόξαι πρὸς ταῦτα ἔτι τόδε [ποιῆσαι]· νόμον εἶναι κτλ. Legrand post Stein: τοῖσι δὲ... [ἔτι τόδε ποιῆσαι]· κτλ. Stein: lacunam ante καὶ statuit Powell

καὶ τριηκοστῶι Αἰακῶι τέμενος ἀποδέξαντας ἄρχεσθαι τοῦ πρὸς Αἰγινήτας πολέμου, καί σφι χωρήσειν τὰ βούλονται· ἢν δὲ αὐτίκα ἐπιστρατεύων-
ται, πολλὰ μέν σφεας ἐν τῶι μεταξὺ τοῦ χρόνου πείσεσθαι, πολλὰ δὲ καὶ
ποιήσειν, τέλος μέντοι καταστρέψεσθαι. ταῦτα ὡς ἀπενειχθέντα ἤκου-   3
σαν οἱ Ἀθηναῖοι, τῶι μὲν Αἰακῶι τέμενος ἀπέδεξαν τοῦτο τὸ νῦν ἐπὶ τῆς
ἀγορῆς ἵδρυται, τριήκοντα δὲ ἔτεα οὐκ ἀνέσχοντο ἀκούσαντες ὅκως χρεὸν
εἴη ἐπισχεῖν πεπονθότας πρὸς Αἰγινητέων ἀνάρσια.
Ἐς τιμωρίην δὲ παρασκευαζομένοισι αὐτοῖσι ἐκ Λακεδαιμονίων   **90**
πρῆγμα ἐγειρόμενον ἐμπόδιον ἐγένετο. πυθόμενοι γὰρ Λακεδαιμόνιοι τὰ
ἐκ τῶν Ἀλκμεωνιδέων ἐς τὴν Πυθίην μεμηχανημένα καὶ τὰ ἐκ τῆς Πυθίης
ἐπὶ σφέας τε καὶ τοὺς Πεισιστρατίδας συμφορὴν ἐποιεῦντο διπλήν, ὅτι τε
ἄνδρας ξείνους σφίσι ἐόντας ἐξεληλάκεσαν ἐκ τῆς ἐκείνων, καὶ ὅτι ταῦτα
ποιήσασι χάρις οὐδεμία ἐφαίνετο πρὸς Ἀθηναίων. ἔτι τε πρὸς τούτοισι   2
ἐνῆγόν σφεας οἱ χρησμοὶ λέγοντες πολλά τε καὶ ἀνάρσια ἔσεσθαι αὐτοῖσι
ἐξ Ἀθηναίων, τῶν πρότερον μὲν ἦσαν ἀδαέες, τότε δὲ Κλεομένεος κομίσαν-
τος ἐς Σπάρτην ἐξέμαθον. ἐκτήσατο δὲ ὁ Κλεομένης ἐκ τῆς Ἀθηναίων
ἀκροπόλιος τοὺς χρησμούς, τοὺς ἔκτηντο μὲν πρότερον οἱ Πεισιστρατίδαι, ἐξελαυνόμενοι δὲ ἔλιπον ἐν τῶι ἱρῶι· καταλειφθέντας δὲ ὁ Κλεομένης
ἀνέλαβε.
Τότε δὲ ὡς ἀνέλαβον οἱ Λακεδαιμόνιοι τοὺς χρησμοὺς καὶ τοὺς Ἀθη-   **91**
ναίους ὥρων αὐξομένους καὶ οὐδαμῶς ἑτοίμους ἐόντας πείθεσθαι σφίσι,
νόωι λαβόντες ὡς ἐλεύθερον μὲν ἐὸν τὸ γένος τὸ Ἀττικὸν ἰσόρροπον τῶι
ἑωυτῶν ἂν γίνοιτο, κατεχόμενον δὲ ὑπὸ τυραννίδος ἀσθενὲς καὶ πειθαρ-
χέεσθαι ἕτοιμον, μαθόντες [δὲ] τούτων ἕκαστα μετεπέμποντο Ἱππίην τὸν
Πεισιστράτου ἀπὸ Σιγείου τοῦ ἐν Ἑλλησπόντωι ἐς ὃ καταφεύγουσι οἱ Πεισιστρατίδαι. ἐπείτε δέ σφι Ἱππίης καλεόμενος ἧκε, μεταπεμψάμενοι καὶ   2
τῶν ἄλλων συμμάχων ἀγγέλους ἔλεγόν σφι Σπαρτιῆται τάδε· "ἄνδρες
σύμμαχοι, συγγινώσκομεν αὐτοῖσι ἡμῖν οὐ ποιήσασι ὀρθῶς· ἐπαρθέντες
γὰρ κιβδήλοισι μαντηίοισι ἄνδρας ξείνους ἐόντας ἡμῖν τὰ μάλιστα καὶ
ἀναδεκομένους ὑποχειρίας παρέξειν τὰς Ἀθήνας, τούτους ἐκ τῆς πατρίδος
ἐξηλάσαμεν, καὶ ἔπειτα ποιήσαντες ταῦτα δήμωι ἀχαρίστωι παρεδώκα-
μεν τὴν πόλιν, ὃς ἐπείτε δι' ἡμέας ἐλευθερωθεὶς ἀνέκυψε, ἡμέας μὲν καὶ
τὸν βασιλέα ἡμέων περιυβρίσας ἐξέβαλε, δόξαν δὲ φύσας αὐξάνεται, ὥστε
ἐκμεμαθήκασι μάλιστα μὲν οἱ περίοικοι αὐτῶν Βοιωτοὶ καὶ Χαλκιδέες,
τάχα δέ τις καὶ ἄλλος ἐκμαθήσεται ἁμαρτών. ἐπείτε δὲ ἐκεῖνα ποιήσαντες   3
ἡμάρτομεν, νῦν πειρησόμεθά σφεα ἅμα ὑμῖν ἀκεόμενοι. αὐτοῦ γὰρ τούτου εἵνεκεν τόνδε τε Ἱππίην μετεπεμψάμεθα καὶ ὑμέας ἀπὸ τῶν πολίων,
ἵνα κοινῶι τε λόγωι καὶ κοινῶι στόλωι ἐσαγαγόντες αὐτὸν ἐς τὰς Ἀθήνας
ἀποδῶμεν τὰ καὶ ἀπειλόμεθα."

92 Οἱ μὲν ταῦτα ἔλεγον, τῶν δὲ συμμάχων τὸ πλῆθος οὐκ ἐνεδέκετο τοὺς λόγους. οἱ μέν νυν ἄλλοι ἡσυχίην ἦγον, Κορίνθιος δὲ Σωκλέης ἔλεξε τάδε·
α "ἦ δὴ ὅ τε οὐρανὸς ἔνερθε ἔσται τῆς γῆς καὶ ἡ γῆ μετέωρος ὑπὲρ τοῦ οὐρανοῦ, καὶ ἄνθρωποι νομὸν ἐν θαλάσσηι ἕξουσι καὶ ἰχθύες τὸν πρότερον ἄνθρωποι, ὅτε γε ὑμεῖς, ὦ Λακεδαιμόνιοι, ἰσοκρατίας καταλύοντες τυραννίδας ἐς τὰς πόλις κατάγειν παρασκευάζεσθε, τοῦ οὔτε ἀδικώτερόν ἐστι
2 οὐδὲν κατ' ἀνθρώπους οὔτε μιαιφονώτερον. εἰ γὰρ δὴ τοῦτό γε δοκέει ὑμῖν εἶναι χρηστὸν ὥστε τυραννεύεσθαι τὰς πόλις, αὐτοὶ πρῶτοι τύραννον καταστησάμενοι παρὰ σφίσι αὐτοῖσι οὕτω καὶ τοῖσι ἄλλοισι δίζησθε κατιστάναι· νῦν δὲ αὐτοὶ τυράννων ἄπειροι ἐόντες καὶ φυλάσσοντες τοῦτο δεινότατα ἐν τῆι Σπάρτηι μὴ γενέσθαι, παραχρᾶσθε ἐς τοὺς συμμάχους· εἰ δὲ αὐτῶν ἔμπειροι ἔατε κατά περ ἡμεῖς, εἴχετε ἂν περὶ αὐτοῦ γνώμας
β ἀμείνονας συμβαλέσθαι ἤ περ νῦν. Κορινθίοισι γὰρ ἦν πόλιος κατάστασις τοιήδε· ἦν ὀλιγαρχίη, καὶ οὗτοι Βακχιάδαι καλεόμενοι ἔνεμον τὴν πόλιν, ἐδίδοσαν δὲ καὶ ἤγοντο ἐξ ἀλλήλων. Ἀμφίονι δὲ ἐόντι τούτων τῶν ἀνδρῶν γίνεται θυγάτηρ χωλή· οὔνομα δέ οἱ ἦν Λάβδα. ταύτην Βακχιαδέων γὰρ οὐδεὶς ἤθελε γῆμαι, ἴσχει Ἠετίων ὁ Ἐχεκράτεος, δήμου μὲν ἐὼν ἐκ Πέτρης,
2 ἀτὰρ τὰ ἀνέκαθεν Λαπίθης τε καὶ Καινείδης. ἐκ δέ οἱ ταύτης τῆς γυναικὸς οὐδ' ἐξ ἄλλης παῖδες ἐγίνοντο· ἐστάλη ὦν ἐς Δελφοὺς περὶ γόνου. ἐσιόντα δὲ αὐτὸν ἰθέως ἡ Πυθίη προσαγορεύει τοισίδε τοῖσι ἔπεσι·

> Ἠετίων, οὔτις σε τίει πολύτιτον ἐόντα.
> Λάβδα κύει, τέξει δ' ὀλοοίτροχον· ἐν δὲ πεσεῖται
> ἀνδράσι μουνάρχοισι, δικαιώσει δὲ Κόρινθον.

3 ταῦτα χρησθέντα τῶι Ἠετίωνι ἐξαγγέλλεταί κως τοῖσι Βακχιάδηισι, τοῖσι τὸ μὲν πρότερον γενόμενον χρηστήριον ἐς Κόρινθον ἦν ἄσημον, φέρον τε ἐς τὠυτὸ καὶ τὸ τοῦ Ἠετίωνος καὶ λέγον ὧδε·

> αἰετὸς ἐν πέτρηισι κύει, τέξει δὲ λέοντα
> καρτερὸν ὠμηστήν· πολλῶν δ' ὑπὸ γούνατα λύσει.
> ταῦτά νυν εὖ φράζεσθε, Κορίνθιοι, οἳ περὶ καλὴν
> Πειρήνην οἰκεῖτε καὶ ὀφρυόεντα Κόρινθον.

γ Τοῦτο μὲν δὴ τοῖσι Βακχιάδηισι γενόμενον πρότερον ἦν ἀτέκμαρτον, τότε δὲ τὸ Ἠετίωνι γενόμενον ὡς ἐπύθοντο, αὐτίκα καὶ τὸ πρότερον συνῆκαν ἐὸν συνωιδὸν τῶι Ἠετίωνος. συνέντες δὲ καὶ τοῦτο εἶχον ἐν ἡσυχίηι, ἐθέλοντες τὸν μέλλοντα Ἠετίωνι γίνεσθαι γόνον διαφθεῖραι. ὡς δ' ἔτεκε ἡ γυνὴ τάχιστα, πέμπουσι σφέων αὐτῶν δέκα ἐς τὸν δῆμον ἐν τῶι

---

92 Σωκλέης ABC, Plut. *Mor.* 86of, *P. Oxy.* 1012 fr. 9. 55: Σωσικλέης PDRSV   92 α 2
αὐτῶν Weber 1940: αὐτοὶ DSUV: αὐτοῦ A   92 β 1 οὗτοι codd.: οἱ vel οἱ τότε Madvig

κατοίκητο Ἠετίων ἀποκτενέοντας τὸ παιδίον. ἀπικόμενοι δὲ οὗτοι ἐς τὴν 2
Πέτρην καὶ παρελθόντες ἐς τὴν αὐλὴν τὴν Ἠετίωνος αἴτεον τὸ παιδίον·
ἡ δὲ Λάβδα εἰδυῖά τε οὐδὲν τῶν εἵνεκα ἐκεῖνοι ἀπικοίατο καὶ δοκέουσά
σφεας φιλοφροσύνης τοῦ πατρὸς εἵνεκα αἰτέειν φέρουσα ἐνεχείρισε αὐτῶν
ἑνί. τοῖσι δὲ ἄρα ἐβεβούλευτο κατ᾽ ὁδὸν τὸν πρῶτον αὐτῶν λαβόντα [τὸ
παιδίον] προσουδίσαι. ἐπείτε ὦν ἔδωκε φέρουσα ἡ Λάβδα, τὸν λαβόντα 3
τῶν ἀνδρῶν θείηι τύχηι προσεγέλασε τὸ παιδίον, καὶ τὸν φρασθέντα
τοῦτο οἶκτός τις ἴσχει ἀποκτεῖναι, κατοικτίρας δὲ παραδιδοῖ τῶι δευτέρωι,
ὁ δὲ τῶι τρίτωι, οὕτω τε διεξῆλθε διὰ πάντων τῶν δέκα παραδιδόμενον,
οὐδενὸς βουλομένου διεργάσασθαι. ἀποδόντες ὦν ὀπίσω τῆι τεκούσηι τὸ 4
παιδίον καὶ ἐξελθόντες ἔξω, ἑστεῶτες ἐπὶ τῶν θυρέων ἀλλήλων ἅπτοντο
καταιτιώμενοι καὶ μάλιστα τοῦ πρώτου λαβόντος, ὅτι οὐκ ἐποίησε κατὰ
τὰ δεδογμένα, ἐς ὃ δή σφι χρόνου ἐγγινομένου ἔδοξε αὖτις παρελθόν-
τας πάντας τοῦ φόνου μετίσχειν. ἔδει δὲ ἐκ τοῦ Ἠετίωνος γόνου Κορίν- 5
θωι κακὰ ἀναβλαστεῖν. ἡ Λάβδα γὰρ πάντα ταῦτα ἤκουε ἑστεῶσα πρὸς
αὐτῆισι τῆισι θύρηισι· δείσασα δὲ μή σφι μεταδόξηι καὶ τὸ δεύτερον λαβόντες τὸ παιδίον ἀποκτείνωσι, φέρουσα κατακρύπτει ἐς τὸ ἀφραστότατόν
οἱ ἐφαίνετο εἶναι, ἐς κυψέλην, ἐπισταμένη ὡς εἰ ὑποστρέψαντες ἐς ζήτησιν
ἀπικνεοίατο, πάντα ἐρευνήσειν μέλλοιεν· τὰ δὴ καὶ ἐγένετο. ἐσελθοῦσι δὲ 2
καὶ διζημένοισι αὐτοῖσι ὡς οὐκ ἐφαίνετο, ἐδόκεε ἀπαλλάσσεσθαι καὶ λέγειν
πρὸς τοὺς ἀποπέμψαντας ὡς πάντα ποιήσειαν τὰ ἐκεῖνοι ἐνετείλαντο. οἱ
μὲν δὴ ἀπελθόντες ἔλεγον ταῦτα· Ἠετίωνι δὲ μετὰ ταῦτα ὁ παῖς ηὐξάνετο, ε
καὶ οἱ διαφυγόντι τοῦτον τὸν κίνδυνον ἀπὸ τῆς κυψέλης ἐπωνυμίην Κύψελος οὔνομα ἐτέθη. ἀνδρωθέντι δὲ καὶ μαντευομένωι Κυψέλωι ἐγένετο
ἀμφιδέξιον χρηστήριον ἐν Δελφοῖσι, τῶι πίσυνος γενόμενος ἐπεχείρησέ τε
καὶ ἔσχε Κόρινθον. ὁ δὲ χρησμὸς ὅδε ἦν· 2

ὄλβιος οὗτος ἀνὴρ ὃς ἐμὸν δόμον ἐσκαταβαίνει,
Κύψελος Ἠετίδης, βασιλεὺς κλειτοῖο Κορίνθου,
αὐτὸς καὶ παῖδες, παίδων γε μὲν οὐκέτι παῖδες.

τὸ μὲν δὴ χρηστήριον τοῦτο ἦν, τυραννεύσας δὲ ὁ Κύψελος τοιοῦτος δή
τις ἀνὴρ ἐγένετο· πολλοὺς μὲν Κορινθίων ἐδίωξε, πολλοὺς δὲ χρημάτων
ἀπεστέρησε, πολλῶι δέ τι πλείστους τῆς ψυχῆς.
Ἄρξαντος δὲ τούτου ἐπὶ τριήκοντα ἔτεα καὶ διαπλέξαντος τὸν βίον ζ
εὖ διάδοχός οἱ τῆς τυραννίδος ὁ παῖς Περίανδρος γίνεται. ὁ τοίνυν
Περίανδρος κατ᾽ ἀρχὰς μὲν ἦν ἠπιώτερος τοῦ πατρός, ἐπείτε δὲ ὡμίλησε
δι᾽ ἀγγέλων Θρασυβούλωι τῶι Μιλήτου τυράννωι, πολλῶι ἔτι ἐγένετο
Κυψέλου μιαιφονώτερος. πέμψας γὰρ παρὰ Θρασύβουλον κήρυκα ἐπυν- 2
θάνετο ὅντινα ἂν τρόπον ἀσφαλέστατον καταστησάμενος τῶν πρηγ-
μάτων κάλλιστα τὴν πόλιν ἐπιτροπεύοι. Θρασύβουλος δὲ τὸν ἐλθόντα

παρὰ τοῦ Περιάνδρου ἐξήγαγε ἔξω τοῦ ἄστεος, ἐσβὰς δὲ ἐς ἄρουραν
ἐσπαρμένην ἅμα τε διεξήιε τὸ λήιον ἐπειρωτῶν τε καὶ ἀναποδίζων τὸν
κήρυκα κατὰ τὴν ἀπὸ Κορίνθου ἄπιξιν, καὶ ἐκόλουε αἰεὶ ὅκως τινὰ ἴδοι
τῶν ἀσταχύων ὑπερέχοντα, κολούων δὲ ἔρριπτε, ἐς ὃ τοῦ ληίου τὸ κάλ-
3 λιστόν τε καὶ βαθύτατον διέφθειρε τρόπωι τοιούτωι. διεξελθὼν δὲ τὸ
χωρίον καὶ ὑποθέμενος ἔπος οὐδὲν ἀποπέμπει τὸν κήρυκα. νοστήσαν-
τος δὲ τοῦ κήρυκος ἐς τὴν Κόρινθον ἦν πρόθυμος πυνθάνεσθαι τὴν ὑποθήκην ὁ Περίανδρος· ὁ δὲ οὐδέν οἱ ἔφη Θρασύβουλον ὑποθέσθαι, θωμάζειν
τε αὐτοῦ παρ' οἷόν μιν ἄνδρα ἀποπέμψειε, ὡς παραπλῆγά τε καὶ τῶν
ἑωυτοῦ σιναμωρόν, ἀπηγεόμενος τά περ πρὸς Θρασυβούλου ὀπώπεε
η <ποιευμένα>. Περίανδρος δὲ συνεὶς τὸ ποιηθὲν καὶ νόωι σχὼν ὡς οἱ
ὑπετίθετο Θρασύβουλος τοὺς ὑπερόχους τῶν ἀστῶν φονεύειν, ἐνθαῦτα
δὴ πᾶσαν κακότητα ἐξέφαινε ἐς τοὺς πολιήτας. ὅσα γὰρ Κύψελος ἀπέλιπε
κτείνων τε καὶ διώκων, Περίανδρός σφεα ἀπετέλεε, μιῆι δὲ ἡμέρηι ἀπέδυσε πάσας τὰς Κορινθίων γυναῖκας διὰ τὴν ἑωυτοῦ γυναῖκα Μέλισ-
2 σαν. πέμψαντι γάρ οἱ ἐς Θεσπρωτοὺς ἐπ' Ἀχέροντα ποταμὸν ἀγγέλους
ἐπὶ τὸ νεκυομαντήιον παρακαταθήκης πέρι ξεινικῆς οὔτε σημανέειν ἔφη
ἡ Μέλισσα ἐπιφανεῖσα οὔτε κατερέειν ἐν τῶι κεῖται χώρωι ἡ παρακατα-
θήκη· ῥιγοῦν τε γὰρ καὶ εἶναι γυμνή· τῶν γάρ οἱ συγκατέθαψε εἱμάτων
ὄφελος εἶναι οὐδὲν οὐ κατακαυθέντων· μαρτύριον δέ οἱ εἶναι ὡς ἀληθέα
ταῦτα λέγει, ὅτι ἐπὶ ψυχρὸν τὸν ἰπνὸν Περίανδρος τοὺς ἄρτους ἐπέβαλε.
3 ταῦτα δὲ ὡς ὀπίσω ἀπηγγέλθη τῶι Περιάνδρωι (πιστὸν γάρ οἱ ἦν
τὸ συμβόλαιον, ὃς νεκρῶι ἐούσηι Μελίσσηι ἐμίγη), ἰθέως δὴ μετὰ τὴν
ἀγγελίην κήρυγμα ἐποιήσατο ἐς τὸ Ἥραιον ἐξιέναι πάσας τὰς Κορινθίων
γυναῖκας. αἱ μὲν δὴ ὡς ἐς ὁρτὴν ἤισαν κόσμωι τῶι καλλίστωι χρεώμε-
ναι, ὁ δ' ὑποστήσας τοὺς δορυφόρους ἀπέδυσέ σφεας πάσας ὁμοίως, τάς
τε ἐλευθέρας καὶ τὰς ἀμφιπόλους, συμφορήσας δὲ ἐς ὄρυγμα Μελίσσηι
4 ἐπευχόμενος κατέκαιε. ταῦτα δέ οἱ ποιήσαντι καὶ τὸ δεύτερον πέμψαντι
ἔφρασε τὸ εἴδωλον τὸ Μελίσσης ἐς τὸν κατέθηκε χῶρον τοῦ ξείνου τὴν
παρακαταθήκην. τοιοῦτο μὲν ὑμῖν ἐστι ἡ τυραννίς, ὦ Λακεδαιμόνιοι, καὶ
5 τοιούτων ἔργων. ἡμέας δὲ τοὺς Κορινθίους τό τε αὐτίκα θῶμα μέγα εἶχε
ὅτε ὑμέας εἴδομεν μεταπεμπομένους Ἱππίην, νῦν τε δὴ καὶ μεζόνως θωμά-
ζομεν λέγοντας ταῦτα. ἐπιμαρτυρόμεθά τε ἐπικαλεόμενοι ὑμῖν θεοὺς τοὺς
Ἑλληνίους μὴ κατιστάναι τυραννίδας ἐς τὰς πόλις. οὔκων παύσεσθε ἀλλὰ
πειρήσεσθε παρὰ τὸ δίκαιον κατάγοντες Ἱππίην; ἴστε ὑμῖν Κορινθίους γε
οὐ συναινέοντας."

92 ζ 3 ποιευμένα suppl. Wilson

Σωκλέης μὲν ἀπὸ Κορίνθου πρεσβεύων ἔλεξε τάδε, Ἱππίης δὲ αὐτὸν **93**
ἀμείβετο τοὺς αὐτοὺς ἐπικαλέσας θεοὺς ἐκείνωι, ἦ μὲν Κορινθίους μάλιστα
πάντων ἐπιποθήσειν Πεισιστρατίδας, ὅταν σφι ἥκωσι ἡμέραι αἱ κύριαι
ἀνιᾶσθαι ὑπ' Ἀθηναίων. Ἱππίης μὲν τούτοισι ἀμείψατο οἷά τε τοὺς 2
χρησμοὺς ἀτρεκέστατα ἀνδρῶν ἐξεπιστάμενος· οἱ δὲ λοιποὶ τῶν συμμάχων τέως μὲν εἶχον ἐν ἡσυχίηι σφέας αὐτούς, ἐπείτε δὲ Σωκλέος ἤκου-
σαν εἴπαντος ἐλευθέρως, ἅπας τις αὐτῶν φωνὴν ῥήξας αἱρέετο τοῦ Κοριν-
θίου τὴν γνώμην, Λακεδαιμονίοισί τε ἐπεμαρτύροντο μὴ ποιέειν μηδὲν
νεώτερον περὶ πόλιν Ἑλλάδα. Οὕτω μὲν ταῦτα ἐπαύσθη. Ἱππίηι δὲ ἐνθεῦτεν ἀπελαυνομένωι ἐδίδου **94**
μὲν Ἀμύντης ὁ Μακεδὼν Ἀνθεμοῦντα, ἐδίδοσαν δὲ Θεσσαλοὶ Ἰωλκόν.
ὁ δὲ τούτων μὲν οὐδέτερα αἱρέετο, ἀνεχώρεε δὲ ὀπίσω ἐς Σίγειον,
τὸ εἷλε Πεισίστρατος αἰχμῆι παρὰ Μυτιληναίων, κρατήσας δὲ αὐτοῦ
κατέστησε τύραννον εἶναι παῖδα ἑωυτοῦ νόθον Ἡγησίστρατον, γεγονότα
ἐξ Ἀργείης γυναικός, ὃς οὐκ ἀμαχητὶ εἶχε τὰ παρέλαβε παρὰ Πεισιστράτου. ἐπολέμεον γὰρ ἔκ τε Ἀχιλληίου πόλιος ὁρμώμενοι καὶ Σιγείου ἐπὶ 2
χρόνον συχνὸν Μυτιληναῖοί τε καὶ Ἀθηναῖοι, οἱ μὲν ἀπαιτέοντες τὴν
χώρην, Ἀθηναῖοι δὲ οὔτε συγγινωσκόμενοι ἀποδεικνύντες τε λόγωι οὐδὲν
μᾶλλον Αἰολεῦσι μετεὸν τῆς Ἰλιάδος χώρης ἢ οὐ καὶ σφίσι καὶ τοῖσι ἄλλοισι,
ὅσοι Ἑλλήνων συνεπρήξαντο Μενέλεωι τὰς Ἑλένης ἁρπαγάς.

Πολεμεόντων δέ σφεων παντοῖα καὶ ἄλλα ἐγένετο ἐν τῆισι μάχηισι, ἐν **95**
δὲ δὴ καὶ Ἀλκαῖος ὁ ποιητὴς συμβολῆς γενομένης καὶ νικώντων Ἀθηναίων
αὐτὸς μὲν φεύγων ἐκφεύγει, τὰ δέ οἱ ὅπλα ἴσχουσι Ἀθηναῖοι καί σφεα
ἀνεκρέμασαν πρὸς τὸ Ἀθήναιον τὸ ἐν Σιγείωι. ταῦτα δὲ Ἀλκαῖος ἐν μέλεΐ 2
ποιήσας ἐπιτιθεῖ ἐς Μυτιλήνην ἐξαγγελλόμενος τὸ ἑωυτοῦ πάθος Μελανίππωι ἀνδρὶ ἑταίρωι. Μυτιληναίους δὲ καὶ Ἀθηναίους κατήλλαξε Περίανδρος
ὁ Κυψέλου· τούτωι γὰρ διαιτητῆι ἐπετράποντο· κατήλλαξε δὲ ὧδε, νέμεσ-
θαι ἑκατέρους τὴν ἔχουσι. Σίγειον μέν νυν οὕτω ἐγένετο ὑπ' Ἀθηναίοισι.

Ἱππίης δὲ ἐπείτε ἀπίκετο ἐκ τῆς Λακεδαίμονος ἐς τὴν Ἀσίην, πᾶν χρῆμα **96**
ἐκίνεε, διαβάλλων τε τοὺς Ἀθηναίους πρὸς τὸν Ἀρταφρένεα καὶ ποιέων
ἅπαντα ὅκως αἱ Ἀθῆναι γενοίατο ὑπ' ἑωυτῶι τε καὶ Δαρείωι. Ἱππίης τε 2
δὴ ταῦτα ἔπρησσε καὶ οἱ Ἀθηναῖοι πυθόμενοι ταῦτα πέμπουσι ἐς Σάρδις
ἀγγέλους, οὐκ ἐῶντες τοὺς Πέρσας πείθεσθαι Ἀθηναίων τοῖσι φυγάσι.
ὁ δὲ Ἀρταφρένης ἐκέλευέ σφεας, εἰ βουλοίατο σόοι εἶναι, καταδέκεσθαι
ὀπίσω Ἱππίην. οὐκ ὦν δὴ ἐνεδέκοντο τοὺς λόγους ἀποφερομένους οἱ Ἀθη-
ναῖοι· οὐκ ἐνδεκομένοισι δέ σφι ἐδέδοκτο ἐκ τοῦ φανεροῦ τοῖσι Πέρσηισι
πολεμίους εἶναι.

97 Νομίζουσι δὲ ταῦτα καὶ διαβεβλημένοισι ἐς τοὺς Πέρσας ἐν τούτωι δὴ τῶι καιρῶι ὁ Μιλήσιος Ἀρισταγόρης ὑπὸ Κλεομένεος τοῦ Λακεδαιμονίου ἐξελασθεὶς ἐκ τῆς Σπάρτης ἀπίκετο ἐς τὰς Ἀθήνας· αὕτη γὰρ ἡ πόλις τῶν λοιπέων ἐδυνάστευε μέγιστον. ἐπελθὼν δὲ ἐπὶ τὸν δῆμον ὁ Ἀρισταγόρης ταὐτὰ ἔλεγε τὰ καὶ ἐν τῆι Σπάρτηι περὶ τῶν ἀγαθῶν τῶν ἐν τῆι Ἀσίηι καὶ τοῦ πολέμου τοῦ Περσικοῦ, ὡς οὔτε ἀσπίδα οὔτε δόρυ νομίζουσι εὐπετέες

2 τε χειρωθῆναι εἴησαν. ταῦτά τε δὴ ἔλεγε καὶ πρὸς τοῖσι τάδε, ὡς οἱ Μιλήσιοι τῶν Ἀθηναίων εἰσὶ ἄποικοι, καὶ οἰκός σφεας εἴη ῥύεσθαι δυναμένους μέγα· καὶ οὐδὲν ὅ τι οὐκ ὑπίσχετο οἷα κάρτα δεόμενος, ἐς ὃ ἀνέπεισέ σφεας. πολλοὺς γὰρ οἶκε εἶναι εὐπετέστερον διαβάλλειν ἢ ἕνα, εἰ Κλεομένεα μὲν τὸν Λακεδαιμόνιον μοῦνον οὐκ οἷός τε ἐγένετο διαβάλλειν, τρεῖς δὲ μυριά-

3 δας Ἀθηναίων ἐποίησε τοῦτο. Ἀθηναῖοι μὲν δὴ ἀναπεισθέντες ἐψηφίσαντο εἴκοσι νέας ἀποστεῖλαι βοηθοὺς Ἴωσι, στρατηγὸν ἀποδέξαντες αὐτέων εἶναι Μελάνθιον, ἄνδρα τῶν ἀστῶν ἐόντα τὰ πάντα δόκιμον. αὗται δὲ αἱ νέες ἀρχὴ κακῶν ἐγένοντο Ἕλλησί τε καὶ βαρβάροισι.

98 Ἀρισταγόρης δὲ προπλώσας καὶ ἀπικόμενος ἐς τὴν Μίλητον, ἐξευρὼν βούλευμα ἀπ᾽ οὗ Ἴωσι μὲν οὐδεμία ἔμελλε ὠφελίη ἔσεσθαι (οὐδ᾽ ὦν οὐδὲ τούτου εἴνεκα ἐποίεε, ἀλλ᾽ ὅκως βασιλέα Δαρεῖον λυπήσειε), ἔπεμψε ἐς τὴν Φρυγίην ἄνδρα ἐπὶ τοὺς Παίονας τοὺς ἀπὸ Στρυμόνος ποταμοῦ αἰχμαλώτους γενομένους ὑπὸ Μεγαβάζου, οἰκέοντας δὲ τῆς Φρυγίης χῶρόν τε καὶ κώμην ἐπ᾽ ἑωυτῶν, ὃς ἐπειδὴ ἀπίκετο ἐς τοὺς Παίονας, ἔλεγε τάδε·

2 "ἄνδρες Παίονες, ἔπεμψέ με Ἀρισταγόρης ὁ Μιλήτου τύραννος σωτηρίην ὑποθησόμενον ὑμῖν, ἤν περ βούλησθε πείθεσθαι. νῦν γὰρ Ἰωνίη πᾶσα ἀπέστηκε ἀπὸ βασιλέος, καὶ ὑμῖν παρέχει σώιζεσθαι ἐπὶ τὴν ὑμετέρην αὐτῶν· μέχρι μὲν θαλάσσης αὐτοῖσι ὑμῖν, τὸ δὲ ἀπὸ τούτου ἡμῖν ἤδη μελή-

3 σει." ταῦτα δὲ ἀκούσαντες οἱ Παίονες κάρτα τε ἀσπαστὸν ἐποιήσαντο καὶ ἀναλαβόντες παῖδας καὶ γυναῖκας ἀπεδίδρησκον ἐπὶ θάλασσαν· οἱ δέ τινες αὐτῶν καὶ κατέμειναν ἀρρωδήσαντες αὐτοῦ. ἐπείτε δὲ οἱ Παίονες

4 ἀπίκοντο ἐπὶ θάλασσαν, ἐνθεῦτεν ἐς Χίον διέβησαν. ἐόντων δὲ ἤδη ἐν Χίωι κατὰ πόδας ἐληλύθεε Περσέων ἵππος πολλὴ διώκουσα τοὺς Παίονας· ὡς δὲ οὐ κατέλαβον, ἐπηγγέλλοντο ἐς τὴν Χίον τοῖσι Παίοσι ὅκως ἂν ὀπίσω ἀπέλθοιεν. οἱ δὲ Παίονες τοὺς λόγους οὐκ ἐνεδέκοντο, ἀλλ᾽ ἐκ Χίου μὲν Χῖοί σφεας ἐς Λέσβον ἤγαγον, Λέσβιοι δὲ ἐς Δορίσκον ἐκόμισαν· ἐνθεῦτεν δὲ πεζῆι κομιζόμενοι ἀπίκοντο ἐς Παιονίην.

99 Ἀρισταγόρης δέ, ἐπειδὴ οἵ τε Ἀθηναῖοι ἀπίκοντο εἴκοσι νηυσί, ἅμα ἀγόμενοι Ἐρετριέων πέντε τριήρεας, οἳ οὐ τὴν Ἀθηναίων χάριν ἐστρατεύοντο ἀλλὰ τὴν αὐτῶν Μιλησίων, ὀφειλόμενά σφι ἀποδιδόντες (οἱ γὰρ δὴ Μιλήσιοι πρότερον τοῖσι Ἐρετριεῦσι τὸν πρὸς Χαλκιδέας πόλεμον συνδιήνεικαν, ὅτε περ καὶ Χαλκιδεῦσι ἀντία Ἐρετριέων καὶ Μιλησίων

Σάμιοι ἐβοήθεον), οὗτοι ὧν ἐπείτε σφι ἀπίκοντο καὶ οἱ ἄλλοι σύμμαχοι
παρῆσαν, ἐποιέετο στρατηίην ὁ Ἀρισταγόρης ἐς Σάρδις. αὐτὸς μὲν δή 2
οὐκ ἐστρατεύετο ἀλλ᾽ ἔμενε ἐν Μιλήτωι, στρατηγοὺς δὲ ἄλλους ἀπέδεξε
Μιλησίων εἶναι τὸν ἑωυτοῦ τε ἀδελφεὸν Χαροπῖνον καὶ τῶν ἄλλων ἀστῶν
Ἑρμόφαντον.

Ἀπικόμενοι δὲ τῶι στόλωι τούτωι Ἴωνες ἐς Ἔφεσον πλοῖα μὲν 100
κατέλιπον ἐν Κορησσῶι τῆς Ἐφεσίης, αὐτοὶ δὲ ἀνέβαινον χειρὶ πολλῆι,
ποιεύμενοι Ἐφεσίους ἡγεμόνας [τῆς ὁδοῦ]. πορευόμενοι δὲ παρὰ ποταμὸν
Καΰστριον, ἐνθεῦτεν ἐπείτε ὑπερβάντες τὸν Τμῶλον ἀπίκοντο, αἱρέουσι
Σάρδις οὐδενός σφι ἀντιωθέντος, αἱρέουσι δὲ χωρὶς τῆς ἀκροπόλιος
τἆλλα πάντα· τὴν δὲ ἀκρόπολιν ἐρρύετο αὐτὸς Ἀρταφρένης ἔχων ἀνδρῶν
δύναμιν οὐκ ὀλίγην.

Τὸ δὲ μὴ λεηλατῆσαι ἑλόντας σφέας τὴν πόλιν ἔσχε τόδε. ἦσαν ἐν τῆισι 101
Σάρδισι οἰκίαι αἱ μὲν πλεῦνες καλάμιναι, ὅσαι δ᾽ αὐτέων καὶ πλίνθιναι
ἦσαν καλάμου εἶχον τὰς ὀροφάς. τουτέων δὴ μίαν τῶν τις στρατιωτέων
ὡς ἐνέπρησε, αὐτίκα ἀπ᾽ οἰκίης ἐπ᾽ οἰκίην ἰὸν τὸ πῦρ ἐπενέμετο τὸ ἄστυ
πᾶν. καιομένου δὲ τοῦ ἄστεος οἱ Λυδοί τε καὶ ὅσοι Περσέων ἐνῆσαν ἐν τῆι 2
πόλι, ἀπολαμφθέντες πάντοθεν ὥστε τὰ περιέσχατα νεμομένου τοῦ πυρὸς
καὶ οὐκ ἔχοντες ἐξήλυσιν ἐκ τοῦ ἄστεος, συνέρρεον ἔς τε τὴν ἀγορὴν καὶ
ἐπὶ τὸν Πακτωλὸν ποταμόν, ὅς σφι ψῆγμα χρυσοῦ καταφορέων ἐκ τοῦ
Τμῶλου διὰ μέσης τῆς ἀγορῆς ῥέει καὶ ἔπειτα ἐς τὸν Ἕρμον ποταμὸν ἐκδιδοῖ, ὁ δὲ ἐς θάλασσαν· ἐπὶ τοῦτον δὴ τὸν Πακτωλὸν καὶ ἐς τὴν ἀγορὴν
ἀθροιζόμενοι οἵ τε Λυδοὶ καὶ οἱ Πέρσαι ἠναγκάζοντο ἀμύνεσθαι. οἱ δὲ 3
Ἴωνες ὁρῶντες τοὺς μὲν ἀμυνομένους τῶν πολεμίων, τοὺς δὲ σὺν πλήθεϊ πολλῶι προσφερομένους ἐξανεχώρησαν δείσαντες πρὸς τὸ ὄρος τὸ
Τμῶλον καλεόμενον, ἐνθεῦτεν δὲ ὑπὸ νύκτα ἀπαλλάσσοντο ἐπὶ τὰς νέας.

Καὶ Σάρδιες μὲν ἐνεπρήσθησαν, ἐν δὲ αὐτῆισι καὶ ἱρὸν ἐπιχωρίης θεοῦ 102
Κυβήβης, τὸ σκηπτόμενοι οἱ Πέρσαι ὕστερον ἀντενεπίμπρασαν τὰ ἐν
Ἕλλησι ἱρά. τότε δὲ οἱ Πέρσαι οἱ ἐντὸς Ἅλυος ποταμοῦ νομοὺς ἔχοντες προπυνθανόμενοι ταῦτα συνηλίζοντο καὶ ἐβοήθεον τοῖσι Λυδοῖσι.
καί κως ἐν μὲν Σάρδισι οὐκέτι ἐόντας τοὺς Ἴωνας εὑρίσκουσι, ἑπόμενοι 2
δὲ κατὰ στίβον αἱρέουσι αὐτοὺς ἐν Ἐφέσωι. καὶ ἀντετάχθησαν μὲν οἱ
Ἴωνες, συμβαλόντες δὲ πολλὸν ἑσσώθησαν. καὶ πολλοὺς αὐτῶν οἱ Πέρσαι 3
φονεύουσι, ἄλλους τε ὀνομαστούς, ἐν δὲ δὴ καὶ Εὐαλκίδην στρατηγέοντα
Ἐρετριέων, στεφανηφόρους τε ἀγῶνας ἀναραιρηκότα καὶ ὑπὸ Σιμωνίδεω
τοῦ Κηίου πολλὰ αἰνεθέντα. οἳ δὲ αὐτῶν ἀπέφυγον τὴν μάχην ἐσκεδάσθη-
σαν ἀνὰ τὰς πόλιας.

100 τῆς ὁδοῦ om. PSVU

103 Τότε μὲν δὴ οὕτω ἠγωνίσαντο· μετὰ δὲ Ἀθηναῖοι μὲν τὸ παράπαν ἀπολιπόντες τοὺς Ἴωνας ἐπικαλεομένου σφέας πολλὰ δι᾽ ἀγγέλων Ἀρισταγόρεω οὐκ ἔφασαν τιμωρήσειν σφι. Ἴωνες δὲ τῆς Ἀθηναίων συμμαχίης στερηθέντες (οὕτω γάρ σφι ὑπῆρχε πεποιημένα ἐς Δαρεῖον) οὐδὲν

2 δὴ ἧσσον τὸν πρὸς βασιλέα πόλεμον ἐσκευάζοντο. πλώσαντες δὲ ἐς τὸν Ἑλλήσποντον Βυζάντιόν τε καὶ τὰς ἄλλας πόλις πάσας τὰς ταύτηι ὑπ᾽ ἑωυτοῖσι ἐποιήσαντο, ἐκπλώσαντές τε ἔξω τὸν Ἑλλήσποντον Καρίης τὴν πολλὴν προσεκτήσαντο σφίσι σύμμαχον εἶναι· καὶ γὰρ τὴν Καῦνον πρότερον οὐ βουλομένην συμμαχέειν, ὡς ἐνέπρησαν τὰς Σάρδις, τότε σφι καὶ αὕτη προσεγένετο.

104 Κύπριοι δὲ ἐθελονταί σφι πάντες προσεγένοντο πλὴν Ἀμαθουσίων· ἀπέστησαν γὰρ καὶ οὗτοι ὧδε ἀπὸ Μήδων. ἦν Ὀνήσιλος Γόργου μὲν τοῦ Σαλαμινίων βασιλέος ἀδελφεὸς νεώτερος, Χέρσιος δὲ τοῦ Σιρώμου

2 τοῦ Εὐέλθοντος παῖς. οὗτος ὁ ἀνὴρ πολλάκις μὲν καὶ πρότερον τὸν Γόργον παρηγορέετο ἀπίστασθαι ἀπὸ βασιλέος, τότε δέ, ὡς καὶ τοὺς Ἴωνας ἐπύθετο ἀπεστάναι, πάγχυ ἐπικείμενος ἐνῆγε. ὡς δὲ οὐκ ἔπειθε τὸν Γόργον, ἐνθαῦτά μιν φυλάξας ἐξελθόντα τὸ ἄστυ τὸ Σαλαμινίων ὁ Ὀνήσιλος

3 ἅμα τοῖσι ἑωυτοῦ στασιώτηισι ἀπεκλήισε τῶν πυλέων. Γόργος μὲν δὴ στερηθεὶς τῆς πόλιος ἔφευγε ἐς Μήδους, Ὀνήσιλος δὲ ἦρχε Σαλαμῖνος καὶ ἀνέπειθε πάντας Κυπρίους συναπίστασθαι. τοὺς μὲν δὴ ἄλλους ἀνέπεισε, Ἀμαθουσίους δὲ οὐ βουλομένους οἱ πείθεσθαι ἐπολιόρκεε προσκατήμενος.

105 Ὀνήσιλος μέν νυν ἐπολιόρκεε Ἀμαθοῦντα, βασιλέϊ δὲ Δαρείωι ὡς ἐξαγγέλθη Σάρδις ἁλούσας ἐμπεπρῆσθαι ὑπό τε Ἀθηναίων καὶ Ἰώνων, τὸν δὲ ἡγεμόνα γενέσθαι τῆς συλλογῆς ὥστε ταῦτα συνυφανθῆναι τὸν Μιλήσιον Ἀρισταγόρην, πρῶτα μὲν λέγεται αὐτόν, ὡς ἐπύθετο ταῦτα, Ἰώνων οὐδένα λόγον ποιησάμενον, εὖ εἰδότα ὡς οὗτοί γε οὐ καταπροΐξονται ἀποστάντες, εἰρέσθαι οἵτινες εἶεν οἱ Ἀθηναῖοι, μετὰ δὲ πυθόμενον αἰτῆσαι τὸ τόξον, λαβόντα δὲ καὶ ἐπιθέντα ὀιστὸν ἄνω πρὸς τὸν οὐρανὸν

2 ἀπεῖναι, καί μιν ἐς τὸν ἠέρα βάλλοντα εἰπεῖν· "ὦ Ζεῦ, ἐκγενέσθαι μοι Ἀθηναίους τείσασθαι", εἴπαντα δὲ ταῦτα προστάξαι ἑνὶ τῶν θεραπόντων δείπνου προκειμένου αὐτῶι ἐς τρὶς ἑκάστοτε εἰπεῖν· "δέσποτα, μέμνεο τῶν Ἀθηναίων."

106 Προστάξας δὲ ταῦτα εἶπε, καλέσας ἐς ὄψιν Ἱστιαῖον τὸν Μιλήσιον, τὸν [ὁ Δαρεῖος] κατεῖχε χρόνον ἤδη πολλόν· "πυνθάνομαι, Ἱστιαῖε, ἐπίτροπον τὸν σόν, τῶι σὺ Μίλητον ἐπέτρεψας, νεώτερα ἐς ἐμὲ πεποιηκέναι πρήγματα· ἄνδρας γάρ μοι ἐκ τῆς ἑτέρης ἠπείρου ἐπαγαγὼν καὶ Ἴωνας σὺν αὐτοῖσι τοὺς δώσοντας ἐμοὶ δίκην τῶν ἐποίησαν, τούτους ἀναγνώσας ἅμα

ἐκείνοισι ἔπεσθαι Σαρδίων με ἀπεστέρησε. νῦν ὦν κῶς τοι ταῦτα φαίνε-   2
ται ἔχειν καλῶς; κῶς δὲ ἄνευ τῶν σῶν βουλευμάτων τοιοῦτό τι ἐπρήχθη;
ὅρα μὴ ἐξ ὑστέρης σεωυτὸν ἐν αἰτίηι σχῆις." εἶπε πρὸς ταῦτα Ἱστιαῖος·   3
"βασιλεῦ, κοῖον ἐφθέγξαο ἔπος, ἐμὲ βουλεῦσαι πρῆγμα ἐκ τοῦ σοί τι ἢ
μέγα ἢ σμικρὸν ἔμελλε λυπηρὸν ἀνασχήσειν; τί δ᾽ ἂν ἐπιδιζήμενος ποιοῖμι
ταῦτα, τέο δὲ ἐνδεὴς ἐών; τῶι πάρα μὲν πάντα ὅσα περ σοί, πάντων
δὲ πρὸς σέο βουλευμάτων ἐπακούειν ἀξιεῦμαι. ἀλλ᾽ εἴπερ τι τοιοῦτο οἷον   4
σὺ εἴρηκας πρήσσει ὁ ἐμὸς ἐπίτροπος, ἴσθι αὐτὸν ἐπ᾽ ἑωυτοῦ βαλόμενον
πεπρηχέναι. ἀρχὴν δὲ ἔγωγε οὐδὲ ἐνδέκομαι τὸν λόγον, ὅκως τι Μιλήσιοι καὶ ὁ ἐμὸς ἐπίτροπος νεώτερον πρήσσουσι περὶ πρήγματα τὰ σά· εἰ
δ᾽ ἄρα τι τοιοῦτο ποιεῦσι καὶ σὺ τὸ ἐὸν ἀκήκοας, ὦ βασιλεῦ, μάθε οἷον
πρῆγμα ἐργάσαο ἐμὲ ἀπὸ θαλάσσης ἀνάσπαστον ποιήσας. Ἴωνες γὰρ   5
οἴκασι ἐμέο ἐξ ὀφθαλμῶν σφι γενομένου ποιῆσαι τῶν πάλαι ἵμερον εἶχον·
ἐμέο δ᾽ ἂν ἐόντος ἐν Ἰωνίηι οὐδεμία πόλις ὑπεκίνησε. νῦν ὦν ὡς τάχος
ἄφες με πορευθῆναι ἐς Ἰωνίην, ἵνα τοι κεῖνά τε πάντα καταρτίσω ἐς τὠυτὸ
καὶ τὸν Μιλήτου ἐπίτροπον τοῦτον τὸν ταῦτα μηχανησάμενον ἐγχειρίθε-
τον παραδῶ. ταῦτα δὲ κατὰ νόον τὸν σὸν ποιήσας θεοὺς ἐπόμνυμι τοὺς   6
βασιληίους μὴ μὲν πρότερον ἐκδύσεσθαι τὸν ἔχων κιθῶνα καταβήσομαι ἐς
Ἰωνίην πρὶν ἄν τοι Σαρδὼ νῆσον τὴν μεγίστην δασμοφόρον ποιήσω."

Ἱστιαῖος μὲν δὴ λέγων ταῦτα διέβαλλε, Δαρεῖος δὲ ἐπείθετο καί μιν   107
ἀπίει, ἐντειλάμενος, ἐπεὰν τὰ ὑπέσχετό οἱ ἐπιτελέα ποιήσηι, παραγίνεσ-
θαί οἱ ὀπίσω ἐς τὰ Σοῦσα.

Ἐν ὧι δὲ ἡ ἀγγελίη τε περὶ τῶν Σαρδίων παρὰ βασιλέα ἀνήιε   108
καὶ Δαρεῖος τὰ περὶ τὸ τόξον ποιήσας Ἱστιαίωι ἐς λόγους ἦλθε καὶ
Ἱστιαῖος μεμετιμένος ὑπὸ Δαρείου ἐκομίζετο ἐπὶ θάλασσαν, ἐν τούτωι
παντὶ τῶι χρόνωι ἐγίνετο τάδε· πολιορκέοντι τῶι Σαλαμινίωι Ὀνησίλωι
Ἀμαθουσίους ἐξαγγέλλεται νηυσὶ στρατιὴν πολλὴν ἄγοντα Περσικὴν
Ἀρτύβιον ἄνδρα Πέρσην προσδόκιμον ἐς τὴν Κύπρον εἶναι. πυθόμενος δὲ   2
ταῦτα ὁ Ὀνήσιλος κήρυκας διέπεμπε ἐς τὴν Ἰωνίην ἐπικαλεύμενός σφεας.
Ἴωνες δὲ οὐκ ἐς μακρὴν βουλευσάμενοι ἧκον πολλῶι στόλωι. Ἴωνές τε δὴ
παρῆσαν ἐς τὴν Κύπρον καὶ οἱ Πέρσαι νηυσὶ διαβάντες ἐκ τῆς Κιλικίης
ἤισαν ἐπὶ τὴν Σαλαμῖνα πεζῆι· τῆισι δὲ νηυσὶ οἱ Φοίνικες περιέπλεον τὴν
ἄκρην αἳ καλεῦνται Κληῖδες τῆς Κύπρου.

Τούτου δὲ τοιούτου γινομένου ἔλεξαν οἱ τύραννοι τῆς Κύπρου, συγ-   109
καλέσαντες τῶν Ἰώνων τοὺς στρατηγούς· "ἄνδρες Ἴωνες, αἵρεσιν ὑμῖν
δίδομεν ἡμεῖς οἱ Κύπριοι ὁκοτέροισι βούλεσθε προσφέρεσθαι [ἢ Πέρσηισι ἢ
Φοίνιξι]. εἰ μὲν γὰρ πεζῆι βούλεσθε ταχθέντες Περσέων διαπειρᾶσθαι, ὥρη   2
ἂν εἴη ὑμῖν ἐκβάντας ἐκ τῶν νεῶν τάσσεσθαι πεζῆι, ἡμέας δὲ ἐς τὰς νέας

109.1 ἢ...Φοίνιξι om. SVU

ἐσβαίνειν τὰς ὑμετέρας Φοίνιξι ἀνταγωνιευμένους· εἰ δὲ Φοινίκων μᾶλλον
βούλεσθε διαπειρᾶσθαι, ποιέειν χρεόν ἐστι ὑμέας, ὁκότερα ἂν δὴ τούτων
ἕλησθε, ὅκως τὸ κατ' ὑμέας ἔσται ἥ τε Ἰωνίη καὶ ἡ Κύπρος ἐλευθέρη."
3 εἶπαν Ἴωνες πρὸς ταῦτα· "ἡμέας [δὲ] ἀπέπεμψε τὸ κοινὸν τῶν Ἰώνων
φυλάξοντας τὴν θάλασσαν, ἀλλ' οὐκ ἵνα Κυπρίοισι τὰς νέας παραδόντες αὐτοὶ πεζῆι Πέρσηισι προσφερώμεθα. ἡμεῖς μέν νυν ἐπ' οὗ ἐτάχθημεν
ταύτηι πειρησόμεθα εἶναι χρηστοί· ὑμέας δὲ χρεόν ἐστι, ἀναμνησθέντας
οἷα ἐπάσχετε δουλεύοντες πρὸς τῶν Μήδων, γίνεσθαι ἄνδρας ἀγαθούς."
Ἴωνες μὲν τούτοισι ἀμείψαντο.
110 Μετὰ δὲ ἡκόντων ἐς τὸ πεδίον τὸ Σαλαμινίων τῶν Περσέων διέτασσον
οἱ βασιλέες τῶν Κυπρίων τοὺς μὲν ἄλλους Κυπρίους κατὰ τοὺς ἄλλους
στρατιώτας ἀντιτάσσοντες, Σαλαμινίων δὲ καὶ Σολίων ἀπολέξαντες τὸ
ἄριστον ἀντέτασσον Πέρσηισι. Ἀρτυβίωι δὲ τῶι στρατηγῶι τῶν Περσέων
ἐθελοντὴς ἀντετάσσετο Ὀνήσιλος.
111 Ἤλαυνε δὲ ἵππον ὁ Ἀρτύβιος δεδιδαγμένον πρὸς ὁπλίτην ἵστασθαι
ὀρθόν. πυθόμενος ὦν ταῦτα ὁ Ὀνήσιλος, ἦν γὰρ οἱ ὑπασπιστὴς γένος
μὲν Κάρ, τὰ δὲ πολέμια κάρτα δόκιμος καὶ ἄλλως λήματος πλέος, εἶπε
2 πρὸς τοῦτον· "πυνθάνομαι τὸν Ἀρτυβίου ἵππον ἱστάμενον ὀρθὸν καὶ ποσὶ
καὶ στόματι κατεργάζεσθαι πρὸς τὸν ἂν προσενειχθῆι. σὺ ὦν βουλευσά-
μενος εἰπὲ αὐτίκα ὁκότερον βούλεαι φυλάξας πλῆξαι, εἴτε τὸν ἵππον εἴτε
3 αὐτὸν Ἀρτύβιον." εἶπε πρὸς ταῦτα ὁ ὀπέων αὐτοῦ· "ὦ βασιλεῦ, ἕτοιμος
μὲν ἐγώ εἰμι ποιέειν καὶ ἀμφότερα καὶ τὸ ἕτερον αὐτῶν καὶ πάντως τὸ
ἂν σὺ ἐπιτάσσηις· ὡς μέντοι ἔμοιγε δοκέει εἶναι τοῖσι σοῖσι πρήγμασι
4 προσφορώτερον, φράσω. βασιλέα μὲν καὶ στρατηγὸν χρεόν εἶναί φημι
βασιλέϊ τε καὶ στρατηγῶι προσφέρεσθαι (ἤν τε γὰρ κατέληις ἄνδρα
στρατηγόν, μέγα τοι γίνεται, καὶ δεύτερα, ἢν σὲ ἐκεῖνος, τὸ μὴ γένοιτο,
ὑπὸ ἀξιοχρέου καὶ ἀποθανεῖν ἡμίσεα συμφορή), ἡμέας δὲ τοὺς ὑπηρέτας
ἑτέροισί τε ὑπηρέτηισι προσφέρεσθαι καὶ πρὸς ἵππον. τοῦ σὺ τὰς μηχανὰς
μηδὲν φοβηθῆις· ἐγὼ γάρ τοι ὑποδέκομαι μή μιν ἀνδρὸς ἔτι γε μηδενὸς
στήσεσθαι ἐναντίον."
112 Ταῦτα εἶπε, καὶ μεταυτίκα συνέμισγε τὰ στρατόπεδα πεζῆι καὶ
νηυσί. νηυσὶ μέν νυν Ἴωνες ἄκροι γενόμενοι ταύτην τὴν ἡμέρην ὑπερε-
βάλοντο τοὺς Φοίνικας, καὶ τούτων Σάμιοι ἠρίστευσαν. πεζῆι δέ, ὡς
2 συνῆλθον τὰ στρατόπεδα, συμπεσόντα ἐμάχοντο· κατὰ δὲ τοὺς στρατηγοὺς ἀμφοτέρους τάδε ἐγίνετο. ὡς προσεφέρετο πρὸς τὸν Ὀνήσιλον ὁ
Ἀρτύβιος ἐπὶ τοῦ ἵππου κατήμενος, ὁ Ὀνήσιλος κατὰ συνεθήκατο τῶι
ὑπασπιστῆι παίει προσφερόμενον αὐτὸν τὸν Ἀρτύβιον· ἐπιβάλλοντος δὲ

111.3 προσφορώτερον Macan et Wilson: προφερέστερον codd.: προσφερέστερον Stein

τοῦ ἵππου τοὺς πόδας ἐπὶ τὴν τοῦ Ὀνησίλου ἀσπίδα, ἐνθαῦτα ὁ Κὰρ
δρεπάνωι πλήξας ἀπαράσσει τοῦ ἵππου τοὺς πόδας· Ἀρτύβιος μὲν δὴ ὁ
στρατηγὸς τῶν Περσέων ὁμοῦ τῶι ἵππωι πίπτει αὐτοῦ ταύτηι.

Μαχομένων δὲ καὶ τῶν ἄλλων Στησήνωρ, τύραννος ἐὼν Κουρίου, προ-   113
διδοῖ ἔχων δύναμιν ἀνδρῶν περὶ ἑωυτὸν οὐ σμικρήν. οἱ δὲ Κουριέες οὗτοι
λέγονται εἶναι Ἀργείων ἄποικοι. προδόντων δὲ τῶν Κουριέων αὐτίκα
καὶ τὰ Σαλαμινίων πολεμιστήρια ἅρματα τὠυτὸ τοῖσι Κουριεῦσι ἐποίευν.
γενομένων δὲ τούτων κατυπέρτεροι ἦσαν οἱ Πέρσαι τῶν Κυπρίων.
τετραμμένου δὲ τοῦ στρατοπέδου ἄλλοι τε ἔπεσον πολλοὶ καὶ δὴ καὶ   2
Ὀνήσιλός τε ὁ Χέρσιος, ὅς περ τὴν Κυπρίων ἀπόστασιν ἔπρηξε, καὶ ὁ
Σολίων βασιλεὺς Ἀριστόκυπρος ὁ Φιλοκύπρου, Φιλοκύπρου δὲ τούτου
τὸν Σόλων ὁ Ἀθηναῖος ἀπικόμενος ἐς Κύπρον ἐν ἔπεσι αἴνεσε τυράννων
μάλιστα.

Ὀνησίλου μέν νυν Ἀμαθούσιοι, ὅτι σφέας ἐπολιόρκησε, ἀποταμόν-   114
τες τὴν κεφαλὴν ἐκόμισαν ἐς Ἀμαθοῦντα καί μιν ἀνεκρέμασαν ὑπὲρ τῶν
πυλέων. κρεμαμένης δὲ τῆς κεφαλῆς καὶ ἤδη ἐούσης κοίλης ἑσμὸς μελισσέων ἐσδὺς ἐς αὐτὴν κηρίων μιν ἐνέπλησε. τούτου δὲ γενομένου τοιού-   2
του (ἐχρέωντο γὰρ περὶ αὐτῆς οἱ Ἀμαθούσιοι) ἐμαντεύθη σφι τὴν μὲν
κεφαλὴν κατελόντας θάψαι, Ὀνησίλωι δὲ θύειν ὡς ἥρωι ἀνὰ πᾶν ἔτος, καί
σφι ποιεῦσι ταῦτα ἄμεινον συνοίσεσθαι.

Ἀμαθούσιοι μέν νυν ἐποίευν ταῦτα καὶ τὸ μέχρι ἐμεῦ. Ἴωνες δὲ οἱ ἐν   115
Κύπρωι ναυμαχήσαντες ἐπείτε ἔμαθον τὰ πρήγματα τὰ Ὀνησίλου διεφ-
θαρμένα καὶ τὰς πόλις τῶν Κυπρίων πολιορκεομένας τὰς ἄλλας πλὴν
Σαλαμῖνος, ταύτην δὲ Γόργωι τῶι προτέρωι βασιλέϊ τοὺς Σαλαμινίους
παραδόντας, αὐτίκα μαθόντες οἱ Ἴωνες ταῦτα ἀπέπλεον ἐς τὴν Ἰωνίην.
τῶν δὲ ἐν Κύπρωι πολίων ἀντέσχε χρόνον ἐπὶ πλεῖστον πολιορκεομένη   2
Σόλοι, τὴν πέριξ ὑπορύσσοντες τὸ τεῖχος πέμπτωι μηνὶ εἷλον οἱ Πέρσαι.

Κύπριοι μὲν δὴ ἐνιαυτὸν ἐλεύθεροι γενόμενοι αὖτις ἐκ νέης κατεδεδούλ-   116
ωντο. Δαυρίσης δὲ ἔχων Δαρείου θυγατέρα καὶ Ὑμαίης τε καὶ Ὀτάνης,
ἄλλοι Πέρσαι στρατηγοί, ἔχοντες καὶ οὗτοι Δαρείου θυγατέρας, ἐπιδιώξ-
αντες τοὺς ἐς Σάρδις στρατευσαμένους Ἰώνων καὶ ἐσαράξαντές σφεας ἐς
τὰς νέας, τῆι μάχηι ὡς ἐπεκράτησαν, τὸ ἐνθεῦτεν ἐπιδιελόμενοι τὰς πόλις
ἐπόρθεον.

Δαυρίσης μὲν τραπόμενος πρὸς τὰς ἐν Ἑλλησπόντωι πόλις εἷλε μὲν Δάρ-   117
δανον, εἷλε δὲ Ἄβυδόν τε καὶ Περκώτην καὶ Λάμψακον καὶ Παισόν (ταύτας
μίαν ἐπ᾽ ἡμέρηι ἑκάστηι αἵρεε), ἀπὸ δὲ Παισοῦ ἐλαύνοντί οἱ ἐπὶ Πάριον
πόλιν ἦλθέ οἱ ἀγγελίη τοὺς Κᾶρας τὠυτὸ Ἴωσι φρονήσαντας ἀπεστάναι

117 μίαν Powell: μὲν codd.

ἀπὸ Περσέων. ἀποστρέψας ὦν ἐκ τοῦ Ἑλλησπόντου ἤλαυνε τὸν στρατὸν ἐπὶ τὴν Καρίην.

118 Καί κως ταῦτα τοῖσι Καρσὶ ἐξαγγέλθη πρότερον ἢ τὸν Δαυρίσην ἀπικέσθαι. πυθόμενοι δὲ οἱ Κᾶρες συνελέγοντο ἐπὶ Λευκάς τε Στήλας καλεομένας καὶ ποταμὸν Μαρσύην, ὃς ῥέων ἐκ τῆς Ἰδριάδος χώρης ἐς 2 τὸν Μαίανδρον ἐκδιδοῖ. συλλεχθέντων δὲ τῶν Καρῶν ἐνθαῦτα ἐγίνοντο βουλαὶ ἄλλαι τε πολλαὶ καὶ ἀρίστη γε δοκέουσα εἶναι ἐμοὶ Πιξωδάρου τοῦ Μαυσώλου ἀνδρὸς Κινδυέος, ὃς τοῦ Κιλίκων βασιλέος Συεννέσιος εἶχε θυγατέρα. τούτου τοῦ ἀνδρὸς ἡ γνώμη ἔφερε διαβάντας τὸν Μαίανδρον τοὺς Κᾶρας καὶ κατὰ νώτου ἔχοντας τὸν ποταμὸν οὕτω συμβάλλειν, ἵνα μὴ ἔχοντες ὀπίσω φεύγειν οἱ Κᾶρες αὐτοῦ τε μένειν ἀναγκαζόμενοι γινοίατο 3 ἔτι ἀμείνονες τῆς φύσιος. αὕτη μέν νυν οὐκ ἐνίκα ἡ γνώμη, ἀλλὰ τοῖσι Πέρσῃσι κατὰ νώτου γίνεσθαι τὸν Μαίανδρον μᾶλλον ἢ σφίσι, δηλαδὴ ἢν φυγὴ τῶν Περσέων γένηται καὶ ἑσσωθέωσι τῆι συμβολῆι, ὡς οὐκ ἀπονοστήσουσι ἐς τὸν ποταμὸν ἐσπίπτοντες.

119 Μετὰ δὲ παρεόντων καὶ διαβάντων τὸν Μαίανδρον τῶν Περσέων ἐνθαῦτα ἐπὶ τῶι Μαρσύηι ποταμῶι συνέβαλόν τε τοῖσι Πέρσῃσι οἱ Κᾶρες καὶ μάχην ἐμαχέσαντο ἰσχυρὴν καὶ ἐπὶ χρόνον πολλόν, τέλος δὲ ἑσσώθησαν διὰ πλῆθος. Περσέων μὲν δὴ ἔπεσον ἄνδρες ἐς δισχιλίους, Καρῶν δὲ ἐς 2 μυρίους. ἐνθεῦτεν δὲ οἱ διαφυγόντες αὐτῶν κατειλήθησαν ἐς Λάβραυνδα ἐς Διὸς Στρατίου ἱρόν, μέγα τε καὶ ἅγιον ἄλσος πλατανίστων. μοῦνοι δὲ τῶν ἡμεῖς ἴδμεν Κᾶρές εἰσι οἳ Διὶ Στρατίωι θυσίας ἀνάγουσι. κατειληθέντες δὲ ὦν οὗτοι ἐνθαῦτα ἐβουλεύοντο περὶ σωτηρίης, ὁκότερα ἢ παραδόντες σφέας αὐτοὺς Πέρσῃσι ἢ ἐκλιπόντες τὸ παράπαν τὴν Ἀσίην ἄμεινον πρήξουσι.

120 Βουλευομένοισι δέ σφι ταῦτα παραγίνονται βοηθέοντες Μιλήσιοί τε καὶ οἱ τούτων σύμμαχοι. ἐνθαῦτα δὲ τὰ μὲν πρότερον οἱ Κᾶρες ἐβουλεύοντο μετῆκαν, οἱ δὲ αὖτις πολεμέειν ἐξ ἀρχῆς ἀρτέοντο. καὶ ἐπιοῦσί τε τοῖσι Πέρσῃσι συμβάλλουσι καὶ μαχεσάμενοι ἐπὶ πλέον ἢ πρότερον ἑσσώθησαν· πεσόντων δὲ τῶν πάντων πολλῶν μάλιστα Μιλήσιοι ἐπλήγησαν.

121 Μετὰ δὲ τοῦτο τὸ τρῶμα ἀνέλαβόν τε καὶ ἀνεμαχέσαντο οἱ Κᾶρες· πυθόμενοι γὰρ ὡς στρατεύεσθαι ὁρμέαται οἱ Πέρσαι ἐπὶ τὰς πόλις σφέων, ἐλόχησαν τὴν ἐν Πιδάσωι ὁδόν, ἐς ἣν ἐμπεσόντες οἱ Πέρσαι νυκτὸς διεφθάρησαν καὶ αὐτοὶ καὶ οἱ στρατηγοὶ αὐτῶν, Δαυρίσης καὶ Ἀμόργης καὶ Σισιμάκης· σὺν δέ σφι ἀπέθανε καὶ Μύρσος ὁ Γύγεω. τοῦ δὲ λόχου 122 τούτου ἡγεμὼν ἦν Ἡρακλείδης Ἰβανώλλιος ἀνὴρ Μυλασεύς. οὗτοι μέν νυν τῶν Περσέων οὕτω διεφθάρησαν, Ὑμαίης δὲ καὶ αὐτὸς ἐὼν τῶν ἐπιδιωξάντων τοὺς ἐς Σάρδις στρατευσαμένους Ἴωνας, τραπόμενος ἐς τὴν Προπον-2 τίδα εἷλε Κίον τὴν Μυσίην. ταύτην δὲ ἐξελών, ὡς ἐπύθετο τὸν Ἑλλήσποντον ἐκλελοιπέναι Δαυρίσην καὶ στρατεύεσθαι ἐπὶ Καρίης, καταλιπὼν τὴν

Προποντίδα ἐπὶ τὸν Ἑλλήσποντον ἦγε τὸν στρατόν, καὶ εἷλε μὲν Αἰολέας πάντας ὅσοι τὴν Ἰλιάδα νέμονται, εἷλε δὲ Γέργιθας τοὺς ὑπολειφθέντας τῶν ἀρχαίων Τευκρῶν. αὐτός τε [Ὑμαίης] αἱρέων ταῦτα τὰ ἔθνεα νούσωι τελευτᾶι ἐν τῆι Τρωιάδι.

Οὗτος μὲν δὴ οὕτω ἐτελεύτησε· Ἀρταφρένης δὲ ὁ Σαρδίων ὕπαρχος καὶ **123** Ὀτάνης ὁ τρίτος στρατηγὸς ἐτάχθησαν ἐπὶ τὴν Ἰωνίην καὶ τὴν προσεχέα Αἰολίδα στρατεύεσθαι. Ἰωνίης μέν νυν Κλαζομενὰς αἱρέουσι, Αἰολέων δὲ Κύμην.

Ἁλισκομένων δὲ τῶν πολίων, ἦν γάρ, ὡς διέδεξε, Ἀρισταγόρης ὁ Μιλή- **124** σιος ψυχὴν οὐκ ἄκρος, ὃς ταράξας τὴν Ἰωνίην καὶ ἐγκερασάμενος πρήγ- ματα μεγάλα δρησμὸν ἐβούλευε ὁρῶν ταῦτα· πρὸς δέ οἱ καὶ ἀδύνατα ἐφάνη βασιλέα Δαρεῖον ὑπερβαλέσθαι· πρὸς ταῦτα δὴ ὦν συγκαλέσας **2** τοὺς συστασιώτας ἐβουλεύετο, λέγων ὡς ἄμεινον σφίσι εἴη κρησφύγετόν τι ὑπάρχον εἶναι, ἢν ἄρα ἐξωθέωνται ἐκ τῆς Μιλήτου, εἴτε δὴ ὦν ἐς Σαρδὼ ἐκ τοῦ τόπου τούτου ἄγοι ἐς ἀποικίην, εἴτε ἐς Μύρκινον τὴν Ἠδωνῶν, τὴν Ἱστιαῖος ἐτείχεε παρὰ Δαρείου δωρεὴν λαβών. ταῦτα ἐπειρώτα ὁ Ἀρισταγόρης.

Ἑκαταίου μέν νυν τοῦ Ἡγησάνδρου, ἀνδρὸς λογοποιοῦ, τουτέων μὲν ἐς **125** οὐδετέρην στέλλειν ἔφερε ἡ γνώμη, ἐν Λέρωι δὲ τῆι νήσωι τεῖχος οἰκοδομη- σάμενον ἡσυχίην ἄγειν, ἢν ἐκπέσηι ἐκ τῆς Μιλήτου· ἔπειτα δὲ ἐκ ταύτης ὁρμώμενον κατελεύσεσθαι ἐς τὴν Μίλητον.

Ταῦτα μὲν δὴ Ἑκαταῖος συνεβούλευε· αὐτῶι δὲ Ἀρισταγόρηι ἡ πλείστη **126** γνώμη ἦν ἐς τὴν Μύρκινον ἀπάγειν. τὴν μὲν δὴ Μίλητον ἐπιτρέπει Πυθαγόρηι ἀνδρὶ τῶν ἀστῶν δοκίμωι, αὐτὸς δὲ παραλαβὼν πάντα τὸν βουλόμενον ἔπλεε ἐς τὴν Θρηίκην καὶ ἔσχε τὴν χώρην ἐπ᾽ ἣν ἐστάλη. ἐκ **2** δὲ ταύτης ὁρμώμενος ἀπόλλυται ὑπὸ Θρηίκων αὐτός τε ὁ Ἀρισταγόρης καὶ ὁ στρατὸς αὐτοῦ, πόλιν περικατήμενος καὶ βουλομένων τῶν Θρηίκων ὑποσπόνδων ἐξιέναι...

122.2 Ὑμαίης del. Wilson   126.2 post ἐξιέναι lacunam statuit Maas

COMMENTARY

1–16 THRACE AND THE PAIONIANS

At first sight, the opening chs. of bk. 5 'belong' more with bk. 4 than with the Ionian revolt narrative which follows: cf. Hdt. 4.80.2 (confrontation between Sitalkes, son of the Thracian king Teres, and Oktamasades, brother of Skyles of Skythia and son of Teres' daughter). This part of the world was topical at the beginning of the Peloponnesian War (431–29 BC), when Hdt. was still active: Th. 2.29, 95–7, 4.105.1 and 7.29.4. In addition to Th., another possible literary intertext is the undatable Pindar *Paian* 2, for the Abderites; this exploited the verbal similarity 'paian' / 'Paionians' in a way comparable to Hdt., see below. (Radt 1958: 60, cf. 14f.; Rutherford 2001: 43f., 116, 27of.; Archibald 1998: 86 n. 36).

But there are also important pointers forward to the Ionian revolt narrative proper (which begins only at **28.**1): earlier relations between Dareios and Histiaios (**11.**1), and the first suggestion that the conflict is a freedom fight (**2.**1). Immerwahr 1966: 110–11 sees the whole section 4.143–4 and 5.1–27 as a link between the Skythian campaign and the Ionian revolt.

1–2 The Paionians and the Perinthians

The two early Paionian episodes (the second will be at **11–15**) frame the Thracian ethnographic *logos* (**3–10**); then we pass to the subjugation of Macedon (**16–22**). The Paionian episodes balance each other in small ways: ἀντικατιζομένων δὲ τῶν Περινθίων will be picked up by προκατιζόμενον ἐς τὸ προάστιον at **12.**2). The first Paionian episode (**1–2**) introduces the Thracian *logos* (so rightly AHG), noting that like the Egyptian logos it 'precedes its survey of epichoric *nomoi* with a backward-looking ('analeptic') anecdote concerning inter-cultural linguistics, whose resolution establishes the dominance of one nation over another, and involves misunderstanding or un-understanding'. The corresponding Egyptian anecdote is the '*bekos*' experiment with children at bk. 2 ch. 2).

In the larger architecture of the *Histories*, the Paionians have a continuing and long-term importance: their story continues beyond their uprooting and transportation into Asia (**15.**3 and **98**) until, after serving in Xerxes' army (7.185), they acquire and humiliatingly dispose of his sacred chariot after his defeat (**15.**3n., citing 8.115.3–4): symbolic revenge and reversal. This is the *Histories* in a nutshell.

The Paionian-Perinthian story is set in an unascertainable past time (πρότερον at the beginning and end of the narrative loop, **1.**1 and

2.1). The story was perhaps contrived just for the sake of the verbal similarity between 'paian' and 'Paionians' (AHG). There are also historically
improbable features: Propontic Perinthos was a long way from the approximate seat of the Paionian tribe, and that seat was on the Axios river, not
the Strymon to the east of it.

An argument for the story's historicity might point (a) to Plutarch
Quaest. Graec. 57 (see below, n. on πρώτους...: undated but archaic help by
Samians to their daughter-city Perinthos against Megarian colonial neighbours, a story probably derived from one of Aristotle's lost *Constitutions*),
and (b) to the Samian colonial origins of the Perinthians (Plutarch again),
whom Hdt. praises for their efforts on behalf of freedom (below, 2.1). He
is well informed about Samian affairs (see bk. 3 and 6.14.1, cf. Pelling
2011) and could have been told on Samos about heroic Perinthian and
Samian struggles with Perinthos' Greek and non-Greek neighbours.

1.1 οἱ δὲ ἐν τῆι Εὐρώπηι: the δέ balances ἡ μέν (Pheretime's excessive
revenge) at 4.205, the immediately preceding ch., but the narrative content resumes 4.144. μέν – δέ is often used as a device to stress both continuity and the element of transition; cf. Brock 2003: 7. Biographical items
tend to be placed at the end of sections of narrative (see e.g. 6.17 for
Dionysios of Phokaia, and cf. Macan on 6.1.1, discussing the death of
Aristagores which closes bk. 5). The book divisions into which Herodotus'
text is divided are probably not his own (see Introduction §1), and the second half of the *Histories*, which has much less by way of foreign ethnography than the first half, can be regarded as starting later than ch. 1, perhaps
with **17** (the Macedonian narrative), or even with **27**.

The revenge theme forms the powerful closure to bk. 4: the horrible
end of Pheretime is said by Hdt. to show that the gods do not like excessive
acts of revenge (see Introduction p. 35 n. 117). The theme will be crucial
to the narrative both of Marathon in 490 (revenge for the Ionian revolt)
and of Xerxes' campaign of 480, which was in revenge for Marathon and –
again – for the Ionian revolt and the burning of Sardis. Note esp. the proleptic **102.**1 with its Persian focalisation: the burning of the Greek temples
(in 480) was 'reciprocal-burning' (ἀντενεπίμπρασαν) for the burning of the
temple of Kybebe at Sardis. See n. there, and cf. **15.**3, where the Paionians
are themselves a signifier for delayed revenge.

1.1 (cont.) τῶν ὁ Μεγάβαζος ἦρχε: an important individual, highly valued
by Dareios (4.143), possibly an Achaemenid (Burn 1962: 335, Badian
1994: 110. Burn sorts out the various Megabazoi and their possible inter-
relationships; add Lewis 1984: 621 and 1985: 115 [= 1997: 358]). Names
in Baga- or Baka- are theophoric, from the Persian word for 'god'; see
Schmitt 2000: 141. As at the similar 7.233.1, the relative clause serves not
so much to tell us who the commander was but to 'remind us which force

is being referred to' (Dover 1960: 61 n. 2). **πρώτους μὲν Περινθίους**: Perinthos, on the north coast of the Propontis (Hdt.'s word 'Hellespontine' is loose), was a colony of the Samians (Isaac 1986: 199 and nn. 239, 205; *IACP*: no. 678 at p. 920, both citing Plut. *Quaest. Graec.* 57 (= *Mor.* 303–4): archaic Samians help their daughter-city against aggression from the Megarian colonies to the east). But Hdt. does not mention the colonial link, although he is much interested in Samos (cf. Pelling 2011); see Introduction §4 for such unstated kinship links. **κατεστρέψαντο**: the word is 'marked', because it was used, at the opening of the narrative proper (1.6.2), to describe Kroisos' subjugation of the Greeks. By this verbal repetition, Hdt. is announcing the approximate (see above n. on οἱ δέ...) opening of the second half of his work. But there is continuity with bk. 4 as well, see 4.144.3 τοὺς μὴ μηδίζοντας κατεστρέφετο. See Introduction §1. **περιεφθέντας... τρηχέως**: this expression for 'treated roughly' (aorist passive of περιέπω) recurs in similar form at 6.15.1, where it is used of the Chians at the battle of Lade: περιέφθησαν τρηχύτατα. The combination of words is a favourite of Hdt., starting with 1.114.3 (the boy Kyros' harsh treatment of Artembares' son). This frequency weakens Irwin's nevertheless interesting idea (2007: 52f.) that there is 'thematic and structural parallelism' between the present passage and the Theban/Aiginetan story at **81.1** (Thebans roughly handled, τρηχέως περιεφθέντων, by the Athenians).

1.2 οἱ γὰρ ὦν ἀπὸ Στρύμονος Παίονες: the Paionians were a Thracian tribe. In prehistoric times (Early Bronze Age) they controlled Upper Macedonia and perhaps even Emathia in Lower Macedonia as well, but were then pushed eastwards towards the Axios (Vardar) river: *HM* I: 418–9 and Walbank on Polyb. 23.10.4 (Emathia). Hdt. here and at **13**.2 (focalised through the Paionian brothers) places the Paionians on the Strymon, the river which flows out near Amphipolis, but this is inaccurately far east. In fact they occupied the middle reaches of the Axios, roughly the vicinity of the later city of Stobi (*HM* I: 78; *Il.* 2.848–9, whence Strabo 7 frr. 20 and 23, but frr. 34 and 41 speak also of the Strymon; *Barr.* maps 49 and 50). See Archibald 1998: 86, who however notes 'some [Paionian] penetration' in the Strymon direction, south of the Rupel defile, for which see *Barr.* map 49 B2, east of the later Herakleia Sintike; cf. also *HM* I: 418. This is well within range of social contact with Greeks. Archibald 108 suspects that 'Greek sources report most information about those tribes which happened to be closest to colonies'. It is surprising to find the Paionians threatening Perinthos, so far away on the Propontis, even allowing for the small westward Perinthian territorial extension noted at *IACP*: p. 920. Apsinthians, not Paionians, would be more obvious and local enemies of the Perinthians (Asheri 1990: 155–6). Hdt., by locating the Paionians further east than they actually were (Strymon not Axios), reduces the difficulty, but perhaps not consciously.   χρήσαντος τοῦ θεοῦ: this could be either Apollo (cf. the paian, usually associated with Apollo, and despite ch. 7 where Apollo is not one of the gods worshipped by Thracians) or Dionysos. Or perhaps (some commentators) '*their* god'. But it is pointless to inquire, because the story arose from the joke.   ἀντικατιζό-μενοι...Περίνθιοι...ὀνομαστί: these words would fit easily into a hexametrical Greek oracle – perhaps a further indication that the story is essentially a Greek concoction.   καὶ ἦν μὲν...ἐπικαλέσωνταί...μὴ ἐπιχειρέειν 'and if...the Perinthians called on them by shouting their name they should attack, but if they did not shout it, they should not attack'. For the 'apodotic' use of δέ in ἦν μέν...τοὺς δὲ ἐπιχειρέειν, cf. 1.13.1, ἦν μὲν τὸ χρηστήριον ἀνέληι μιν βασιλέα εἶναι Λυδῶν, τὸν δὲ βασιλεύειν, ἢν δὲ μή etc., with Powell, δέ E I (1).   μουνομαχίη τριφασίη 'a triple duel'. τριφάσιος and διφάσιος are found in no classical author apart from Hdt., but they were clearly good Ionic words, cf. διφάσια [μ]ελίχματα δίφασια in the archaic Milesian cultic calendar Rehm 1914: no. 31 (= Sokolowski 1955: no. 41) line 2; for the date (?last quarter of the 6th cent.) see *LSAG*² : 334–5 and 343 no. 33.   ἵππον ἵππωι: this ought to mean a horse fighting another horse, which (despite the fighting horse of **111–12**) is much harder to visualise than a dog-fight or a human duel, but perhaps (Chris Carey in class discussion, 2008) it means a horse-race.

1.3 νικώντων δὲ τὰ δύο τῶν Περινθίων: it is not clear which two contests of the three are meant, or why Hdt. does not tell us this. Perhaps the article (τά) means the two out of three needed for a victory, or perhaps the first two, if they were sequential not simultaneous.   ὡς ἐπαιώνιζον κεχαρηκότες 'when in joy (perf. part. of χαίρω) they began to sing a paian'. For the paian as victory song (paians had several other uses as well, cf. *OCD*⁴ 'paean'), see *Il.* 22.391. See also Rutherford 2001: 42–4, but the present passage is not an example of a pre-battle paian; it is a paian for an abnormal victory. The paian itself, because of the peculiar circumstances, precipitated a battle of a normal sort.   καὶ εἶπάν κου παρὰ σφίσι αὐτοῖσι 'they surely (or 'perhaps') said to each other'. For this sense of the enclitic particle κου see Powell 2(a). With this speculative story-teller's idiom – 'well, I expect they all got the point' – contrast another and more confident story-telling device, the 'one man who eventually understands' a riddle, κοτὲ μαθών τις, at **80**.1 and 6.37.2.

2.1 τότε δέ...ἐπεκράτησαν πλήθει: despite 'fighting bravely for their freedom', the Perinthians are overwhelmed by numbers, πλήθει. Contrast the outcome of the main Persian wars. This is perhaps the first explicit mention of the notion that the fight against the Persians is a freedom-fight. The idea is, however, implicit at 4.136–42 (esp. 136.4 and 137.1, ἐλεύθεροι, ἐλευθεροῦν Ἰωνίην), but there the Ionians are persuaded by Histiaios not to accept the Skythian liberation plan. For the link between being brave men, ἄνδρες ἀγαθοί, and fighting for freedom and/or rejecting slavery, cf. 1.95.2 (the Medes) and 1.169.1 (the Ionians).

2.2 ἡμερούμενος βασιλέϊ: the verb, which in Hdt. is always used of Persian imperial subjugation, effects a link to bk. 4; see the speech of the Skythians at 4.118.5 (also in the middle voice, cf. 7.5.2 for the active) where they outline Dareios' plans of northern conquest. The root idea is 'taming', and perhaps carries a justificatory hint at a Persian civilising mission – assuming that the nuance reflects actual Persian thinking.

3–10 *The Thracian logos*

3.1 μέγιστόν ἐστι μετά γε Ἰνδούς: Hdt. has already said this at 3.94.2.   **εἰ δὲ ὑπ' ἑνός ἄρχοιτο ἢ φρονέοι κατά τὠυτό** 'if it were ruled by one person or had a united purpose' (lit. 'were minded in the same way'). By contrast, Th. was to say (2.97. 6) that there is no ἔθνος which could resist the *Skythians* if they were united, ὁμογνωμονοῦσι. This, then, is either an ethnographic commonplace (cf. Paus. 1.9.5, about the Kelts, with Asheri 1990: 137) or implied disagreement with Hdt. For the relation between Hdt. and Th. here, see Schneege 1884: 13, cf. *CT* II: 142. We may be meant to reflect on Greek disunity, as hinted at by Xerxes at 7.101.2.   **ἀμήχανον μή κοτε ἐγγένηται** 'it is impossible that it should ever happen'.

3.2 οὐνόματα δ' ἔχουσι πολλά κατά χώρας ἑκάστων 'the tribes have many names, according to the regions inhabited by each of them'. This translates Wilson's suggestion ἑκάστων, itself an improvement on Nenci's emendation ἑκάστου for the MSS' ἕκαστοι, which produces an oddly condensed piece of Greek.   **πλὴν Γετέων καὶ Τραυσῶν καὶ τῶν κατύπερθε Κρηστωναίων οἰκεόντων:** for the Getai, see next n. The Trausoi have not been mentioned in bk. 4 at all, and they hardly feature in later writers, but they have not been invented for the purpose of the anecdote at **4**.2 about their unusual attitudes to birth and death: see Livy 38.41.6 describing Manlius Vulso's return from Asia Minor to Greece in 188 BC, with Briscoe 2008: 147. The precise location of the Trausoi is unknown. From Livy's itinerary, they ought to be between Ainos on the Hebros river and Maroneia; but such peoples moved around over the centuries. Krestonia, by contrast, is a well-attested district N. of the later Thessalonike, see *Barr.* map 50 CD3; Th. 2.99.6; *HM* I: 179–82. Xerxes' camels were attacked by lions here, see below 7.125. In the present context κατύπερθε means 'inland of' (Powell II (3)), which here means in effect 'to the north of'.

4.1 τούτων δὲ τὰ μὲν Γέται οἱ ἀθανατίζοντες ποιεῦσι, εἴρηταί μοι 'of these, I have already described what the immortalising Getai do'. The reference is to Γέτας τοὺς ἀθανατίζοντες at 4.93–4, and the story which follows (men thrown onto spear-points to send messages to the god Salmoxis). τὰ μέν means 'the things which'. This time (contrast **3.**1) the internal cross-reference to the 'immortalising Getai' is explicit, and follows a common Herodotean form, unusually borrowed by Th. at 6.94.1, ὥσπερ καὶ πρότερόν μοι εἴρηται. See Brock 2003: 8–9, collecting many such 'marker phrases' in Hdt., and noting their function as advising us of the 'status and movement of the narrative'; see also, for general discussion of such cross-referencing formulae in ancient historians, *CT* II: 422–3 on Th. 5.1.1. For the Getai (= Goths) see Hartog 1988: 84–109.

4.2 τὸν μὲν γενόμενον...ὀλοφύρονται: the same thought is found in the *Kresphontes* of Euripides (*TrGF* fr. 449): 'It would be better for us to gather and weep for a newborn baby for all the ills (κακά) he is entering into, but when he dies and rests from toil, to send him from home with joy and cries of good omen'. The play was probably produced about 425, so Hdt. could have known it. The general gloomy idea that not to be born is best is found elsewhere in Greek literature (e.g. Thgn. 425–8, Bacchyl. 5.155–62); the parallel between Hdt. and Eur. consists in similar elaboration of detail.   **ἀναπλῆσαι κακά:** a Homerism, cf. e.g. *Il.* 15.132. The verb is from ἀναπίμπλημι, here 'I endure'.   **ἀπηγεόμενοι** 'recounting'. The MSS have ἀνηγεόμενοι, but this verb is found nowhere else in Hdt.; otherwise only in Pindar, e.g. *Nem.* 10.19. If the text is sound, it might be thought appropriate to the poetic flavour of the passage, see previous n. But Bekker, followed by Wilson, emends to ἀπηγεόμενοι.

5 κρίσις γίνεται μεγάλη: but Hdt. does not tell us how the 'judging' between the women was decided.   **ἐγκωμιασθεῖσα...σφάζεται ἐς τὸν τάφον:** this is the first use by any Greek author of the verb ἐγκωμιάζω, and it implies the existence of the noun ἐγκώμιον; but Pindar had already used the adjective ἐγκώμιος at e.g. *Ol.* 2.47. Much of the detail and decor of this description, notably the rivalry between the wives for the honour, recurs in the accounts of Indian suttee in Diodorus (19.33–4, the wife of Keteus, cf. 17.91.3), except that Diodorus adds a non-Herodotean explanation of the practice (it was introduced so as to stop wives poisoning their husbands; cf. Strabo, 15.1.30). See J. Hornblower 1981: 94 and n. 71, 151 n. 200. It was not a Greek custom (absent from Homer, and Diod. 19.34.6 says 'some of the Greeks' criticised it as barbarous and cruel). But Euripides has Euadne throw herself on the funeral pyre of Kapaneus: *Supp.* 980–1071 with West 2007: 500, who notes that suttee was an 'old-established rule' in Vedic India.   **αἱ δὲ ἄλλαι συμφορὴν μεγάλην ποιεῦνται** 'the others consider it a great misfortune'.

6.1 πωλεῦσι τὰ τέκνα ἐπ᾽ ἐξαγωγῆι 'they sell their children for export'. For the sale of slaves on condition of export out of the territory of their *polis* cf. ML 32 line 39 (from Hdt.'s native Halikarnassos), as well as Hdt. 7.156.2. It was common for enslavement to take place 'across the Tiber' (as the Romans would put it). Nobody wanted the continuing and uncomfortable presence of a degraded former fellow-citizen.   ἐῶσι τοῖσι αὐταὶ βούλονται ἀνδράσι μίσγεσθαι: the relative (τοῖσι) is attracted into the dative case of ἀνδράσι.   ὠνέονται τὰς γυναῖκας ... χρημάτων μεγάλων: with such wife-purchase cf. Xen. *Anab.* 7.2.38, where Seuthes tells Xen. he will give him his daughter, and continues, if you have a daughter, 'I will buy her according to Thracian custom', ὠνήσομαι Θραικίωι νόμωι. Xen. expected his readers to pick up the Herodotean allusion. Compare the similar marital customs of the Lydians (1.93.4 with Asheri 1990: 143).

6.2 τὸ μὲν ἐστίχθαι: the verb means to 'prick', and this is tattooing and not branding. See C. P. Jones 1987: 139–55 at 145, classifying the present passage as non-Greek decorative (as opp. penal) tattooing. Tattooing is a 'badge of ethnic identity among foreign nations': Lightfoot 2003: 530–1 and n 16.   τὸ δὲ ἄστικτον: understand εἶναι.   ἀργὸν εἶναι κάλλιστον 'to do no work is considered the finest thing'. ἀργός (i.e. ἀ- ἔργον) means unoccupied, as a member of the leisure class. Cf. 2.167.1–2 for speculation as to where the Greeks (with the partial exception of the Korinthians) derived their contempt for manual labour: the Thracians are offered as one candidate.

7 θεοὺς δὲ σέβονται ... Ἄρεα καὶ Διόνυσον καὶ Ἄρτεμιν: the perceived connection between war-god Ares and Thrace is at least as old as Homer: *Od.* 8.362, Ares departs for Thrace after he and Aphrodite have been freed by Hephaistos from the bed-trap. As for the other two, the present passage is a typical case of 'Greek interpretation' (Dionysos linked with fertility and vegetation, Artemis embodying the female principle): see *OCD*[4], 'religion. Thracian'.   λέγουσι γεγονέναι ἀπὸ Ἑρμέω ἑωυτούς: similarly, the Skythian kings were supposedly descended from Herakles (4.8–10); for other such divine genealogies see Darbo-Peschanski 1987: 30. This Hermes may be H. Psychopompos, given the Thracian preoccupation with burial and the afterlife (AHG).

8 The funerary rites here described are reminiscent of the Homeric funeral of Patroklos, *Il.* 23.252–7 (cf. Petropoulou 1986–7 and 1988: 492–3; also Richardson 1993: 200 and Munson 2001: 167).   ταφαί 'burials', as opp. τάφοι, 'graves' (note the different accents).   τὰ μέγιστα ἄεθλα: so too in Homer (*Il.* 23.257ff.) the athletic and equestrian contests for Patroklos follow immediately after the funeral; Richardson 1993: 166–7. The holding of funeral games after a funeral is attested for other Indo-European peoples, for instance in Irish narratives. See West 2007: 501–2, with an interesting guess as to the origin of the practice: on the Eurasian steppes, men rode their horses from long distances to attend the funeral of a great man, and at the gathering it would be natural for them to challenge each other to races.   **κατὰ λόγον <εὐδαιμονίης διὰ> μουνομαχίης** 'in proportion to wealth, by single combat'. This is Wilson's attractive emendation; as he says, the context deals with burial rites for the wealthy. The MSS' reading κατὰ λόγον μουνομαχίης is usually taken to mean something like 'in the category of one-to-one combat'. But that is a strange expression; those Greek words ought to mean 'by analogy with one-to-one combat', but that makes poor sense here. For μουνομαχίη, cf. 6.92.3, Sophanes. If we do not emend, the best solution may be, with Legrand, to take μουνομαχίης (not with κατὰ λόγον but) with τίθεται: 'les prix les plus importants sont proposés, avec raison, aux vainqueurs en combat singulier'. But this word order is unattractive.

9.1 τὸ δὲ πρὸς βορέω ἔτι τῆς χώρης 'the region to the north of this country'. That is, of Thrace. ἔτι, indicating extent, is usually found with comparatives such as μᾶλλον, but for its use with positives cf. expressions such as ἀνέκαθεν ἔτι at **62**.3 and 6.53.2.   **μούνους δὲ δύναμαι πύθεσθαι … Σιγύνναϛ:** Hdt.'s Transdanuvian knowledge is limited, his inquiries have been unsatisfactory ('nobody can say with accuracy', οὐδεὶϛ ἔχει φράσαι τὸ ἀτρεκέϛ) and his language is hesitant. The Sigynnai are obscure. Ap. Rhod. (4.320) brackets them uninformatively with the Skythians, but may be merely drawing on Hdt. Strabo 11.11.8 puts them between the Caspian and the Caucasus, but crams the *Kresphontes* reference (**4**.2n.) into the same ch.

The whole of **9**.1–2 is reported speech (a series of infinitives) following δύναμαι, and this same construction is continued at the beginning of **9**.3 by λέγουσι, as the source of information becomes more specific.

9.1 (cont.) ἐσθῆτι δὲ χρεωμένους Μηδικῆι: the Median dress is here offered as mere evidence of borrowing, not of common origin, but in **9**.3 we will learn that the Sigynnai themselves claim Median origin. Hdt. is uneasy about this second claim. For the link between barbarian dress and ethnicity see 88.1 and Th. 1.6; cf. also **49**.3n. Cf. Munson 2001: 92 and n. 147.

9.2 λασίους ἄπαν τὸ σῶμα 'their bodies are shaggy all over'. Strabo too (see **9**.1n. on μούνους) has this detail about the horses.   **πρὸς ταῦτα** 'because of this'.   **κατήκειν … τοὺς οὔρους** 'their boundaries … extend'.

9.3 γένοιτο δ' ἂν πᾶν ἐν τῶι μακρῶι χρόνωι: the idea that everything can happen in the course of time recalls the long view taken at 1.5.4, great cities become small and vice versa; but the exaggeration here is nonetheless startling. For the thought, cf. Soph. *Phil.* 305f.   **σιγύννας δ' ὢν … τὰ δόρατα** 'anyway, *sigynnai* is what the Ligyes, who live north of Massilia, call shop-keepers but the Cypriots call spears'. This is, surprisingly, Hdt.'s only mention anywhere of the important Greek city of Massilia, mod. Marseille in Provence (*IACP*: no. 3, 'Massalia'). It is from Th. (1.13.6) that we learn that it was a Phokaian foundation. The 'Ligyes' are the Ligurians.

This little excursus about the meaning of *sigynnai* is baffling, but the sentence should not be deleted; see Wilson. Nenci 1990a: 314 and 1990b tried to combine the Ligurian and Cypriot data by suggesting that Cypriot spear-heads were used by merchants as units of exchange, like *obeloi* (spits). Burkert 1990 was unconvinced, partly on the grounds that, in Homer, δόρυ is the shaft of a spear. Lykoph. *Alex.* 555, in the course of the poem's Cypriot section, uses the word σίγυμνος [sic] to mean a spear, probably with Hdt. in mind.

10 μέλισσαι...δοκέουσι λέγειν οὐκ οἰκότα: here, Hdt.'s rejection does not give rise to an alternative theory or explanation of his own, contrast e.g. 4.31 (feathers or snow?) with Darbo-Peschanski 1987: 131. For Hdt.'s interest, shared with contemporaries like Demokritos and the Hippokratic medical writings, in the effect of climate on animals, see Thomas 2000: 150–1, cf. also Munson 2001: 88 n. 131.   **τὰ γὰρ ζῷα ταῦτα φαίνεται εἶναι δύσριγα** 'for these creatures appear to be intolerant of cold'.

11.1 Δαρεῖος δὲ ὡς...ἀπίκετο ἐς Σάρδις: for Sardis as satrapal capital of Lydia, see **25.**1n. The date is around 512 BC.   **ἐμνήσθη τῆς ἐξ Ἱστιαίου τε τοῦ Μιλησίου εὐεργεσίης καὶ τῆς παραινέσιος τοῦ Μυτιληναίου Κώεω:** Histiaios has featured before, 4.137–9 and 141, but his patronym Lysagores will not be given until **30.**2; see nn. there. The name Histiaios itself is theophoric, formed from the goddess Hestia: see Bechtel 1917: 528 ('property of Hestia') and Parker 2000: 56; cf. also **37.**1n. on Histiaios son of the Karian Tymnes. The name, whether spelled as in Hdt. or as Ἑστιαῖος (see Introduction p. 44), is common everywhere, but there is a noticeable abundance at Miletos itself (nine classical bearers of the name Ἱστιαῖος) and at its colonies, such as Olbia, Odessos, Sinope and Pantikapaion. The prominence of the cult of Hestia at Miletos is displayed by the long Molpoi decree from the mid 5th cent. (Rehm 1914: no. 133 = *Syll.*[3] no. 57, Eng. tr. at Gorman 2001: 176–82 at 179, and Herda 2006: 10–14 with German tr.); see line 13 for sacrifices to Hestia, with Herda 2006: 81. There are many theophoric names, including Histiaios, formed from Hestia at Miletos and Milesian colonies; the connection between the cults of Apollo Delphinios and Hestia was probably tied to the custom of obtaining sacred fire from the mother-city (Ehrhardt 1988: 175–6).

A Histiaios made an offering at Didyma, the great sanctuary of Miletos, Tod: no. 9: Ἱστια[ῖος ἀνέθ]ηκε τὠπόλλωνι. There is no patronym or ethnic, and this perhaps (Tod; Tozzi 92 and n. 89) means that the dedicator was a leading Milesian. Epigraphically, the date is right for the famous Histiaios:

*LSAG*² 334 and 343, no. 32 ('*c.* 525–500?'; cf. Rehm 1958: 9 no. 14: before 513?). But the stone itself is lost.

As for εὐεργεσίης, the 'benefaction' was to arrange for the Persian army to get back from Skythia over the (only partly demolished) pontoon bridge over the Danube; before this he had spoken successfully against the Athenian Miltiades' proposal that the Greeks should adopt the Skythians' offer to help liberate Ionia.

The reader or hearer has met Koes, too, before: see 4.97.2, where he was introduced as son of Erxandros and general (not yet tyrant) of the Mytilenaians on Lesbos. The name Erxandros is not otherwise attested in *LGPN* vol. I (the islands), but see vol. VA ('coastal Asia Minor: Pontus to Ionia'), for two early Hellenistic bearers of the name, one from Smyrna, one from the Troad, both of them areas of Aiolian settlement, as was Mytilene. There is no other Koes in either vol. At **37**.1 Koes will again get his patronym. His advice to Dareios was to leave the Danube bridge intact in the first place.

The whole sentence is elegantly constructed, with a chiastic ABCCBA arrangement at the centre, framed by two mentions of Sardis: Dareios arrives at Sardis, where he remembers (A) Histiaios the (B) Milesian's (C) benefaction and the (C) advice of the (B) Mytilenaian (A) Koes, so summons them to Sardis and gives them a choice. (For this stylistic device see Nünlist 2009: 326–37.) The different choices made by the two men will be significant later in the narrative: Koes will be stoned to death by the Mytilenaians (**38**), whereas Histiaios' adventures continue well into bk. 6. It is only natural that the present passage – linking as it does the bk. 4 Skythian episode with the Ionian revolt narrative – should be constructed with particular care.

The Asiatic Greeks who had supported Dareios at the Danube bridge received their rewards at Athens' expense: the Strymon and the Troad (where the Mytilenaians had territory as a *peraia* on the mainland) were two of the main Athenian interests in the north. The other was the Chersonese, the location of Miltiades' tyranny, and this was the object of the ambitions of the Lampsakenes, with whom Hippias of Athens formed an alliance after he had broken off his friendship with Miltiades (6.37). For all this see Wade-Gery 1958: 161.

11.2 **αἰτέει δὲ Μύρκινον τὴν Ἠδώνων, βουλόμενος ἐν αὐτῆι πόλιν κτίσαι**: here, as often in bk. 5, there is an implied allusion to bk. 1, and perhaps a causal and chronological link as well. Peisistratos drew financial resources from the mineral resources of the Strymon region (1.64), and we will learn at **23**.1 that Myrkinos was on the Strymon. It is even possible that the end of Peisistratid control in this region coincided with the territorial concession to Histiaios (Myres 1953: 196).   **Μύρκινον**: though called a mere 'place' (χῶρος) at **23**.1, Myrkinos qualifies for inclusion as a *polis* in *IACP* (no. 633) on the strength of the present passage and also (more securely) Th. 4.107.3, Μύρκινος...Ἠδωνικὴ πόλις. Its location is unknown, and just when it became a *polis* is hard to fix. At **24**.3 Dareios urges Histiaios to leave his 'newly-founded *polis* in Thrace', but his fortification of Myrkinos is implied to be incomplete at **124**, and its last mention in Hdt. (Aristagores ἔσχε τὴν χώρην ἐπ' ἧν ἐστάλη, **126**) is a very vague one. This *polis* was in fact a mixed Greco-Thracian settlement, ruled by members of a non-Greek royal family (Th. as above).

For the Edonians see introd. n. to **124–6** and **126**.2n.   ὁ δὲ **Κώης...αἰτέει Μυτιλήνης τυραννεῦσαι**: Koes' request for a tyranny, like the similar ambition of the Paionian brothers in **12**.1 below, prepares us for the ambitions of some of the main players in the Ionian revolt. Such Persian support of tyrannies was normal practice by the time of Dareios: see Austin 1990: esp. 304; and for earlier Mytilenaian tyrannies, notably that of the poet Alkaios' enemy Pittakos, see *IACP* no. 798 at pp. 1027f. With δημότης, 'commoner' as opp. ruler, cf. 2.172.2 and 5; at Tyrt. fr. 4.5 West, the 'common men' are listed in third place after the kings and the *gerontes*.

12–15 The Paionian brothers and their multi-tasking sister

A similar story is told by Nikolaos of Damascus – writing in the time of Augustus but using much older material – about Alyattes of Lydia and the wife of a 'Thracian' (*FGrHist* 90 F 71, from Constantine Porphyrogennetos). Most likely, the story is of a folkloric type whose details could be adjusted according to narrative need, and it is futile to ask which version is primary and which secondary. (Hdt.'s version has been rejected on the grounds that (a) he got his story from the version used by Nikolaos, (b) the names Pigres and Mastyes are not authentically Thracian; it is true that each name is without Thracian parallel in *LGPN* iv, but that is not decisive. So Will 1967; Jacoby and others have thought Nikolaos derivative from Hdt.) The best discussion is by Griffiths 2001: 82f., who notes that this resembles tales of entrapment with a view to snaring a husband, and compares Genesis 24 (the industrious Rebecca, with Alter 2011: 64).

12.1 οὗτοι μὲν κατὰ τὰ εἵλοντο ἐτράποντο 'so they made their way to the places which they had chosen' (lit. 'they went on their way according to what they had chosen'). And to their different fates, see **11**.1n. on ἐμνήσθη...   **Δαρεῖον δὲ συνήνεικε πρῆγμα τοιόνδε ἰδόμενον** 'now it happened that Dareios saw the following thing'. Ring composition: we are here told in advance (*prolepsis*) that Dareios gave the order to uproot the Paionians to Asia, because of something he saw; then the something is described; then (**14**.1) he gives the uprooting order; then (**17**.1) the

Paionians are taken off to Asia.   ἀνασπάστους ποιῆσαι 'to lead off into captivity' (lit. 'make drawn or dragged up'); a favoured Persian policy, cf. 3.93.2 and (for the full expression with ποιέειν as here) 4.204, **106**.4 and 6.32.   ἦν Πίγρης καὶ Μαστύης ἄνδρες Παίονες: for this use of ἦν, singular (instead of plural ἦσαν), usually found at the beginning of sentences, see LSJ εἰμί A (V). Compare *Il.* 7.386, ἠνώγει Πρίαμός τε καὶ ἄλλοι Τρῶες ἀγαυοί. So there are no good grounds for doubting the text (see app. crit., and Wilson).

For the names, see introd. n. above. These two chancers prefigure the various Greeks who meddle in a self-interested way, always disastrously either for their fellow-countryfolk or for themselves. Their tyrannical ambitions pick up those of Koes in **11**.2.

12.1 (cont.) μεγάλην τε καὶ εὐειδέα: compare Phye at 1.60.4, described in markedly similar language (cf. Irwin 2007: 51); and see **12**.2n. on σκευάσαντες. As often, bk. 5 echoes bk. 1: two beginnings. There may also be an intended similarity between the Paionians of bk. 5 and the similar-sounding Paiania, the deme or village from which Phye came. See Griffiths 2001: 86f. (who also notes the consonantal similarities between the names Pigres/Mastyes and Peisistratos/Megakles).

Hdt., like Homer but unlike Th. (who in this respect was perhaps reacting against Hdt.), sometimes describes or at least refers to the personal appearance and/or dress of individuals and groups. For other refs. in Hdt. to female beauty see 1.8.1 (Kandaules' wife), 3.1.3, 6.61.5, and various ethnographic passages. For the looks (handsome and/or tall) of male individuals see **47**.1 (Philippos of Kroton), 6.127.4 and n. on Hippokleides of Athens, and for non-Greeks see 3.3.1 (Kambyses and the other children of Kyros by Kassandane) and 7.187.2 (Xerxes); both these are tall and good-looking. See Pohlenz 1937: 45f. and 46 n. 1. Tall Persians: 9.25.1 (Masistios' corpse) and 96.2 (Tigranes). Here, as with Phye, we are told about both looks and dress. For Th. see *TT*: 18 n. 82, suggesting that the exceptions are from passages where he adopts Herodotean colouring, e.g. 1.130, the 'Median' dress of Pausanias the Regent. Sometimes, but not always, and not here, such comments on height or beauty suggest heroic or divine status (see Introduction §6 and n. 130). See also Osborne 2007: 92 n. 7: beauty in Hdt. tends to signify trouble for someone.

12.2 φυλάξαντες δὲ Δαρεῖον προκατιζόμενον ἐς τὸ προάστιον 'they waited until Dareios was seated in state in front of the town'; for the echo of ἀντικατιζομένων at **1**.2 see introd. n. to **1–2**.   σκευάσαντες τὴν ἀδελφεὴν ὡς εἶχον ἄριστα 'they dressed their sister in the best clothes they could'. See 1.60.4, again of Phye, but there the woman was dressed in full armour by the men, σκευάσαντες πανοπλίηι.   ἐπ' ὕδωρ ἔπεμπον ἄγγος ἐπὶ τῆι κεφαλῆι ἔχουσαν: carrying the water-pot on her head, like Elektra in Euripides' play of that name (lines 55–6). At modern Lefkada (Leukas), a festival in August includes women dancing while carrying water-pots on their heads, a display of female skill.

12.3 ὡς δὲ παρεξήιε ἡ γυνή 'as the woman passed by' (from παρεξέρχομαι). Cf. Hdt. 4.168: the girls are paraded in front of the king. **οὔτε πρός τῶν ἐκ τῆς Ἀσίης οὐδαμῶν**: what she does is neither Persian nor Lydian 'nor characteristic of Asiatics generally' (for this use of πρός see Powell II (2), also adducing 7.153.4); this is a kind of priamel or paratactic comparison: see *OCD⁴* 'priamel'. Female industriousness is, however, something that *Greeks* prize (Goff 2004: 54). However, it was not necessarily the individual tasks which were un-Asiatic in Dareios' opinion, but the virtuoso combination of them. That is the marvel, but Greeks – no less than Dareios – would have found that marvellous, so that the comment is not quite logical.

12.4 ἦρσε . . . ἄρσασα: both are from ἄρδω, 'I water' an animal or piece of land. The verb is used at *Homeric Hymn to Artemis* 3 of Artemis watering horses near Smyrna. The combination of indicative verb and participle of the same verb is a feature of the λέξις εἰρομένη, the 'strung-out' i.e. continuous or running style. It is Homeric (e.g. *Il.* 22.33–4 ᾤμωξεν . . . οἰμώξας, about Priam, with de Jong 2012: 68), and frequent in Hdt.

13.1 τά τε ἤκουσε . . . καὶ τά αὐτὸς ὥρα: the king sees the woman walking past; he orders his spies to follow her (out of sight of the king, we have to assume) and to tell him what she does with the horse; they do so. So he marvels both (a) at what (τά τε) they tell him, and (b) at what (καὶ τά) he had already seen for himself. That is, (a) supplements (b). **οὐ κῃ πρόσω σκοπίην ἔχοντες τούτων** 'who were keeping a watch on all this from somewhere not far off'. κῃ is Ionic for πῃ or που, and σκοπίην ἔχω is Homeric, see *Od.* 8.302.

13.2 With Dareios' threefold Homeric question compare *Il.* 1.170, τίς πόθεν εἷς ἀνδρῶν; πόθι τοι πόλις ἠδὲ τοκῆες; cf. also Hornblower and Matthews 2000: 10, on *Od.* 7.238. For similarly-formulated questions put by Persians, see **73.2** (Artaphrenes), cf. also **105.2** (Dareios again) with nn. Note that in what follows, the Paionian brothers do all the talking. **δώσοντες σφέας αὐτούς**: the Paionians understand how the Persian system works: they want to be tyrants over the Paionians (**12.1**), but they know that their own surrender to Persia is a precondition for this. **εἴη δὲ ἡ Παιονίη ἐπὶ τῶι Στρύμονι ποταμῶι πεπολισμένη**: the participle derives from πόλις and is surprising, as applied to the vast area which was Paionia, although **15.2** does speak of the Paionian *poleis*, plural. In all the other five places that Hdt. uses the verb πολίζω, it is combined with the root-noun πόλις, usually as part of the phrase πόλις πεπόλισται (e.g. of Sousa at **52.**6), an expression of the double

type known as *figura etymologica*; this is true even of 7.199, where πεπόλισται is used of Trechis, which was called a πόλις three lines further up. The
verb here adds to the generally Greek decor. Or perhaps we are meant to
remember that at *Il.* 20.217 the words πεπόλιστο, πόλις μερόπων ἀνθρώπων
were used about Troy itself, the city from which the brothers are about
to claim the Paionians were descended as colonists. For the inaccuracy
of 'Strymon', see **1.2**n.   **οὐ πρόσω τῆς Ἑλλησπόντου** 'not far from the
Hellespont'.   **εἴησαν δὲ Τευκρῶν τῶν ἐκ Τροίης ἄποικοι:** for the Paionians
fighting on the Trojan side see Homer, *Il.* 2.848–9: Pyraichmes leads the
'Paionians with their curved bows'; also 16.287–8: Pyraichmes is killed by
Patroklos. But there (see Janko's n.) the Paionians are called 'arrangers of
chariots', ἱπποκορυσταί (cf. also 21.205). For Paionians as horsemen, see
also Mimnermos fr. 17, Παίονας ἄνδρας ἄγων, ἵνα τε κλειτὸν γένος ἵππων.
   The claim of Trojan colonial descent must be based on the Homeric
passages. A similar claim was made by the people of 'Teukrian Gergis',
see **122.2**n., cf. 7.42.2. For the mysterious Teukroi, see 7.20 (Mysian and
Teukrian invasion of Europe before the Trojan War). By Virgil's time, their
name was a standard synonym for 'Trojans', as at e.g. *Aen.* 2.48, *equo ne
credite, Teucri*. In mythology, Teukros son of Skamandros (who later became
a river god) is a local ruler of the Troy region, who makes a pact with
Dardanos the ancestor of the Trojan kings. See Lykoph. *Alex.* 1303–4 (the
poet makes Teukros come from *Krete*); M. L. West 1985: 97 and Gantz
1993: 560–1.

13.3 οἱ μὲν δὴ ταῦτα ἕκαστα ἔλεγον: the imperfect refers to the whole of
a long reply.   **οἱ δὲ καὶ τοῦτο ἔφασαν προθύμως οὕτω ἔχειν· πάντα γὰρ ὢν
τούτου εἵνεκα καὶ ἐποιέετο** 'they eagerly said that they were; and indeed that
was the point of everything they had been doing'. For the text see app. crit.;
πάντα is a great improvement on αὐτοῦ. The final comment is authorial.

14.1 ἐνθαῦτα Δαρεῖος γράφει γράμματα Μεγαβάζωι: the tenses in this ch. are
a lively mix of past and present.   **ἐξαναστῆσαι ἐξ ἠθέων** 'to remove them
from their native land'. For this as a separate sense of ἤθεα (Powell ἤθεα
(2)), cf. 1.15. But the pattern – royal notice taken of a population group,
then order given for mass-deportation and uprooting – is a regular Persian
one (Asheri 1990: 158) and the ambiguity between 'customs' (the other
sense of ἤθεα) and 'native land' reflects the imperial reality: the deracina-
tion was meant to be cultural as well as geographical.

14.2 αὐτίκα δὲ ἱππεὺς ἔθεε φέρων τὴν ἀγγελίην: a horseman sped off with the
letter; the verb is from θέω, 'I run'. The detail generates a sense of urgency.
See, for some other examples of this literary device, *CT* III: 789 on Th.
8.11.3.   **βυβλίον** 'letter', lit. 'strip of Egyptian papyrus', βύβλος, hence
any document.

15.1 πρὸς θαλάσσης 'towards the sea'.

15.2 ἐρήμους: usually (as here) two-termination in Hdt., but sometimes the fem. is in -η.   **οἷα δὲ κεινῇσι** 'inasmuch as they were empty' (Attic would be κεναῖς; see Introduction p. 44).

15.3 οἱ δὲ Παίονες ὡς ἐπύθοντο ἐχομένας τὰς πόλιας: the *polis* motif is continued from **13.**2, see n. there on εἴη δέ...for πολίζω used of Paionia as a whole. When the Paionians realise they have lost their cities, they just give up, as if they were Greeks without the Skythian guerilla option.   **Σιριοπαίονες:** for such 'composite ethnics' see Fraser 2009: 142–5, noting (143 and n. 78) that the present passage is an early example of a formation generally found (a) in the Imperial period and (b) in Syria and neighbouring countries. Usually at least one of the two parts is descriptive of a non-Greek people. Here both of them are: for a Paionian place or region called Siris, modern Serres, see below 8.115.2 and Steph. Byz. Σῖρις· ἔστι καὶ Σῖρις ἐν Παιονίαι, ἧς τὸ ἐθνικὸν ἀπὸ τῆς γενικῆς Σιριοπαίονες. Fraser, who cites Steph. Byz. at n. 78, remarks that Hdt. 'knows of both elements [of Siriopaiones] separately'.   **μέχρι τῆς Πρασιάδος λίμνης:** Lake Prasias: *Barr.* map 51 B3, on the usual and preferable location, mod. Lake Tachinos. (Hammond identified Lake Prasias with mod. Lake Butkova further up the Strymon, and regarded Lake Tachinos as the ancient Lake Kerkinitis. See *HM* I: 193–4 and II: 55).   **ἐς τὴν Ἀσίην:** such transportations are attested also in the Persepolis Fortification Tablets; Lewis 1977: 6–7 cites some Egyptian workers moved from Sousa to Tamukkan, 'a place from which people do not seem to come back', and some other Thracians 'moved around in some quantity'. In fact, the Paionians were taken to Phrygia, as Hdt. will explain, by a Homeric technique of 'increasing precision', at **98**. At 7.185 the Paionians are found serving in Xerxes' army. (For this technique see *TT*: 75–6 and n. 40. The classic example is the progressively more detailed predictions in the *Iliad* of Achilles' death.) But their final appearance is significant in that it amounts to a kind of revenge for their bk. 5 treatment: at 8.115 they get hold of Xerxes' 'sacred chariot of Zeus' and hand it over to some Thracians further up the Strymon.

16 The fish-eating pile-dwellers

Unconquered, self-sufficient 'socially marginal' fish-eaters are a favourite of ancient Greek ethnography; see Asheri 1990: 140–1 and cf. Arr. *Ind.* 29.8–16 for the Ichthyophagoi encountered by Nearchos in Gedrosia (see *Barr.* map 3 H4 for this region).

16.1 With οἱ δέ..., understand Παίονες, i.e. the reference is to Παιόνων at **15.**3: the pile-dwellers of Lake Prasias are thought of by Hdt. as Paionians.

This is consistent with Hdt.'s placing of the Paionians on the Strymon, whatever view we take of the location of Lake Prasias (**15**.3n.).

The Doberes and Odomantoi are mentioned again at 7.112–13, where they again feature in the context of the gold and silver mines of Pangaion, to the south and east of them respectively; it was the wealth from these mines which made possible the career of Philip II. For the Doberes and Odomantoi see *HM* I: 200–1 and 193, citing Strabo bk. 7 fr. 36. For the Agrianes, frequently mentioned as skirmishers in Alexander the Great's campaigns (e.g. Arr. *Anab.* 4.25.6), see Th. 2.96.3. They are normally found much further north than Pangaion, but see *HM* II: 56 n. 1, citing Strabo bk. 7 fr. 41 for Agrianes as far south as Pangaion.

16.1 (cont.) ἐξαιρέειν 'capture, wipe out' (Powell). For the verb cf. Xen. *Hell.* 2.2.19 of the desire of the Korinthians and others at the end of the Peloponnesian War to destroy the Athenians.   ἴκρια ἐπὶ σταυρῶν ὑψη-λῶν ἐζευγμένα ἐν μέσηι ἕστηκε τῆι λίμνηι 'in the middle of the lake there are decking-planks secured [lit. 'tied across'] on tall posts'. The word for 'planks', ἴκρια, is found here only in Hdt., but the technical context calls for unusual vocabulary. For archaeological evidence of pile-dwellers in this region (actually from Lakes Malik and Kastoria to the west) see *HM* I: 230–1.

16.2 ἐξ ὄρεος τῶι οὔνομά ἐστι Ὄρβηλος 'from a mountain whose name is Orbelos', Hdt. speaks as if of some distant wonder, but Mt Orbelos, some 50 km. NW of the later Amphipolis (Map 3), must have been a familiar feature of the skyline to many Greeks who had visited that colonial part of the world.

16.3 καλύβης...θύρης καταρρακτῆς 'hut'... 'trap door'.   δέουσι τοῦ ποδὸς σπάρτωι: the genitive means they tie the child *by the foot* with cord.

16.4 τοῖσι δὲ ἵπποις καὶ τοῖσι ὑποζυγίοισι παρέχουσι χόρτον ἰχθύς 'they give their horses and baggage-animals fish as fodder'. Athenaios (345e) says that the Mossynoi of Thrace have oxen which eat fish. These are presumably the same as Hdt.'s Mossynoikoi or palisade-dwellers of 3.94.2 and 7.78. For the word μόσσυν as a wooden house or tower see Xen. *An.* 5.4.26 and Aen. Tact. 33.3. The whole of *An.* 5.4 is about the Mossyn-oikoi, but those people lived on the SE coast of the Black Sea, W of Trapezous. For fish-eating oxen see also Plin. *HN* 11.281, from Theophr. fr. 281.   σπυρίδα κεινήν 'an empty basket'; for κεινήν cf. **15**.2n. πάπρακάς τε καὶ τίλωνας: these species of fish are obscure, but Hdt. is evi-dently and understandably proud of knowing their names. Chantraine 1968–80: 3.856 thinks *paprax* is an indigenous Thracian name, a safe enough guess, and gives hospitality to the theory that it is onomatopoeic, from the sound the fish made. (Not completely absurd: noisy or vocal fishes were favourites of paradoxographers, i.e. collectors of marvels. See Badino 2010: 95–8 on Philostephanos fr. 9 = Ath. 331e). The *tilon* may be mentioned for its spawning habits by Aristotle, *Hist. an.* 568b25, but there are other possible readings for the name, and the present passage of Hdt. has probably influenced editors.

17–22 THE MACEDONIANS AND ALEXANDROS

(In this comm., the leading figure of these chs. is spelt *Alexandros*, to distinguish him from *Alexander* the Great, who is naturalised in English under that spelling). The Macedonian theme will be important in later books; see esp. 8.137–44 with A. Bowie; also 9.45.2. For Hdt.'s motive in splitting up his material in this way, see below, **22**.1n. On the present episode see esp. Badian 1994, Fearn 2007b (and more briefly 2007a: 30–4) and Zahrnt 2011.

Although the story has been comprehensively doubted (Errington 1981), and certainly contains motifs of a traditional story-telling type, we can accept the basic fact that the Macedonian king Amyntes gave not only earth and water to the Persian king (**18**.1) but his daughter in marriage to a high-ranking Persian (see **21**.2nn. on Γυγαίη and Βουβάρηι), and in fact became a vassal of the Persian king; so rightly Badian 1994, Green 1996: 13 and Zahrnt 2011: 765 and n. 10 (stressing, with citation of Zahrnt 1984, that the Macedonian kingdom at this time was small, weak and in no position to resist the Achaemenid giant). The centrepiece of the story, the banquet at which the cross-dressing Macedonian youths kill the Persians, is a wonderfully constructed narrative, but not historically believable; it is a later fiction, designed to palliate Macedonian submission. If it were true, we would have expected the Macedonians to offer stiff resistance when the Persians next appeared in the area, but at 6.44.1 Mardonios' reduction of the Macedonians to slavery will be recorded in a mere six words, Μακεδόνας...προσεκτήσαντο. The implication of this apparent need to re-establish control over Macedon at that later date may well be that Macedonian submission to Persia had lapsed in the eventful intervening years; so Badian 1994: 116–17 and Zahrnt 2011: 765.

17.1 ἑπτὰ Πέρσας: the anonymity of all these seven is surprising, especially given that 'they' are given more than one speech in the narrative which follows. They must have had a leader and spokesman. By contrast, Hdt. is able and willing to tell us (**21**.2) the name of Boubares, the Persian who comes to look for the missing men. The effect is to focalise the main part of the story through the Macedonians. The cultural interplay ('our custom is this'; 'but our custom is the opposite') works well with this focalisation: the

Macedonian custom of female segregation is essentially Greek and thus familiar, whereas that claimed – whether sincerely or not – by the Persians is alien and shocking. (That the whole banquet story is likely to have been invented is not – despite Badian 1994: 108 – a complete explanation of the anonymity: good stories often include circumstantial details: the 'effects of the real'.)

The number seven is that of the Persian conspirators at 3.71.1 (and, we can add, of the Chian conspirators against Strattis at 8.132.2), so the number seven has been seen as one of the 'obvious marks of fiction' in this story (Badian 108). That may be right, but in the present passage the seven are appointed by the king as a delegation; the famous 'seven' of bk. 3 were self-appointed.

17.1 (cont.) γῆν τε καὶ ὕδωρ: earth and water confer formal and symbolic rights. In Hdt., the demand is usually made to Greeks (but not always: see 4.126, the Skythians). See Kuhrt 1988, and AHG (cf. Griffiths 1988), who notes that the demand was tailored to Greeks, 'adopting their own imagery and turning it against them' (similarly but independently S. West 2011), and that the words form the end of a Greek hexameter, cf. *Od.* 3.300, ἄνεμός τε καὶ ὕδωρ. There are many Greek examples of clods of earth which confer rights, though usually in colonial contexts and as part of a gift-exchange relationship (see Gottesman 2010); note esp. Lykoph. *Alex.* 1379, Neileus and the potter's daughter who gives Neileus the clay, i.e. earth and water, which is the token of his right to Miletos, which he then founds. See **39–48n.**

17.2 ἐκ τῆς Πρασιάδος λίμνης: for Lake Prasias see **15.3n.   σύντομος κάρτα ἐς τὴν Μακεδονίην** 'a short cut to Macedon'. This is an ellipse: with σύντομος, a two-termination adjective, understand ἡ ὁδός. Cf. Xen. *Hell.* 7.2.13, ὥστε γὰρ τὴν σύντομον πρὸς τοὺς Πελληνέας ἀφίκεσθαι.   **ἔχεται τῆς λίμνης...ἐφοίτα** 'next to the lake is the mine, from which, at a later time, Alexandros derived a talent of silver a day'. For this sense of φοιτῶ (the accruing of revenue) cf. 3.90.3 and 115.2. The amount – a talent or 6000 drachmas a day – is colossal, and the time-indicator ('later') signals, perhaps, the period in the 'pentekontaetia' (*c.* 480–430) when the Athenians seized the mainland mine and markets which had been exploited by the islanders of Thasos: Th. 1.100.2 (460s). Alexandros' mines are not identical with this mine, but the mineral resources of the region were highly topical in the later 5th cent. See 6.46 for the mineral resources of Thasos and its *peraia*.

Note (a) the 'temporal complexity' of this sentence, which refers to time present (ἔχεται), time future (ὕστερον τούτων) and – in a way – time past (ἐφοίτα); and (b) the seemingly gratuitous mention of Alexandros, which neatly introduces the developed story of the 'disappeared' envoys (for these two points, Fearn 2007b: 100).

This is Alexandros I, the so-called Philhellene, son of Amyntes and father of Perdikkas. Here, at his first mention, he gets no patronymic. That is saved for **19**.1, where it has special significance.

17.2 (cont.) μετὰ δὲ τὸ μέταλλον Δύσωρον καλεόμενον ὄρος ὑπερβάντι <ἔξεστι> εἶναι ἐν Μακεδονίηι 'then after the mine you have only to cross a mountain called Dysoron and you can be in Macedonia' ('only' is not in the Greek, but that is the idea). The name of the mountain (here only in Hdt., but for a restored epigraphic mention see *SEG* 34.664 B line 10 = Ager 1996: no. 5 B line 25, Philippi, 335 BC) appears, in adjectival form, as one of a long list of weather-words in Pollux (5.109), and means something like 'unseasonable'. So, a bad *nomen omen* for the Persians? Especially if we recall how close the omega and omicron sounds are (in Doric we find mountains actually spelt that way, so that Hermes is said to arrive ἀπ' ὤρεος at Theok. 1.77, a Doricism for Homeric οὖρ-), in which case the compound word here might at a recitation have conveyed 'ill-mountain', cf. *Od.* 23.97 (imitated by Lykoph. *Alex.* 1174), μῆτερ ἐμή, δύσμητερ. Further ominous hints will follow at **18**.2 below.

18.1 ἐλθόντες ἐς ὄψιν τὴν Ἀμύντεω: the story which follows will feature a lot of seeing (Fearn 2007b: 112–13). The formula (ὄψις = 'sight, presence': Powell) is appropriate to Persian monarchical or satrapal practice: cf. 3.128.3 (Oroites), **24**.3 and **106**.1 (Dareios). (At 6.134.1 it is used of a Parian priestess coming into the presence of a Greek, though an autocratic one; cf. also 3.42.1, the fisherman and Polykrates.) For restricted access to Persian kings see generally Brosius 2007: 39–40. It is ambiguous, whether the Macedonians are more like Persians or more like Greeks (as at **22**). It may be that Alexandros is meant to come across as neither 'obviously Greek' nor 'entirely Eastern' either (Fearn 2007b: 108). If so, compare Th.'s view of the Macedonians as neither Greek nor barbarian; see *CT* II: 392 on 4.124.1.   ὁ δὲ ταῦτά τε ἐδίδου: even if we take the verb to mean 'was ready to give' rather than 'gave', imperfect not aorist, the fact of willing submission is clear.   ἐπὶ ξείνια καλέει: the expression is usually used in Hdt. about invitations to hospitality issued by Greeks (6.34.2, 9.15.4 and 89.1, but cf. 2.115.4). This is one of the banqueting episodes in Hdt. in which 'the Greek colour' has been felt to be dominant (A. Bowie 2003: 106).

18.2 ὡς δὲ ἀπὸ δείπνου ἐγίνοντο, διαπίνοντες εἶπαν οἱ Πέρσαι: cf. the almost identical formulation at 9.16.2, the banquet of Attaginos of Thebes: ὡς δὲ ἀπὸ δείπνου ἐγίνοντο, διαπινόντων τὸν Πέρσην etc. That banquet, too, will be ominous (like the last banquet of the suitors in the *Odyssey*). ἀπὸ δείπνου means 'after dinner', and διαπίνω conveys the idea of competitive drinking (Fearn 2007b: 101 n. 6). See Lightfoot 2003: 409 (citing also 2.78 and

6.129.2, which have the initial ἀπὸ δείπνου formula): 'Significant questions are often posed or dangerous propositions canvassed after dinner.' There are echoes of this Macedonian dinner in the narrative of the feast given by Kleisthenes of Sikyon for Agariste's suitors (6.129.2); cf. **19**.1 on οὐδαμῶς and μηδὲ λιπάρεε τῆι πόσι). For the Macedonians as (Greek) Lapiths to the drunken Persian centaurs, see Scaife 1989: 131.   **ξεῖνε Μακεδών**: on the form of address here, see **72**.3n. on ὦ ξεῖνε Λακεδαιμόνιε. Here the speakers' continuation ('our Persian customs are different from yours') surely gives extra point to the ethnic, although in general the addition of an ethnic to the vocative ξένε does not alter the usage of the address and 'has no perceptible significance of its own': Dickey 1996: 175.

18.3 **κεχωρίσθαι ἄνδρας γυναικῶν**: separation of the sexes was Greek sympotic practice. But Hdt.'s Amyntes is surely right that it was Macedonian also, at least in the Hellenistic period: for the symposion as an important Macedonian institution, see Cameron 1995: 73–4. Only the Etruscans are known to have mixed the sexes at symposia.

18.4 **εὐμόρφους**: mentions of beauty in Hdt. are often bad news for somebody: see **12**.1n. citing Osborne.   **οὐδὲν εἶναι σοφόν**: the tone is good-humouredly aggrieved, and the final word is, by a clever echo, picked up authorially at **21**.2, to describe the cunning or guile (σοφίη) by which Alexandros bought off Boubares. Note the plurality of 'speakers' (perhaps we are to imagine they spoke through an interpreter).   **καὶ μὴ παριζομένας ἀντίας ἵζεσθαι** 'not to sit next to them but to sit opposite'. **ἀλγηδόνας σφίσι ὀφθαλμῶν**: cf. the similar language (an echo?) at Plut. *Alex.* 21.10 (Alexander the Great jokingly calls some Persian women ἀλγηδόνες ὀμμάτων) with *Mausolus*: 221. The eyes are the place where desire enters; see also ὄψει…ἀλγεινά at Th. 7.75.2 with *CT* III: 708.

18.5 **ἀναγκαζόμενος**: the 'compulsion' is something more than mere bowing to the demands of etiquette, something less than *force majeure*.   **καὶ κού τις καὶ φιλέειν ἐπειρᾶτο** 'and one or other of them would try to kiss…' The final word need not mean more than that the anonymous representative Persian 'tried' to do some kissing, but in the context it is relevant – as also at **20**.5 below – that, when used absolutely and in the active, πειρῶ can mean 'I make a pass at'; see *CT* III: 443 on Th. 6.54.3.

19.1 **Ἀλέξανδρος δὲ ὁ Ἀμύντεω**: Alexandros gets his patronym now (rather than at his first mention at **17**), partly to emphasise the contrast with his more cautious father, partly because he now steps centre-stage. Compare, for Th., *TT*: 93.   **ἅτε νέος τε ἐὼν καὶ κακῶν ἀπαθής**: almost a hendiadys: the young – it is implied – do not know the meaning of suffering. For the second element, cf. 1.32.6, the string of words used by Solon to Kroisos, ἄπηρος δέ ἐστι, ἄνουσος, ἀπαθὴς κακῶν, εὔπαις, εὐειδής, and the authorial description of the Ionians before the battle of Lade (6.12.2) as ἀπαθέες ἐόντες πόνων. **οὐδαμῶς ἔτι κατέχειν οἷός τε ἦν**: the young man could no longer contain himself. Cf. the similarly worded description of an older man's reaction, Kleisthenes of Sikyon's disapproval of the upside-down dancing of Hippokleides (6.129.4): οὐκέτι κατέχειν δυνάμενος εἶπε. **σὺ μὲν, ὦ πάτερ**: the – surely by now adult – Macedonian prince and his father (see **19.**2, ὦ παῖ) address each other like ordinary family members. Cf. the way in which e.g. Spartan kings are normally addressed by name not title. See Dickey 1996: 237 and **49.**2n. **εἶκε τῆι ἡλικίηι**: compare Telemachos ordering his mother Penelope upstairs to bed (*Od.* 1.256–9 and 19.344–53 with Fearn 2007b: 107, who however notes some obvious differences: Telemachos is, as Fearn puts it, not 'actually able to do away with the suitors', and Amyntes is not a woman). The exchange between father and son makes clear that the father, who after all possesses the royal authority, has a very good idea (συνιείς) of what his son plans to do, but does nothing to stop him. The question of responsibility is thus cleverly blurred. **μηδὲ λιπάρεε τῆι πόσι**: lit. 'and do not persevere with the drinking'. For the noun cf. 6.129.2, προιούσης δὲ τῆς πόσιος (Kleisthenes of Sikyon again). **πάντα τὰ ἐπιτήδεα παρέξω τοῖσι ξείνοισι**: the ambiguity is beautifully amusing, and sinister: he will 'take care of the guests'/'give the (importunate) strangers the appropriate treatment'. In the epic *Kypria*, Menelaos, who has to go to Krete for a family funeral, tells Helen to provide their guests with appropriate treatment, τοῖς ξένοις τὰ ἐπιτήδεια παρέχειν, in his absence. This is from Proklos' prose summary (arg. 2b, cf. West 2013: 89), so the curious closeness of wording cannot be pressed far; and Menelaos' injunction is innocent of intentional ambiguity; nor does the role of the Trojan Alexandros i.e. Paris correspond to that of his Macedonian namesake. But the two texts share the irony that the reader/hearer knows that both Helen and the Macedonian Alexandros have unusual ideas of the appropriate way to behave with guests: elopement, murder. Hdt. may have had this passage at the back of his mind. (The reverse is also just possible i.e. Proklos' wording was influenced by Hdt. But not the thought behind it).

19.2 συνιείς: see **19.**1n. on εἶκε...Amyntes knows perfectly well what is going to happen (the repetition below, συνίημι, rubs in the point) and thus has some responsibility for it, despite his parting admonition to his son to avoid causing trouble. **ὦ παῖ**: see on ὦ πάτερ, **19.**1n. **νεώτερα πρήγματα πρήξειν ... ποιέειν τι νεώτερον ... νεοχμῶσαι**: all these νεο-expressions indicate 'doing mischief'; compare **93.**2 and **106.**4; also Th. 1.102.3 for both the noun νεωτεροποία ('revolutionary tendencies'), and the common Thucydidean verb νεωτερίζω. It says something about Greek political conservatism that compounds in 'new' should have such negative connotations.   ἀνακαιομένου: usually in Hdt. (nine times) this verb means 'kindle' in the literal sense, but here only it means 'flare up (in anger)', 'burn' (with indignation). There is no need to emend; see Wilson, citing Eur. *Or.* 609, μᾶλλον μ' ἀνάψεις.

20.1 χρηίσας τούτων 'after asking this', with gen. of object.   γυναικῶν τουτέων…ἔστι ὑμῖν πολλὴ εὐπετείη: lit. 'there is great availability of these women', i.e. 'they are all yours'. The portentous noun is found here only in Hdt.; it adds to the humour which is undoubtedly a feature of the story.

20.2 τῆς κοίτης ὥρη προσέρχεται 'bed-time is approaching'. A far from innocent time-indicator. There are two additional meanings: sex, and (ironically aimed at the audience) the 'big sleep'.   καὶ καλῶς ἔχον-τας…μέθης 'you have drunk a good deal' lit. 'you are well off in respect of strong drink'; a polite way of saying 'you are drunk'.

20.3 λειογενείους τῆι τῶν γυναικῶν ἐσθῆτι σκευάσας καὶ ἐγχειρίδια δούς: the cross-dressing story-type (armed young men dressed as women to carry out some daring deed) recurs; it is a 'roving anecdote'. See Paus. 4.4.12 (Messenians and Spartans); Polyainos 1.30 (Athenians and Megarians); Xen. *Hell.* 5.4.6 (liberation of the Theban Kadmeia in 379, where it is given as one of two variant stories); and Cawkwell 1978: 24 n. sees here a forerunner of the mixed marriages organised by Alexander the Great, at Susa. For the motif of killing guests at a banquet after getting them drunk, cf. 1.106.2, Kyaxares and the Medes do this to a large number of Skythians and so recover their empire; for the parallel see Wesselmann 2011: 269–82, noting that in that much briefer story there are no women and no cross-dressing.

The immediate resonance of σκευάσας in the present passage is with **12.2** above, where the Paionian brothers dressed up, σκευάσαντες, their sister as smartly as they could.

20.4 οἴκατε πανδαισίηι τελείηι ἱστιῆσθαι 'you seem to have had a perfect feast'. οἴκατε is from οἶκα, Ionic for ἔοικα. πανδαισίη is a 'complete banquet at which no one and nothing fails': LSJ. Cf. μᾶζα καῖ πανδαισία, 'cakes and Easy Street', at Ar. *Pax* 565, as translated by Silk 2000: 145 n. 99, who says πανδαισία is 'semi-abstract and has connotations of the fabulous' and comments of the present passage that it 'reads like an ironic allusion to perfection'. The 'exotic' πανδαισίη here may suggest abundance of the sort associated with tyranny (Fearn 2007b: 105 n. 14, for whom Hdt.'s Macedonians are quasi-tyrannical). τελείη may, given the range of meanings in τέλος words (see Powell sense (3), 'death'), add to the ominous ambiguities of this section. ἱστιῆσθαι is passive inf. ('to be feasted) of ἱστιῶ, Attic ἑστιῶ; for the change of vowel see **11.1**n. on the theophoric name Histiaios i.e. Hestiaios.   καὶ πρὸς τὰ οἶά τε ἦν ἐξευρόντας παρέχειν 'and in addition (καὶ πρός) everything (τά = 'the things which') we were able to obtain for you'. As often in this speech, there is irony and ambiguity here, given what the Macedonians really intend to do to their guests.   τάς τε ἑωυτῶν μητέρας καὶ τὰς ἀδελφεὰς ἐπιδαψιλευόμεθα ὑμῖν 'we lavish upon you our own mothers and sisters'. The unique multi-syllabic word here (found nowhere else in Hdt., and here for the first time in any author) underscores the preposterousness of the 'gift' from a Greek (or any other) perspective, as does the unexpected 'mothers' (rather than 'daughters'). The root adjective δαψ-ιλῆς is itself not common in Hdt. (only 2.121 δ 5 and 3.130.5).   τιμώ-μενοι πρὸς ἡμέων τῶν πέρ ἐστε ἄξιοι 'honoured by us as you deserve', lit. 'honoured by us in respect of the things of which you are worthy'. More ambiguity and irony; see Pelling 2008: 549.   ἀνὴρ ῞Ελλην, Μακεδόνων ὕπαρχος: Alexandros means his father, Amyntes. Badian 1994: 114 renders this 'a Greek man, satrap of the Macedonians', as part of his view that Macedonian submission to the Persian king was indeed voluntary and complete; but the whole speech is palpably insincere and ironic, so not usable as evidence for political reality. Nevertheless it is likely that the Macedonians did indeed accept vassal status (Zahrnt 2011: 765). Μακεδών, the reading of some MSS, is defended by Nenci. It is true that this produces a neat chiasmus, but ὕπαρχος is usually followed in Hdt. by a genitive of one sort or another.

20.5 Πέρσηι ἀνδρὶ ἄνδρα Μακεδόνα: the ABBA order neatly allows Hdt. to place man next to (disguised) man.   **ὡς γυναῖκα τῶι λόγωι...διεργάζοντο**: another neat touch: this verb for 'killed', a compound of ἐργ-, answers τῶι λόγωι, deed following word.   **ψαύειν ἐπειρῶντο**: see **18**.5n. on καὶ φιλέειν...

21.2 κατέλαβε σοφίηι 'restrained them by guile' i.e. he made sure they never got to the bottom of the mystery. The verb occurs twice running in this form (and see below for a third occurrence).   **Γυγαίη**: Alexandros has after all avoided making a 'lavish present' of the mothers and sisters of the Macedonians to the drunken Persians, but now he gives his own sister to a Persian after all – surely a gesture of submission. That he and not his father gives her away in marriage is not proof that he was already king, as opposed to acting as his father's agent or emissary: so rightly Badian 1994: 112.

It is possible that the name Gygaia recurs a century later in the Macedonian royal house, as the wife of Amyntas, father of Philip II: Just. *Epit.* 7.4.5, with *LGPN* IV, 83 and Beloch 3². 2.66f. But the name in Justin is the result of a 16th-cent. emendation, surely influenced by Hdt. (the MSS have e.g. 'cignea', 'chigeam', 'ichea'). The name in Hdt. may (Fearn 2007b: 115–16) indicate an 'eastern-looking Macedon' because of the Lydian Lake Gygaia at 1.93.5, for which lake see Robert 1989: 296ff.

21.2 (cont.) δούς δὲ ταῦτα κατέλαβε...στρατηγῶι: the sentence is notable for its dislocated word-order, perhaps enacting the disorientation of the search-party, lit. '[it was by] giving those things [that] he restrained them, Alexandros did, [that is by giving them] to Boubares, a Persian man, [who was] of-the-ones-who-were-inquiring-after-the-lost-men the commander'. More generally, it has been well said that one of the most powerful determinants of word order in Hdt. is 'the desire to achieve variety so far as this is consistent with the principles shared by him with other Greek writers and the stock of models available to him' (Dover 1960: 67–8).   Βουβάρηι: on this point, as on others (notably Alexandros' genealogy), the material at the end of bk. 8 amplifies the present section. There we will learn (8.136.1) that the son of this marriage, who was called Amyntes after his maternal grandfather, was given 'Alabanda in Phrygia, a great city' for its revenues. (The city gifted to this younger Amyntes cannot have been the well-known Alabanda, which is in Karia – 7.195 and *IACP*: no. 870 – and the correct place-name for the gifted place may have been Blaundos: see *Mausolus* 218f. n. 2). Boubares himself was son of Megabazos, Dareios' general in Thrace (but we have to wait until 7.22.2 to be told the filiation), perhaps therefore an Achaemenid (**1.1n.**). If so, he was a good match for a Macedonian princess at this early date (see Badian 1994: 110–11, though some of his Persian prosopography is speculative).   θάνατος οὕτω καταλαμφθεὶς ἐσιγήθη: see LSJ under καταλαμβάνω v.2: '*inquiries about their death being checked...*', the death was kept secret.

22 *The Greekness of the Macedonian kings*

22.1 ἐν τοῖσι ὄπισθε λόγοισι ἀποδέξω ὡς εἰσὶ "Ελληνες: the promise will be kept at 8.139, the genealogy of the Macedonian kings, starting with the Argive Perdikkas I. But the placing of it there has been thought artful and subversive, because it appears 'precisely before Alexandros' most conspicuous act of medism': Badian 1994: 119–20, who thinks a malicious motive explains the splitting up of the story into two widely separated sections.   καὶ οἱ τὸν ἐν Ὀλυμπίηι διέποντες ἀγῶνα Ἑλλήνων 'the people who managed (from διέπω) the Greek contest at Olympia'. That is, the officials known as the Hellano- or (Ionic) Hellenodikai, for whom see below; and some MSS actually read Ἑλληνοδίκαι here instead of Ἑλλήνων. Of the four great panhellenic festivals and contests, the quadrennial Olympian was the most prestigious (see the opening of Pind. *Ol.* 1), sacred to Zeus the king of the gods; see *OCD*[4] 'Olympian games', and Instone 2007, stressing the military origins of many of the events. Olympia was in the territory of Elis in the western Peloponnese, and the festival and contests were organised and supervised by the Eleians, who announced the holding of the games and the Olympic truce (*IACP*: p. 496): see 2.160.4, where the Egyptians say that in that case the Eleians ought not to compete themselves (because of what we would call conflict of interest). The actual rule-enforcers were the Hellenodikai or Hellanodikai, who were Eleian officials. For these 'Greek judges' or 'judges of the Greeks', see Paus. 5.9.5, N. Jones 1987: 142–5 with 152–3 (nn. 1–18), and *IACP*: pp. 496–7; cf. **22.2**n. on φάμενοι . . .

For Hdt.'s frequent mention of Olympic and other prestigious athletic and equestrian victories by prominent individuals, see the list at **47**.1n. (Philippos of Kroton).

22.2 βουλομένου γὰρ Ἀλεξάνδρου ἀεθλεύειν 'when Alexandros wished to compete'. See app. crit. for the alternative reading here, ἑλομένου and a different word-order. In the context 'he wished' makes better sense than 'he chose' (so rightly Wilson).   **καταβάντος ἐπ' αὐτὸ τοῦτο**: the verb here means he 'entered the ring', lit. 'went down'.   **οἱ ἀντιθευσόμενοι Ἑλλήνων** 'those Greeks who were going to run against him'.   **φάμενοι οὐ βαρβάρων . . . ἀλλὰ Ἑλλήνων** 'saying that the competition was not for barbarian competitors [from ἀγωνιστής] but for Greeks'. For the rule about Greekness as a condition for entry, see 2.160.3, where the Eleians tell the Egyptians that the contest at Olympia is open to themselves and to 'any Greek who wishes', though that passage does not explicitly contrast Greeks with other ethnic groups (so rightly Hansen, *IACP*: p. 107 n. 7). The very name 'Hellan- (or Hellen-)odikai' for the judges of the contests (see **22.**1n. on καὶ οἱ τόν . . .) perhaps also implies that one of their functions was to adjudicate about Greekness.   **Ἀλέξανδρος δὲ . . . συνεξέπιπτε τῶι πρώτωι**: the last three Greek words surely mean that he ran a dead heat, i.e. came first equal (there is no great difficulty in understanding e.g. νικήσαντι with τῶι πρώτωι), rather than that he 'was drawn in the same heat as the winner': it would be ridiculous to suppose that Hdt. would provide 'an uninteresting detail about which heat Alexandros ran in, but not say what really mattered, what the result was' (so rightly Roos 1985: 165). Borza 1990: 111–12 is sceptical about the entire tradition; so also Hunt 2010: 82 and n. 61. The main trouble has been felt to be that Alexandros' name does not appear in the Olympic victory lists, by which is really meant Eusebius (text at Christesen 2007: 392). Moretti 1957 excluded Alexandros despite the plain statement of Hdt. The most attractive solution is that the story reflects divided opinion about Alexandros' eligibility (Golden 2008: 146 n. 40). This would mean that someone, not necessarily Hdt. himself, was faced with a clash between an oral (Macedonian or Argive?) tradition that Alexandros won, and another tradition (also oral, but anti-Macedonian?) that he did not. After all, Hdt. makes clear that Alexandros' eligibility was disputed.

In conclusion: Alexandros did compete and he won; but his enemies did not leave the matter there. Note in any case that any decision about Alexandros' own Greekness did not extend to the Macedonians at large. Indeed the kings may have promoted the idea of their Greekness partly so as to elevate themselves above their own Macedonian subjects: Hornblower 2008: 56.

Alexandros surely made his claim to Greekness early in the proceedings. Hdt.'s account implies the sequence: Alexandros expresses a desire to enter – challenge by other Greeks – dispute settled in Alexandros' favour – Alexandros duly competes – Alexandros comes first (equal). Note esp. the order of the vital words ἐκρίθη τε εἶναι Ἕλλην καὶ ἀγωνιζόμενος στάδιον etc. (Roos 1985: 163–4 thinks 'the victory came first and the proclamation of origin after it'. He argues from the analogy of Th. 5.50.4, the announcement that the Boiotian state had won the chariot race in 420 BC. But this was just an announcement that a Greek team had won; there would have been no trouble if the Spartan Lichas had not shattered the deception under which the team had entered.)

Now for the date – assuming the story is true. We do not know, but the usually favoured date of 496 (recently defended by Zahrnt 2011: 766) is on the late side for a running race: Alexandros would then have been about thirty-four years old. (Roos 1985: 167). Perhaps 500 or 504? Hardly as late as 476 (Kertesz 2005).

For the Argive-Macedonian kinship connection, see *Greek World*: 84 and 94, with the 5th-cent. inscribed tripod illustrated at 94 (a prize won at the games to Hera at Argos, but found in a Macedonian royal tomb); also Th. 5.80.2 with *CT* III: 203–4 (Th., speaking of Alexandros' son Perdikkas, echoes Alexandros at Hdt. 9.45.2, αὐτός τε γὰρ Ἕλλην γένος εἰμὶ τὦρχαῖον). See also Hall 2001: 168; Thomas 2001: 219; Fantuzzi in Fantuzzi and Hunter 2004: 394 and n. 140.

23–24 DAREIOS SUMMONS HISTIAIOS

The speeches of Megabazos to Dareios, and of Dareios to Histiaios, at **23–4** are similar in detail and phrasing to the exchange between Dareios and Histiaios at **106**, after the Sardis sack; see nn. on both passages, esp. **106**.3n. on ἢ μέγα ἢ σμικρόν for the possibility that Hdt. is attempting a Greco-Persian idiolect. We are not meant to ask what language they really spoke in, or if they used interpreters. At 6.29.2 Histiaios tells his captor his name and ethnic 'in the Persian tongue'. Speeches become more frequent from now on, as the subject matter becomes more 'historical' (Solmsen 1943: 194). For these chs. see Greenwood 2007.

23.1 ἅτε δὲ τειχέοντος ἤδη Ἱστιαίου 'Histiaios was by now fortifying', lit. 'inasmuch as he was...'; the construction continues, after a long parenthesis, with μαθών: 'when Megabazos discovered what Histiaios was doing...' **ἔτυχε δωρεὴν <ἅτε> μισθόν:** we do not need μισθόν and δωρεήν, so edd. have deleted one or the other. Wilson's <ἅτε> elegantly retains both. **ἐόντος δὲ τοῦ χώρου τούτου παρὰ Στρυμόνα ποταμόν, τῶι οὔνομά ἐστι Μύρκινος** 'this place, whose name is Myrkinos, is by the river Strymon'. Hdt. postpones the detail about the Strymon until now, although we have already been told briefly (**11**.2) that Histiaios asked for 'Myrkinos of the Edonians' as his reward. The topographic amplification prepares us for Megabazos' enumeration of the area's valuable resources (**23**.2). This explains the handling of the Strymon, but not 'whose name is Myrkinos', as if even the place-name were new. Perhaps the clue lies in μαθών: Megabazos 'learned' what was being done by Histiaios, and we are told not only what he learned, but the expository way in which he learned it from his informant ('the place is on the Strymon, and its name is Myrkinos'). This approach is better than assuming (with Macan) that we have here evidence of separate composition dates. For Myrkinos see further **124**.2: Aristagores contemplates it as a refuge.

23.2 κοῖόν τι χρῆμα ἐποίησας 'what a thing to do!' lit. 'what sort of a thing you have done!' One might punctuate with a question mark at the end of the long sentence (after νυκτός), but an exclamation is politer. Megabazos is saying to the king, in effect, 'you are a fool to have done what you did', but he gets away with it, and Dareios takes it very well (**24**.1, where he is 'easily persuaded'). Crossing or correcting his more impulsive son Xerxes was riskier, as we will find in bk. 7. (11.1 etc.); in any case, Megabazos was in high favour with the king (see 4.143.2, where he says he would like as many Megabazoi as there are seeds in a pomegranate), and this helps to explain how he can get away with such plain speaking. Megabazos is right that Histiaios is dangerous, but it is Dareios' acceptance of this advice that will cause the problem. As at Th. 1.23.6, fear produces actions which bring on what is feared.

For the precise expression used here cf. the Macedonian foundation-myth at 8.138.1, where the king is told what the young Perdikkas has so strangely done with his cloak and the sunshine, οἶόν τι χρῆμα ποιήσειε ὁ παῖς. With the exclamatory κοῖον compare the Homerism κοῖον ἐφθέγξαο ἔπος, 'what a word you have uttered!' (**106**.3, Histiaios himself, addressing – again – Dareios). **ἀνδρὶ Ἕλληνι δεινῶι τε καὶ σοφῶι** 'a dangerous and cunning Greek'. Dareios will amusingly adapt Megabazos' description when addressing Histiaios himself (**24**.3, συνετός τε καὶ εὔνοος, 'an intelligent and well-disposed friend'). See Greenwood 2007: 134.

ἵνα ἴδη τε ναυπηγήσιμος 'where there is ship-building timber...' The noun ἴδη gave its name to Mt Ida, for whose timber see Th. 4.52.3 and *CT* II: 213. Cf. Th. 4.108.1, about Amphipolis in the same region as Myrkinos, ξύλων τε ναυπηγησίμων πομπή.   ὅμιλός τε πολλὸς μὲν Ἕλλην περιοικέει, πολλὸς δὲ βάρβαρος: the anaphora (πολλός) is both a possible attempt at characterisation, and also keeps the Greeks and barbarians in perfect balance.   καὶ ἡμέρης καὶ νυκτός: this expression, or variants of it, seem to have struck Greeks as specially appropriate in a Persian context. Cf. the letter of Xerxes at Th. 1.129.3, μήτε νύξ μήθ' ἡμέρα, which Wilamowitz 1902: 27 thought 'a poetic expression, one which carries the stamp of authenticity'; by 'poetic' he was presumably referring to more than the iambic rhythm there. In the present passage, the sing-song redundancy of 'by night and day' adds rhetorical strengthening, like the anaphora above (πολλός ... πολλός). See further **106**.3n. on the comparable ἢ μέγα ἢ σμικρόν.

23.3 ἵνα μὴ οἰκηίωι πολέμωι συνέχηι 'so that you are not entangled with a war near home'. There is a similar expression at Th. 1.118.2: the Spartans were hampered by wars near home, οἰκείοις πολέμοις ἐξειργό-μενοι.   ἐπεὰν δὲ αὐτὸν περιλάβηις 'when you get hold of him'.   ποιέειν ὅκως μηκέτι κεῖνος ἐς Ἕλληνας ἀπίξεται 'make sure he never reaches any Greeks'. At **23**.2 Greeks and barbarians were carefully balanced, but now the emphasis is firmly on the Greeks, who are the eventual narrative target.

24.1 εὐπετέως ἔπειθε: with the easy persuasion, cf. **107** below.   ὡς εὖ προορῶν τὸ μέλλον γίνεσθαι: but this prediction turns out correct only because Megabazos' advice, and Dareios' acceptance of it, ensure its fulfilment.   τοῖσι ἐμοῖσι πρήγμασι: cf. **106**.4.

24.2 ἐπινοέω γὰρ πρήγματα μεγάλα κατεργάσασθαι: Herodotean great deeds are typically accomplished by 'kings, tyrants, heroes, or massive forces of nature': Lightfoot 2003: 405.   ἵνα τοι αὐτὰ ὑπερθέωμαι: the verb is from ὑπερτίθημι, 'communicate'; in the middle, it is specially used where, as here, advice is sought.

24.3 ἐξ ὀφθαλμῶν: cf. **106**.5 for exactly these words, and **106**.1n. on καλέσας ἐς ὄψιν... for the stress on the visual (also **18**.1n.). Of the other two uses of ἐξ ὀφθαλμῶν in Hdt., 1.120.6 is put into the mouths of the Magi advising Astyages to send the boy Kyros away out of his sight to Persia; 3.52.6 (authorial but focalised through the agent) is thematically similar but in a Greek tyrannical context: Periandros sends his son Lykophron away to Kerkyra, out of his sight.

With Dareios' extravagant praise of Histiaios in this section, cf. 4.143, said with apparently greater sincerity about Megabazos himself (the pomegranate story, **23**.2n.).

24.4 Μίλητον μὲν ἔα 'Forget Miletos'.   **ἐς Σοῦσα**: the first mention of Sousa in this bk.; see 1.188 and **49**.7 (Aristagores to Kleomenes) for its wealth. For Sousa, 'city of lilies', see *Barr.* map 93 D1; *OCD*[4]; Harper, Aruz and Tallon 1992. In Hellenistic times it became Seleukeia on the Eulaios, for which city see Fraser 2009: 370. The Greek inscriptions are at *SEG* 7.1–34.   **σύσσιτος ἐὼν καὶ σύμβουλος** 'sharing my table and my confidence'. The idea of 'fellow-diner' is authentically Achaemenid: see *FGrHist* 689 Herakleides (4th-cent. author of a *Persika* or work about Persia) F 2 for the king's σύνδειπνοι. See *Mausolus*: 147. It is the role that Histiaios wanted, but he gets more than he bargained for. Histiaios the clever speaker is allowed to say nothing in reply.

25 APPOINTMENTS OF ARTAPHRENES AND OTANES. OTANES' THRONE MADE FROM HIS FATHER'S SKIN

25.1 Ἀρταφρενέα ἀδελφεὸν ἑωυτοῦ ὁμοπάτριον ὕπαρχον εἶναι Σαρδίων: that is, he made him satrap of Lydia, whose capital was Sardis; but for Otanes' parallel role see below on Ὀτάνην ... ἀνδρῶν. Sardis runs right through the *Histories*. It features in every one of the nine books, starting at 1.7.2 (Kandaules is 'tyrant' of Sardis) and ending with 9.108.1: it was at Sardis that Xerxes fell in love with Masistes' wife. So the burning of Sardis towards the end of bk. 5 (**102**.1) is central both to the *Histories* and to the story of Sardis itself. But for Dareios' administrative arrangements, the important earlier passage is 1.153.3: Sardis is put by Kyros under the command of Tabalos a Persian, but the city's treasury is entrusted (unwisely) to Paktyes, a Lydian. Alexander the Great was surely aware of these precedents for divided commands at Sardis (see Arr. *Anab.* 1.17.7, three co-ordinate appointments). Lydia and Sardis were too wealthy and too dangerous, especially at crisis times, to be placed in a single pair of hands.   **Ὀτάνην δὲ ἀποδέξας στρατηγὸν εἶναι τῶν παραθαλασσίων ἀνδρῶν**: for this Otanes (not the same as the advocate of *isonomie* at 3.80), see further **116** and **123**, where he commands in an early phase of the Ionian revolt. For the 'generalship of the coastal men' (or similar expressions), which, as this passage and others show, could be held alongside the jurisdiction of the territorial satrap at Sardis, cf. Th. 8.5.4, Tissaphernes, with *CT* III: 764–71.   **τῶν βασιληίων δικαστέων**: for these 'royal judges' cf. 3.31.1–2, where Griffiths notes that stories like the present passage and that at 7.194 (in both of which royal judges are horribly punished for injustice) explain why in the bk. 3 passage the judges are so eager to please.   **ἀπέδειρε πᾶσαν τὴν ἀνθρωπηίην** 'he flayed him'. The noun ἀνθρωπηίη here has a special meaning 'human hide' (Powell). This analeptically inserted story indicates, in its horrible way, a concern for rectitude and forensic justice, manifested in deeds and words, on the part of the 'tyrant' Kambyses (Xerxes will also be portrayed in a less than simple way, sometimes behaving tyrannically, sometimes excelling Greeks in magnanimity). 'Good' king Dareios, by contrast, has just resorted to a deception. For morally impeccable sentiments in the mouth of a dubious speaker (note Kambyses' final admonishment), compare 6.86, where we cannot take too seriously the Spartan king Leutychides' parable-lecture about oath-keeping versus perjury, given that the Athenians he is lecturing have not actually sworn to anything at all, and that Leutychides himself will shortly be done for embezzlement (see *TT*: 157f.).

For Persian kings demonstrating their power by mutilations and other types of violence against the body, see Hartog 1988: 332–4 and Munson 2001: 154 and n. 54. For the persistence of flaying as an extreme Persian punishment, and more than a Greek literary commonplace, see Rollinger and Wiesehöfer 2012: 500; also (giving earlier near eastern, esp. Assyrian examples) Rollinger 2010: 593, cf. 605; for an earlier treatment of the topic in English see Rollinger 2004: 141–2 n. 40. Hdt. uses some outré vocabulary to describe this outré procedure: this is a form of 'stylistic enactment', for which notion see *CT* III: 36.

25.1 (cont.) σπαδίξας 'peeled off'. A most unusual verb, found here only in Greek. It may (Stein) be related to σπάδιξ, a bark stripped from the root of the holm-oak; see LSJ σπάδιξ, end of entry. But Stein suggested that the meaning is rather 'tanning' ('gerben'), using oak-root bark, and AHG prefers this.   **ἱμάντας ἐξ αὐτοῦ ἔταμε καὶ ἐνέτεινε τὸν θρόνον ἐς τὸν ἵζων ἐδίκαζε** 'he cut thongs (from ἱμάς, ἱμάντος) from it and *strung* the throne on which he (Sisamnes) used to sit and give judgment'.

25.2 ἐντανύσας δὲ ὁ Καμβύσης… 'So, after *stringing* it, Kambyses…'. ἐντανύσας is from ἐντανύω, a poetic and Ionic variant for ἐντείνω just before, which is the usual word for stringing or bending or drawing a bow, i.e. he stretched the strips of skin tightly as if drawing a bow.

26–27 CONQUESTS OF OTANES IN PROPONTIC THRACE, THE TROAD AND THE ISLANDS OF THE NE AEGEAN

26.1 Βυζαντίους τε εἷλε καὶ Καλχηδονίους: the picturesque double story of the foundations of Byzantion and Kalchedon, both Megarian colonies, was given fairly recently, at 4.144. They are *IACP*: nos. 674 (Byzantion) and 743 (Kalchedon).   **εἷλε δὲ Ἄντανδρον…, εἷλε δὲ Λαμπώνιον:** for Antandros, see *IACP*: no. 767 and *CT* III: 1051 (suggesting that Th.'s statement that the Antandrians 'are Aiolians' may be silent correction of Hdt. 7.42, who had said that Antandros was Pelasgian). The name of Lamponion, also in the Troad (*IACP*: no. 783, 'Lamponeia'), is variously given in the ancient sources. It too was Aiolian (Strabo 13.1.58). The systematic rapidity of the campaign is enacted by the repeated εἷλε. **εἷλε Λῆμνόν τε καὶ Ἴμβρον, ἀμφοτέρας ἔτι τότε ὑπὸ Πελασγῶν οἰκεομένας**: the island of Imbros is mod. Imroz, part of Turkey. Lemnos (mod. Limnos, part of Greece) was an island with two *poleis*, Myrina and Hephaestia. In the classical period the two islands were Athenian dependencies, and are often bracketed together, as at Th. 7.57.2, on which see *CT* III: 661. See *IACP*: no. 483 (Imbros), pp. 756–7, 'LEMNOS', and nos. 502 and 503 (the Lemnian *poleis*).

Pelasgians were a mysterious people, thought of by the Greeks themselves as pre-Greeks; see *OCD*[4] 'Pelasgians' and Fowler 2003b. Hdt.'s mention here of Pelasgians on Lemnos both looks back to 4.145.2 (descendants of the Argonauts driven out of Lemnos by Pelasgians) and also prepares us for the sinister story of Miltiades, his capture of Lemnos, and the 'Lemnian deeds' at 6.137ff. For Pelasgians on Lemnos see also Th. 4.109.4 (with *CT* II: 348): the inhabitants of the Akte (Athos) peninsula in the Chalkidike include 'Pelasgians descended from the Etruscans who once inhabited Lemnos and Athens'.

27.1 οἱ Πέρσαι ὕπαρχον ἐπιστᾶσι Λυκάρητον τὸν Μαιανδρίου τοῦ βασιλεύσαντος Σάμου ἀδελφέον: a back-ref. to 3.143.2, where Lykaretos is mentioned in the course of the Maiandrios narrative.

27.2 οὗτος ὁ Λυκάρητος ἄρχων ἐν Λήμνωι τελευτᾶι … αἰτίη δὲ τούτου ἥδε: this has seemed to many editors to be inconsequential or even meaningless as it stands, and a lacuna after τελευτᾶι has often and probably rightly been suspected.   **πάντας ἠνδραποδίζετο καὶ κατεστρέφετο**: there may be an allusion to these sufferings of the Lemnians, at the harsh hands of Otanes, in Aesch. *Cho.* 635–6. See Garvie 1986: 219.   **τοὺς μὲν λιποστρατίης**: this word for military desertion is found here only in Hdt., but see Th. 6.76.3 with *CT* III: 479. The refs. in this section of Hdt. are to the bk. 4 narrative, e.g. 4.142.   **τοὺς δὲ σίνεσθαι** 'others of inflicting casualties on …' αἰτιῶμαι, 'I accuse', can take either a genitive or an infinitive. Hdt. varies the construction by using both.   **ἀποκομιζόμενον** 'returning'.

28–38.1 ORIGINS OF THE IONIAN REVOLT

The causes of the Ionian revolt are discussed in the Introduction, §2.

28 μετὰ δὲ οὐ πολλὸν χρόνον ἀνανέωσις κακῶν ἦν, καὶ ἤρχετο τὸ δεύτερον ἐκ Νάξου τε καὶ Μιλήτου Ἴωσι γίνεσθαι κακά 'after a short time there was a renewal of troubles, and for the second time troubles began to arise for the Ionians from Naxos and Miletos'. This is an emended text, containing one of the two most historically important textual difficulties in bk. 5 (see **48** for the other). To sum up the following discussion, ἀνανέωσις κακῶν is better than any alternative, but it is not certain.   **ἀνανέωσις κακῶν:** the problem centres on the MSS' ἄνεος or ἄνεως, which make no sense.

(1) The preferable line of emendation in modern times assumes that the MS readings conceal some νέος-based word for 'renewal', e.g. ἀνανέωσις (as much of a Herodotean hapax as ἄνεσις would be, but an obvious formation). The second and third parts of the sentence now say ' . . . there was a resumption of misfortunes, and it was from Naxos and Miletos that misfortunes began again for the Ionians' (so Munson 2007: 150 and n. 23). That is, καί is now explanatory, and introduces a development of a simple thought.

(2) But AHG improves on the main idea of this by suggesting that εως conceals an original Ἴωσι, and offers νέα Ἴωσι κακὰ ἦν (for the combination νέα . . . κακά see Soph. *OC* 1448–9): 'But not long after there were fresh troubles for the Ionians, and for a second time it was from Naxos and Miletos that troubles came to the Ionians'. For the repetition cf. 6.42.1, and for amplification after μετὰ οὐ πολλὸν χρόνον cf. 7.15.2. One improvement thus effected is, by the early introduction of the Ionians, the achievement of a much less abrupt and bewildering transition from the opening words, which were about Otanes' generalship.

(3) A commonly favoured, but here rejected, emendation is ἄνεσις κακῶν (it goes back to Scaliger in the 16th cent., see Powell 1938b: 58). The noun ἄνεσις hardly occurs anywhere, but is supposed to mean 'remission, abatement', a metaphorical extension of the literal meaning 'loosening, relaxing' (of strings etc.). If that is right, μετά must be taken adverbially, so that μετὰ οὐ πολλὸν χρόνον is taken to mean 'afterwards, for a short time' (Stein, Legrand and Maas); or else καί has adversative force, as apparently in Waterfield's rendering 'there was a brief respite, but troubles . . . '. But both of these result in awkward Greek, and the sense required for ἄνεσις is difficult. This supposed respite, a matter of historical and chronological importance, is built entirely on the emendation.

(4) A final possibility is kept for the end of this discussion. If we look at the balance of this sentence from μετά to κακά, and compare it with the more obviously balanced and longer sentence which immediately follows (Naxos the most prosperous of the *islands*, then Miletos the jewel of *Ionia*, here used in the sense of the mainland), we need to reproduce the same balance in the earlier and shorter sentence. It is possible that ανεοσ might conceal e.g. ἀνὰ τὰς νήσους (ἀνὰ νήσους would be closer to the MSS, but

the article is better). The sense we should be looking for is e.g. 'there was [something bad] throughout the *islands*; and trouble began for the *Ionians* out of Naxos and Miletos for the second time'. It may be objected that Naxos is an island and yet features in the second and mainland half of the sentence. But it does so only as one of the places from which the trouble for the mainland originated.

28 (cont.) ἤρχετο τὸ δεύτερον ... γίνεσθαι κακά 'so for the second time the troubles began' This is the first appearance of the important ἀρχὴ κακῶν theme, cf. **30**.1 and above all **97**.3, the twenty Athenians ships sent to help the Ionians. The model is Homeric, see *Il.* 5.63 (the ἀρχέκακοι ships which stole Helen) and 11.604 (about Patroklos, κακοῦ δ᾽ ἄρα οἱ πέλεν ἀρχή); cf. also Th. 2.12.3 with *CT* I, 250, citing Ar. *Pax* 435–6. The ambiguity of ἀρχή (beginning/empire) has often been noted.

The words raise a difficulty affecting the entire *Histories*. Even with the addition here of τὸ δεύτερον (for which see below), the repeated insistence on the 499 revolt as an ἀρχὴ κακῶν implies that the 'trouble' which will culminate in the Persian Wars started or at any rate became serious only now; but the message of the first four books has been the relentless and inevitable expansion of Persian power, and the logic of that expansion indicated that mainland Greece and the Aegean islands were next in line. Hdt. does not here mean to deny any of this; he is saying that from now on the chain of troubles becomes linear and sustained. This will be treated in the Introduction to bk. 6 (Pelling). τὸ δεύτερον, 'for the second time', refers by implication to an earlier occasion. This was the Persian subjugation of Ionia in 546, narrated in bk. 1. Cf. 6.32: 'so for the third time the Ionians were enslaved, first by the Lydians, then twice in succession by the Persians'. This is consistent with 1.169, where the original Persian conquest of Ionia was said to be the second enslavement. But Hdt. regards the *second* enslavement as the *first* set of troubles, i.e. for this purpose the Lydian conquest is ignored, perhaps because it was not part of the direct causal chain which led *via* Marathon in 490 to the Persian wars of 480/79. At the otherwise resumptive **30**.1, τὸ δεύτερον is not repeated.

But in the present passage Hdt. is not implying that Naxos or even Miletos were prominent in the coercion of Ionia in 546: they were not. The Naxians do not feature in bk. 1 at all (except incidentally at 64.1, part of the story of Peisistratos) and the Milesians are twice said to have stayed neutral because of their special treaty with Kyros (143.1 and 169.2). In the present passage, Naxos and Miletos are singled out because they provide the link to the Ionian revolt narrative proper. The point is 'so for the second time trouble afflicted the Ionians, and it all started at Naxos and Miletos'. Naxos and Miletos are balanced and opposed as island and mainland Ionian places, but this is not just schematic and literary: their historical fates will become intertwined at **30**.1, when the 'fat cats' of Naxos flee to Miletos.

28 (cont.) εὐδαιμονίηι τῶν νήσων προέφερε: splendid dedications at Delos and Delphi, and marble quarries on the island itself, are an index of this archaic Naxian prosperity: see *IACP* no. 507 at p. 763 (G. Reger) and Constantakopoulou 2007: 44–6; also Stewart 1991: 19–42, esp. 25 for the two giant statues on the island, never scooped out, but left in their quarries and still *in situ* today.   **αὐτή τε ἑωυτῆς μάλιστα δὴ ... ἀκμάσασα**: with this description of Miletos as 'exceptionally (lit. 'more than itself', cf. 1.203.1) flourishing' cf. 6.127.1 (Sybaris ἤκμαζε τοῦτον τὸν χρόνον). The echo is significant as indicating an awareness that east and west Mediterranean events are connected, and because these two great cities illustrate the opening statement (1.5.4) about the precariousness of the greatness of cities; see Hornblower 2007a: 175f. and *Th. and Pi.* 306 n. 55; cf. below, introd. n. to **39–48** for the Dorieus affair (in which the Sybaris-Kroton war features) as integrated into the Ionian revolt narrative, not a digression. The comment on Milesian prosperity is ominous (Lateiner 1982); the passage is relevant to the question of the causes of the revolt. The prosperity of Miletos was due to its role as agricultural producer (it had an extensive territory, see 6.20) and port of trade, rather than to manufacture. So rightly Greaves 2002: 97.   **κατύπερθε δὲ τούτων ἐπὶ δύο γενεάς**: the story of the Parian 'adjusters' runs from here to the first words of **30**.1, which end the excursus in words close to those which began **28**. Its inclusion puzzled Macan: 'a good story which has no obvious bearing on the situation'. It explains how the Milesians became prosperous, and the account of their earlier *stasis* works as a foil to this. The partial model is from bk. 1, mirrored as so often by bk. 5. The 'two generations' are probably intended to take us back to before the Persian conquest of 546, but not much before; see Greaves 2002: 92; but Gorman 2001: 120 wants to push the *stasis* back to the 7th or even 8th cent.   **νοσήσασα ἐς τὰ μάλιστα στάσι** 'suffered [lit. 'was sick'] particularly from *stasis* (Attic dative would be στάσει), to the most extreme extent of her history'. The chiastic word order (ABBA) is emphasised by an internal rhyme: μάλιστα δὴ ... ἀκμάσασα ... νοσήσασα ἐς τὰ μάλιστα. The force of αὐτή τε ἑωυτῆς (above) may be carried over from that first μάλιστα to this second one, i.e. Hdt. is not just saying 'particularly' but also 'to the most extreme extent [etc.]'; the Greek is ambiguous, so the above tr. has it both ways. Compare 1.65.2, where the shift of the early Spartans from bad to good is also signalled by a verbal similarity: from being κακονομώτατοι they changed to εὐνομίη as follows (introducing the story of Lykourgos).

The medical way of looking at politics is natural and old, at least as old as Solon F 4.17 West, 'an unavoidable wound comes to the whole city' (followed by *stasis* at line 19). See Th. 6.14, Nikias' appeal to the Athenian *prytanis* to act like a good Hippokratic doctor and 'help or at least do no harm' (with Brock 2000 and 2004: 169, and other ancient and modern material cited at *CT* III: 337).

Hdt. says no more about the nature of the *stasis*, or about the factions involved, and attempts have been made to supplement or explicate him from other literary sources. Plutarch, *Quaest. Graec.* 32 (= *Mor.* 298c) asks 'who are the perpetual sailors, ἀειναῦται, among the Milesians?' and answers himself with a narrative. 'After the tyrants Thoas and Damasenor were overthrown, τῶν περὶ Θόαντα καὶ Δαμασήνορα τυράννων [or better, despite Gorman 2001: 118, τυράννους] καταλυθέντων, two factions (ἑταιρεῖαι) held the city, called Ploutis and Cheiromacha. The powerful men (δυνατοί) prevailed...' and after that they instituted a strange system of decision-making, involving putting out to sea on ships and ratifying their decisions there before sailing back to land; hence the name 'perpetual sailors'. See *IACP* no. 854 at p. 1084: 'it is widely assumed that Thrasyboulos' reign [for Thrasyboulos, see below **92 ζ 1**n.] was followed by the rule of...' Thoas and Damasenor, and that Plutarch's *stasis* and Hdt.'s are identical; see however below for the second point.

Athenaios 524a quotes Herakleides Pontikos (fr. 50 in Wehrli 1969) for a different story, according to which the propertied class (οἱ τὰς οὐσίας ἔχοντες) were engaged in strife with the popular party (οἱ δημοταί), who were called the Gergithes. (These Gergithes are different from the Gergithes from Gergis in the Troad (**122.2**n.). Halliday (1928: 146) thought that in both areas they were a native element in the population, and that at Miletos they formed some sort of Karian under-class. This is rightly rejected by Gorman 2001: 107; there is no evidence for such an under-class at Miletos, and the Karian indigenes were called Leleges.)

Hdt. hints at none of these class or ethnic (?) tensions, and it is possible that his *stasis* is not identical with those described by either Herakleides or Plutarch (whose source in *Quaest. Graec.* is often one of the lost *polis* 'Constitutions' of Aristotle), neither of whom, for their part, show knowledge that they are talking about the same events as those in Hdt. The modern tendency is to run the three sources together as evidence for a single 6th-cent. episode (Halliday 1928: 145–6, Wehrli 1969: 76, *IACP* as above, and even Gorman 2001: 120, though see previous n. for her early dating). But we know very little about archaic Greek history, and it is incautious to think we can bring all our few scattered pieces of evidence into close relation with each other.

28 (cont.) κατήρτισαν ... καταρτιστῆρας: the root meaning is 'adjusting', or 'restoring'. This Parian activity resembles, but is not quite the same as, arbitration or the use of foreign judges, for which cf. **95** below (Periandros of Korinth) and 6.108 (the Korinthians generally), where the verb is καταλάσσω both times. The noun καταρτιστήρ was used at 4.161.2 about Demonax of Arkadian Mantineia, the 'adjuster' of *stasis*-affected Kyrene; but Hdt. was there surely reproducing the poetic and hexametric reply of the oracle at Delphi, ἐκ Μαντινέης... καταρτιστῆρ(α) ἀγαγέσθαι. The vocabulary of the present passage may be influenced by bk. 4, especially since the Parians were supposedly colonised from Arkadia (*IACP* no. 509 at p. 764, citing Herakleides Lembos fr. 25, from Aristotle's *Constitution of the Parians*); but it may also continue the medical language of νοσήσασα just above. Hdt. amusingly makes Histiaios use the word about Miletos at **106**.5 below, where he undertakes to 'sort everything out' there. See Pelling 2007: 181 n. 7.   **ἐκ πάντων Ἑλλήνων εἵλοντο**: emphatic, as if to underline the honour thus paid to the Parians. (In Hdt. the Korinthians are commonly found as arbitrators; in the classical period this role was often performed by the Argives, and in the Hellenistic period the Rhodians were popular as 'foreign judges'; see **95**.2n.) For Parians as arbitrators at an even earlier date see Plut. *Quaest. Graec.* no. 30 (= *Mor.* 298 a-b), dispute between Chalkidians and Andrians over Akanthos, early 7th cent., cf. *IACP* p. 765. The Parian judges favoured the Chalkidians, but the Samians and Erythraians favoured the Andrians. The story of this Parian 'adjustment' has some credibility. It has been doubted as a mere political parable, inserted to illustrate the merits of oligarchy; it is that too, but that does not necessarily make it a floating story.

29.1 δεινῶς οἰκοφθορημένους 'economically ruined'.   **τὴν Μιλησίην** 'Milesian territory', as at 1.17.2 and Th. 8.24.1.   **< ἐν > ἀνεστηκυίηι τῆι χώρηι** 'in the devastated territory'.   **τοῦ δεσποτέω τοῦ ἀγροῦ**: this phrase ('master of the field') may suggest slave labour (Macan).

29.2 καὶ τῶν δημοσίων...ὥσπερ τῶν σφετέρων: for the idea that the man who looks after his own property will also be the best guardian of the interests of the state, lit. 'public things', cf. Nikias at Th. 6.9.2, who speaks of the likely civic excellence of the man who looks after his own property and person. For the present passage as the first example of the image 'state as household' see Brock 2004: 169–70.

30.1 Πάριοι μέν νυν Μιλησίους οὕτω κατήρτισαν· τότε δὲ ἐκ τουτέων τῶν πολίων ὧδε ἤρχετο κακὰ γίνεσθαι τῆι Ἰωνίηι: for the resumptive language (but here with the omission of τὸ δεύτερον) see on **28.1**. If we had only this sentence, it would be natural to assume that the *poleis* are the just-mentioned Miletos and Paros (the latter of which is another one-*polis* island, like Naxos). But (i) the verbal correspondence with **28.1** makes clear that the ref. must be to Miletos and *Naxos* and that τουτέων τῶν πολίων means '*those* afore-mentioned cities'; as does (ii) the continuation (emphatic asyndeton, no particle) ἐκ Νάξου ἔφυγον... **ἔφυγον ἄνδρες τῶν παχέων ὑπὸ τοῦ δήμου**: the παχέες are, as we would say, 'the fat cats'. Compare **77**.2n. (Chalkis, where the category is identified with the *hippobotai*); 6.91.1 (Aigina), and 7.156.2 (Syracuse). Cf. also Ar. *Vesp.* 288 and *Pax* 639. Murray 1988: 475 plausibly remarks that the recent Athenian example (i.e. the changes introduced by Kleisthenes) 'prompted the reforms on Naxos', though 'upheavals' or *stasis* might be better descriptions than 'reforms'.

These Naxian exiles have been seen as exemplifying a story pattern by which exiled or alienated Greek groups or individuals 'induce Persian incursions against fellow citizens' (Boedeker 1987: 191–2; she lists half a dozen other such cases). But this is more than a mere story pattern. It was a standard move in times of *stasis*, as inscriptions and Th. confirm. See ML 40 line 27 for an out-group at Ionian Erythrai 'fleeing to the Mede', and Th. 1.115.4 for mobilisation of Persian forces by such an Ionian out-group.

30.2 Ἀρισταγόρης ὁ Μολπαγόρεω 'Aristagores the son of Molpagores'. The name is too common everywhere to bear any weight of inference, though the suffix –gores is (as we shall see) a feature of these Milesian names. And note the Hellenistic historian Aristagoras, probably of Miletos, *FGrHist* 608, with Fornara's 1994 comm., *FGrHist* C fasc. 1.

The patronym Molpagores is more informative (Tozzi 1978: 97 and 138): it occurs in the great series of inscriptions from the Delphinion (temple of Apollo) listing the annual *stephanephoroi* or eponymous magistrates of the city of Miletos (Rehm 1914: nos. 122–8). They are called *stephanephoroi* ('crown-wearers') by modern scholars for convenience; actually the first six lists, covering the archaic to Hellenistic periods, are headed 'these of the Molpoi acted as *aisymnetes*', οἵδε μολπῶν αἰσύμνησαν, and then no. 128, which starts in AD 21, calls them '*stephanephoroi* who were also *aisymnetai*'. But they were all *stephanephoroi*. Note that the datings in Rehm 1914 are now thought to be 'out' (too high) by three years for the period up to 406/5 BC, after which they are out by two years until 394, and thereafter out by one year. See Rhodes 2006. In what follows, adjustment has been made.

For the sacred officials called the Molpoi of Miletos see Herda 2006 with Parker 2008: 178, who notes that they are remarkable as 'a perhaps unique case of a religious grouping that also exercised real political power'. The name Molpoi means roughly 'Singers' and derives from μολπή, 'dance or rhythmic movement with song' (LSJ). Sons of a Molpagores held the office of *stephanephoros* in 495/4 and again in 489/8 (they are called Daphnis – an Apolline name, see Graf 1979 and Philippe 2005 – and Leanax respectively); a Molpagores son of Mandragores is *stephanephoros* himself in 484/3, another Molpagores (son of Hekatonymos) in 441/0, and a Phyleos son of Molpagores three years later, 438/7. It is tempting to speculate prosopographically about the possible relationships of these epigraphically attested people to each other, or to the individuals named in Hdt., but there can be no certainties.

Names in –agores (from ἀγορεύω, I speak) are common everywhere, but seem specially so at Miletos. Oligarchs do as much speaking as democrats, so there is no special left-wing connotation (see below, and note Peithagores the monarchical ruler of Sicilian Selinous at **46**.2). In addition to the present two and Lysagores just below, see **37**.1 (Ietragores) and **126**.1 (Pythagores), with nn.: Ietragores and Pythagores both have Apolline flavours, as does Molpagores.

The position of *stephanephoros* was evidently a liturgy, i.e. a semi-voluntary form of taxation of the rich. So these men belong to the Milesian elite. The name Molpagores/oras is virtually unattested in the Greek world except at Miletos itself; at Milesian colonies (Sinope, Kyzikos, Pantikapaion and neighbours, Olbia, and the Kian at Polyb. 15.21.1); and at Hellenistic Amorgos (in the eastern Kyklades) where we know Milesians settled: a remarkable example of *polis*-specific name-diffusion. See also Jones 1988: 194 (Sinope).

30.2 (cont.) γαμβρός τε ἐὼν καὶ ἀνεψιός: Aristagores the ἐπίτροπος (vicegerent or acting governor) of Miletos is both son-in-law and first cousin of Histiaios, who seems to have appointed him. At any rate, in his slippery speech at **106**, Histiaios uses the word three times about Aristagores, twice calling him '*my* deputy', ὁ ἐμὸς ἐπίτροπος, admittedly in a context where he needs to stress his control over his wayward deputy so as to convince Dareios that he will sort everything out, πάντα καταρτίσω (see **28**n. for this word). This was a close family. At **99**.2 below, we will learn that Aristagores has a brother Charopinos, whom he appoints to co-lead the army against Sardis.   **Ἱστιαίου τοῦ Λυσαγόρεω**: Histiaios' patronym is revealed only now, although the man himself has featured several times already, including in bk. 4; contrast the ancient scholarly expectation that a standard Homeric first introduction would include a man's patronymic (Nünlist 2009: 52). Hdt.'s aim is partly to balance 'Aristagores son of Molpagores', partly to stress the interconnectedness of this family, and partly to add solemnity to the opening of the Ionian revolt narrative proper.

The name Lysagores is not uncommon (plenty on Thasos in particular, and see 6.133.1 for a man from Thasos' mother-city Paros). It is borne by only one other Milesian, who features as *stephanephoros* in 401/0. But there are some more in Milesian colonies (Sinope; Kyzikos).

30.3 ἀπικόμενοι δὲ οἱ Νάξιοι ἐς τὴν Μίλητον: a standard move in Greek *stasis* or factional strife: the exiled party appeals to an outside power to reinstate it. Compare the start of the Peloponnesian War, Th. 2.2.1: a Plataian faction invites in the Thebans. Thus both the Ionian revolt and the main Peloponnesian war begin with an act of *stasis*, though on neither occasion is the actual word used; see also Th. 6.19.1 for exiles at Leontini (i.e. *stasis* there) as a cause of the Sicilian Expedition of 415 (for detailed examination of the parallels between Hdt. on the Ionian revolt and Th. on the Sicilian expedition, see Kallet 2001: 87–94). See further **104**.3n. (the Cypriot Gorgos 'flees to the Medes'). ὁ δὲ ἐπιλεξάμενος ὡς 'he, considering/reflecting that...' σκῆψιν δὲ ποιεύμενος τὴν ξεινίην τὴν Ἱστιαίου: that is, using Histiaios' guest-friendship with the Naxians as a pretext; a good example of Hdt.'s ability to distinguish between true cause and pretext – which is not to say that the pretext need have been false or insincere (cf. **102**.1n.): such guest-friendships were serious currency. For abstract nouns in – σις cf. 6.25.2., ἔκλειψιν.

30.4 Αὐτὸς μὲν ὑμῖν οὐ φερέγγυος 'I am not capable of...', 'I cannot undertake to'. The final word is a solemn one, found only here and at 7.49.2 (Artabanos); at Th. 8.68.3 (in the superlative, and his only use of the word) it is even heavier; and see Aesch. *Eum.* 87. It is derived from ἐγγύη, and means literally 'giving surety/guarantees'. Here it is pompous talk, designed to impress with its weightiness. πλοῖα μακρὰ πολλά: this must mean warships (unusually, cf. LSJ). Cf. 2.102.2. That Naxos had a strong naval tradition is true, but it is hard to believe in the 'eight thousand shield' i.e. soldiers. μηχανήσομαι: it is entirely appropriate that this word for cunning devising should be put into the mouth of the tricksy Aristagores; see Th. 5.45.2 (with *CT* III: 105–7) on another wily operator, Alkibiades. See further **37**.1, **62**.2, **70**.1, and **106**.5.

30.6 ὡς αὐτοὶ διαλύσοντες 'which they themselves would pay'.

31.1 μεγάθεϊ μὲν οὐ μεγάλη ... καὶ ἀγχοῦ Ἰωνίης: neither statement is strictly true: Naxos is not small (it is the largest of the Kyklades), and is not very close to mainland Ionia. See further **31**.3n. χρήματα δὲ ἔνι πολλά: see on Σύ ... below for ἔνι. καὶ ἀνδράποδα: these 'slaves' (the word is used as an inducement by Aristagores again at **49**.4, addressing Kleomenes) are ambiguous as between people who are already slaves, and those who will become so after a Persian takeover. Σὺ ὦν: note the seamless transition from indirect speech in **31**.1 (λέγει ... ὡς Νάξος εἴη) to direct. It is smoothed by ἔνι, 'there is in it' (not ἐνείη) just above.

31.2 πάρεξ τῶν ἀναισιμωμάτων 'except for the expenses'. Cf. the compound verb προσαναισίμωτο at **34**.3. ἡμέας τοὺς ἄγοντας: neatly ambiguous: the participle could just mean 'we who are guiding/conducting you to your objective' or 'we who are in command' (ἄγω as in στρατηγός, 'leader-of-army'). The ambiguity will be relevant to Aristagoras' speech which so angers Megabates (**33**.4).

31.3 εὐπετέως: this word for 'easily', like ῥαδίως in Th., is often ironically self-cancelling. For 'it will be easy' as an ironic indicator that things will be anything but that, see *CT* 1 : 241; also Rood 1998: 34 n. 30, giving Herodotean as well as Thucydidean examples, and noting that 'only gods do things with ease', and citing e.g. Homer *Il.* 15.361–6. (But not all Homeric gods, cf. the exertions of Hephaistos the blacksmith; West 2011a: 350.) Cf. also **49**.4 and **49**.8 with Solmsen 1943: 199, who remarks 'in fact "easy" is the keyword of the speeches' i.e. those of Aristagoras in this section.   **οὐκ ἐλάσσονι Κύπρου:** not for the first time in this speech, Aristagoras' geography is – perhaps by deliberate choice on Hdt.'s part – astray. Cyprus is not far short of three times the size of Euboia (9,251 as opp. 3,657 km²). Admittedly, ancient Greek sailors would have had a better notion of total length than of area, and here the difference is less (225 as opp. 180 km.).

31.4 διηκόσιαι: compare the two hundred triremes offered by Gelon at 7.158.4, with Fehling 1989: 230 (who thinks such powers of ten are specially associated with autocrats, perhaps because such people are prone to expansiveness and exaggeration).   **δεῖ δὲ τούτοισι καὶ αὐτὸν βασιλέα συνέπαινον γίνεσθαι:** the mild συνέπαινος, 'agreeable', raises the question of the limits of satrapal initiative. On this occasion, Artaphrenes does indeed consult the King, who agrees to the plan. Cf. Diod. 15.41.5 (from Ephoros) 'Persian generals, not being plenipotentiaries, refer to the King about everything, and await his replies'. But sometimes, in the best-documented periods (the Peloponnesian War and the 4th cent.), satraps seem to enjoy extensive latitude of independent decision-making, though it may occasionally have been convenient for them to allege a need for royal approval. See *Mausolus*: 152–3.

32 περιχαρής: this word for 'overjoyed' is sinister (Chiasson 1983: esp. 115). It usually conveys a warning: the joy tends to be short-lived, misplaced or premature.   **Μεγαβάτην ἄνδρα Πέρσην τῶν Ἀχαιμενιδέων, ἑωυτοῦ τε καὶ Δαρείου ἀνεψιόν:** Megabates is closely related to the other Persian principals in the affair, just as his antagonist Aristagoras is closely related to the other Greek principal, Histiaios. He may, though Hdt. never says so, be the father of Megabazos the admiral mentioned at 7.97 (Burn 1962: 335. This man is not identical with the Megabazos of **1**.1 above). The build-up of Megabates is lengthy and impressive; here – contrast **30**.2n. on Histiaios – Hdt. follows the lead of Homer, who gives extensive introductions to important characters (Nünlist 2009: 56). Megabates' high status (for

Achaimenes as supposed founder of the dynasty see 3.75 1 and 7.11.2) is important as background to what follows: Aristagores was picking a dangerous quarrel. 'Megabates [Bakabada] the admiral' is attested at Persepolis late in the reign of Dareios: Lewis 1985: 115 [= 1997: 358–9], citing *PT* 8, cf. Murray 1988: 473. This is interesting as showing that his behaviour now (outrageous, as Hdt. describes it) did not bring a stop to his career.   τοῦ Παυσανίης...ὑστέρωι χρόνωι τούτων ἡρμόσατο θυγατέρα: this and the connected statement – below – that Pausanias the Spartan regent wanted to be tyrant over the Greeks (startling if we have not read Th. – see esp. 1.95.3 – but assumed here as a matter of general knowledge), form an external *prolepsis*. That is, they refer forwards to events outside Hdt.'s own narrative, and – more important – to a different Pausanias from the young Greek patriot who will dominate bk. 9 and who at virtually his last important appearance will comment incredulously on Persian luxury (9.82.3). The Pausanias of the present passage is, so to speak, Th.'s Pausanias, who has become an object of suspicion to his fellow-countrymen (not only Spartans but other Greeks) and who looks to Persia instead. It is not quite Hdt.'s first mention of Pausanias before bk. 9 (see 4.81.3 for an obviously impressive but neutrally and casually mentioned bronze bowl which he dedicated at the mouth of the Black Sea), nor will it be the last: at 8.3.2, in another and equally significant external prolepsis because it anticipates the Athenian empire, we will be told that the Athenians seized the hegemony using Pausanias' ὕβρις (deliberately violent and insulting behaviour, cf. Th. 1.95.1) as an excuse. The three prolepses thus form a progression; the first merely arouses our curiosity and is there only because Pausanias' bowl is six times smaller than the wondrous Skythian bowl made of arrowheads, but the second and third disclose how Pausanias' glory, still untarnished at the end of Hdt.'s *Histories* proper, will turn to disgrace outside their main time-frame. On Hdt.'s ambivalent presentation of Pausanias, see Munson 2001: 68–70.

The positioning just here of the story of Megabates' daughter is neat and natural enough (part of the biographical introduction of Megabates) but has an extra point: Megabates and Aristagores are signifiers for a clash of cultures, but by and after the end of the *Histories* the opposition between Greeks and Persians will seem less straightforward. Lewis 1977: 148 remarked that 'it seems to me to be a theme of the History that the Persians gradually discover what the Spartans are like'; see also Pelling 2013.

32 (cont.) ἡρμόσατο θυγατέρα: Th. 1.128.9 says that Pausanias *proposed* marriage to the daughter (not of Megabates but) of Xerxes, an even grander match; but though Th. surely had Hdt. in mind at that point, he is not necessarily in outright contradiction of Hdt. because the verb ἁρμόζομαι indicates a definite *betrothal*. See LSJ ἁρμόζω I. 2. Med. 'betroth to one-self, take to wife'. Those might seem to us different things, and at Hdt. 3.137.5 and 5.47.1 the context makes it clear that events might indeed intervene to prevent a betrothal developing into a full marriage; but in Greek states (including Pausanias' native Sparta, and also – we are meant to assume – Persia) a betrothal, more usually ἐγγύη, was a formal contract between father and groom, and a necessary first element of marriage; see 6.130.1 and *OCD*⁴, 'marriage law, Greek' and 'betrothal, Greek'. Note however that Hdt. expresses himself cautiously: he is not sure the story is true.   ἔρωτα σχὼν τῆς Ἑλλάδος τύραννος γενέσθαι: this is the position that Demaretos the Spartan wanted (6.70), so that Pausanias 'allows him-self to be pushed down the very path that his victory [sc. at Plataia in 479] had closed off for Demaretos'. So Burkert 2001b: 104.   The erotic lan-guage is here applied to Pausanias' desire for power rather than for the young woman. (For Pausanias' same-sex relationship with 'the Argilian', see Th. 1.132.5.)

33.1 τὴν Ἰάδα στρατίην 'the Ionian army'. For Ἰάς as the fem. adj. 'Ionian', cf. e.g. 1.92.3 and Th. 4.61.2, τῆι Ἰάδι ξυγγενείαι. For the masc. adj., the 'ktetic' form Ἰωνικός does duty; the Ionian κοινόν or league (**109**.3) did not give rise to an ethnic, see Fraser 2009: 139.   **ἐς Καύκασα**: perhaps at Volissos on the SE of Chios: *IACP* p. 1060 and *Barr.* map 56c, following Chamoux 1980.

33.2 καὶ οὐ γὰρ ἔδεε τούτωι τῶι στόλωι Ναξίους ἀπολέσθαι: for positively expressed authorial foreknowledge and acknowledgment of the role of fate, compare 1.8.2, χρῆν γὰρ Κανδαύληι γένεσθαι κακῶς, 4.79.1, ἐπείτε δὲ ἔδεε οἱ [i.e. to Skyles] κακῶς γένεσθαι, **92** δ 1 below, ἔδει δὲ ἐκ τοῦ Ἠετ-ίωνος γόνου Κορίνθωι κακὰ ἀναβλάστειν, and 6.135.3, δεῖν γὰρ Μιλτιάδεα μὴ τελευτᾶν εὖ (but this is a negatively-put variant). A poetic model for the species of 'presentation by negation' found here was Hom. *Il.* 5.674–5: οὐδ' ἄρ' Ὀδυσσῆι μεγαλήτορι μόρσιμον ἦεν|ἴφθιμον Διὸς υἱὸν ἀποκτάμεν ὀξέι χαλκῶι: it was fated for Odysseus to kill Sarpedon (because that was reserved for Patroklos to do later).

The present passage surely implies that it was fated for Naxos to per-ish on some other expedition. Macan assumes that the reference is to the 'next expedition' at **96** below, but there may be, alternatively or in addition, a hint at the Athenian 'enslavement' of Naxos in the 470s (Th. 1.98.4); so rightly Munson 2007: 159.

33.2 (cont.) ἐπὶ νεὸς Μυνδίης ... τὸν ἄρχοντα ταύτης τῆς νεός, τῶι οὔνομα ἦν Σκύλαξ: this episode is not trivial: the humiliating physical punishment of the Myndian ship's captain Skylax, and the strong reaction to it on the part of Aristagores, is a signifier for a clash of cultures; and the quarrel between the Greek Aristagores and the high-ranking Achaimenid Megabates illustrates the difficulties which can arise when forces are mixed and the lines of authority are not entirely clear, or can be argued to be unclear. (See **31**.2n. and below, **33**.4n. on ὁ δὲ εἶπε.)

Skylax is introduced slowly, so that it is only from the anonymous informant in **33**.3 that we learn that he was a guest-friend of Aristagores. Though this coincidence is not marked by Hdt. in any way, the personal relationship was surely a large part of the reason for Aristagores' indignation. But there is a more general aspect as well: the rough punitive treatment of the Karian Greek Skylax by Megabates was not at all in the usual Greek way.

Skylax is a Greek 'animal-name' from a root meaning dog or puppy (cf. the more famous Skylax from nearby Karian Karyanda, Hdt. 4.44.1, 'old sea-dog Skylax', as Myres 1953: 1 called him). The name may have been popular in Karia because of the link between the Karian goddess Hekate (**36**.2n.) and dogs, bitches and puppies (so E. Sittig, *R.-E.* VII 'Hekabe' [sic] col. 2662). For another Karian Skylax (patronym, Athens, late 6th cent. BC) see *IG* i³ 1344.

Myndos in Karia (*IACP* no. 914) was situated at the western tip of the Halikarnassos peninsula. The Myndians claimed that their city was Greek, founded, like Halikarnassos, from Troizen (Paus. 2.30.9). A direct Troizenian origin for Myndos is not likely, but there could have been secondary settlement from Halikarnassos; or else (Bean and Cook 1955: 111) the Myndian claim was made in imitation of Halikarnassos. Most likely the population of Myndos, again like Halikarnassos, was a mix of Greek and Karian (for Karian commanders in this fleet see **37**.1: Oliatos son of Ibanollis and Histiaios son of Tymnes, where all the names except Histiaios are Karian). So Skylax was a Greek of sorts, and Aristagores certainly was Greek. The story of Skylax of Myndos thus illustrates an important difference between Greek and Persian attitudes to military discipline: see *CHGRW* I. 36 (Greek military discipline generally lax and nonphysical). If Skylax had indeed neglected to place a watch on his ship, that was a serious lapse of military discipline, and Aristagores' intercession on behalf of Skylax, and then his release of Skylax on his own initiative, cannot have been prompted by any sense of absolute injustice. First, he felt obliged to act in defence of his guest-friend, right or wrong; and second, he found the punishment degrading. To these motives a third became relevant at the point when his intercession failed: as often in coalition armies and navies (*TT*: 240), questions of authority and control are delicate, and Aristagores directly challenges the Persian Megabates' authority (**33**.4, 'did not Artaphrenes send you to obey me?' See n. there for the financial promises which made this position not entirely absurd).

33.2 (cont.) τοῦτον δῆσαι διὰ θαλαμίης διέλκοντας τῆς νεὸς κατὰ τοῦτο 'to tie him up through the lowest oarport of the ship, dragging him through in such a way that…' On the MSS reading διελόντας, the participle is from διαιρέω: 'dividing him up in such a way that…' (Powell's conjecture διέχοντας would mean 'thrusting him through'). The 'thalamian oarport' was at the lower level (the *thalamos* was the hold) and was wider than those higher up (Morrison, Coates and Rankov 2000: 41, cf. 131–2).

33.3 λυμαίνοιτο 'maltreat'. The word is strong (perhaps implying that Skylax was left to die slowly), and underlines what a Greek would regard as the very Persian nature of the punishment. Plut. *Artax.* 16 (the revolting slow death by torture known as 'boating') is different from this.

33.4 ὁ δὲ εἶπε: only Aristagores is given a direct speech, and a very cool and insolent one. Megabates by contrast comes across as inarticulately angry, and one can understand why: it is hardly likely that Artaphrenes specifically subordinated his kinsman Megabates to the deputy of a local Greek city-ruler. On the other hand, the story as Hdt. tells it involves a partial financial bluff on the part of Aristagores, a bluff which has not yet been called: he has promised to bankroll the entire expedition (**31.**2), a promise which replicates that made to him by the Naxian exiles (**30.**6). And the promises are not entirely bluff, because **34.**3 shows that Aristagores had spent money of his own in addition to the costs incurred by the Persians. On these premises, for Aristagores to present himself as in some sense an independent operator and entitled to be consulted about the treatment of his fellow-countryman (and a personal guest-friend) is not wildly absurd. But he goes preposterously further than that.   ὁ δὲ θυμωθεὶς τούτοισι, ὡς νὺξ ἐγένετο, ἔπεμπε ἐς Νάξον…: Megabates loses his temper, and then we are told, almost incredibly, that he betrays the expedition by sending a secret night-time message to the Naxians. As we saw above (**32**n.), Persian evidence shows Megabates still holding high naval office some years later, and this might be thought to tell against the historicity of the story, as might the approximate similarity to Themistokles' secret message to Sikinnos at 8.75. Dewald 1998: 669 remarks that the Naxians hardly needed a message from Megabates to tell them that an invasion was impending, but Hdt. foresaw this objection and is anxious to assure us that they were indeed ignorant at first (**34.**1). It is possible that the stratagem (a feigned move against Chios and then a swoop down from the north) worked for a while.

34.1 For such a scramble to get everything inside the walls in a military emergency compare Th. 4.103.5 – 104.1 (Amphipolis) with *CT* II: 331. τὸ τεῖχος ἐσάξαντο: the middle of σάσσω means 'strengthen'.

34.1–2 παρεσκευάσαντο δὲ ὡς πολιορκησόμενοι…καὶ οὗτοι μὲν παρεσκευά-ζοντο ὡς παρεσομένου τοῦ πολέμου…πρὸς πεφραγμένους προσεφέροντο καὶ πολιόρκεον μῆνας τέσσερας: 'stylistic enactment' (cf. **25**.1 ἀπέδειρε πᾶσαν…and **26**nn.): the repeated polysyllabic plosive words enact the long tedious siege. For another siege 'enacted' in something like this way see Th. 7.6.3–4 with *CT* III: 552–3.

Naxos town (the *chora* in mod. Greek parlance), located in the middle of the western side of the island, is exceptionally well placed to withstand a long drawn-out siege such as characterised the pre-artillery age before about 400 BC: the Venetian kastro, complete with water-cistern, occupies the strong site of the ancient acropolis.

34.3 καὶ αὐτῶι τῶι Ἀρισταγόρηι προσαναισίμωτο πολλά: Aristagores does put up large amounts of money, so his earlier speech was not pure bluster: see **33**.4n. The verb (meaning 'had been spent in addition') is found here only, but see **31**.2 for ἀναισιμώματα. κακῶς πρήσσοντες: this pithy expression for failure is repeated in reverse order at **35**.1, πρήξαντος κακῶς.

35.1 οὐκ εἶχε 'he was not able' to carry out his promise. For this sense of ἔχω, common in Hdt. (esp. when saying what he himself is able or not able to say with certainty, ἀτρεκέως), see Powell IV (2) 1. τὴν βασι-ληίην τῆς Μιλήτου ἀπαιρεθήσεσθαι 'to be deprived of the kingship of Mile-tos' (but it could be taken, alternatively or in addition, to mean 'robbed of the kingship he had been so sure of establishing', i.e. prospective as much as actual). The word 'kingship' is remarkable (there is no such cult magistrate at Miletos). At **30**.2, Aristagores was a mere *epitropos* or deputy governor, and at **37**.2 he renounces his tyranny. The focalisation may help to explain it: Aristagores is presented as giving himself airs, and as liking to think of himself as a royal personage. There is no inconsistency between the motive given here and **37**.1 (the abdication), provided we accept that Hdt. is here merely offering inferred motivation, and that the inference is part of a generally hostile portrait. As for king/tyrant, the words are in general not so far apart as they would later become; see **44** n.

35.2 ἀρρωδέων δέ: for participle following an indicative form of the same verb see 12.4n. συνέπιπτε γὰρ καὶ τὸν ἐστιγμένον τὴν κεφαλήν: the main facts and key words are given briefly in this introductory sentence; then there follows the explanatory narrative; then the ring is closed at the end of **35**.3, with the cross-reference ὡς καὶ πρότερόν μοι εἴρηται, for which see n. there. The opening word συνέπιπτε prepares us for the magnificent three-fold statement of contingency at **36**.1.

The story was popular: for example, it is quoted in the 4th cent. BC by Ain. Tact. ch. 38 (just after a citation of the message-on-the-feathered-arrow story at Hdt. 8.128, Potidaia), as part of a section about how to send secret messages. But it was perhaps already famous in Hdt.'s own time, hence '*the* man with the tattooed head', as if we know who he is. The sheer entertainment value of such stories (and thus the motive of giving pleasure by recounting them) should not be forgotten, and that goes for Aineias too, who is too often treated as a kind of military and political manual and no more. Th., also, was an admirer of ingenious stratagems; see 5.45.2 (Alkibiades' trick on the Spartan envoys at Athens) with *CT* III: 105–6, citing other examples.

With the present story, compare 1.123.3–4 (message concealed inside a hare, cf. Erbse 1992: 38) and 7.239.4 (Gorgo and the apparently blank wax tablet); cf. Gorman 2001: 135.

35.2 (cont.) σημαίνοντα ἀπίστασθαι: this verb for what the head 'disclosed' is very choice. How many letters were inscribed? Perhaps, as in a modern text-message on a mobile phone, some vowels were omitted. (Aineias, in the same chapter, has suggestions as to how to go about this.)

35.3 καὶ ἀνέμεινε ἀναφῦναι τὰς τρίχας 'he waited for the hair to grow'. So it would seem that the message was after all not very urgent. But we are not meant to press the story too hard. (For instance, if the man were tortured, he would say 'shave my head'; or perhaps he himself knew what was inscribed on it. But at least he would be able to get past a guard-post which was interested only in checking documents.)   **ὥστε φυλασσομένων τῶν ὁδῶν** 'because the roads were guarded'. Here ὥστε = ὡς; see Powell ὥστε I (1) and cf. 4.136.2.   **τὰ δὲ στίγματα ἐσήμαινε, ὡς καὶ πρότερόν μοι εἴρηται, ἀπόστασιν:** for such explicit back-references see on **36.4**; but that will direct us to bk. 1, whereas the present passage takes us back an unusually short distance – just a few lines, to **35.2**.

35.4 ταῦτα...ἐποίεε συμφορὴν ποιεύμενος μεγάλην '[Histiaios] did this because he considered it a great misfortune...' The closely juxtaposed forms of ποέω were presumably not felt by Hdt. to be awkward; for the whole expression συμφορὴν ποιέεσθαι see **5**n. Here the sense is almost 'he resented' ('hated': Waterfield).   **ἀποστάσιος ὢν γινομένης πολλὰς εἶχε ἐλπίδας μετήσεσθαι ἐπὶ θάλασσαν** 'he had great hopes that in the event of a revolt he would be released (the verb is from μετίημι) towards the sea' i.e. the western or coastal satrapies. So he assumes that Dareios will trust him; but Hdt.'s readers/hearers know that, thanks to Megabazos, Dareios did not trust him; and yet Dareios will eventually (**107**) let him go. Hdt. may be reading motives back from what actually happened.   **μὴ δὲ νεώτερόν τι ποιεύσης τῆς Μιλήτου οὐδαμὰ ἐς αὐτὴν ἥξειν ἔτι ἐλογίζετο** 'whereas he calculated that if there were no revolution in Miletos he would never get back there'. For this use of μή with a participle in hypothetical conditional sentences, see Powell C (II) 1.

36.1 Ἀρισταγόρηι δὲ συνέπιπτε τοῦ αὐτοῦ χρόνου πάντα ταῦτα συνελθόντα: for the triple expression of simultaneity – lit. all these things (1) falling together, (2) at the same time, (3) came together – see *Th. and Pi.*: 301–6, esp. 302. The three locutions enact the three separate occurrences or causal strands denoted by πάντα ταῦτα (Skylax's humiliation; Aristagores' lack of money; the slave sent by Histiaios). Compare Orestes at Aesch. *Cho.* 299 (cf. *TT:* 10 n. 47): πολλοὶ γὰρ εἰς ἓν συμπίτνουσιν ἵμεροι, where the 'desires' (really 'motivating factors') are then enumerated. In Hdt. himself, compare 7.3.1 and 7.6.1. See also Dover 1974: 225.

The idea of causation here is not Thucydidean; but for something more like Th.'s notion of layered causes (as at Th. 1.23.6) see Hdt. 4.167 with *TT:* 12. As often in Hdt. (Immerwahr 1966: 68–9), the present passage addresses only immediate not underlying causes.

36.1 (cont.) ἐβουλεύετο ὧν μετὰ τῶν στασιωτέων: no large decision-making body is meant by these στασιῶται or partisans (Tozzi 1978: 138). They are surely elite Milesians rather than the Ionians as a whole. Only in the course of **37**.2 is the revolution extended to the rest of Ionia. Contrast the federal Ionian meeting at the Panionion, 1.170, cf. 141.4, and for the Panionion and Panionian festival in Hdt. see *TT:* 178–81, cf. 6.7. The Ionians act collectively at **103**, and we hear (with a small analepsis) of a decision by τὸ κοινὸν τῶν Ἰώνων at **109**.3, but even that expression is not decisive as evidence for the formal, federal, entity, 'the Ionian league'; see **109**.3n.

It is remarkable that, at this grave moment of decision, Branchidai is mentioned as only a possible financial resource: nothing is said about Milesian or general Ionian consultation of the oracle there, to which we were introduced as long ago as 1.46.2 and 158.1. Another source (Demon, see **36**.3n. on the sanctuary of Branchidai) suggests that there was a consultation of the oracle at about this time, but by the Karians, who were contemplating war with the Milesians. See Introduction, p. 35 for human as opposed to divine factors in the revolt, and for the delayed mention of the oracle about the Milesians given by Apollo at (not Branchidai but) Delphi, recorded at 6.19 and 77.2.

36.2 οἱ μὲν δὴ ἄλλοι...Ἑκαταῖος δ': for this Homeric focussing device, cf. **92**.1 and *Od.* 8.532f.; also Th. 5.27.2 with *CT* III: 60. **Ἑκαταῖος δ' ὁ λογοποιός:** the noun will be used again about Hekataios at **125** (where again he gives advice), but elsewhere in Hdt. only of Aisop, 2.134.3, and the implied comparison is perhaps not intended politely. For Hekataios see S. West 1991. He has featured already by name in Hdt.'s bk. 2 (143), but he underlies other passages in that bk. also: with 2.5.1; 70–3; 156 compare *FGrHist* 1 FF 301, 324A, 305.

The name is theophoric, from Hekate, who is probably Karian by origin (for doubters, see Fontenrose 1988: 134 and n. 21). The Karian form of the personal name is 'Krais'. See Herda 2006: 288 and esp. Parker 2000: 69–70, whose discussion begins with Hekataios of Miletos: 'the East Greek bias in theophoric names formed from Hekate is quite unusually marked'. As he says, the earliest evidence for the cult of Hekate comes from, precisely, Miletos, namely the 6th-cent. dedication Rehm 1914: no. 129, cf. West 1966: 278 (on Hes. *Theog.* 404–52) and Fontenrose 1988: 133 and n. 20. In the cultic 'Molpoi decree' from the mid 5th cent., already discussed above at **11.1** n. in connection with Hestia, an offering is to be placed at the sanctuary of Hekate, and a paian is to be sung there (Rehm 1914: no. 133 = *Syll.*³ no. 57, tr. at Gorman 2001: 179 at lines 25 and 28). Hekataios is not a rare name and is widely dispersed. But statistics from the unpublished Karian files are astonishing: 32 bearers of the name from Miletos, 44 from Iasos, 15 from Mylasa, 12 from nearby Olymos, etc. We are not here told Hekataios' patronymic Hegesandros; see **125** and n.

For such advice by a famous local sage compare 1.27–8 (advice to Kroisos by Bias of Priene or possibly Pittakos of Mytilene) or 1.170, the advice given to the Ionians by Bias of Priene and by Thales of Miletos. (Bias advocates Ionian emigration *en masse* to Sardinia, and Thales is then reported for an earlier suggestion of a move to central Ionian Teos.) The structural implication is important: as often (Introduction, §1), there are thematic and verbal correspondences between bks. 5 and 1. But there are important differences: Hdt. explicitly praises the advice of both Bias and Thales, but Hekataios' is reported without adjudication; and the advice is different in both content and degree of complexity.

It is not clear whether Hekataios was right (or rather whether Hdt. thought he was right, or wanted us to think he was right) to believe that Persian power, the δύναμις of Dareios as he calls it, was irresistible. In the short term he was right in that the Ionian revolt failed (and the double mention of κακῶν . . . κακά at **28**.1 prepares for this, just as the 'folly' or ἀγνωμοσύνη at 6.10 reinforces it retrospectively); but in the longer term he was wrong, in that the Persian wars were a Greek victory.

As for his second-best advice to seize the treasures of Branchidai, it is even harder to be sure what we are meant to think, because the advice has several components, including a conditional prediction that the Persians will seize the treasures if the Ionians do not. That prediction was not borne out by Datis' behaviour at Delos (6.97): so far from looting the sanctuary, he made a lavish dedication of frankincense (not to mention his dedications in Athena's sanctuary at Rhodian Lindos, if they are historical: Higbie 2003: 44–5, 142, 146). But Hekataios did not necessarily believe the prediction himself. The present passage is indirect speech and intended to be persuasive rhetoric. 'If you don't do it, someone else will' is often a good line.

It has been thought (Dewald 1998: 669) that Hdt. wants us to think that Hekataios' advice should have been heeded, and even that Hekataios here speaks for Hdt. But there is no single piece of advice. Unlike the simpler proposals of Bias and Thales, the 'advice' of Hekataios was complex and partly conditional, as we have seen, and the beauty of a focalisation through him, rather than an unequivocal authorial judgment, is that it leaves several matters open.

36.2 (cont.) καταλέγων τά τε ἔθνεα πάντα τῶν ἦρχε Δαρεῖος: this is a very briefly reported 'catalogue' (the English noun is from the Greek καταλέγω) of the peoples ruled by Dareios, compared with Aristagores' lengthy description at **49** and Hdt.'s own even longer one at **52–4**. Aristagores' motive is different: he will enumerate the easy pickings to be had from the Persian empire, whereas Hekataios wants to show how formidable it is. As for the contrast with **52–4**, this has metatextual implications: Hdt. will not allow Hekataios a full length speech; he does the job himself, and not just there, but through the whole geography-rich text of the *Histories*. **δεύτερα συνεβούλευε ποιέειν ὅκως ναυκρατέες τῆς θαλάσσης ἔσονται** 'as the next best thing he advised them to use their ships to become commanders of the sea'. ναυκράτεες τῆς θαλάσσης is a partly redundant and thus emphatic expression ('of the sea' is not needed after ναυκράτεες, which means the same as ναυκράτορες on its own at 6.9.1). For the 'second-best' option cf. Bacchyl. 5.160–2; also Th. 6.11 and *CT* III: 331.

36.3 *The sanctuary of Branchidai*

To sum up what follows, the sanctuary of Branchidai was in every way close to Miletos, but its oracle was capable of taking an independent line.

For the great temple at what is more usually called Didyma, south of Miletos, see Rehm 1958; Fontenrose 1988: ch. 2; Gorman 2001: 186–96; Greaves 2002: 109–29; for the oracle, not here mentioned, see **36.1**n. on ἐβουλεύετο . . . For the Branchidai see Parke 1985a: 1–22 and 1985b: 59–61. The sanctuary has usually been thought to take its name Branchidai – a family name of a partly religious type familiar at Athens and elsewhere – from its hereditary operators: Hdt. never calls it Didyma, except at 6.19.2–3 where he is first quoting then elucidating a Delphic oracular response (Piérart 2003: 287–8). Indeed it has been doubted whether the supposed family, the Branchidai, existed at all in historical times: even Hdt. 1.158.1, where uniquely in Hdt. we find the masculine form οἱ Βραγχίδαι, can be understood as referring to a place not a family: Ehrhardt 1998: 15 16, esp. n. 15. This problem is bound up with that of the alleged massacre of the Branchidai by Alexander the Great and Greeks in his army: Curt. 7.5.28–35, esp. *gens Branchidarum* at 30. This massacre is probably historical (Parke 1985b) and the status of the Branchidai as an interrelated religious group has not been disproved.

The sanctuary had close links with Miletos (so rightly Ehrhardt 1998, against Tuchelt 1988; *IACP*: p. 1083; Gorman 2001: 187 n. 35 and Herda 2006: 447–57). To be sure, a Sacred Way links Didyma to Miletos, so to that extent archaeology indicates a more than physical closeness; see also *SEG* 30.1283 (sacred law from the Sacred Way, with Milesian features). But Parke 1985a: 18–20 with 203, and 1985b: 61, noted some early oracular i.e. literary evidence unfavourable to the Milesians; particularly relevant to the present passage of Hdt. is an oracle in which Apollo, presumably of Didyma, warned the Karians against joining the Milesians against the Persians at what appears to be the time of the Ionian revolt: *FGrHist* 327 Demon F 16 and Diod. 10.25 (but see Parke 1985b: 61 n. 11. Fontenrose 1988: 214–15 regarded the oracle as 'not genuine').

Branchidai was a 'priest-state functioning independently within local territory' (Parke 1985b: 61, cf. 1985a: 2–3 for Branchidai as a community centred on a local deity). 'Branchos' may be a pre-Greek name, though Branchos was made the subject of an eponymous myth, for which see Kall. frr. 194.28 and 229 Pf., with D'Alessio's comm.).

36.3 ἄλλως μέν νυν οὐδαμῶς ἔφη λέγων ἐνορᾶν ἐσόμενον τοῦτο... εἰ δέ 'he said that the only way he could see this could happen was if...' **ἐπίστασ-θαι... ἀσθενέα**: but we were told at **28** that Miletos was flourishing, not weak. However, the verb does not necessarily imply actual knowledge i.e. it does not guarantee truth, but may express mere confident belief on the part of Hekataios: **42.1**n. Or rather, a pose of such belief: this is still Hekataios' rhetoric: see **36.2**n. In any case, Milesian resources were indeed weak, relative to those of the entire Persian empire. **πολλὰς εἶχε ἐλπίδας**: the hopes are false, or at least unreasonable.

36.4 ὡς δεδήλωταί μοι ἐν τῶι πρώτωι τῶν λόγων: that is, at 1.92.2. The usual cross-referencing formula (copied by Th. at 5.1.1, see *CT* ii: 422–3) is here made more precise by the addition of 'in my first *logos*'. But this does not mean 'in my bk. 1'. Book-numbers are a 4th-cent. innovation (see Introduction: §1). **οὐκ ἐνίκα ἡ γνώμη**: for exactly this metaphorical formula for 'be defeated' see **118.**3, and cf. 6.109.2, ἐνίκα ἡ χείρων τῶν γνωμέων. The imperfect of νικᾶν is often used to refer to a single event, as at Th. 3.8, athletic victory. See Rood 1998: 242f. on ἐνίκων in Th.: 'an imperfect denoting a state, not a complete action ('they were victorious')'. **ἐδό-κεε δὲ ὅμως ἀπίστασθαι**: that is, by deciding to revolt (and leave the treasury alone), they prefer what Hekataios had called the 'second-best option' at **36.**2. **ἕνα τε αὐτῶν πλώσαντα ἐς Μυοῦντα**: in fact the Milesian (**36.1**n. on ἐβουλεύετο...) chosen for this mission will be Ietragores, below **37.**1.

For Myous, about 15 km NE of Miletos, see 1.142.3, where it features in a list of the Ionian cities running south to north and beginning Miletos, Myous, Priene. Myous is *IACP*: no. 856 (*Barr.* map 61 E2). At Lade, it provided a mere three ships to Priene's twelve (6.8.1), and it was absorbed in Miletos by the Hellenistic period. But it was still independent enough in *c.* 390 to engage in a boundary dispute with its great neighbour Miletos, R/O no. 16 (for possibly 'invented traditions' of ancient hostility between the two cities, see Kall. fr. 80 Pf. with Harder 2012: 2.671–4).

37.1 Ἰητραγόρεω: the reader has not met Ietragores by name before, and Hdt. introduces him without explanation or patronymic, but he is the one στασιώτης sent to Myous at **36.4**. Hdt. does not actually say here that he was a Milesian in so many words. But his Milesian identity surely follows from the preceding narrative (see **36.**1n. on ἐβουλεύετο...and **36.**4n. on ἕνα...), and the name, though exceptionally rare elsewhere (no examples in any published vol. of *LGPN*), is in fact attested at 5th-cent. Miletos. See Rehm 1914: no. 122 for a Diomedon son of Ietragores, who was *stephanephoros* at Miletos in 417/16. (Otherwise, unpublished *LGPN* files show that there is just one other attested anywhere, and he too is from Karia: *I. Iasos* no. 56 line 7, spelling the name Iatro-.) Diomedon is perhaps too young to be the son of Hdt.'s Ietragores, but he could be another close relative (for such 'floating kindreds', see Hornblower 2000: 131 and n. 7). For the name in –agores, see **30.**2n., and for the prefix it is relevant (see again **30.**2n.) that Apollo was the healer god, and at Lykoph. *Alex.* 1207 and 1377 is actually given the title Ἰατρός. See Isaac 1986: 247. But it is possible (Ehrhardt 1983: 147 and n. 561) that there was a separate hero at Miletos called Iatros, who came over with the original Athenian settlers. Indeed Apollo's son Asklepios was called Iatros at Kyrene, and even Poseidon was Iatros (at Tenos: *FGrHist* 328 Philochoros F 175). But Apollo is the main Iatros. Ὀλίατον Ἰβανώλλιος Μυλασέα καὶ Ἱστιαῖον Τύμνεω Τερμερέα: Hdt. does not call these two tyrants in so many words, merely 'commanders' (στρατηγούς), but they are in tyrannical company (Koes, Aristagores of Kyme), and the context is anti-tyrannical, so it seems reasonable to assume that they were. Their names and patronyms are precious, as showing Hdt.'s careful researches at the level of detail. With Oliatos, compare the Karian name Ολετας, gen. Ολεταδος (Masson 1990b: 21). For the Karian name Ibanollis see also **121** (Herakleides son of Ibanollis, and so possibly brother of Oliatos, see n.); and compare with it Aridolis at 7.195, and some of the many 5th-cent. BC Karian names preserved in *Syll.*[3]: no. 46, Halikarnassos; also no. 45 (=ML 32), also Halikarnassos, law about disputed property. Note e.g. (no. 45 = ML 32, lines 12–13) Κάσβωλλις, and, from *Syll.*[3] 46, Ἀκταύσσολλος. Ὕσσωλλος, Πονύσσωλλος, etc. For 'la grande liste d'Halicarnasse' (Robert 1963: 159), see esp. Masson 1990b (orig. 1959). From the 4th cent., see the Karian names in *Syll.*³ 167 (= Tod no. 138 and R/O no. 55, Mylasa) and 169 (Iasos).

For Tymnes of Termera, known from his mixed (Greek and Karian) coinage, see *Mausolus*: 24 and n. 144, cf. 340. In the 5th cent., the Athenian tribute lists attest payments of half a talent (3000 drachmai) by 'the Karians whom Tymnes rules', Κᾶρες ὦν Τύμνης ἄρχει, *ATL*: 1.495. But it is not certain that this is a descendant of Hdt.'s dynast, because the area the *ATL* man controls seems to be up in the Iasos region to the north of Karia. As for Histiaios, the name is Greek and is familiar from the famous Milesian in the present bk. (**11.1**n.), but we should recall that Miletos was itself half-Karian. Histiaios might be both a theophoric Greek name (**11.1**n. again) and a hellenised form of a Karian name.

Inland Mylasa (mod. Milas, *IACP*: no. 913; see esp. 1.171.6 and Strabo 14.2.23) was the capital of Karia until Mausolos moved it to Halikarnassos (no. 886) in the 370s (but after Alexander's death the Macedonian satrap Asandros may have moved it back again to Mylasa: *Mausolus*: 99–100). For Mausolos' ethnic Μυλασεύς, as here, see *Syll.*³ 168 (Erythrai = Tod 155 = R/O no. 56). Mylasa's sanctuary was Labraunda, for which see **119**.2 and n.

Termera (*IACP*: no. 937, *Barr.* map 61 E4) was towards the western end of the stubby Myndos peninsula, in the middle of which is Halikarnassos. It was one of the six Karian communities merged by Mausolos into Halikarnassos as part of his 4th-cent. synoikism (*FGrHist* 124 Kallisthenes F 25, from Strabo).

37.1 (cont.) Κώην Ἐρξάνδρου: see **11.1**n. for name and patronym.   καὶ Ἀρισταγόρην Ἡρακλείδεω Κυμαῖον: already mentioned as tyrant of Kyme at 4.138.2. For Aiolian Kyme (*IACP*: 817, L. Rubinstein), see below **123**n., discussing its role in the Ionian revolt. At 4.138.1, Hdt. names a third Aristagores, tyrant of Kyzikos, a Milesian colony (*IACP*: 747). We are not told what happened to him, but 6.33.3 (the Kyzikene treaty with Oibares satrap of Daskyleion) may suggest he held on to power. It would be tempting, therefore, to use these onomastic coincidences to suggest that at least the Milesian and Kyzikene tyrants called Aristagores were related, since the same personal names are often found in mother and daughter cities. But the name Aristagores is too common for such an argument to be worth much, and Kyme is not a Milesian foundation.   καὶ ἄλλους συχνούς: see 7.164.1, with Macan's n. (at p. 229) for the possibility that the tyrant of Kos, Kadmos son of Skythes, was among these 'many others' arrested by Ietragores; cf. 6.23–4.   πᾶν ἐπὶ Δαρείωι μηχανώμενος: for the verb see **30**.4n. (Aristagores again), and for the full πᾶν ἐπί...formula, cf. **62**.2n.

37.2 λόγωι μετεὶς τὴν τυραννίδα ἰσονομίην ἐποίεε τῆι Μιλήτωι 'he pretended to lay down his tyranny and proclaimed *isonomie* in Miletos'. The word *isonomie* means equality under the law, or perhaps equal access to it for all

(Vlastos 1953 and 1964, and cf. Pelling 2002: 137 n. 44). It is not quite identical with democracy, but it can be predicated of it, as resoundingly by the Persian Otanes at 3.80.6, πλῆθος δὲ ἄρχον πρῶτα μὲν οὔνομα κάλλιστον ἔχει, ἰσονομίην; closer to an outright identification is 3.83.1, where Otanes is said authorially to have been advocating ἰσονομίη i.e. in effect democracy, though Hdt. does not call it that, despite having the vocabulary to do so (see 6.131.2: Kleisthenes introduced 'the tribes and the democracy' at Athens). So too at Th. 3.82.8, πλήθους τε ἰσονομία πολιτική is said to be the 'specious name' used by the democrats, balancing the ἀριστοκρατία σώφρων of the oligarchs. But ἰσονομία can also, and more surprisingly, be predicated of oligarchy, as by some Theban speakers only twenty chs. earlier in Th. (3.62.3, an admittedly tendentious piece of rhetoric); see *CT* I: 455f., discussing other early uses, such as *PMG* no. 896 = Fornara no. 39A, and the medical writer Alkmaion of Kroton, DK 24 B4. See Ostwald 1969: 155, 157.

The particular claim here about Aristagores' action and motive is difficult. The problem is λόγωι, 'in word', with its imputation of insincerity or unreality. Later in the sentence Hdt. says that Aristagores *did the same* elsewhere in Ionia, driving out some of the tyrants and handing others over to their cities. This makes no sense except on the supposition that Aristagores really did resign his local powers. So it is not easy to see how his abdication can have been a pretence. One might stress the purpose-clause which follows (ὡς ἄν...): to stress the public announcement explains why the bid for goodwill and support was successful, i.e. λόγωι should be taken literally, and emphasises that he 'made a *speech* renouncing...' (if so, compare Maiandrios at Samos at 3.142.3, another proclaimer of *isonomie*). Another solution (Waterfield) ingeniously takes the pretence to refer to the proclamation of *isonomie*, as if there were commas before and after μετεὶς τὴν τυραννίδα. But this is a forced hyperbaton (unnatural word-order); we would expect λόγωι to form part of the expression it qualifies. Yet another possibility is that Hdt. means that Aristagores, who is strictly no more than an *epitropos* or deputy (30.2), now publicly renounces all claim on the tyranny. But at 49.1 he is called 'tyrant of Miletos', without qualification; i.e. Hdt. has by then, and perhaps already now, forgotten about his deputy status. AHG comments 'I can't make any sense out of λόγωι. <τῶι> λεῶι (LSJ μεθίημι 1.2c)?' i.e. relinquished it 'to the people'; he compares τῶι δήμωι at 4.161.3, Demonax's arrangements at Kyrene. Replying to this, Wilson, equally radically and ingeniously, counter-suggests that Aristagores made his renunciation 'in a public meeting', πρῶτα μὲν <ἐν συλ> λόγωι.

It is possible that another east Greek tyrant, Kadmos son of Skythes of Kos, resigned his tyranny voluntarily at this time, and went to Sicily. See 7.164.2 with Macan on that passage. It is not certain, whether this man's father Skythes is the same as the king of Sicilian Zankle at 6.23.1.

37.2 (cont.) ὡς ἂν ἕκοντες αὐτῶι οἱ Μιλήσιοι συναπισταίατο 'in order that the Milesians would willingly join him in revolt'. This is strong evidence for a desire for freedom, or at least 'constitutional government', as one of the causes of the revolt – not a motive much stressed by Hdt., but see. 4.137.2, where Histiaios claims that all the Ionian cities would prefer to be ruled democratically rather than tyrannically. See Raaflaub 1985: 98; Munson 2007: 161 and n. 63.   τοὺς μὲν ἐξελαύνων: the narrative technique here is notable. The reader will find out only much later, with explicit back-reference to Aristagores, what happened to the tyrants thus 'driven out': they fled to the Persians (ἔφευγον ἐς Μήδους) and joined in the expedition against Miletos (6.9.2). They will have an important role at that point in the narrative, up to 6.10: they send messengers to their respective cities, urging capitulation. At 6.13.2 Hdt. reveals, with another explicit back-reference to Aristagores' depositions, that one of them was Aiakes son of Syloson, and ex-tyrant of Samos. Hdt. has decided to hold back much of this until he needs it.

38.1 ἐξαγαγόντες κατέλευσαν: for stoning as the archetypal collective punishment, see *TT*: 273–4 (biblical parallels), and see *CT* III: 158 on the attempted stoning of Thrasylos at Th. 5.60.6 (citing Fehling 1974: 63 n. 262 and Parker 1983: 195 n. 20), and 992–4 on Astyochos at 8.84.2–3. For the sequence 'attempted stoning–fleeing to an altar' (attested in the epic cycle and tragedy, and for Thrasylos and Astyochos), see *TT*: 148 n. 28. But there is no such sequence in the present passage of Hdt. Perhaps the assailants were too quick for Koes. Contrast **46**.2 and n.: Euryleon flees to an altar, but no mention of stoning.   Κυμαῖοι δὲ τὸν σφέτερον: that is, Aristagores, see **37**.1 and 4.138.2. It is curious that he is not named here, as was Koes of Mytilene in the first part of the sentence, and as he himself was at **37**.1. Perhaps naming him now would have been confusing in a detailed narrative about the more famous Aristagores.

38.2 τυράννων μέν νυν κατάπαυσις ἐγίνετο . . . ὡς τοὺς τυράννους κατέπαυσε: but in that case the question arises, how Mardonios is able to do exactly the same six years later, at 6.43, the Persian settlement after the failure of the revolt. (Note the closely similar language, τοὺς γὰρ τυράννους τῶν Ἰώνων καταπαύσας.) A possible answer is that the Persian declaration was no more than a mere good-will gesture, although καταπαύσας seems too strong a word for that, and some features of the settlement described in that section are historical enough (see 6.42.1 for the arbitration arrangements). One possibility is that Hdt. is generalising from a single instance, and means no more than that Aiakes of Samos, who was briefly reinstated at 6.25.2, was deposed again at 6.43. See Austin 1990: 306.   κελεύσας: here 'urged' not 'ordered'. He no longer has power, *potestas*, to give orders (there is no reason why other cities should obey a Milesian anyway), but his prestige, *auctoritas*, enables him to advise. Gorman 2001: 140–1 wonders by what right Aristagores was allowed to go to the mainland, and why he is able to appoint generals at **99**.2 (see n. there); she suggests that he enjoyed some sort of authority conferred on him by the Ionian league, although that body is not obviously in evidence until the end of bk. 5, see **109**.3n. Or perhaps (AHG) he was re-elected to some sort of command straight after resigning his tyranny.   δεύτερα: here just 'next'.   ἐς Λακεδαίμονα: Sparta is inserted very abruptly into the narrative.   ἔδεε γὰρ δὴ συμμαχίης τινός οἱ μεγάλης ἐξευρεθῆναι lit. 'it was necessary for him that some great alliance should be found'. This explanatory sentence, with its heavyweight closing passive infinitive and its unexpected word-order (the dative singular οἱ goes with ἔδεε, from which it is separated by four words, and συμμαχίης is detached from the deliberately postponed μεγάλης) seems designed to emphasise the greatness of the alliance needed. The long thematic and spatial leap from Asia Minor to the extended section on Spartan affairs is thus prepared for.

39–97.1 MAJOR EXCURSUS ON SPARTAN AND ATHENIAN AFFAIRS, WITH MINOR EXCURSUSES INSERTED: DORIEUS IN SICILY; THEBES; SIKYON; AIGINA; KORINTH

The following section, until **54**, is the first part of an enormous two-part excursus about Spartan then Athenian affairs, which continues right up to **97**.1. The second part (the Athenian) begins when Aristagores, expelled from Sparta, makes his way to Athens at **55**, first sentence. The essential narrative device is similar to that used in bk. 1, a bk. which as so often is recapitulated or mirrored in bk. 5: an inquiry or a visit by a man from the east (Kroisos, Aristagores) is the peg from which is hung a pair of excursuses, one about Athens, the other about Sparta. But in bk. 1, the order of treatment is Athens, then Sparta (1.59.1 and 65.1): a true 'mirror' effect. In both bks., the excursuses enable the easy feeding in of much explanatory and background information about the two great powers, Ionian and Dorian. The device was re-used by Th. in his bk. 1 (the Pausanias and Themistokles material), but he dispenses with the 'man from the east', as does Xenophon, in whose *Hellenika* the Arginousai trial (1.7) and the Kinadon affair (3.3) introduce us in like manner to Athenian and Spartan ways. Hdt. had the opportunity in bk. 3 to feed in some of the bk. 5 material, but on the whole he did not take it. (For an example of avoidance, see **39**.1n. on Anaxandrides.)

It is possible that the Skythian invitation to Kleomenes to join in an invasion of the Persian empire (6.84) belongs, if there is anything in it at all, in the present context (Busolt: 2^2 528 n. 1 and Berve 1937: 58).

39–48 The Dorieus of Sparta episode

This section is relevant to the Ionian revolt and to the structure of the whole *History*: the historical and historiographical parallels between Miletos and Sybaris (see **28**n. and 6.21.1 for the close kinship between the two cities) not only effect the integration of the present story into the surrounding Ionian revolt narrative, but offer the fates of the two places as illustrations of the generalisation at 1.5.4 about the vicissitudes of cities. See Hornblower 2007a, and *Th. and Pi.*: 107–13 and 301–6. Beyond bks. 5–6, Dorieus' failure and death in Sicily will be needed for our understanding of Gelon's anti-Spartan gibe (7.158.2); and his death, and Kleomenes' lack of a male heir (**48**n.), will be needed at 7.205, which explains how Anaxandrides' son Leonides came to be king at the time of Thermopylai, despite starting out in life with two older brothers (on the succession, see Griffith-Williams 2011). So rightly Pohlenz 1937: 88.

The Dorieus narrative is thus organically connected to the main line of narration; but is at the same time easily detachable and book-ended by opening and closural repetition. It is what ancient rhetorical theory would have called a *diegema* inside the *diegesis* of the *Histories* as a whole. For this distinction see Cameron 2004: 73, citing Hermogenes *Progymnasmata* 2 (p. 4.9–15 Rabe): 'the history of [Hdt.] is a *diegesis*, his account of Arion [1.23–4] a *diegema*'.

The myth in Pindar's long Kyrenaian ode, the mini-epic *Pyth.* 4 (at 36–49), about the 'clod of earth' (see **17**.1n.) washed overboard after being given to the Argonaut Euphemos (whom Pindar treats as a Spartan, lines 44, 49 with Malkin 1994: 176), may show knowledge of the story that is differently given by Hdt.: the Spartan Dorieus led unsuccessful colonial expeditions to a part of Libya near Kyrene, and to Sicily. See esp. Niese 1907, Malkin 1994: 169–218, and Hornblower 2004: 108f. Note however that Malten 1911: 132 and n.2 protested against Niese that the Kinyps region is not near enough to Kyrene (they are separated by the entire Gulf of Syrtes) for the Pindaric myth to be relevant.

Diod. 4.23.3 (=10.18.6) is a brief and unreliable account of Dorieus in Sicily. Diodorus says Dorieus actually founded a city Herakleia (hence *IACP* no. 20, 'Herakleia (1)'). But this Diodoran version looks like the result of a careless reading of or remembering of Hdt., and the supposed Karthaginian destruction of the flourishing city and the motive given for it (desire not to be overshadowed) are incompatible with Hdt., whose account implies that Dorieus' failure was immediate and catastrophic. See

Stauffenberg 1960: 190 (but he is too inclined to believe Diodorus); also Munson 2006: 261–2 (Dorieus' expedition 'dangerous and misguided from beginning to end'). Dorieus' first departure was probably in about 514 BC (the Sybaris-Kroton war of 44 was *c.* 510, Diod. 11.90.3), therefore some years after his half-brother's accession (48n.). See Cawkwell 2011: 77f.n.8. For a suggestion that Dorieus' career has a mythical prototype in traditions about Menelaos' wanderings in the west, see Braccesi 1999: 69–76.

39.1 Ἀναξανδρίδης μὲν ὁ Λέοντος οὐκέτι περιεὼν ἐβασίλευε ἀλλὰ ἐτετελευτήκεε: Hdt. has not mentioned Anaxandrides, here said to be 'no longer living and ruling but dead', since 1.67.1 – except in passing as the patronym of Kleomenes at 3.148.1, the attempted bribery by Maiandrios of Samos in *c.* 520 BC. Hdt. might have told us in bk. 3 that Anaxandrides was dead, which is the implication of the statement there that Kleomenes was king, but instead chooses to do so now. See Introduction p. 6 for this choice, and the reasons for it. In narrative terms, Anaxandrides is not 'dead' at all, because he is about to feature analeptically as a vigorous agent who takes two wives after a fairly good-natured confrontation with the ephors.

The negative-then-positive formulation, a good story-telling device, will be used again in regard to his son Kleomenes at **42**.1, 'not in his right mind but slightly mad': see n. there, and for such polar expressions see Nünlist 2009: 222. For 'not alive but dead' in particular, cf. Soph. *OT* 956 (Iokaste about Polybos). Anaxandrides' father Leon was mentioned at 1.65.1 as one of the two Spartan kings at the time of the Spartan reverses in their struggle against the Tegeans of Arkadia, but in bk. 1 Hdt. did not spell out the filiation as he does here, now that Anaxandrides is about to be central to the narration; and it will not be until 7.204 and Leonides' genealogy that he will position the two kings, father and son, in the whole 'Agiad' line: see **41**.3n. for this delay. For the other, 'Eurypontid', royal line see 8.131: Leutychides' genealogy. But the genealogies are not quite king-lists, so that for instance the Eurypontid line as given by Hdt. does not include King Ariston or his son Demaretos, who was replaced as king by his cousin Leutychides. Ariston's death and succession by Demaretos will be described at 6.64 in language similar to the present passage.

39.1 (cont.) οὐ κατ᾽ ἀνδραγαθίην: the negative presentation is surprising, as if manly qualities ever constituted a claim on the Spartan kingship, which they did not. See Hornblower 2007a: 170 and further below, on **42**.1.

39.1–41 Anaxandrides and his two wives

This story has features in common with the biblical theme, played out in recurrent 'type-scenes', of the barren favoured wife and her bitter conflict with the fertile but spurned co-wife or concubine: Sarah and Hagar, Rachel and Leah, Hannah the mother of Samuel and Peninnah. (See Alter 2011: 58 and 104.) Often the previously childless wife conceives after the second has done so. In Hdt., the king loves his first wife but she has no children, so he takes another, who gives birth to Kleomenes; the first wife then gives birth to three sons in rapid succession (including Dorieus). But the story diverges from the biblical type because the king's bigamy is explicitly commented on as un-Spartan, whereas in some of the biblical stories it is taken for granted as normal.

The story forms in some respects a pair with that of Demaretos and his parents, Ariston and his unnamed wife, in the middle of the next bk. (6.61–70): the difficulties of both Kleomenes and Demaretos, it has been said, 'have their roots in their fathers' problems' (Dewald 2011: 61).

39.1 (cont.) ἔχοντι γυναῖκα ἀδελφέης ἑωυτοῦ θυγατέρα: for such close Spartan kin-marriage, here uncle-niece, as a device for concentrating property and power, see Hodkinson 2009: 101f. and Millinder 2009, but we should not forget that Hdt. insists that he loved her. The phenomenon, in its economic aspect, is not confined to ancient Sparta: for an anthropological study of the rationale for cousin-marriages and other consanguineous marriages in 19th-cent. bourgeois England, see Kuper 2009. Neither of Anaxandrides' wives is named.   καὶ ἐούσης ταύτης οἱ καταθυμίης 'and although he was very happy with her', lit. 'and she being pleasing to him'. The participle is concessive and οἱ is dative singular.

39.2 οὐ περιοπτέον: 'we must not over*look*' – in the sense of 'neglect' – say the ephors (ἔφοροι) or over*look*ers – in the sense of 'super-visors'. ἐξίτηλον: the ephors share Hdt.'s own anxiety to avoid oblivion and extinction in human affairs: the word is found only here and in the proem. ἔξεο 'divorce her!', from ἐξίημι (middle). Compare ἐκπέμπειν at 1.59.2 (Chilon to Hippokrates). Only the ephors, who take the initiative throughout, are given direct speech (as here); Anaxandrides' reactions are in indirect speech or else reported (συνεχώρησε, 'he agreed to this', **40.2**).   οὐ καλῶς συμβουλεύειν: the simple but effective expression of disapproval οὐ (or μή) καλῶς is noticeably frequent in Spartan-related contexts: see 6.69.2, and Th. 3.32.3, 93.2, 5.12.1, 52.1, 57.1.

40.1 οἱ ἔφοροι καὶ οἱ γέροντες: without explanation, but as an evident index of the increasing gravity of the matter, the *gerousia* of thirty senior life-members (twenty-eight without the kings) is now added to the ephors. But not much can be inferred from the present episode about the formal roles of these two groups. See Andrewes 1966: 4: 'once this story is read attentively, it is clear that no one has exercised any constitutional power at all or done anything but offer advice'; there is a threat, to be sure, but it is vaguely expressed and is about what the Spartiates as a whole might do if Anaxandrides does not budge at all, and he does budge. (Luther 2004: 94–9 presses the story too hard as evidence for formal judicial decision-making.) With the good-humoured outcome of this story contrast the otherwise comparable 9.111.2–3 with 112–13: the terrible fate of the Persian Masistes when he disobeys Xerxes' instruction to divorce his wife and marry Xerxes' daughter instead.

40.1 περιεχόμενόν σε ὁρῶμεν τῆς ἔχεις γυναικός 'we see you are reluctant to let go of / you cling to your present wife'. περιέχομαι takes the genitive, and the relative pronoun is attracted into the genitive of the antecedent γυναικός, dependent upon περιεχόμενον. **ἀλλοῖον**: a euphemism for 'something unpleasant' (lit. 'something different'). **βουλεύσωνται** 'resolve'. But no such resolution is necessary in the event.

40.2 διξὰς ἱστίας οἴκεε lit. 'he inhabited two separate hearths'. Cf. 4.68.2, the most solemn Skythian oaths are sworn by the 'king's hearths'; also 6.86 δ, no hearth is considered to be that of Glaukos (i.e. his line has been extinguished). **ποιέων οὐδαμῶς Σπαρτιητικά**: not conventional or even legal Spartan behaviour, to be sure (MacDowell 1986: 82–3), but we will be told at 6.57.1 that Spartan kings get double rations of *food*. John Carey, discussing the character of George Cannon in Arnold Bennett's 1911 novel *Hilda Lessways*, observes 'there is a connection between bigamy and second helpings, of course': Carey 1992: 176.

41.1 ἡ ἐσύστερον ἐπελθοῦσα γυνή, <ἐοῦσα θυγάτηρ Πρινητάδεω τοῦ Δημαρμένου>, τίκτει: the information about the woman's paternity might be better provided at her first mention, rather than at **41**.3 below. Hence Maas' transposition, accepted by Wilson and here followed; but AHG thinks the delay of the information can be justified as a device which makes for brisk story-telling, and he would even defend the repetitious material at **41**.3 (for the patronymics as a closural slowing-down device he compares 1.45.3 or 3.69.3). No name is given for the woman herself (unlike Perkalos the wife of Demaretos, but like the first wife, Anaxandrides' niece); but she gets both a patronym and a papponym. Call her x. The name Prinetades/ -as is not otherwise attested at Sparta or anywhere else; Demarmenos (listed in *LGPN* IIIB under its Doric form Damarmenos) is commoner, though the other two Spartan bearers are many centuries later. Damarmenos is the patronym of Chilon (6.65), and if this is the same Damarmenos, then Kleomenes is interestingly related through x to the other royal line: Chilon is father of Perkalon, who was betrothed to Leutychides but then 'snatched away' by Demaretos (6.65; the correct form of the girl's name is in -on). That the onomastic information about x's ancestry is, in the present passage, postponed as it is (rather than being placed at roughly the start of **41**), might mean that it is significant i.e. that we are invited to remember it when we get to bk. 6, and therefore that Damarmenos is the same man both times; but that is not certain. The family tree at Poralla 1913: 56 contains a mistake – corrected by H. T. Wade-Gery in his personal copy – in that it makes x the wife of Kleomenes rather than of his father Anaxandrides. Wade-Gery (handwritten marginal notes) offered a different genealogy, involving two men called Damarmenos, and making better generational sense (but e.g. niece-marriage shows that we must not be too rigid about this). He comments on the difficulty that according to Poralla's scheme (as corrected), Kleomenes is 'a generation later [than his actual contemporary Damaretos] if Damarmenos is the same man in the 2 cases'. Below is Wade-Gery's improved tree (in which, incidentally, the anonymity of x leaps off the page. The equally anonymous first wife is omitted).

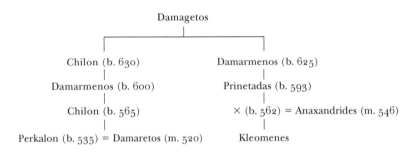

Damagetos

Chilon (b. 630)   Damarmenos (b. 625)

Damarmenos (b. 600)   Prinetadas (b. 593)

Chilon (b. 565)   X (b. 562) = Anaxandrides (m. 546)

Perkalon (b. 535) = Damaretos (m. 520)   Kleomenes

ἔφεδρον βασιλέα: 'heir-apparent' (Powell). The adjective is a metaphor from athletics: it refers to a competitor who waits to fight whoever emerges as victor in the first round. Cf. e.g. Pind. *Nem.* 4.96 for the straight athletic sense, and for an equally but differently metaphorical use cf. Xen. *An.* 2.5.10 (Klearchos to Tissaphernes: πρὸς βασιλέα τὸν μέγιστον ἔφεδρον ἀγωνιζοίμεθα); see *CT* iii: 889, discussing ἀναστάς ποτε διαγωνίσασθαι at Th. 8.46.2.   συντυχίηι ταύτηι χρησαμένη 'by coincidence'. Powell tr. 2: 706 conjectures συντυχίηι θείηι, 'by divine/marvellous chance', as at 92 γ 3.

41.2 ἔχουσαν δὲ αὐτὴν... οἱ τῆς ἐπελθούσης γυναικὸς οἰκήιοι πυθόμενοι ὤχλεον 'although she really was pregnant, when the relatives of the second wife heard about it, they began to make trouble...' With ἔχουσαν understand ἐν γαστρί (as at 3.32.4 and 4.30.2), itself an abbreviated expression for 'having [a child] in the womb'. This whole sentence gives a glimpse of the role of gossip in small-town life. Compare Nausikaa's fears of spiteful talk at *Od.* 6.273ff., or Pind. *Pyth.* 11.28, 'townsmen are evil-tongued', κακολόγοι δὲ πολῖται.   φάμενοι αὐτὴν κομπέειν ἄλλως βουλομένην ὑποβαλέσθαι 'saying she was merely (ἄλλως) boasting, and was intending to substitute a child'.

The force of ἄλλως is 'with no substance behind it'. With ὑποβαλέσθαι cf. 1.137.2, where ὑποβολιμαῖα means 'supposititious children'.

41.3 ἰθέως ἴσχει Λεωνίδην 'she immediately conceived Leonides'. The genealogy of the Agiad Spartan kings is postponed to 7.204 (Hdt. is there building up to Thermopylai). See Baragwanath 2008: 65. Much later in the *Histories*, Dorieus will be said to have died ἐν Σικελίαι (7.205.1), a statement which would be mystifying without the present passage, 5.41–2.

42.1 ὡς λέγεται, ἤν τε οὐ φρενήρης ἀκρομανής τε: 'not-x-but-the-opposite' expressions are favoured by Hdt. generally (for such polar expressions see **39.**1 n. and **72.**3; also 3.74.2 and 9.106.4); they are specially used for defects: cf. the very similar 3.25.2 on Kambyses, ἐμμανής τε ἐὼν καὶ οὐ φρενήρης (but that was confident authorial assertion, whereas this is a report of what was said); also 9.55.2 about another Spartan, Amompharetos, μαινόμενον καὶ οὐ φρενήρεα. Hdt. confines the word φρενήρης (always in negated form) to these three individuals. The parallel between Hdt.'s presentation of Kleomenes and of Kambyses is elaborated in convincing detail by Griffiths 1989. See also **42.**2n. on φρονέων. The theme of Kleomenes' supposed insanity is picked up, with a less cautious formulation, at 6.75.1, ἐόντα καὶ πρότερον ὑπομαργότερον. The text has been needlessly doubted. **εὖ τε ἠπίστατο κατ' ἀνδραγαθίην αὐτὸς σχήσων τὴν βασιληίην** 'he firmly believed that he would have the kingship, judged by manly qualities'. The reference to ἀνδραγαθίη picks up **39.**1 (referring to Kleomenes), part of a sustained presentational comparison and contrast between Kleomenes and Dorieus throughout this episode: see Hornblower 2007a: 170 for the pointedly negative presentation in the present passage, and 169 with 172 for Dorieus as foil to Kleomenes generally. ἐπίσταμαι can mean 'I know that *p*', but it does not always, even with the strengthening additive εὖ, entail the truth of proposition *p*: as 3.139.3 and 6.139.4 show, it can mean confident but wrong belief (Hornblower 2007a: 171; see Powell, listing the present passage under ἐπίσταμαι 3 'of mistaken knowledge, *suppose*', and cf. Burnyeat 2011: 11 n. 28. Burnyeat 2011 argues, surprisingly, that the verb, and the noun ἐπιστήμη, should be kept separate). This reduces, though it does not remove, the difficulty that talk of manly qualities implies an elective kingship as opposed to one based on primogeniture, whereas there is no evidence for an elective kingship before the time of Lysandros and the daring proposals he made in about 400 BC (Hornblower 2007: 170 and n. 17, citing Diod. 14.13.2–8 and Plut. *Lys.* 24–26; misunderstood by Griffith-Williams 2011: 50 and n. 13).

42.2 φρονέων: there may be a deliberate echo here of **42.**1 above: Kleomenes was there said to be not in his right 'mind' (according to some), but Dorieus was 'minded' in the way which has just been described.

Nevertheless he will turn out to have been wrongly 'minded'.   οἱ
Λακεδαιμόνιοι χρεώμενοι τῶι νόμωι ἐστήσαντο βασιλέα τὸν πρεσβύτατον: so
the method of selection was the usual and legal, or at least customary,
one (the hereditary principle), and manly qualities were irrelevant. The
admittedly formal word ἐστήσαντο need not imply 'some election or rati-
fication' (Macan). The reference may rather be to the kind of inaugural
'choruses and sacrifices' attested in this context by Th. 5.16.3.   δεινόν
τε ποιεύμενος: Dorieus' discontent is expressed in three separate ways: by
this expression, by οὐκ ἀξιῶν just after it, and a few lines later by οἷα δὲ
βαρέως φέρων. But the expedition is most unlikely to have been officially
frowned on (he is granted a troop of men by the Spartiates or possibly a
Spartiate troop, see next n.). For a close parallel see 6.35.3, Miltiades 'fed
up' with the rule of Peisistratos. The difference is that the Dorieus story
is one of specifically fraternal friction, and Hdt. has perhaps exaggerated
this aspect so as to bring it within the scope of the Brothers' Quarrel motif
which often explains colonial departures. See Burnett 1988: 149f., giving
mythical and historical examples, and noting the social truth behind such
stories: younger brothers did not inherit, and might need to make a new
life overseas.   αἰτήσας λεὼν Σπαρτιήτας: though this is strictly ambiguous, the meaning is likely to be 'he asked the Spartiates for a troop of
men' rather than 'he asked for a troop of Spartiate men'. The suggestion
that he took with him settlers from perioikic Anthana in Lakonia (*IACP*
no. 324) rests on a bold emendation in Paus. 3.16.4; see Lobel 1927: 50
with Huxley 1962: 79 and 140 n. 552.   οὔτε τῶι ἐν Δελφοῖσι χρηστηρίωι
χρησάμενος... οὔτε ποιήσας οὐδὲν τῶν νομιζομένων: the negative presentation
is emphatic, and the meaning is that he did not, as you would expect/he
did not, as he ought to have done, consult the oracle at Delphi about
this colonial venture. Cicero (*Div.* 1.1.3) asked rhetorically what Greek
colony was ever sent to the Aiolid, Asia, Sicily, or Italy without an oracle
from Delphi, Dodona or Ammon. This implied generalisation was not literally true (Londey 1990), but the present passage shows that consultation
was accepted practice, and its omission thought dangerous, even at this
late date, though many of the relevant surviving oracular replies may not
be genuine. For Spartan consultation of Delphi even later (the 420s) in
connection with another Herakleia (Trachinia) see Th. 3.92.5 and Parker
2000: 86 (that particular consultation said to be not 'an absolute formality'); at 85–7 he cites other classical examples, but notes that there is little Hellenistic evidence for oracular consultation before the dispatch of
colonies.

42.3 ἀπικόμενος δὲ ἐς Κίνυπα οἴκισε χῶρον κάλλιστον παρὰ ποταμόν: for
the river Kinyps near the later Lepcis Magna (*Barr.* map 35 C2), see
4.175.2 and 198.1. Here and at **43**, it is surprising that Hdt. gives no hint

that he has talked about these regions already, and not long ago in his narrative. Kinyps was described in the 4th cent. BC by Ps.-Skylax (109.4) as 'a fine locality and a city, which is deserted', and on the strength of this modern authorities both award it full *polis* status, and conjecture that Dorieus may possibly have left behind him a short-lived settlement (Shipley 2011: 191, and more hesitantly *IACP*: no. 1027, cf. p. 1237 col. 1). ὑπὸ Μακέων: for the Makai (*Barr.* map 37 A-C), see 4.175.1.

43 Ἀντιχάρης ἀνὴρ Ἐλεώνιος: Eleon or Heleon near Tanagra in Boiotia was not a *polis*, but one of the 'four villages' (*tetrakomia*) which formed part of the *chora* or territory of the polis of Tanagra. See Strabo 9.2.14 with *IACP*: p. 453 (part of no. 220, Tanagra); also Toepffer 1889: 294. The oracle-collector Bakis also came from this same tiny place: a remarkable coincidence, or else informative about the intense religious culture of the locality (Parke 1988: 181 and 189 n. 25.) The name Antichares is not rare; it is specially common at Delphi. The only other probably Boiotian bearer of the name (no. 2 in *LGPN* IIIB, 'THEBES?') is himself attested in a 2nd cent. BC Delphic inscription, *SGDI* 2032.11. ἐκ τῶν Λαΐου χρησμῶν: these 'oracles of Laios', father of Oidipous in myth, have been found incredible (they are not otherwise attested), and some edd. prefer Λάσου (for Lasos' activity at Athens see Hdt. 7.6.3 and generally *OCD*[4] 'Lasus') or Ἰάμου (for the famous Iamid family of seers, see 44.2 and Pind. *Ol.* 6). But we know too little about ancient Greek divination at the local level to deny that a collection of oracles might have been ascribed to Laios. The Boiotian connection makes Theban Laios appropriate enough. Ἡρακλείην τὴν ἐν Σικελίηι κτίζειν: either understand πόλιν with τήν or else translate 'Herakleia, the one in Sicily' (there was a Herakleia Minoa in the S. of the island, *IACP*: no. 20, and 46.2n.). Expansion to γῆν τήν is neither necessary nor desirable. The entire context is about city foundations, and the name Herakleia is regularly used of Spartan cities. Spartan colonial city foundations tended, unimaginatively, to be called Herakleia, after the god-hero from whom both royal houses traced descent: two such foundations in the second half of the 5th cent. were Herakleia Trachinia in central Greece (Th. 3.92), and Herakleia in south Italian Lucania (Strabo 6.1.14 = *FGrHist* 555 Antiochos F 11). But for a city in the west of Sicily, Herakles was a specially appropriate patron because of his struggle against the local wrestler Eryx. τὴν Ἔρυκος χώρην πᾶσαν εἶναι Ἡρακλειδέων αὐτοῦ Ἡρακλέος κτησαμένου: Eryx was eponymous mythical founder of the city and sanctuary (for which see Th. 6.2.1 and 46.3; it was at the western end of Sicily). He was an indigenous ruler whom Herakles defeated in a wrestling match, and thus acquired possession of Eryx' territory. This is a foundation myth asserting Greek rights over western Sicily as against Phoenician (Gantz 1993: 409; Malkin 1994: 217). For the myth see Diod. 4.23 and 83, also

Lykoph. *Alex.* 866; cf. Malkin 1994: 203–18 and 2011: 123–4 and 133–6 (stressing the relevance of the Phoenician cult of Melqart/Herakles in W. Sicily; cf. also Davison 1992: 388) and Battistoni 2010: 124 and n. 58. It is attractive to suppose that the poet Stesichoros of Sicilian Himera gave some of this material in his *Geryoneis* (Malkin 1994: 206–11), but Hdt. does not mention his poetry anywhere, not even at 2.112ff. where a mention would have been highly appropriate (the various versions of the story of Helen). And Hdt. here, in his report of Antichares' advice, shows no awareness of the traditions which linked Eryx to the Trojans and esp. Aineias, and which have been speculatively traced to Stesichoros (Gruen 1990: 8f. and 14 with n. 40; 1993: 14).

44–45 *The war between the Sybarites and Krotoniates*

This episode is a small *diegema* inside the larger *diegesis* which is the Dorieus episode as a whole (for these rhetorical terms see above, introd. n. on **39–48**). It is notable for its length (Munson 2006: 261), for the semi-religious character of the arguments used (gifts of sacred land and so on), and for Hdt.'s refusal to adjudicate between the two versions, Sybarite and Krotoniate (**45**.2, end). Nevertheless most scholars have suspected that Hdt., who in one ancient tradition settled at Sybaris' successor city Thourioi (Munson 2006: 257, citing Arist. *Rhet.* 1409a34), favoured the version of his own adoptive 'townsmen', as Macan puts it at p. 186. The people of Kroton naturally prefer the version according to which they had help only from the seer Kallies (i.e. god was on their side); the Sybarites equally naturally make out that the Krotoniates prevailed only because of the assistance of the energetic visiting Spartan.

44.1 ὡς λέγουσι Συβαρῖται: the Achaian (perhaps also Troizenian) foundation Sybaris is, unlike Kroton, new to us, but is introduced here casually via its plural ethnic, with no further explanation. It is at *Barr.* map 46 E2 and is *IACP*: no. 70, a complex entry with several subdivisions. For the city's fate as structurally important in the *Histories* for the reason given above, see introd. n. to **39–48**.   **Τῆλυν τὸν ἑωυτῶν βασιλέα** 'their king, Telys'. This is authorial description; but at **44**.2, he will be called ὁ Συβαριτέων τύραννος. The focalisation makes a difference: the second occurrence is more disparaging, because it is put into the mouth of the Krotoniates. So this ch. as a whole does not prove that the two nouns βασιλεύς and τύραννος were interchangeable, or that τύραννος was not yet a bad word. Better support for the idea of interchangeability is at **46**.2 (Selinous), but there the two words are τυραννίς and μούναρχος (not βασιλεύς). See n. there on αὐτὸς τυραννίδι.   **ἐπὶ Κρότωνα:** Kroton, also an Achaian foundation, is *IACP*: no. 56. Note *IACP*: p. 267 on the foundation: 'Spartan participation (Paus.

3.3.1) is a tradition probably no older than the victory over Sybaris and the expedition of Dorieus.' Kroton is familiar to us because of the story of the doctor Demokedes, 3.131.1 and 136–8.

44.2 Καλλίην τῶν 'Ιαμιδέων μάντιν 'Ηλεῖον: for the Iamid family of seers, *manteis*, see 9.33–5 and Pind. *Ol.* 6, in which – as here – there is a west Greek (actually Syracusan), as well as an Eleian (and Arkadian), aspect: *Th. and Pi.*: 184 n. 212. (Elis: the poem is for an Olympic victory and the Eleians managed the Olympic festival.) For the Iamidai generally see Kett 1966, Flower 2008b, Hornblower 2012: 97–102; for the present episode, Flower 2008a: 156 and 2008b: 195; Hornblower 2012: 99; for the Krotonian aspect, see Giangiulio 1989: 73f. and Malkin 1998b: 133 (also 1998a: 219), suggesting that it was at the instance of the Iamidai that the Krotoniates exploited the mythical traditions about Philoktetes' presence in the region so as to help them prevail over Sybaris (see Lykoph. *Alex.* 911–29) and that this explains the rewards the Iamidai received at Kroton (**45.2**). Kallies (Kett 1966 no. 41) may be the unnamed Eleian seer of 3.132.2.   **ἐπείτε οἱ τὰ ἱρὰ οὐ προεχώρεε χρηστὰ θυομένωι ἐπὶ Κρότωνα** 'since he did not get good omens for the attack on Kroton'. Kallies' switch of sides needed explaining (though summoned by the ruler of Sybaris, he defects to the Krotoniates). It has been suggested that the imperfect tense of οὐ προεχώρεε should be pressed: he *repeatedly* tried to get good sacrificial omens for the Sybarites, but when he failed, 'the will of the gods was clear' so it was all right for him to desert – or so he made out afterwards in self-exculpation. (See Flower, as in previous n.) But this underrates the extent to which Greek sacrifices must often have been repeated.

Note the long-term implications: at 8.47 we will learn that the people of Kroton were the only west Greeks to come over and fight with the Greeks in their time of peril (Salamis), so the divine will was already starting to work itself out when Kallies made his sacrifices.

45.1 ταῦτα δ' ὧν οὗτοι λέγουσι 'so that is what they say'. The MSS' οὐχ or οὐκ must be wrong, and Wilson, following de la Barre, assumes corruption of ὧν, first to οὖν and then to οὐκ.   **'Αθηναίηι ἐπωνύμωι Κραθίηι:** the Krathis was a river in the Sybarite interior: 1.145 for its naming after the river Krathis in Achaia, the metropolis of the Sybarites; cf. Lykoph. *Alex.* 919 (Italian Krathis the site of the tomb of Philoktetes). Athena's divine *epiklesis* or cult-epithet Krathaia or –aie (Ionic) is not otherwise attested; but for possible archaeological evidence for an Athena cult at Sybaris see *IACP* pp. 296 and 297 (under no. 70, Sybaris I and II), and note the part-metrical agonistic inscription dating from the later 6th cent., discovered at Sybaris, honouring the Olympic victor Kleomrotos [*sic*], who made a dedication to Athena (not to Zeus, patron of the Olympic festival): Ebert pp. 251–5,

CEG no. 394 and Colvin 2007: no. 62; detailed discussion at Hornblower 2007b. 'Krathie' is here a divine cult epithet, for which Hdt. uses the word ἐπώνυμος. Another word for the same thing is ἐπίκλησις, but although *epiklesis* is a convenient modern word where there was actual cult, the Greek equivalent is not a technical term for a cult epithet (as opposed to a poetic adjective for a god). It is found only once in Hdt. in this sense: 1.19.1, also about Athena: Ἀθηναίης ἐπίκλησιν Ἀσσησίης, where, as also here, the epithet derives from a place or topographical feature (see *IACP* p. 1058 for Milesian Assesos). ἐπώνυμος has the same meaning in the present passage, and implies cult, no less than does 1.19. Hdt. makes no clear distinction between the two terms or their respective cognates, as shown by a passage where he uses both in the same breath: 2.112.2, ξείνης Ἀφροδίτης ἐπώνυμόν ἐστι· ὅσα γὰρ ἄλλα Ἀφροδίτης ἱρά ἐστιν, οὐδαμῶς ξείνης ἐπικαλέεται. **εἷλε ἂν τὴν Ἐρυκίνην χώρην καὶ ἑλὼν κατέσχε**: the counterfactual statement could have been extended further and deeper: if the Spartans had established themselves securely in western Sicily before the Persian wars and spread out from there, the history of the 5th cent. would have been different; but in the event they confined their ambitions largely to mainland Greece (Stadter 2012: 6). Largely but not entirely: for Sicily as object of imperialist ambitions by both Spartans and Athenians in the entire period late 6th cent to early 4th, see *CT* III: 5–12, discussing the present episode at 6–7; add Whitehead 2008 for a possibly relevant 4th-cent. episode.

45.2 ἐξαίρετα 'perquisites', i.e. specially allocated plots of land. For these rewards see **44.2**n. on Καλλίην... **τὰ καὶ ἐς ἐμὲ ἔτι ἐνέμοντο οἱ Καλλίεω ἀπόγονοι**: 'down to my time' is most naturally taken as evidence of a personal visit by Hdt., and interrogation by him of Kallies' descendants, at whatever period we take 'my time' to be: presumably but not quite necessarily after the late 440s and the foundation of Thourioi. For such formulae as creating intimacy with the reader, see **58**.3n.   **τοῖσι Δωριέος ἀπογόνοισι**: it would come as a surprise to be told that Dorieus the Spartan had descendants *who settled in south Italy*; but Hdt. is not saying that he did, and indeed their non-existence strengthens his point. The negative formulation merely balances, with emphatic fulness, what has just been said about Kallies and his descendants. The sense is 'but nothing of the sort happened to Dorieus – or his descendants'.   **τοῦ Συβαριτικοῦ πολέμου**: for the use of such 'ktetics' or possessive adjectives to describe wars, see Fraser 2009: 35–6 and n. 55.   **καὶ πάρεστι, ὁκοτέροισί τις πείθεται αὐτῶν, τούτοισι προσχωρέειν**: after an exceptionally full account of the arguments on both sides, Hdt. leaves the choice open; see introd. n. to **44–45**.

46.1 Θεσσαλὸς καὶ Παραιβάτης καὶ Κελέης καὶ Εὐρυλέων: the names mean 'Thessalian', 'warrior who stands next to the charioteer', 'courser' (from κέλης, a race-horse), 'wide (i.e. 'far-reaching'?) lion'. The names here specified are of interest (as is the specification itself, as showing the importance Hdt. attached to this episode). They all have a definite athletic/equestrian flavour: *Th. and Pi.* 305 for details (in particular Paraibatas has 'horsey' connotations and is well attested at Kyrene, colony of the Spartan colony Thera). For the name Thessalos (Thessaly was a famous horse-breeding country, cf. 7.196), see Lavelle 1985; Sickinger, comm. on *BNJ* 373 Heliodoros F5. Travelling groups of five men (here four + Dorieus himself) are found in Spartan contexts on other occasions: see e.g. 1.67.5 for the 'agathoergoi', and Th. 3.52.3 for the five judges sent to Plataia. **ὑπό τε Φοινίκων**: by 7.158, when Gelon reminds the Spartans of their failures in western Sicily, the Phoenicians have 'disappeared' and Dorieus is said to have been defeated by the Egestaians alone. The Egestaians were perhaps topical when Hdt. was active. They were important in the run-up to the Sicilian expedition of 415, and might for all we know have played a similar role earlier, e.g. in the Athenian expedition to Sicily of 427–424. See *TT*: 284. **τούτου τοῦ πάθεος**: cf. 6.18: an equivalent *pathos* or disaster befalls Miletos. For the 'only one survivor' motif, specially common in poetry, see below, **85**.2n.

46.2 ἔσχε Μινώην τὴν Σελινουσίων ἀποικίην: for this city, otherwise called Herakleia Minoa (but Hdt. avoids the longer name, perhaps to avoid confusion?), see *IACP* no. 21, listing it as 'Herakleia (2)'. (*IACP*'s Sicilian 'Herakleia (1)' is Dorieus' colony near Eryx, but see above on **39–48**: this city never got off the ground.) Selinous, in the far west of the south coast of Sicily (*IACP* no. 44), was a colony of Sicilian Megara (*IACP* no. 36), which was in turn a colony of 'Nisaian' Megara in central Greece (*IACP* no. 225). These four colonial 'generations' Megara-Megara-Selinous-Minoa are remarkable, but not unparalleled (cf. the sequence Sparta-Thera-Kyrene-Euesperides, with *CT* III: 641 on Th. 7.50.2). Hdt. mentions Selinous only in this ch. **καὶ συνελευθέρου Σελινουσίους τοῦ μουνάρχου Πειθαγόρεω**: the verb means he 'helped to liberate' them. *IACP* p. 222 says that 'Selinous was mostly governed by tyrants', but apart from Peithagores and Euryleon in the present passage, there is not much hard evidence. An undatable story at Polyainos 1.28.2 (with Luraghi 1994: 54–5) features a Theron son of Miltiades who, during a war against the Carthaginians, uses a force of slaves to acquire the tyranny over the Selinountines by trickery. The story may be reliable, though both name and patronym are suspiciously the same as well-known 'tyrannical' figures at Akragas and Athens respectively. **αὐτὸς τυραννίδι ἐπεχείρησε Σελινοῦντος καὶ ἐμουνάρχησε χρόνον ἐπ' ὀλίγον**: the cynical opportunism of these spoiling Spartan individuals is staggering, and gives a no doubt correct picture of a certain type of rampant archaic Greek individualism: *Th. and Pi.*: 305. For Euryleon's activity in western Sicily see Malkin 2011: 137–41.

The vocabulary for these periods of one-man rule displays more interchangeability between terms ('tyranny', *mounarchos*) than that found at **44** above, although '*mounarchoi*' will be applied to the tyrannical Bacchiadai of Korinth at **92** β 2 (oracle).   ἀπέκτειναν καταφυγόντα ἐπὶ Διὸς Ἀγοραίου βωμόν: fleeing to an altar was often a recourse against stoning: for the combination of the two, cf. the material (including poetic) at *CT* III: 158–9 and 992–4 on Th. 5.60.6 and 8.84.3. But Euryleon, unlike them, does not escape with his life. Contrast **38**.1n. (Koes): stoning, but no mention of fleeing to an altar.

Agoraios, 'of the agora', was one of the commonest and most geographically widespread *epikleseis* (cult epithets) of Zeus.; see *OCD*[4], 'Zeus', and, for the full details, Schwabl 1978: cols. 256–9. But this is Hdt.'s only mention of this Zeus.

47.1 ἁρμοσάμενος: for the verb, see **32**n.   **ψευσθεὶς δὲ τοῦ γάμου** 'cheated of his marriage', i.e. foiled or disappointed in his marriage hopes. **οἰκηίηι τε τριήρεϊ καὶ οἰκηίηι ἀνδρῶν δυνάμι**: on the text (Powell's clever δυνάμι, not the MSS' δαπάνηι) see Wilson: 'expense of men' would be an odd expression. The repetition of οἰκηίηι is emphatic on either reading. With this privately-owned and manned ship cf. the similar (and similarly emphatic) language used at 8.17 about Kleinias the son of Alkibiades at Artemision (surely a substantive parallel between these two larger-than-life athletic/equestrian individuals is intended): δαπάνην οἰκηίην παρεχόμενος ἐστρατεύετο ἀνδράσι τε διηκοσίοισι καὶ οἰκηίηι νηί (but the similarity is slightly less without δαπάνηι in the present passage). See also Th. 6.50.1 (the younger Alkibiades) with *CT* III: 425–6. For the hop from Sicily to Kyrene or in reverse, see Th. 7.50.2, and, for routine traffic between Sicily and Libya, Theok. 1.24 and 3.5.   **Ὀλυμπιονίκης**: for Krotonian athletic success see Miller 2000, and cf. Phayllos at 8.47 below. Philippos is Moretti no. 135. Hdt. frequently mentions past athletic or equestrian successes of individuals, much more frequently than does Th. (*Th. and Pi.*: 10). He is aware of the link between war and athletic/equestrian contests. Hdt. shows his awareness of contests as warlike most obviously at 9.33.2–3 (Teisamenos of Elis) where the ambiguity of *agon*, 'contest', is spelt out and exploited: οὐκ ἐς γυμνικοὺς ἀλλ' ἐς ἀρηίους ἀγῶνας. See **22**.2n. (Alexandros of Macedon), **71**n. (Kylon of Athens), **72**.4n. (Timesitheos of Delphi), **102**.3n. (Eualkides of Eretria), 6.70.3. (Demaretos of Sparta), 103.2 (Kimon of Athens), 122.1 (Kallias of Athens, unless interpolated), 125.5 (Alkmaion of Athens), 126.2 (Kleisthenes of Sikyon), 8.47 (Phayllos of Kroton, with Tod: no. 21), 9.33.2 (Hieronymos of Andros). Cf. also 6.127.3 for Pheidon of Argos' usurped presidency of the Olympic festival.

47.2 διὰ δὲ τὸ ἑωυτοῦ κάλλος ἠνείκατο παρὰ Ἐγεσταίων τὰ οὐδεὶς ἄλλος: the verb ἠνείκατο means 'he won for himself', aorist middle, from the verbal form ἐνείκ- (Attic ἐνεγκ-) which does duty for some of the past tenses of φέρω; and we must understand with it a noun such as 'a prize/tribute'. τά is relative: 'such things as nobody else has won'. As for διὰ δὲ τὸ ἑωυτοῦ κάλλος, Homer *Iliad* 2.673–4 commented pathetically on Nireus, most beautiful of all the Greeks who came to Troy; in Hdt. cf. 9.96.2, Tigranes. But athletes in particular were often good-looking boys and men, so perhaps this is a mere expansion of the athletic point above. The generalisation was, however, not always true. Here is Pindar on a physically unimpressive athlete, 477 BC: 'it was not his fortune to inherit the stature of Orion; he was paltry to look at. But his wrestling strength...': Pind. *Isthm.* 4.49–50 on Melissos of Thebes. (The model may be *Il.* 5.810, Tydeus.)   ἐπὶ... τοῦ τάφου αὐτοῦ ἡρώιον ἱδρυσάμενοι θυσίηισι αὐτὸν ἱλάσκονται: the hero-cult is notable because the Egestaians are not Greek (cf. 2.50.3 for hero-cult as Greek). But see Th. 6.19.1 for the Egestaians' knowledge of another distinctively practised Greek ritual, supplication. See Currie 2005: 120 and n. 2: Phoenician influence has been suggested, not very plausibly. These look like hellenisers.

It is often said that the words θυσίαι and (verb) θύειν are appropriate for celestial, Olympian sacrifice, whereas ἐναγίσματα and (verb) ἐναγίζειν are appropriate for 'chthonian' hero-cult: cf. (the classic text) Hdt. 2.167.2 on Herakles. It would be better to say that θυσίαι and θύειν (lit. 'making smoke') are the more general words; cf. Arist. *Eth. Nic.* 1134b24 (Brasidas), where comparison with Th. 5.11.1 shows that hero-cult is meant. This sort of lexical overlap does not justify extreme modern arguments tending to deconstruct the entire notion of hero-cult.

For 'propitiation' [lit. 'to make cheerful'], ἱλάσκεσθαι, see Burkert 1985: 195, and 273. The anger of the dead, and especially of heroes, who are often malign, needs to be appeased. Currie 2005: 120. Boedeker 1987: 190 thinks that Philippos belonged to the category of posthumously disgruntled 'hero-athletes' in need of appeasement, a category identified by Fontenrose 1968 in a classic structuralist study. Cf. below, n. on **114.1** (Onesilos).

48 οὐ γάρ τινα πολλὸν χρόνον ἦρξε ὁ Κλεομένης, ἀλλ' ἀπέθανε ἄπαις: chronologically problematic. If Kleomenes was still king shortly before Marathon in 490, as he certainly was, but was already king at the time of the events described and dated to 519 at Th. 3.68.5 (cf. below, Hdt. 6.108), how can Hdt. say here that he 'ruled for no long time'? One solution has been to emend the relevant numeral in Th., but there is no justification for this (see *CT* 1: 465). Another (see Nenci) is to take Hdt. to mean that there was no long interval between the deaths of Dorieus and of Kleomenes, but in that case Hdt. has expressed himself with unusual and almost Thucydidean compression. (Wilson suggests emending to οὐ γὰρ ἔτι πολλὸν χρόνον...,

so that Hdt. would be saying that Kleomenes did not live much longer.)
A clever and palaeographically tiny solution was propounded by Griffiths
1989: 54. He changes Hdt.'s οὐ to εἰ 'for while it is true that Kleomenes had
a pretty long reign, still he died without an heir'; here ἀλλά is 'apodotic'
as at e.g. **39**.2, cf. Denniston 1954: 11–13. Pelling 2007: 192 n. 43 is not
convinced, partly because it is hard to see what τινα is doing before πολλὸν
χρόνον, partly because such protases are usually negative (cf., again, **39**.2).
Griffiths' solution is attractive. Nevertheless the MSS' reading is here hesitantly preferred.   ἄπαις, θυγατέρα μούνην λιπών, τῆι οὔνομα ἦν Γοργώ:
'childless, leaving only a daughter' sounds to us like comically blatant sex-
ism, though it is said (oral information provided by UCL female MA students in 2008–10) that some Greek fathers nowadays still speak in this
way, naming only their sons when asked the number of their παιδιά. At
7.205.1, we have a longer form which spells out what Hdt. obviously means
in the present passage, viz. 'without a male heir': ἀποθανόντος δὲ Κλεομένεος ἄπαιδος ἔρσενος γόνου (cf. also 6.71.2, Leutychides). For another use
of ἄπαις on its own to mean 'without a male heir', see **67**.4 (Polybos of
Sikyon).

The name 'Gorgo', carefully withheld until the end of the *diegema*, is a
narrative seed: see **51**; also 7.239, where she and her cleverness close the
whole bk., and she is denominated as 'Kleomenes' daughter and Leonides'
wife: Gorgo': note the climactic position of the name. The name 'Gorgo',
the 'grim one', is, as Gow 1950. 2: 266 says, 'not uncommon' (cf. Theokri-
tos' chatty Syracusan woman in *Id.* 15). It is an apotropaic name, designed
to ward off malignant demons: cf. Hes. *Theog.* 274 and Bechtel 1917: 564.
The adjective γοργός also has military connotations at Sparta in particular;
see Harman 2008: 79 n. 36.

49–51 *Aristagores and Kleomenes*

See Solmsen 1943: 196–200 and esp. Pelling 2007.

49.1 Ἀπικνέεται ... ἀρχήν: Aristagores is called 'tyrant' (he no longer actually is that, having resigned his tyranny, but the designation has stuck
to him), but Kleomenes 'has the *arche*'. This too is misleading, but in a
different way: it ignores the partly collective realities of decision-making
at Sparta: see on **49**.9 below. Hdt. wants us to think that both are autocrats for the purposes of this head-to-head encounter, but at the same
time he drops a hint (again **49**.9, but see **50**.1n.) that this was not the
whole truth, as far as Kleomenes was concerned. Note in particular that
Hdt. completely ignores, for the moment, the existence of the other
Spartan king. He is saving up Demaretos until the tensions described at
75.1.   ἔχων χάλκεον πίνακα ἐν τῶι γῆς ἁπάσης περίοδος ἐνετέτμητο 'bringing with him a bronze tablet on which was engraved a map of the whole
world'.   πίνακα: the word πίναξ, which comes to be used for a list (hence

'pinakographer', a compiler of lists), means a (painted) panel or (bronze) tablet, perhaps of the kind implied at Ar. *Nub.* 206. It cannot have been large if Aristagores carried it round with him on his help-raising journey as a visual aid. It must (despite Brodersen in Dueck and Brodersen 2012: 107–8) have done more work than a mere list or itinerary would have done, if only in the sense that its main function was as a spectacular visual adjunct to Aristagores' more detailed rhetoric. Aristagores points to it at **49**.5 (δεικνύς) and uses 'deictic' words such as οἵδε or ἥδε ('here are', 'here is') about the Lydians and Phrygians at **49**.5, about Cyprus and the sea round it, the Kilikians, the Armenians, and the land (χώρη) of the Matienoi at **49**.6, and the river Choaspes and Sousa at **49**.7. [Longinus] *Subl.* 26.2 commented that Hdt.'s geographical descriptions enable the reader to visualise the places in question; the present passage would have been a very good illustration of this (cf. Nünlist 2009: 155).

The first person to have drawn the inhabited world on a map is said to have been the philosopher Anaximandros from Anaxagores' city of Miletos: Strabo 1.1.11, citing Eratosthenes; so too Agathemeros (*GGM* 2.471, date uncertain), who adds 'after him the much-travelled, πολυπλανής, Hekataios [another Milesian] corrected it'. Agathemeros goes on to say that Hellanikos wrote his history without one, ἀπλάστως, *sine tabula*, as Müller translates it. See Dilke 1985: 23–4 and *OCD*[4], 'maps'. Dilke 23 acutely notes that since Kleomenes has to ask how many days the journey would take (**50**.1), the map presumably had no indication of scale (but the question is necessary preparation for the punch-line at **50**.3, and may not have been guileless on the part of Kleomenes, or, if one prefers, of Hdt.). See also Dilke 112: Aristagores' map may have depended on the Persian courier system, and will probably (Dilke 23) have included the Royal Road, about to be described below. Maps were not everyday items in the ancient world (Shipley 2011: 10), and part of the reason why Hdt. writes up this episode may be because Aristagores' map was a famous curiosity. (For the remarkable maps included in a recently discovered papyrus of what appears to be a post-classical Greek geographical text, see *OCD*[4] 'Artemidorus (2)' and bibliography: the authenticity of the papyrus is disputed.)

49.1 (cont.) γῆς … περίοδος: the word περίοδος is lit. a 'going-round' or 'circuit'. Here, as also at Ar. *Nub.* 206 and at **49**.5 below, γῆς περίοδος really means a physical *map* of the whole world; so also at the polemical 4.36.2.

Hekataios of Miletos (**36**.2n.) is immediately suggested to us by the two words γῆς περίοδος, which, in the order περίοδος γῆς, form the title often given in modern times to his literary work of geographical description. The more usual ancient title of Hekataios' work was, however, περιήγησις; see Jacoby 1956: 188, who suggested that the title περίοδος γῆς may have been taken from Hdt. 4.36.2 by a partial misapplication.

49.2 Κλεόμενες: Aristagores does not address him as βασιλεῦ, because that would be too deferential (it was normally avoided for Greek kings, cf. Dickey 1996: 92; but see her 237 for an exception, a Spartan king addressed as such by his mother in unusual circumstances, Plut. *Ag. and Kleom.* 43.7). For Greek kings, the name is usually used (Dickey 236), but see the address of the Athenian priestess to Kleomenes at **72.3**. With the form of address with no ὦ, contrast the opening of Kleomenes' reply at **50.3**, ὦ ξεῖνε Μιλήσιε. Though it is generally impossible to say whether it is the presence or the absence of ὦ which indicates the greater formality (Dickey reaches no conclusion: 199–206), Kleomenes' tone at **50.3** is displeased and even threatening.   **ὅσωι προέστατε τῆς Ἑλλά-δος:** 'inasmuch as you are the leaders of Greece'. Cf. (with Pohlenz 1937: 34 and n. 2) 1.69.2, ὑμέας γὰρ πυνθάνομαι προεστάναι τῆς Ἑλλάδος (Kroisos, as reported by his messengers at Sparta). The flattering rhetoric is less anachronistically exaggerated on the present occasion, half a century later.

49.3 νῦν ὦν...ῥύσασθε ῎Ιωνας ἐκ δουλοσύνης, ἄνδρας ὁμαίμονας 'so now, by the Greek gods, save from slavery the Ionians, your kinsmen', i.e. 'save the Ionians, your fellow-Greeks' (the Greek does not mean 'save your fellow-Ionians'). See **97.2** for Aristagores' version of kinship rhetoric at Athens, the mother-city of the speaker's native Miletos; there he says that the Ionians are 'colonists of the Athenians'. At Sparta, it would seem that he can invoke only Greekness of a general sort. If so, it is interesting that he attempts 'kinship diplomacy' (Jones 1999) at all. Aristagores is, in fact, pushing rhetoric as far as it will go (and that is why he stresses the gods of the Greeks etc.).

But there is an alternative way of taking 'kinship' here: Hdt. perhaps makes Aristagores allude unspecifically to a tradition otherwise ignored in the *Histories*, according to which Miletos was founded by Sarpedon from Dorian Krete (*FGrHist* 70 F 127, from Strabo 14.1.6; cf. Huxley 1969: 87, who suggests a link with the Kretan Milatos or Miletos in the Homeric Catalogue of Ships: *Il.* 2.647; Paus. 7.2.5 has a relevantly similar story, and says this was the Milesians' own account). Aristagores, who was quite clever enough to have exploited this kinship connection at Dorian Sparta, preferred to keep things vague. But we cannot be sure that this tradition antedates Ephoros (mid 4th cent.); Hdt. does know a story of Kretan immigration to Asia Minor under Sarpedon, but to Lykia not Miletos (1.173). The decisive objection, however, is that Aristagores is talking here about the Ionians generally, not about Miletos in particular, contrast **97.2**, his reported speech at Athens. At best, we might suppose that Hdt. has here abbreviated a report of a longer speech in which the Milesians featured specifically, and that this memorable (and surprising) detail survived. See Introduction, n. 51.

49.3 (cont.) εὐπετέως δὲ ὑμῖν ταῦτα οἷά τε χωρέειν ἐστί 'you will easily be able to succeed in this' lit. 'for you this can be easy to succeed in'. The word 'easily' (here and at paras. 4 and 8 below, and again at **97**.1) practically warns us of its own falseness: see **31**.3n. ἥ τε μάχη αὐτῶν ἐστι τοιήδε: the description of Persian fighting methods ignores their impressive cavalry, and this makes it suspect to us, the readers or hearers. ἀναξυρίδας... κυρβασίας 'trousers'... 'stiff peaked caps'. Trousers were regarded by Greeks as 'weird and theatrical', so that Alexander the Great avoided them (and the tiara) even when in other ways he adopted items of Median dress: Plut. *Alex.* 45 and *Mor.* 329f–330a = *FGrHist* 241 Eratosthenes F30. For the stiff peaked caps or *kyrbasiai* (the same as the tiara) see 7.64 and Ar. *Av.* 487 with Dunbar 1995: 333. Greeks were fascinated by the differences between Asiatic and Greek clothing; see Hordern 2002: 218 on Περσίδα στολήν at Timoth. *Pers.* 167.

49.4 ἀπὸ χρυσοῦ ἀρξαμένοισι 'including [lit. 'beginning with'] gold'. ἐσθὴς ποικίλη 'embroidered clothes'. Cf. Aesch. *Ag.* 923. We are dangerously close to the arrogance of Agamemnon (see **49**.7n. on τῶι Διί...). The mention of ἐσθής looks not only backwards from Aeschylus but forwards, to Hdt.'s own description of the terror inspired at Marathon by ἐσθὴς ποικίλη (6.112.3 with Pelling 2007: 194). Here, by contrast, Persian clothing is merely one species of desirable booty, as it will be again after Plataia (9.80.2). τὰ θυμῶι βουλόμενοι αὐτοὶ ἂν ἔχοιτε 'you could have whatever your heart desires of all this'.

49.5 δεικνὺς δὲ ἔλεγε ταῦτα ἐς τῆς γῆς τὴν περίοδον 'and he pointed to the map of the world as he spoke'. The direct speech is interrupted for the authorial insertion about the *pinax*. Direct speech is then resumed with the emphatic double expression ἔφη λέγων. But (see next n.) Herodotus's authorial presence will continue to be felt. πάντων τῶν ἐγὼ οἶδα: Aristagores is made to use a characteristically Herodotean expression (1.142 etc.; see Shimron 1973 for πρῶτος τῶν ἡμεῖς ἴδμεν, and cf. below, 119.2n.). This helps to create a stereophonic effect in the geographical paragraphs which follow: there are really two speakers, Aristagores and Hdt. himself. But in **52** Hdt. will supplement this, e.g. by mentioning the great rivers Halys, Euphrates and Gyndes, here omitted. And it is possible that despite the 'stereophony', **52** seeks to correct **49** in some respects. See **52**.2n.

49.6 Κίλικες, κατήκοντες ἐπὶ θάλασσαν τήνδε, ἐν τῆι ἥδε Κύπρος νῆσος κεῖται: Kilikia's nearness to Cyprus will soon have a reality 'off the map'. See **108**.2 and n., citing Casabonne 2004, for Kilikia as the naval base from which the Persian attack was launched on rebel Cyprus. Ἀρμένιοι οἵδε: for Armenia see *Barr.* map. 89 and bk. 4 of Xen. *Anab.*, and for Matiene/Matiane map 89 H4.

49.7 Κισσίη, ἐν τῆι δὴ παρὰ ποταμὸν τόνδε Χοάσπην κείμενά ἐστι τὰ Σοῦσα ταῦτα: the climax: wealthy Sousa as magnet for greed. The river Choaspes was described more elaborately, and as a kind of 'marvel', at 1.188–9 (the king drinks from no other water, and chariots carrying its water trundle after him with it). But in the present rhetorical context, the marvel is naturally not repeated (contrast the authorial **101**.2, which repeats information from bk. 1 about the gold-bearing Paktolos; see n. there). Cf. Munson 2001: 9 and 11. Sousa itself was introduced elaborately at 1.188. See **25.**1n.   **τῶι Διὶ πλούτου περὶ ἐρίζετε:** the comparison, even restricted as it is to riches, would make a Greek reader or listener gasp, and is the clearest signal in the speech that Aristagores goes much too far. Homer's Apollo warns Diomedes against fighting against the gods (*Il.* 5.440–2, cf. *Od.* 4.78, Ζηνὶ βροτῶν οὐκ ἄν τις ἐρίζοι), and even Aeschylus' Agamemnon realises the danger of putting himself on a level with gods by walking on the purple (though he does it all the same): *Ag.* 922–4.

49.8 ἀλλὰ περὶ μὲν χώρης ἄρα οὐ πολλῆς οὐδὲ οὕτω χρηστῆς: there is a pre-echo here of the final ch. of the *Histories* (9.122), with its choice between good land and bad land (Pelling 2007: 194).   **πρός τε Μεσσηνίους ἐόντας ἰσοπαλέας καὶ Ἀρκάδας τε καὶ Ἀργείους:** the word ἰσοπαλής, 'equally matched' (a metaphor from wrestling, πάλη), occurs elsewhere in Hdt. only at 1.82.4, in a relevantly similar context, a battle between Spartans and Argives. For the perennial Spartan-Argive hostility, see *CT* iii: 66, n. on Th. 5.29.1, citing Tyrtaios fr. 23a West (it mentions Arkadians also). The present passage has been, not very convincingly, pressed to prove that the crushing Spartan defeat of the Argives at Sepeia could not have occurred before 500 BC, or Aristagores would not have spoken of the Argives as a threat; for the chronological problems of Sepeia, see 6.76.1n., citing Macan on that passage. For 5th-cent. Spartan conflicts with all three groups here mentioned, see 9.35.2. Before we dismiss Aristagores' knowledge of Spartan history as inconceivable, we should recall 3.47.1, the Milesians' enemies the Samians helped the Spartans against the Messenians (perhaps in the 7th cent., see Cartledge 1982: 247, 258–9); and generally cf. the trans-Aegean archaic alignments implied at **99**, the Lelantine War (see n. there).   **παρέχον δέ:** impersonal acc. abs. expression: 'when it is possible'.   **εὐπετέως:** that delusive word again (above, **49**.3 and 4).

49.9–54 *The Aristagores-at-Sparta story continued*

49.9 ὦ ξεῖνε Μιλήσιε: Aristagores is not named. The tone is severe, given that he knows the addressee's name: see on **49**.2 for the form of address, citing Dickey.   **ἀναβάλλομαί τοι ἐς τρίτην ἡμέρην:** the two full days (with which cf. 6.86 β 2: Glaukos) need explaining. Perhaps, if we can press the historical accuracy of the detail, the delay is so that Kleomenes can consult the Spartan authorities (but see **50.**1n.). If so, Hdt. passes lightly over this aspect, partly because he wishes to keep the spotlight on Kleomenes, whom he represents, here and elsewhere, as in sole control, a sort of tyrant (see **49.**1n.). At the same time, the story is a story, and needs these calibrated intervals of time for the build-up to the climax at **51** (Gorgo's surprise intervention).

Periods of three days (here 'on the third day') are common in Hdt., e.g. **8.**1 (funerals among Thracians); see Fehling 1989: 221 and Nenci. We are about to get a mention of a period of three months.

50.1 εἴρετο ὁ Κλεομένης τὸν Ἀρισταγόρην ὁκοσέων ἡμερέων ἀπὸ θαλάσσης: for the possible implications of this for the physical map, see **49.**1n. If there was a standing rule about how far armies could be taken from Sparta, perhaps Kleomenes did not need to consult more widely before giving his reply; so Richer 1998: 402. But the existence of such a firm rule is conjectural.

50.2 διαβάλλων 'taking him in' (Waterfield). The verb can sometimes mean 'to slander', sometimes 'to deceive'. It is as slippery as the behaviour it describes. See Pelling 2007: 183–5; and nn. on the word at **96.**1 and **97.**2 below. See also the other modern material cited at *CT* III: 338, n. on Th. 6.15.2 (Alkibiades complaining about Nikias' 'slanders').

Aristagores is given indirect speech so as to enable Hdt. to make the comment about his folly. He should have been *more* deceitful! (cf. δια-βάλλων above). As Syme 1995: 6 neatly put it, Aristagores 'supported his case and ruined his argument by exhibiting a map'. Cf. also Pelling 2007: 183.

50.3 πρὸ δύντος ἡλίου: cf. 7.149.3, a similarly worded Argive ultimatum to some Spartan representatives. οὐδένα γὰρ λόγον εὐπρεπέα λέγεις Λακεδαιμονίοισι...: Maas' suggestion εὐπρέπεα, for εὐεπέα in the MSS, is here followed; on this emendation, Kleomenes is describing Aristagores' suggestion as 'unbecoming', 'unattractive' or 'inappropriate'. εὐεπής is very rare in classical Greek, and not otherwise used by Hdt. (or Th.). The noun εὐέπεια occurs at Soph. *OT* 932, where it has the meaning 'welcome words' (LSJ), which is possible but not quite right for the present passage.

There is a hint here of the usual myth about Spartans shrinking from the wider world. It is a myth because, as we were told long ago, they had sent a deputation to Sardis to buy gold for a statue of Apollo, whereupon Kroisos gave it them for nothing (1.69.4:), and cf. Hegetorides the Koan guest-friend of Pausanias the Regent (9.76.3). See also Cartledge 1982 for the 'special relationship' between Sparta and Samos in the archaic period, and Catling 2010 (Sparta and Ephesos); add the early visit of the Milesian to Glaukos of Sparta, if historical: 6.86. But taking an army so far inland was a more serious matter, especially if there was helot trouble in the 490s (ML 22 = Fornara 8), the usual reason or excuse for Spartan nervousness in foreign affairs.

51.1 ὁ δὲ Ἀρισταγόρης λαβὼν ἱκετηρίην 'Aristagores took a suppliant bough'. For these suppliant boughs, see Andok. 1.110 and *Ath. Pol.* 43.6 with Rhodes. Hdt.'s story of Aristagores is in three stages of ascending seriousness and insistence: the first approach, the return after the specified two days, then the ritual supplication. The main focus and climax of the story is the role of Gorgo. See Naiden 2006: 144, who, however, goes beyond what Hdt. tells us; thus Hdt. does not say or imply that Aristagores 'barges into the house without any formalities'. And Naiden's comparison of Gorgo's role here to the use of children in acts of supplication – as at Th.1.136.3 – is forced and unhelpful.

The chapter has a forward function: it prepares us not only for the later role of Gorgo (7.239), but more immediately – and very neatly – for the description of the Royal Road at **52–4** below. 'Aristagores was not able to tell the Spartan king about the road; but I, the omniscient narrator, now will'. See **52.1**n. for the hard-working γάρ.

51.1 (cont.) τῆι οὔνομα ἦν Γοργώ· τοῦτο δ' οἱ καὶ μοῦνον τέκνον: the daughter's name, and the information that she was Kleomenes' only child, has already been supplied as recently as **48** above, whose preparatory function now becomes clearer.

51.2 πάτερ: the ordinary family address. See Dickey 1996: 237 (cf. above, **19.1**n.).   **διαφθερέει σε ὁ ξεῖνος** 'the stranger will corrupt you'. At 3.148, Kleomenes had avoided corruption by another foreigner, Maiandrios; but on that earlier occasion (in real time as well as in Hdt.'s text) he did not need anyone else to stiffen his resolve, though Pelling 2011: 10 n. 31 is right that he may have felt a twinge of temptation. It is possible that Hdt., who there praises Kleomenes' justice, means us to think of a gradual deterioration in his character. On character-change in ancient writers, see Hands 1974 and other modern refs. at *CT* I: 130.

51.3 οὐδέ οἱ ἐξεγένετο: impersonal: 'he did not succeed in'.

52–54 The Royal Road

The name is Hdt.'s (see **53**, ἡ ὁδὸς ἡ βασιληίη). Though he evidently regards it as special, it was in fact one of a number of such roads throughout the Achaemenid empire, as is shown by letters written in Aramaic and Elamite tablets from Persepolis, which also attest a tight system of control, and of elaborately monitored access to rations in depots along the route (Kuhrt 2007: 730–41, and more briefly *OCD*⁴ 'Royal Road'). One trunk road across Asia Minor has been identified and traced (French 1998), but it is surely not what Hdt. thought he was describing here; see **52**.2n. It is possible that some kind of map like that of Aristagores underlay Hdt.'s description (so Kuhrt 2007: 739), but that map was evidently something of a marvel (see **49**.1 on πίνακα), and a written source for Hdt. cannot be excluded.

An interesting 3rd-cent. AD papyrus commentary on **52–5**, *P.Oxy.* 4455 (1998), notes discrepancies from Kyros' route in Xen. *Anab.* 1, and comments on vocabulary and other matters. The author evidently re-did Hdt.'s sums and queried one of his results (see **54**.2n.).

52.1 σταθμοί: the remains of one of these 'stages' or 'way-stations', a six-columned, wooden roofed lodge, have been found: Mousavi 1989 and Kuhrt 2007: 738 (figs 15.2, a and b).   **τείνοντες:** the verb (assuming the text is sound, see app. crit.) is used of the 'stretching' i.e. extension of geographical features.   **παρασάγγοι:** a parasang was thirty stades, according to 2.6.3; see **53** and n. for Hdt.'s emphatic repetition of this, and for the variability of both stades and parasangs.

52.2 καὶ οὕτω διεκπερᾶν τὸν ποταμόν: the verb is most naturally taken to refer to actual crossing of the river Halys ('traverse': Powell, cf. 3.4.3). It has been argued (French 1998: 16, in the course of a study which seeks to show that the route of Hdt.'s Royal Road did not cross the Halys, or take a northerly route through Asia Minor) that it means 'pass alongside' the river.   **μέχρι οὔρων τῶν Κιλικίων:** since Hdt.'s road evidently runs from west to east through the *northern* part of the great Anatolian rectangle, the mention of Kilikia is very surprising (see map at Calder 1925: 8), and the extension to the Euphrates is explicable only on the assumption that Kilikia at Hdt.'s time (or in Hdt.'s head) had a much larger extension than we are accustomed to. Or else (Casabonne 2004: 27–8, cf. 22) Hdt. has confused two separate senses of Kilikia, or rather two Kilikias, a Cappadocian Kilikia (for which see Strabo 12.2.7) and a sub-Tauric Kilikia in the Tarsos region. This seems the likelier of the two main historical solutions. But it is possible that Hdt. intends authorial 'correction' of the brief information about Kilikia which he put into Aristagores' mouth at **49**.6. See Pelling 2007: 196 and n. 58. (Theories which discount altogether the clear evidence, at the beginning of **52**, for a northern first stretch of the road, should be rejected; so rightly Graf 1994: 178–9, who also rejects a compromise solution of Lendle 1987, which involves increasing Hdt.'s Kilikian distances by emendation. Calder 1925 argued that Hdt. simply made an error, and confused the route of the Royal Road with other routes in his *Histories*, those at 1.73–9 and 7.26.)

52.5 Γύνδης: for Kyros' punitive violence against this river, an anticipation of Xerxes' punishment of the Hellespont (7.35), see 1.189 with Munson 2001a: 153 n. 51.   τὸν Κῦρος διέλαβέ κοτε ἐς διώρυχας ἑξήκοντα καὶ τριηκοσίας 'which Kyros divided into three hundred and sixty channels'. See 1.190.1, which the language here closely echoes.   ἐκ δὲ ταύτης τῆς Ἀρμενίης ἐσβάλλοντι ἐς τὴν Ματιηνὴν γῆν σταθμοί εἰσι τέσσερες < καὶ τριήκοντα, παρασάγγαι δὲ ἑπτὰ καὶ τριήκοντα καὶ ἑκατόν >: the words in angled brackets were added by de la Barre in the 18th cent. to make the numbers add up right (for the totals, see **54.**2); and Stein then transposed everything, from ἐκ δὲ ταύτης to the end of the sentence, to this position. In the MSS the sentence comes at the end of **52.**3, after ἐν αὐτοῖσι. Both changes are improvements, but we cannot be sure that they represent exactly what Hdt. found in his source, whatever or whoever that was.

52.6 Σοῦσα πόλις πεπόλισται: for πολίζω, see **13.**2n. (Paionia).

53 εἰ δὲ ὀρθῶς…ὁ παρασάγγης δύναται τριήκοντα στάδια, ὥσπερ οὗτός γε δύναται ταῦτα: Hdt. has already stated firmly that a parasang was thirty stades (2.6.3), but from his 'strange insistence' on the point here, it has been argued (Rood 2010: 53) that he was aware that the measurement was disputed in his own time, as it certainly was later: Strabo 11.11.5 and Poseidonios fr. 203 Edelstein/Kidd give alternative estimates, up to sixty stades. The uncertainties do not end there, because it has been shown (Bauslaugh 1979: 5–6) that even Thucydides, so punctilious about chronology, did not operate with anything like a fixed stade (the fluctuation within Th.'s range of stades is from about 150 to 260 metres!). But the name derives from the running track or stadion at Olympia, which was 192.3 metres long, and this was supposed to be the canonical stade. See Hornblower 1994: 26–7. ἐς τὰ βασιλήια τὰ Μεμνόνεια καλεόμενα: for Sousa as Memnon's capital, cf. 7.151, and for Memnon himself (Ethiopian ruler, actually mythical) see 2.106.5. In myth he was a victim of Achilles, see e.g. Pind. *Isthm.* 5.40–1. ἡμέραι ἀπαρτὶ ἐνενήκοντα 'exactly ninety days'. This is the only certain use of the rare word ἀπαρτί in Hdt. (at 2.158.4 it comes down by an indirect tradition); it was thought worth comment in *P.Oxy.* 4455 (see introd. n. to **52–4**), col. ii.

In this ch. Hdt. compromises between an older method of computation (by time taken to cover a distance, 90 days) and a newer and more accurate method (by spatial measurement, 150 stades); see Dueck and Brodersen 2012: 71. But note that even Th., when in ethnographic mode, can use the 'older' method: 2.97.1 with *CT* II: 372.

54.1 τὴν γὰρ ἐξ Ἐφέσου ἐς Σάρδις ὁδόν: that is, the route along the river Kayster, mentioned not here, but at **100.**1. The present passage looks like an innocent statement of an additional stretch of road, but is at the same time a narrative 'seed', anticipating the opening campaign of the Ionian revolt.

54.2 τρισὶ ἡμέρῃσι: the papyrus commentary *P.Oxy.* 4455 appears to point out in col. ii that if travel is at 150 stades a day, 450 not 540 stades will be covered in three days.

55–65 *The Peisistratids of Athens*

On the place of this excursus within the structure of bk. 5 as a whole, see introd. n. to **39–97**. Hdt.'s account of the killing of Hipparchos and the subsequent fall of the Peisistratid tyranny allows us, unusually, to place a detailed Herodotean and a Thucydidean narrative of the same event(s) side by side, and to see how Th. (6.54–9) both imitates Hdt.'s manner, and also corrects and supplements him on the homosexual angle to the tyrannicide – an aspect prominent in Th. but wholly absent in Hdt. See *CT* III: 433–53, esp. 435–8, and see further **65.**1n. on νῦν δὲ συντυχίη ...

55 ἤιε ἐς τὰς Ἀθήνας: but he may not have gone directly to Athens from Sparta but have visited Argos in between (so Bury 1902): it would not be much of a detour by the land route. Hdt., on this view, did not explicitly record the Argive visit in its obvious place in the narrative i.e. here at **55.**1 (perhaps because he did not wish to take away from the clean Sparta-Athens polarity), but supplied us with indirect evidence which implied that the visit took place. That evidence is the so-called 'epicene' (i.e. 'shared', 'in common', ἐπίκοινα used adverbially, 6.77.2) oracle which Hdt. gives in two halves, at 6.19 and 77. This view presupposes that the oracle was authentic and datable to about 500, rather than being a product of the atmosphere after 494, when the Milesians were defeated. The authenticity of the oracle has been challenged. Piérart 2003: 294 and 296 leaves open the possibility of a consultation in 500. But he argues that the word 'Argives' in the oracle has the Homeric sense 'Greeks' generally, in which case the oracle would provide no support for Bury's theory.

Visits by Aristagores to cities of south mainland Greece other than Sparta and Athens are not impossible, quite apart from the evidence of the oracle. Those two were not the only states with substantial armies or navies. Thus Bury 1902: 18 suggested a personal visit to Eretria, in view of the five triremes of **99.**1. A visit to Korinth, with its long-standing eastern commercial connections from the port of Kenchreai, is also possible. There was no way for Aristagores to travel from Sparta to Athens direct, and the normal land route would take him through Korinthian territory, and indeed close to the decision-making *polis* centre. Not everything that is not in Hdt. (or Th.) did not happen, and Hdt.'s Aristagores was up to the task of adjusting his rhetoric for Korinthian consumption.

55 (cont.) γενομένας τυράννων ὧδε ἐλευθέρας: Hdt. recounts the rise of the Peisistratids in bk. 1 and their fall here in bk. 5, but says almost nothing about the decades in between, i.e. about their long period in power from 546 to 514 (**94** implies a very little). Compare Th. on the regime of the Four Hundred in 411 BC: *CT* III: 963 and 1007.

The narrative now moves back in time by a decade and a half, to the assassination of Hipparchos (514), and the liberation of Athens and its consequences (see esp. the statement of method at **65**.5). In particular, Hdt.'s narrative will now take us up to the triumph of confident democratic *isegorie* 'equality of speech', a state of affairs whose excellence is celebrated authorially, and with rhetorical exaggeration, at **78**. Aristagores' arrival at Athens at this watershed moment might be regarded as historical contingency, except that one stimulus for the Ionian revolt was precisely the example of the Kleisthenic reforms at Athens (see **37**.2n. on *isonomie*). That is, there was direct causal connection between political events in Athens and Ionia.

55 (cont.) ὄψιν ἐνυπνίου τῶι ἑωυτοῦ πάθει ἐμφερεστάτην 'a dream which was very like what was going to happen to him'. For the text, see app. crit. and Wilson: ἐμφερής is a favourite word of Hdt.: nine occurrences, apart from this emended passage, including four uses of the superlative, at 2.76.3, 3.37.2, 4.74 and 192.2. By contrast, the MSS' ἐναργεστάτην, 'very clear', or better (since the meaning of the vision was not really clear at all in the sense ἐναργής has at 7.47.1) 'vivid', required the undesirable deletion of τῶι ἑωυτοῦ πάθει. The dream resembled i.e. corresponded to his own fate because it said that the lion would suffer (Hipparchos would be killed) but that those who inflicted injustice would pay for it (this refers either to the killing of the tyrannicides themselves, or to that of Hipparchos himself. See **56**.1n.). By 'very like' Hdt. does not mean that this was what the dream-writer Artemidoros (1.2 = Harris-McCoy 2012: 49) would later call a 'directly perceived' (θεωρηματικόν) dream, as opposed to an 'allegorical' or symbolic one. That is, Hdt. is not saying that Hipparchos went on straightforwardly and exactly to experience what he had dreamed about (obviously not: he was not really a lion). Hdt.'s use of the word for 'riddling', αἰνίσσεσθαι (**56**.1 and n.) makes clear that this is the allegorical type of dream; for this verb as indicating allegorical dreams see Harris-McKoy 2012: 419. The simpler distinction between true and false dreams was known to Homer's Penelope (*Od.* 19.562–7).

Dreams in Hdt. happen either to barbarians or tyrants; they are associated with 'a sinister world of lawless power', and Hdt. distances himself from them. So Harris 2009: 146–7 (cf. Schubert 2011 for the 'tyrannical' aspect of Hipparchos' dream). Harris concedes that Agariste the younger at 6.131.2 fits this schema only imperfectly, through her *kinship* with tyrants.

55 (cont.) Ἀριστογείτων καὶ Ἁρμόδιος: the two heroic tyrannicides will recur, in reverse order, at 6.109.3, where Miltiades, before Marathon, tells Kallimachos the polemarch that he has it in his power to liberate Athens more truly than did Harmodios and Aristogeiton; see also 6.123.2, the Alkmaionids indeed liberated Athens more than did Harmodios and Aristogeiton. **γένος ἐόντες τὰ ἀνέκαθεν Γεφυραῖοι:** for ἀνέκαθεν (and ἄνωθεν) as adverbs indicating descent, usually 'from a remote, not always historical, individual or famous city', and found at all periods of ancient Greek history (and about the Alkmaionidai at **62**.3 below), see Fraser 2009: 34. For the *genos* of the Gephyraioi see Toepffer 1889: 293–300; *APF*: 472–3; Parker 1996: 288–9, and below on **57**.1.

It is hard to see why Hdt. dwells at such length on the origins of the Gephyraioi, or to be confident about his view of them. It can be argued that he wants to degrade them so as to write up the Alkmaionids, the real liberators of Athens; or that he wants to present them in an impressive light so as to 'enhance the status of their victim' (Gray 215). A more promising approach is in terms of immigrant status: Hdt., himself a species of immigrant, is stressing that, except for the Alkmaionids, the great families who made or unmade Athens – Peisistratidai, Gephyraioi – were immigrants: Immerwahr 1966: 117 n. 119; Pelling 2007: 198 n. 70. S. West 1985: 290 complained that the origins of the tyrannicides were 'of the most marginal relevance to sixth-century Athenian history', and suggests that Hdt. dragged them in only because he wanted to contribute to a topical controversy about the origins of the alphabet. But there must be more to it than that. Hdt. is certainly interested in background and lineage for its own sake: Gray 2007: 201. Here the lengthy material serves in part to amplify the importance of the deed of tyrannicide – except that the deed itself is not narrated! Th. felt this gap, and filled it.

55 (cont.) μετὰ ταῦτα ἐτυραννεύοντο ... οὐδὲν ἧσσον ἀλλὰ καὶ μᾶλλον ἢ πρὸ τοῦ: Th. agrees that the tyranny became harsher, χαλεπωτέρη, after the assassination (6.59.2), but Hdt.'s language is less explicit (Strasburger 1982: 611): they were 'ruled tyrannically more than before'. Nevertheless, Hdt. may, no less than Th., be correcting the popular version which made Harmodios and Aristogeiton the liberators.

56.1 ἐν τῆι προτέρηι νυκτὶ τῶν Παναθηναίων: the annual Panathenaia festival, celebrated every four years as the 'Great Panathenaia', took place in the month Hekatombaion (approx. August), and was the greatest civic festival of Athens; see Parker 2005: 253–69 and in *OCD*[4] 'Panathenaea';

ThesCRA 7 (2011), see index; and *CT* III: 449 on Th. 6.57.2 (giving other modern refs.). Th. specifies, as Hdt. does not, that this was the Great Panathenaia (of 514/13).

The distraction provided by festivals made them good opportunities for daring political actions such as the attempting of *coups d'état*: see 6.138.1 (the Pelasgians knew well the dates of the Athenian festivals and exploited one). Writers on sieges, and on how to capture cities, were well aware of the risk or opportunity presented by religious festivals. See Ain. Tact. 17.1 and the Hellenistic military expert Philon of Byzantion (Fraser 1972: 1.433 with Greek quotation at 2.628 n. 476); real-life examples include Th. 3.3.3 and 3.56.2.

56.1 (cont.) ἄνδρα οἱ ἐπιστάντα μέγαν καὶ εὐειδέα 'a tall, good-looking man standing over him'. In epiphanies (divine self-manifestations, often as here in dreams; see Introduction p. 34), gods regularly 'stand over' the human recipient. See Hom. *Od.* 20.32 (Athena), στῆ δ᾽ ἄρ᾽ ὑπὲρ κεφαλῆς καί μιν πρὸς μῦθον ἔειπε, and other Homeric passages cited by Said 2011b: 205 and n. 27; Hdt. 7.12.1 (all six words identical to those used in the present passage), cf. 7.14; and the epiphany of Athena in the '*anagraphe* from Lindos' ('Lindian Chronicle'), *FGrHist* 532 (= Higbie 2003: p. 43) D lines 13–14: 'the goddess, standing over one of the rulers in his sleep ...', ἁ μὲν θεὸς ἐνὶ τῶν ἀρχόντων ἐπιστᾶσα καθ᾽ ὕπνον.... The inscription dates from 99 BC, but the epiphany supposedly took place in the Persian Wars.   αἰνίσσεσθαι τάδε τὰ ἔπεα 'spoke these riddling words'. For the significance of the verb, see **55**n. on ὄψιν...The noun can mean 'hexameters', and is so classified by Powell here; but since Hdt. specifies hexameters at **60**, a less precise tr. is preferable.   τλῆθι λέων ἄτλητα παθὼν τετληότι θυμῶι᾽ | οὐδεὶς ἀνθρώπων ἀδικῶν τίσιν οὐκ ἀποτίσει 'endure, lion! you who have suffered the unbearable with enduring heart. No-one who commits injustice will escape retribution.'

We should probably write ἀδικῶν (sing. participle, agreeing with οὐδείς); but ἀδίκων (genitive plural adjective, understand e.g. ἔργων, and dependent on τίσιν, or perhaps agreeing with ἀνθρώπων) would also be possible. However, this is a riddling oracle, and the ambiguity should perhaps be respected, unless the phantom's pronunciation is to be thought of as following the word's accent.

The tall and handsome dream-man (for these often divine or heroic physical qualities see Harrison 2000: 163 and n. 20) speaks in hexameters, and generally like a regular oracle. Animal imagery is characteristic of oracular discourse in literature. Thus in the second Pythian oracle at **92**.β 3, an eagle will give birth to a lion (in that passage there is extra point to the word for 'eagle').

For lions in 5th-cent. literature, see esp. Aesch. *Ag.* of 458/7 BC, lines 717–36. Lion-derived personal names were common everywhere and at all periods, including some notable classical Spartan bearers of the simple name Λέων (*Th. and Pi.* 235–6 and n. 422), not to mention Leonides: the lion was Herakles' animal and Herakles was special at Sparta.

Except in north Greece between the rivers Nestos and Acheloos (Hdt. 7.125–6), real-life lions were not familiar to Greeks, but were 'on the verge of extinction in the fourth century BC in Greece': Sallares 1991: 401, who notes the discovery of two lion-bones in an LH IIIB level at Tiryns (Peloponnese). Lions in Homeric similes do not roar (Edwards 1991: 36 n. 43), though one groans (*Il.* 20.169). See Hainsworth 1993: 201 on *Il.* 10.485 ('lions, it is said, do not roar when actually attacking prey'). This may suggest that knowledge was growing indistinct.

Lion symbolism is always ambiguous (Thomas 1989: 271). There is further ambiguity in the prediction that the 'wrongdoer' will pay requital. This could be either Hipparchos himself, or his assassins (whose death would be described by Th. 6.57.4, but not by Hdt., who on this view took knowledge of it for granted). So Powell's tr. 'no man that harmeth thee' is wrong, because it eliminates the ambiguity. By the aorist participle παθών Hipparchos is not implied to have already endured the unendurable; presumably the meaning is simply that both the suffering and the enigmatic requital lie in the future. Despite this difficulty, we should not emend λέων to λεώς i.e. 'people' (so Vollgraff 1895: 129). The vision surely addresses the person it stands over, not the Athenian *demos* as a whole.

The lines are cleverly constructed; note (1) the variation on the τλη- and τι- roots, perhaps influenced by Aesch. *Ag.* 408, ἄτλητα τλᾶσα ('daring to do what she should not have dared', which is followed in the next line by a mention of 'seers in the house', δόμων προφῆται), unless Hdt.'s was a historical oracle and the influence was the other way, or it was merely a common oracular turn of phrase; and (2) internal rhymes in a menacingly long 'o' sound: λέων/παθών and then ἀνθρώπων/ἀδικῶν. This points to a sophisticated and well-read composer; on the other hand, the alliteration thus produced is characteristic of 'popular genres', including oracles: Silk 1974: 184 and n. 9, 224, citing Parke-Wormell 1956: xxiv (cf. *CT* III: 324 on Th. 6.9.1); cf. **92 β** 2n.

56.2 φανερὸς ἦν ὑπερτιθέμενος ὀνειροπόλοισι 'he was seen communicating it to the dream-interpreters'. It has been neatly said that 'in sleep every individual becomes a kind of seer' (Parker 2011: 66), but in practice one needed help. From the context alone, it would have been clear that ὀνειροπόλοι must here mean dream-interpreters, but in any case the word is – despite some ancient doubts about the authenticity of the line – a good Homeric one; see *Il*. 1.62–3 ('let us ask some seer or priest or ὀνειροπόλος, for a dream too is from Zeus', with Pulleyn 2000: 142–3, citing a closely parallel Hittite text from the 14th cent. BC) and *Il*. 5.149; cf. also Aesch. *Cho*. 44 for ὀνειρομάντεις. The -πολ- part of the word is related to Latin 'colo', and means to attend to something; at Plato *Leg*. 909d, θεοπολεῖν means 'to do god business' (Parker 2011: 59). In Hdt. himself, ὀνειροπόλος is otherwise found in non-Greek contexts; note esp., for a full formulation exactly similar to that used here, 1.107.1 and again 108.2, Astyages communicates his dream to the dream-interpreters, ὑπερθέμενος... τοῖσι ὀνειροπόλοισι (but this may be one of the 'Greek' touches identified by Pelling 1996: 74 in his treatment of Astyages' dreams). In ordinary Greek life, dream-divination was institutionalised in the form of incubation in sanctuaries such as those of Asklepios (see R/O no. 102) or the Amphiaraion at Oropos. See Näf 2004: 46.

Gray 2007: 209 calls this a 'near-miss', and compares **65**.1 (συντυχίη). Interestingly similar in a different way is 4.79.2: Skyles is sent a divine warning (a thunder-bolt destroys his house) but nevertheless proceeds with his Dionysiac initiation *because it was necessary/fated for him to end badly*. So we may wonder about the status of these supernatural warnings. Perhaps the message is 'the god gives and the god takes away'. **ἀπειπάμενος τὴν ὄψιν:** he rejected or dismissed the vision, but we are not told whether this was in spite of the dream-interpreters, or because they had reassured him, like the magi at 1.120 (AHG).

56.2 (cont.) ἔπεμπε τὴν πομπήν 'he conducted the procession'. For this particular combination of verb and related noun ('figura etymologica'), see *CT* III: 449, discussing πομπὴν πέμψοντας at Th. 6.56.2. **ἐν τῆι δὴ τελευτᾶι:** the innocent reader or hearer surely assumes that this is proleptic, and that Hdt. will return to the matter and recount the killing. But in fact this is all we get, and we have to go to Th. to find how it happened in detail.

57.1 The Gephyraioi had moved from Eretria on Euboia to Tanagra (*IACP*: no. 220) in eastern Boiotia; for Tanagra as a magnet for immigration in the archaic period see Fossey 1988: 468. The Phoenician story is fiction – perhaps explicable in part by politics, the bad relations between Athenians and (some) Boiotian cities after 519; so *APF*: 472–3. The close links between Eretria and the mainland opposite (Tanagraian territory and Oropos) mean that Eretria fits plausibly into the story; and the further move to Athens could have been the result of 'Theban expansionism in southern and eastern Boiotia' i.e. population pressure causing southwards displacement. For both these points see Schachter 1994: 304. See also Gray 2007: 205–18. **ἦσαν Φοίνικες... ἐς γῆν τὴν νῦν Βοιωτίην**

καλεομένην: according to Th. 1.12.2, the older name for Boiotia was Kadmeis, and Hdt. presumably has this in mind here. Even further back, pre-Greek Boiotia and Boiotians were supposed to have been called Temmikia and Temmikoi: Strabo 7.7.1 and 9.2.3; Lykoph. *Alex.* 644 and 786.

By tradition, Kadmos the Phoenician settled in Boiotia. He had left Phoenicia to search for his sister Europa, who had been abducted by Zeus in the shape of a bull: see M. West 1985: 83 and n. 115. Euripides (fr. 819, from the mostly lost play *Phrixos*) has Kadmos leaving the citadel of Sidon, and coming to Thebes. He was (the fr. continues) born Phoinix (this is ambiguous between 'he was called Phoinix', and 'he was born a Phoenician') but changed his *genos* to Greek. But sometimes Kadmos was son of Phoenix (rather than, as usual, of Agenor). The present passage has been seen as an exception to the general principle that most Greeks gave 'foreigners' good Greek genealogies (Price 2008: 176); but the family line becomes purely Greek at **59–60** (Darbo-Peschanski 1987: 31). For the link between 'Kadmos the Phoenician' and Boiotia see Edwards 1979 (generally seeking to retain as much of the myth as possible for history); also Gantz 1993: 209–10 and 467, West 1997: 448–50, and Kühr 2006.

Hdt.'s interest in early Phoenicians, here and at 6.47 (Thasos), is partly to be explained by Phoenician prominence in the suppression of the Ionian revolt, starting at **108** below, and in the main Persian War narrative.

57.2 <ὀλίγων> τεων καὶ οὐκ ἀξιαπηγήτων ἐπιτάξαντες ἔργεσθαι: they 'imposed on them a requirement of abstention' from a few unimportant rituals (see app. crit. for the text); this is not so much religious reticence on Hdt.'s part, as a refusal to expand on unimportant details. It remains curious that he should have bothered to mention the restrictions at all. This is not quite like **72.**4, where he says that he could (if he wanted to) list the deeds of Timesitheos of Delphi (but he does not).

58 The Greek alphabet a Phoenician import

The structure of Hdt.'s account resembles other excursuses describing the introduction, from outside Greece, of foundational Greek institutions, e.g. Melampous' inauguration of Dionysiac ritual at 2.48–9 (Kadmos featured there too, 2.49.3); see Gray 2012: 184–5. Cf. **58.**2n. for the 'small changes' which are regularly made to such imports.

58.1 ἄλλα τε πολλά . . . ἐσήγαγον διδασκάλια ἐς τοὺς Ἕλληνας καὶ δὴ γράμματα: διδασκάλια are accomplishments ('things taught'). The Phoenician origin or identity of the Gephyraioi may indeed be suspect, but that is a separate question from the role of Phoenicians in the Greek adaptation of 'Phoinikeia' or 'Phoenician letters' (**58**.2 below) so as to produce the alphabet. Here Hdt. was partly right, and corroborative proof was published in 1970, an inscription of *c.* 500 BC from Kretan Lyttos, *SEG* 27.631 = Colvin 2007: no. 52 (Spensitheos). This mentions a *p(h)oinikastes* who from the context is a remembrancer ('scribe', LSJ Suppl.). But the alphabet probably did not come direct from Phoenicia, but via Cyprus. Cf. Pfeiffer 1968: 17–24. On the transmission of the alphabet from Phoenicia to Greece, see Willi 2005, esp. 170, noting the insistence, in the Greek tradition, on the role of votive offerings (as here in Hdt., and as in the record of the mythical dedication by Kadmos 'in Phoenician letters' at Rhodian Lindos: *FGrHist* 532 B15-17, 99 BC). **οὐκ ἐόντα πρὶν Ἕλλησι ὡς ἐμοὶ δοκέειν**: in parenthetical clauses, the infinitive δοκέειν often replaces δοκέει; see e.g. 6.95.2, 9.113.2.

This negative formulation, and the personal nature of the comment, may imply (S. West 1985: 295) that other inquirers such as Hekataios, and maybe some poets, did indeed think that the Greeks were literate even before the time of Kadmos, which was itself several generations before the Trojan War on any of the available Greek genealogical systems. See Edwards 1979: 166 for a chart of these.

58.2 μεταρρυθμίσαντές σφεων ὀλίγα 'after changing a few of their shapes'. Compare 2.49.2 (of Melampous): ὀλίγα αὐτῶν παραλλάξαντα. **ἐφάτι-σαν . . . Φοινικήια κεκλῆσθαι** 'they spoke of them by the name of Phoenician' (LSJ). With the semi-redundant κεκλῆσθαι cf. **68**.2, τὴν ἐπωνυμίην ποιεύμενοι κεκλῆσθαι. The verb φατίζω is not used elsewhere by Hdt., who evidently felt it precisely appropriate to this linguistic discussion. For φοινικήια, 'Phoenician things', meaning 'letters' (of the alphabet), see ML 30 = Fornara 63, from Ionian Teos *c.* 470 BC, lines 37–8, curses against anyone erasing the letters of the inscription or making them otherwise unreadable. New frr. of the Teos text include φοινικογραφέων, 'being a secretary': *SEG* 31.985 D lines 19–21 and ML, p. 310, and Soph. fr. 514 *TrGF* mentioned φοινίκια γράμματα (Pfeiffer 1968: 21 and n. 8). **ὥσπερ καὶ τὸ δίκαιον ἔφερε** 'as was only right'; for this idiom cf. 7.137.2 and Powell φέρω II (3).

58.3 The dossier of 5th-cent. BC Aramaic leather documents from Achaemenid Egypt (Driver 1957), shows that Hdt. was correct about early writing on leather by one influential group of non-Greeks; see also *FGrHist* 688 Ktesias F5 = Diod. 2.32.4, and Driver 1957: 1–3 for other leather documents, starting in 2000–1788 BC, 12th dynasty Egypt. Hdt. was probably right about the Ionians also (Pfeiffer 1968: 19; cf. 236 on Hellenistic Pergamon and parchments).

On the tone of author-reader intimacy lent by expressions like ἔτι δὲ καὶ τὸ κατ' ἐμέ, 'even in my time', see Dewald 1987: 154–5.

59–61 The 'Kadmeian' inscriptions

The excursus on the 'Kadmeian' inscriptions at **59–61** is prompted by the mention of the Gephyraioi but has a didactic function going well beyond the needs of the context. See S. West 1985: 289–95 (too severe on Hdt. for his naïve treatment of the inscriptions. She doubts his claims to autopsy).

59 εἶδον δὲ καὶ αὐτός: there is no good reason to doubt the claim to autopsy here, but as often (Dewald 1987: 155–9) such claims to eye-witness investigation are used to introduce material which Hdt. knew was controversial. For the vocabulary for autopsy see Lightfoot 2003: 164 (Hdt. prefers tenses of ὁράω to the other verbs available).   ἐν τῶι ἱρῶι τοῦ Ἀπόλλωνος τοῦ Ἰσμηνίου: this sanctuary was south-east of the Kadmeia, on the Ismenion hill: *IG* 7.2455 and *SEG* 22.417 (both 6th-cent.) and other evidence: Schachter 1981–94: 1.77–85. For offerings in this temple see also 1.52 and 92.1.   τὰ πολλὰ ὅμοια ἐόντα τοῖσι Ἰωνικοῖσι: the supposed similarity to Ionic script is fatal to modern attempts to argue that what Hdt. saw was not Greek at all but some form of Linear B: Edwards 1979: 178. If we wish to maintain the link between 'Kadmos' (as a way of referring to a Phoenician import) and the introduction of the alphabet, we must suppose that Hdt. has put the alphabet several centuries too early. Mavrojannis 2007 seeks to avoid chronological conflict by pushing the origins of the alphabet back to the 10th cent., but this lacks support from epigraphy.   Ἀμφιτρύων ... ἀπὸ Τηλεβοάων: for Amphitryon and the Teleboians see Apollod. 2.4.6–7 with Frazer, Loeb ed. vol. I: 173 n. 3. The Teleboians inhabited the Taphian islands, which were probably situated between Leukas and the Akarnanian mainland (Strabo 10.2.20 and *Barr.* map 54 C4). Herakles' mortal father Amphitryon made war on the Teleboians because Alkmene, daughter of Elektryon, refused to marry him unless he avenged the deaths of her brothers at the hands of the Teleboians. Before that, Elektryon had himself planned to carry out the revenge against the Teleboians, but Amphitryon accidentally killed him, for which he was purified by Kreon at Thebes.

Schachter 1981–94: 1.82 n. 2 thinks that the Amphitryon and Laodamas dedications 'could have been forgeries, or, more probably, falsified transcriptions'. The closest parallel would be some of the early dedications in the Lindian *anagraphe* of 99 BC: Higbie 2003: 23 = *FGrHist* 532 A III, report of a dedication: 'Kadmos, a bronze cauldron, inscribed with Phoenician letters, as Polyzalos describes in Book Four of his investigations'; no. V (Higbie, as above) says that another was inscribed 'Herakles, from the Meropes, the [shield] of Eurypylos'. The tripods: Papalexandrou 2008.

59 (cont.) ...μ' ἀνέθηκεν †ἐών† ἀπὸ Τηλεβοάων: the MSS' reading ἐών, 'being from...', makes poor sense (though Hude seems to have been happy with it), and there have been many emendations. Nenci prints Bentley's ἀνέθηκε νέων, 'dedicated this on returning from . . .'. This is said to be justified by *Hom. Hymn Dem.* 395, νέουσα, but that too is a doubtful reading, see Richardson 1974: 282–3, citing the present passage of Hdt. among others and concluding: 'the active is thus only dubiously attested'. Wilson suggests νεῶν, 'from the ships', since the Teleboiai were pirates.   ταῦτα ἡλικίην εἴη ἂν κατὰ Λάιον 'that would date from the time of Laios'. The synchrony arises because Amphitryon was purified by Kreon, whose sister Iokaste was married to Laios.

60 Σκαῖος πυγμαχέων . . . ἄγαλμα: this looks like a regular late archaic or early classical agonistic dedication: Schachter 1981–94: 1.82 n. Hdt. was unhappy at identifying the dedicant with the mythical son of Hippokoon, supposedly a contemporary of Oidipous, and so suggests here that the epigram commemorated some other Skaios. He was on the right track, though the personal name Skaios is not historical, or at any rate not attested in any published *LGPN* vol. But σκαιός means 'left-handed', so perhaps it was a nick-name from the boxing-ring, 'Southpaw', borne by a boxer whose real name is lost. (Note the different accent. Accents often change when a word is used as a personal name, thus Ἀθηναῖος ethnic, Ἀθήναιος name.) The supposed patronymic Ἱπποκόωντος does not feature in the epigram, although it would have fitted metrically.   τεΐν: here and at **61.1**, this is the disyllabic Doric and epic dative of σύ.

61.1 Λαοδάμας . . . μουναρχέων: Laodamas was, in myth, son of Eteokles and grandson of Oidipous. Were it not for the title μουναρχέων (three long syllables, by synizesis of the last two vowels) we might think, as with Skaios above, of dedication by a real-life late archaic Laodamas. (The name Laodamas is not all that rare; there are two historical men of that name just in the pages of Hdt.: 4.137, the late 6th-cent. tyrant of Phokaia and 4.152, the patronym of Sostratos of Aigina.) But μουναρχέων is decisive: it takes us into the mythical world. μόναρχος is found as the title of a routine magistrate, but only at Kos after the synoikism of the 360s.   τεΐν: see **60**n.

61.2 For the Encheleis see *Barr.* map 49 ('Illyricum') A1. Apollod. 3.5.4 says that these people had been helped by Kadmos in their struggle against the Illyrians.   καὶ σφι ἱρά ἐστι ἐν Ἀθήνησι ἱδρύμενα: see Parker 1996: 289. If the Gephyraioi 'were indeed a *genos* in the technical sense', perhaps Hdt. should have said that they had a special, rather than an exclusive, relation with certain cults.   καὶ δὴ καὶ Ἀχαιίης Δήμητρος ἱρόν τε καὶ ὄργια 'in particular a temple of Achaian Demeter, with secret rites'. For Hdt.'s specification of the cults of an individual Athenian *genos* compare **66.1**, the family of Isagores are said to sacrifice to Karian Zeus. The cult of Achaian Demeter is attested in Boiotia generally, and at Boiotian

Thisbe and Thespiai, but not certainly at Boiotian Tanagra in historical times (Schachter 1981–94: 162–3 and 169–1; cf. also Parker 1996: 288 n. 11). The link with Achaia is obscure.

62.1 The Spartan expulsion of the Peisistratids of Athens; the Alkmaionids and Delphi

Hdt. says nothing about the Spartans' motives for deposing Hippias, beyond citing their obedience to the oracle, itself said to have been conditioned by their greater respect for 'the things of the god than for the things of men' (**63**.2). At **92**.α 1, he will make the Korinthian Soklees allude, by implication, to principled Spartan hatred of tyranny, but that is clever and flattering rhetoric. Two self-interested Spartan motives can be conjectured; both of them arise from Peisistratid friendships with definite or possible Spartan enemies. (1) Peisistratos had links with the Argives: see 1.61.4 for the Argive mercenaries who helped him to power and 5.**94**.1 for his Argive wife. This must be set against the Spartan guest-friendship with the Peisistratids, mentioned at **63**.2 and **91**.2 and presumably rooted in fact of some sort. (2) Hippias had married his daughter to a medising tyrant of Lampsakos (Th. 6.59.3). This may be relevant to Kleomenes' moves against suspected Aiginetan medisers (6.50.1). Forrest 1980: 79–83 puts the possibilities concisely.

On this section see Thomas 1989: 247–51 (Hdt. used oral traditions, not all pro-Alkmaionid, cf. also Develin 1985) and Sánchez 2001: 84–91, 'La reconstruction du temple et la liberation d'Athènes'.

62.1 ἀναλαβεῖν τὸν κατ' ἀρχὰς ἦια λέξων λόγον 'to take up again the story which I embarked on'. ἦια is the epic and Ionic imperfect of εἶμι, 'I shall go'.

62.2 Ἀλκμεωνίδαι, γένος ἐόντες Ἀθηναῖοι καὶ φεύγοντες Πεισιστρατίδας: yet again, bk. 5 picks up a story and a theme where Hdt. left it in bk. 1, with verbal markers to help us remember. The account of Peisistratos' acquisition of power closed with the statement that 'Peisistratos proceeded to rule as tyrant over Athens; some Athenians had fallen in the battle [of Pallene], while others, including the Alkmaionidai, were in exile from their homeland': 1.64.3. Even earlier (1.61.1) we were told, with no explanation, that the Alkmaionidai, into whose family Peisistratos married, were under a curse. The explanation of the curse will come at **71** (again with a verbal marker).

Hdt.'s Alkmaionid material is in fact distributed over three bks. not just two. The last and longest section on the family is climactically inserted in the context of Marathon. It is an excursus, which also reaches back farthest in time (Alkmaion and Kroisos) and closes by looking forward to Perikles: 6.121–31. For the present purposes, we may note only the repeated claim that the family were 'tyrant-haters', μισοτύραννοι (6.121.1 and 123.1), a claim supported according to Hdt. by their absence in exile during the tyranny, but undermined or (deliberately?) challenged by the epigraphically-preserved archon-list from the Athenian agora, inscribed *c.* 425 BC. It shows Kleisthenes was archon in 525/4, early in the reign of Hippias: ML 6 (= Fornara 23), c line 6.

62.2 (cont.) Λειψύδριον τὸ ὑπὲρ Παιονίης τειχίσαντες: Leipsydrion, the 'water-lacking place', has not been securely identified, but was probably north of Acharnai in central Attica, and close to a poorly-attested deme Paionidai. For this deme see Traill 1975: 47. See also Rhodes 1981: 235.

Hdt. reports this episode back to front: first he says that the Alkmaionidai and other exiles tried to return but failed badly, then that they had fortified Leipsydrion, evidently in preparation for the failed attempt he has just narrated. Arist. *Ath. Pol.* essentially repeats Hdt.'s order, but adds – for us preciously, though the song must have been famous in the 5th cent. – four lines of a drinking song or *skolion* lamenting those who fell at 'Leipsydrion the comrade-betrayer' (19.3, whence *PMG* 907).

62.2 (cont.) ἐνθαῦτα οἱ Ἀλκμεωνίδαι πᾶν ἐπὶ τοῖσι Πεισιστρατίδηισι μηχανώμενοι: the strenuousness of the family's efforts is conveyed by πειρώμενοι and πειρωμένοισι for their direct attempts, then μηχανώμενοι for the indirect and cunning plan involving Delphi. For the latter verb (which will be used again at **90**.1, in the form μεμηχανημένα, about the Alkmaionid treatment of the Pythia) see **30**.4 n., and for πᾶν ἐπὶ [x in dative] μηχανώμενος cf. **37**.1 n. The verb was used of the Alkmaionidai in bk. 1 (60.3), about the ruse jointly perpetrated by the Peisistratids and the Alkmaionid Megakles. At 6.121.2, embedded in a passage whose theme is subsequent Alkmaionid hatred of the tyrants, it will be used of the hostile machinations of another aristocratic enemy of Peisistratos, Kallies: καὶ τἆλλα τὰ ἔχθιστα ἐς αὐτὸν πάντα ἐμηχανᾶτο.

ἐνθαῦτα conceals a chronological problem. It suggests that the Alkmaionid contract, to rebuild the temple at Delphi splendidly, was taken out only after the debacle at Leipsydrion. The killing of Hipparchos and the fortification of Leipsydrion and the defeat there happened in 514, and Hippias was expelled in 510. During those four years, the Spartans were persistently urged by the oracle to liberate Athens (**63**.1). But Forrest 1969 showed that this rapid sequence is impossible: it takes more than four years to commission and build such a temple. Either the building went on for many years after 510, or the Alkmaionid contract antedated 514. Of these options, the second is likelier, despite Sánchez 2001: 90 (sceptical of all modern attempts to fix the chronology of the financial transactions and building works).

62.2 (cont.) τὸν νηόν: the temple which burnt down was supposedly the fourth in a sequence of which the first three were conceived in mythical, almost magical terms (e.g. no. 2 was made by bees out of wax and feathers): Paus. 10.5.12, drawing on Pindar's *Paian* 8, of which we have frr.: see Rutherford 2001: 217–19 for discussion. Hdt. has already told us (2.180.1) that the previous temple at Delphi had burnt down αὐτόματος, i.e. by accident not arson; this word may be a reply to those who alleged, improbably, that the fire was the work of the Peisistratids (scholion on Pind. *Pyth.* 7.10–11, Drachmann 1910: 203–4). This fire was in about 548/7 (Paus. 10.5.13 gives that exact year; two different versions of Eusebius' *Chronicle,* Jerome's and the Armenian, give 549/8 and 547/6: Frazer 1898: 5.328). Hdt. tells us that Amasis the Pharaoh of Egypt contributed to the 300 talents needed (a huge sum for the temple but not enough for the entire building works, see Sánchez 2001: 90 for the problem), for which the Delphians made appeal. He died in 526, so the appeal was launched earlier than that (and could have continued later than that, cf. De la Coste-Messelière 1946: 280). This has a bearing on the date of the Alkmaionid involvement in the rebuilding: the fund-raising seems to have gone on for decades, so the family's grand gesture can without difficulty be put some years earlier than 514, though we cannot say how many years elapsed between pledge and either completion or the moment at which it became clear that this rebuilding was to be spectacularly lavish. The Alkmaionid contribution related only to the façade of the temple, and this could have been done between 514 and 510 (De la Coste-Messelière 1946: 285). The motif (horses) on the pediment may have some reference to the Alkmaionid equestrian successes at the international contests, as attested by Pind. *Pyth.* 7 and perhaps Hdt. 6.122 (Athanassaki 2011: 245–9).

The Delphic Amphiktiony ('group of neighbours') was an organisation of communities which looked after the sanctuary, administered justice in limited spheres (with the sanction of declaring 'sacred wars' in the event of non-compliance or other outrage), and ran the Pythian games and festival every four years; these were its three most important regular responsibilities: Lefèvre 1998: 223–56 and 2011: 121; also Sánchez 2001: 44–57; Aeschin. 2.115 is a key text. For its more occasional role in putting the rebuilding of the temple out to tender, see Lefèvre 1998: 257 and 260. We know most detail about the rebuilding of the Delphi temple after another great fire (and/or earthquake), in 373 BC: Tod no. 140 (R/O no. 45) and comm. at p. 121. For the frequency and ease with which ancient Greek temples burnt down see *CT* II: 411–14, on Th. 4.133.2: fire which burnt down the Argive Heraion, 423 BC; Higbie 2003: 8–9: fire at temple of Athena at Lindos on Rhodes 392/1 BC.

Hdt. mentions the Amphiktiony (apart from these two connected passages in bks. 2 and 5) in a cluster of refs. late in bk. 7 (200.2; 213.2; 228.4). This contrasts with Th.'s non-mention of the Amphiktiony as such (the 'sacred war' narrated briefly at 1.112.5 may be an implicit mention), and is an example of what Th. chooses not to tell us about religion and its intersection with politics, and a difference between him and Hdt. See *TT*: chs. 1–2, but note Mari: 2006.

62.3 οἷα δὲ χρημάτων εὖ ἥκοντες καὶ ἐόντες ἄνδρες δόκιμοι ἀνέκαθεν ἔτι: the sources of Alkmaionid wealth will be revealed in the excursus about Alkmaion's visit to Kroisos, which begins at 6.125.1; there the repetition of ἀνέκαθεν (for which word see **55n.**) back-refers to the present passage. That ch. of bk. 6 begins by saying that the family were λαμπροί from the beginning, ἀνέκαθεν, and became still more so as a result of the Lydian and Sikyonian episodes which are then narrated.   **τὸν νηὸν ἐξεργάσαντο τοῦ παραδείγματος κάλλιον**: the meaning of παράδειγμα is unclear: it could be the Amphiktionic instructions as shown to the Alkmaionid family; or the latter's own blueprint; perhaps even a model of the earlier temple. **συγκειμένου σφι πωρίνου λίθου ποιέειν τὴν νηόν, Παρίου τὰ ἔμπροσθε αὐτοῦ ἐξεποίησαν** 'although it had been agreed [gen. abs.] that they should make the temple from tufa, they made the front from Parian marble' (lit. 'from Parian', understand λίθου). For the famous marble of Kykladic Paros, see Berranger 1992: 294–7. There is verbal play here (πωρ-/παρ-), which might even go back to some boast by the Alkmaionids themselves.

63.1 ὡς ὦν δὴ οἱ Ἀθηναῖοι λέγουσι: here ὦν δή is progressive rather than adversative. The text has been doubted, but we can avoid emending if we accept that 'the Athenians' whom Hdt. cites are not 'all the Athenians' but non-Alkmaionid Athenians. ('[Hdt.] seems deliberately to be adding awkward and non-Alcmaeonid confirmation of the Alcmaeonid claim to have liberated Athens': Thomas 1989: 248–9.) The MSS' reading has therefore been retained here. Forrest 1969a: 281, following an old suggestion of Valckenaer, then Schweighäuser, proposed to change οἱ Ἀθηναῖοι to οἱ Λακεδαιμόνιοι, cf. too Macan and Rhodes 1981: 236. The reason for the change is that otherwise this passage would, it is said, be the only reliable *Athenian*-derived evidence for good relations between Spartans and Peisistratids (Forrest 281 n. 7 puts it too strongly: 'with this change all evidence for friendship between the Spartans and the Athenian tyrants disappears'; see Rhodes 1981: 237). By contrast it would be only natural for the *Spartans*, after the (from their viewpoint) alarming developments which rapidly succeeded the overthrow of the tyranny at Athens in 510, to rewrite history so as to claim they had been duped by fraudulent oracles into getting rid of the stable Peisistratid regime. Palaeographically, the error would be a polarity mistake of a type common in hastily-written student examination scripts, i.e. you write the opposite of what you mean, 'Athenians' not 'Spartans' and so on. Against the emendation, see Kinzl 1975: 194–5 n. οὗτοι οἱ ἄνδρες...ἀνέπειθον τὴν Πυθίην χρήμασι: 'these men' is plural and indeterminate; not until **66**.1 do we learn that the one man said to have done the deed was Kleisthenes. The imperfect ἀνέπειθον implies that Delphi took some persuading/bribing.

The whole expression (combination of 'persuasion'-word with 'money'-word) means bribery: Harvey 1985: 79 and n. 10. Sánchez 2001: 85–6 n. 26 rightly rejects attempts to argue that the lavish building work and the 'persuasion of the oracle' were the same. There was nothing improper about the building work, whereas the bribery of the oracle was a famous stain, one of only two successful manipulations of the Pythia (Parker 1985: 318 and 325). The other was that described, in the manner of Hdt., at Th. 5.16.2. The manipulation at Hdt. 6.66.2–3 was successful only for a time, and the sanctions taken against the culprits show rather the oracle's general incorruptibility. The present passage is unique as an example of successful bribery in the strict financial sense, as opposed to persuasion of the 'no such thing as a free lunch' variety.

4th-cent. BC writers, perhaps influenced by contemporary events (the rebuilding of the temple after the destruction of 373; the prominence of the Amphiktiony thereafter, in the period of its political manipulation by the Thebans; and the Third Sacred War of 355–46 BC) introduced new and surprising elements into the story. *Ath. Pol.* 19.4 hints at outright embezzlement by the Alkmaionids of the building money. None of this is in Hdt., or is of any evidential value, except for the contemporary drinking-song already discussed above. For the later traditions, see Forrest 1969a, helpfully summarised by Rhodes 1981: 236–7; also Thomas 1989: 251–7 and Zahrnt 1989 (who rejects the 4th-cent. material, but thinks, following Wells 1923: 88, that not only the Alkmaionids but also the Spartans themselves, perhaps Kleomenes in particular, might have induced the Pythia to take the line she did).

63.1 (cont.) εἴτε ἰδίωι στόλωι εἴτε δημοσίωι: στόλος can sometimes mean an army, but here the phrase must mean something like 'whether on a private or a public *mission*'. For Spartan connections with Delphi – always close – see below, 6.57.2 and 4 on the high status of the 'Pythioi', Spartan oracle-consulters whose functions included the sharing, with the kings, of knowledge of oracles (perhaps only Delphic ones, as their title implies; for 4th-cent. BC Spartan state consultation of Zeus' oracle at Dodona, see Eidinow 2007: 272–3 n. 37). So the Pythioi must have scrutinised the oracles mentioned in the present passage.

63.2–4 *The expedition of Anchimolios*

The best discussion of this from the military (esp. cavalry) point of view
is Worley 1994: 51–3, esp. 52–3 (the Spartans were few in number, had
no screening force, and were inexperienced at dealing with cavalry. One
thousand – the Thessalian total – is a huge force).

63.2 Ἀγχιμόλιον τὸν Ἀστέρος: Mr Close-at-hand, son of Star (see Bechtel
1917: 599 for Aster as one of a category of names formed from expressions for light and sound; see also now C. B. Kritzas in *Onomatologos*: 239
on the newly attested Argive name Ἀστροβίων). Anchimolios or Anchimo-
los (the form preferred in *LGPN* IIIA and see Rhodes 1981: 237) is a rare
name anywhere. For names in Ἀγχι-, see Faulkner 2008: 261, on ἀγχίθεοι at
line 200 of *Homeric Hymn to Aphrodite*, discussing Anchises, 'close to a god',
i.e. Aphrodite, who slept with him; cf. Hom. *Od.* 5.35, the Phaiakians are
in a different way 'close to the gods'. Aster is also rare until the Imperial
period; but there are derivatives such as Asteriskos, Asterion, Asteropos,
etc. (Bechtel as above, and for the 'speaking' Spartan name Asteropos in
particular Nafissi 2008: 65–72), and two classical bearers of Aster itself:
(1) the archer who deprived Philip II of an eye in 353 BC (*LGPN* IV no.
1); and (2) a pupil of Plato, *FGE* lines 584–5. A Spartan 'Mr Star' might –
like Asteropos, above – be a 'speaking' name, from the ephors' role as
sky-watchers. The Spartans did not send a king first time, perhaps because
of a taboo on kings operating militarily by sea, at least before the Persian
wars (Lewis 1977: 45, cf. Cartledge 1987: 47).   **ἐξελῶντα Πεισιστρατίδας...ὅμως καὶ ξείνους σφι ἐόντας τὰ μάλιστα:** Peisistratos and Hipparchos
are dead, so Hippias is now sole tyrant. But in the present context Hdt.
continues to think of the family in the plural, even speaking of the 'children of the Peisistratidai' at **65**.1; and at **63**.3–4 he attributes political and
military decisions to the Peisistratidai collectively. (Contrast **91** and **93–94**,
where Hippias alone features, perhaps because only he is summoned by
the Spartans at **91**.) We know from Th. that Hippias had five children:
Th. 6.55.1. Th. 6.54.6–7 shows that one of these was a younger Peisistratos (II), son of Hippias, who held the archonship (Davies, *APF* 450–1);
Davies thinks this man's family should be the 'Peisistratidai' of Hdt. 7.6 and
7.52.2. Additional to the five sons was a daughter, Archedike, for whom see
Th. 6.59.3.

  Although there has been no source-statement since οἱ Ἀθηναῖοι at the
start of **63**.1, an implied shift of focalisation should be extracted from
ἐξελῶντα, a future participle of purpose after πέμπουσι. This looks tendentious and Spartan-derived (it is repeated at **90**.1, a more obviously Spartan piece of focalisation). Most of Peisistratid foreign policy, in particular
the Argive alignment, was uncongenial to the Spartan decision-makers;
and Kleomenes' rejection of the Plataian appeal in 520 is said to have

been motivated by desire to make trouble, πόνοι, between Athenians and Boiotians other than Plataians, i.e. (mainly) the Thebans: 6.108.3. It is tempting to take ξεῖνοι here to indicate ritualised friendship in the technical sense, but this was normally between individuals and families (cf. that between Perikles and the Spartan king Archidamos at Th. 2.13.1, for the likely origin of which in 479 see *CT* I: 251). If a relationship of this private sort is behind the words here used, it is beyond capture.

63.2 (cont.) τὰ γὰρ τοῦ θεοῦ πρεσβύτερα ἐποιεῦντο ἢ τὰ τῶν ἀνδρῶν: this is a precious comment on Spartan religiosity (comparable to 9.7.1 on the Hyakinthia festival: the Spartans 'considered it of utmost importance to prepare the things of the god', περὶ πλείστου δ' ἦγον τὰ τοῦ θεοῦ πορσύνειν, with Flower and Marincola). It provides a good reply to any nowadays who think that ancient Greeks did not have the concept of superstition, or a separate notion of the religious as opposed to the secular sphere. Against the latter modern misconception see also Th. 5.70, the Spartans march in step 'not for religious reasons', οὐ τοῦ θεοῦ χάριν; and against the former see also Th. 7.50.4, Nikias said to be 'excessively' given to 'divination and the like', with *CT* III: 186–7 and 642–4 on the two passages.

It is not obvious who in the present passage are the focalisers. The remark is not likely to represent the Spartans' own view of themselves, so it is either an Athenian or a Herodotean view. (See Parker 1989: 154 = Whitby 2000: 164 and n. 11.) Of these alternatives, the second is preferable.

63.2 (cont.) πέμπουσι δὲ τούτους κατὰ θάλασσαν πλοίοισι: the land-loving Spartans send this expedition *by sea*; but it fails (cause and effect, some Spartans may have thought) and we are expressly told that the next is by land not sea, **64**.1, and is led by a king, not an ordinary Spartiate. The decisions to send (1) a small expedition and (2) by sea are connected: few troops and no horses could be conveyed on ship-board (Worley 1994: 52). Decision no. (2) entailed no. (3), which was to send a private individual in command: cf. above on Anchimolios. The Spartans' initial military calculations must have looked inadequate with hindsight, but the unexpected element, from their point of view, was the presence on the Peisistratid side of a large Thessalian cavalry force. (Unexpected, that is, at the time of the Spartan decision to send the force they did send. In the immediate run-up to the battle, Anchimolios cannot have been unprepared – certainly by the time he saw the condition of the plain, see **63**.4 on κείραντες. See Worley 1994: 51–2.) Cf. also **63**.3n. on ἐπεκαλέοντο.

63.3 ἐς Φάληρον: Phaleron ('the white place') was the main Athenian harbour before Piraieus was developed in the time, and at the initiative, of

Themistokles; see 6.116. Piraieus was unavailable as long as Salamis opposite was in Megarian control: *CT* I: 139 on Th. 1.93.3.   οἱ δὲ Πεισιστρατίδαι...ἐπεκαλέοντο: the appeal was presumably made rapidly and by
sea to Pagasai, the main Thessalian harbour town.   ἐπεποίητο γάρ σφι
συμμαχίη πρὸς αὐτούς: note the pluperfect: the alliance was long-standing,
perhaps as old as the 540s. See Forrest, *CAH* 3². 3: 298 and 317, who
also noted that the friendship continued past 510 (**94**.1, Thessalians offer
Iolkos to Hippias). The name of Peisistratos' son Thettalos shouts out
the connection: Th. 1.20.2 and 6.55.1 with Lewis *CAH* 4² 297.   κοινῆι
γνώμηι: at most the present passage is evidence for 'some rudimentary
kind of federal organisation' in Thessaly (Forrest *CAH* 4²: 298). Helly
1995: 144 and *IACP*: p. 680 take it as early evidence of a full-dress federal
decision-making Thessalian body. But κοινόν and associated words can be
vague expressions for collective decision-making, see *CT* II: 260 on Th.
4.78.3 (also Thessaly), citing Tréheux.   τὸν βασιλέα τὸν σφέτερον Κινέην
ἄνδρα Κονδαῖον: this probably means no more than that he was their leader
or commander. Larsen 1968: 14 n. 6 regarded 'king' or βασιλεύς here as
an imprecise equivalent of *tagos*, supposedly the supreme Thessalian magistrate; but Hdt. is unlikely to have been accurate about Thessalian titles,
and the whole idea of *tagos* is dubious, attested as it is once only, for Jason
of Pherai in the 370s (Helly 1995: 15–68 and *OCD*⁴ '*tagos*'). Helly thinks
the supreme figure was called ἄρχων (or similar) and that βασιλεύς was
used by the great aristocratic families like the Aleuadai. For the present
passage of Hdt. see Helly 1995: 221–2: Kineas was simply, as a member of
a great Thessalian family, leader of a cavalry corps from Pelasgiotis, where
Helly thinks Kondaia was situated. But much of this rests on an emended
ethnic.

   The Thessalian name Kineas (eleven Thessalians out of fourteen individuals in *LGPN* IIIB) occurs in a four-line elegiac Greek poem (*c.* 300
BC) inscribed at Ai Khanoum in Afghanistan by Aristotle's pupil Klearchos
of Soloi; see Robert 1969–90: 5.510–15 and 1973: 211. Klearchos says
he has inscribed Delphic precepts in the *temenos* or sacred precinct of
Kineas, the oikist or city-founder (Κινέου ἐν τέμενει, line 4). Robert 1973:
219–22 demonstrated the high probability that the oikist Kineas was a
Thessalian, like Hdt.'s homonymous king, for whom see Robert 1973: 219.
The king is *LGPN* no. 7 and the oikist is no. 13.

   In Hdt., Κονιαῖον should probably be emended, most plausibly to Κονδαῖον, the ethnic of the Thessalian city Kondaia (firmly attested only in
the Hellenistic period). See Robert 1973: 219 and n. 73; *IACP* 694 no.
399 (where however it is noted that the Hellenistic ethnic is Κονδαιεύς).
This emendation is preferable to the more violent emendation Γονναῖον
or Γοννεῖον (see *IACP*: 723 on no. 463, 'Gonnos'). Helly 1995: 103 (and

222–3) puts Kondaia at mod. Magoula kastri (marked by that name with a star at *Barr.* map 55 C1, north of Larisa and south of Mopsion). Jeffery 1976: 82 n. 5 suggested Κονιαῖον might be a patronymic (cf. her 72 for such patronyms in -ιος; and there is in fact a Thessalian name Κόνας in *LGPN* IIIB, from Krannon in Pelasgiotis, 3rd-cent. BC). Her suggestion was anticipated by Maas (a marginal note published only recently); see Wilson 2011: 66, '[ἄνδρα] Κονιαῖον, filium Coniae'.

63.4 κείραντες . . . καὶ ἱππάσιμον ποιήσαντες 'they manicured the plain and made it suitable for cavalry' (the tr. 'manicured' is taken from Worley 1994: 52). For Attica as poorly suited to cavalry operations, see 9.13.3, where this is given as one reason for Mardonios' withdrawal northwards into Boiotia in 479. The best region of Attica for cavalry was Marathon, cf. 6.102: Bugh 1988: 9–10. For similar pre-battle preparations cf. Arr. *Anab.* 3.8.7, the Persians before Gaugamela, 331 BC, where too the word ἱππάσιμα is used, perhaps with the present passage of Hdt. in mind. (Th. does not use the word, and the context at Xen. *Cyr.* 1.4.14 is different.) **ταφαί:** see **8**.n. for this word. Alopeke was near Phaleron. Cartledge 1987: 337 shows that Spartans other than kings were buried on the spot where they died, and gives other examples. The Kynosarges gymnasium had an epigraphically attested precinct in honour of Herakles, who (along with Hermes) was the patron of gymnasia. See Travlos 1971: 340. It is relevant that Alopeke was a deme with Alkmaionid connections: Bicknell 1970: 131 (cf. 1972: 39) and Sancisi-Weerdenburg 2000: 90 n. 27. This may be further evidence that the family's exile was not complete.

64.1 μέζω στόλον στείλαντες . . . ἀποδέξαντες βασιλέα . . . οὐκέτι κατὰ θάλασσαν στείλαντες ἀλλὰ κατ' ἤπειρον: in effect a triple piece of negative presentation, though only the third is expressed in explicit 'not x but y' form: 'not under a private individual but a king; not a small force like before but a bigger one; not by sea but by land'. For expressions like στόλον στείλαντες (noun and related verb) see **56**.2n. on ἔπεμπε τὴν πομπήν.

64.2 οὐ μετὰ πολλὸν ἐτράπετο: this military reverse (esp. after the military success of **63**, against an admittedly smaller and under-equipped force), and Hdt.'s comment on its rapidity, may imply treachery. Certainly Thessalian politics and political divisions will be important later: see esp. 7.172.1.   **ἀπεργμένους ἐν τῶι Πελαργικῶι τείχει:** the 'Storks' wall' or 'Storkade' (Dunbar 1995: 497 on Ar. *Av.* 832) on the Acropolis, a name derived from πελαργός, or 'the Pelasgic wall', Πελασγικῶι, the form found in most MSS here (as also some of those of Th. 2.17.1) and also used by a Hellenistic chronological list, the 'Parian marble', when describing the present episode: *FGrHist* 239 A45. 'Storks' wall' is probably the older form, derived from religion or myth; the name 'Pelasgian' displaced it out of a vague sense of Pelasgian antiquity. Or one can have it both ways. The historian and mythographer Myrsilos of Methymna (?3rd cent. BC) said that when the Pelasgians were driven out of Thessaly and founded Etruria, they changed their name to Πελαργοί, Storks, in their wanderings, because they settled in flocks over Greek and barbarian lands: *FGrHist* 477 F 9, from Dion. Hal., *Ant. Rom.* Behind this may lie a metamorphosis myth of a familiar foundational type: founders of new colonies were thought of as originating from creatures such as wasps (Cyprus) or ants (Aigina): Buxton 2009: 68–9 and Bowie 1993: 159–60.

The Pelargic wall in its original form goes back to the 13th cent., but the name was also given to a second and lower wall or enclosure on the western part of the Acropolis; see Travlos 1971: 52; Dunbar 1995: 497 on Ar. *Av.* 832. The Peisistratids probably fortified this area towards the end of the tyranny: Lewis *CAH* 4²: 300.

65.1 οὐδέν τι πάντως ἂν ἐξεῖλον: the counterfactual assertion is linked to the comment on contingency which follows; see below on νῦν δὲ συντυχίη…Such authorial comments are part of the rhetoric of narrative. They are focussing devices, designed to draw attention to the importance of the chance occurrence, and the more important the 'path not taken', the greater the elaboration (a famous example is 7.139 – what if the Athenians in 480 had fled or surrendered? – and see *CT* III: 1030–1 on Th. 8.96.4). If the Peisistratids had not been dislodged as a result of the accident that their children were captured, the course of Greek history in the 5th cent. would have been different. **σίτοισι καὶ ποτοῖσι εὖ παρεσκευάδατο:** the water-supply in this area mainly consisted of the Asklepieion spring and the Klepsydra; see Travlos 1971: 52. The verb is Ionic 3rd pers. pl. pluperfect passive of παρασκευάζω. **νῦν δὲ συντυχίη τοῖσι μὲν κακή … τοῖσι δὲ ἡ αὐτὴ αὕτη σύμμαχος:** 'a piece of very bad luck for them, but helpful to the others' (lit. 'this same chance was helpful'). An expression of contingency (see **56.**2n.). Th.'s account of the tyrannicide also stressed contingency, and with the same word, but combined with an adjective, and a significant one: ἐρωτική ξυντυχία (6.54.1). Th. preferred to stress the accident of a same-sex love affair. **ὑπεκτιθέμενοι:** 'removed to safety'. **οἱ παῖδες τῶν Πεισιστρατιδέων:** see **63.**2n. on ἐξελῶντα…

65.2 παρέστησαν δὲ ἐπὶ μισθῶι τοῖσι τέκνοισι, ἐπ᾽ οἷσι ἐβούλοντο οἱ Ἀθηναῖοι 'they surrendered on whatever terms the Athenians wanted, in return for their children' (lit. 'for a reward, namely their children'). For the verb in this sense, see LSJ παρίστημι (B) (III). **ἐν πέντε ἡμέρηισι:** the period of grace is half of the (mild) allowance of ten days accorded to ostracised persons before they had to be out of Attica: *FGrHist* 328 Philochoros F 30. The period may have some traditional significance which escapes us.

65.3 ἐξεχώρησαν ἐς Σίγειον τὸ ἐπὶ τῶι Σκαμάνδρωι: 'Trojan Sigeion' (*IACP*: no. 791; also *OCD*[4], 'Sigeum') has been mentioned already, but only incidentally and as a geographical indicator: 4.38.2. The Trojan connection made it an appropriate bolt-hole for a family with Homeric pretensions (**65**.4n.); compare the Thessalian offer to Hippias of Iolkos (**94**.1n.).

Hdt. delays giving the earlier background (Peisistratos' conquest of Sigeion) until **94–5**, when he will relate (**94**.1) that Hippias returned there after the failure of the last and most dramatic Spartan attempt to restore him. See also Th. 6.59.4 with *CT* III: 452 for the numismatic evidence for Hippias' presence in the region (an owl coin with ΗΙΠ, see Head 1911: 377); and for mid 5th-cent. Athenian claims on the place, which may be reflected in Aesch. *Eum.* 399–402. Hdt.'s refs. thus had a topical interest. But Th., though otherwise echoing Hdt.'s language, ignores the other Peisistratids and says that Hippias went (*singular*) to Sigeion *and Lampsakos*, ἐχώρει ὑπόσπονδος ἔς τε Σίγειον καὶ παρ' Αἰαντίδην ἐς Λάμψακον. The closing words of **95**.2, 'so Sigeion came under Athenian control', and also the coin, raise the question of how and why Hippias was able to go there if it was sovereign Athenian territory. He must have been *persona grata* in an overseas Athenian possession, though not at Athens itself. This is lenient treatment, and is consistent with the five days' grace.

The narrative delay is notable (Hdt. has chosen not to tell us *here* about Peisistratos' conquest of Sigeion) and calls for explanation. The present ch. is, as we have it, an effective piece of composition: from the humiliating bargain by which the family negotiated its exile in 510 BC we jump back to romantic figures from Homer (Nestor) and from very early mythology (Kodros etc.). Hdt. did not wish to spoil this long view by inserting intervening episodes. The excursus on the family's antiquity also serves as a kind of αὔξησις or rhetorical amplification, designed to point up the solemnity of the moment at which its members ceased to rule Athens. For speculation as to the positive motives for, and advantages of, narrating the background at **94**, see introd. n. there.

The Peisistratids may eventually have settled on Chios: see **65**.4n. If so, Hdt. could have spoken to them there.

65.3 (cont.) ἄρξαντες μὲν Ἀθηναίων ἐπ' ἔτεα ἕξ τε καὶ τριήκοντα: the chronology of Peisistratos' career as a whole is disputed, but the most natural candidate for these 36 years is 546 (the date of Peisistratos' third and final seizure of power) to the end of the tyranny in 510: Rhodes 1976: 224 and 230; 1981: 194; and 2003: 63.   ἀνέκαθεν Πύλιοί τε καὶ Νηλεῖδαι 'originally Pylians and Neleidai'. By calling the Peisistratids 'Pylians', Hdt. here subscribes to the view, which has been seen as 'essentially an Athenian imperial fiction of the 5th cent.', that the colonisation of Ionia by people from Pylos, in the Peloponnese, took place not directly from Pylos but after an intermediate stay in Athens (*OCD*⁴, 'Codrus'). Hdt. has already, as so often in bk. 5, prepared the way for this in bk. 1, but in more general terms: see 1.147.1 for some early kings of the Ionians as 'Kaukones from Pylos, descended from Kodros son of Melanthos'. See Kearns 1989: 107; Smarczyk 1990: 328–59, esp. 336–7 n. 16. It is consistent with this imperial inflation of the role of Kodros that his Athenian cult is not attested before the later 5th cent.: Parker 2005: 446 and n. 110, citing *IG* 1³ 84 (418/7) and Kearns 1989: 107, as above.

A ch. of Strabo (14.1.3) is important evidence for the traditions about the colonisation of Ionia; it would be good to be sure how far it derives from Pherekydes of Athens (mid 5th cent. BC), whom he cites at the beginning (*FGrHist* 3 F 155 and in Fowler *EGM* I: 355). Others, such as Panyassis (a kinsman of Hdt., perhaps), and Ion of Chios treated the topic, and Hdt. could have used their works – or talked to them.

As for 'Neleidai', the descent is from Neleus, son of Poseidon and Tyro, and father of Homer's Nestor, for whom see **65**.4.

65.3 (cont.) ἐκ τῶν αὐτῶν γεγονότες καὶ οἱ ἀμφὶ Κόδρον τε καὶ Μέλανθον 'from the same ancestors as (καί) Kodros and Melanthos'. The relevant genealogical line ran as follows, according to Hellanikos F 125 Fowler (323a F 23   Jac.; slightly differently given in Paus. 2.18.8): Neleus (son of Poseidon and Tyro) – Periklymenos – Boros – Penthilos – Andropompos – Melanthos – Kodros – Neileos. So Hdt. is saying that the Peisistratidai had the same ancestors as Melanthos and Kodros, and so they did, namely Neleus and his wife Chloris; but the two lines came from different sons of Neleus, viz. Periklymenos and Nestor. Hdt. looks back to the patriarch Neleus because it is Nestor's son Peisistratos who is relevant to the naming of the Athenian tyrant (**65**.4).

Hdt.'s mention of the Neleidai and Kodros might well have reminded his hearers of Neleus' descendant, and Kodros' son, Neileos the oikist of Miletos, for whom see below 9.97 (spelling him Νείλεως), and for his foundation of Miletos cf. Lykoph. *Alex.* 1378–87. (The names Neleus and Neileos are both thought to be essentially the same as Mycenaean ne-e-ra-wo = *Nehelawos (Neleus being a shortened form), meaning 'bringing the army back safely'; the name Nestor comes from the same root. I am grateful to Martin West for help with all these genealogical and onomastic matters.) Although Miletos is never actually mentioned in the present passage, Hdt. has thus cleverly reminded them and us, in the middle of an excursus apparently about the Peisistratids and pre-Persian wars Athens, of the colonial kinship ties which embroiled the Athenians in the Ionian revolt which is the main narrative trunk from which these branches and twigs ramify; see esp. **97**.2, where the Milesian Aristagores appeals to the Athenians on the explicit grounds that Μιλήσιοι τῶν Ἀθηναίων εἰσὶ ἄποικοι. Athenian colonisation of Miletos was first mentioned at 1.146. See also **97**.3n. for the significance of the name of the Athenian commander Melanthios.

For ἀνέκαθεν see on **55**, and for such Athenian aristocratic genealogies or pseudo-genealogies, see Thomas 1989: 155–95.

65.4 ἐπὶ τούτου δὲ ... τὴν ἐπωνυμίην 'Hippokrates gave his son the name Peisistratos, in memory of Peisistratos son of Nestor' (lit. 'Hippokrates acted in memory of this when he gave his son the same name Peisistratos, calling him after Peisistratos son of Nestor'). ἀπομνημονεύω, 'I do something in memory of', appears to take the infinitive, here θέσθαι οὔνομα, and one meaning of ἐπί with the genitive is naming 'after' something or someone. But the whole sentence is difficult and clumsy (Bravo 2008: 100 is right to that extent), and there may be textual corruption; Wilson suggests ἀπομνημονεύ<ων ἠθέλη>σε, 'in memory... he wanted (i.e. decided) to give him the name ...'.

Peisistratos son of Nestor features only in *Odyssey* bks. 3–4 – part of the so-called *Telemachy* – and 15, starting at 3.36 (he is not mentioned in the *Iliad* or the list of Nestor's sons at Hes. fr. 35 Merkelbach/West; for the possible significance of this, see below). It is unusual to find an ancient author commenting specifically, as Hdt. does here, on the (conjectured) reason for a choice of personal name drawn from myth, though homonymity with a grandfather is sometimes commented on (6.131.1, Kleisthenes; Th. 6.54.6, the younger Peisistratos; see esp. Dem. 43.74 for the general practice), and see Th.'s comment (8.6.3) on a famous Athenian name resulting from a guest-friendship with a Spartan family: Alkibiades. The Peisistratids continued to care about their names, and were onomastically conservative after their fall, as exiles often are. From the frequency of Peisistratid names attested epigraphically at Chios, including several Peisistratoi, a Hippias, a Hipparchos, a Neleus or Neileus and a Thessalos, Forrest 1981 suggested that the family ended up there (after leaving Sigeion?): 'the Peisistratidai of Hdt. viii 52.2 will have had to settle somewhere'. For another link between the Peisistratids and Chios, see Graziosi 2002: 208–28 (the Homeridai, rhapsodes based on Chios).

Because Peisistratos features only in the *Odyssey*, some have wondered whether the relationship between Homer and the Peistratids was the reverse of that asserted by Hdt., that is, that Peisistratos son of Nestor was an invented figure, inserted into the Homeric text at the time of the edition prepared under Peisistratean patronage (the 'Peisistratean recension'). But in view of the importance of Peisistratos in the *Telemachy*, this theory would involve a drastically low dating of the *Odyssey* to the mid 6th cent., or at least a radical reworking of a role originally played by another of Nestor's sons, whose name was perhaps changed as a compliment to the tyrant. See S. West 1988: 162, comm. on *Od.* 3.36, and M. West 2013: 305 n. 25. Pausanias (2.18.9) implies, in apparent contradiction of Hdt., that the Homeric Peisistratos did not come to Athens, unlike the other Neleidai, and says he does not know where he went. This version can be explained as due to a desire in some quarters to deny the tyrants a noble pedigree (Nilsson 1951c: 62 n. 43).

65.5 οὕτω ... ὅσα δὲ ἐλευθερωθέντες ἔρξαν ἢ ἔπαθον ἀξιόχρεα ἀπηγήσιος: after some closural words ('that is how the Athenians were liberated from the tyrants'), Hdt. continues by undertaking to describe 'what they did or had done to them after they had been liberated, as far as it is worth recording ... '. The formulation ἔρξαν ἢ ἔπαθον anticipates, and may even have influenced, Aristotle's epigrammatic claim (*Poetics* 1451b10–11) that the 'particular', τὸ καθ' ἕκαστον, with which history is concerned, is τί Ἀλκιβιάδης ἔπραξεν ἢ τί ἔπαθεν. But the model for Hdt. himself is *Od.* 8.490, ὅσσ' ἔρξαν τε πάθον τε. With 'as far as it is worth recording', and with the long clause as a whole, compare Th.'s admission of selectivity at 3.90.1, the first Athenian expedition to Sicily, ἃ δὲ λόγου μάλιστα ἄξια ἢ μετὰ τῶν Ἀθηναίων οἱ ξύμμαχοι ἔπραξαν ἢ πρὸς τοὺς Ἀθηναίους οἱ ἀντιπολέμιοι, τούτων μνησθήσομαι. **πρὶν ἢ Ἰωνίην τε ἀποστῆναι ἀπὸ Δαρείου καὶ Ἀρισταγόρεα ... χρηίσαι σφέων βοηθέειν, ταῦτα πρῶτα φράσω:** the last three words mean 'I will narrate all this first' i.e. before going back to the Ionian revolt from the point where I left it at **38**.2; the Peisistratid material is an analepsis of a few years. πρῶτα is probably neuter plural not adverbial, but the idea is the same (or we might emend to πάντα, 'I will set forth all': Powell tr. 2: 707). Such signposting by Hdt. is not in itself unusual (cf. e.g. 1.194.1, 2.147.1, 8.55.1, all involving some future form of φράσω), but the degree of explanation for an excursus, and the specificity with which its temporal scope is defined, is here very full. The period about to be narrated covers everything until **97**.1, Aristagores' arrival: in our terms, the decade roughly 510–499 BC.

66.1 ἐοῦσαι καὶ πρὶν μεγάλαι, τότε ... ἐγένοντο μέζονες: the Athenian greatness he is talking about is surely political and military, not physical or cultural. But it is not clear what previous period Hdt. has in mind with καὶ πρίν. His line in bk. 1 was that when Kroisos of Lydia made his inquiries, the Athenians were oppressed and fragmented under the tyranny of Peisistratos (1.59.1 and 65.1). Peisistratos' Aegean and other successes, narrated rapidly at 1.64, should be understood proleptically, i.e. as having happened only *after* the time of Kroisos' inquiry, so that 1.65.1 is a return to the time of 1.59.6. In that case, the 'previous' greatness of the present passage might apply to the years of Peisistratos' established tyranny. (For further foreign policy successes of Peisistratos see **94**.1: Sigeion). Or the reference might rather be to long-past and mythical greatness. At **78** he goes even further, and denies all military success to the Peisistratid tyranny; see n. there. ἐδυνάστευον... περὶ δυνάμιος (para. 2): verb and noun are cognate. The verb will be used of another prominent Athenian, Miltiades, at 6.35.1, and usually means prominence inside a city (as at 9.2.3). Only once in Hdt. is it applied to a city – Athens itself, at 5.97.1. Κλεισθένης τε ἀνὴρ Ἀλκμεωνίδης: see *APF*: 375–6. For the moment, Hdt. tells us no more than that he was an Alkmaionid (see **62.**2nn.), and that he was thought to have been behind the bribery of the Pythia. ὅς περ δὴ λόγον ἔχει τὴν Πυθίην ἀναπεῖσαι: note the artful delay of the detail that the man behind it was alleged to be Kleisthenes (or rather still is in Hdt.'s own day, ἔχει not εἶχε); this detail creates continuity with the story already told at **62–3** above, where the Alkmaionidai were kept anonymous. Even now, the biographical detail will be surrendered slowly: at **67.**1 we will learn that Kleisthenes' maternal grandfather was Kleisthenes the tyrant of Sikyon, and only at **69.**1 will Hdt. say explicitly (what any Greek could have guessed, **65.**4n.) that his name derived from his grandfather. At 6.131.1 he adds that the younger Kleisthenes was the man who set up 'the tribes and the democracy' at Athens. Hdt. never tells us that Kleisthenes had a prominent career under the Peisistratids, but he held an eponymous archonship in 525/4: ML 6, c3. The inscription was a physical product of the 420s and may be part of an argument about which families were or were not compromised by involvement with the tyrants. So it is not neutral documentary evidence, though it may also reflect the sort of interest in exact chronology that is also shown by Th. 5.20 and by the researches of Hippias on the Olympic victors. The fact of the archonship is probably correct. Ἰσαγόρης Τεισάνδρου: the 'speaking' name might seem encouraging politically (though see **30**n. for –*gores* names), but in the event it was Kleisthenes who introduced *isegorie*: **78** below. *Ath. Pol.* 20.1 calls Isagores a *philos* of the tyrants; but the opening of that ch. is closely Hdt.-derived; moreover, Isagores is said to have been a *xeinos* or guest-friend of Kleomenes 'from the siege of the Peisistratidai' (**70.**1). For the delay of this item, see n. there. The patronym Teisandros should probably not be connected to that of the Philaid Hippokleides at 6.127.4 (Lewis 1997: 81 and *APF*: 296). οὐκ ἔχω φράσαι: contrast Hdt.'s confidence about the Gephyraioi. θύουσι δὲ οἱ συγγενέες αὐτοῦ Διὶ Καρίωι: Miletos was part-Karian, so family links with the Athenian daughter-city (**97.**2) are possible. The epithet has been emended, ingeniously, to Ἰκαρίωι, after the Attic deme Ikaria: Rhodes at Lewis 1997: 82 n. 46. But there is no reason why Hdt. should mention Isagores' worship of an Attic deme god. He means foreign ties. 'Karian Zeus' certainly existed at later dates (Strabo 14.2.23), and is attested epigraphically (e.g. *BCH* 12 (1888) 250 no. 3, dedication to 'Karian Zeus and Hera' from Panamara in inland Karia). For the cult see Debord 2001 and Ismard 2010: 61.

66.2 ἐσσούμενος...τὸν δῆμον προσεταιρίζεται: the last three words could mean either he 'took the people into partnership' or 'he made it part of his ἑταιρεία (i.e. political club or association)'; or even both simultaneously, perhaps. The second sense is not out of the question (it is rejected firmly by Rhodes 1981: 243), but would be daring anachronism, not inappropriate for a political innovation of the first importance: for such political clubs (in 411 BC, but admittedly implying their somewhat older existence), see Th. 8.54.4 (with *CT* III: 916–20), calling them by a derogatory title 'sworn associations', ξυνωμοσίαι. In favour of the first sense, however, is the only other occurrence of the verb in Hdt., which is at 3.70.2: the Persian conspirators decided that each of them should recruit or associate, προσεταιρίσασθαι, one trustworthy individual. Also, the differently-worded recapitulation at **69**.2, πρὸς τὴν ἑωυτοῦ μοῖραν προσεθήκατο, slightly favours the first sense.

The *Ath. Pol.* paraphrases, and adds nothing to, Hdt.'s account, except that at 21.1 it refers to Isagores as archon in 508/7. This, combined with another item of non-Herodotean evidence that Kleisthenes had already held the archonship in the 520s (**66**.1n. on ὅς περ...) has been thought to lie behind Hdt.'s unelaborated word ἐσσούμενος, 'worsted', 'defeated'. Isagores' election may have constituted Kleisthenes' 'defeat': if we assume that the later rule about non-iteration of the archonship already applied, Kleisthenes may have wanted the post for a political associate rather than for himself. (See Rhodes 1981: 243–4.) So he took the people into association instead. But Hdt. may have had in mind something different, and we should not assume we have all the evidence.

66.2 (cont.) μετὰ δὲ τετραφύλους ἐόντας Ἀθηναίους δεκαφύλους ἐποίησε: a Greek *phyle* is the largest sub-division of the citizen-body. Dorian states were traditionally divided into three tribes (named in **68**), Ionian into four, which are those named here. Membership was by descent. See Davies 1977.

A number of Mediterranean communities reorganised themselves in the later 6th cent. BC, as a response to immigration or *stasis* or both. Cf. the tribal changes at Kyrene (4.161.3): Delphi told the Kyrenaians to send for Demonax of Mantineia as a καταρτιστήρ (**28** n.), and he made them 'three-tribal', τρίφυλοι. Since Kyrene was Dorian, it had three tribes already, but Hdt. makes clear that the membership of the new tribes was to be based this time not on descent, but on geographical origins. Similarly, the Romans switched from a three-tribe system based on descent to one based in part on residence, and consisting (eventually) of thirty-five tribes. The Roman system resembled and perhaps imitated the counter-clockwise arrangement of the Athenian urban tribes after Kleisthenes: Taylor 1960: 72.

There is much that Hdt. does not tell us about the Athenian reforms; yet he was aware of their importance for the strong new democracy (**78** and 6.131.1). Key facts became known from the Aristotelian *Ath. Pol.* Above all we learn from there (21.3) that Kleisthenes replaced Solon's old preparatory council of Four Hundred members, presumably drawn from the old four tribes, by a new one of Five Hundred. Fifty councillors (*bouleutai*) were drawn from each of the ten new tribes; see further **69**. In recent times, historians have sought to show that Kleisthenes used this reorganisation so as to break up traditional religiously-based centres of influence (Lewis 1963) or actually to confer electoral advantages on his own family, the Alkmaionids (Bicknell 1972). The arguments use epigraphic evidence, the inscribed lists of members of the Council of Five Hundred (so-called 'bouleutic lists') from each of the 139 demes which made up the ten tribes; demes were allocated to one of three 'thirds' or trittyes, city, coastal, inland (*Ath. Pol.* 21.4). Different tribes had different, sometimes widely different, numbers of councillors, and the lists give the detail. The general effect (and surely aim) of the system was to make sure that the number of councillors from each deme was in proportion to the size of the deme's population. This was done partly for military reasons (see esp. Siewert 1982 for the military aspect to Kleisthenes' changes, and for tribes as military units see e.g. Th. 6.98.4 with *CT* III: 528).

66.2 (cont.) τῶν Ἴωνος παίδων: Ion was supposedly son of Xouthos, but actually of Apollo, according to the developed version of the myth found in Eur. *Ion* (*c.* 412 BC). For Ion's (somewhat precarious) mythical links with Athens see Parker 1987: 206. The 'best that could be done' (Parker) was to make him a general summoned from outside to command the Athenians in war (against the Thracians, in the time of Eumolpos, 8.44.2).   ἀπαλλάξας τὰς ἐπωνυμίας: in fact, an inscription shows that the old four tribes continued to have ritual functions at Athens, in the celebration of the festival of the Synoikia, which celebrated the political unification of Athens and Attica by Theseus: *IG* 1³ 244, col. 2 line 16 (end of 5th cent.). Kleisthenes did not change the essential religious structures, and the Aristotelian *Ath. Pol.* 21.6 – Kleisthenes permitted everyone to retain their *gene* or clans and phratries, 'brotherhoods' (see *OCD*⁴) and priesthoods according to ancestral custom, κατὰ τὰ πάτρια – is not contradicted by Aristotle himself in the *Politics*. There he says (1319b20ff.) that measures like those of Kleisthenes at Athens or the democrats at Kyrene (date uncertain) are useful in extreme democracies. He goes on to say new tribes and phratries should be established and private rituals restricted and made public, all with a view to mixing up the citizens; but he is there recommending, not describing in detail what Kleisthenes did. So rightly Rhodes 1981: 258 and Kearns 1985: 190–1. Differently Murray 1990: 14–15, preferring the

Politics version (which he takes to mean a 'deliberate remodelling' of the phratry system). Hdt.'s order of treatment is as follows: tribal reorganisation (ten not four, reform briefly stated), then renaming (reform elaborated). At **69**.2 he neatly reverses the procedure.   ἐξευρὼν δὲ ἑτέρων ἡρώων ἐπωνυμίας ἐπιχωρίων: this implies that Kleisthenes chose the ten eponymous heroes himself, but *Ath. Pol.* 21.6 says he submitted them to the Pythian oracle at Delphi. This is not a serious contradiction: either the oracle was invited to choose from a longer list, or else Kleisthenes made the choice and put to Apollo a request on the lines 'is it better and more good?' for this to happen. See Kearns 1985: 199. The ten are males from Athenian mythical history, but Theseus is noticeably absent: he was too great and powerful a symbolic figure to be annexed by any one of the ten tribes. Athenian mythology had its self-sacrificing mythical heroines, but the close link between citizenship and military service presumably excluded the use of female icons for this purpose. The new tribes (for which see esp. Kron 1976) had already become objects of emotional attachment by the time Th. makes Nikias address his troops, in a desperate military plight in Sicily, by their names, their fathers' names *and their tribes* (Th. 7.69.2); and in the 4th cent. the Demosthenic funeral oration ([Dem.] 60.27ff.) shows what rhetorical play could be made with the deeds of the ten heroes. See *CT* III: 692. The altar of the eponymous heroes in the agora functioned as a tribal notice-board.   πάρεξ Αἴαντος . . . ἀστυγείτονα καὶ σύμμαχον: the point is that Ajax was associated with the neighbouring island of Salamis, an Athenian cleruchy or military settlement of Athenians, for which see ML 14 = Fornara: 44B; and for Ajax's Salaminian contingent in the Homeric Catalogue of Ships, where they are ranged with suspicious explicitness next to the Athenians (a result of early Athenian tampering with the text?), see *Il.* 2.557–8. This co-opting of 'neighbour Ajax' may have been compensation to the Salaminioi for not being a deme in the full sense. See *IACP*: no. 363, where Salamis is treated as a separate *polis* (preferable to Taylor 1997, according to whom the Salaminians were registered in the 139 demes).

Hdt. is brief and enigmatic here; the full importance of the present narrative 'seed', especially the description of Ajax as an ally of the Athenians, will become clear at 8.64, where the Salaminian connection is spelt out: before the battle of Salamis and after an earthquake, the Athenians called on Ajax and Telamon from Salamis, and sent a ship to fetch Aiakos and the other Aiakidai from Aigina. On that passage see Bowie, citing Parker 1996: 153–4 (the festival of the Aianteia commemorated Ajax's help).

67–68 *Kleisthenes of Sikyon*

Hdt.'s account of the tribal reforms of Kleisthenes of Sikyon is a puzzle: it is not easy to see why he gave it at such length. The Alkmaionid link is one line of explanation, and the present excursus should be seen as half of a pair whose other half is the excursus at 6.126–31 (Megakles at Sikyon), where the link between the Alkmaionidai and the tyrants of Sikyon is explored in a different way. Kleisthenes' imitation of his grandfather is the frail peg on which the present story is hung. Other authorial motives were no doubt simultaneously in play. Gray 2007: 224 suggests that Hdt. is keen to stress the Athenian Kleisthenes' anti-Ionianism (the reminder of which 'gives piquancy to the decision of the Athenians to accept the appeal of Aristagores') and that this is one reason for the elaboration of the parallel. For Osborne (2002: 503–4), Hdt.'s archaic Sikyonian material exemplifies his tendency to relate early Greek history only in order to explain later events.

Kleisthenes of Sikyon was unusual among ancient Greek leaders in having a 'religious policy' (Parker 2011: 47 n. 22). The request to the Thebans for Melanippos, whatever exactly it meant (**67**.2), is unusual in having so obviously political a motive (anti-Argive). But in other ways it is not abnormal. The mobility of the Aiakidai (**80–1**) and of Damie and Auxesie (**82–6**) illustrates the role played by such tutelary figures and cult-objects in archaic inter-state relations.

67.1 ταῦτα δέ…ἐμιμέετο ὁ Κλεισθένης οὗτος τὸν ἑωυτοῦ μητροπάτορα Κλεισθένεα τὸν Σικυῶνος τύραννον: the story of how Megakles, father of the Athenian Kleisthenes, married Agariste the daughter of Kleisthenes of Sikyon, will be told at 6.126–31. The tyranny of Kleisthenes of Sikyon lasted *c.* 595–75: Griffin 1982: 44. For the 100-year tyrannical rule of his family, known to modern scholars as the Orthagorids, see Griffin 40–59, Lolos 2011: 61–5.

The 'imitation' (the verb is repeated closurally by ἐμιμήσατο at **69**.1, see n. there for the compositional ring) seems to us not much more than nominal. Kleisthenes of Sikyon inherited a traditional Dorian three-tribe system (Hylleis, Pamphyloi and Dymanes), supplemented by one apparently non-Dorian one, his own; in what sounds like a mainly dissimilar operation from that at Athens, he re-named them all, but on the evidence of Hdt. made no other changes. His motives are said to be (a) the wish that Sikyonians' tribe names should not be the same as those of the Argives, with whom Kleisthenes was at war; and (b) a contempt for the Ionians, which he shared with Kleisthenes of Athens (this, at any rate, is the obvious meaning of the Greek of **69**.1; but see n. there on καὶ οὗτος ὑπεριδὼν Ἴωνας for the difficulty of this). Given the evidence for widespread tribal changes in this period (**66**.2n. μετὰ δέ), it is tempting to suppose that Hdt.'s 'imitation' is a personalising description of an adhesion to a wider trend; but that would mean the Sikyonian changes were more radical and organisational than Hdt.'s account of them, as opposed to his comments about imitation, entitles us to say. R. P. Legon's statement at *IACP*: 469 (under no. 228) that 'the tyrant Kleisthenes reformed the tribal structure' is too confident and categorical. He refers only to N. Jones 1987: 103–6 among modern works. But Jones' suggestion (105) that the name-change 'masks some more substantial alteration in the nature of the public apparatus' rested on an unacceptable interpretation of **68**.1 (see n. there on οὗτοι μὲν…). It is possible that Korinth, not Sikyon, was the Athenian Kleisthenes' real model; see Salmon 2003.

67.1 (cont.) ῥαψωιδοὺς ἔπαυσε ἐν Σικύωνι ἀγωνίζεσθαι τῶν Ὁμηρείων ἐπέων εἵνεκα: rhapsodes recited poetry for a living, especially but not only the works of Homer. The word means 'song-stitchers' (see *OCD*[4] 'rhapsodes'), but Greeks themselves derived it from ῥάβδος, a staff; both associations may be relevant to the Greeks' own perceptions (Graziosi 2002: 18–40 at 23). The word is first attested on a mid 5th-cent. BC tripod from Dodona, dedicated to Zeus Naios by 'Terpsikles the rhapsode' *SGDI*: 5786 with Graziosi 25: Terpsikles means 'famed for giving pleasure' and may be a professionally assumed name (though see *SGDI* 5505: Miletos). But already in the 6th cent., Herakleitos (DK 22 B42) had recommended that Homer should be expelled from the contests and beaten with a staff (ῥαπίζεσθαι), and Graziosi 29 (see also 221) ingeniously sees here a coded reference to rhapsodes, and notes the similarity to what Kleisthenes of Sikyon actually did. In particular, both items feature an explicit element of competition. It is thought that the Sikyonian contests were dedicated to Apollo, and that Kleisthenes transferred them to a Sikyonian version of the Pythian festival (Griffin 1982: 158, cf. 53–4). These local 'Pythia' are not mentioned by Hdt., but are known from the victory ode which Pindar wrote for Chromios of Aitna (Sicily) to celebrate his victory at the Sikyonian Pythia: *Nem.* 9.9 with the scholia (Drachmann 1910–27: 3.149 and 152). These Pythia were founded by Adrastos according to Pindar, but by Kleisthenes according to the scholia. For the importance of Homeric recitations at Sikyon and (not much later) at Athens, see further **67.5** n. χορούς…
ὅτι Ἀργεῖοί τε καὶ Ἄργος…ὑμνέαται: Homer was capable, within fewer than a hundred lines, of using 'Argos/Argives' to mean both Greece and the Greeks generally and also the particular *polis* of Argos and the Argives: *Il.* 6.66 and 159 with Graziosi and Haubold; see also *Il.* 2.108 (Agamemnon 'king of many islands and all Argos') and the paraphrase at Th. 1.9.4. This extended use of 'Argives' in the main epics is annoying enough, from Kleisthenes' point of view, to explain his ban on Homer. It is also possible, though not necessary, to see here a ref. to those parts of the Epic Cycle in which the Argives were prominent, such as the *Thebais* and the *Epigoni* (Wilamowitz 1884: 352). In any case, there was presumably a blanket ban on Homer and all poems thought to be Homeric. ἡρώιον γάρ

ἦν καὶ ἔστι ἐν αὐτῆι τῆι ἀγορῆι τῶν Σικυωνίων Ἀδρήστου τοῦ Ταλαοῦ: for the myth, see *OCD*[4], 'Adrastus'. He led the 'Seven against Thebes', an expedition intended to reinstate his son-in-law Polyneikes on the Theban throne. The hero-shrine which Hdt. here mentions does not feature in Paus.'s account of Sikyon in his bk. 2 (at 1.43.1, he says that Adrastos died at Megara), and had presumably disappeared by the 2nd cent. AD, though Hdt. is here emphatic that it was still there in his day. For a daring suggestion that the Seven were originally an Akkadian-influenced 'outbreak from hell' of infernal demons, led by A-drastos 'the Inescapable', see Burkert 1992: 108–9; the hero-cult i.e. chthonic worship attested in the present passage of Hdt. might be adduced in support, though Burkert in fact cites the tragic choruses of **67.5**.

For hero-cult in the agora or city-centre (heroes were non-polluting), see Parker 1983: 42–3, discussing the behaviour of, precisely, the Sikyonians when in the 3rd cent. they wanted to bury their liberator Aratos within the walls (Plut. *Arat.* 53.2–4). Nilsson 1951b: 94 remarked that whereas Adrastos was buried in Megara, he had a cenotaph in Sikyon.

67.1 (cont.) ἐόντα Ἀργεῖον: the Argives built a hero-shrine to Adrastos in their city at just this time: Pariente 1992 with Osborne 2009: 267.

67.2 ἐλθὼν δὲ ἐς Δελφούς: this raises the question of the Sikyonian Kleisthenes' relations with Delphi. Hdt. never mentions the 'First Sacred War', supposedly fought for control of Delphi in the 590s–80s, by the members of the Amphiktiony under the leadership of Kleisthenes of Sikyon, to put a stop to a usurpation by the people of Krisa. For a simple statement of Kleisthenes' role see Paus. 10.37.4, but there is other evidence, notably some scholia to Pindar's Pythian odes. Davies 1994 analysed the traditions about the war, and defended them cautiously against extreme modern scepticism. Th.'s silence is as complete as Hdt.'s, but is less surprising, given that Th.'s information and his silences about early Greek history replicate those of Hdt.: *CT* II: 125–6. The literary evidence closest in time to the war is *Hom. Hymn Apollo*, lines 540–3; see Richardson 2010: 151–2. These lines have been seen (Forrest 1956: 39) as post-war propaganda against the old management of oracle and sanctuary; and the rash or idle word (τηύσιον ἔπος, 540) as a ref. to the rude word λευστήρ, for which see next n.

It would not have been hard for Hdt. to have fitted the war into his structurally dominant picture of close Alkmaionid relations with Kleisthenes of Sikyon: the leader of the Athenian forces was Alkmaion, according to Delphi's own records. We are told this by Plutarch (*Sol.* 11), who was in a good position to obtain reliable information about Delphi and the Amphiktiony (he was a priest there, *Mor.* 992f, and an executive official of the Amphiktiony, *Syll.*[3] 829A). Alkmaion's visit to Sardis may be connected with the First Sacred War (cf. 6.125.5 n.) but, again, Hdt. does not say so, and the connection is a modern inference. Kleisthenes' participation in the Sacred War may have been 'a response to Delphi's rejection of his [Adrastos'] policy' (Griffin 1982: 54).

67.2 (cont.) Ἄδρηστον μὲν εἶναι Σικυωνίων βασιλέα, ἐκεῖνον δὲ λευστῆρα: the first part of the oracle's reply, up to the comma, recalls Homer, *Il.* 2.572, καὶ Σικυῶν' ὅθ' ἄρ' Ἄδρηστος πρῶτ' ἐμβασίλευεν. The final word of the oracle is enigmatic. In its original hexameter form, the oracle surely included the word βασιλεύς in the nominative (e.g. Ἄδραστος βασιλεύς Σικυώνιος, ἀλλὰ σὺ λευστήρ, though the ethnic in this reconstruction is not quite what we want), so that βασιλεύς is picked up by the first syllable of λευσ-τῆρα. Gray (2007: 222 n. 51) cites Aesch. *Eum.* 179–97 for the tremendous denunciation (by Pythian Apollo, as here) of the arbitrary and bloodthirsty punishments, including stonings, inflicted by the Erinyes. It has been suggested (Ogden 1993 and 1997: 100–4) that the obviously abusive final word λευστήρ ('he who performs or suffers an act of stoning') refers to the *pharmakos* ritual, by which a polluted person, often a criminal, was driven out of the community with stones (Douglas 2004: 38–60). Another interpretation (see LSJ⁹) is that 'stone-thrower' is a rough synonym for ψιλός, a light-armed non-hoplite soldier, cf. Diomedes' taunt at Paris as a mere archer, τόξοτα, at *Iliad* 11.585.   ἐφρόντιζε μηχανὴν τῇ αὐτὸς ὁ Ἄδρηστος ἀπαλλά-ξεται: Sikyon will be made so disagreeable for Adrastos that he will leave of his own accord, a sort of 'constructive dismissal'. This expulsion is abnormal manipulation of hero-cult, because such exploitation is usually positive: the acquisition of a hero's bones or of his otherwise manifested presence, as below with Melanippos (Ekroth 2007: 112). Parker 2011: 118, protesting against reductivist views of hero-cult as legitimation or identity politics, rightly observes that Adrastos here is 'a real presence...who retains the affections and antipathies of his mortal existence'.   ὡς δέ οἱ ἐξευρῆσθαι ἐδόκεε 'when he thought he had found it'. That is, a μηχανή or device for getting rid of Adrastos.   πέμψας ἐς Θήβας: there were ancient mythical ties between Sikyon and Thebes; see *OCD⁴* 'Antiope', who was mother of Amphion and Zethos, builders of Thebes, by either Zeus or Epopeus of Sikyon. But shared hostility to Adrastos is also relevant, if the Thebans shared the view of the Boiotian Pindar (*Pyth.* 8.48–55, composed for an Aiginetan victor) that Adrastos took part in the expeditions against Thebes of both the Seven and the Epigonoi; see Huxley 1969: 49. Kleisthenes could have derived poetic justification for his actions from anti-Argive poetry of the kind exemplified by Stesichoros' poem about Eteokles and Polyneikes (see Burnett 1988: 147. The poem is fr. 222(b) *PMGF*, tr. at Burnett 109–10).   Μελάνιππον τὸν Ἀστακοῦ: Melanippos the Theban, son of 'Lobster-man', featured memorably in the story of the Seven against Thebes because of the horrible behaviour of Tydeus, father of Diomedes, who killed Melanippos (as in Hdt., see below, but another version has Melanippos killed by Amphiaraos) and then sucked out his brains and ate them. Athena in disgust withheld from Tydeus the intended gift of immortality (Shapiro 1993: 34–6). See Apollod. 3.6.8 with Frazer's n. 4 (Loeb edn).   οἱ δὲ Θηβαῖοι ἔδοσαν: the tomb of Melanippos was on the road from Thebes to Chalkis (Euboia): Paus. 9.18.1; Schachter 1981–94: 2.125. It is not clear whether the 'fetching' of Melanippos to Sikyon was thought of as involving his permanent departure from Thebes, or whether he could thereafter be in two places at once. Heroes (Adrastos himself is an example) could have cult in several places; but such rival cults were a form of inter-state competition, so that does not solve the matter. For the 'multilocality' of heroes in this competitive sense, see Ekroth 2007: 111. It is not plausible that the Thebans would say goodbye to Melanippos as casually as this: they could have allowed the Sikyonians to have a cult-image (so rightly Demand 1982: 58). Hdt. does not here specify bones (as he does at 1.67.2, Orestes, cf. Plut. *Kim.* 3.7, Theseus), and Farnell 1921: 335 cannily wrote of Kleisthenes inviting from Thebes the 'spirit' of Adrastos' enemy Melanippos. See Kearns 1989: 47 'a hero's physical remains are not indispensable to his presence' (discussing Aiakos at **8g**, for which see n. there); at 46 she says of the summoning of Aiakos in 480 (8.64, discussed above at **66**.2n.) 'it is not clear in what form he was supposed to be brought'. ἔδοσαν surely refers to the giving of more than 'permission' (Waterfield), in fact to the 'giving' of Melanippos himself.

The Sikyonian approach to the Thebans is not obviously backed up by a kinship or other tie of closeness like that which could be held to link Thebes and Aigina at **80** (and see introd. n. to **82–8**). Perhaps the myth of the Seven against Thebes, and the ancestral Theban hostility towards Argos which it implied, were felt to be enough.

67.3 τέμενός οἱ ἀπέδεξε ἐν αὐτῶι τῶι πρυτανηίωι: οἱ is dative singular. Melanippos' location in the prytaneion is obviously meant to be even more central and prestigious than Adrastos' in the agora.   Hdt. gives the facts first (request for Melanippos and establishment of cult for him at Sikyon), then the explanation for it only a few lines later (Melanippos' strong hostility to Adrastos), with a story-teller's interactive word to hearer/reader, 'I need to explain that . . .', καὶ γὰρ τοῦτο δεῖ ἀπηγήσασθαι. Hdt. 'needs' to tell whatever enables understanding, see Pohlenz 1937: 57.

67.4 ἡ γὰρ χώρη ἦν αὕτη Πολύβου . . . θυγατριδέος: the background is given more fully by the early Hellenistic Sikyonian historian Menaichmos, quoted by the scholiast on Pind. *Nem.* 9.30 (*FGrHist* 131 F9): Pronax and Adrastos are sons of Talaos, king of Argos, and of Lysimache, daughter of Polybos king of Sikyon. Pronax dies and Adrastos flees to Sikyon. He

inherits Polybos' kingdom. See Gantz 1993: 507–8 for variants.   ἄπαις:
see 48n.

67.5 τραγικοῖσι χοροῖσι ἐγέραιρον, τὸν μὲν Διόνυσον οὐ τιμῶντες: this is the
only mention of 'tragic choruses' in Hdt., or indeed of 'tragic' as an adjective; but for a 'drama' (a tragedy, clearly) about the fall of Miletos, see
6.21.2. 'Tragic' means what it says. Macan says 'presumably dithyrambic',
but if Hdt. had meant dithyrambs, he had the vocabulary to say so: see
1.23 about Arion, and cf. Pickard-Cambridge 1927: 127, 137 and Nilsson
1951b: 94 against attempts to take τραγικοί here in any sense other than
'tragic'.

It is frustrating not to be able to make more of Hdt.'s early reference
here to early tragic institutions, and moreover at a *polis* other than Athens
(the usual ancient account involved the Athenian Thespis). The non-
Athenian dimension is the most important feature of the present passage
for the student of the origins of tragedy, and it is possible that Hdt. was
contributing, consciously but indirectly, to an argument about the cradle
of tragedy, and was quietly discounting or qualifying Athenian claims. It is
also possible that early theatrical institutions were more widespread than
our limited, mainly Athens-centred, knowledge allows us to see. It would
not, for instance, be a surprise if relevant epigraphic evidence were to turn
up from 6th-cent. Sicily; see Dubois 1989: no. 134 (with Eidinow 2007:
157–8 and 294–5 nn. 2, 9 and 10) for an early 5th-cent curse-tablet from
Sicilian Gela mentioning a *choregos* and contests of some sort. And the Sicilian Epicharmos influenced Attic comedy rather than the other way round,
and may also have mentioned the *choregia*.

The presentation by negation (οὐ τιμῶντες) is an emphatic way of anticipating the account of what Kleisthenes did, and of underlining its importance: before him, the Sikyonians did not honour Dionysos in this way, but
after his changes they did.

**67.5 (cont.) χορούς μὲν τῶι Διονύσωι ἀπέδωκε, τὴν δὲ ἄλλην θυσίην Μελανίπ-
πωι:** Hdt. is remarkably well informed on the detail. But it is surprising
that the Sikyonian Kleisthenes did not transfer everything to Melanippos,
choruses as well as sacrifices. Presumably this was because tragic choruses
were already thought of as appropriate for association with Dionysos, so
we have here an important contribution to the problem of the origin of
tragedy. Seaford 1994: 326 suggests that the choruses now celebrated the
'sufferings' of Dionysos.

68.1 φυλὰς δὲ τὰς Δωριέων ... μετέβαλε ἐς ἄλλα οὐνόματα: this sentence, with
its explicit mention of Dorian tribes, and the assumed non-Dorian character of Kleisthenes' own tribe, are the only hints at the 'racial factor'
which Andrewes 1956: 54–65 saw as the key to Kleisthenes' tyranny. And

yet (a) Hdt. continues – as he did over Adrastos in **67** – to present Kleisthenes' motive as political hostility towards the Argives rather than anti-Dorianism as such; and (b) the changes are said by Hdt. to be name-changes only, however much modern historians hanker after interpretations which impute to Kleisthenes a structural and sweeping reform of the system. For this sentence as the possible centre of the structural ring formed by the excursus, see **69**.1n. on ἐμιμήσατο.   **ἔνθα καὶ πλεῖστον κατεγέλασε τῶν Σικυωνίων**: this must mean 'in this way more than in any other he made them laughing-stocks', rather than that he himself was laughing at them. Kleisthenes wanted to get rid of Argive features, not to make his own people ridiculous in the eyes of other Greeks, although that is what he actually did. (For the actual names and their implications, see end of next n.) So we may ask why Hdt. did not say καταγελάστους ἐποίησεν, as at 8.100.4. Perhaps there is a clue in πλεῖστον; it normally accompanies a verb, and here helps to fix the non-intentional sense. The combination πλεῖστον κατεγέλασε is easier to take as 'he made them very ridiculous' than as 'he [deliberately] derided them very much'.   **ἐπὶ γὰρ ὑός τε καὶ ὄνου < καὶ χοίρου> τὰς ἐπωνυμίας μετατιθείς**: the usual emendation is probably right, and is dictated by the sequence Ὑᾶται Ὀνεᾶται Χοιρεᾶται below. It is also easy to explain the corruption: a copyist's eye might well jump over the second pair of words ending in -ου. Bicknell 1982 suggested instead that the mismatch found in the MSS (two animal names, three animal-derived tribe names) should be solved not by generating three animal names but by the elimination of ἕτεροι δὲ Χοιρεᾶται below, producing two animal-names and two animal-derived tribe names. (Against this, see N. Jones 1987: 125 n. 8; cf. also Lolos 2011: 63 n. 27.) Bicknell's idea should probably be rejected, though see n. on ἕτεροι...below. He does, however, make a different and good point about the names. It is obvious that they lent themselves to ridicule, but they had positive features. Thus the donkey symbolises stubbornness in the memorable simile about Ajax at *Il.* 11.558–65, though that too has its comic side; and for donkeys as sexually voracious see Pind. *Pyth.* 10.36. Pigs and swine are not so easy. Boars indicate ferocity, as Bicknell says, and σῦς (the Homeric form of ὗς) can mean a boar, but only with extra qualifiers such as κάπριος or ἀγρότερος. As for χοῖρος, it is just a young pig or hog, though the Aristophanic sense (female genitals) might add to the humour, cf. above on donkeys.   **οὗτοι μὲν δὴ Ἀρχέλαοι ἐκαλέοντο**: the 'Herrenvolk', unless it means 'leaders of the people'. The natural way of taking this is as a renaming of an existing tribe. But N. Jones 1987: 105 thought that this fourth tribe was a new 'creation' by Kleisthenes, on the grounds that it is 'difficult to imagine what would have been...the constituency of such an extra-Dorian phyle'. On Jones' hypothesis, the changes would indeed have amounted to a radical tribal reorganisation, but the hypothesis does too much violence to Hdt.'s language. 'Except for his own tribe' (πλὴν τῆς ἑωυτοῦ φυλῆς, see above) surely implies the pre-existence of that tribe. Hdt. does not say what the tribe was called before Kleisthenes changed its name.   **ἕτεροι δὲ Χοιρεᾶ-ται**: see above on ἔνθα...: these words should probably not be deleted (with Bicknell), though it is true that the order ἕτεροι...ἄλλοι...ἕτεροι is odd, and Wilson expresses some sympathy with the deletion.

68.2 λόγον σφίσι δόντες 'after deliberating among themselves'.   **τετάρ-τους δὲ αὐτοῖσι προσέθεντο... Αἰγιαλέας**: 'Pelasgian Aigialees' or 'Pelasgian Men of the Shore' is said at 7.94 to have been an old name for Ionians. But Hdt. evidently does not think that the name of the fourth Sikyonian tribe indicated Ionianism (which would have produced a very surprising civic blend within one *polis*), because he derives it instead from the Argive hero Adrastos' son Aigialeus, for whom see Apollod. 1.9.13. This renaming looks like a post-tyrannical gesture of friendship towards the Argives. If Aigialees had been the name of the Archelaoi before Kleisthenes changed it, then the mythical association with Adrastos would have been an obvious motive for Kleisthenes to call it something else. And yet Hdt. saves the information about the link with Adrastos until now, rather than providing it at the earlier point where he mentions the Archelaoi; and this order of narration implies *either* that there was no fourth tribe at all before Kleisthenes (the view rejected above) *or* that there was a fourth tribe (usually assumed to be non-Dorian because distinct from the three Dorian ones), which was called neither Archelaoi nor Aigialees but by some lost name. That is the best solution. The wording of the present passage certainly suggests, without quite saying so, that the name Aigialeis was not a mere reversion. That tribe was specially associated with Kleisthenes, so this was a clear break with the tyranny.   **τὴν ἐπωνυμίην ποιεύμενοι κεκλῆσθαι**: cf. **58.2**n.

69 Kleisthenes of Athens again

69.1 καὶ τὸ οὔνομα ἐπὶ τούτου ἔχων... τὸν ὁμώνυμον Κλεισθένεα: the onomastic point, here made with the emphasis of a repetition within a couple of lines, will be repeated yet again at 6.131.1; and see **67.1**n. Naming is curiously prominent hereabouts. Hdt. may mean us to reflect that two men, whose names were the same as each other's, nevertheless made the names of their tribes different. For ἐπὶ τούτου see **65.4**n.   **καὶ οὗτος ὑπεριδὼν Ἴωνας**: the point here must be 'he was another person with a low opinion of others – in his case the Ionians' (Waterfield). This must be the right idea, whether that meaning can actually be extracted from the Greek (as is doubtful), or whether (the better view) we have to accept that Hdt. expressed himself in an over-condensed way. The literal meaning of the Greek is 'He too despising the Ionians...' i.e. 'Kleisthenes the Athenian also, i.e. like his Sikyonian grandfather, despised the Ionians.' But his grandfather did not despise the Ionians, or at least did not do what he did because he despised them. He was getting at the Argives. (The continuation here 'so that the tribes should not be the same for them and for the Ionians' exactly parallels **68.**1, 'so that the tribes should not be the same for the Sikyonians and for the Argives'.)   **ἐμιμήσατο**: the verb closes a narrative ring begun at **67.**1, ἐμιμέετο. Ring composition often entails a 'well-marked turning point' (Douglas 2007: 37 on 'central loading', cf. Immerwahr 1966: 72), and here the central point is the first sentence of **68.**1, beginning φυλὰς δέ..., tribal names changed at Sikyon.

69.2 **τὸν Ἀθηναίων δῆμον πρότερον ἀπωσμένον πάντως τότε πρὸς τὴν ἑαυτοῦ μοῖραν προσεθήκατο**: again this is resumptive: it picks up προσεταιρίζεται at **66.**2, but with the extra idea that the people had been previously 'pushed away'. As for μοῖρα, 'side' is a better tr. than 'political party', which suggests too modern and organised a concept. A full commentary on the statement that 'the people had previously been discounted' would be a history of early Athenian democracy, but it should be remembered that Hdt. is here speaking only of the political means for the capture and exercise of power. He is presumably thinking of the period of the Peisistratid tyranny, rather than making a point about Solon. But in any case he treats Solon as a legislator (1.29–32) rather than a populist politician or proto-democrat, and indeed Solon's own remarks about the people do not imply that he saw them in any way as partners or 'on his side': 'I gave the demos as much γέρας as was sufficient, neither taking away nor adding any element of τιμή' (F 5.1–2 West), he says firmly, and claims that anyone else but himself 'would not have been able to restrain the demos' (F 36.22 West). The Greek is not easy and the text has been suspected. Perhaps (a) πάντως is wrong, and (b) an important word has dropped out, e.g. τότε <μεταδιδοὺς τῶν> πάντων, 'giving them [the people] a share of everything'; so Stein, followed by Forrest 1979: 321 n. 24.   **τὰς φυλὰς μετωνόμασε καὶ ἐποίησε πλεῦνας ἐξ ἐλασσόνων**: at **66.**2, Hdt. had described this same programme, but in reverse order, i.e. he there said Kleisthenes made the Athenians δεκαφύλους instead of τετραφύλους, and that he renamed the tribes; then with an easy transition Hdt. expanded on the second half of this, by the long analogy with Sikyon. Now Hdt. reverses the order of presentation: Kleisthenes renamed the tribes, and he made them many instead of few, and again Hdt. glides on to an expansion of the second half.   **δέκα τε δὴ φυλάρχους ἀντὶ τεσσέρων ἐποίησε, δέκαχα δὲ καὶ τοὺς δήμους κατένειμε ἐς τὰς φυλάς**: the MSS have δέκα twice, which would produce 100 demes. But there were 139. So unless we suppose that Hdt. did not know what he was talking about, we should, instead of the second δέκα, read δέκαχα, 'by tens' (cf. ML 94, Athens, 405 BC, line 33, Samians to be distributed among demes and tribes δέκαχα). Bravo 2008: 107 thinks this would have been too obvious to be worth saying, and regards this sentence – and much else in Hdt. on archaic Greek history – as the interpolated work of an 'editore falsario'. But not all Hdt.'s envisaged readers were Athenians.

The old four phylarchs were presumably infantry (hoplite) commanders, and if we had no other evidence we would assume that the same was true of their successors the ten phylarchs. The assumption is probably right, but we shall see below that Hdt. may have mis-named them. He correctly says nothing here about the ten generals (στρατηγοί): they were introduced only in 502/1: *Ath. Pol.* 22.2 with Rhodes 1981: 262–3. The big difference was that the new generals were elected *by all Athenian males*, from (usually) each of the ten tribes. So the period of the tribal supremacy of the 'phylarchs' was short, a very few years. There is, however, a complication. By the 4th cent. BC, phylarchs at Athens were purely cavalry commanders: see *Ath. Pol.* 61.5 (*c.* 330 BC): there were ten phylarchs and ten taxiarchs (for whom see also 61.3), and the former led the cavalry and the latter the hoplites in each tribe. This means that taxiarchs were the more important, since late archaic and classical Athens was not a cavalry power (see **63**.3 above for the request for Thessalian cavalry); at any rate, Athenian taxiarchs are mentioned in Th. (e.g. 7.60.2, the Sicily campaign), phylarchs never. It seems likely that Hdt. has been over-attracted by the prefix φυλ- and has produced a balanced sentence by mis-naming the taxiarchs as phylarchs. (See Rhodes 1981: 684–5 against the old view that taxiarchs were not introduced until after the Persian Wars.) Bugh 1988: 5 n.14 states confidently that 'phylarchs' in the present passage of Hdt. means purely civil magistrates, not cavalry commanders of the later sort. The second half of this is right, but the first part is too extreme and one-sided. The Athenian tribes were militarily important in Kleisthenes' arrangements: see above **66**.2n. on μετὰ δὲ τετραφύλους..., citing Siewert. This is not to deny the 'phylarchs' of 508–2 (i.e. the taxiarchs) some non-military functions (e.g. religious) as well.

69.2 (cont.) ἦν τε τὸν δῆμον προσθέμενος πολλῶι κατύπερθε τῶν ἀντιστασιωτέων: 'after winning over the people, he was was more powerful than (lit. 'on top of') his political opponents'.

70–79 *Kleomenes of Sparta and his interventions*

Hdt.'s presentation of Kleomenes is discussed fully in the Introduction to bk. 6. Among modern works see esp. Griffiths 1989 (the madness of K.); Cawkwell 1993; Parker 1998; Ste. Croix 2004b.

70.1 ξεῖνον ἀπὸ τῆς Πεισιστρατιδέων πολιορκίης: another delayed item; see **66**.1 (with n.) for the introduction of Isagores and **65** for the siege. But it is only here that the personal connection with Kleomenes becomes relevant. τὸν δὲ Κλεομένεα εἶχε αἰτίη φοιτᾶν παρὰ τοῦ Ἰσαγορέω τὴν γυναῖκα 'Kleomenes was accused of (lit. 'blame had it that he had had') a sexual relationship with (lit. 'having frequented', a euphemism) Isagores' wife'. One might have thought that this (if the rumour were true, or even if untrue but known to Isagores) would make Isagores less rather than more keen to ask help from Kleomenes. In any case, contrast the reticence of Th. in this sort of matter, if the reason for the personal enmity between Agis and Alkibiades in 412/11 BC (8.12.2 and 45.1) was the latter's affair with Agis' wife Timaia, a piece of gossip known from Plutarch: *CT* III: 790.

70.2 ἐξέβαλλε Κλεισθένεα καὶ μετ᾽ αὐτοῦ ἄλλους πολλοὺς Ἀθηναίων, τοὺς ἐναγέας ἐπιλέγων 'he tried to banish Kleisthenes and many other Athenians with him, choosing those under a curse' The imperfect tense means he *tried* to do this. It is picked up at **72**.1, after the analeptic material about Kylon. Such religious accusations were no doubt worrying, but might be no more than diplomatic point-scoring. The Spartans used the Alkmaionid curse again on the eve of the main Peloponnesian War (Th. 1.126.2, where the target is Perikles, a maternal Alkmaionid), and that famous re-use will surely have been in Hdt.'s mind and the minds of his hearers and readers.

The Alkmaionid family curse was mentioned as long ago as 1.61.1, where it was given as the reason or pretext for Peisistratos' abnormal sexual relations with Megakles' daughter; but the explanation and background are given only now (and in the continuation at para. 2 below), in a remarkably long postponement. The word ἐναγής is used by Hdt. in these two passages only (though 6.56.1 ἐν τῶι ἄγει ἐνέχεσθαι comes close), and this is a clear form of non-specific back-reference; this postponement may imply that Hdt. was already planning what we call bk. 5 when he wrote about Peisistratos in bk. 1. The motive for the postponement is not easy to see. It is not possible to argue *either* that it is only here that it becomes properly relevant (it was already relevant in bk. 1, though in a different way) *or* that Hdt. takes it for granted that everyone knew about something so famous (in that case why explain it now?). The curse was highly topical in the run-up to the Peloponnesian War, and that is why Th., too, narrates the Kylon episode (1.126), with divergences. The parallel between the situations in 432 and 508 (Spartan demands for expulsion) may explain the positioning of the Kylon story just here; as may the desire for structural balance between bks. 1 and 5 (Introduction §1).

The Kylon episode, after which the city was purified by the Kretan Epimenides (*Ath. Pol.* 1 and Plut. *Sol.* 12; cf. Develin 1989: 34), has been thought to resemble the situation in the *Oresteia* (esp. the *Eumenides*) of Aeschylus (so Seaford 1994: 92–9). The hard link is the mention of the Semnai – the solemn/awful goddesses, i.e. the Eumenides – in Th.'s account of Kylon, 1.126.11. As Seaford remarks, it cannot have been true that all the family were implicated in Kylon's killing, or that all the killers were Alkmaionids. But pollution is thought of as extending outwards from the one affected individual to his or her entire kin.

71 Kylon

71.1 ἦν Κύλων τῶν Ἀθηναίων ἀνὴρ Ὀλυμπιονίκης: the chronology of this (actually not many years after 640 BC) has been obscured by Hdt.'s final remark (**71.2**) that 'this happened before the age, ἡλικίη, of Peisistratos'. Scholars have wondered why he did not say 'before the time of Solon' (590s), if he meant the 7th cent. But he means 'this unsuccessful attempt at a tyranny happened some time before the successful one of Peisistratos'.

The chronological clue is contained in the Olympic victory, which the victory-list preserved by Eusebius puts in 640 (cf. *CT* I: 204, which however worried too much about 'before the time of Solon'; see above).

The link between athletic or equestrian success and political aspirations was long-standing in Greek and Macedonian history, as we have seen already: see **22.2**, Alexandros I of Macedon, and **47.1**, Philippos of Kroton, with nn.

By Th., but not by Hdt., we are told that Kylon was son-in-law of Theagenes, tyrant of Megara. Intermarriage between tyrannical and other elite families was common at all periods of Greek history (cf. 6.128.2); so there is no reason to doubt the fact of Kylon's marriage (it has been seen – picturesquely but unnecessarily – as a detail added to the tradition later, e.g. as part of a folklore motif (hand of princess and half the kingdom), or so as to make Kylon a traitor who brought in foreigners: Lang 2011: 29).

This sentence and the next (οὗτος ἐπί…) open abruptly i.e. without particles. Such asyndeton is a feature of story-telling mode, and is used by poets and prose authors to introduce an excursus or radically new section of narrative (here the excursus is short, but the jump back in time is enormous). Cf. 1.6.1, Κροῖσος ἦν Λυδὸς μέν γένος, with Dion. Hal. *Comp.* 4; **82.1** Ἐπιδαυρίοισι ἡ γῆ…and **104.1** (Onesilos); or Th. 1.24.1, Ἐπίδαμνός ἐστι πόλις…, and there were Homeric precursors, e.g. *Il.* 6.152. Th.'s own asyndetic opening to his Kylon excursus matches Hdt.'s almost exactly, Κύλων ἦν Ἀθηναῖος ἀνὴρ Ὀλυμπιονίκης but thereafter his account diverges sharply for the most part (there is one further echo, see below on προσποιησά-μενος…), and is much fuller.

71.1 (cont.) ἐπὶ τυραννίδι ἐκόμησε 'he grew his hair long for a tyranny'. It is possible that the lit. sense of the verb (κομῶ, LSJ κομάω) remains present, and should not be squeezed out, as in such metaphorical trs. as 'set one's heart on', 'plume oneself, give oneself airs' (Powell; LSJ); cf. e.g. Ar. *Nub.* 545. To be sure, if Kylon planned a secret and deceitful putsch, to be carried out when most Athenians were absent at a festival, the meaning would have to be metaphorical, he 'set his heart on' (hidden mental state) 'a tyranny'. But that impression of deceit and surprise derives essentially from Th. (1.126), and Th. seems to have wanted to put Hdt. straight on details. So it is worth considering whether Hdt. meant bold and public swaggering over a period of time, symbolised by literal hair-growing 'with a view to (as it turned out) a tyranny'. For young men growing their hair sym- bolically, see *SvT* 523 line 43 (Anaktorion, *c.* 216 BC) = Sokolowski 1962: no. 45 line 43, with Chaniotis 2005: 54: regulations governing a procession for Apollo include a stipulation that the (young male) participants should be allowed to grow their hair long, καὶ τὰγ κόμαν τρέφειν. This exceptional permission reflected the normal need to control young male aggression. For hair-growing as an assertion of physical (and sexual) vitality, see Leitao 2003: 119 and for hairiness = wildness see Berman 1999. Hdt. was alert to the symbolism of male hair-growing and of short hair. See 1.82.7–8: the Argives, after their defeat by the Spartans, swear not to grow their hair, while the Spartans do the opposite and start to grow their hair, not hav- ing done so before. (This prepares us for the Spartan hair-combing before Thermopylai, 7.208.3.) Interest in physical appearance is as characteristic of Hdt. as lack of interest in it is characteristic of Th., who in his longer account finds no place for Kylon's growing of the hair. (See Lightfoot 2003: 531 and n. 1 for interest in 'tonsure' as characteristic of Herodotean ethnography.) **προσποιησάμενος δὲ ἑταιρηίην τῶν ἡλικιωτέων**: in Hdt., Kylon seems to act on his own initiative. For once it is Th. (1.126) not Hdt. who provides the most religious detail: consultation of the Delphic oracle, Apollo's advice to seize the acropolis during the greatest festival of Zeus, detail about the Athenian Diasia. Hdt. and Th. agree, however, on one crucial religious point: there was a formal act of supplication, and it was violated. The violation was essential to explain pollution and curse.

The *hetaireia* of age-mates is a precursor of the later political clubs, char- acterised by Th. at 8.54.4. Hdt. perhaps presents Kylon's action as planned in the context of a symposion, and reinforced by a pledge, *pistis*. For such pledges (ritual cementing of partnership in crime) by a *hetaireia* or συν- ωμοσία in classical Athens, see Andok. 1.67, with Burkert 1993: 184 and n. 41 (cf. *CT* III: 369 on the affairs of the Herms and Mysteries, and 972 on Th. 8.73.3). See also **66**.2n. on ἐσσούμενος τὸν δῆμον προσεταιρίζεται.

For ἡλικιῶται (really just 'contemporaries') as an age-group of young aggressive males, cf. Th.'s οἱ ἐν ἡλικίαι who are so full of optimism and of longing for the unknown (6.24.3, the departure of the fleet for Sicily), and (with Doric alpha) ἅλιξιν σὺν ἄλλοις at Pind. *Pyth.* 4.187, Jason and the Argonauts; cf. *Th. and Pi.*: 334.

But Th. seems tacitly to reject this picture – as anachronistic? – when he emphasises instead the role of the Delphic oracle. His adoption (1.126.4) of Hdt.'s exact phrase καταλαβεῖν τὴν ἀκρόπολιν underscores this disagreement, because of the different use to which he puts it: in Th., it is part of the oracle's instruction. It is sometimes said (see Introduction p. 32) that bk. 5 is without gods. The present passage might be thought to support that idea; but Hdt.'s account is very brief, and oracular consultation is not quite excluded. On the relation between the accounts in Hdt. and Th. see esp. Rood 2013.

71.1 (cont.) ἱκέτης ἵζετο πρὸς τὸ ἄγαλμα: a physical 'approach' was one of the three steps a suppliant needed to take for a valid act of supplication, and altars were a frequent choice of destination (Naiden 2006: 30–43 and 36–41; and see briefly *OCD*⁴ 'supplication, Greek'). But statues were also possible, and Kylon (like Kassandra in myth, when threatened by Lokrian Ajax: Lykoph. *Alex.* 359–64 and Naiden 49) supplicates Athena's statue.

71.2 ἀνιστᾶσι μὲν οἱ πρυτάνιες τῶν ναυκράρων, οἵ περ ἔνεμον τότε τὰς Ἀθήνας: the 'prytanies of the naukraries' are surely naval, though the prefix ναυ- could strictly be from 'temple' or 'ship' (van Wees 2013: 44–53). This statement that they 'governed Athens at that time' seems expressly contradicted by Th., who says that at that time the archons had most of the conduct of affairs, 1.126. 8. (but we do not know who else in the 5th cent. had treated the topic). For the history of the problem, see Lambert 1986; Figueira 1986 [= Figueira 1993: 151–72]; *CT* I: 209. Lambert's own ingenious but not compelling solution is to stress τότε: the prytanies were *temporarily* in charge of the city during the festival. Develin 1989: 30–1 does not register the 'prytanies of the naukraries' as Athenian officials; he merely notes the discrepancy between Hdt. and Th.

It has often been thought that Hdt. here exculpates the Alkmaionids (because Megakles was an archon) and that Th. puts him straight; but Thomas 1989: 278 rightly denies this, mainly on the grounds that Hdt. says no more than that the prytanies were responsible for the offer of safe conduct, and does not associate them with the sacrilege. If so, Th.'s disagreement is limited to the question of who ran Athens at the time.

71.2 (cont.) ὑπεγγύους πλὴν θανάτου 'liable to any penalty except death'. This entire narrative (note the plural here, and φονεῦσαι δὲ αὐτούς below) clearly implies that everyone was killed, Kylon as well as his followers, whereas Th. (1.126.10) says that Kylon and his brother escaped. Naiden 2006: 194 thinks the word ὑπεγγύους, 'liable', 'hints at some [legal] proceeding they [the Kylonian conspirators] would undergo', and that 'the evaluation of the suppliants now belongs to a court'. Possibly; but attempted tyranny, seizing the acropolis, and so on, were crimes enough (presumably attempting a tyranny was some sort of indictable offence). **αἰτίη ἔχει**: cf. **70.**1n., and esp. αἰτίη δὲ ἔσχε at 6.1 15, the shield-signal: again, 'blame' will attach to the Alkmaionids.   **πρὸ τῆς Πεισιστράτου ἡλικίης**: for chronology, see first n. on **71.**1 (ἦν Κύλων...). The word ἡλικίη here has a purely chronological sense, as at **59** above; but the extra nuance (young male group of contemporaries) conveyed by Kylon's ἡλικιῶται may be hovering here too.

72.1 ἐξέβαλλε: see **70.**2n. on the tense of this word.   **ὑπεξέσχε** 'slipped out of the country'. Like Kleomenes in his turn, slipping away to Thessaly (same verb) at 6.74.1.   **ἀγηλατέει ἑπτακόσια ἐπίστια** 'he expelled seven hundred households as accursed'. The noun here must mean 'households', though it can sometimes mean 'suppliants'. The prominence of supplication in the preceding chs. perhaps subconsciously influenced Hdt.'s choice of word. The total is almost incredibly large. For Fehling 1989: 226 it is formulaic (he notes that the number recurs at **77.**2 for the total of Boiotian prisoners); but the problem here is the scale of the eviction, given that the base figure needs to be multiplied two or three times to give the number of individuals.   **τὴν βουλὴν καταλύειν ἐπειρᾶτο**: Hdt. does not specify which council. Kleisthenes' new Council of Five Hundred (see **66** n.) was appointed in a complicated way from the tribes and demes, and it would be surprising if it was already up and running so as to be actually capable of physical resistance, though that cannot be ruled out. Another possibility (Pleket 1969: 30 n. 39) is the old Solonian Council of Four Hundred. The Areopagus could have been described as 'the Council' and is another possibility (Pleket, as above); but it was composed of ex-archons from many previous years, who were thus presumably former Peisistratid supporters (but may have nimbly changed sides, as happens in such situations).

72.2 Ἀθηναίων δὲ οἱ λοιποὶ τὰ αὐτὰ φρονήσαντες ἐπολιόρκεον αὐτούς... 'the rest of the Athenians united and besieged them'.

72.3–4 *Kleomenes on the Athenian Acropolis*

72.3 ἐπετελέετο...ἡ φήμη: this is an effective little analepsis: Hdt. has the Spartans leaving the acropolis under truce before he tells us of the 'prophetic saying' (Powell) which the priestess had uttered to Kleomenes on his arrival there, and which was now fulfilled. For the reason for this, see below, n. on ὁ δὲ εἶπε...On the noun φήμη see Garvie on Aesch. *Cho.* 343; '[it] lacks a one-word equivalent, an omen in the form of something

said' (Parker 1998: 1).   ἄδυτον: the negative prefix ἀ- has special point
here: 'the area which should *not* be entered'.   ὡς προσερέων: he wanted
to 'address' Athena; cf. Aesch. *Ag.* 811–12, where Agamemnon says it is
right for him 'first to address Argos and the local gods'. Hdt. does not
say what business Kleomenes had with Athena, or what he intended to
say to her, but the answer is surely political. Such gestures were politically
assertive, as well as pious: Kleomenes, like other conquerors and would-
be conquerors (e.g. the Spartan Derkylidas at Skepsis in 399 BC, Xen.
Hell. 3.1.21), wanted to show that he could sacrifice even in normally forbidden places. See Parker 1997: 24–5.   ἡ δὲ ἱερείη: this was the priestess of Athena Polias, the protecting goddess of the city, who outranked
all other priests: Garland 1984: 92. She has a star role here, but she is
not named; contrast Th.'s naming of Chrysis the priestess who accidentally burnt down her temple near Argos: 4.133.2–3, or Hdt.'s own naming
of Periallos the promantis at Delphi, 6.66.3, and of the three priestesses
at Dodona, 2.55.3. It is inconceivable that the name of the priestess of
Athena Polias on the present occasion was lost from memory. Her family,
the Eteoboutadai (Garland 1984: 92 and Parker 1996: 290–3), will have
kept her memory green. Non-naming of women may be merely respect-
ful, and naming them may be insulting (cf. Schaps 1977). But not all the
mentions above are disrespectful, and there may be more to the anonymity
here: by not naming the priestess, Hdt. enhances her authority. She speaks
for Athena, and for Athena's city.

Hdt. assumes knowledge of the layout of the temple, probably the 'old
temple of Athena' i.e. Athena Polias between Parthenon and Erechtheion,
though it is not agreed whether it was Peisistratid or a little later. (Athena
Parthenos, housed in the Parthenon and its predecessors, had no separate priestess, though it is possible that the same priestess served Athena
in both manifestations: Garland 1984: 91–2. See Travlos 1971: 143; Mee
and Spawforth 2001: 52.) There were two cellas or inner rooms; this is
what Hdt. means by the *adyton*. One of these cellas (the east one) contained the simple cult statue of Athena; the other, western, one had three
compartments and served other deities (Mee/Spawforth). This area was
evidently marked off by double doors, to which the priestess held the key,
perhaps even in the literal sense of brandishing it (large keys are the usual
attribute of priestesses in iconography, cf. Connelly 2007: 92–104 and
Arat. *Phain.* 192 with D. Kidd 1997: 253–4 and fig. 2). The priestess sat outside these doors, perhaps in the porch, waiting on her ceremonial throne.
Kleomenes could have walked through the archaic Propylaia and climbed
the steps of the platform at the east end, thereby arriving at the porch and
the doors. The priestess stood up and advanced to bar the king's passage.
Presumably there were temple attendants on the scene (see Garland 1984:
93–4 for the female assistants of the priestess of Athena Polias), and it was
one of these, or even the priestess herself, who told the story.

72.3 (cont.) ἐξαναστᾶσα ἐκ τοῦ θρόνου πρὶν ἢ τὰς θύρας αὐτὸν ἀμεῖψαι: ἀμείβω here means 'I pass through'. Like English 'throne', θρόνος implies something grand and solemn; the word is not uncommon in Hdt., but this is the only time he uses it of a priest's chair. Unsurprisingly, Th. never has occasion to mention one. We may perhaps get an idea of its appearance from the 4th-cent. dedicated thrones from the sanctuary of Nemesis and Themis at Rhamnous in Attica: Travlos 1988: 389 with 399, plates 500 and 501, where no. 500 is an imaginative reconstruction by the Dilettanti in 1817. Such thrones were perhaps assigned to priestesses, see Connelly 2007: 202 (illustration of the Rhamnous throne at 203).

Like Telesilla of Argos later (6.77), the woman splendidly prevails, at least morally, over the super-tough Kleomenes where the men had not (and compare the assertiveness of Aristophanes' Lysistrata, who is probably intended as priestess of Athena Polias). Parker 1997: 4 remarks 'it is rather startling to find a woman issuing orders to Cleomenes' but he continues 'she is only standing up for principles that her male fellow citizens would have endorsed'. This is not the only occasion when Kleomenes is involved with females who say decisive things (see **51.**2 for Gorgo).

72.3 (cont.) ὦ ξεῖνε Λακεδαιμόνιε: not the vocative Κλεόμενες as at **49.**2 (Aristagores), although she can hardly have been unaware of what was going on or who he was: the terrified women of the various sanctuaries will have watched the Spartan soldiers winding their way up the acropolis to the clank of armour. For the form of address see Dickey 1996: 146–9, 'ξένε', esp. 148: it is not often used to one whose name the speaker knows, as the priestess surely does here. It is dignified and not necessarily hostile or even impolite, nor is foreignness necessarily uppermost in the characteristically Herodotean combination of ξεῖνε and ethnic, for which see Dickey 149. But in the context of the priestess's attempted exclusion and her rebuke about Kleomenes' Dorianism, we can hardly fail to detect a reference to his outsider status. Such a reference is needed so as to enable his neat reply.   πάλιν χώρει μηδὲ ἔσιθι ἐς τὸ ἱρόν: the emphatic positive+negative expression is semi-colloquial, and a favourite of Hdt.; see **42.**1n.   οὐ γὰρ θεμιτὸν Δωριεῦσι παριέναι ἐνθαῦτα: compare 6.81, Kleomenes again: he tries to sacrifice at Argos but the priest, this time a man, forbids him because it is not right, lit. 'pious', for a foreigner to do so, οὐκ ὅσιον εἶναι ξείνωι αὐτόθι θύειν. A religious prohibition against Dorians in particular is attested epigraphically and in a relevant context: *IG* 12.5.225 = Sokolowski 1969: no. 110 (Paros, 5th cent. BC): 'it is not lawful, ωὐ [*sic*] θέμις, for a Dorian stranger or a slave to [be a spectator of] the rites of Kore of the city', with Jeffery 1976: 48 n. 4, cf. 44. Ionian Paros was in some sense a colony of Athens (R/O: no. 29 lines 5–6, 4th cent. BC), and will thus have shared some religious features, perhaps including this one, with the metropolis. For θεμιτόν, cf. 3.37.3, it is not right, θεμιτόν, for anyone but the priest to enter the sanctuary of the Kabeiroi at Memphis (and cf. Richardson 1974: 244 on οὐ γὰρ θεμιτόν at *Hom. Hym. Dem.* 27); but the shorter word is usual in sacred laws, as above (Paros) and e.g. Sokolowski 1969: no. 96 (Mykonos, *c.* 200 BC) line 9, γυναικὶ οὐ θέμις, or no. 114 (5th cent. BC, Thasos). See Versnel 2011: 112 n. 324. For a Delian prohibition on foreigners (perhaps Athenians) entering the sanctuary of the founder-hero Anios, see *SEG* 44.678, 400–375 BC (ξένωι οὐχ ὁσίη ἐσιέναι).   ὁ δὲ εἶπε· "ὦ γύναι, ἀλλ' οὐ Δωριεύς εἰμι ἀλλ' Ἀχαιός": a celebrated reply, which might seem to give Kleomenes the better of the exchange for the moment, except that Hdt. has already informed us that Kleomenes was going to be worsted by being forced to withdraw under a truce; this, as we now see, is the point of the reverse order of narration. The form of address is polite (Dickey 1996: 86–9 'γύναι'; also 244, 'the only way of addressing a respectable unrelated woman'); see also Barrett 1955: 159 on John 2.4. Dickey 86 treats the present use as an example of an addressee possessing higher status than the speaker. It is perhaps more like a clash of high but different statuses.

For the emotionally charged postponement of the first ἀλλά (as a strong adversative, it would normally come first in the sentence) see Denniston 1954: 23. The doubling of ἀλλά reinforces the indignation.

As for 'Dorian', we have, yet again, a strong allusion to bk. 1, this time to a cult of relics, namely the 6th-cent. Spartan appropriation of the bones of (Achaian) Orestes at 1.67. (But we should not take too seriously Kleomenes' temporary denial of Dorianism, because Spartans and all Greeks were able to have it both ways in this area of mythical exploitation, with no discomfort; cf. Buxton 1994: 196.) There is also, as many have noted, an ambiguity 'I am not [my brother] Dorieus', whose name was certainly programmatic.

There was, in an Athenian context, a positive side to the Spartan king's claim to be an Achaian, in view of the kinship ties between the Ionian Athenians and the Achaians of the northern Peloponnese (for the complicated sibling-relationship between Ion and Achaios in myth, see *OCD*[4] 'Ion (1)'; and note Th. 3.92.5, both the Ionians and Achaians are excluded from the new Spartan-led colony at Herakleia in Trachis). For this aspect to Kleomenes' reply, see the excellent discussion of Fragoulaki forthcoming: ch. 6, arguing that, by stressing his Achaian origin, Kleomenes hoped to make himself seem less polluted and more acceptable to the Athenians.

72.4 τῆι κληδόνι 'omen of a spoken word'. Hdt. does not treat the priestess as the direct agent of the god's will (as many who heard the story, including Kleomenes' numerous enemies at Sparta, will have assumed she was), but rather as the vehicle of an omen. κληδών can mean a 'chance' utterance which turns out to be an omen (as at 9.91.1), but on this occasion the priestess' utterance was deliberate, not accidental. At *Od.* 20.120 a κληδών (a prayer by a female corn-grinder) is combined with an omen of thunder.   ἐπεχείρησε 'made the attempt'. It would appear from this choice of verb that Kleomenes did persist in entering the sanctum, and did offer sacrifice.   μετὰ τῶν Λακεδαιμονίων: he left with Isagores too, as we will learn at **74**.1, and with some oracles left behind by the Peisistratidai in the sanctuary, as we will learn at **90**.2.   κατέδησαν τὴν ἐπὶ θανάτωι 'they imprisoned them for execution', understand δέσιν with τήν.   ἐν δὲ αὐτοῖσι καὶ Τιμησίθεον τὸν Δελφόν: the emendation for ἀδελφεόν ('brother') is certain, because of the evidence of Paus. (next n.) and because *LGPN* shows that the name is much commoner in Central Greece than in the Peloponnese (there is no Spartan of the name). It is interesting to find a Delphian entangling himself with Kleomenes. As a panhellenic victor he would have moved around internationally in elite circles, and in any case Spartan kings had institutional links with Delphi (6.57.2). For Kleomenes' relations with another prominent Delphian (Kobon) see 6.66.2.   τοῦ ἔργα χειρῶν τε καὶ λήματος ἔχοιμ᾽ ἂν μέγιστα καταλέξαι: see Paus. 6.8.6 for a statue at Olympia of Timasitheos the Delphian, twice Olympic and three times victor in his home place (at the Pythia): Smith 2007: 100 (but for '510' read '508') and 137; Thomas 2007: 56. Paus. goes on to tell the story of his death at the hands of the Athenians. This seems reprised from Hdt. (for Paus.' use of and fondness for Hdt. see Habicht 1985: 133), except that Paus. connects him with Isagores rather than with Kleomenes. The source for the athletic successes (spelt out by Paus., implied by Hdt.) could have been the same statue-base, inspected at an interval of over half a millennium.

'I could tell, but I won't'. The word for telling, καταλέγω, can mean either 'recount at length', or 'list' (hence our 'catalogue'); both nuances are appropriate for a frequent victor in the games. Hdt.'s refusal to expand is clever rhetoric (see **57**.2n. on ἐπιτάξαντες ...) and deliberately tantalising (is it trailed so as to invite an encore at recitation?). If he had wanted to, he knew how to convey succinctly the athletic information, at least; cf. 8.47.1, Phayllos of Kroton is called ἀνὴρ τρὶς πυθιονίκης. True, Timesitheos was more than an athlete, but so too was Phayllos. Unlike Dorieus, the Rhodian athletic phenomenon a century later (Xen. *Hell.* 1.5.19), Timesitheos was not such a star that the Athenians were moved to acquit him.

73.1 ἠπιστέατο 'they knew' (Ionic 3rd pers. plural of ἐπίσταμαι). See **74**.1n. on Κλεομένης ... ἐπιστάμενος.   **ἐκπεπολεμῶσθαι** 'had become their enemies'.

73.2 καὶ λεγόντων τὰ ἐντεταλμένα: Hdt. does not tell us what language these Athenians spoke. Perhaps (Raaflaub 2009: 89) they hired interpreters in Ionia.   **Ἀρταφρένης ὁ Ὑστάσπεος Σαρδίων ὕπαρχος**: the fullness of description is a focussing device at this weighty moment. Hdt. is not absent-mindedly under the impression that he is telling us something new by specifying name, patronym and title (see already **25**.1 and **30**.5), nor do we need to postulate different sources for the two sections.   **ἐπειρώτα τίνες ἐόντες ἄνθρωποι καὶ κῆι γῆς οἰκημένοι**: for this recurrent type of Persian question, see **13**.2 and **105**.1 with nn.   **ἀπεκορύφου** 'gave them this answer in a nutshell' (Powell, under ἀποκορυφῶ). The unusual choice of verb (here only in Hdt.) serves to highlight the satrap's response; so S. West 2011: 10.   **γῆν τε καὶ ὕδωρ**: see **17**.1n.

73.3 ἐπὶ σφέων αὐτῶν βαλόμενοι 'on their own initiative', lit. 'putting it on themselves'.   **διδόναι ἔφασαν** 'they promised to give', not 'they gave', ἔδοσαν. To undertake to do something is not the same as to do it (S. West 2011: 19). But the *volte-face* of the Spartan allies implies that the Athenians were indeed regarded as having, in effect, submitted to Persia (**75**.1n. on Κορίνθιοι...).   **αἰτίας μεγάλας εἶχον** 'they were held in great blame'. The mildness of this response to their own envoys' action proves that the Athenians medised. See Berve 1937: 71 n. 1, Schachermeyr 1973: 213 and Badian 1994: 125–6 (with n. 19): the 'vague phrase about their blaming the envoys...reveals [Hdt.'s] technique when he has something to hide'; he concludes that Athens became for a few years a city of the Great King (Kramer 2004, who argues against this, ignores Badian 1994). So far from showing that the Athenians at home disavowed their envoys' subservient action, as has been assumed (by e.g. Ostwald, *CAH* 4²: 308), these three words indicate the exact opposite. See Tamiolaki 2010: 63 n. 159.

Badian suggests that Alexandros I of Macedon brokered the submission to Persia, and that this, rather than or as well as the provision of ship-building timber, was the reason why Alexandros was honoured as *proxenos* and benefactor of the Athenians: 8.136.1. But at **94**.1 below, which is subsequent to **73**.3 in real time as well as in Hdt.'s text (i.e. it is not part of an analepsis), it is Amyntes, not Alexandros, who offers Anthemous to Hippias after the Spartans finally abandon their attempts to reinstate him (this abandonment was the result of Soklees' speech). Badian 126 argues that Alexandros 'on a realistic estimate of Hippias' chances of returning, decided to transfer his family connection with the Athenian tyrants to the new Athenian *demos*', and so gave the Athenians the idea of turning to the [Persian] King, and 'supported their improbable plea at Sardis' (the present passage). But **94**.1 shows not only that Amyntes was still on the Macedonian throne after the Soklees episode, but that the family connection with the tyrants still subsisted at that time (see n. there). It is no help to say that Alexandros was crown prince not king at the time of **73**.3, because **94**.1 still implies the family connection, and shows that Macedonian policy had not yet changed.

74.1 Κλεομένης δὲ ἐπιστάμενος: here (as at **73**.1n, ἠπιστέατο) the meaning is close to 'knowing' or 'realising', with an implication of truth.   **οὐ φράζων ἐς τὸ συλλέγει** 'not saying for what purpose [ἐς τό] he was gathering it together'. This seems to imply automatic military obligations on the Spartans' allies to 'follow wherever the Spartans might lead', in the language of Xen. *Hell.* 2.2.20, unless there was 'some prevention of gods or heroes': Th. 5.30.1 and 3. See Ste. Croix 1972: 109. It is doubtful whether the formal obligations are as old as the time of Kleomenes. But even a strong-minded figure like Kleomenes could not expect people to march like this into the unknown, unless they were under antecedent obligations. **συνεξῆλθε γὰρ οἱ οὗτος**: see **72**.4n. for this delayed item.

74.2 ἐσέβαλε ἐς Ἐλευσῖνα: Eleusis was a key point on the main route into Attica for a land army invading from the Peloponnese. This is the reason for the heavy fortifications there, and the (later) presence of a garrison of ephebes: see Th. 2.19.2 (Archidamos' first invasion) with *CT* I: 272, citing *Syll.*[3] 485 and 957 lines 61–2, also Dem. 18.177 with Wankel 1976: 875; for ephebes, see *OCD*[4]. Eleusis is mentioned on the inscribed pillar from Thebes, alluding to these events; see Aravantinos 2006: 373 (text) and 374 (discussion), noting that the inscription appears to show that the Boiotians also (not only the Peloponnesians) got as far as Eleusis. See further **77**.4n.

When narrating Kleomenes' horrible death, and the reasons for it which were aired at the time, Hdt. will say that the Athenian explanation was that Kleomenes had felled trees in the sacred precinct of Eleusis: 6.75.3. This is an analeptic ref. to the present section of narrative, where, however, there is nothing about sacred trees. Hdt. saves it up for the time being, perhaps because he wishes the evidence for Kleomenes' supposed irreligious outrages to emerge cumulatively (the defiance of the Athenian priestess at **72**.3 above has already put us on notice, but at least he does not flog her, as he will the male Argive priest at 6.81).

74.2 (cont.) ἀπὸ συνθήματος: this specification of agreement in the case of the Boiotians indicates that the Peloponnesian allies 'were bound to come when summoned'. See further Schachermeyr 1973: 215.   **Οἰνόην αἰρέουσι καὶ Ὑσιάς, δήμους τοὺς ἐσχάτους τῆς Ἀττικῆς**: see *Barr.* map. 58 E1 for Oinoe and Hysiai, shown in one square. Hdt. nearly always uses 'deme' non-technically in the sense of 'village': Whitehead 1986: 48 and, on the present passage, n. 39 (but contrast 9.73.1, Sophanes said to be ἐκ δήμου Δεκελεῆθεν). Hdt. is loose here twice over. There was *no* Kleisthenic deme Hysiai, and there were *two* Kleisthenic demes called Oinoe, one near

Marathon in the tribe Aiantis, the other in Hippothontis. Hdt. means the second, for which see also Th. 2.18.2 (describing it as 'on the borders, ἐν μεθορίοις, of Attica and Boiotia') with *CT* I: 271 for the probable location at Myoupoli.

Hysiai, for which see also 6.108.6 (a joint mention with Plataia) and 9.15.3, was S. of the river Asopos and SW of Erythrai. It was Boiotian in the later 5th and the 4th cents. (Th. 3.24.1 with *CT* I: 408 for the location). But Hysiai and Eleutherai were 'so dependent on Athenian protection that [they] could sometimes be considered villages of Attica': Buck 1979: 123, cf. 99 for Plataian expansion in the direction of Hysiai and other Ionic-speaking frontier places (7th–6th cents.?). Hdt. here says that 'the Boiotians' seized, αἱρέουσι, Oinoe and Hysiai – a hostile act, one would have thought, unless the verb means that Hysiai, already in a sense Boiotian, was now *occupied militarily* and without a necessary implication of a formal transfer from Athenian to Boiotian control. With border settlements, especially those which fell outside the Kleisthenic scheme for Attica, it may be best not to press the matter of political affiliation too exactly.

The inscribed column from Thebes (above, n. on ἐσέβαλε) seems to add the information that the frontier fort of Phyle was captured, in addition to Oinoe and Hysiai.

74.2 (cont.) Χαλκιδέες τε ἐπὶ τὰ ἕτερα ἐσίνοντο ἐπιόντες χώρους τῆς Ἀττικῆς: Hdt. is oddly unspecific about the localities so ravaged. For the close connection at all times between Boiotia and Euboia see **57.**1n.   **ἐσύστερον ἔμελλον μνήμην ποιήσεσθαι** 'they decided to postpone thinking about them' (lit. 'they intended to remember them later'). With these admiring words, Hdt. prepares us for the general comments at **78** below about the superiority of democracy. With this Athenian nonchalance when faced with a double threat, compare Th. 1.105.4, 'they did not move their army from Aigina' when invaded by the Korinthians in the Pentekontaetia.

75.1 Κορίνθιοι ... δόντες λόγον ὡς οὐ ποιοῖεν τὰ δίκαια: the Korinthians play this role twice (see **92** below, Soklees' great speech), but here they are given no speech by Hdt., though λόγος makes it clear that one was delivered. There is some intensification between here and the grand federal gathering of **92**; here the Korinthians are merely considering among themselves (σφίσι αὐτοῖσι). Although at **74.**1 the Spartans' allies did not know where they were being led, by this time they have either been told or have worked it out for themselves: the 'unjust' reason for the expedition is presumably the restoration of a tyrant. Hdt. does not yet wish to elaborate on this theme: he is working up to his grand climax at **92**. See Salmon 1984: 248 on the Korinthian motives, which may well have included alarm at the growth of Spartan power, as well as outrage at the proposed 'injustice'; cf. also Stickler 2010: 80.

The allied change of mind has seemed puzzling, and the high-minded motive here given ('injustice') unconvincing. It seems likely that the real reason why the invasion was called off was because news had just arrived of the Athenian submission to the Persian king (Schachermeyr 1973: 216–17; cf. above **73**.3 and n.). The Spartan allies, and especially the Korinthians, in Hdt.'s presentation, did not want to risk Persian reprisals. Δημάρητος ὁ Ἀρίστωνος: the first mention of this important figure, who will be so prominent in bk. 6 in a Spartan context, and then in bk. 7 as an adviser figure ·in Xerxes' retinue. It is likely that his descendants were still living in NW Asia Minor in Hdt.'s time, and therefore that he could have spoken to them: see 6.70.2 (grant to Demaretos of land and cities by Dareios), with Xen. *Hell* 3.1.6 for a descendant in 399 BC.   καὶ οὐκ ἐὼν διάφορος ἐν τῶι πρόσθε χρόνωι Κλεομένεϊ: the immediate function of this remark is merely to underline the seriousness of the διχοστασίη (Demaretos opposed him now, despite never having quarrelled with him before); but διάφορος also looks forward to Kleomenes' spectacular deposition, κατάπαυσις, of Demaretos at 6.64 (which will specifically back-refer to the present incident as providing part of Kleomenes' motivation) and 67.1.

75.2 ἐτέθη νόμος: for foreigners seeking to invoke this rule against the Spartans see 6.73.2 (Aiginetans) and 86.1 (Athenians). The Spartan indirect speech at 7.149.2 ignores the existence of the rule. 6.56 says that the Spartan kings (plural) could make war on any land they chose ('almost certainly false for his own day', acc. Cartledge 1987: 105); but see Ste. Croix 1972: 149–51. The introduction of the 'one king' rule increased the risk of competition and friction between the kings (Cartledge 1987: 206).   παραλυομένου δὲ τούτων τοῦ ἑτέρου...εἵποντο 'and since one of the kings was discharged from active duty, one of the Tyndaridai should also stay behind. Before that, they had both followed them as allies [lit. 'called in' sc. as allies]'. The Tyndaridai are the Dioskouroi, the divine twins Kastor and Polydeukes (Pollux), who are here said to have, in some shape or form, accompanied Spartan armies in the field as allies (ἐπίκλητοι). In Simonides' elegiac poem which narrated the battle of Plataia in 479 BC, described by Hdt. in bk. 9, the Spartans set out with 'the horse-taming sons of Zeus, the Tyndarids, and with Menelaos' (fr. 11.30 W²). This could be a divine epiphany, or it might in both Hdt. and Simonides mean statues (but the difference is not great because, in a real sense, a statue *was* the god). If we take seriously the 'law' here mentioned – after 506, only one king and one Dioskouros might leave Sparta on campaign – the two Dioskouroi ought not to have left Sparta in 479, as Simonides says they did. See Hornblower 2001, esp. 141 for a suggested solution to the 'two kings' problem (it is there suggested that the under-age Pleistarchos was not present on the Plataia campaign), and 142 for Menelaos, whose presence surely makes it likely that we should think in terms of actual epiphany.

76 The four Dorian visits to Attica

The two expeditions 'for the good of the mass of Athenians' were the two which got rid of the Peisistratidai, nos. 2 and 3. (The abortive Spartan attempt at **72** above is omitted.) There would be another visit (no. 5, a friendly one) within Hdt.'s own text: see 9.19.2, the Spartans under Pausanias arrive at Eleusis on their way to the battlefield of Plataia (an event also recorded by Simonides, fr. 11 W², as above, **75**n.). And Hdt. and his audience, whether Athenian or not, surely had in their minds the (hostile) arrival in Attica of further groups of Dorians – the armies led by the Spartan kings Pleistoanax in 446 BC (Th. 1.114.2 and 2.21.1 = no. 6) and Archidamos in 431 (Th. 2.19.1) and later years (these more or less annual invasions might be numbered nos. 7, 8, 9 etc.). The present expedition is twice said to be no. 4, and is 'for war', like no. 1.

No. 1 in the series, the first Dorian visit and the first unfriendly one, is said to have been an invasion whose most lasting result was the foundation of Megara from the Peloponnese. The present passage is the earliest evidence for this version of the origins of Megara, but Strabo 9.1.7 (from Ephoros?) gives a fuller account. 'Dorians' in this version may really mean 'Argives'; so Hanell 1934: 69–91. (The alternative tradition was that Megara was founded by Boiotians from Onchestos under an eponymous oikist Megareus: Hanell 24–35, citing *FGrHist* 4 Hellanikos F 78, cf. *CT* II: 240.) For Hdt., this event from the mythical past – the time of Kodros – is not qualitatively different from the invasions he has recounted so recently in the present bk.

The enumeration of the four visits emphasises the importance of the present moment in Athenian history, when the emerging democracy showed itself a match for its neighbours in combination (**78** is the climax of this line of thought).

77.1 ἀκλεῶς: a very strong word for that most unusual event, a Spartan military setback, though not an actual defeat. It is found only here in Hdt.; but the adjectival form was used in the proem ('so that the deeds of Greeks and barbarians should not become ἀκλεᾶ'). **Ἀθηναῖοι τίνυσθαι βουλόμενοι**: see **79**.1n. **Βοιωτοὶ δέ**: at **79**.1, they will have become just 'the Thebans', whose domination of their neighbours begins around this time.

77.2 ἑπτακοσίους: see **72**.1 n. on the seven hundred Athenian families. **τετρακισχιλίους κληρούχους ἐπὶ τῶν ἱπποβοτέων τῆι χώρηι**: these cleruchs (i.e. Athenians settled on land overseas) were detailed by the Athenians at the time of the Marathon campaign to help the Eretrians: 6.100.1, where

Hdt. describes the cleruchs in language similar to that here, except that there he uses the verbal form κληρουχέοντες. (These cleruchs went across to Attica: 100.2, and did not go back, in the view of Brunt 1966: 87 = 1993: 132.) These are Hdt.'s only refs. to the institution; Th. also mentions cleruchs just once (3.50.2), and see ML 14 = Fornara 44B, Salamis, line 1 (restored, but very probably). This late 6th-cent. inscription sets out the two basic duties of cleruchs, to pay taxes and perform military service. The Salamis cleruchy makes sense in terms of military security after the Athenians had broken with the Spartans, and the contemporary Chalkis cleruchy can be seen in the same light. Moreno 2007: 93 and 2009: 213 disputes this view of cleruchs (performers of useful garrison functions) as too rosy, and sees cleruchies as essentially exploitative. That is more likely to be true of the developed imperial system than of these late 6th-cent. cleruchies. But Moreno (2007: 102; 2009: 213) notes archaeological evidence which may indicate the presence of non-Athenian mercenary archers at Vrachos on the edge of the Lelantine plain in western Euboia. This site is thought to be associated with the first cleruchy at Chalkis i.e. that mentioned in the present passage of Hdt., and is taken by Moreno to show absentee exploitation by cleruchs even in 506–490. None of Moreno's evidence excludes military functions by cleruchs. Salomon 1997 believes in garrisoning functions for cleruchs.

For the *hippobotai* or 'horse-feeders' at Chalkis as a census-based 'aristocracy' i.e. oligarchy, see Arist. fr. 603, cf. *Pol.* 1289b36ff. for the horse-breeding oligarchies of Eretria and Chalkis. The word is peculiar to Chalkis (at Eur. *Or.* 1000, the preferable spelling is ἱπποβώτα, see Willink's comm.). See *IACP*: 649 (no. 365). After the present expropriation, they must have returned before 446, when they are again found at Chalkis, and are again thrown out, this time by Perikles (unless the eviction was in two stages, 506 and 446, cf. Stadter 1989: 232): Plut. *Per.* 23 3, where they are 'wealthy and distinguished', πλούτωι καὶ δόξηι διαφέροντες.

77.2 (cont.) παχέες: see 30.1n.

77.3 ἔλυσάν σφεας δίμνεως ἀποτιμησάμενοι: 'they released them after putting a price of two minas on them'. See **77.4**n. for the recently published inscription which may mention this ransoming. Two minas are 200 drachmai, and this figure recurs at 6.79.1; for these and other testimonia for ransoming see *GSW* 5: 247–55.   **αἵ περ ἔτι καὶ ἐς ἐμὲ ἦσαν περιεοῦσαι:** with the favourite expression καὶ ἐς ἐμέ (cf. **45**.2, **88**.3), Hdt. does not quite say that he saw the objects himself (so ML), contrast the explicit formula εἶδον δὲ καὶ αὐτός at **59**; but the assumption of autopsy is a reasonable one, given the amount of detail he provides. Cf. below, **89**.3 for another such Athenian topographic allusion. Nevertheless it is optimistic to use these passages as evidence for Hdt.'s personal biography, e.g. to argue for a redaction of his text in Thourioi after a stay in Athens (so Schwartz 1969: 369). A 'period of extended residence' by Hdt. at Athens is a mere inference (S. West in Bowie 2007: 27–8).   πυρὶ ὑπὸ τοῦ Μήδου: see 8.53.2. ἀντίον δὲ τοῦ μεγάρου τοῦ πρὸς ἑσπέρην τετραμμένου: this is, probably, the cella of the old temple to Athena known as the Hekatompedon.

77.4 τὸ δὲ ἀριστερῆς χειρὸς ἕστηκε πρῶτα ἐσιόντι ἐς τὰ προπύλαια τὰ ἐν τῆι ἀκροπόλι: 'it is immediately on the left as one enters the Propylaia of the Acropolis'. For 'on the left hand as you enter', cf. 2.169.4 and 4.34.2. In other words, within or even outside the entrance to the Acropolis (for Mnesikles' magnificent Propylaia or ceremonial gateway see ML 60 = Fornara 63, building accounts of 434/3). But Paus. (1.28.2), when mentioning this chariot, appears to position it inside the acropolis complex, near the statue of Athena by Pheidias, and there is a visible rock-cutting in an appropriate position. To save Hdt.'s accuracy, ML: 29 suggest that it was originally there, then moved outside for some reason (that is, at the time which Hdt. refers to), then back again. See S. West 1985: 283ff.   ἔθνεα Βοιωτῶν...: the inscription survives, twice over, but in fragmentary form both times. See ML no. 15 = *CEG* 179 = *IG* 1² 501. It was re-carved in the mid 5th cent. after the Persian sack; the two hexameters were then transposed, perhaps so as to begin in a more direct and specific way with the reference to the Boiotians and Chalkidians. Hdt. quotes the second version, the inscribed form of which is in 'stoichedon' i.e. strict checker-board layout, which allows exact calculation of the number of letters.   δεσμῶι ἐν ἀχνυόεντι is an emendation for the MSS.' ἀχνυνθέντι, ἀχνυθέντι or ἀχλυόεντι (this requires that one of the iotas shared a stoichos or box with another letter). Hude printed the last of these, but it is not easy to get the required sense from a word which means 'dark' or 'misty'; cf. S. West 1985: 283). The problem word must mean something like 'unpleasant'. We should probably (with West) accept the emendation and a derivation from a rare noun, ἀχνύς, 'pain'.   τῶν ἵππους 'from whom these horses'.

A fragmentary dedication on a small inscribed column, found at Thebes, appears to commemorate these same events as successes (see line 3 for the ?ransoming which Hdt. records at **77**.3), and thus gives a different view from that 'imposed on posterity by the [Athenian] victors' (so Knoepfler, alluding to ML 15; for other views and dates see Figueira 2010). See Aravantinos 2006 (= *SEG* 56.521) with D. Knoepfler, *BE* 2008: no. 237. It may be partly verse, partly prose. (Cf. the Kleomrotos inscription from Sybaris, above, **45**.1n. on Ἀθηναίηι ἐπωνύμωι Κραθίηι.) Here it is, as printed at Aravantinos 373, with the correction of some obvious typos:

———ος Ϝοινόας καὶ Φυλᾶς
———hελόντες κέλευσῖνα
———ΑΙ Χαλκίδα λυσάμενοι (or λυσαμένοι i.e. λυσαμένωι, dat. sing.)
———μοι ἀνέθειαν

('capturing Oinoe and Phylai...and Eleusis...Chalkis...ransoming
(??)...dedicated')

78 Authorial praise of Athens

The admirably plain simplicity of the Greek of this ch. contrasts with Th.'s
guarded, carefully but obscurely qualified, and thus controversial praise of
the regime of the Five Thousand at 8.97.2. Nevertheless we shall see that
there is room for disagreement about the exact scope of Hdt.'s praise.

**78 δηλοῖ δὲ οὐ κατ᾽ ἓν μοῦνον ἀλλὰ πανταχῇι ἡ ἰσηγορίη ὡς ἐστὶ χρῆμα
σπουδαῖον:** for σπουδαῖος as 'excellent', see 8.69.2 (Xerxes' opinion of
Artemisia) and Baragwanath 2008: 197 n. 76, noting that it often suggests excellence *in* or *at* something; she stresses (196, cf. 198) the purely
military character of the excellence in the present passage (but note the
introductory and reinforcing words 'not in one respect only but in every
respect'). The form of the comment recalls that of Periandros to his son
Lykophron (3.53.4): τυραννὶς χρῆμα σφαλερόν.

ἰσηγορίη derives from the verb ἀγορεύω and thus puts the emphasis on
equality of *speech*. Griffith 1966 argued that the term was not really introduced until after 462, though Hdt. evidently associated it with Kleisthenes;
see also Fowler 2003a: 315 ('this celebrated passage lies at the heart of the
Histories in every way'), noting that *isegorie* implies a more radical and artic-
ulate form of democracy than does *isonomie*.

78 (cont.) εἰ καὶ Ἀθηναῖοι τυραννευόμενοι: this use of εἰ is not concessive; it
means 'since', 'because', and the addition of καί here does not affect this
(see the parenthesis at LSJ καί B (8)).   **τῶν σφέας περιοικεόντων:** from the
echoing Spartan speech at **91**.2 (ἐκμεμαθήκασι μάλιστα μὲν οἱ περίοικοι αὐτῶν
Βοιωτοὶ καὶ Χαλκιδέες), it appears that this is meant to apply to the Boiotians
and Chalkidians only. But what follows has a wider scope.   **ἀπαλλαχθέντες δὲ τυράννων μακρῶι πρῶτοι ἐγένοντο:** Hdt. has here gone beyond Athens'
military capacity to handle hostile immediate neighbours and has shifted
to a wider generalisation (he leaves it vague how far forward he is looking).
In this rhetorical passage he both underrates Peisistratid military compe-
tence and exaggerates the military strength and confidence of liberated
Athens: the homage of earth and water promised to Persia by the Athenian envoys was criticised on their return, but not repudiated (**73**.3n.). On
the first point (under-rating of the Peisistratids), Th. 6.54.5 corrects Hdt.,
see *CT* III: 444–5, and indeed Hdt. himself supplies contrary evidence;
see 1.64.2 for Peisistratos' intervention on Naxos and his 'purification' of
Delos, and **94**.1 for his capture of Sigeion. For all this see esp. D. M. Lewis,
CAH 4²: 297.

We have now more or less reached the point from which Hdt. diverged
at **55**, so as to tell us analeptically how the Athenians got rid of their tyrants

and what they did after that (see **65**.5). We are nearly ready for the arrival
of Aristagoras. But first comes the story of the Athenian clashes with the
Aiginetans, their main naval rivals.

78 (cont.) ἐλευθερωθέντων: Hdt.'s admiration is directed at least as much
towards freedom as opposed to despotism, as towards democracy as such.
For Fornara 1971: 48f., ἐλευθερωθέντων is 'the key word' of the whole passage, democracy is secondary to freedom, and Hdt. is thus able without
inconsistency to admire the freedom of the Spartan system even more
intensely than he does Athenian democracy. This tilts things a little too
far. Hdt. could have made that point here without so politically specific a
word as ἰσηγορίη; and note that the two pro-Spartan passages adduced by
Fornara are both from speeches: Soklees on Spartan opposition to tyranny
at **92** α, Demaretos at 7.104. The assertion 'Demaratus is plainly speaking
for [Hdt.]' (Fornara 49 n. 22) is too confident. In any case (Fowler 2003a:
315) we are not to forget 'what Athens did with that democracy and freedom' later on; this may give a special edge to μακρῶι πρῶτοι above, depending how far forward Hdt. is looking.   ἐργαζόμενοι … <τι> κατεργάζεσθαι:
the contrast is between 'working for' a master and 'achieving something'
(the prefix κατά adds a positive sense). The addition of τι is due to Powell
1938a: 216.

79–89 *Thebes and Aigina*

A long but much-interrupted excursus about (mainly) Aiginetan affairs is
distributed between bks. 5 and 6. Two reasons for the heavy weight of Aiginetan history do not become clear until later. (1) it was, in Hdt.'s view,
the long-drawn-out war against the Aiginetans which gave the Athenians
their large navy at Salamis, because Themistokles persuaded them to use
a financial windfall from the Laurion silver mines to build a navy for 'the
war', sc. against the Aiginetans. But in the event it was available for defence
against the Persians: 7.144, cf. Pohlenz 1937: 40. In other words, this was
contingency on a large scale: the Athenians were ready for the Persians at
sea, but for unrelated, or rather not obviously related reasons ('not obviously' because Greek squabbles, or some of them, turn out paradoxically
to be the saving of Greece). (2) The Aiginetans won the collective prize for
bravery at Salamis (8.93), whereas the Thebans medised (so that the twin
sisters Thebe and Aigina went separate ways; see **80** for the sisterhood, and
Immerwahr 1966: 228 for the political divergence between the two states).
Hdt. tells us by slow degrees how it came about that Aiginetans eventually
fought on the Greek side alongside their bitter and long-standing enemies the Athenians. This outcome was astonishing, and contrary to the
principle about neighbourly rivalries which Hdt. implies at 8.30.2: 'if the

Thessalians had taken the Greek side, I think the Phokians [their secular enemies] would have medised'. Nobody would have bet in advance on a Greek victory, given these animosities between neighbours. The miraculous repulse of the Persian invasion was largely due to the temporary and partial abandonment of those animosities at e.g. Aigina. See Stadter 2006: 251–2.

Two other motives are relevant. (3) The Athenian reduction of Aigina to tributary status in 458/7 (and perhaps also the utter catastrophe of 431, Th. 2.27.1) must have enhanced the topical interest which Aiginetan history had for Hdt. and his hearers. Finally (4), Hdt. is often willing to expand on the background to the aetiology of a ritual or other practice, and here there are two distinct such aetiologies (kneeling statues; the wearing or not of pins by women). See **86.**3n. on ἐς γούνατα..., citing e.g. 3.48.3, the aetiology of the Samian cake-festival. For expansion on the origin and etymology of a non-ritual practice, the drinking of unmixed wine, 'Skythian style', cf. 6.84.3. Desire to explain etymologies, or the origins of proverbial sayings, can be part of the reason for an excursus. Examples are **92** ε 1, the name Kypselos, 6.129.4, οὐ φροντὶς Ἱπποκλείδηι, and the 'Lemnian deeds' of 6.138.4. From the Hebrew Bible, cf. Gen. 10.9 'therefore it is said, Even as Nimrod the mighty hunter before the Lord' (proverb) or Exod. 15.23 (origin of the name of Marah, the place of undrinkably bitter water), with Bolin 1999: 135.

The present excursus (**79–89**) is book-ended at the extremes by Delphic oracles, at **79.**1 and **89.**2; the story of the Theban appeal to the Aiginetans for help encloses the Aiginetan material at **82–8**; and inside that section there is Epidaurian and Argive material at **82–6**. For chronology see below on **81.**2, καὶ ἐχθρῆς παλαιῆς...

79.1 Θηβαῖοι δὲ μετὰ ταῦτα ἐς θεὸν ἔπεμπον: the 'Boiotians' of **77** have now become 'the Thebans', who are the real agents. **βουλόμενοι τείσασθαι Ἀθηναίους** 'wanting to punish the Athenians'. Cf. **77.**1 (same verb), where it was the Athenians who wanted to do the punishing. The theme of τίσις or requital is a governing principle of the *Histories* (Gould 1989). At the important **105.**2, using language closely similar to the present passage, Hdt. will make Dareios pray to 'Zeus' that it may be possible for him Ἀθηναίους τείσασθαι. **ἐς πολύφημον δὲ ἐξενείκαντας:** the 'many-voiced one' is the people or Assembly (the ἁλίη of **79.**2); cf. *Od.* 2.150 ἀγορὴν πολύφημον (and Wilson would like to supplement <ἀγορήν>, but this is not necessary). The oracle perhaps began ἐσφέρετ' ἐς πολύφημον...For the verb in this political sense, but in a prosaic context, cf. 9.5.1 (Athens), ἐξενεῖκαι ἐς τὸν δῆμον.

79.2 ἁλίην: the Ionian-Athenian equivalent is Heliaia, but at Athens it was the name for the popular lawcourt. **οὐκ ὦν ἄγχιστα ἡμέων οἰκέουσι**

Ταναγραῖοί τε καὶ Κορωναῖοι καὶ Θεσπιέες; There is a significant omission in this Theban-focalised list of three neighbouring and always helpful Boiotian *poleis*, namely Plataia. Plataia was geographically much closer to Thebes than were either Tanagra or Koroneia, and slightly closer than Thespiai. Th. makes his Thebans claim – and complain – that they had actually founded Plataia: 3.61.2, but see 7.57.5 for the later hostile relationship. In fact, Hdt. does not mention Plataia anywhere until the analeptic 6.108 (Kleomenes and some Spartans encourage the Plataians to ally themselves with the Athenians in 519 BC), an excursus inserted to explain their presence on the Athenian side at Marathon; it also explains the Theban-Plataian hatred which underlies Th.'s Plataian debate (3.52–69); and it explains the non-mention of the Plataians as Theban allies in the present context, *c.* 504 BC (see **81.2n.**), fifteen years or so after their alliance with the Athenians. In view of the cardinal importance of Plataia in bk. 9, where it is the scene of the climactic battle of the Persian Wars, Hdt.'s decision as to where and how to introduce the Plataia theme can hardly have been casual, and attentive listeners or readers might have noticed the significant absence of the Plataians here.

Hdt. also here omits 'Minyan Orchomenos', for which see 1.146.1. Orchomenos was not only further away than any of the three places here listed; it was also a rival to Thebes in prestige.

For Tanagra, in eastern Boiotia, see **57.**1n.; for Koroneia, on the eastern shore of Lake Kopais, see *IACP*: no. 210. Seven hundred men of Thespiai (*IACP*: no. 222) took part in the battle of Thermopylai on the Greek side alongside four hundred from Thebes; see 7.202.1 (at 222 they are said to be willing fighters, unlike the reluctant Thebans).

See S. Larson 2007: 191 for the kind of military co-operation, perhaps short of formal alliance, here implied.

79.2 (cont.) ἀλλὰ μᾶλλον μὴ οὐ τοῦτο ἦι τὸ χρηστήριον 'but that is probably not what the oracle meant'. μὴ οὐ with the subjunctive expresses tentativeness; with ἦι cf. above **1.**3, the Paionians realised that that was what the oracle meant, τὸ χρηστήριον αὐτὸ τοῦτο εἶναι.

80.1 εἶπε δή κοτε μαθών τις: the motif of the one anonymous clever man or woman who 'eventually understands', i.e. sees the truth of a riddle when others are perplexed, is a well-established story-telling device. Compare 6.37.2: the Lampsakenes are baffled by Kroisos' threat to wipe them out like a pine-tree, but then one of the older citizens sees the truth, μόγις κοτὲ μαθὼν τῶν τις πρεσβυτέρων εἶπε τὸ ἐόν. Gorgo at 7.239.4 is the only one to see 'beneath the surface' of the riddlingly blank wax tablet. From the Bible, Belshazzar and the 'writing on the wall': Daniel 5.8, 'then came in all the king's wise men, but they could not read the writing, nor make known to the king the interpretation thereof'. Then the queen says (verse 11) 'There is a man in thy kingdom . . .' etc. – and Daniel is brought in and solves it (but let us not forget the queen's role). The Thebans gather repeatedly to solve the Sphinx's riddle, until along comes Oidipous (Apollod. 3.5.8; for this sub-type of story – death for failure to solve – cf. Calaf in Puccini's *Turandot*. See Eidinow 2011: 63–4 for such 'neck riddles', as they are called). At Verg. *Aen.* 2.31ff., only Laocoon, priest of Apollo (the mantic god), sees 'beneath the surface' of the wooden horse. Often in the ancient Greek world it will have been a *mantis* or seer who could do the trick, using his special powers to replace a literal with a metaphorical interpretation, and so penetrate to the deeper meaning. Hdt. 9.33.2–3 (with 35.2) inverts this: the seer Teisamenos gets it wrong and then the Spartans get it right. See also 7.142–3, where Themistokles, introduced at 143.1 with a τις formula, refers the oracle correctly to the fleet.

The anonymous τις here for the one clever Theban may be a joke involving ethnic stereotyping (Boiotians are famously slow-witted); or it may be a dramatising 'button-holing' device for engaging the listener/reader and making the interpretation-debate more lively: better than the boring 'That was the oracle. The Thebans duly realised that their "nearest" meant . . .' etc. The addition of κοτε (here 'at last', 'eventually', see Powell) contributes to the effect: a long baffled silence, and then someone sees the light.

80.1 (cont.) Ἀσωποῦ λέγονται γενέσθαι θυγατέρες Θήβη τε καὶ Αἴγινα: the nymphs Thebe and Aigina were twin sisters, daughters of the river-god Asopos (Pind. *Isthm.* 8.16–18 and Bacchyl. 9.53–5; S. Larson 2007: 81–3; Nagy 2011: 44. Asopos had nine daughters according to Korinna 654 col. iii 21 *PMG* with Bowra 1953: 54–65: the others included Kerkyra and Tanagra, and the total from all sources was far larger than nine). Hdt.'s Aiginetans, like other early sources, ignore the difficulty that Thebe was daughter of a Boiotian river Asopos, Aigina of a Peloponnesian; see M. West 1985: 100. Note also the significant but characteristically 'unmarked' pairing of Thebes and Aigina, as victims of Athenian aggression, in the Thebans' speech at Th. 3.64.3 (*CT* I: 458–9 and II: 74, and Indergaard 2011: 305 n. 42). Hdt., equally characteristically, spells it out. For an Aiginetan *proxenos* at Boiotian Plataia, see 9.85.3.   **Αἰγινητέων**: see further **81.2n.** for Aigina and the Aiginetans. With the nymph Aigina, and this plural ethnic, Hdt. opens a long phase of narrative in which Aiginetans will be prominent, culminating at Salamis, but continuing right through to the exchange between the Aiginetan Lampon and Pausanias at 9.78–80.1.

80.2 καὶ οὐ γάρ τις ταύτης ἀμείνων γνώμη: instead of exclaiming with joy and admiration at this obviously right approach, the dull Thebans are merely said to be (grudgingly?) unable to improve on it. Hdt.'s Athenian audience perhaps rolled their eyes upwards at this.   **τοὺς Αἰακίδας**

συμ<πεισθέντας> πέμπειν ἔφασαν 'they said that they were persuaded and
were sending the Aiakidai'. The usually accepted reading συμπέμπειν has
to be taken to mean 'we are sending'. But the variant συμπείθειν points to
the solution.

Here (contrast, perhaps, the Tyndaridai at **75** above) cult objects or
statues are clearly meant, because they get 'returned' to Aigina at **81**.1
(and see 8.84 and 86 for a ship conveying the Aiakidai in 480); but the
word ἀγάλματα is not explicitly used here, as it will be at **84–6** (Damie
and Auxesie). Hdt. does not specify which 'Aiakidai' are meant; probably
(to anticipate the conclusion below) Telamon and Peleus, but there are
complications. What follows assumes that the request named names, or at
any rate that it was understood on both sides which Aiakidai were meant;
but it is just possible that the request for 'Aiakidai' was vaguely put, leaving
it for the Aiginetans to interpret it as they liked.

The Aiakidai, in the strict patronymic sense of 'sons of Aiakos', are
Telamon (father of Ajax and Teukros, and himself an Argonaut); Peleus
(father of Achilles, and himself a participant in the Kalydonian boar-
hunt); Menoitios (acc. Hes. fr. 212a, accepted by Nagy 2011: 52, but see
Gantz 1993: 222 for his alternative father Aktor); and Phokos (father
of Panopeus and eponym of Phokis), who was killed by his half-brothers
Peleus and Telamon, who were exiled by Aiakos from Aigina for this. (See
Apollod. 3.12.6; this exile and that of Teukros are myths of colonial identity.) But 'Aiakids' can also mean 'remoter descendants of Aiakos', as at
8.64 where Ajax is certainly one, and as at Lykoph. *Alex.* 53, where Αἰάκειοι,
the 'ktetic' form of the patronymic, may in the context include Neoptole-
mos, son of Achilles, and even Epeios the builder of the wooden horse,
who was son of Panopeus.

The present passage has to be taken with 8.64.2. There the Athenians
in 480 decide to 'pray to the gods and to ask for the Aiakidai as allies'; this
turns out to involve sending to Salamis for Ajax and Telamon (for Ajax
as 'helper' of Athens see **66**.2n.), and to more distant Aigina for Aiakos
καὶ τοὺς ἄλλους Αἰακίδας where ἄλλους must mean 'and the Aiakidai in addition' rather than 'the other Aiakidai'. If 'Aiakidai' in the present passage
includes Telamon, he is somehow thought of as living on both Salamis
(8.64) and Aigina, and this is not impossible (cf. **67**.2 n. for Melanippos).
But in that case the question arises whether Telamon is on both islands at
8.64 too. On this see Nagy 2011: 51.

So the Aiakidai in the present passage are probably the undisputed and
high-profile pair of Aiakos' sons, Telamon and Peleus (but probably not
Phokos), unless Telamon is regarded as fixed on Salamis, in which case
another Aiakid, in the wider sense of 'descendant of Aiakos', is needed to
accompany Peleus. Of these, Ajax is one possibility, but if so, it is surprising
that he is not named (as he is at **66**.2). Teukros is another, despite the myth

which sent him to found a new Salamis on Cyprus (Lykoph. *Alex.* 450ff. and Hor. *Carm.* 1.7.27–9). For Aigina as the island of the Aiakidai see Pind. *Ol.* 8.23–4, 13.109, etc.

For Hittite precedents for this sort of summoning of talismanic statues, see Faraone 1992: 27 and 34 n. 77.

81.1 τρηχέως περιεφθέντων: see **1.1**n. for this expression.   τούς μὲν Αἰακίδας σφι ἀπεδίδοσαν, τῶν δὲ ἀνδρῶν ἐδέοντο: either the heroes have proved useless, so that the Thebans, in a notably secular spirit – or as recorded by Hdt. in a secular spirit – give them back and ask for men instead, or else, perhaps, the heroes are to be thought of as deliberately unhelpful because they are already too sympathetic to Athens (How and Wells). See **80.2**n. on the Aiakidai, citing 8.64. For the Athenian sanctuary to Aiakos see **89.2** and 3nn.

Haubold 2007: 228 sees a gender-opposition between the women Thebe and Aigina and the men who are now requested. But the men are to replace (δέ) the Aiakidai (μέν), who are also males.

81.2 Αἰγινῆται δὲ εὐδαιμονίηι τε μεγάληι ἐπαρθέντες: the prosperity and success of Aigina (for which island neighbour of Athens see Figueira 1981 and now *IACP* no. 358, Figueira again) have been hinted at by Hdt. more than once already (Irwin 2011 discusses the bks. 1–4 passages). See 2.178.3 for an Aiginetan presence at Egyptian Naukratis (a precinct to Zeus in this panhellenic trading emporium, and see *IACP*: 622 for Aiginetan colonies of the more usual sort); 3.59 for a 6th-cent. defeat of the Samians by a combined Aiginetan-Kretan fleet (this reversed a previous Aiginetan naval defeat at the hands of the Samians); 3.131 for the Aiginetan hiring of the doctor Demokedes for the huge salary of one talent (though he later went elsewhere); and esp. 4.152.3 (with *LSAG²*: 439 no. E and *SEG* 48.370; cf. Kowalzig 2011: 161) for the fabulous fortune acquired by Sostratos of Aigina in – as we now know from an inscribed stone anchor – central Italy. On 9.80.3 (the origins of Aiginetan wealth lay in their purchase on the cheap of Persian booty after Plataia) see Ste. Croix 2004c: 388–9: at best this is a wild exaggeration, in view of the present passage and much other evidence for early Aiginetan wealth. Aiginetan prosperity rested on trade (cf. Ar. *Pol.* 1291b24). Its population was much larger than could have been sustained from local resources alone, though the standard figure of 35–45,000 for total population (*IACP*: 620) has been lowered to 20,000 (Hansen 2006: 12. He thinks the Aiginetans made extensive use of hired foreign rowers as opp. citizens, but the proportions must be conjectural). There are two non-literary indicators of late archaic Aiginetan prosperity: its early and influential silver coinage (*IACP*: p. 622 and Osborne 2009: 243–4; unduly minimised by Ste. Croix 2004c: 392) and its expensively decorated temple of Aphaia (Podlecki 1976: 405–8; Ohly 1977, Burnett 2005: 29–44 and Osborne 2009: 308, and Watson 2011).

In Hdt., ἐπαρθέντες, 'encouraged', is often a word with disquieting implications in the long run: people are 'encouraged' in foolish or undesirable courses by oracles (1.90.3 and 5. **91.**2) or dreams (7.18.4). In his *Histories*, it is not a good idea to be carried away by prosperity and success. The Aiginetans take a long time to learn this lesson, but in the end are subjected by the Athenians (458/7) and then lose their independence completely in 431, when their island is evacuated by the Athenians (Th. 2.27.1).

81.2 (cont.) καὶ ἔχθρης παλαιῆς ἀναμνησθέντες: the double statement of motive is characteristic of Hdt. (but an either-or formulation is commoner), and as often the more compelling motive is placed second.

On the history of Athenian-Aiginetan relations, Amit 1973: 9–60 (esp. 17–29); Figueira 1993: 409–18. At one end, παλαιή does not have the same associations as our 'ancient' (it can refer to fairly recent history), but that is the only indicator of time which Hdt. supplies for the origins of the hostility, apart from the equally unspecific ἐξ ἀρχῆς at **82.**1. Figueira (*IACP*: 621) takes the 'heraldless war' to begin only in 506.

At the other end, the natural and preferable implication of Hdt.'s presentation is that all the Athenian-Aiginetan hostilities recounted in bks. 5 and 6 (see esp. the Nikodromos episode at 6.87–93, where 87 explicitly back-refers to the present episode of Aiginetan help to the Thebans) are over by the time of Marathon in 490; see Hammond 1955: 406–11. The Boiotian defeat of **77** may be put in 505; the Theban defeat of **81.**1 (τρηχέως περιεφθέντων), and the Aiginetan raid on Phaleron, can then both be put in 504, and the Peloponnesian refusal to co-operate with Kleomenes (**91**ff.) in 503. See Buck 1979: 128.

(Not everyone has been happy with this. Figueira 1993: 113–49 puts the Nikodromos episode in the early 480s, cf. Andrewes 1936/7: 4 complaining that to squeeze everything in before Marathon was 'intolerable compression'; so too Amit 1973: 26. It has often been suggested that the oracle at **89** – the Athenians are advised to abstain from attacking the Aiginetans for thirty years – is a 'prediction after the event' and shows knowledge of the decisive Athenian coercion of the Aiginetans in 458/7. This would take us back to 487, three years after Marathon. The conclusion is not necessary, however: cf. Podlecki 1976: 397–8; and the oracle – which the Athenians disobeyed – probably means that it took more than thirty years to bring down the Aiginetans. See Buck 1979: 127.)

The pre-history of the Athenian-Aiginetan hostility, involving the Epidaurians and then Argives, is much harder to date, and takes us into a earlier period: note the 'once upon a time' flavour of κατὰ χρόνον κεῖνον at **82.**2. It seems likely (Figueira 1993: 9–33 and 35–60) that the period of Aiginetan dependence on Epidauros (**83**.1) should be dated to the second half of the 7th cent. (see also Buck 1981: 12) and that the Aiginetans broke away from this dependence in around 610 (see **83**.2). The early hostilities between Athenians and Aiginetans (those involving the cult-statues of Damie and Auxesie) might then be put in the 590s. (Figueira 1993: 409 suggests 595–90? as the period of 'significant [Aiginetan] estrangement with Athenians'.) The mention of the trireme at **85**.1 (see n. there) is compatible with an early 6th-cent date for the Athenian landing on Aigina. It also forbids us to push the story back into the mists of myth.

81.2 (cont.) πόλεμον ἀκήρυκτον 'truceless war', lit. 'without heralds'. The expression is used only here in Hdt.; Th. uses adverbial forms: ἀκηρύκτως μέν, ἀνυπόπτως δὲ οὔ (1.146) and ἐπεμείγνυντο ἔτι ἀκηρυκτεί (2.1). The meaning in the present passage is not exactly 'sudden' (LSJ), but rather 'truceless' (Andrewes 1936/7: 2). The 'unheralded war' begins in 506, but the origins of the bad blood between Athenians and Aiginetans are older.

81.3 κατὰ μὲν ἔσυραν Φάληρον: for Phaleron see **63**.3n. and esp. 6.116 (the pre-Piraieus harbour of Athens). The verb is from κατασύρω (cf. 6.33.2), but the two halves are here separated (by 'tmesis'), though note the continuation with κατὰ δέ.

82–88 The back-history of Aiginetan-Athenian bad blood; Epidauros

The early history of the four poleis here considered (Aigina, Athens, Epidauros, Argos) is presented in terms of cult, and of cult objects, which are requested, lent, stolen, demanded back. This is reminiscent of the Sikyonian request to Thebes for 'Melanippos' at **67**.2. But the interrelation between the four poleis of the present section is more complicated, and it is tempting to look for a connecting thread between them. All four were members of the 'Kalaureian amphiktiony', a network which had for its centre the sanctuary of Poseidon at Kalaureia, part of the mod. double-island of Poros (Strabo 8.6.14: the Argives participated via Nauplia, which they controlled. See Tausend 1992: 12–19, Constantakopoulou 2007: 29–37, and *IACP* no. 360, 'Kalaureia' for the members and history). Hdt. never mentions this organisation, but its existence might help to explain the various religious requests, and the reactions to those requests, which he here narrates; it might also explain why identical but unusual cults were found on both Aegina and Epidauros (**83**.3). Membership may have involved obligations to other members on what in private matters is called the ἔρανος principle (there is an obligation to lend, but also an obligation to repay when you can). As particular archaic states, notably Aigina and Athens, expanded in wealth and international standing, any original equality which may have characterised the amphiktiony could have come to seem irksome, and certainly the Aiginetans, now a 'thalassocratic' power (**83**.2) no longer felt their subordination to their amphiktionic fellow-member Epidauros to be tolerable (**83**.1). The amphiktiony was no mere Hellenistic fiction; see *OCD*[4] 'Calauria': the inclusion of Nauplia and Prasiai, both of which later succumbed to larger neighbours, looks authentic.

Some aspects of the conflicts and tensions here narrated are not 'archaic' at all, but would remind contemporaries of the symbolic obligations imposed on, and perhaps resented by, subject allies of the Athenians in their 5th-cent. empire (see esp. **82**.3 for the offerings to Athena Polias and Erechtheus, and **84**.1 for Athenian anger when these dues were no longer paid). Again, the application to Aigina of the word 'thalassocracy' (**83**.2n.) anticipates the Athenian thalassocracy. See also, for a late 5th-cent. religious dispute which escalated into hostilities, Th. 5.50 and 53 (also involving Epidauros).

In the Athenian version, the Athenians who have been sent to take the statues go mad and kill each other; in the Argive/Aiginetan version, the statues miraculously fall to their knees when the Athenians try to remove them (Hdt. himself doubts whether this actually happened). It is not easy to say which of these explanations is the more religious, despite Haubold, who thinks the Athenian version is more explicitly religious and calls this whole section 'an astonishing narrative experiment' (2007: 239 and 244). The excursus is unexpected and has uncanny features, but is not obviously more daring and experimental than the Dorieus excursus at **42–8**, with its juxtaposed alternative accounts of the Sybaris/Kroton war at **44–5**, both of which involve religious evidence; or the analeptic narrative at 3.48–53, which, like the present passage, seeks to explain long-standing antipathies (Samos, Kerkyra, Korinth).

There are parallels to the punishment of the Athenian sacrilege at **85** and (variant) **86**, after they attempt to drag the statues away. In Hdt. himself, one version of the reason for Kleomenes' death is suicide when suffering from an insanity inflicted as a result of his impious tree-felling in the sacred precinct at Eleusis (6.75). Mythical examples include the punishment of Erysichthon for a similar offence. If, like the Athenians in the present narrative, you attempt to bind gods, you are asking for trouble (Pentheus, and the pirates in *Hom. Hymn* (7) *Dionysos*). It is typically Demeter and Dionysos who exercise this power to punish, and (see on **82**.1), there is some connection between Damia and Demeter. But note also that the assault on Kassandra, witnessed by the statue of Athena, leads to the destruction of Ajax and his crew; and that Hera foils the attempted theft of her statue at Samos by immobilising the guilty ship (*FGrHist* 541 Menodotos F1, with How and Wells). This is the *aition* for a binding ritual. (This para. is indebted to AHG. Other aspects, and some problematic details, are dealt with in the commentary below.)

On the whole section **82–88** see Buck 1981.

82.1 ἡ δὲ ἔχθρη ἡ προοφειλομένη: the choice of verb is unexpected when applied to negative feelings (for the literal financial sense 'owe something already' see 6.59). Th. uses the compound form as a metaphor, but applies it to positive notions like benefits: 1.32 (a speech), cf. 1.137.4 (letter of Themistokles) for the simple form of the verb.   **Ἐπιδαυρίοισι ἡ γῆ...**the abrupt mention of the Epidaurians comes as a surprise; we have not heard of Epidauros (*IACP* no. 348) since the Korinthian Periandros' invasion and his deposition of the tyrant Prokles: 3.52.7. For the storytelling asyndetic opening, often used to introduce excursuses about the remoter past, cf. **71.1**n. on ἦν Κύλων...With this ch. contrast the faster **79.   περὶ ταύτης ὦν τῆς συμφορῆς**: consultation of oracles about crop failure is attested in Hdt. (4.151.1, Thera), other prose sources (Strabo 6.1.6; Paus. 2.29.7), and tragedy (Eur. *Ion* 303, Ion asks Kreousa if her consultation was about crops or children, similar problems; for worries about children cf. **92 β** 2, 9.33.2, and inscribed Dodona questions, Eidinow 2007: 87–93, cf. 346 no. 8, concern for good crops, not necessarily indicative of famine).   **Δαμίης τε καὶ Αὐξησίης ἀγάλματα**: these were ancient Greek goddesses, but their names and functions are deeply obscure. Whatever their exact nature, they belong (Parker 2011: 72) to a puzzling category of figures who are unknown to myth (leaving aside Troizen, see below) but who have 'an importance in cult normally only available to major gods'. Their statues were (like that of Artemis at Tauris and the Palladion, Athena's sacred image) examples of cultic statues disputed between cities and sanctuaries: *ThesCRA* II: 467 (= 5. G no. 491, Noelle Icard-Gianolio). Auxesie was clearly a goddess of (agricultural) 'increase' or 'growth' – the literal meaning of αὔξησις. Cf. Dionysos' Arkadian cult epithet Αὐξίτης (Jost 2005: 399), and cf. R/O 88.18 (4th-cent. Athenian ephebic oath) for Αὐξώ and Ἡγεμόνη as two of the witnessing gods, along with personified Wheat, Barley etc. Sophocles (fr. 981 *TrGF* and Pearson) says Ἀζησία was a cult epithet of Demeter (cf. Kowalzig 2011: 139 on Paus. 2.30.4); this might fit what is said at **83**.3 about female reviling. Cf. generally Wilamowitz 1931–2: 2.100–2.

Damie is more of a puzzle: the root may be δεμ-, 'house', and the meaning δέσποινα: Nilsson 1906: 414 n. 5; or perhaps the root is δαμ-, and Damia is 'the Enforcer' (from δαμάζω): Wilamowitz 1931–2: 101; or else the word is connected to Ge, 'Earth' (West 2007: 174f.). Festus p. 60 Lindsay (entry under 'Damium') connects Damia with the Italian Good Goddess or *Bona dea*, for whom see *OCD*[4] (vines and other plants were a feature of her cult, so she too was agricultural). Damie and Auxesie are epigraphically attested on Aigina, under the names Μνία and Αὐζεσίη (*IG*4.2². 787, a temple inventory from the 431–404 Athenian kleruchy on the island, with Dunbabin 1936/7: 85 and Hallof's 2007 comm.), and similarly at Epidauros (*IG*4.1². 386 etc.). The Aiginetan inventory shows the statue of Mnia was of cypress-not olive-wood, as Hdt. would lead us to expect; see **82.**2n.

The goddesses' kneeling position (**86.**3, recounted as miraculous, but presumably an aetiology for an unusual feature of the statues) may have indicated goddesses of childbirth (cf. Hes. *Theog.* 460 with West's n.). See also Wilamowitz 1893: 2.282 and Figueira 1993: 37 n. 4. The lexicographer Hesychius knew of a festival Δάμεια at Taras in S. Italy, Sparta's best attested historical colony (cf. also the 1st-cent. AD Spartan inscription Sokolowski 1969: no. 62 line 2: Αὐξη?]σίαι καὶ Δαμοίαι), and this, with the rest of the evidence above, might suggest a widespread Dorian cult. Paus. 2.32.2 tells of two Kretan (i.e. Dorian) girls Damie and Auxesie who were stoned to death at Troizen by mistake, after which a festival of 'Stone-throwing' or λιθοβολία was instituted: Nilsson 1906: 412. But the stoning means they were not goddesses (Wilamowitz 100); in fact, these girls look more like heroines of a familiar sort (J. Larson 1995: 15–16 and 140). There may (Figueira 1993: 58) be an affinity between this and the ritual abuse of **83.**3 below, but that abuse is directed at local not foreign women. The Troizen festival is part of a different tradition altogether.

Henderson 2007: 305 and n. 54 sees in Damie and Auxesie a ref. to the 'augmentation' of the Athenian 'demos' (αὐξόμενοι and δῆμος are used about Athens at **91**). But the alpha of Δαμίη is not long, as in δῆμος (Doric δᾶμος), but short, if the root is δεμ- or δαμ- as in δαμάζω (above).

82.2 οὐδέτερα τούτων: there are Homeric precedents for this type of two-pronged question and doubly dissenting reply ('is it that *x* or is it that *y*?'; answer: 'it is not *x* or *y*, but...'; see Macleod 1982: 41 and n. 4, citing e.g. *Il.* 1.62–7 with 93–4). **ἡμέρης ἐλαίης**: ἡμέρης 'cultivated', but AHG suggests ἱρῆς, 'sacred'; cf. below, ἱρωτάτας. For small statues of olive wood see Meiggs 1982: 309. But there is a crucial difficulty: in the inscribed inventory *IG* 4.2². 787 (see above), line 6, Mnia's statue is made from cypress-wood. Perhaps (AHG) the change of wood was symbolic and took place at the time of the Aiginetan surrender to Athens in 458/7. Whatever the date, it is strange that Hdt. does not mention the change, if change there was.

82.3 ἔτεος ἑκάστου τῆι τε Ἀθηναίηι τῆι Πολιάδι ἱρὰ καὶ τῶι Ἐρεχθεῖ: similar offerings were expected from Athenian tributary allies in the 5th cent.: ML 40.2–8 (Erythrai) or 46.41–3. Athena Polias was the goddess of the Athenian acropolis (**72.**3n. on ἡ δὲ ἱερείη), and the mythical early Athenian king Erechtheus, sometimes identified with Poseidon, was supposedly reared by Athena and installed by her in her 'rich temple', where he received animal sacrifice: Hom. *Il.* 2.546–51 and *OCD*⁴ 'Erechtheus'.

83.1 τοῦτον δ’ ἔτι τὸν χρόνον καὶ πρὸ τοῦ Αἰγινῆται Ἐπιδαυρίων ἤκουον: this perhaps refers to a period from around 650 BC. An Epidaurian hegemony over Aigina (ἀκούω here means ‘obey’) is thought to be possible at a time when Aiginetan commerce had not got started properly, i.e. around the middle of the 7th cent.: Epidauros has four times as much agricultural land as Aigina. See Figueira 1993: 19 cf. 46. In any case, on the foundation story accepted by Hdt. (8.46.1), Aigina was colonised directly by the Epidaurians, who would expect deferential treatment from a daughter-city, cf. Th. 1.25.4.   δίκας διαβαίνοντες ἐς Ἐπίδαυρον ἐδίδοσάν τε καὶ ἐλάμβανον παρ’ ἀλλήλων οἱ Αἰγινῆται: ‘giving and receiving δίκαι’ etc. ought to refer to arbitration between individual Aiginetans, as at Th. 1.140.2 (Perikles on Spartan state refusal of arbitration): δίκας μὲν τῶν διαφορῶν ἀλλήλοις διδόναι καὶ δέχεσθαι or Ager 1996: no. 13. II line 43, Teos *c.* 303 BC (partly restored, but with great probability); admittedly both these refer to inter-state arbitration. See also Gauthier 1972: 349–5 and Figueira 48 n. 32. Note the hyperbaton or unexpected word-order, with the Aiginetan subjects postponed to the last place in the sentence.   ἀγνωμοσύνηι χρησάμενοι ἀπέστησαν ἀπὸ τῶν Ἐπιδαυρίων: it is not necessary to look for anti-Aiginetan informants, so as to explain the strongly condemnatory ἀγνωμοσύνη, which was the converse of συγγνώμη, ‘fellow-feeling’, ‘indulgence’ (see 6.10). Aiginetan independence, here inaugurated with ‘foolish arrogance’, was curtailed at the hands of the Athenians in 458 and then ended in 431. For the date of the Aiginetan revolt from Epidaurian control, perhaps around 600 BC, see above on **81.**2, καὶ ἔχθρης παλαιῆς ἀναμνησθέντες. Aiginetan greatness (or pretensions, depending on viewpoint) lasted a century and a half.

83.2 ὥστε δὴ θαλασσοκράτορες ἐόντες: the main word here is a powerful one, used elsewhere in Hdt. only of the mythical Minos and of Polykrates of Samos (both 3.122) – but the real comparison is surely with the 5th-cent. Athenians. ‘Thalassocracy lists’ were compiled in antiquity (perhaps even in the 5th cent.) on the basis of this sort of evidence (Forrest 1969b: 95–106). Diod. 7 fr. 11, from Eusebius, is the main evidence. Here the Aiginetans are given the 17th and last thalassocracy, lasting ten years until Xerxes’ invasion, i.e. from 490–80.   Οἴη: not a *polis* (so not in *IACP*), and ‘unlocated’ acc. *Barr.* map-by-map Directory: 915; but it may (Dunbabin 1936/7: 85) have lain east of the city, because the temple inventory mentioned at **82.**1n. above (*IG* 4.2² 787) was found in that direction. See also Müller 1987: 742.

83.3 θυσίηισί τέ σφεα καὶ χοροῖσι γυναικηίοισι κερτόμοισι ἱλάσκοντο: the female reviling suggests the Demeter cult, and indeed there is slight evidence (e.g. Sophocles, see **82.**1n.) linking Auxesie and Demeter. For such reviling by women, compare the Thesmophoria (festival for Demeter), where it is connected with Iambe, who made the mourning Demeter laugh; see *OCD*[4] 'Iambe'.   **χορηγῶν ἀποδεικνυμένων ἑκατέρηι τῶν δαιμ-όνων δέκα ἀνδρῶν**: Hdt. is very well informed about the detail of the cult (the total of twenty chorus members etc.); he uses the word χορηγός here only. It evidently has the literal sense of 'chorus-leader', rather than alluding to financial arrangements (i.e. *choregia* as a 'liturgy' or form of taxation). For the institution of the *choregia* at Athens, see Wilson 2000. Male chorus-leaders of female choruses, as specified here, are normal in Alkman and Pindar. See Calame 1997: 64.   **ἄνδρα μὲν οὐδένα, τὰς δὲ ἐπιχωρίας γυναῖκας**: very emphatically expressed by the negative-positive formulation; cf. Parker 2011: 207 (and n. 131), noting that this may imply that one would have expected the women to abuse men, as at Anaphe and Pellene. Women as objects (not only perpetrators) of reviling are an unusual feature.   **ἦσαν δὲ καὶ τοῖσι Ἐπιδαυρίοισι αἱ αὐταὶ ἱρουργίαι· εἰσὶ δέ σφι καὶ ἄρρητοι ἱρουργίαι** 'the Epidaurians have the same rites; they also have secret rites'. See introd. n. to **82–88** for the significance of the shared cult. ἱρουργίαι occurs only here (twice) in Hdt. The god for whom the mystery cult (secret rites) were performed is not named; in classical and Hellenistic times, Epidauros' main deity was Asklepios, and this cult can be traced to the 6th cent.: *IG* 4.1² 1136. But that was not a mystery cult requiring initiation.

σφι probably refers to the Epidaurians (Stein and Waterfield). But it may possibly be ambiguous; cf. Parker 2011: 207 n. 131 'they (the Aeginetans? both? [i.e. the Epidaurians as well]) also have secret rites'.

84.1 ἐμήνιον 'were angry with', as at 9.7.β.2.   **οὐ δίκαιοι εἶναι ἀποφέρειν ἔτι**: for such a personal construction see 9.27.6 (the Athenians before Plataia), ἆρ' οὐ δίκαιοί εἰμεν ἔχειν ταύτην τὴν τάξιν.

84.2 σφίσι τε καὶ Ἀθηναίοισι εἶναι οὐδὲν πρῆγμα: lit. 'they had no business with the Athenians', i.e. the Athenians should mind their own business. This rude Aiginetan reply is the first hostile move.

85.1 τριήρει μιῆι τῶν ἀστῶν †τούτους†: the mention of a trireme (and cf. τριηρῖται at **85**.2) is a clue to the date of the whole ἔχθρη παλαιή episode, on the reasonable assumption that Hdt. meant what he said by the word 'trireme' (Wallinga 1993: 142 n. 36 does not accept this). Triremes are thought to have been invented about 650 BC and to have come into use slowly thereafter (Morrison, Coates and Rankov 2000: 40). A date in the 590s (**81**.2n.) for the Athenian raid on Aigina is thus possible on this dating of the invention of the trireme, but not on a date for the trireme in the 530s (as argued for by Wallinga 1993: 103–29). In place of the probably corrupt τούτους Wilson and Griffiths (see app. crit.) hanker for the meaning 'picked men', perhaps with a numeral (Griffiths' λ' αἱρετούς would mean thirty of these).

85.2 βροντήν τε καὶ ἅμα τῆι βροντῆι σεισμὸν ἐπιγενέσθαι: the combination of thunder and a downpour, even without accompanying earthquake, was enough to give the Athenians in Sicily forebodings of destruction: Th. 7.79.3. The earthquake here briefly mentioned by Hdt. is the first of a historiographical type identified by Chaniotis 1998: 407–11: an imaginary (or originally real but embellished) quake which works as an instrument of a higher power, and which punishes a sinner. **ἀλλοφρονῆσαι** 'they went out of their wits'. The verb means 'to be stunned, concussed' at *Il.* 23.698 (Epeios knocks out Euryalos in the boxing event) but cannot mean that here. At 7.205.3, the preferable reading is ἄλλα φρονέοντες not ἀλλοφρονέοντες. Some compounds in –*phron* mean 'out of one's *phren(es)* or mind' (Padel 1992: 23 and n. 44, though she does not discuss this one). For other exx. of divinely induced insanity after sacrilege, see introd. n. to **82–88**. **παθόντας δὲ τοῦτο κτείνειν ἀλλήλους ἅτε πολεμίους** 'and in that state they started killing each other as if they were enemies'. Like the 'earthborn men' in the story of Jason and the Argonauts: Ap. Rhod. 3.1373ff., or like Kadmos' Spartoi (the 'sown men') at Thebes: Apollod. 3.4.1. an appropriate myth in this narrative of Theban/Aiginetan relations. **ἐκ πάντων ἕνα λειφθέντα ἀνακομισθῆναι αὐτόθεν ἐς Φάληρον** 'there was only one left of all of them, and he made his way from there to Phaleron'. For the text see app. crit. and Wilson, and for the common literary motif of the solitary survivor, see Haubold 2007: 239, citing *Hom. Hymn (7) Dionysos* 53; see also *CT* III: 605–6 on the one Korinthian survivor at Th. 7.32.2, citing other parallels. Cf. **46.**1n. A modern example is the 'Messenger of Death' Dr. Brydon, celebrated (not quite accurately) as the only survivor of the massacre on the retreat from Kabul in 1842, near the end of the First Anglo-Afghan War (Hopkirk 2006: 267–70).

86.2 συγγινωσκόμενοι: in effect 'realising' (lit. 'admitting to themselves').

86.3 ἐμοὶ μὲν οὐ πιστὰ λέγοντες, ἄλλωι δέ τεωι: the build-up is carefully managed, making clear that something astonishing is to come, while continuing to withhold it. For the explicit expression of personal disbelief see next n., and for this exact formulation of it in religious contexts, see 1.182.1, 4.5.1 and other passages collected at Baragwanath and Bakker 2012: 13 n. 49; contrast 8.39.1, where the supernatural intervention of the heroes Phylakos and Autonoos in defence of Delphi is recorded with a non-committal 'the Delphians say' (and see 8.38.2 for Persian stories which tend in the same direction). See also 6.117.2, the vision of Epizelos at Marathon, reported without explicit incredulity. Hdt. seems to find such 'heroic' battle epiphanies easier to credit than he does an epiphany involving an outright suspension of the laws of nature, as in the present passage, or indeed fully 'divine' epiphanies of any sort (see 6.105 for his caution about Pan). For Hdt.'s doubts about or rejection of epiphanies of the divine sort, see Scullion 2006: 201, with a partial list of passages at 207 n. 36; also Introduction pp. 33–4. **ἐς γούνατα γάρ σφι αὐτά πεσεῖν, καὶ τὸν ἀπὸ τούτου χρόνον διατελέειν οὕτως ἔχοντα**: this kind of formula ('from that time onwards', 'down to the present day') foreshadows aetiologies in Hellenistic poetry, cf. e.g. Ap. Rhod. 4.1770: ἔνθ' ἔτι νῦν... See also **88.**3n. on ἔτι καὶ ἐς ἐμέ, **115.**1 (the hero-cult for Onesilos), and 3.48.2 for the Samian festival τῇ καὶ νῦν χρέωνται κατὰ ταὐτά. See also E. Kearns, 'aetiology' in *OCD*[4], with good bibliography.

Cf. 2.131.2–3: the attendants of Mykerinos' daughter had their hands cut off for betraying the girl to her father, and the hands of their statues were also missing. As here, Hdt. disbelieves it, but records it. See Griffiths 2006: 139 for such explanations of peculiarities. The aetiologies, both this one and the reasons for the changes in national costume at **87.**3–88, may help to explain the inclusion of the entire long excursus.

Kneeling statues are occasionally attested archaeologically. See Hampe and Simon 1981: pl. 328 a (Mykenai, 14th cent., Demeter and Kore with ?Ploutos); Pipili 1987: 58 (Lakonia). Pausanias (8.48.7) knew of a kneeling statue of Auge, who fell to her knees before giving birth to Telephos, at Tegea in Arkadia. (It is also possible that Damie and Auxesie are kneeling in supplication, to give the villains one last chance to avoid catastrophe (AHG).)

86.4 Ἀθηναίους μὲν δὴ ταῦτα ποιέειν, σφέας δὲ Αἰγινῆται λέγουσι 'the Aiginetans say that that is what the Athenians did, but that they themselves...' The second part of this, despite referring to what the Aiginetans say about themselves, is in accusative (not nominative) and infinitive construction, because attracted by the first part.   **ἑτοίμους Ἀργείους ποιέεσθαι**: a sudden mention of an Argive alliance for which we have not been prepared in any way.   **ὑποταμομένους ἀπὸ τῶν νεῶν**: ὑποτέμνω, used here in the middle voice, is found here only in Hdt., and has the same metaphorical sense as the English equivalent: 'they *cut them off* from the ships'. See app. crit.: the MSS τὸ ἀπὸ τῶν νεῶν makes no sense, although Powell (under ἀπό C. V. 4) translated it as '[cutting off] the retreat to the ships'.   **τὴν βροντὴν τε γενέσθαι καὶ τὸν σεισμόν**: *the* thunder and *the* earthquake. Cf. **85.**2: this is the moment when they happened.

87.2 Ἀθηναῖοι δὲ τοῦ δαιμονίου 'but the Athenians said it was due to the god' (this is succinctly expressed; the genitive resumes the genitives of αὐτῶν... διαφθειράντων i.e. 'the Athenians said it was the god [who destroyed the Athenian camp]'). For the Athenian religious explanation see introd. n. to **82–88**. That the Athenian losers should put a reverse down to divine displeasure rather than their own military incapacity makes sense in a way, but for a pious Greek observer it would imply an admission of the injustice of their cause.   **πυθομένας δὲ τὰς γυναῖκας**: the gruesome story finds a partial parallel at 9.5.3, the collective stoning of the wife and children of Lykides by the women of Athens; cf. also the 'Lemnian deeds' at 6.138.4. The use of brooches, a very female punishment, recalls Euripidean revenges, as in *Hek.* 1035ff.

87.3 τὴν δὲ ἐσθῆτα μετέβαλον αὐτέων ἐς τὴν Ἰάδα: in the 6th cent. there was a change from pinned peplos to unpinned chiton; see Figueira 1993: 41–2. These assertions of Hdt. seem to have provoked Th. to a reply (1.6.2–3), but he appears to have in mind a change from Ionic to the simpler Doric dress, and to be thinking of men rather than women. See *CT* I: 25–6 and Geddes 1987.

88.1 Ἰάς...Κάειρα: these are the female forms of the ethnic (cf. 1.92.3, Kroisos was ἐκ Καείρης γυναικός while Pantaleon was ἐξ Ἰάδος) but are here used as if they were ktetics. Hdt. might have said Καρική, as at 7.97, Καρικὴ στρατιή, but for some reason always avoids the feminine ktetic form of 'Ionian' viz. Ἰωνική, and that appears to have here affected his choice of word for 'Karian'.

88.2 τοὺς δὲ Ἀργείους...: the text seems disturbed here, and has been variously emended. The general meaning (the Argives and Aiginetans adopted the following custom ...) is not in doubt, though Wilson inclines to Powell's suggestion of a lacuna before καὶ, and that would produce radical uncertainty.   **τὰς περόνας ἡμιολίας ποιέεσθαι τοῦ τότε κατεστεῶτος μέτρου:** the pattern of symmetrical aetiological reversal – the Argive and Aiginetan women lengthen their pins as the Athenian women are deprived of theirs – resembles that at 1.82.7–8 (discussed above, **71.**1n. on ἐπὶ τυραννίδι ἐκόμησε ...): the Argives decide not to cut their hair, so the Spartans establish the opposite custom, τὰ ἐναντία τούτων ἔθεντο νόμον, and grow theirs.   **καὶ ἐς τὸ ἱρὸν τῶν θεῶν τουτέων περόνας μάλιστα ἀνατιθέναι τὰς γυναῖκας:** the inventory (*IG* 4.2². 787) confirms this, by listing large numbers of dedicated pins (lines 10–12): Mnia has 120 iron pins and Auxesia 180. So the story of the death by pins (**87.**2–3) 'will stand in some aetiological relation to the established fact': AHG, who compares 2.135, spits dedicated by Rhodopis at Delphi. See Dunbabin 1936/7; Jacobsthal 1956: 97–100; Morris 1984: 107–15.   **Ἀττικὸν δὲ μήτε τι ἄλλο προσφέρειν πρὸς τὸ ἱρὸν μήτε κέραμον:** the scope of this ban is limited to the sanctuary of Damie and Auxesie, and since that has not been located, let alone excavated (see on Οἴη at **83.**2 above), there is as yet no archaeological confirmation.

88.3 ἔτι καὶ ἐς ἐμέ: for such closural formulae in the giving of aetiologies, see **86.**3n.

89.1 τῆς δὲ ἔχθρης...ἀρχή: this echoes **82.**1, the start of an enormous ring.

89.2 ἦλθε μαντήιον ἐκ Δελφῶν: despite the language used, this was presumably not a spontaneous utterance by Apollo (see ML 5, Kyrene, line 24 for αὐτοματίζω as the word for this, and see below **92** β 2n. for ἰθέως). Delphi had already been consulted, and then the reply arrived just at this moment. Perhaps this was a double oracle, if the mechanics of state consultation by publicly appointed consulters allowed this. The first might have said e.g. 'wait thirty years and you'll win' and the second was in reply to a follow-up query 'what if we don't?' See further Bowden 2005: 115. For the chronological implications (or not) of the thirty-year period, see **81**.2n. on ἔχθρη παλαιή.   **πολλὰ μέν ... πείσεσθαι ... πολλὰ δὲ καὶ ποιήσειν:** the opposing pair 'suffering/doing', for which see **65**.5n., is here ascribed to the oracle. But the second part may be a mere polar expression, to be discarded; cf. 7.52.1 'destroy or save' (AHG).

89.3 τῶι μὲν Αἰακῶι τέμενος ἀπέδεξαν τοῦτο τὸ νῦν ἐπὶ τῆς ἀγορῆς ἵδρυται: the site of this *temenos* of Aiakos has recently been fixed with virtual certainty, thanks to work prompted by an important epigraphic discovery. It was on the south side of the agora, next to the south stoa and not far from the council-chamber or *bouleuterion* (it is no. 13 on the excellent American School Athenian agora website. The relevant building was previously identified as the Heliaia or Law-court). See above all Stroud 1998: 85–104. It appears to have had no roof or door in 374/3 BC, judging from the new text, an inscribed law of that year taxing Lemnos etc., R/O no. 26 (*SEG* 48.96) lines 14–16, where it is stipulated that grain shall be piled up in the Aiakeion and that the city will make available the Aiakeion στέγον δὲ καὶ τεθυρωμένον. The physically minimal state of the *temenos* would help to explain why it survived the Persian sack of 480. Intriguingly, it seems that the marble used was the same as that used for the Aiakeion on Aigina itself, which it resembled in other ways also (Stroud 1998: 101).

This *temenos* (precinct), unusually, did not purport to contain the hero's tomb or remains. For the hero-cult of Aiakos see **67**.2n. on οἱ δὲ Θηβαῖοι ἔδοσαν; Kearns 1989: 47. Paus. 2.29.8 implies that the Aiginetans kept it a secret that an altar in their territory was the tomb of Aiakos: they anticipated an attempt to remove the bones. See also Nagy 1990: 178; Parker 2010: 133 and n. 18.

For another reference to a topographic feature of Athens still visible in Hdt.'s day see **77**.3, καὶ ἐς ἐμέ ... and n. (neither passage is much use for reconstructing Hdt.'s biography). The reference here to the continued existence of the *temenos* of Aiakos down to Hdt.'s own time has been thought a way of saying that it was surprising that the cult of an Aiginetan hero should have survived the long period of hostility between the Athenians and Aiginetans (so Nenci). But that is not how Greek religion worked: continuance of the cult of a powerful hero is not surprising at all. Rather, its discontinuance could be dangerous. Of the two explanations offered by Stroud (1998: 102) for the at first sight startling use of a centrally located sacred place as a grain dump, the first (Aiakos was a suitable hero to mind the grain because he saved the world from famine, cf. Gantz 1993: 221) is more attractive than the second (Aiakos' Athenian worship had come to an end by the 370s). See Kowalzig 2007: 211–13, explaining Athenian-Aiginetan mythical rivalry in terms of historical competition over the 'grain-chain'.

90–93 *The Spartans propose to intervene at Athens again but fail*

The narrative introduction (**90–91**.1) and the Spartan address to their allies in direct speech (**91**.2–3) are to a large extent recapitulatory, in that they recycle material familiar from the middle part of the bk. ('almost as if they have "read the text"', as Moles 2007: 247 puts it). The main new elements are (1) stress on Spartan resentment at Athenian 'ingratitude', and (2) the oracles at **90**.2, an item held back from **72**.This volume of thematic repetition makes the innovative long story-telling speech of Soklees (**92**) stand out by contrast. Then follows a short indirect speech by Hippias (**93**.1), so that we have a triad of speeches, the first two in direct speech, the third in indirect. **91–93** is a 'challenge-response-synthesis' triad; it resembles 3.80–2, the Persian debate, in having three separate speakers ABC, not AB (Lang 1984: 104–5). Nevertheless, Soklees' vast speech (see introd. n. on **92**) is the dominant member of the three and could stand on its own as an attractive recitation unit; see **92** γ 1n. on δέκα.

90.1 ἐκ Λακεδαιμονίων πρῆγμα ἐγειρόμενον ἐμπόδιον ἐγένετο 'trouble arose from Sparta and prevented them' from taking revenge on the Aiginetans (lit. 'trouble, arising from the Spartans, was an obstacle'). Hdt. is here using a kind of 'break-off' formula to dramatise the multi-directional threats faced by the Athenians. He will resume the story of Aiginetan/Athenian relations at 6.49.1.   μεμηχανημένα: the verb is picked up from **62**.2 above. See n. there.   ὅτι τε ἄνδρας ξείνους σφίσι ἐόντας: this virtually repeats **63**.2, which was also explicitly Spartan-focalised.   καὶ ὅτι ταῦτα ποιήσασι χάρις οὐδεμία ἐφαίνετο πρὸς Ἀθηναίων: this – unlike much in the present section – is a new notion, but not a surprising one. Hand in hand with reciprocity (**79**.1n.) goes expectation of gratitude for benefits. For Spartan foreign policy methods see Th. 1.19, making clear what Spartans meant by 'gratitude', and from whom they expected it: 'they took care that [their allies] should be governed by oligarchies in the exclusive interest of Sparta', κατ' ὀλιγαρχίαν δὲ σφίσιν αὐτοῖς μόνον ἐπιτηδείως ὅπως πολιτεύσουσι θεραπεύοντες.

90.2 τοὺς χρησμούς, τοὺς ἔκτηντο πρότερον οἱ Πεισιστρατίδαι, ἐξελαυνόμενοι δὲ ἔλιπον ἐν τῶι ἱρῶι: cf. the way Greek hexameter oracles were kept on the Capitol at Rome in the regal period, and for the same probable reason: it was 'almost the only secure place of storage' (Parke 1988: 77).

Peisistratos and his sons were keenly interested in oracles and divination generally, but of a non-Delphic sort (see Lewis and Parker below). The sequence perhaps starts with the portentous sacrifice made by Peisistratos' father Hippokrates at Olympia: 1.59.1–2. Then see 1.62.4–63.1 for the inspired utterance, delivered to Peisistratos θείηι πομπῆι, by Amphilytos the Akarnanian before the battle of Pallene (with Flower 2008: 79); also 1.64.2, Peisistratos 'purified' Delos ἐκ τῶν λογίων; **56**.2 for Hipparchos and the ὀνειροπόλοι; 6.107–8.1, Hippias' prophetic dream before Marathon; and esp. the partly retrospective story at 7.6.3–5 of Peisistratid dealings with Onomakritos. See Lewis *CAH* 4² (1988) 297; Parker 1996: 87 and nn. (Peisistratos' nickname 'Bakis'; no public consultation of Delphi, at least in later Peisistratid period); Eidinow 2007: 29 and nn. The resumption in bks. 5–6 of themes from bk. 1 is, as often, noticeable.

Many less well documented Greek tyrants and aristocrats at this period – and their non-Greek imitators like Kroisos, 1.46 – went in for both informal divination and formal consultation of oracular sanctuaries. (At **92** ε 2 below, the Korinthian Kypselos consults the Pythia at Delphi, at **92** η 2, his son Periandros consulted the Oracle of the Dead at Ephyra (see nn. on **92** η for the reason), and Kleisthenes of Sikyon was presumably not expecting the rebuff he received when he approached the Pythia at **67**.2; see also Schachter 1994 for elite Athenians at the Boiotian oracular sanctuary of the Ptoion.) But Hdt. in his handling of the Peisistratids stresses this motif with particular insistence: **93**.2 is explicit that Hippias' knowledge of oracles was exceptionally good.

90.2 (cont.) καταλειφθέντας δὲ ὁ Κλεομένης ἀνέλαβε: this must have been during his visit at **72**.3–4, the occasion of his verbal duel with the priestess, but Hdt. reserves it for now. It looks forward as well as back, because there is a heavy concentration of oracular material in what follows, culminating in the remark about Hippias at **93**.2.

91.1 οἱ Λακεδαιμόνιοι 'the Spartans', and so throughout this section. That is, Kleomenes – who was mentioned at **90**.2, but only analeptically – is not the speaker or agent in what follows, though it is sometimes assumed that he must be. On the contrary, the other Spartans were now seeking to reverse Kleomenes' expulsion of Hippias. (See Ste. Croix 2004b:

424.) Indeed Kleomenes disappears now entirely from Hdt.'s narrative until 6.50, when he acts against Aiginetan medisers, and is given a full formal 'introduction' with patronymic and title. (97.1 is a mere analeptic and recapitulatory reference to his dismissal of Aristagoras.) ὥρων αὐξομένους: with this (and 91.2, δόξαν δὲ φύσας αὐξάνεται) cf. Th. 1.23.6: Athenian expansion, and Spartan fear of it, as the 'truest cause', the ἀληθεστάτη πρόφασις, of the Peloponnesian War (for the exact verb of 'growing', cf. Th. 1.89.1, the Athenians ἦλθον ἐπὶ τὰ πράγματα ἐν οἷς ηὐξήθησαν). For these intertexts, see Wecowski 1996: 246 and n. 125.   ἐλεύθερον μέν...κατεχόμενον δὲ ὑπὸ τυραννίδος: the balance and contrast reproduce, from a Spartan perspective, the thought, though not the language, of the authorial ch. 78.   μετεπέμποντο Ἱππίην τὸν Πεισιστράτου ἀπὸ Σιγείου τοῦ ἐν Ἑλλησπόντωι: see 65.3 for 'Sigeion on the Skamandros' as the Peisistratid refuge, but the full story of Sigeion is reserved for 94. Strictly neither specification is needed, patronym or location in the Hellespont, but the moment is a solemn one.

For the singular Hippias (not 'the Peisistratidai') see 63.2n. on ἐξελῶντα Πεισιστρατίδας. The Spartans sent for him, not the whole family, but this enables Hdt. to put Hippias under the spotlight in 93–4.

91.2 ἄνδρες σύμμαχοι...: at fifteen lines this speech is about the same length as Megabyzos' advocacy of oligarchy at 3.81, and nothing like as short as the Spartan Kleomenes' three-line reply to Aristagoras at 50.3. Not, therefore, specially brief or 'laconic' (as claimed by Moles 2007: 247), except perhaps by comparison with Soklees; and the rhetoric is cleverly manipulative. It takes an outstanding and unusual reply by Soklees the Korinthian to defeat it.   συγγινώσκομεν αὐτοῖσι ἡμῖν οὐ ποιήσασι ὀρθῶς 'we admit that we did wrong'. The opening verb, when it means to admit or confess something, usually takes the infinitive (as, twice, at 6.92.2), but the accumulated datives here provide the emphasis of reiteration.   κιβδήλοισι: for this word used of 'counterfeit' oracles, see 1.66.3 and 1.75.2 (the only other instances in Hdt. of this word, which he never uses *except* of oracles), with Kurke 2009, who argues that the numismatic metaphor should be taken seriously (see also Kroll 2000: 89). The first of the three oracles, that which concerned Tegea, is particularly important because it involved the Spartans in a policy mistake, just as here, and so constitutes yet another pairing between bks. 1 and 5. But in bk. 1 the word means 'deceptive' whereas here it means 'spurious' (Powell). The problem with the bk. 5 oracle is not one of faulty interpretation but of bribery. δήμωι ἀχαρίστωι: cf. Gelon on the *demos* at 7.156.3 (with Gray 1996: 384). ἐλευθερωθεὶς ἀνέκυψε: this choice of verb (including the syllable -κυψ) hints that the liberated Athenians went on to do a Κύψελος i.e. behave tyrannically themselves in their 5th cent. empire (Gray 1996: 386; Dewald

2003: 31). There may also be an echo of 3.82.4, the Constitutions Debate, συγκύψαντες, and the mentions of *hubris* at 3.80.2. and 81.1, with which compare περιυβρίσας here.   **δόξαν δὲ φύσας αὐξάνεται** 'their pride has grown along with their power', lit. 'it [the *demos*] increases, after generating pride'.

91.3 ἐπείτε δὲ ἐκεῖνα ποιήσαντες ἡμάρτομεν, νῦν πειρησόμεθά σφεα ἅμα ὑμῖν ἀκεόμενοι 'when we did that we made an error, and we will now, with your help, try to remedy it'. Cf. 1.167.2, βουλόμενοι ἀκέσασθαι τῆν ἁμαρτάδα. The rhetoric for this intended U-turn is excellent.   **ἀποδῶμεν τά καὶ ἀπειλόμεθα**: 'give back what we took away'.

92 The long narrative speech of Soklees

Hdt.'s decision to use an otherwise unknown but (we are invited to believe) astonishingly gifted Korinthian narrator to provide his hearers and readers with so much material about the Kypselid tyranny is extraordinary, especially when we consider the context. (For the tyranny, see below.) Soklees is supposed to be addressing an army, which then sits down and listens to a story about a baby being passed from hand to hand, etc. To appreciate the full flavour, one only has to imagine by contrast what a Thucydidean speech delivered in such circumstances would look like. It, too, would be long (Soklees' speech is the longest in Hdt.); but it would also be difficult, full of abstractions and generalisations, of which there are few traces in Hdt. 5.92 apart from the gnomic τοῦ οὔτε ἀδικώτερον...at **92 α 1.** Conversely, there would be less use of past or mythical paradigms, whereas virtually all of Soklees' speech is one very long paradigm. The Plataian-Theban exchange at Th. 3.53–67 comes closest in that respect because it proceeds largely by an examination of the past record of each side, indeed 3.55.1 recycles factual 6th-cent. material from Hdt. 6.108; and at Th. 1.41.2 some later Korinthian compatriots of Soklees appeal to the Athenians by invoking their own past benefactions involving Aigina and Samos.

The only comparable speech in Hdt. himself is the shorter 6.86 (the story of Glaukos). Both stories involve traffic between the Peloponnese and Miletos (see **92 ζ 1**ff. for Thrasyboulos the tyrant of Miletos), and this may be no accident in view of the recent visit to the Peloponnese of the Milesian ex-tyrant Aristagores, a man we are not meant to forget for long.

The exceptional length of the speech needs an explanation. Hdt. was emphasising the moment as a historical hinge: this was the last opportunity when another Greek state or coalition of states could have put a stop to the growth of self-confident democratic Athens, whose policies would affect so many lives in the next decades. In fact, there was no terminal Athenian break with the Spartans because the two *poleis* fought alongside each other in the Persian wars (with some friction), and remained allies until the late 460s.

The obvious precedent for such 'story-telling speeches' (as they are called by Johnson 2001) is Homer, esp. *Il.* 9.530 for Phoinix' story of Meleagros and Kleopatre. But epinikian poetry, with its use of exemplary and warning figures, not all of them mythical, should also be borne in mind. Pind. *Pyth.* 2 offers Ixion as a negative model for the kingship of Hiero of Syracuse, and *Pyth.* 1.94–6 opposes good Kroisos and bad Phalaris of Akragas, two real-life autocrats from the mid 6th cent.

The desire to explain the name Κύψελος (**92** ε 1 and n.) is part of the motive for the elaboration of this section of the story; cf. introd. n. to **79–89**, motive (4).

Structurally, the present exploration of tyranny comes at a pause point, like two other tyranny sections, the story of Deiokes in bk. 1 and the Constitutional Debate in bk. 3; so Dewald 2003: 32. It is also a further retardation of the moment when the rebellious Ionians and their allies will finally come to blows with the Persians: like Homer, Hdt. is 'ever fertile in means of retarding his climaxes' (West 2011a: 373, on the *Iliad*, and for retardation in Homer see also Nünlist 2009; 78, 151).

From another point of view, it continues and partly elucidates a rich but intermittently presented sequence of Kypselid material which began very early in the *Histories*: Kypselos is introduced at 1.14.2: Gyges' dedications are not really in the Korinthian treasury, but in that of 'Kypselos son of Eetion' (not called a tyrant). Then (1.20) comes the guest-friendship between Kypselos' son Periandros (not called tyrant) and the tyrant (τυραννεύοντι) Thrasyboulos of Miletos, which caused Periandros to send a helpful message to Thrasyboulos (this anticipates the present passage, except that at **92** ζ-η 1 Thrasyboulos does a good turn to Periandros, i.e. 1.20 is a return favour). Next, Arion and his dolphin (1.23–4) are attached to their Lydian context by means of Periandros (see de Jong 2001: 95, also Myres 1953: 83, 'he will see justice done to a Lesbian, even if the villains are Corinthian'); and here the Kypselids' tyranny is mentioned, ἐτυράννευε, 1.23.1. After that there is a long gap until 3.48–53, the narrative of Periandros, his son Lykophron, and the Kerkyraians. (3.50.1–3, describing Periandros' killing of Melissa, his wife and the mother of Lykophron, and Lykophron's reaction, are important for present purposes, as complementing and preparing for **92**.The fact of her killing is not repeated at **92** η, where Periandros' offences against her are necrophilia and failure to give proper burial, indignities which in their turn retrospectively deepen our understanding of Lykophron's sense of outrage in bk. 3.) Looking forward in bk. 5, at **95**.2, Periandros the Sage arbitrates between the Mytilenaians and Athenians, very soon after we have shuddered at him as necrophiliac monster. There is no Kypselid or other Korinthian suitor at the betrothal of Agariste of Sikyon near the end of bk. 6; but the initially successful Hippokleides of Athens is 'related by descent to the Kypselids of Korinth', 6.128.2; for another elite Athenian 'Miltiades son of Kypselos' see 6.34.1.

In its more local context (the central part of the *Histories*), the Kypselid tyrannical material balances that about the Peisistratids and about Kleisthenes of Sikyon earlier in bk. 5 and at the end of bk. 6. The rule of the Peisistratids became 'more of a tyranny' after the murder of Hipparchos (55), and Periandros' rule also changed for the worse after a good start: 92 ζ 1. Within the Ionian revolt narrative, the rejection of tyranny in favour of freedom (see 93.2n. on ἐλευθέρως) has obvious general relevance to the situation of the east Greeks after 500 (see 37.2n. on ὡς ἂν ἔκοντες...), and the reluctance of the Milesians to oblige the Chians by taking back a tyrant after having once tasted ἐλευθερία (6. 5.1) has some parallels with the situation of the Athenians, the Spartans and Hippias, except that the Athenians, unlike the Milesians, play no direct role in their own escape from a renewal of tyranny.

A much favoured modern line of interpretation takes its cue from Hippias' prediction at 93.1 that the Korinthians would one day miss the Peisistratids, and argues that Hdt. here, through the mouth of Hippias, anticipates tensions which would become acute only in the Periklean period. On this view, Soklees' speech is actually less important than what frames it. Strasburger (below) even dismissed Soklees' speech as a mere repetition of what had been said about tyranny in more lapidary form at 3.80. Other and more recent inquirers have extended this line of analysis ('irony') so as to include 92 and Soklees' speech itself. To be sure, there is an obvious irony in having a late 6th-cent. Korinthian performing a restraining function (Soklees stops the Spartans from attacking Athens), in view of the role played by the Korinthians in precipitating the main Peloponnesian war of 431–404 (they urged the Spartans to attack Athens). There is, however, a risk of over-interpretation in some of this. First, we do not need to go down as far as the 430s to find strong enmity between Korinthians and Athenians: Th. dates the start of the 'vehement hatred' between them to the 460s (1.103.5; cf. Baragwanath 2012: 46f.). Second, the concept of 'irony' can be made to work too hard (Gould). In any case, if the Korinthians really did stop the Spartans in 506, the basic irony is one of history, not of Hdt.'s creation, though, to be sure, Hdt. chose what to record and how to arrange it. (For the 'favoured line' see esp. Strasburger 1982: 601, 607–10, 617–18 [= Marg 1965: 583, 589–92, 599–600, but originally 1955]; Dewald 2003: 30–2; Gray 1996; Wecowski 1996; Johnson 2001; Fowler 2003a: 310–13; Giangiulio 2005: 100–1; Pelling 2006: 101–3 and 2007: 106–8; Moles 2002: 40 and 2007. For reservations, see Gould 1989: 118–20, a lively protest against seeing Hdt.'s text as a mere set of coded messages for his contemporaries, and Fowler 2003a: 312–13.)

Much of Soklees' speech is about what has been called 'the *internal* impact of a tyrant, in this case the outrages committed by Cypselus and Periander against their fellow-citizens' (Pelling 2006: 107). On the other hand, there is a foreign policy aspect as well. The advice given by Thrasyboulos of Miletos to Periandros (his 'special guest-friend' as we were told as early as 1.20) makes the point that tyrants stick together, even across long geographical distances: allow in a tyrant, and you do not land yourselves with just one, or with just one family, but you risk having to cope with an entire international network. Hdt. himself at 8.142.5 makes the Spartans say 'tyrants collaborate with tyrants' (cf. Gray 1996: 384).

Some supposed inconsistencies in the speech – which argues against tyranny but with (it has been thought) apparent uncertainty of touch and wobbling over detail – are either not serious or can even be explained away completely. It is not necessary or desirable to think in terms of imperfectly reconciled oral sources. Delphi might have been such a source, but is not a solution, and perhaps there is no problem in need of one.

Attempts to extract Hdt.'s own views about tyranny or anything else from the particular arguments in the speech are misguided. It is rhetoric, not a personal authorial manifesto. No responsible political scientist uses Th.'s speeches in this way, and Hdt.'s ability to construct τὰ δέοντα – to use the language of Th. 1.22.1 to describe what was rhetorically necessary or appropriate – should also be respected (Versnel 2011: 531 notwithstanding. Hdt.'s views can never be straightforwardly identified with those of his speakers: Munson 2001b).

For the historical value of the material in **92** see introd. n. on **92** β 1–η 4.

92.1 οἱ μὲν νυν ἄλλοι ἡσυχίην ἦγον, Κορίνθιος δέ...: this focussing device ('all the others kept silent; but so-and-so...') is Homeric: see e.g. *Od.* 8.532–3. Hdt. uses it again at 7.10.1 ('the other Persians were silent, but Artabanos...') with Johnson 2001: 7, and cf. Th. 5.27.2, where, as it happens, the exception is again Korinthian ('the others went home, but the Korinthians...') with *CT* III: 60. Cf. Gray 1996: 383 n. 53, Moles 2007: 248 n. 22 and Pelling 2006: 101 and n. 68.   **Σωκλέης**: the name, which is not a rare one generally in the Peloponnese (*LGPN* IIIA no. 16, listing him under Σωκλῆς), is given as Σωσικλέης in one group of MSS, including the Parisinus, and this is still preferred by some commentators (and by Rosén); but Σωκλέης has better MS authority (and is the reading of *P. Oxy.* 1012 fr. 9.55), is what Plutarch's MSS read (*Mor.* 86of), and is attested at Korinth on a vase of the 7th or 6th cents. BC: Amyx 1988: 595, no. Gr. 5a line 4 (= *LGPN* no. 15). So maybe this man did exist and speak, though we cannot say if he was really a narrator in the Hdt. class. At **93**.1, he will be described as ἀπὸ Κορίνθου πρεσβεύων. Moles 2002: 40 and 2007: 264 sees Soklees as a speaking name ('saver-of-fame' – his own fame, and that of the tyrant-hating Spartans), and this cannot be excluded, but such onomastic arguments ought always to consider area-specific frequency of attestation.

92 α 1 ἢ δή: an epic opening formula, cf. e.g. *Il.* 1.518 (Zeus addresses Thetis), as noted by Pelling 2006: 101–2 and n. 69.   ἄνθρωποι νομόν ἐν θαλάσσηι ἕξουσι καὶ ἰχθύες τὸν πρότερον ἄνθρωποι 'men will dwell (lit. 'have their province', note the accent: not νόμον) in the sea, and fishes will change places with men'. πρότερον is adverbial, and τόν is relative, lit. 'and fishes (will have) that thing (the province) which previously men (had)'. The *adynaton* or 'when pigs have wings' motif was a favourite in Greek literature of all periods, and no doubt in popular speech as well; see esp. Archil. fr. 122 W² lines 7–9 on dolphins changing places with wild beasts, from which Hdt. perhaps took the word νομόν (μηδ᾽ ἐὰν δελφῖσι θῆρες ἀνταμείψωνται νομόν | ἐνάλιον). See also Theok. *Id.* 1.134ff. with Gow's n., and Lykoph. *Alex.* 83–4 (land-sea reversals at the time of the great flood); and Verg. *Ecl.* 1.59–60 (with Coleman 1977: 85) is close to the present passage. A related but distinct type of explicit or implied *adynaton* is that used in solemn oaths and treaties – 'until this metal weight floats to the surface', 'as long as the earth stands firm/the sun stays in the same course' – as at 1.165.3, 4.201.2–3 and 8.143.2; see Wecowski 1996: 212–14. Cf. Hor. *Epod.* 16 lines 25ff.   ἰσοκρατίας καταλύοντες τυραννίδας ἐς τὰς πόλεις κατάγειν παρασκευάζεσθε: *isokratia* is broader than 'democracy' (a word significantly avoided by Soklees) and covers any form of government opposed to tyranny, the Spartans' own system included. Cf. Ostwald 2009b: 37, but it does not mean anything so precise as a bicameral system of council and assembly. The implied claim here, that the Spartans were antipathetic to tyranny, has been thought wrong or at best anachronistic, a reflection of the mood in the run-up to 431, when some later Korinthian speakers appealed to the Spartans against the 'tyrant city' Athens (Th. 1.122.3). It is true that the 'tradition of Spartan opposition to tyranny abroad, despite Thucydides (1.18.1), is of dubious historicity' (Johnson 2001: 11; cf. *CT* I: 51 citing Bernhardt 1987). But we must remember that Soklees is offering not history but would-be persuasive rhetoric. In particular (a) the recent and spectacular Spartan deposition of the Athenian Hippias is quite enough to form the grounds for a generalisation, and it is clever of Soklees to ignore what the Spartans have just said about the 'counterfeit oracles' of **91**.2 (not to mention the anti-Argive and anti-Persian aspects to the deposition of Hippias, for which see **62**.1n.) and instead give the Spartans credit, by implication, for ideologically principled action. This leads to (b): Soklees, whose audience is the Spartans as well as their allies, does well to flatter the Spartans by pretending to be shocked at their temporary deviation from noble anti-tyrannical attitudes. See above, introd. n. on 92, on the general question of 'irony' i.e. implied awareness by Hdt. of much later developments.   τοῦ οὔτε ἀδικώτερόν ἐστι οὐδὲν κατ' ἀνθρώπους οὔτε μιαιφονώτερον: for this type of gnomic political expression, which tends to be found in speeches i.e. heavily rhetorical contexts, cf. Megabyzos at Hdt. 3.81.1 (ὁμίλου γὰρ ἀχρηίου οὐδέν ἐστι ἀξυνετώτερον οὐδὲ ὑβριστότερον, cf. also Otanes at 80.5 ἀναρμοστότατον δὲ πάντων), and the Theban speakers at Th. 3.62.3, describing their city's Persian Wars regime: we were ruled, they say, by a narrow family clique, than which nothing is more opposed to law and moderate government, or is closer to tyranny.

For Periandros as more bloodthirsty than Kypselos, Κυψέλου μιαιφονώτερος, see below, ζ 1.

92 α 2 παραχρᾶσθε ἐς τοὺς συμμάχους: 'you are indifferent to your allies'. **εἰ δὲ αὐτῶν ἔμπειροι ἔατε** 'if you had experience of them' sc. 'of tyrants'; see app. crit. and Wilson for the text (the MSS have the emphatic αὐτοί, as in the preceding sentence, but this is less apt here). The verb is from εἰμί (the Attic form of the 2nd pers. pl. impf. would be ἦτε).

92 β 1–η 4 *The Kypselids*

The central, narrative, part of the speech falls into two halves, the stories of Kypselos, and then of his son and successor Periandros. Both concentrate on short episodes (one for Kypselos, two for Periandros), with only a minimum of linkage and of more general information and comment. The Kypselos-as-baby narrative belongs to a category of more or less miraculous stories in which special infants are saved from death by exposure, or at the hands of jealous would-be killers, because they are reserved for future greatness or at least prominence, sometimes sinister, sometimes not. See Binder 1964 with Murray 1967 and 2001: 30; Wesselmann 2011: 201–26, and chart of standard narrative features at 205. Thus in Hdt. himself, there are clear parallels with Kyros at 1.108ff. (Murray 2001: 38, Gray 1996: 367–8 and others); outside Hdt. there are Oidipous, Paris, Moses, Sargon, Romulus and Remus, Jesus Christ (saved from Herod). Often the reason for the attempted violence is an oracle or other supernatural prediction. For further parallels between the Kypselids and the mythical stories of Oidipous and his family (physical disabilities, sexually transgressive behaviour) see Vernant 1982; see also Lightfoot 1999: 484f. (discussing Parthenios *Erotika pathemata* no. XVII, a late Hellenistic fictional story which explains Periandros' character-deterioration in terms of the effects of his incest with his mother, not of his association with Thrasyboulos).

As for the historicity of the material, it will be seen (next n.) that much of the other literary evidence for the Kypselids of Korinth is late and unreliable. This leaves Hdt. as the prime source for the dynasty, and he is so treated by e.g. Salmon 1984 and by many other historians. But the three stories which Hdt. tells through the mouth of Soklees are in many respects 'roving anecdotes', or else conform to mythical patterns. Kypselos' seizure of power took place more than two hundred years before Hdt. can be supposed to have been gathering and shaping his information, and the dynasty lasted for only three-quarters of a century after that. The long time-lag imposed huge difficulties on him – especially with regard to the reign of Kypselos. (This particular asymmetry is reflected in his distribution of attention: not only is there the 1:2 ratio mentioned above, but the Kypselid material in bks. 1 and 3 all relates to Periandros, not his father.) Roving anecdotes have their uses for the historian, but in the severely limited respect that they assign a man to a category: that is how Periandros was perceived and remembered. We can safely believe that Kypselos was a mixture of insider and outsider, and that this combination enabled him to overthrow the Bacchiads; that Delphi (with which Kypselos at least was on good terms) played a decisive role by turning against the Bacchiads but then also and later against the Kypselids; that both Kypselos and Periandros retained power by savage repression of the old elite; that Periandros had cordial relations with another autocrat, Thrasyboulos of Miletos; and that he confused sex and the exercise of power. Smiling babies, vandalised corn-fields, and naked shivering female ghosts are illustrative, and their truth is symbolic not literal. Soklees' speech is 'a creation, not a recollection' (Fowler 2003a: 312); it is one long *paradeigma* (illustrative story about the past). Since such stories were often, in the poets, taken from myth (Nünlist 2009: 261–4), the audience would not have been surprised to find mythical features in the narrative.

92 β 1 ἦν ὀλιγαρχίη, καὶ οὗτοι Βακχιάδαι καλεόμενοι ἔνεμον τὴν πόλιν, ἐδί-δοσαν δὲ καὶ ἤγοντο ἐξ ἀλλήλων: Hude obelised οὗτοι, but Rosén reasonably explains it as referring to the implied ὀλίγοι in ὀλιγαρχίη. For the language used here for intermarriage ('they gave and they led away'), cf. Th. 8.21: after a revolution at Samos in 412, the wealthy *geomoroi* or 'landholders' are henceforth forbidden οὔτε ἐκδοῦναι οὐδ' ἀγαγέσθαι παρ' ἐκείνων, where the last two words refer to the *demos*. Cf. also the marriage stipulations, using διδόναι and λαμβάνειν in the marital sense, at *SEG* 47.1563 (4th-cent. treaty from Karia) 21–5, with van Bremen 2003: 316.

On the present passage, see Gernet 1981: 293–4: tyrants tended to marry each others' daughters, but the Bacchiads were endogamic. The breakdown of the old closed endogamic marriage system led to the establishment of the tyranny.

On the Bacchiads generally see Oost 1972 and Salmon 1984: 55–74. Our detailed knowledge – such as it is – is derived from sources later and less reliable than Hdt., esp. Diodorus (7.9.6) and Nikolaos of Damascus in the time of Augustus (*FGrHist* 90 F 57, on Kypselos' rise to power but naturally including Bacchiad material), both of whom drew on the 4th-cent. Ephoros (*FGrHist* 70). But despite Hdt.'s picture of paranoid Bacchiad insularity, the main achievement of the archaic Korinthians, their important colonies at Syracuse (733) and Kerkyra (733 or 706), took place under the Bacchiad regime and with Bacchiad oikists or founders (Salmon 1984: 65 and n. 40); the third great colony, Potidaia, dates from the time of Periandros. As Strabo put it, the Bacchiads 'reaped the harvest of commerce unstintingly': 8.1.20. Korinth controlled two great passages, the north-south land-route via the Isthmus which joined the Peloponnese to central Greece; and the east-west sea-route: the harbours of Lechaion in the west and Kenchreai in the east were connected by the stone *diolkos* or pathway, a sensational engineering feat of the Bacchiad period. Cargoes and even light ships could be hauled along it.

The Bacchiads were preceded by a hereditary monarchy which fell in about the mid 8th cent. (Salmon 1984: 56). Ancient literary evidence for the chronology of the Kypselids who succeeded them is not unanimous, but epigraphic evidence has settled the matter in favour of the traditional and higher chronology for the whole tyranny, *c.* 657–584. (Arist. *Pol.* 1315b22ff. gives the total period of the tyranny as seventy-three years and six months: thirty for Kypselos – this is from **92 ζ 1**; forty years and six months for Periandros; three for Psammetichos son of Gorgos). The traditional start date of 657, at e.g. Diod. 7.9.3, has no precise validity (Jacoby 1902: 151–5), but a mid 7th-cent date is about right. Decisive for the higher chronology is the Athenian archon list which gives Kyphselos [sic], surely grandson of the Korinthian tyrant, as archon in 597; see ML: p. 11 (and Oost 1972: 16 n. 26), cf. Hdt. 6.34.1 for the Athenian Miltiades son of Kypselos who must be son of the archon.

On Kypselos and his overthrow of the Bacchiads, see Salmon 1984: 186–95 (Periandros will be dealt with separately below). Nikolaos' statement (*FGrHist* 90 F 57 para. 5) that Kypselos was a *polemarchos*, and acquired popularity in that office through the manner in which he exercised his judicial powers, is unusable. It is surely contaminated by the much later role of the *polemarchos* as a judicial magistrate at e.g. Athens; see ML: 31 lines 9–10 (460s). Aristotle, too, struggled to find hard evidence for the archaic tyrants, and was unduly, though not uncritically, influenced by tyrants of his own 4th-cent. day, above all the Sicilian Dionysios I, of whom his own teacher Plato had such bitter experience (for salutary remarks about the dubious utility of such 4th-cent. analyses, see Osborne 2009: 182). At *Pol.* 1310b29, Aristotle ascribes Kypselos' success to his 'demagogy', bracketing him with Peisistratos and – suspiciously – Dionysios. Attempts to make Kypselos a beneficiary of a 7th-cent 'hoplite revolution' in warfare find no more support than do similar attempts to explain other early Greek tyrannies. In particular, the military historian Th. knows of no such general linkage (1.13.1; so rightly Cawkwell 2011: 47–8, in the course of an attack on this 'hoplite theory' of tyranny). Aristotle says (*Pol.* 1315b28) that Kypselos 'had no bodyguard' (he was ἀδορυφόρητος, lit. 'without spear-bearers'), and this ought to have knocked any military theory on the head; it shows that Aristotle realised that there were limits to the viability of his own 4th-cent. model. (At **92 η 3**, Periandros has a bodyguard, but he was agreed to have been worse and more aggressive than his father.)

In conclusion, we cannot say how or why Kypselos succeeded in toppling the Bacchiads, except that it is a plausible bet that he exploited their unpopularity and perhaps disunity, and had some moral help from Delphi: Aristotle shrewdly remarked that 'an oligarchy which is at unity is not easily destroyed from within' (*Pol.* 1306a9–10): Hdt. shows that Kypselos' maternal grandfather Amphion, at least, was a Bacchiad insider, and 'Cypselus the Bacchiad' is the provocative title of Oost 1972.

92 β 1 (cont.) θυγάτηρ χωλή· οὔνομα δέ οἱ ἦν Λάβδα: the marginal status of Labda is relevant to Kypselos' story. Her name may suggest the crooked Greek letter la(m)bda and thus also her physical condition. For the motif of the physical defect which marks out the future autocrat see Ogden 1997, esp. 87–94 for Kypselos. But in Hdt. it is Kypselos' mother who is lame. (Ogden 90 ingeniously but implausibly argues that Kypselos himself was lame: κύψελος is a martin, see below ε 1n., and this bird is said by Aristotle, *Hist. an.* 618a31, to have another name, the 'footless one', ἄπους.)

It is possible but unnecessary to see a metaphor here, rather than literal lameness: having married 'outside' (or 'married out', as we would say), the girl came to be called 'the lame one'. Gernet 1981: 293 (cf. also Vernant 1982: 26). It has been intriguingly suggested that the deformities of the feet of some of the dancers depicted on Korinthian archaic vases are subversive, an anti-tyrannical allusion to Kypselid deformity: Ziskowski 2012.

92 β 1 (cont.) Ἠετίων ὁ Ἐχεκράτεος, δήμου μὲν ἐὼν ἐκ Πέτρης: 'Eetion son of Echekrates, a commoner from Petra'. For this as the right meaning of δήμου μὲν ἐών, see Powell 1935: 159.

The name Echekrates and derivatives such as Echekratidas are not rare in the Peloponnese (sixteen bearers of all periods in *LGPN* IIIA), and are specially common in Thessaly. The Lapith Echekrates may have belonged to the ruling house of Thessalian Larisa: Sordi 1958: 26 n. 2 (cf. Vannicelli 1993: 118 n. 32). For Lapiths see below.

Eetion is listed in *LGPN* IIIA in the form Ἀετίων. There are several other historical bearers of this name (in *LGPN* I, there are a Rhodian and a Samian, both Hellenistic, and an Αἰετίων from Delos, 364/3 BC; in VA there is another Ἀετίων from Pontus, 1st cent. BC). Andromache's father and other Homeric bearers of the name Ἠετίων are all connected with Troy; see Graziosi and Haubold 2010: 190 on *Il.* 6.395 (and cf. Jacoby on *FGrHist* 328 F 72 for the mythical Athenian Eetion who gave his name to Eetioneia in Piraieus). They cite von Kamptz 1982: 135 and 372 for the non-Greekness of the name, but he ignored Hdt.'s Eetion and the other epigraphically attested names cited above. Note in any case that Quint. Smyrn. 6.639 has an Eetion on the Greek side at Troy.

As for the etymology, the Delphic oracle (below, β 3) treated it as a Vogelname or 'bird name' (from 'eagle', ἀετός, epic and Ionic αἰετός), like that of Kypselos himself. But this is considered by the experts to be false etymology: Patrick James, to whom (and to Anne Thompson) I am indebted for help with this point, tells me that Ionic eta cannot correspond to a long alpha in Attic that has developed relatively recently.

92 β 1 (cont.) ἀτὰρ τὰ ἀνέκαθεν Λαπίθης τε καὶ Καινείδης: for the favourite formula in ἀνέκαθεν see **55**n. The Lapiths were pre-Greeks from Thessaly, and 'descendants of Kaineus' are a sub-set, because of the Lapith leader Kaineus (or in female form Kainis); see Hom. *Il.* 1.264 and Gantz 1993: 277–81 and *OCD*[4] 'centaurs'. There may (Gray 1996: 374) be a hint at the root for 'slaughter', καίνειν.

The link between the Kypselids and the Athenian family of Hippokleides, a link which so impressed Kleisthenes of Sikyon (6.128.2), has a bearing on the present passage. The mythical ancestor of the family of the famous Miltiades and Kimon (to which Hippokleides also belonged) was Philaios, who was grandson of the Lapith Koronos: Steph. Byz. Φιλαί-δαι. See Toepffer 1889: 276 and Thomas 1989: 167 n. 28. It has been suggested that this mythical connection was manufactured at the time of the 6th-cent. marriage between an older Miltiades and a daughter of the Korinthian Kypselos (cf. Hdt. 6.34.1 for Miltiades son of Kypselos); see Davies *APF*: 295.

92 β 2 ἐστάλη: 'he set out for' his destination.   **περὶ γόνου:** see **82**.1n. for oracular consultations about fertility and children.   **ἰθέως** 'immediately', i.e. before he had had time to put his question. Compare 1.65.2: as soon as Lykourgos entered the *megaron*, ἰθύς the Pythia spoke, with a statement about the good qualities of a ruler, whereas here the oracle stresses the bad character of the Bacchiads.   **ἡ Πυθίη προσαγορεύει:** Delphi itself was perhaps a source for some of this material, even those parts of the responses which seem most obviously tampered with after the event (Delphi might have wished to ingratiate itself with Kypselos or Periandros in their days of power, though it is surprising that the Kypselids play no part in the tradition about the early 6th-cent. First Sacred War, fought for the possession of Delphi). For the oracles in **92**, and their interrelation, see McGlew 1993: 61–74. The order in which Hdt. reports the two 'ante-natal' oracular responses is the reverse of the real-time chronology: the meaning of the 'eagle', αἰετός, of the first-given but later-narrated response becomes clear and specific only after the slight shift of letters to Ἠετίων. **Ἠετίων, οὔτις σε τίει πολύτιτον ἐόντα**: as in the oracular response at **56**.1, there is heavy alliteration here (compounded by the introductory τοισίδε τοῖσι ἔπεσι, cf. at **56**.1 τάδε τὰ ἔπεα), and also ingenious and incantatory variation of words with the same root. For the personal name, see β 1n. above: there is an obvious play on the Greek word for eagle, philologically unjustified though the connection is thought to be. Like the 'common oracle' at 6.19 and 77, this one's language is heavily influenced by Homer, cf. Zeus to Poseidon at *Od.* 13.143–4, promising his brother-god requital if there is any man who dishonours him, ἀνδρῶν δ᾽ εἴ πέρ τίς σε βίηι καὶ κάρτει εἴκων | οὔ τι τίει, σοὶ δ᾽ ἐστὶ καὶ ἐξοπίσω τίσις αἰεί. **ὀλοοίτροχον**: a round rock or boulder, partly alluding to Eetion's home place Πέτρη, the Rock (cf. also the first line of the second oracle, β 3 below). The word in this lengthened form is Homeric, see *Il.* 13.137: Hektor compared ὀλοοίτροχος ὡς ἀπὸ πέτρης. Many hearers of the Herodotean oracle will have mentally completed the Homeric quotation, and its final word will have suggested Πέτρη even more clearly than did ὀλοοίτροχον. At 8.52.2, the Athenians on the Acropolis will roll ὀλοίτροχοι (*sic*, four syllables) down on the Persians. On the symbolism of this frightening and out-of-control object (the first half of the word suggests ὀλοός, 'deadly'), see McGlew 1993: 65: 'an object of fear as well as a tool of destruction'. **ἐν δὲ πεσεῖται | ἀνδράσι μουνάρχοισι, δικαιώσει δὲ Κόρινθον**: for the 'men who rule alone', see (with McGlew 1993: 65–6) the severely negative uses at Thgn. lines 51–2 and Solon fr. 9W lines 3–4 ('through ignorance, the people fall into slavery to a μόναρχος').

δικαιώσει ought to mean 'he will punish', on the analogy of 1.100.2 (Stein, and see Gray 1996: 374). But the root is δίκη, 'justice', and this sits oddly in a narrative illustrating the ills of tyranny. It is hard to believe that δικαιώσει has no flavour of commendation at all. Against this idea, the protest of Moles 2007: 257 n. 58 seems justified; and McGlew 1993: 73 is right that the Kypselids, like some other tyrants, saw themselves, and could be seen by others such as Delphi, as agents of justice.

92 β 3–γ 1 ταῦτα χρησθέντα τῶι Ἠετίωνι . . . καὶ τὸ πρότερον συνῆκαν ἐὸν συνῳδὸν τῶι Ἠετίωνος 'this oracle, which had been given to Eetion, had

somehow been reported to the Bacchiadai, who had received an earlier
and unintelligible one, which had the same meaning as Eetion's oracle
and went as follows [four-line text of oracle]...this had been obscure to
the Bacchiads before, but they now realised that it referred to Eetion, and
understood that it was one of a matching pair with that of Eetion'. The
earlier oracle, whose existence is only now disclosed, was ἄσημον, 'unintelligible', lit. 'unmarked', used of bullion; for the numismatic metaphor
cf. κιβδήλοισι at **91**.2 above, with n., citing Kurke 2009. After the text
of the earlier oracle has been given, the same idea is conveyed by a
more immediately 'intelligible' word for 'unintelligible', ἀτέκμαρτον, here
translated 'obscure'. Hdt.'s roundabout form of elucidation demands an
effort of concentration from the listener/reader, and involves Hdt. in this
resumptive phrasing πρότερον...ἄσημον/πρότερον...ἀτέκμαρτον. If Hdt.
had wanted to enact the process of *Bacchiad* comprehension stylistically, he
would have begun with the more general and obscure, as well as chronologically earlier, 'eagle oracle' and proceeded to the 'Eetion oracle' which
solved the puzzle. But the heavy weight of biographical and personal material about Eetion and Labda in β 1 imposes initial focalisation through
the individual, Eetion, who presumably (as a non-Bacchiad) did not know
about the eagle oracle. For him, the 'Eetion oracle' was the only one, so it
is narrated first. This way of managing the two responses has the extra and
crucial advantage that we, the listeners/readers, already know the 'Eetion
oracle' and can therefore take in the 'eagle oracle' comprehendingly.
Thanks to the omniscient narrator, we are in a better position than either
Eetion or the Bacchiads.   **αἰετὸς ἐν πέτρηισι κύει, τέξει δὲ λέοντα | καρτερὸν
ὠμηστήν**: see **56**.1n. on τλῆθι λέων' both for the animal imagery, common
in oracular responses, and for the connotations of lions in particular. This
lion is unambiguously bloodthirsty.   **πολλῶν δ' ὑπὸ γούνατα λύσει**: the
two halves of ὑπολύσει are separated (by 'tmesis'). 'Loose the knees' is a
Homeric expression for 'kill', as at *Il.* 11.579, εἴθαρ δ' ὑπὸ γούνατ' ἔλυσεν,
cf. 13.360 : the knees were the seat of physical power.   **καλήν | Πειρήνην**:
the spring or fountain Peirene, which helped to give the Akrokorinth or
city citadel its ability to withstand sieges, is used to designate Korinth at
Pind. *Ol.* 13.61, 'city of Peirene'. For the myth of its origin (the spring
gushed out when the winged horse Pegasos, also featured in Pind. *Ol.* 13,
stamped his hoof), see Strabo 8.6.21. See generally Robinson 2011.

92 γ 1 συνῆκαν ἐὸν συνωιδόν: the literal meaning of 'putting together'
(συνίημι) is specially appropriate here, where it is a question of putting
two oracles together to make sense of them. The other obviously available
verb σύνοιδα would have produced too close an assonance with συνωιδόν
(used here only by Hdt., and a tragic and Aristophanic word before the
4th cent.).   **δέκα**: the *ten* men need explaining, and we should think in

terms of recitation. At **92 γ 3** below, a passage of great comic potential, especially if delivered aloud to an audience, the first man passes the baby to the second, the second to the third, and so on through the whole circle of ten. There was no more natural way to recite this than to the accompaniment of a pantomime involving counting them off on the ten fingers. For counting on the fingers, see 6.63.2, Ariston king of Sparta, and cf. πεμπάζω, 'I count [on the five fingers]', at Plut. *Mor.* 387e.

Other explanations are feeble; for instance, the number ten is said to be formulaic (Fehling 1989: 217, 226–31), but most such 'tens' in Hdt. occur as periods of time: days, years etc. There were ten new Kleisthenic tribes at Athens (**69.**2), but it is not likely that Hdt. means us to think that the ten Korinthians represent the Bacchiad elite, because Korinth had the usual three Dorian tribes, and the only other civically important number there was eight; anyway, Bacchiad government was not representative.

92 γ 2 φιλοφροσύνης: the word is found here only in Hdt., and once only in Homer: *Il.* 9.256, φιλοφροσύνη γὰρ ἀμείνων. That is Odysseus sanctimoniously admonishing Achilles by quoting the latter's father Peleus on the virtues of friendship. Achilles' reply opens by denouncing insincerity (lines 312–13), so we, as Hdt.'s hearers or readers, are put on notice that here, too, apparent φιλοφροσύνη will turn out treacherous.   **προσουδίσαι** 'dash on the ground'. A shocking word, especially coming straight after the account of Labda's trusting reception of the visitors. The harsh juxtaposition is cleverly set up by a small analepsis: the ten *had already* decided en route, κατ' ὁδόν, to kill the child in this horrible way, for which cf. Psalm 137 ('By the waters of Babylon') verse 9: 'happy shall he be, that taketh and dasheth thy little ones against the stones' – another arresting juxtaposition of nice and nasty ideas; also perhaps *Il.* 24.734–5: Andromache predicts that one of the Achaians may throw her child Astyanax from a tower. Cf. West 1997: 393 on *Il.* 22.73f.

92 γ 3 θείηι τύχηι προσεγέλασε τὸ παιδίον: the uncanniness of this should not be diluted. It is said that new-born babies do not smile: see Moles 2007: 259 n. 70 and the *TLS* review (22.5.09) of Hrdy 2009; also Coleman 1977: 149, discussing the invocation of the wonder-child at Verg. *Ecl.* 4.60: 'incipe, parve puer, risu cognoscere matrem'. But others say that new babies smile (or appear to do so) if suffering from wind. This all assumes that the baby was born yesterday, so to speak, but it is possible that the news took a while to travel, or that the usual risks of infant mortality meant that the parents did not announce the birth straight away.

θείη τύχη is 'divine chance', for which cf. Eidinow 2011: 105. In Hdt., see esp. 3.139.3, where it describes the impulse which made Syloson give his cloak away to young Dareios. This acknowledgment by Hdt. of contingency does not negate the responsibility of the would-be assassins, who 'misread' the smile and then make further errors (e.g. allowing themselves to be overheard and pretending they had killed the baby): Moles 2007: 261.

92 γ 3 (cont.) κατοικτίρας δὲ παραδιδοῖ τῶι δευτέρωι, ὁ δὲ τῶι τρίτωι, οὕτω…δέκα: κατοικτίρας picks up οἶκτος, in an example of the 'running style', suitable for story-telling. See above, γ 1n. on δέκα: the hypothesis of comic oral recitation of the present passage, the reciter enumerating the cowardly men by using all ten of his fingers, explains the number of Bacchiads in the story. Compare also (with Gray 1996: 368) the passing of the baby Kyros from Harpagos to herdsman to wife (1.110).

92 γ 4 κατὰ τὰ δεδογμένα: an amusingly formal word for the decision. **πάντας τοῦ φόνου μετίσχειν:** collective responsibility, as in stoning.

92 δ 1 ἔδει δὲ ἐκ τοῦ Ἠετίωνος γόνου Κορίνθωι κακὰ ἀναβλαστεῖν: for similarly expressed statements of inevitability in Hdt. cf. 4.79.1 and **33**.2n.; Wecowski 1996: 254 n. 143. The biological metaphor in ἀναβλαστεῖν ('sprout', 'spring up', cf. 3.62.4 for the metaphorical use) continues, with verbal reminiscence, the idea in περὶ γόνου at β 2 and γόνον διαφθεῖραι at γ 1 above.   **φέρουσα κατακρύπτει ἐς τὸ ἀφραστότατόν οἱ ἐφαίνετο εἶναι, ἐς κυψέλην** 'she carried the child and hid it in the most unlikely place she could think of: a chest'. A κυψέλη was a chest or λάρναξ (the usual interpretation both now and in antiquity, cf. Paus. 5.17.5 for the 'chest of Kypselos' exhibited at Olympia). An alternative tr. is 'beehive' (cf. Plut. *Mor.* 601c). For this intriguing possibility, not here followed, see Roux 1963 and Griffiths 2006: 141, suggesting that the quasi-miraculous concealment of Kypselos belonged originally to a class of story involving a hero-figure who is saved by helpful animals. It is certainly true that a beehive is a less likely hiding-place than a chest, but 'chest' is how Paus. understood the word.

92 ε 1 ἀπὸ τῆς κυψέλης ἐπωνυμίην Κύψελος οὔνομα ἐτέθη: the derivation from the word for 'chest' is part of the point of the story. But in fact the name is an animal name, a *Tiername*, or rather a bird-name or *Vogelname*; see Bechtel 1917: 583. It means a martin of some sort. Compare bird-names like Κορυδαλλός at 7.214.1 below, or Ὄρτυξ and Πέρδιξ, (lark, quail and partridge respectively) and indeed Ὀρνιθίων: all from Bechtel 580–8; see also Robert 1963: 191–2 for 'falcon' names. The names Κύψελος and Κύψελις are historically attested in a small way (mainland Greece, Krete, Cyrenaica), but Κύψελος did not enter the enormous *Athenian* name-pool, despite the archon of 597 (**92** β 1, first n.).

The giving of the supposed etymology is important for Hdt., and is one reason for the elaboration of the story: see introd. n. to **92**, and Wecowski 1996: 216 and n. 28.   **ἐπεχείρησέ τε καὶ ἔσχε Κόρινθον:** this is very brief; as

with the Peisistratids, the main period of power is passed over with hardly
a word. Hdt. probably had difficulty finding much to say about Kypselos.
With this use of ἔχω for tyrannical seizure or control, cf. 6.36.1, ἔσχε τὴν
χώρην (Miltiades' seizure of the Thracian Chersonese).

92 ε 2 ὄλβιος οὗτος ἀνὴρ ὅς . . .: cf. ὄλβιος, ὅς . . . at Hom. *Hymn Dem.* 480 with
Richardson 1974: 313–14 (a 'traditional formula of μακαρισμός' i.e. blessing, beatitude, specially associated with initiatory cults, and with a strong
implication of material prosperity); Bion frag. XII line 1 with Reed 1997:
176. Korinth itself is ὀλβία at Pind. *Ol.* 13.4.   **παῖδες, παίδων γε μὲν οὐκέτι
παῖδες:** see 3.48ff. for the story of the third Kypselid generation (the unhap-
pily alienated Lykophron, and the anonymous brother who was not up
to the job). From other sources, we know that Periandros was briefly succeeded by his nephew Psammetichos son of Gorgos, another son of Kypselos (see further **92 β 1**, first n. The name Psammetichos indicates intermarriage or other close connection with the Egyptian ruling family). It is sometimes thought that this third line of the response is additional to an earlier and more positive couplet, but that is not necessary. The whole oracular response would appear to have been composed with hindsight. The
final line should not be connected with Periandros' necrophilia, regarded
as a signifier for absence of children. Periandros had sons, as we know
from bk. 3, though the family was dysfunctional.   **πολλοὺς μὲν Κορινθίων
ἐδίωξε, πολλοὺς δὲ χρημάτων ἀπεστέρησε, πολλῷ δέ τι πλείστους τῆς ψυχῆς:**
the actions which make Soklees' point about the badness of tyranny are
set out briefly, but with rhetorically effective anaphora. Exiles and killings
('deprivation of life') recur at η 1 below in reverse order: Kypselos did
these things to 'many' and 'much the greatest number', Periandros did
them to the rest. See **92 η 1**n. for the handling there of the middle item
here, deprivation of property.

92 ζ 1 ἐπὶ τριήκοντα ἔτεα: for chronology, see **92 β 1**, first n.   **διαπλέξαντος τὸν βίον εὖ:** an almost exact, but opposite, repetition of 4.205.1: the
same emphatically did not happen to Pheretime. The formula need not
mean more than that Kypselos died in his bed; no moral approval is conveyed by εὖ, and in any case a Greek would want to 'look to the end', and to
the fate of a man's descendants. Cf. Alkman fr. 1 lines 37–9 *PMG*: ὁ δ᾽ ὄλβιος,
ὅστις εὔφρων ἁμέραν [δι]απλέκει ἄκλαυτος.   **διάδοχος οἱ τῆς τυραννίδος ὁ παῖς
Περίανδρος γίνεται:** this was in *c.* 627, and he continued in power until
c. 585. For Periandros' reign, see Salmon 1984: 197–205 and 221–9. He
was one of the Seven Sages, all 6th-cent. figures (see *OCD*[4] 'seven sages').
The canon may have formed by the beginning of the 5th cent., but is first
explicitly attested in Pl. *Prot.* 343a (4th cent.). Periandros' bad reputation
seems to have caused him to be dropped from some lists, including Plato's,
where he appears to have been replaced by Myson; but he was reinstated

by Kall. (*Iambus* 1; on the replacement see explicitly Diod. 9.7 with Busine 2002: 35). There were despairing ancient attempts to posit two Periandroi, tyrant and sage, but see Martin 1993: 111 and Busine 2002: 22. Periandros' inclusion in the list of Seven Sages may be due to his arbitration between Athens and Mytilene (**95**.2n.), but this – in effect, he favoured Athens – was not conspicuously fair. If the list was of Athenian origin, we see why Periandros was thought a 'sage'. Martin 1993: 116–17 tries to find other examples of Periandros' sagacity.

Periandros continued his father's close control of Korinthian overseas colonies and territories, but that aspect plays little part here, except that the oracle of the dead was situated not far from NW Greek places under Korinthian influence.

As a figure in Hdt., Periandros is already familiar for his cruelty – re-emphasised here by the word μιαιφονώτερος – from bks. 1 and (esp.) 3, where he sends Kerkyraian boys to Sardis to be castrated (48.2) and kills his wife Melissa (50.1). Diog. Laert. 1.94 has him kick her while pregnant (cf. Lightfoot 1999: 485 and n. 254), but Hdt.'s language is compatible with accidental killing; see Loraux 1993: 15–18. For Periandros as tyrant constructed on the mythical model of the Labdakids of Thebes, including deviant sexual behaviour, see Vernant 1982: 33–4 (summary).

92 ζ 1 (cont.) ἐπείτε δὲ ὡμίλησε δι᾽ ἀγγέλων Θρασυβούλωι τῶι Μιλήτου τυράννωι: for the importance of the underlying motif – tyrants stick together – see introd. n. to **92** (Soklees' speech). Readers have already been told that Periandros and Thrasyboulos were ξεῖνοι (1.20), but that was already an established relationship (note ἐς τὰ μάλιστα there), and so pre-sumably post-dates the present episode in real time, although described much earlier in Hdt.'s text (unless the two men were in contact during Kypselos' life-time, or the relationship was inherited from Kypselos). Indeed, the guest-friendship might have been generated by the 'tallest poppies' advice now given.

Thrasyboulos, like Periandros, makes an early appearance in the *Histories* for his cleverly-achieved treaty with Alyattes of Lydia: 1.20–3 with Bauslaugh 1991: 88–90: the language (esp. *xeinoi*, 1.22.4) may indicate a personal relationship between the rulers and a public one between their states. If so, Thrasyboulos had *xenia* relations with the rulers of Korinth and Lydia. Otherwise, little is known about him; but the Miletos connection reminds us of the Milesian material earlier in bk. 5, and of Aristagores, who will reappear soon (**97** below). For the foreign policy alignments of Miletos, Samos, Korinth and others, see below on **99**. Miletos and Korinth were both prosperous commercial cities with extensive colonial networks, Korinth in the W. Mediterranean and N. Aegean, Miletos in the Black Sea region (e.g. 4.78.3, Milesian origins of Borysthenes-Olbia).

92 ζ 1 (cont.) μιαιφονώτερος: the word picks up Soklees' gnomic generalisation at α 2 above; and see above n. on διάδοχος.

92 ζ–η 1 *Pruning the tallest poppies (actually ears of corn)*

The story recurs in Livy's account of Tarquinius Superbus, the last king of Rome, *c.* 534–510 BC (see 1.54, where the recipient of the advice is his son Sextus at Gabii); it is not the only point of resemblance between Livy bk. 1 and Hdt.'s presentation of Greek tyrants. See Ogilvie 1965: 765, index entry 'Greek: episodes adapted from Greek mythology and history'. Aristotle (*Pol.* 1284a26ff. and again 1311a20ff.) tells Hdt.'s story the other way round: Periandros advises Thrasyboulos. The story is a 'roving anecdote', illustrating the perennial hostility between tyrants and oligarchs; unless Livy imitated, and Aristotle carelessly relied on his memory of, Hdt. 5.92.   There is a similarity with the story of Histiaios and the 'tattooed head' (**35**.2), in that in each case an exceptionally smart man communicates with another by means of, but also (in one case literally as well as metaphorically) 'over the head of', an ordinary man; and the story of Gorgo and the 'blank' wax tablet falls into this category (7.239). Thrasyboulos' cleverness has already been illustrated at 1.20–3. See Gray 1996: 378.   The present passage reverses **28** above, where power went to those (Naxian oligarchs) who looked after their estates best. But in a tyranny the answer is not to encourage but to eliminate the most successful.

92 ζ 2 ἀναποδίζων τὸν κήρυκα κατὰ τὴν ἀπὸ Κορίνθου ἄπιξιν 'he repeatedly questioned him about his visit ['arrival'] from Korinth'; that is, about the reasons for it. The verb lit. means 'make to step back', then 'call back and question', 'cross-examine' (Aeschin. 3.192); compare mod. English idiom 'put someone on the back foot'.   **καὶ ἐκόλουε αἰεὶ ὅκως τινα ἴδοι τῶν ἀσταχύων ὑπερέχοντα** 'and whenever he saw an ear of corn protruding above the others, he would cut it off'. With the language and thought here, cf. 7.10 ε, φιλέει γὰρ ὁ θεὸς τὰ ὑπερέχοντα πάντα κολούειν. Thrasyboulos disposes like the god. For the non-verbal communication here see Lateiner 1987: 99.

92 ζ 3 ἦν πρόθυμος πυνθάνεσθαι τὴν ὑποθήκην ὁ Περίανδρος 'Periandros was eager to know what the advice was'. We have to wait until the end of the sentence for the name Periandros to arrive, just as he had to wait impatiently for the advice to arrive: stylistic enactment. For word-order in Hdt., see **21**.2n. on δοὺς δέ...   **παραπληγά τε καὶ τῶν ἑωυτοῦ σινάμωρον** 'crazy and a wanton destroyer of his own property'. With the metaphorical use of the rare word παραπλήξ, lit. 'struck sideways' (Homer, *Od.* 4.518), cf. the related word at Soph. *Aj.* 230, παραπλήκτωι χειρί, 'with frenzied hand'. For σιναμωρέειν, an extremely strong verb, see 1.152.3.

ὀπώπεε <ποιεύμενα>: ὀπώπεε is pluperfect of ὁρῶ. The addition of ποιεύμενα improves the sense of an otherwise odd expression (Wilson).

92 η 1 συνεὶς τὸ ποιηθέν: the verb picks up συνῆκαν at γ 1 above (see n. there). Tyrants are as much of a riddle as are oracles.   **κακότητα**: this recalls δ 1 above, the κακά which were bound to grow from the seed of Eetion. With the whole expression πᾶσαν κακότητα ἐξέφαινε cf. 3.158.1 about Zopyros (AHG).   **ὅσα γὰρ Κύψελος ἀπέλιπε κτείνων τε καὶ διώκων**: the participles refer to deaths and enforced exiles, and, as we saw at ε 2n. above, they repeat in reverse, and with surely deliberate symmetry, the first and third of the list there (Kypselos' misdeeds). But Hdt. has not forgotten the second item in that earlier list, the *property* of which Kypselos deprived the Korinthians. What Periandros did in that department is about to be narrated. See next n. for the women as property. For the manner of expression compare the Renaissance witticism about a great but destructive Roman family, *quod non fecerunt barbari, fecerunt Barberini*.   **μίηι δὲ ἡμέρηι ἀπέδυσε πάσας τὰς Κορινθίων γυναῖκας**: the stripping of the married women (not just the citizen wives, see η 3 n. below) would come as no anti-climax to a Greek (male) hearer; note the possessive genitive plural Κορινθίων rather than a feminine ethnic form in the accusative plural. These women are male property, and Periandros' spoliation corresponds to Kypselos' thefts. The story is told in a ring: first the climax (the stripping, succinctly narrated), then what led to it, then the stripping again in more detail.   **διὰ τὴν ἑωυτοῦ γυναῖκα Μέλισσαν**: for Melissa's death at Periandros' hands (it is not mentioned here at all) see 3.50.1–3 and 52.4 with ζ 1n. above on διάδοχος..., and for Melissa herself, wife and daughter of tyrants, like the Peisistratid Archedike at Th. 6.59.2, see Loraux 1993. Melissa was daughter of Prokles, tyrant of Epidauros (3.50.2, further evidence for tyrannical intermarriage), but this, too, is ignored in the present context. There are three separate outrages against her: the killing (if deliberate), the failure to give proper burial (the importance of which is a theme not only of the last books of the *Iliad* but of much tragedy, such as Sophocles' *Ajax* and *Antigone*), and the necrophilia.

92 η 2–4 Periandros, the Oracle of the Dead, and Melissa's ghost

This section of Hdt. is the best evidence for oracles of the dead and their consultation. For this one, the Thesprotian or Acheron oracle, see Ogden 2001, esp. 17–21, 43–60, 51 and 54–60; on the present passage see also Johnston 1999: vii–viii and 27 n. 68 ('one of our oldest ghost stories': vii); and *OCD*[4] 'ghosts'. Other well-attested Greek oracles of the dead were at Tainaron in southern Lakonia, Herakleia on the Black Sea (Herakleia Pontike) and Lake Avernus in Campania (Italy).

The literary precursor is Odysseus' visit to the underworld in *Od.* 11 to consult Teiresias (a visit clearly located in or inspired by Thesprotia, see

Paus. 1.17.5); but this was presumably generated in its turn by actual Greek beliefs about the dead. And if Odysseus had been able to consult an oracle of the dead, he would not have needed to go down to the underworld himself (Stengel 1920: 77).

Dying people were thought to possess prophetic powers, see Most 1993: 108–9 and Janko 1992: 420 on *Il.* 16.852–4 ('dying was held to bring precognition') and the texts he cites; compare also John of Gaunt in Shakespeare's *Richard II* ('methinks I am a prophet new inspired | and thus expiring do foretell of him'). From this it is a natural step to a wish to consult the actual dead, ouija boards and so on.

The story may be unhistorical, but can be accepted as good evidence for the existence and functioning of the oracle, perhaps as late as Hdt.'s own day (Ogden 2001: 51). AHG compares Periandros' mythical predecessor as Korinthian ruler, 'rascally old Sisyphos'. He persuaded his wife not to give him proper funerary rites, then pleaded successfully with Hades for a reprieve and return to the world of the living. See *OCD*[4], 'Sisyphus'.

92 η 2 πέμψαντι γάρ οἱ ἐς Θεσπρωτοὺς ἐπ᾿ Ἀχέροντα ποταμὸν ἀγγέλους ἐπὶ τὸ νεκυομαντήιον: the nekyomanteion or nekromanteion in Thesprotia was at Ephyra in Epeiros (*IACP*: no. 96, *Barr.* map 54 C3). But it is doubtful whether the remains at mod. Xylokastro, which are exhibited as the nekyomanteion, have much to do with the oracle. The building in question is now thought to be an aristocratic residence of the 4th–3rd cents. BC: Baatz 1999; Mee and Spawforth 2001: 382–4; *IACP*. But the nekyomanteion must have been close to the building, which could have formed part of a larger sanctuary complex, even if the excavated machinery (ratchets etc.) was part of a catapult system rather than of fairground-style devices for simulating clanking ghostly apparitions, as Dakaris 1993 argued.

The double ἐπί is a kind of hendiadys: the river Acheron somehow *was* the oracle, and we might imagine a water-side ritual of necromancy, as a preliminary to a night of incubation (Ogden 2001: 47, cf. 46). There is no good evidence for descent into a cave at Ephyra, as there is at other oracles of the dead. For the river Acheron, see *Od.* 10.513 and *OCD*[4].

Periandros did not visit the oracle himself; he sent messengers. Hence the need for Melissa to offer proof of her identity (Johnston 1999: viii). The consultation probably took place through incubation, as at healing sanctuaries like Oropos or Epidauros: you slept in the sanctuary overnight and hoped to see a god or hero in your dreams (Ogden 2001: 18–19, 75).

92 η 2 (cont.) παρακαταθήκης πέρι ξεινικῆς 'about a friend's deposit'. This hints at Periandros' mercenary greed. Inquiries about lost property (e.g. 'did Dorkilos steal the cloth?') are well attested from inscribed tablets found at the oracular sanctuary at Dodona, not far away from Ephyra; for examples see Eidinow 2007: 116–18, 'past/present concerns'. Rather than going to the oracle of the dead, Periandros might have consulted Dodona, the oldest oracle in Greece. As it stands, the story of the lost or hidden deposit implies a routine consultation, at which Melissa's epiphany (ἐπιφανεῖσα) was as much of a surprise as was her response about the cold loaves. But it has been suggested (Eidinow 2007: 262 n. 60, comparing the story of Pausanias the Spartan regent and Kleonike at Paus. 3.17) that behind the story lies a wish on the part of Periandros to appease the ghost of the woman he had killed. This is attractive; we would have to suppose that a different sort of story has been blended with the one we have. The plurality of messengers is certainly odd as it stands, unless they were meant to check up on each other. Perhaps Melissa's ghost did the rounds and appeared to all of them in the night, or to one, or to some. **οὔτε σημανέειν … οὔτε κατερέειν:** that is, she would tell them the answer neither by non-verbal nor by verbal indicators. But she evidently knew what had been going on in the upper world – at least as far as her own body was concerned – in the time since she had died (Johnston 1999: viii). Contrast the ignorant dead who need to ask for news of the living, such as Achilles in *Od.* 11.492 and 494; or those for whom special postal arrangements need to be made, cf. Pind. *Ol.* 14 lines 20–1 with Segal 1985. **ῥιγοῦν τε γάρ … κατακαυθέντων** 'she was cold and naked: the clothes which had been buried with her were no use because they had not been burnt'. The burial was clearly inadequate, but we are not told how. The clothes-burning, or lack of it, is not easy to understand. Melissa's demand shows that the dead are 'generally thought to be in much the condition they had been in during life' (Kurtz and Boardman 1971: 207), in other words the dead need clothes, and consumption by fire somehow makes the clothes available to those who have been consumed by death. See also Richardson 1993: 162 (on *Il.* 22.510–14, cf. de Jong 2012: 192), discussing the present passage in connection with distraught Andromache's plan to burn Hektor's clothes. 'I will burn them all in the blazing fire, not for your profit [ὄφελος, as here], since you will never lie in them, but to be an honour for you in the sight of the men and women of Troy.' There the negated reason – 'not for your profit' – indicates the expected and familiar one. For the burning of Hektor's clothes see Bruck 1926: 29f., treating it together with the burning of a Homeric hero's weapons at burial. **ἐπὶ ψυχρὸν τὸν ἰπνόν** 'into a [lit. 'the] cold oven'. Both of the Periandros stories have him seeing the point of a riddle, like Oidipous solving the riddle posed by the sphinx. And both involve corn, first raw, then cooked (AHG). But this time (contrast the mystified messenger who returns from Thrasyboulos), the messengers would need to be slow-witted not to grasp the meaning. The point of the 'evidence' or 'trustworthy token' (μαρτύριον, πιστὸν συμβόλαιον) was to convince Periandros of her identity, because he and only he knew the *truth* of the necrophilia allegation. But as soon as she spoke the 'token' to the messenger(s), he or they surely knew the *fact* of the allegation about necrophilia.

92 η 3 ἐς τὸ ῞Ηραιον ἐξιέναι πάσας τὰς Κορινθίων γυναῖκας: this is the excavated sanctuary of Hera at Perachora, in the N. Korinthia, at the tip of the small peninsula running westward into the Korinthian gulf (*Barr.* map 58 D1). For the sanctuary, see Salmon 1972. It is at the edge of Korinthian territory, like many sanctuaries of Hera (de Polignac 1995), and was used as a place of refuge in time of trouble (Xen. *Hell.* 4.5.5 with Sinn 1993: 103). That is, it was a lonely spot (note ἐξιέναι), ideal for playing a monstrous trick on unprotected married women; and the connection with Hera, goddess of marriage, made this a special outrage (unless Periandros hoped that this aspect would work conjugally in his favour. At any rate, Melissa now becomes co-operative and Periandros gets his friend's property back, unlike the men of Korinth). Note πάσας τὰς Κορινθίων γυναῖκας, *all* the Korinthian women, slaves as well as free. This expands Κορινθίων γυναῖκες at **92.** η 1, but still wives i.e. property are meant, and Hera is the archetypal wife.   **ὑποστήσας τοὺς δορυφόρους ἀπέδυσέ σφεας** 'he placed his bodyguards in ambush and stripped the women'. This, in full and shocking view of the bodyguards, deprived the women of their αἰδώς; cf. the horrified Gyges to Kandaules at 1.8.3, the only time that powerful noun (as opp. the verb αἰδέομαι) is used in Hdt., but it is surely implied here.   **συμφορήσας δὲ ἐς ὄρυγμα Μελίσσηι ἐπευχόμενος κατέκαιε** 'he had them taken to a pit and burnt, while he invoked Melissa in prayer'. The partly dactylic rhythm has led to a speculation that Hdt. might have drawn on a hexametric account (Ogden 2001: 57).

92 η 4 τοιοῦτο μὲν ὑμῖν ἐστι ἡ τυραννίς: the end of the stories and the return to the main theme are abrupt, and effected by a kind of 'break-off formula', in the manner of a Pindaric ode after the telling of a lengthy myth (as at Pind. *Pyth.* 4.247).

ὑμῖν is a so-called 'ethic dative'. Here it corresponds exactly to an English idiom: 'well, that's tyranny for you'.

92 η 5 θῶμα μέγα: the peroration begins by reasserting more succinctly the message of the opening *adynaton* (α 1 n.), but then switches to the language of open and urgent appeal.   **ἐπιμαρτυρόμεθά τε ἐπικαλεόμενοι ὑμῖν θεοὺς τοὺς Ἑλληνίους:** for the formula of divine invocation in the second part of this, cf. Aristagores at **49.**3, πρὸς θεῶν τῶν Ἑλληνίων ῥύσασθε ῎Ιωνας ἐκ δουλοσύνης where the context is similar: a plea to avert enslavement. (Note the pointed adverb ἐλευθέρως at **93.**2, with n.) This might (esp. in view of the dative in Λακεδαιμονίοισι ἐπεμαρτύροντο in **93.**2) be hyperbaton, emphatically dislocated word order, i.e. ὑμῖν really goes not with ἐπικαλεόμενοι but with ἐπιμαρτυρόμεθα, but has been postponed. It is not obvious who is being 'called to witness' in the first word: the gods, the allies, or (more likely) both. See Pelling 2006: 102 n. 70.   ἴστε ὑμῖν Κορινθίους γε οὐ συναινέοντας: Soklees ends his speech as he began it, with an expression borrowed from Homeric epic, but with small and significant differences from Homer. When Zeus contemplates saving Sarpedon from death, Hera says 'do it, but we other gods will not all approve you', ἔρδ᾽· ἀτὰρ οὔ τοι πάντες ἐπαινέομεν θεοὶ ἄλλοι, *Il.* 16.443; cf. also 4.29 and Athena to Zeus at 22.181 – Zeus wonders whether to save Hektor – with Pelling 2006: 102–3, esp. 103 n. 71 on the rhetorically artful prefix συν- (as opp. Homer's invariable ἐπ-). This prefix by implication accuses the other states of acquiescence, and thus needles them into the decisive rejection which follows. Note also the absence in Hdt. of an equivalent to Homer's ἔρδ᾽· ἀτάρ. That is, Zeus can do it if he wants (he can always throw a few other gods out of Olympos first), but the Spartans cannot so defy their allies. ἴστε ὑμῖν Κορινθίους... (no particle or other connecting word) is a strong final warning, which lacks some of Hera's – possibly gendered and subtle – concessiveness.

The Homerisms in Soklees' speech, including this closing flourish, beckon towards the Homeric and Trojan-war content of **94–5** below (Sigeion, Helen, Menelaos etc.); see also **93**.1n. on ἐπιποθήσειν.

93.1 πρεσβεύων: see **92**.1n. on Σωκλέης.   **τοὺς αὐτοὺς ἐπικαλέσας θεούς**: that is, the gods of the Greeks, just invoked by Soklees; see **92** η 5n. for the cluster of invocation-words hereabouts.   **ἦ μέν**: an untranslatable phrase, used to introduced solemn oaths, as at 6.74.1, where Kleomenes makes the Arkadians swear to follow him.   **ἐπιποθήσειν**: the rare compound form (used only here in Hdt., though the simple ποθέω is found, as is πόθος) enhances the portentousness. The root of the word is another Homeric allusion: Achilles knows that all the sons of the Greeks will miss him when things start to go badly for them, ἦ ποτ᾽ Ἀχιλλῆος ποθὴ ἵξεται υἷας Ἀχαιῶν | σύμπαντας (*Il.* 1.240–1). See Pelling 2006: 103; and cf. **92** η 5n. on ἴστε... for the placing of these Homerisms.

This prediction is the best card in the hands of the 'irony' school of Herodotean interpreters, inviting us as it does to contemplate the bumpy relations between Athenians and Korinthians in the following hundred years.

93.2 τούτοισι ἀμείψατο: cf. 9.28.1, οἱ μὲν ταῦτα ἀμείβοντο (picking up ὑπερκρίναντο at 27.1).   **οἷά τε τοὺς χρησμοὺς ἀτρεκέστατα ἀνδρῶν ἐξεπιστάμενος** 'inasmuch as he had a uniquely accurate understanding of oracles'. See above, **90**.2nn. for Peisistratids and oracles, and other types of divination. The longer form of ἐπίσταμαι means 'know full well'; the prefix ἐξ- suggests exegesis, exegetes, and other words for religious interpretation.   **οἱ δὲ λοιποὶ τῶν συμμάχων τέως μὲν εἶχον ἐν ἡσυχίηι σφέας αὐτούς**:

this subtly adapts and varies the sentence used to introduce the ring of Soklees' speech (**92**.1): 'the others remained silent, but Soklees...' / 'the others had remained silent up till now (τέως) but when Soklees had spoken so freely, they burst out...' etc. It is odd that here Hdt. ignores Hippias' speech.   **εἴπαντος ἐλευθέρως**: more ambiguity: Soklees had spoken 'in favour of freedom', but also 'like a free man'. There is a similar and surely deliberate instability of meaning in a famous sentence of Th. (2.65.8), Perikles led the Athenians ἐλευθέρως (Parry 1989: 144–5).   The reading of some MSS would mean 'he bade them liberate, ἐλευθερῶσαι', but this is inappropriate. The Athenians are already free (cf. ὅσα δὲ ἐλευθερωθέντες ἔρξαν... at **65**.5), so do not need liberation. The Spartans have been proposing to remove that freedom.   **ἅπας τις αὐτῶν φωνὴν ῥήξας** 'everyone, crying out', lit. 'breaking voice'. The expression is a strong one; it was used at 1.85.4 about Kroisos' hitherto dumb son, who miraculously cries out 'don't kill Kroisos'.   **Λακεδαιμονίοισί τε ἐπεμαρτύροντο** 'they implored the Spartans'. But the idea of witnessing is still vestigially present (see next n. for the echo of Soklees' peroration), and only the gods can be meant. See **92** η 5n.   **μὴ ποιέειν μηδὲν νεώτερον περὶ πόλιν Ἑλλάδα**: see **19**.2n. on νεώτερα πρήγματα. The formulation περὶ πόλιν Ἑλλάδα recalls the 'Greek gods' of Soklees' peroration; but 'a Greek city' looks forward to the Persian Wars and the crucial theme of Greek unity. That idea is reinforced by the choice of the proper noun Ἑλλάδα. For the adjectival use of the substantive Ἑλλάς with πόλις cf. 7.22.3 and Th. 6.62.2 with *CT* iii: 463–4.

94–95 *Hippias retires to Sigeion; the Athenian conquest of Sigeion*

Hdt. has already said (**65**.3) that Hippias went to Sigeion after his expulsion, so he is now merely returning to it, and Hdt. could have found a way of telling us there about the history of Athenian interest in and possession of the place. See **65**.3n. for the decision not to expand at that point. The positive gains achieved by the placing here include (1) a building of the tension still further by this final insertion of a pause before Aristagores' arrival at Athens and the military narrative of the Ionian, Karian and Cypriot revolts, and a covering up of the chronological hiatus between the departure of the Spartans and the arrival of Aristagores (see **97**.1n. on ἐν τούτωι δὴ τῶι καιρῶι). In addition (2), the arbitrating activity of Periandros at **95**.2 continues the Kypselid theme of **92**, although he now appears in a different and less lurid light as international brokering statesman, although his fairmindedness is suspect. Finally (3), the mention at **94**.1 of the offers to Hippias of residences by two later medising powers, Macedonian and Thessalian, builds on the panhellenic motif touched on at the end of **93**.2 (περὶ πόλιν Ἑλλάδα, see preceding n.) and prepares us for

Hippias' own role as mediser and would-be Persian puppet ruler of Athens (**96**.2 etc.).

Hdt.'s Sigeion excursus narrative here is drawn on by Strabo (13.1.38), who, however, adds details, one of which is chronologically important: see **94**.2n. on ἐπολέμεον γάρ.

94.1 ἐδίδου μὲν Ἀμύντης ὁ Μακεδὼν Ἀνθεμοῦντα, ἐδίδοσαν δὲ Θεσσαλοὶ Ἰωλκόν: the imperfects ἐδίδου and ἐδίδοσαν mean 'tried to give him'; 'offered'.

Anthemous (*IACP*: no. 562) was south of the site of the later Thessalonike; the present passage and Th. 2.99.6 indicate that in the 5th cent. it was a Macedonian-controlled district (and a river); it became a *polis* only in the 4th. The relations of the Macedonian kings with the Athenian democracy were ambiguous. But there is no doubt that Amyntes is still king of Macedon and is still friends with the Peisistratids: the imperfect tense (above) cannot yield the sense 'Amyntes had given him Anthemous at an earlier date'. See above **73**.3n. Hippias left Athens permanently at **65**.3 when he went to Sigeion for the first time. Therefore Amyntes' offer of Anthemous to Hippias postdates the Athenian submission, by tokens of earth and water, to the Persian king, and neither Amyntes nor Alexandros as his 'father's envoy' (Badian 112) can have helped to bring about that Athenian submission.

Iolkos (mod. Volos, on the ancient gulf of Pagasai) is a name splendid in myth, and the offer by Achilles' fellow-Thessalians was appropriate for a family with Homeric pretensions (**65**.4 and n.; or was this offer just mid 5th-cent. big talk by Peisistratid exiles on Chios? For whom see – again – **65**.4n.). For 'famous Iolkos', see Pind. *Pyth*. 4.77 and for 'well-built Iaolkos' (*sic*) see *Il*. 2.712–13. Cf. *IACP*: 449 (the present passage is the only evidence that it was a Thessalian dependency in the late 6th cent.); also *OCD*[4], 'Iolcus'. The Thessalians were Peisistratid allies at **63**.3 (though their behaviour at **64**.2 is half-hearted, see n. there); for general Thessalian medism in 480, see 8.30. So all three – Hippias, Macedonian kings, Thessalians – had a pro-Persian future. But the absence here of the definite article might imply that the offer of Iolkos came from only one Thessalian group.

94.1 (cont.) ἀνεχώρεε δὲ ὀπίσω ἐς Σίγειον: see **65**.3n., discussing Hippias' first move to that place, and how this was possible, given that Sigeion was Athenian territory. As also discussed there, the plurals of **63–5** ('the Peisistratidai') have now been replaced by the singular 'Hippias', perhaps because he had left his family behind (see **91**), but also because he has just played a vigorous personal role in **93**.   τὸ εἶλε Πεισίστρατος αἰχμῆι παρὰ Μυτιληναίων: this military success is at variance with the negative judgment on the tyranny at **78** above, and there is other evidence too. See

n. there on ἀπαλλαχθέντες...For the chronology and oscillating fortunes of the Athenian involvement at 6th-cent. Sigeion see **94.**2n. on ἐπολέμεον γάρ.   **κατέστησε τύραννον εἶναι παῖδα ἑωυτοῦ νόθον...ἐξ Ἀργείης γυναικός:** the use of junior members of the family to rule outlying or colonial places is well-attested tyrannical policy; the Korinthian Kypselids did this, and by a political anachronism Th. even has Minos do it (1.4).

At 9.91, Hdt. will make the Spartan king Leutychides, in a verbal exchange with another Hegesistratos (of Samos), exploit the literal meaning of the latter's name: 'leader of the army'. The name is also apt for its Peisistratid bearer, because he (re-)takes Sigeion 'not without fighting', οὐχ ἀμαχητί. But it was perhaps not his only name. *Ath. Pol.* 17.4 says that Peisistratos' son by his morganatic Argive wife was called Hegesistratos, but had a nickname as well, Thettalos. This is probably wrong: Thettalos (or Thessalos) and Hegesistratos were distinct sons. Hippias, Hipparchos and Thettalos (whose name surely indicates good relations with Thessalians, see above on Iolkos) were sons of an Athenian mother, Hegesistratos and Iophon of an Argive; hence the supposed illegitimacy of the latter two under Athenian law. See *APF:* 445–50 and Rhodes 1981: 225. ('Supposed' because children by foreign women were not actually illegitimate at Athens until 451. Hdt. appears to have retrojected the later situation into the 6th cent.)

For Peisistratid contacts with Argos, see 1.61.4 and *Ath. Pol.* 17.4. The friendly connection was surely one reason for the Spartan deposition of Hippias; see introd. n. to **62.**1.

94.2 ἐπολέμεον γάρ: the date of the war for Sigeion is tied up with that of the poet Alkaios, because at **95.**2 Hdt. says that Alkaios took part in the war, whose first phase should be dated to the late 7th / early 6th cents. (see *OCD*[4] 'Alcaeus': 'the last decade of the [7th] cent.'). The best discussion of the chronology is Page 1955: 152–61.   The material about Alkaios at **95.**2 is embedded in a Peisistratid excursus, and this has been wrongly thought to support a 6th-cent. date for him, or else to show that he lived in the 7th cent. but that Hdt. mistakenly thought otherwise. But γάρ in the present passage is 'elliptic' and is working hard: 'you must know that' for a long time the Athenians and Mytilenaians had disputed possession of Sigeion. (So rightly Page, and already Berve 1937: 27f.) That is, we are being taken back well beyond and behind the Peisistratid era. Strabo (13.1.39) provides the needed chronological fix by his mention of the Athenian Olympic victor Phrynon, who commanded the Athenian forces and died fighting at Sigeion in 606. His Olympic victory was probably in 636 (Moretti 1957: p. 66 no. 58), and he was mentioned by Alkaios (Page 1955: 159–60). All this happened many years before Peisistratos' time. Nevertheless, Peisistratid interest in Homer (see **65.**4 and n., and Graziosi

2002: 205–8, 221–8) will have added urgency to later Athenian military efforts in the region.

94.2 (cont.) ἔκ τε Ἀχιλληίου πόλιος: for this resonantly named *polis*, see *IACP*: no. 766. Strabo (13.1.39) cites Demetrios of Skepsis for criticism of the early 3rd-cent. historian Timaios, who said (*FGrHist* 566 F 129) that Periandros of Korinth used stones brought from Troy to build a wall round 'the Achilleion', as protection against Athenian attacks. But in fact (says Strabo, still drawing on Demetrios) the place was fortified by the Mytilenaians against Sigeion, though not with stones from Ilion, nor by Periandros, which would have been absurd given that he was arbitrator. The Troy region was important in later inter-state politics and the present passage of Hdt. shows that this process began early; see below on Menelaos and the mythically-based argument between Mytilenaians and Athenians. ἀποδεικνύντες τε λόγωι: we should imagine an eloquent deputation – armed with literary texts including and especially Homer – of the sort attested epigraphically in Hellenistic territorial disputes. Thus Lysimachos' letter to the Samians says that the Prieneans 'demonstrated from the histories and other evidences…' etc. (*OGIS* 13; cf. Rehm 1914: no. 155, and for other examples Chaniotis 1988: 274 n. 613; see also the remarks of Momigliano 1980: 373). For another Athenian argument from Homer see 7.161.3, where it is combined with an appeal to their own autochthony. See Graziosi 2002: 228–31 for recognition of the authority of Homer, esp. the Catalogue of Ships, in settling international disputes (with discussion of literary texts which show that the Athenians used Homer in their 6th-cent. dispute with the Megarians over Salamis). οὐδὲν μᾶλλον Αἰολεῦσι … τὰς Ἑλένης ἁρπαγάς 'the Aiolians had no better right to the territory of Ilion than themselves or any other Greeks who helped Menelaos to avenge the abduction of Helen'. μετεόν is impersonal: 'had no greater [right to a] share in'. Ἰλιὰς χώρη means 'the land of Ilion' i.e. the territory of Troy, but the first word on its own can mean the famous poem (as at 2.116.2), and thus has great emotional power. The Athenian argument seems weak (unless, as is possible, it is a rebuttal of a Mytilenaian argument based on the *Iliad*). It admits that any third party from a place or area mentioned in the Greek section of the Catalogue of Ships in *Iliad* 2 (including Periandros' Korinth, see below) would have just as much right to the place as the Athenians. Periandros' arbitration, which in effect favoured the Athenians, looks like expediency (backing the stronger naval power) rather than the act of a 'sage'; see **92** ζ 1 n. on Periandros as one of the Seven Sages, and below, **95**.2n. However, if the Athenian argument is in fact a reply (see above) it was perhaps not unreasonable to think that the burden of proof lay on the Mytilenaians, if they were saying that the Athenians should withdraw.

95.1 ἐν δὲ δὴ καὶ Ἀλκαῖος ὁ ποιητὴς συμβολῆς γενομένης ... αὐτὸς μὲν φεύγων ἐκφεύγει: here συμβολή means 'a battle'. With the apparently redundant expression φεύγων ἐκφεύγει, cf. φεύγων καταφυγῆι at 4.23.5. See LSJ φεύγω I (2): 'the pres. and impf. tenses prop. express only *the purpose* or *endeavour to get away*: hence part. φεύγων is added to the compound verbs ... to distinguish the attempt from the accomplishment'.

The main ancient narrative sources for the 'Sigeian War' other than Hdt. are Strabo 13.1.38 and Diog. Laert. 1.74, but Page 1955: 152–3 considered that 'the poems of Alcaeus were presumably the principal ultimate source of their information'. For the relevant fragmentary poems, such as they are, see fr. 306(f) and 167 Voigt. At fr. 306(f) lines 19–20, μεσί[την, 'mediator', appears to refer to Periandros. For the chronology, see **94**.2n. on ἐπολέμεον γάρ.

Hdt. has already displayed his knowledge of and interest in the older poets. See 1.12.2, Archilochos (unless that is interpolated), 1.23, Arion the dithyrambist, 2.135.1, Σαπφώ ἡ μουσοποιός, 3.121, Anakreon in the company of Polykrates; cf. **113**.2 (Hdt.'s only ref. to Solon as poet, as opposed to lawgiver and general sage), and note the implications of 6.52.1, citing what 'the Spartans say, agreeing with no poet', where in the context the poets cannot include Homer (and Tyrtaios' poem *Eunomia* may be hinted at in 1.65.2). See also, for 5th-cent. epinikian poets, 3.38.4 (Pindar) and **102**.3n. (Simonides). For the non-mention of Archilochos at **99** (the Lelantine War) see n. there; and for Stesichoros (never mentioned at all), **43**n.

95.1 (cont.) καί σφεα ἀνεκρέμασαν πρὸς τὸ Ἀθήναιον τὸ ἐν Σιγείωι: it is possible that some depiction (perhaps a statue or painting in the temple of Athena, the Ἀθήναιον) gave rise to this story (Fehling 1985: 106 n. 240, Schachermeyr, *R.-E.* 'Alkaios'). Alternatively, perhaps Alkaios, like Archilochos, wrote a poem about losing his shield.

95.2 ἐπιτιθεῖ 'he sent'; for the word in this sense, cf. 3.42.4, Polykrates sends a letter to Amasis.   Μελανίππωι ἀνδρὶ ἑταίρωι: Alkaios invites his friend Melanippos to 'drink [and get drunk] with me' in a 13-line poem, fr. 38(a) Voigt; cf. Page 1955: 300–3.   Μυτιληναίους ... τούτωι γὰρ διαιτητῆι ἐπετράποντο: this is one of the earliest historically believable arbitrations; see Tod 1913: 54, though cf. **28–30** above, the Parians and Miletos, whenever exactly that was. The surviving evidence gives the impression that the great age of inter-state arbitration was the Hellenistic, with its proliferation of 'foreign judges', but that may be partly an illusion generated by the large number of relevant inscriptions, for which see Ager 1996. The present passage is an example of what Ager 1996: 8–10 calls 'compromisary arbitration', where there was no pre-existing treaty making arbitration obligatory (cf. *CT* III: 96–7 for such binding but agreed arbitration). In the classical period the Argives are often named as arbitrators (see e.g. R/O no. 82); in the Hellenistic period, the Rhodians had a great reputation, see Polyb. 28.7.9 with *HCP*. It is interesting to find another 6th-cent Korinthian arbitration in Hdt.: below.   κατήλλαξε δὲ ὧδε ... ὑπ' Ἀθηναίοισι: this activity by Periandros may have been what qualified him as a sage (see **92** ζ 1n. on διάδοχος). The decision, which imposed what in diplomacy is called *uti possidetis* (cf. Th. 1.140.2 with *CT* I: 227–8), in effect favoured the Athenians by leaving them in possession of Sigeion, and if the list of the Seven Sages was thought up in Athens, the present decision would help to explain why Periandros was popular enough there to be thought 'sagacious'.   The Korinthians' foreign policy consistently favoured the Athenians up to and beyond the Persian wars, a friendliness most obviously attested by their persistent refusal to intervene against Athens in the present bk. 5, but see also 6.108.5 for the effect of another Korinthian arbitration, that concerning Plataia. Finally, there is the loan of twenty ships to the Athenians for use against Aigina (6.89, cf. Th. 1.41.2). Here is a clue: the Korinthians favoured the Athenians as long as the Aiginetans were a rival to themselves in the Saronic gulf (thus Hdt.'s juxtaposition of Aiginetan and Korinthian themes at **82–92** above is politically apt). It was only with the 460s and the terminal decline of Aiginetan power that the 'great hatred' arose between Korinthians and Athenians (Th. 1.103.4, and see above **93**.1 for Hippias' prediction or 'prediction' of future trouble).

95.2 (cont.) διαιτητῆι: the word is found here only in Hdt., and here for the first time in Greek, unless (as is conceivable) Solon used it to describe himself.

96–126 THE ATHENIANS BREAK WITH PERSIA. MILITARY OPERATIONS IN IONIA, CYPRUS AND KARIA

After a long section of forty chapters during which we have travelled widely and discursively in time and place (Peisistratid Athens, Kadmeian Thebes, early Aigina, Kypselid Korinth), the paths wonderfully converge, the narrative line becomes linear, and it will now proceed with little or no diversion or analepsis (apart from the parenthetically mentioned Lelantine War at **99**.1) until and beyond the end of bk. 5. In particular, ch. **100** will inaugurate a stretch of nearly unbroken military narrative.

See de Jong 2001: 97 for comparison and contrast with smaller-scale Homeric analepses.

96 Hippias' intrigues

96.1 διαβάλλων: the word is insistently repeated in this section (resumptively at **97**.1, and then twice more, though with different nuances from here, at **97**.2). See **50**.2n., citing esp. Pelling 2007: 183–5.   **ὅκως αἱ Ἀθῆναι γενοίατο ὑπ' ἑωυτῶι τε καὶ Δαρείωι:** note the amusing order of mention, with Dareios in second place (compare Otanes at 3.69.2, 'this man who is sleeping with you and having total control over the Persians'). For the suspicion here expressed, cf. **32** above for the comparable but larger ambitions of Pausanias, the Spartan Regent.

96.2 πέμπουσι ἐς Σάρδις ἀγγέλους: the sending of this deputation, and the severe and uncompromising Persian reply, are further indications that for a few years Athens was indeed a 'city of the Great King' (see **73**.3n.): this later embassy was possible only if that earlier submission had not been revoked. See Schachermeyr 1973: 213–14.   **οὐκ ἐῶντες τοὺς Πέρσας** 'asking the Persians not to…'   **εἰ βουλοίατο σόοι εἶναι, καταδέκεσθαι ὀπίσω Ἱππίην:** see n. above for the implication of this instruction; but κελεύειν is not always as strong as 'to order' (cf. **38**.2n.), and this instruction is expressed conditionally, albeit with menacing understatement: 'if they wanted to be *safe*'. This is the first mention of Hippias' restoration as an item of Persian, rather than of Spartan, policy.   **οὐκ ὢν δὴ ἐνεδέκοντο… οἱ Ἀθηναῖοι· οὐκ ἐνδεκομένοισι δέ σφι ἐδέδοκτο… τοῖσι Πέρσηισι πολεμίους εἶναι:** Hdt. applies the brakes. The postponement of the subject, the Athenians, until the end of the first clause, and the weighty repetition, in the second clause, of the polysyllabic key verb of the first, flag the gravity of the moment, and of the Athenian decision. The causal mechanism, which will convey the agents and us right up to the battle of Plataia and the end of the *Histories*, is now in motion, and irreversible.   **ἐδέδοκτο** 'they *had* decided': note the pluperfect, presumably meaning that this was what the refusal of Artaphrenes' terms amounted to, whether or not the Athenians phrased it exactly in this way.

97 Aristagores at Athens

See above on **49–55** for the matching and different-but-similar narrative of his visit to Sparta.

97.1 ἐν τούτωι δὴ τῶι καιρῶι: we have now, at last, reached the narrative point promised at **65**.3. As an expression of contingency the present passage is comparable to, but less extreme than, the three-fold synchronism at **36**.1 (see n. there). In fact, Aristagores hardly arrived on stage just as the Spartans and Soklees left it, but actually a few years later; the insertion of the Sigeion excursus helps to mask this sleight of hand (see introd. n. on

94–5). αὕτη γὰρ ἡ πόλις τῶν λοιπέων ἐδυνάστευε μέγιστον 'because this city was the most powerful of the rest' i.e. the most powerful '*after Sparta*', as Waterfield's tr. explicitly has it. The thought here recalls 1.56.2, where Kroisos ascertains that the Spartans and Athenians are the pre-eminent Greeks; see Introduction, p. 8. There is also a reminder of **78** on Athenian greatness as a result of getting rid of their tyrants.   ἐπελθὼν δὲ ἐπὶ τὸν δῆμον: that is, Aristagores goes immediately to address the Assembly or *ekklesia*, which immediately votes to help the Ionians. But in the developed Athenian democracy at least (cf. (c) below), visiting foreign envoys, or letters from foreign states, would have been taken first to the Council of Five Hundred, the *boule* (introduced by Kleisthenes only a few years earlier), and only after that did they go to the Assembly; a recommendation would have been made by the *boule* in the interim. See Aischin. 2.45–6 (letter from Philip II of Macedon) with *CT* III: 28 and n. 44. There are four ways of explaining Hdt.'s omission, of which (a) is probably the best.

(a) Hdt. has left out an entire constitutional stage, a self-regulating stage tending to make for deliberative caution. Th. does this, either to dramatise events by concentrating on the great collectives, or from anti-democratic prejudice and in order to exaggerate the impetuous folly of the Assembly or People; see *CT* III: 23–31. It is possible that Hdt., too, deliberately omits the role of the Council, and for similar reasons: see below for his censorious comment on the ease with which 30,000 Athenians were persuaded to their own disadvantage.

(b) Hdt., who was not an Athenian like Th., was ignorant of or misunderstood the procedure, or did not think the first constitutional stage worth bothering with.

(c) In these infant days of the Kleisthenic democracy, the role of the *boule* had not yet crystallised, i.e. Hdt. was correct to ignore it. This cannot be disproved.

(d) Aristagores by-passed the *boule* as being full of rich aristocrats (Cagnazzi 1984: 17). But though there was some bias towards the rich, especially before pay for Council attendance was introduced after 460 (Rhodes 1972: 5 and n. 3), the bias was not great. There were social pressures on people to serve, and the *boule* was 'not merely a forum for the politically active and the well-off': Hansen 1999: 249.

If (a) is right, and Hdt. has omitted the *boule*'s actual role, the present passage, like his remarks below about 30,000 men, has a bearing on his attitude to the Athenian democracy. That is, Hdt., no less than Th., exaggerates Athenian impetuosity. See also 6.132 for the hasty Athenian decision to give Miltiades seventy ships.

97.1 (cont.) ταὐτὰ ἔλεγε τὰ καὶ ἐν τῆι Σπάρτηι 'he said the same as he had in Sparta': that is, in the direct speech at **49**. Here we have indirect speech, which is more appropriate for a shorter editorialised version (cf. Th. 2.13 for authorial editorialising). Whereas Homer was happy to repeat speeches *in extenso*, though sometimes with careful and tactful changes suited to a new hearer, Hdt. and Th. use cross-referring flags like the present formula. Compare the periodically adjusted manifesto of Brasidas, delivered at various northern cities, and reported briefly in indirect speech with explicit allusion to the main liberation announcement already made at Akanthos: Th. 4.114.3 and 120.3 with *CT* II: 86–9. Here the main variant from the earlier speech is in **97.2**: see n. there on καὶ πρός . . .   περὶ τῶν ἀγαθῶν: that is, booty. See van Wees 2002: 347.   καὶ τοῦ πολέμου τοῦ Περσικοῦ: *the* Persian war, as if it is already a fact, perhaps resuming the implication of ἐδέδοκτο at **96.2**, see n. there. But it may just mean the war which Aristagores has been talking about before.   ὡς οὔτε ἀσπίδα οὔτε δόρυ νομίζουσι 'they do not customarily use shield or spear'.   εὐπετέες: as often (**31.3**n.) the 'ease' is implied, by an author-reader complicity, to be delusive.

97.2 καὶ πρός τοῖσι τάδε, ὡς οἱ Μιλήσιοι τῶν Ἀθηναίων εἰσὶ ἄποικοι: here Aristagores slightly alters the patter he had used at Sparta (see **97.1**n. on ταὐτὰ ἔλεγε). There (**49.3**, addressing Kleomenes), Aristagores appealed to kinship in general language, ἄνδρας ὁμαίμονας, which was either a reference to the kinship which existed between all Greeks, or just possibly an unspecifically worded hint at the specific tradition that Miletos was founded from Dorian Krete. But against this, see **49.3**n. For the theme of Milesian colonisation from Ionian Athens, see the passages discussed at **65.3**n. on ἐκ τῶν αὐτῶν . . ., esp. 1.146.   καὶ οἰκός σφεας εἴη ῥύεσθαι δυναμένους μέγα: οἰκός (note accent) means 'it is natural that', Attic εἰκός. δυναμένους μέγα probably refers to the Athenians as potential givers (Baragwanath 2008: 168), though it is formally ambiguous and could refer to the Milesians as recipients, who might be strong enough to do the Athenians a good turn in future.   καὶ οὐδὲν ὅ τι οὐκ ὑπίσχετο 'there was nothing he did not promise'.   πολλοὺς γὰρ οἶκε εἶναι εὐπετέστερον δια-βάλλειν . . . ἐποίησε τοῦτο 'it seems to be easier to bamboozle a large number of people than one person, given that Aristagores was not able to do this to Kleomenes the Spartan, but he was able to do it to thirty thousand Athenians'. Here διαβάλλειν must have a different nuance from **96.1**, and is usually but wrongly taken to mean something like 'deceive'; for a better view see Pelling 2007: 183–4: 'there is no suggestion that Aristagoras says anything *false*'. He suggests that the idea is to throw words around so as to wrong someone, and offers the felicitous tr. 'put something across' someone. Cf. ἄνδρα παρελθεῖν at Theok. 16.63. There is nothing conditional here about εἰ. It means 'since', or 'given that'.

This is, among other things, a joke, and would surely have raised as big a laugh at Athens as elsewhere. It should not be pressed as evidence for outright anti-democratic or anti-Athenian sentiments on Hdt.'s part. (On Hdt.'s attitude to Athens see Forrest 1984 and Fowler 2003a.) In any case, on the above interpretation of διαβάλλειν, the Athenians are not being criticised for gullibility (as they are at 1.60.3, the Phye story), but are represented as wronged by Aristagores. Nevertheless there is a serious underlying criticism here of Athenian impetuosity (perhaps not a fair one; see **97.**1n. on ἐπελθών . . .). To make the joke work, Hdt. sacrifices Gorgo's role: Kleomenes was not 'alone' when he resisted Aristagores' διαβολή, **51.**2.

The Pnyx hill, where the Athenian Assembly met, had a capacity of only about 6,000, so Hdt. is here treating the voters as representative of the entire male citizen body (Hansen 1987: 40 and n. 6). With the figure 30,000, compare 8.65.1, the dust cloud from Eleusis made by 30,000 men. It is usual for demographers to dismiss the present figure as a vague, general statement (so e.g. Gomme 1933: 3). But Meiggs 1964 ingeniously combined (a) these two Herodotean mentions of 30,000 Athenians (and that at Ar. *Eccles.* 1132), (b) the evidence for the requirement of 6,000 votes for e.g. ostracism or other *ad hominem* decisions such as citizenship grants and (c) the rule that you need one fifth of the votes to avoid civic dishonour (*atimia*) in certain legal cases, to ask 'Was 30,000 the real total of Athenian adult males enrolled on the deme registers at the time of Cleisthenes' reforms?' Even if it was not that, it might be evidence for Kleisthenes' thinking: a working paper total.

97.3 εἴκοσι νέας: twenty ships may seem a small total compared with the two hundred of 480 BC and Salamis, but the financial windfall from the Laurion silver mines (below 7.144.1 and *Ath. Pol.* 22.7) and Themistokles' consequential building programme fell in between. Note also that at 6.89 the Athenians need to borrow twenty from the Korinthians for use against Aigina, to bring their total up to seventy ships. So the twenty ships sent to Ionia were a heavy commitment, given the small total size of Athens' navy in 500 BC. Were they triremes? See **99.**1n. for this.   ἀρχὴ κακῶν: see **28**nn. for this important and recurring Homerism. The present passage is the most emphatic and powerful expression of it.

On Hdt.'s authorial adverse judgment on the Ionian revolt here, see van Wees 2002: 346. There is no need to look for hostile oral sources, Alkmaionids or whoever, as does Forsdyke 2002: 534 (and as have many others): for Hdt.'s own opinion of the κακά of war, see below, 6.98.2. See rather Fornara 1971: 76 and Harrison 2002: 557. Baragwanath 2008: 170 also has a point (sending the twenty ships was bad because it offered 'a misleading gesture to the Greeks of Ionia, one that implied a degree of Athenian support which would not eventuate').

97.3 (cont.) Μελάνθιον: his patronym was Phalanthos, on the assumption that a surviving ostrakon was cast against this same Melanthios (*AO:* 54). But there is no way of telling if this means that the policy of helping the

Ionians was unpopular, or the execution of that policy, or if the ostraciser disliked him for some quite unrelated, possibly personal, reason. Melanthios' name may have made him specially appropriate for this mission: the name had sentimental significance in Ionian myth (cf. **65**.3n. for Melanthos). It is, however, not rare at Athens (24 bearers in *LGPN* ii, most of them classical).

98 The Paionians again

98.1 βούλευμα ἀπ᾽ οὗ Ἴωσι μὲν οὐδεμία ἔμελλε ὠφελίη ἔσεσθαι 'a plan which was never going to help the Ionians'.   **οὐδ᾽ ὦν οὐδὲ τούτου εἵνεκα** 'and it was *not* for that reason'; a strong and definite negation, rather than a bit of both motives, or even one motive rather than another (cf. **81**.2n. for Hdt. on mixed motives, and on the present 'pointed comment' see Baragwanath 2008: 170). For a different sort of denied motive, see **99**.1. Hdt. presumably means that the Paionians were not likely to send help, although in fact spreading the revolt might not have been a bad idea. **ἐπὶ τοὺς Παίονας ... ὑπὸ Μεγαβάζου**: in effect an internal back-ref.; for these people see **15**.3 and n. on ἐς τὴν Ἀσίην. Cf. Lewis 1977: 67.   **κώμην ἐπ᾽ ἑωυτῶν** 'a village of their own'.

98.2 σώιζεσθαι ἐπὶ τὴν ὑμετέρην αὐτῶν 'to get back safe to your own country'.

98.3 ἀσπαστὸν ἐποιήσαντο 'they welcomed this'.   **ἐς Χίον**: this looks both back and forwards. The theme of 'unhappy Chios' – a place where, or to whose citizens, horrible things happen – begins in bk. 1 (see esp. 1.160.4, the start of a kind of curse), continues in bk. 6 (6.2.2, 16.2, 26–7), and culminates at 8.104–6. See Hornblower 2003 and above, Introduction p. 36 and n.123.

98.4 κατὰ πόδας 'at their heels'.   **ἐκ Χίου μὲν Χῖοί σφεας**: the island is Χίος, acc. Χίον (as above, **98**.3) but the nominative singular of the ethnic adjective is Χῖος with a long iota (from an original Χῖιος, as Σάμος, ethnic Σάμιος).   **ἐς Δορίσκον**: Doriskos, west of the river Hebros in Thrace, will feature extensively in bk. 7, see *IACP*: p. 871.

99 The rebel fleet; Eretria and the Lelantine War

99.1 οἵ τε Ἀθηναῖοι ἀπίκοντο εἴκοσι νηυσί, ἅμα ἀγόμενοι Ἐρετριέων πέντε τριήρεας: for the Athenian total of twenty, see **97**.3 and n. Morrison, Coates and Rankov 2000: 42 argue plausibly that the specification of the Eretrian triremes, coming after the vaguer 'ships' of the Athenians, means that the latter were not triremes. Their further inference that Athens 'was still too poor, or was too much of a landed aristocracy to be willing, to aspire to sea-power' does not follow; in any case, see **85**.1 and n. for the single Athenian trireme during the conflict between Athenians and Aiginetans in perhaps the 590s.

At **31**.3, Aristagores had tried to tempt the Persian Artaphrenes with the prospect of annexing large and prosperous Euboia. But it is possible that soon afterwards he was himself in Euboian Eretria asking for help, and getting it (see **55** n. on ἤιε ἐς τὰς Ἀθήνας).

99.1 (cont.) οὐ τὴν Ἀθηναίων χάριν 'not for the sake of the Athenians'. The presentation by negation means 'not, as you might charitably think...'; with the pointedly denied motive, cf. Th. 7.57.9 (the Argives fought alongside the Athenians in Sicily, not so much because of their alliance with the Athenians, as out of hatred for the Spartans: οὐ τῆς ξυμμαχίας ἕνεκα μᾶλλον ἤ..., with *CT* III: 666). There may be a hint at the old connection of Eretria with Peisistratos: 1.61.2 and 62.1, and see *Eretria*: 27 (J.-P. Descoeudres), for Athens-flattering Theseus themes on the Eretrian temple of Apollo, *c.* 530 BC. In view of this, it might have been expected that the Eretrians would have liked to see his son Hippias reinstated by Persia, and would have had no wish to oblige the Athenians in the new post-tyrannical situation. But no (Hdt. says), they co-operated with the Athenians, though their motive was to oblige not them but the Milesians. Note the usual generalising collective expression, as if Hdt. knew that every Eretrian felt the same. (The same problem arises with Th.'s even more confident statements of inferred motivation.) Here, Hdt.'s denial is too absolute. Some Eretrians were surely not sorry to see their old enemies in Chalkis (below) humiliated by Kleisthenic Athens (**77**). ὀφειλόμενά σφι ἀποδιδόντες: an example of 'good' τίσις, requital for past (sometimes, as here long past) favours. οἱ γὰρ δὴ Μιλήσιοι...Σάμιοι ἐβοήθεον: for this episode of the archaic period, the so-called 'Lelantine war' between Chalkis and Eretria (named after the plain of Lelanton which separated the Euboian cities of Chalkis and Eretria) see Th. 1.15 with *CT* I: 49. Th. says more succinctly and sweepingly that the rest of Greece, καὶ τὸ ἄλλο Ἑλληνικόν, joined in the war, but otherwise does not tell us anything we did not know from Hdt., for whom, by contrast with Th., 'the conflict is part of a pattern of reciprocal action' (Said 2011: 74).

The early war between these two close Euboian neighbours was evidently important, but is frustratingly hard to date, and therefore to place in context. It may have been fought as long in the past as 700 BC, and have had a colonial aspect, in view of the prominent role of these two Euboian cities in early Greek settlement overseas (below). The other main sources for the war are scattered; most of them are conveniently collected and translated at Fornara no. 7. They are Archilochos fr. 3 West (on the fighting methods of the 'spear-famed lords of Euboia'), Strabo 10.1.12 and Plut. *Mor.* 760–1 (Thessalian help for Chalkis); Hes. *Op.* 650–60 boasted of victory in a singing competition at the funeral games of King Amphidamas of Chalkis, who is known to have fought in the Lelantine War (Plut. *Mor.* 153f); this would fit a date for the war around 700 BC, except that Amphidamas and the war are sometimes used to fix Hesiod's own date, and M. West 2011b: 207 is now sceptical about the value of the war (a 'shadowy conflict') for Hesiod's chronology. The later writers may have drawn on a work by a Hellenistic historian called Archemachos of Euboia, *FGrHist* 424 (see esp. F 9): West 1978: 321. Of the earlier writers, Hdt. might conceivably have cited Archilochos here, in view of his mention of him in another context (1.12.2), but that earlier citation may be interpolated, and the allusion in the present passage is vague and indirect. Nevertheless, Archilochos' apparent mention of the war is the best indicator of the war's date, which is left floating by both Hdt. and Th. Archilochos knew of other events around 650 BC (*OCD*[4] 'Archilochus'), so that provides an approximate date earlier than which hostilities had begun. But we do not know how much earlier, or how long the war lasted. By contrast, a link with Euboian colonising activity in the second half of the 8th cent. is plausible, though Ducrey (below) inclined to a lower date ('7th or even 6th century BC'). The war may have been a long one, *c.* 710–650 (V. Parker 1997). The best modern discussion is Boardman, *CAH* 3[2] 1: 754–65, 'Euboia'; and see *Eretria*: 29 (P. Ducrey).

The present passage has always interested historians and archaeologists because it combines (a) east Greek places (Samos, Miletos) with (b) Euboia, always known from literary sources for primacy in colonisation, esp. in west and north. See Livy 8.22.6 for the foundation of Kyme in Italy by Chalkidians in *c.* 750 BC, who 'eventually dared to move their settlement across to the mainland' (*deinde in continentem ausi sedes transferre*) after an initial cautious phase of settlement at Pithekoussai (mod. Ischia in the bay of Naples; see Strabo 5.4.9, Pithekoussai a joint Chalkidian-Eretrian foundation). See also Th. 6.4–5 for the many Chalkidian foundations in Sicily, which explain why in a Sicilian context 'Chalkidian' virtually = 'Ionian' (Chalkis itself was held to be Ionian). For Eretria, see e.g. Th. 4.123.1, Mende in the N. Aegean an Eretrian colony; also (for separate colonising activity by Chalkis and Eretria) Strabo 10.1.8.

Euboians are now known to have been active in the *east* Mediterranean also. The same unusual and distinctive pottery types were found at both Chalkis in Euboia and Al Mina in Syria: Boardman 1957. Then the archaeological picture began to fill out in the W. Mediterranean too: excavations at Pithekoussai produced 'Nestor's Cup' (ML 1), and some more of the same distinctively Euboian pottery. Finally, a rich 9th-cent burial at Lefkandi in the Lelantine plain itself has, since 1980, yielded finds which indicate international contacts at that early date: Cyprus, Egypt etc. See Osborne 2009: 55–60 and 342; for Euboian primacy in early colonising activity see Lane Fox 2008 and (for Chalkis in particular) *TT*: ch. 9, discussing 'Chalkidic Torone' (N. Aegean) at Th. 4.110.1.

Pieces of horse-armour from Syria have been found at Euboia, Samos and Miletos. This distribution pattern may be connected with the present passage of Hdt. See Lane Fox 2008: 118 (and n. 46).

Samians and Milesians were perennial enemies, see Th. 1.115.2 for a 5th-cent war between them, and the Asia Minor parts of Th. bk. 8 presuppose the hostility. The Lelantine War may have been connected with an obscure local mainland Ionian conflict in the Priene region, the 'Meliac War'; and there is epigraphic evidence from the 320s for long-standing friendship between Samos and Chalkis: Habicht 1957: no. 1, part of the large dossier of Samian expressions of gratitude to those who had helped deracinated Samians in the years of the Athenian cleruchy of 365–322. See Shipley 1987: 29–31; 37 and n. 62.

The Korinthians – like the Milesians a great colonising power – can be brought into the picture, though they are not here mentioned by Hdt.: they expelled the Eretrians from Kerkyra before settling it themselves (Plut. *Mor.* 293), probably in the time of Periandros. It is consistent with this that a Korinthian built ships (triremes?) for the Samians at an early date: Th. 1.13.3. But that means that the friendship between Thrasyboulos of Miletos and Periandros of Korinth (see on **92 ζ**) was politically anomalous, and though tyrants may have reversed traditional arrangements almost on principle, and although the present passage of Hdt. shows what long memories Greeks had for favours, it is risky to assign allies 'on the strength of known later alignments and disputes' (Boardman *CAH* 3². 1: 763).

99.1 (cont.) ἐποιέετο στρατηίην ... αὐτὸς μὲν δὴ οὐκ ἐστρατεύετο ἀλλ᾽ ἔμενε ἐν Μιλήτωι: this is close to being 'correction in stride', for which see Lattimore 1958 (a statement or, as here, a natural implication, is immediately qualified or cancelled). The negative presentation in the second sentence has censorious bite: Aristagoras 'bowed out safely ... choosing to remain at Miletos rather than advancing with his army'. So Baragwanath 2008: 169 n. 20; see also her 246, noting the inconsistency with 7.8 β 3, where Aristagoras is incorrectly said by Xerxes to have accompanied the army to Sardis.

99.2 στρατηγοὺς δὲ ἄλλους ἀπέδεξε Μιλησίων εἶναι 'he gave the command to other Milesians' (Waterfield's tr.). Most trs. take the Greek to mean that he appointed the two men to be generals of the Milesians. But the narrative goes on (**100**.1) to speak of military actions by the Ionians generally. It makes a difference: Aristagores is appointing overall commanders (who were Milesians), he was not appointing commanders of the Milesian contingents only. For his powers in the matter (conferred by the Ionian league?) see **38**.2n.   τὸν ἑωυτοῦ τε ἀδελφεὸν Χαροπῖνον καὶ τῶν ἄλλων ἀστῶν Ἑρμόφαντον 'his own brother Charopinos, and another Milesian [lit. 'of the other citizens' in the sense of 'belonging to that category', not that of 'commanding them'] Hermophantos'. That Aristagores had a brother is new information, although **30**.2 showed that Histiaios and Aristagores were related in more than one way, and that these people liked to keep things in the family. Charopinos is not a specially rare name, but the greatest concentrations are at Ephesos (five bearers) and at Miletos: six bearers, all earlier than 200 BC, of whom Hdt.'s man is no. (1); three of the others are in the list of *stephanephoroi*, for which see **30**.2n. It is a 'herophoric' name, formed from the heroic name Χάροψ or Χάροπος (which was e.g. the patronym of Nireus at *Il.* 2.672); see Bechtel 1917: 478.

The name Hermophantos can be either theophoric from Hermes, or else a river-name, Flussname, or 'potamonym', from the Hermos. The suffix–phantos, 'revealed by', is consistent with either. See Hornblower 2003: 45–6 for such ambiguous Herm- or -herm names. The name is specially common in Chios and in Karia: seven bearers at Miletos alone.

100–103 Hostilities open. The burning of Sardis

100 ἐν Κορησσῶι τῆς Ἐφεσίης: Ephesian Koressos or Koresos (both spellings are attested epigraphically) was a military disembarkation point (Xen. *Hell.* 1.2.7) and is actually called a harbour, λιμήν, at *Hell. Oxy.* 1.1 Chambers, a newly discovered Cairo fr. of papyrus narrating events of 409 BC, and mentioning [τὸ]ν λιμένα τὸν Κορησσὸν καλούμενον. That harbour aspect must be meant here. The name was more usually applied to Mt Koressos (mod. Bülbül Dag), which dominated the city of Ephesos. See *IACP*: p. 1060, and Fraser 2009: 346–7. Boardman 1982: 12–13 sees Theseus' exploits against the Ephesos-connected Amazons as a symbol of Athens' help to the Ionian Revolt.   ποταμὸν Καΰστριον: Καΰστριος is the Homeric name of the river (see below for *Il.* 2.461), not an adjective from Κάυστρος; so rightly Powell 1935: 159. The Kayster river is mod. Küçük Menderes or 'small Maeander' as opp. the Büyük Menderes or 'great Maeander', the Maeander proper. This bi-partite conception of the Maeander is of medieval origin (Thonemann 2011: 21). The Kayster is the middle of the three parallel rivers whose valleys have always made western Asia Minor so fertile and desirable. They are, running from north to south, Hermos, Kayster and Maeander. Mt Tmolos separates the Hermos and Kayster.

This is, surprisingly, Hdt.'s only mention of the Kayster (the Ephesos-Sardis route mentioned at **54**.1 would in fact have run along it, see n. there). But the Homerically-minded Athenian troops, as they made their way eastwards along the river, most of them after setting foot on Asian soil for the first time, would surely have seen themselves as re-enacting *Il.* 2.459–65, the simile comparing the Greek army pouring onto the plain of Skamandros to 'the great flocks of flying birds – geese or cranes, or long-necked swans – in an Asian water-meadow, by the streams of Kaystrios, which wheel this way and that in their wings' glory, and the meadow echoes to their cries as they settle in tumult...' The vividness and accuracy of this (cf. Thonemann 2011: 298–301, quoting Th. Wiegand) have been taken to prove the poet's familiarity with the region (see e.g. West 2011: 20).

100 (cont.) ἐπείτε ὑπερβάντες τὸν Τμῶλον ἀπίκοντο: the Tmolos ridge featured in bk. 1, in the narrative of an earlier attack on Sardis (Kyros takes it from Kroisos): 1.84.3, ἔστι δὲ πρὸς τοῦ Τμώλου τετραμμένον τῆς πόλιος. See also **101**.2, where 1.93 is recalled both thematically and verbally. αἱρέουσι Σάρδις οὐδενός σφι ἀντιωθέντος: the blitzkrieg campaign is spectacularly successful – at first; like another Greek invasion of Asia (1920–2). Tozzi 1978: 168–9 speculates that one rebel motive for the attack on Sardis was desire to embroil the Lydians. But if so, there is no sign that they rose against the Persians, and (as Tozzi concedes), we find one prominent Lydian on the Persian side, Myrsos son of Gyges: 5.121 with 3.122.1 for the ethnic. (The Lydians acquiesced in Persian rule. They – as opposed to Lydia's satrap Autophradates – do not feature in the list of peoples who joined in the revolt of the satraps from Persia in the late 360s: Diod. 15.90.3.) The obvious Greek motive, to strike at the administrative nerve-centre and symbolic satrapal seat, is enough. ἐρρύετο 'he saved/defended it' (middle), from ῥύομαι. The acropolis would appear to have been saved; perhaps it was the location of the larger, richer houses (Dusinberre 2003: 215). The damage to the city as a whole may not have been very great: at the beginning of bk. 6, Histiaios arrives at Sardis as if there was nothing wrong with Sardis at all. (But the date of his arrival makes a difference. If several years had passed since the burning, it is not surprising that Sardis was in good shape again, but the length of time-lapse is far from clear. See Introduction p. 20.) There is therefore rhetorical exaggeration at **106**.1; see n. there.

A deposit of carbonised matter at the right level has been taken as archaeological evidence for the conflagration: Hanfmann 1983: 68–9. But this is now disputed. It is now believed (according to Nick Cahill, one of the excavators at Sardis, at a seminar in Oxford, 30 Jan. 2012) that this evidence is unsafe and there is no obvious archaeological evidence for the fire. It seems that the city was relocated as a result of the Persian conquest of 546, after which the inhabited area was outside the city walls and more dispersed. See Cahill 2008b: 118–19, and cf. **101.2**n. for the agora. But Hdt. is nevertheless correct to imply that the damage was to the lower city, not the acropolis.

101.1 τὸ δὲ μὴ λεηλατῆσαι ἐλόντας σφέας τὴν πόλιν ἔσχε τόδε 'what prevented them from looting the city after capturing it was this…' αἱ μὲν πλεῦνες καλάμιναι: this is contingency: if the houses had happened to have been made of different materials and not made of reeds, serious consequences, above all the burning of the Kybebe temple, might have been avoided. For the sack as a matter of chance, but one which had serious consequences as providing delusory evidence that the revolt would succeed, see Baragwanath 2008: 169. ἐπενέμετο 'overspread', or perhaps 'encompassed'. Here only in Hdt., and here for the first time anywhere in this sense; but it may have originated as a medical term for a disease spreading, cf. Hippok. *Epidem.* 3.4 and Th. 2.54.5 (the great plague); or perhaps, as Richard Hunter suggests, it could mean 'fed/grazed on'.

101.2 τὰ περιέσχατα νεμομένου τοῦ πυρός 'the fire was consuming the edges'. Cf. 1.86.5 about another fire at Sardis: the funeral pyre of Kroisos, τῆς δὲ πυρῆς ἤδη ἀμμένης καίεσθαι τὰ περιέσχατα, the only other place where Hdt. uses the word περιέσχατα. Note the way in which, as often, the simple verb-form (νεμομένου) follows the complex (ἐπενέμετο). καὶ ἐπὶ τὸν Πακτωλὸν ποταμόν, ὅς σφι ψῆγμα χρυσοῦ καταφορέων ἐκ τοῦ Τμώλου: the Paktolos was a tributary of the Hermos, and ran down the north slope of the Tmolos mountain from Hypaipa (again *Barr.* map 56 FG5). The Paktolos has not so far been mentioned as such, but its existence was implied at 1.93.1, where the gold dust carried down from the Tmolos was the first of the few wonders, θώματα, of Lydia, and was described in virtually identical language to the present passage: the country – he there says – has no wonders to speak of πάρεξ τοῦ ἐκ τοῦ Τμώλου καταφερομένου ψήγματος. (For the significance of this near-absence for Hdt.'s view of the Lydians and their affinity with the Greeks, see Munson 2001: 193.) The present passage is a back-referring continuation of bk. 1, but with increased precision (the naming of the river). The information about the gold dust was more obviously at home in its bk. 1 context, but it does serve here to emphasise the fabulous wealth of Sardis; cf. Eur. *Bacch.* 154 and Antimachos fr. 191 West = 93 Matthews (*c.* 400 BC), and later writers, e.g. Lykoph. *Alex.* 272, 1351–2 and Prop. 1.6.32 and 3.19.28. διὰ μέσης τῆς ἀγορῆς ῥέει: it is now thought that the Persian city was differently positioned from its Lydian predecessor (**100**n. on αἱρέουσι), and was more dispersed over the plain. If so, the agora was more 'open-plan' than was normal in a city of Greek type, such as is suggested by the word *agora* (cf. 1.153.1). See Cahill 2008b: 118–19.

101.3 πρὸς τὸ ὄρος τὸ Τμῶλον καλεόμενον: it is not clear why Hdt. should have waited until the third mention in bk. 5 (including one in the previous para., and quite apart from those in bk. 1) before adding τὸ καλεόμενον. Perhaps (see on the Kayster at **100**) Hdt. is aware that he is operating with famous names.

102.1 ἐν δὲ αὐτῆισι καὶ ἱρὸν ἐπιχωρίης θεοῦ Κυβήβης: the ancient Anatolian cult of Kybebe or Kubaba was often equated in antiquity with the Phrygian cult of Kybele or the Great Mother, *Meter*, but may originally have been distinct. The 'local' (ἐπιχωρίη) Sardis cult is illustrated by a pottery graffito found at Sardis mentioning Kubaba, and by a votive relief from Sardis, depicting Artemis and Meter. Here too there is a problem of identification: Artemis and the Mother are distinct at Sardis, despite some evidence for conflation elsewhere. The, or a, temple of Kybebe is probably depicted on a marble temple model. The cult of the Mother, despite its exotic flavour, was at home in classical Athens from the 6th cent.: the Metroon or shrine of the mother housed the main city archive; cf. Parker 1996: 159, suggesting that the cult came to Athens from Ionia. For all the above, see Roller 1999: esp. 44–53, 119, 124, 130 fig. 138, 162–9 and 196; also Robert 1989: 322 (Hellenistic Greek dedication to the 'Lydian mother of the gods'); Hordern 2002: 192f.; Lightfoot 2003: 8 n. 7 and 176 n. 408; Kuhrt 2007: 218 and Munn 2006. **τὸ σκηπτόμενοι οἱ Πέρσαι ὕστερον ἀντενεπίμπρασαν τὰ ἐν Ἕλλησι ἱρά:** the double-compound verb is an invention, but its meaning is transparent. It displays Hdt. at his most even-handed, if not φιλοβάρβαρος (Plut. *Mor.* 857a): σκήπτομαι does not automatically imply the *falseness* of the excuse or proffered reason (cf. **30.3**n. on σκῆψιν ...). The Persian firing of the temples on the Athenian Acropolis was to be the pretext for Greek aggression in the east down to the time of Philip II and Alexander the Great (Polyb. 3.6.13, where that is what is meant by Persian παρανομία). But here Hdt. suggests, proleptically, that the Persian impieties of 480 were 'counter-burning'. **νομοὺς ἔχοντες** 'who controlled provinces' (note the noun's accent).

102.2 συμβαλόντες δὲ πολλὸν ἐσσώθησαν: this battle can safely be regarded as historical, although Plutarch denied this on the grounds that there was no mention of it in the parallel account by Charon of Lampsakos (*FGrHist* 262 F 10, quoted by Plut. *Mor.* 861 = *On the malice of Hdt.* 24). See Tozzi 1978: 170 and n. 168 against the modern scepticism of Beloch 2² 2: 11 n. 1. Charon was dated *c.* 400 BC by Jacoby, but Fowler 1996: 67 argued for an earlier date and thought he might have been known to Hdt., as some ancient evidence implies was possible. So Hdt. might here be correcting Charon rather than *vice versa*.

Hdt. does not say so in so many words, but this defeat presumably explains the Athenian withdrawal, about to be mentioned at **103.1** (Tozzi

1978: 170 and Baragwanath 2008: 168: Athens 'belatedly extricates her-self…no doubt regretting having risked her safety over what was clearly *not* going to be an easy task').

102.3 ἄλλους τε ὀνομαστούς, ἐν δὲ δὴ καὶ Εὐαλκίδην…αἰνεθέντα: the Simonides poem is fr. 518 in *PMG*, but that merely reproduces the present passage of Hdt.; evidently more than one poem was written for Eualkides.

The 'crown-bearing' games are the big panhellenic four (cf. 8.26): Olympia, Pythia, Nemea, Isthmia. *IACP*: no. 370 at p. 654 says that the equestrian Olympic victor Krokon in ?492 (Paus. 6.14.4 with Moretti: no. 177) was the only attested Olympic victor from Eretria, and that no Ere-trians won in any of the other major panhellenic games. The first part of this may be true (Hdt. would have specified an Olympic victory, as he does elsewhere), but the second half is falsified by Eualkides. It remains true that the small number of Eretrian victors is surprising. Lysanies of Eretria was a suitor of Agariste of Sikyon, 6.127.4 (in the past in real time, but in the future within Hdt.'s text), and this called for athletic skills, at least from the younger contestants (6.128.1). To the literary evidence, add an inscribed early 5th-cent. bronze cauldron, which identifies itself as a prize from the games for Herakles (Hornblower and Morgan 2007: 41 and n. 167).

For Hdt.'s citation of athletic or equestrian successes by militarily prominent individuals see **47.1n.**

102.3 (cont.) ἀναραιρηκότα: a reduplicated pluperfect of ἀναιρέω, sense I (2) in Powell. Cf. 6.36.1 and Hom. *Il.* 23.736, Achilles tells Odysseus and Miltiades' mythical kinsman Telamonian Ajax to 'take up' equal prizes.

103.1 Τότε μὲν δὴ οὕτω ἠγωνίσαντο: compare *Il.* 24.1, λῦτο δ' ἀγών (after the games in bk. 23). The mention at **102.**3 of the agonistically success-ful Eualkides might have exerted an unconscious pull towards this choice of verb.   **Ἀθηναῖοι…ἐπικαλεομένου σφέας πολλὰ δι' ἀγγέλων Ἀρισταγόρεω οὐκ ἔφασαν τιμωρήσειν σφι:** the alternative reading ἐπικαλεομένους would mean that the Ionians rather than Aristagores did the appealing. But this would reduce the contrast (Baragwanath 2008: 169 and n. 19). See **102.2n.** for the simple reason for the Athenian withdrawal, namely the military defeat. It had nothing to do with the archonship at Athens of the Peisistratid Hipparchos son of Charmos in 496/5 (*AO*: 54); for this expla-nation see Tozzi 1978: 171 n. 172. The eponymous archon was one of an elected college of nine, and in no position to dictate policy. Athens now had a panel of ten elected generals, whose influence will have been much greater. However unavoidable the Athenian withdrawal from the military point of view, Hdt. places much emphasis on the Athenian help to the

Ionians (and makes Xerxes do the same, **105**), but except for the present passage he has little to say about their rapid abandonment of them; see Tamiolaki 2010: 62. The Eretrians probably now withdrew also (Tozzi 1978: 172).

It has been suggested that Miltiades' capture of Lemnos, narrated at the end of bk. 6, was achieved with the help of the returning Athenian fleet on this occasion (Meidani 2010: 172–3).

103.1 (cont.) Ἴωνες δέ...οὐδὲν δὴ ἧσσον τὸν πρὸς βασιλέα πόλεμον ἐσκευά- ζοντο: the negative expression here ('no less') may be purely conventional, a litotic way of saying 'they made preparations for war vigorously'; but there may also be a hint that to continue like this was folly or at least dangerous. The Ionians, in Hdt.'s opinion, *ought* in their own interests to have 'lessened their preparations', i.e. grasped the lesson of the defeat at Ephesos, rather than being elated by the spectacular but accidental burning of Sardis (see **103**.2 for Kaunos, where the Sardis point is made explicitly). But there was no possibility of turning back now.

103.2 πλώσαντες δέ...ἐκπλώσαντές τε...Καρίης τὴν πολλὴν προσεκτήσαντο σφίσι σύμμαχον εἶναι: a brisk crisp piece of military narration (note the neat variation of the verb πλέω, the first time with ἐς, the second time with ἐκ- and ἔξω); if turned into Attic Greek, it could have been written by Th. The last bks. of Hdt., partly because of their military subject matter, draw closer to Th. in manner than the earlier books (e.g. many more speeches). But much of the revolt narrative which follows (up to 6.43) would have been harder to follow without the weight of introductory material provided discursively in bk. 1.

Byzantion was mainly and famously a Megarian colony, but there was a tradition that made it Milesian, perhaps an indication of mixed settlement: Vell. Pat. 2.7.7 (see *IACP*: p. 915 and *CT* III: 986). For the possible relevance of this see **117**n.

The Ionian strategy of spreading the revolt north and south was sound. The adhesion of Cyprus (**104**) had not been planned for by the Ionians, and generated complications. For Karia see **117**n.

103.2 (cont.) καὶ γὰρ τὴν Καῦνον πρότερον οὐ βουλομένην συμμαχέειν... τότε σφι καὶ αὕτη προσεγένετο: see **103**.1n. on οὐδὲν δὴ ἧσσον...Hdt. treated Kaunos separately from Karia at 1.171.1 and 172.1, perhaps because it was on the border with Lykia. For Kaunos (mod. Dalyan), a prosperous though malarial city, see *IACP*: no. 898, adding Robert 1989: 487–520 and Marek 2006: 487–520; cf. also *OCD*[4], 'Caunus' and *CT* III: 864 on Th. 8.39.3. (Malarial: Strabo 14.2.3 and Bean 1971: 166.) Note the almost exasperated force of καὶ αὕτη: 'even Kaunos' (cf. Baragwanath 2008: 169 n. 18).

104 and 108–116 The revolt of Cyprus

On the Cypriot kingdoms (hereditary autocratic monarchies) see F. Maier, *CAH* 6² (1994): 297–306. But they were *poleis* at the same time, and for the particular cities mentioned by Hdt. see *IACP*: nos. 1012 (Amathous), 1016 (Kourion), 1020 (Salamis), 1021 (Soloi): all Maier again. For no. 1019 (Paphos), see below. On Cyprus as a whole, see *Barr.* map 72 and *IACP*: pp. 1223–5.

Cyprus has featured intermittently in the *Histories* so far, most recently in connection with the mysterious *sigynnai* at **9**.3, and at **31**.3, where its size is compared by Aristagores (addressing Artaphrenes) to that of Euboia, and again in Aristagores' speech to Kleomenes, **49**.6. In earlier bks., Hdt. is noticeably interested in the cult of 'Aphrodite' there, 1.105.3 and 199.5. He records that Cyprus was annexed and made tributary by Amasis of Egypt (2.182.2); after that the Persian conquest of Cyprus is not specifically recorded, but it must have taken place as a consequence of Kambyses' conquest of Egypt (probably about 525 BC: Watkin 1987), and is taken for granted at 3.91.1: Cyprus, together with Phoenicia and Palestinian Syria, forms the fifth Persian imperial νομός. For 4.162 (Euelthon ruler of Salamis), see **104**.1n.

For the Cypriot revolt and Hdt.'s narrative of it see Hill 1940: 118–19; Tozzi 1978: 174–86; O. Murray, *CAH* 4² (1988): 483–4; Karageorghis 2004; Petit 2004 (Amathous); Serghidou 2007; Wiesehöfer 2011, stressing the extent to which inter-personal and inter-city rivalries determined the course of Cypriot history in this period. The Cyprus and Karia narratives repeat in miniature the structure of the main 'Ionian' revolt, see Walter 1993: 270 and e.g. below **104**.3n.: Gorgos=Hippias, and **113**.1n. on προδιδοῖ. There is also some anticipation of themes which will recur in the main Persian Wars narrative: see **109**.1n. on ἄνδρες Ἴωνες …

104.1 ἐθελονταί: this is not chance or contingency, because it is made clear at **104**.2 that the Ionian and Karian revolts were infectious. But Cyprus was not part of the Ionian plan.   **πλὴν Ἀμαθουσίων:** Amathous, on the S. of the island, was distinctive and conservative in culture (syllabically written Eteocypriot survived there as the official language until the 4th cent.: Maier, *CAH* 6²: 305, cf. Aupert 2001). The Amathousians are thought to have claimed to be autochthonous in the sense familiar from Greek foundation legends or myths of identity; see Petit 2004.   **ἀπὸ Μήδων:** here and at **104**.3, Hdt. writes 'Medes' not 'Persians', probably because it sounded more solemn and portentous, and is appropriate in situations where formidable military strength and aggression is implied (but this explanation works less well at **104**.2). Powell distinguishes two senses (1) 'Mede' and (2) 'Medo-Persian'. We have met sense (1) already in bk. 5

(see **9**.3, where 'Mede' really does mean 'Mede'), but this is the first use of sense (2) for a long time, in fact since 4.197.1. At **108**.2, **115**.2 etc. below, we are back with 'Persians' in a Cypriot context.   ἦν Ὀνήσιλος Γόργου μὲν ... ἀδελφεὸς νεώτερος, Χέρσιος δὲ ... παῖς: for the asyndeton, see **71**.1n. Names in Onasi- are (like Stas- names, **113**.1n.) characteristic of Cyprus: Mitford 1950: 102 n. 3 and Fraser 1972: 2.146 n. 193. See *LGPN* 1: 349–51, noting esp. 350, the entry for Onasilos (= Onesilos) itself: nineteen Cypriots and one man from Methymna on Lesbos; there are even six men called Onasikypros and one woman called Onesikypra; with these compare the two–kypros names at **113**.2 below. For Gorg-names (not specially Cypriot), see **48**n. Gorgos is the only Cypriot bearer of the name in *LGPN* 1, and the same is true of Chersis.

For Chersis' patronym, Hude's OCT printed the MSS Σιρώμου, and Wilson retains this, because the name occurs in syllabic form on an inscription from an unknown Cypriot city, and on a particularly interesting coin from Paphos; see Egetmeyer 2010: 377 no. 455 and Masson 1990c: 156 (for the coin, which has the name in the form *si-ro-mo-se*). Nöldeke's emendation Εἰρώμου was preferred, both here and at 7.98, at *LGPN* 1: 147 and 174, citing *ICS* 320 and 319.

The last name, Euelthon, suddenly returns us to the bk. 4 Kyrene narrative: for Euelthon as ruler of Cypriot Salamis see 4.162, where we were told that he dedicated a censer at Delphi, and gave hospitality and a golden spindle to Pheretime (mother of Arkesilas III, king of Kyrene *c.* 525–522), but famously not the army she asked for. Euelthon was the first king of Salamis to issue coins.

Salamis is in the east of the island, a little south of the promontory known locally as the 'pan-handle'. It was the largest city in Cyprus, and was a replacement for Bronze Age Enkomi, 5 km. inland: *OCD*[4] 'Salamis' (2). It had an important Greek foundation myth which linked it to the Aiakids. (For the usability of Greek foundation legends about Cypriot cities, see Hornblower 2010.) Teukros, brother of Ajax whom he failed to stop from killing himself, was banished there by his father Telamon, 'exiled by his father's taunts' (Lykoph. *Alex.* 450). Teukros called the city after the Greek island of Salamis, having been promised by Apollo a 'future Salamis in a new land' (Hor. *Carm.* 1.7.29). See **66**.2n. for Ajax and the 'old' Salamis. For Cypriot Salamis see also Isokrates' oration 9, *Evagoras*, which exaggerates the extent to which the place was sunk in barbarism in the 5th cent.

104.2 ὡς καὶ τοὺς Ἴωνας ἐπύθετο ἀπεστάναι: 'Ionians' is surely shorthand for 'the Ionians+Hellespontines+Karians' (cf. **103**.2). Hill 1940:118 was right to stress the relevance, in Cyprus, of the 'adhesion of the Carians to the cause'. For archaeological and other evidence for contacts between Karia and Kypros see *Mausolus*: 15 n. 74, also 21 n. 123 (on Idagygos, an epigraphically attested Halikarnassian mercenary who died at Cypriot Amathous in *c.* 475, and may have gone to Cyprus as part of the Ionian force which went to help Onesilos. See *LSAG²*: 353 and 358 n. 41, with Nikolaou 1971: 13 and pl. ix).   πάγχυ ἐπικείμενος ἐνῆγε 'he applied pressure very energetically indeed'.   ἀπεκλήισε τῶν πυλέων 'he shut him out of the gates' i.e. shut the gates against him.

104.3 Γόργος μὲν δὴ στερηθεὶς τῆς πόλιος ἔφευγε ἐς Μήδους: the family feud (to some extent a contingent causal element) was at least as important a motor of revolt as was the ideology of liberation. It is a kind of *stasis* (note ἅμα τοῖσι ἑωυτοῦ στασιώτηισι above), and – as *stasis* often does – it leads to the involvement of a foreign power (for Homeric precursors, see Said 2011a: 367, citing e.g. Hom. *Od.* 2.326–7, the suitors fear that Telemachos will bring back men to fight for him, from sandy Pylos or Sparta). Cf. 6.88, where Nikodromos of Aigina tries to betray his city to the Athenians; and plentiful later evidence, e.g. Th. 2.2.2, some dissident Plataians wish to hand over their city to the Thebans, and so set off the Peloponnesian War. Gorgos is a Hippias-like figure, except that he will succeed in getting reinstated, thanks to Persian help (**115** below), whereas Hippias will fail.

For 'Medes' (not Persians), see above **104.1n.** In the part of the world close to the Persian empire, 'flying to the Medes' was a standard move for a defeated party in time of *stasis*. See e.g. ML 40 (Erythrai, 450s BC) line 25, or Th. 1.115.4 (Samos, 440 BC). Cf. **30.1n.** and 3n.

104.3 (cont.) Ἀμαθουσίους δὲ … ἐπολιόρκεε προσκατήμενος: for Amathous going its own way, see above, **104.1n.** Sieges are a marked feature of the Cypriot military narrative. Here, the final participle (from προσκάτημαι, lit. 'I sit in front of', cf. Th. 4.130.2 etc.) refers to the usual wearisome siege methods before the invention of non-torsion and then torsion artillery after about 400 BC. Sieges were therefore long and expensive businesses, cf. the staggering 2000 talents spent by the Athenians at Potidaia, Th. 2.70.2. See *CHGRW* I: 237–47 (B. Strauss).

For the Amathous siege in particular, see Petit 2004: 9–14, citing some archaeological evidence for destruction, and discussing at 18–20 the king of the besieged city, whose name, not given by Hdt. but attested on coins, was Rhoikos.

There is archaeological evidence for a siege of Paphos on the west of the island (a ?Persian siege mound and tunnels, illustrated at Tozzi 1978: plate IX, cf. VIII; *CAH* 4² (1988): 485 fig. 42). This is usually associated with the present campaign, though Paphos is not mentioned by Hdt. in this narrative section (it features in passing at 7.195).

105–107 Dareios, Histiaios, and the 'thing with the bow'

The exchange at 106 between Dareios and Histiaios has similarities with the speeches at **23–4**; in both places Hdt. may be seeking to convey a speech-idiom suitable for communication at court: see **106**.3n. on ἐκ τοῦ σοί τι ἢ μέγα ἢ σμικρόν.

105.1 βασιλέϊ δὲ Δαρείωι ὡς ἐξαγγέλθη Σάρδις ἀλούσας ἐμπεπρῆσθαι: there is a narrative delay here (we might have expected this anecdote to come directly after the burning). Tozzi 1978: 178–9 suggests an 'artistic-dramatic' desire to throw Dareios' hostility towards the Athenians into sharp relief. This is possible, but we should also, more prosaically, allow for a time-lag in communication.   **Ἀθηναίων καὶ Ἰώνων**: the post-position of the Ionians is explained by Ἰώνων οὐδένα λόγον ποιησάμενον later in the sentence.   **συνυφανθῆναι** 'had been woven together'. The verb (from the root ὑφαίνω, 'I weave', compare English 'web of intrigue') is found here only in Hdt., but it anticipates the differently expressed metaphor at 6.1.2, where Artaphrenes says to Histiaios 'you sewed the shoe [of the Ionian revolt], and Aristagores put it on'. For the compound verb used metaphorically (in tmesis, i.e. the two parts separated) see *Od.* 13.303: ἵνα τοι σὺν μῆτιν ὑφήνω, cf. Said 2011a: 278 and (on the verb τολυπεύω) n. 107.   **πρῶτα μὲν λέγεται αὐτόν**: such instances of λέγεται are common in Th., who uses them for various purposes, not only to indicate scepticism (see Westlake 1977 and Gray 2011). Here the word may mean little more than that this was a well-known story, cf. below **108**.1n.   **οὐ καταπροΐξονται** 'they would not go unpunished'.   **εἰρέσθαι οἵτινες εἶεν οἱ Ἀθηναῖοι**: Dareios knows the answer, and will know it even better after the battle of Marathon. The exchange is – yet more bk. 1 and 5 correspondence – a thematic and verbal re-run of 1.153.1, where Kyros asks who are the Spartans, ἐπειρέσθαι τοὺς παρεόντας οἱ Ἑλλήνων τίνες ἐόντες ἄνθρωποι Λακεδαιμόνιοι … and when he is told, he makes a witty and defiant reply. Words then, symbolic actions now. (When Dareios asks about the Paionians at **13** above, that looks more like genuine curiosity.) Cf. also Artaphrenes' questions at **73**.2 above.   **αἰτῆσαι τὸ τόξον**: this is the 'thing with the bow' (**108**.1, see n. there). It is possible that when Dareios asked for his τόξον, he did more or less that, because it is an Iranian loan-word (West 2007: 21 n. 52).

105.2 ὦ Ζεῦ: that is, Ahura Mazda. The 'Greek [religious] interpretation' is not in itself a reason for rejecting the story.   **ἐκγενέσθαι μοι Ἀθηναίους τείσασθαι**: compare the similarly expressed **79**.1 (of the Thebans), βουλόμενοι τείσασθαι Ἀθηναίους, with n. there. For the use of the infinitive to express a wish, see (with Stein, and How and Wells) *Il.* 2.413, 7.179, and *Od.* 17.354, all of them from prayers to Zeus, as here. Dareios knew his

Homer! See also below 6.86 α 5, with Lightfoot 2003: 407.   ἐνὶ τῶν
θεραπόντων: at 6.94.1 (the start of the Marathon campaign), Hdt. will
remind us that the servant has been reminding Dareios to remember the
Athenians.

106.1 καλέσας ἐς ὄψιν Ἱστιαῖον: compare Kambyses 'calling [the priests] into
his presence [lit. 'sight']' at 3.28.1. The pompous, visual and spectacular side of the Persian monarchy is often hinted at, cf. also 3.68.2 for the
present expression, and **24**.3 and **106**.5, ἐξ ὀφθαλμῶν. Histiaios has been
'out of the picture' since he sent the man with the tattooed head at **35–6**.1,
having been detained for a long time at court, as Hdt. will now remind us
(χρόνον ἤδη πολλόν).   **ἐκ τῆς ἑτέρης ἠπείρου** 'from the other continent'.
This points discreetly towards the Europe/Asia divide which will be so
important in bk. 7; cf. also 1.4.4.   **τοὺς δώσοντας ἐμοὶ δίκην τῶν ἐποίησαν** 'who will pay me the penalty for what they have done'. The expression
δίκας διδόναι is almost always (but see 6.87) used in speeches, direct or
indirect, and a Persian is usually, as here, one of the interlocutors. See
Lateiner 1980.   **Σαρδίων με ἀπεστέρησε**: for the tense (some MSS have
the perfect, -ηκε) see Wilson. The implication here (and cf. his son Xerxes'
speech at 7.11.2, where ἐνέπρησαν means 'burned down') that Sardis no
longer existed is wrong, or at any rate a great exaggeration of the damage.
See **100**n. on ἐρρύετο.

106.2 βουλευμάτων: cf. **98**.1 (Aristagores' 'plan' which was really designed
to do down Dareios) and n. See also βουλευμάτων at para. 3 below, echoing
the present passage.

106.3 κοῖον ἐφθέγξαο ἔπος: a Homerism, see e.g. Hera at the beginning of
the speech to Zeus discussed above, **92** ἡ 5n.: αἰνότατε Κρονίδη, ποῖον τὸν
μῦθον ἔειπες (*Il.* 16.440). Compare also Hdt. 1.8.3, Gyges to Kandaules,
δέσποτα, τίνα λέγεις λόγον οὐκ ὑγιέα. It is a polite form of contradiction,
often used towards a superior; but not always, thus at 7.103.1 Xerxes uses
it to Demaretos, Δημάρητε, οἷον ἐφθέγξαο ἔπος. It no doubt has its roots
in vernacular speech. A variant is 'what a thing have you done!', as at
23.2 above, Megabazos to Dareios: ὦ βασιλεῦ, κοῖόν τι χρῆμα ἐποιήσας...See
n. there.   **ἐκ τοῦ σοί τι ἢ μέγα ἢ σμικρὸν ἔμελλε λυπηρὸν ἀνασχήσειν** 'which
would result in any harm, great or small, for you' [lit. 'from which any
harm...will result']. Hdt. may have seen this kind of expression as specially suited to Greek spoken in a Persian context (see **23**.2n. for the sing-
song redundancy of καὶ ἡμέρης καὶ νυκτός, and cf. the repetition here of
different cases of πάντα with the varied cases of πολλός there). So this is an
attempt at ethnic characterisation or stereotyping: the clever Greek adopts
elaborate and stylised 'orientalising' courtesies. With this use of ἀνέχω to
mean 'result from', cf. 7.14, τάδε τοι ἐξ αὐτῶν ἀνασχήσει.   **τῶι πάρα μὲν**

πάντα ὅσα περ σοί 'I, who have everything that is yours'. πάρα = πάρεστι.
πάντα … πάντων δέ: for the repeated πάντα see above on ἐκ τοῦ σοί …

106.4 ἐπ᾽ ἑωυτοῦ βαλόμενον 'on his own initiative'.   **νεώτερον πρήσσουσι**
περὶ πρήγματα τὰ σά: cf. Dareios at 24.1, τοῖσι ἐμοῖσι πρήγμασι. Heavy alliteration here, and the last two short words could be spat out indignantly.
ἀνάσπαστον: this word is curiously direct, and also hints at those transfers
of population to which Persian kings were addicted (12.1n.).

106.5 Ἴωνες γὰρ οἴκασι 'the Ionians seem', from οἶκα, Attic ἔοικα, perfect
with present sense.   **ἐξ ὀφθαλμῶν:** cf. 24.3 καὶ σύ μοι ἐγένεο ἐξ ὀφθαλμῶν
and n. there, also 106.1n. on καλέσας ἐς ὄψιν.   **ποιῆσαι τῶν πάλαι ἵμερον**
εἶχον 'to do what they have long yearned for'.   **οὐδεμία πόλις ὑπεκίνησε:**
this verb is found here only in Hdt. It refers to very gentle movement (as
at *Il.* 4.423, the west wind lifting the waves), cf. LSJ ii: 'not a single city
would have stirred a finger'.   **μηχανησάμενον:** for the verb see 30.4n.

106.6 μὴ μὲν πρότερον ἐκδύσεσθαι τὸν ἔχων κιθῶνα καταβήσομαι ἐς Ἰωνίην 'not
to take off the tunic in which I go down to Ionia' (lit. 'the tunic, wearing
which I will go down … '). Compare the extravagant reported promise of
the Persian satrap Tissaphernes that he would 'turn his own bed into silver', i.e. sell it, sooner than see the Athenians short of maintenance: Th.
8.81.3, with *CT* iii: 988 for a similar colourful promise by the younger
Kyros in Xen. At 8.120, Xerxes is said by the Abderites (but Hdt. does not
believe it) to have 'loosed his belt' at Abdera for the first time since retreat-
ing from Athens.   **Σαρδώ:** that is, Sardinia, which will recur at 124.2 as a
possible place of refuge for Aristagores; it was suggested by Bias of Priene
as a possible location for a new pan-Ionian super-*polis* (1.170.1, see next
n.). The island is here chosen for its size (it has a slightly longer coast-
line than Sicily), and because it is just that, an island (Constantakopoulou
2007: 122, cf. Ceccarelli 1996); but Hdt. was perhaps unconsciously influenced by the similar-sounding Sardis at 106.1 (Pelling 2011: 11). Sardinia
does not feature in *IACP*, i.e. no Greek colonies were sent there, despite
what Hdt. says about Bias, Aristagores, and their proposals. It has rich mineral deposits, and was grain-producing, but the climate was bad, at least in
the time of the emperor Tiberius (Tac. *Ann.* 2.85), and this explains why
Greeks steered clear of it in reality, as opposed to fantasy thinking; contrast
Corsica (1.165.1). Nevertheless, there was a marked increase in imports
of Attic pottery to Sardinia after about 500 BC (Davison 1992: 386), and
such growing contacts might help to explain Hdt.'s interest.   **νῆσον τὴν**
μεγίστην: this closely echoes 1.170.2, focalised through Bias, Sardinia said
to be νήσων τε ἁπασέων μεγίστην; and both passages will be picked up at
6.2.1, authorial recapitulation of the present extravagant promise. Translations on the lines of 'largest island in the world' / 'largest island there

is' are unavoidable (ἀπασέων in bk. 1 is stronger than the later formulations), but they heighten the absurdity for us, possessed with 21st-cent. geographical knowledge.

107 διέβαλλε: see **96**.1n. The sense here must be 'deceived' rather than 'slandered' or 'injured'.   **Δαρεῖος δὲ ἐπείθετο:** Hdt. does not add 'easily', εὐπετέως, as at **24**.1, but he might have done, in view of the speed with which Dareios falls for the διαβολή.   **παραγίνεσθαι οἱ ὀπίσω ἐς τὰ Σοῦσα:** contrast Skythes, whom Dareios thought the most honest of men because he *did* come back to him after promising to do so: 6.24.1.

108–115 The Cyprus revolt quashed

108.1 ἐν ὧι δὲ ἡ ἀγγελίη…ἐν τούτωι παντὶ τῶι χρόνωι: this looks like an unusual flag of a time interval 'during which' an extended synchronised series of events occurs, but in fact the first part of the sentence merely summarises the episodes which have just been narrated, and there is no measurement of time intervals (Immerwahr 1966: 59f. and n. 43; 66). **τὰ περὶ τὸ τόξον:** this phrase ('the thing with the bow' is Waterfield's tr.) may be more than a mere back-ref. to **105**.1; the definite articles may also suggest that the story was a well known favourite, cf. ἐστιγμένος, 'the man with the tattoo' at **35**.2, and see above. 105.1n. on πρῶτα μὲν λέγεται αὐτόν. **μεμετιμένος ὑπὸ Δαρείου** 'released by Dareios'. For the verb, see 35.4n. on ἀποστάσιος… **Ἀρτύβιον:** the name (like that of Kypselos' father at **92**) means 'eagle'; see Schmitt 1976: 32.

108.2 ἐπικαλεύμενός σφεας 'summoning them'; at **92**.η. 5 the verb means 'invoke'.   **Ἴωνες δὲ οὐκ ἐς μακρὴν βουλευσάμενοι ἦκον πολλῶι στόλωι:** for the decision-making body, see **109**.3n. The Ionians send zealous and large-scale help, and 'respond in kind to the Cyprians' freedom rhetoric': Baragwanath 2008: 186–7; see **109**.2n. on ἐλευθέρη, and the authorial remark at the opening of **116**. But this positive depiction will soon change. See **113**.1n. on προδιδοῖ.   **ἐκ τῆς Κιλικίης:** for the perennial importance of Kilikia as an Achaemenid Persian naval base, see Casabonne 2004: 93. The link between Cyprus and Kilikia has been hinted at already, in the speech given to Aristagores at Sparta, **49**.6 and n.   **τὴν ἄκρην αἳ καλεῦν-ται Κληίδες τῆς Κύπρου:** these 'Keys' were at the top of the 'pan-handle', ᵗhat is, at the very NE-most tip of Cyprus. There was a temple of Aphrodite ʳaia on the mainland there. See Strabo 14.6.3 (who however applies the ᵖ to a group of offshore islands) and *Barr.* map 72 F1. The relative αἳ ᵗted into the plural form of the name which follows.

ᵗου δὲ τοιούτου γινομένου 'in this situation'.   **ἄνδρες Ἴωνες, ᵗίδομεν:** cf. 7.160.2, Gelon's final offer, which is to help the

Aegean Greeks if he is allowed to lead either the land army or the fleet; and see the angry reply of the Athenian representative in the following ch. **161.** προσφέρεσθαι 'to attack', with dative. ὥρη ἂν εἴη ὑμῖν ἐκβάντας ἐκ τῶν νεῶν τάσσεσθαι πεζῆι 'it would be the moment for you to disembark and form up as infantry ...' After a natural initial dative plural after ὥρη ἂν εἴη, Hdt. switches to an equally natural accusative and infinitive construction, which is then maintained for the rest of the sentence.

109.2 ἐλευθέρη: the Cypriot rhetoric is echoed by the Ionians at the end of **109.**3, οἷα ἐπάσχετε δουλεύοντες.

109.3 ἡμέας ἀπέπεμψε τὸ κοινὸν τῶν Ἰώνων: see **108.**2n. for the Ionian decision. This analeptic reference to themselves as sent by 'the Ionian *koinon*', might mean a formal meeting of the Ionian league at the Panionion, as at bk. 6.7 below (see above **36.**1n. on ἐβουλεύετο); but the expression should not automatically be assumed to indicate a federal entity. Thus at 6.14.3, τὸ κοινὸν τῶν Σαμίων means 'the decision-making Samians' and at Th. 1.89.3, Ἀθηναίων τὸ κοινόν means just 'the Athenians'. ἐπ' οὗ ἐτάχθημεν 'in the task assigned to us'. For this use of ἐπί with the genitive, see Powell A III 'modal' (3), 'in charge of';

110 ἀπολέξαντες τὸ ἄριστον 'they chose the best ...'

111–112 The battles; Onesilos' clever Karian squire

Behind this story lies that of Myrtilos, the mythical archetype of the clever charioteer, who sabotaged Oinomaos' chariot and helped his master Pelops to gain the hand of Hippodameia: Pind. *Ol.* 1, *FGrHist* 3 Pherekydes F 37a (and in *EGM*), Lykoph. *Alex.* 158–67, and Apollod. epit. 2.6. Two clever grooms in Hdt. act, like Myrtilos, in ways which (1) involve horses and (2) trickery, and (3) bring benefit to their masters: at 3.85–7, Oibares helps Dareios to the throne by some sharp practice involving a mare, and in the present passage, Onesilos is cleverly saved by his Karian groom from Artybios' horse. See Köhnken 2006b. It is possible that the present story has been transferred or recycled from another connection altogether, given that the squire's homeland Karia is not cavalry country: Xen. calls it ἄφιππος (*Hell.* 3.4.12 with *Mausolus*: 7 and n. 31).

111.1 δεδιδαγμένον πρὸς ὁπλίτην ἵστασθαι ὀρθόν 'which had been taught to rear upright against a hoplite' (a heavy-armed infantry fighter). ἦν γάρ οἱ ὑπασπιστὴς γένος μὲν Κάρ 'he had a squire, who was a Karian by birth'. It is at first sight surprising that, unlike Oibares in bk. 3 (above, introd. n.), this man is not named, although he is written up so eulogistically (κάρτα δόκιμος etc.). We soon see why the name has been withheld: as he himself is about to explain in para. 4, he is a nobody compared to his master.

(There was a proverb 'try it out on the Karian' meaning a worthless body
for the conduct of an experiment, like 'try it out on the dog'.) For the
Karia-Cyprus link see **104.**2n. on ὡς καὶ τοὺς Ἴωνας…

The noun ὑπασπιστής ('esquire': Powell) is found here only in Hdt.,
and will change its meaning (see LSJ (2)) by the time of Alexander the
Great's 'hypaspists', an elite Macedonian corps of infantry; and see Tod:
no. 183, Alexander's treaty with the Greeks, line 9.

111.2 φυλάξας 'be on your guard' (absolute).

111.3 ὦ βασιλεῦ, ἕτοιμος μὲν ἐγώ εἰμι ποιέειν τὰ ἀμφότερα: compare the
choice offered by the Cypriots to the Ionians at **109**, though the squire
here replies less haughtily than do the Ionians there.

112.1 συνέμισγε 'they joined battle', lit. 'began to engage' (the neuter
plural subject στρατόπεδα takes a singular verb).   **ἄκροι** 'excellent'; cf.
Lykoph. *Alex.* 1128.   **Σάμιοι ἠρίστευσαν:** cf. the Aiginetans after Salamis,
8.93.1. This may refer to a formal post-battle decision and award. At Lade,
the Samian record will be more equivocal (6.14).

113.1 Στησήνωρ: the Ionic form of a good Cypriot type of name. A
later Stasanor (or possibly Stasandros) from Cypriot Soloi was a satrap
of Alexander the Great; see Diod. 18.18.2 with Berve 1926: 2 no. 719,
and Heckel 2006: 255. Stas- names (like Stasinos, the supposed author
of the *Kypria*) are characteristic of Cyprus; see *LGPN* I: 410–11, including
another Cypriot Stasanor from the 5th–4th cents. (from Marion-Arsinoe)
and a Stasikypros, cf. below. Compare also Stasandros, perhaps a relative
of Alexander's Stasanor, Heckel 2006: 255, and cf. Cameron 1995: 8–9 for
the poet Kallimachos' brother-in-law Stasanor.   **προδιδοῖ:** this treachery
(and that of the men of Kourion, προδόντων) anticipates the divisions
at Lade, 6.14; Karageorghis 2004: 3 speaks of the 'discord' between the
Cypriot kings. Baragwanath 2008: 187 notes that it is only through treachery that the Persians prevail on Cyprus, and that this emphasis is part of a
generally positive line towards the whole 'Ionian' revolt on Hdt.'s part. But
this will undergo a subtle change with the beginning of bk. 6 (see 6.10),
when his language becomes more critical.   **οἱ δὲ Κουριέες οὗτοι λέγονται
εἶναι Ἀργείων ἄποικοι:** cf. Tod: no. 194 ('after 331 BC', Nikokreon, king
of Cyprus, claims Argive descent) and Fortin 1980: 40. In reality, archaic
Argos was not a great colonising power (7.150, alleged Argive-Persian
link, is an ambitious piece of 'kinship diplomacy' rhetoric; for Argives
supposedly colonising cities in Egypt, as at Pind. *Nem.* 10.5, see *Th. and
Pi.*: 27 and 206). In the archaic and classical periods, therefore, evidence
for claims to Argive colonisation of places outside the Balkan mainland
(for Macedon, see **22.**2) is in short supply, by contrast with the Hellenistic
period, when many cities sought fictitiously to connect themselves with the

all-powerful Macedonian i.e. Argive-descended monarchies by themselves claiming Argive descent. This may even account for Nikokreon, above. But the present passage is a genuine early claim (Hdt. does not say by whom the claim was made), and is thus of some importance. Cf. also ML: 104–5 on no. 42 (= Fornara: no. 89, mid 5th cent. BC) for Argos as probable colonial mother-city of the Kretan cities Knossos and Tylissos; and for Argos as claimed metropolis of Rhodes, see Th. 7.57.6 and Pind. *Ol.* 7.19ff. with *Th. and Pi.*: 132 n. 7. When assessing some of this, we must remember the old Homeric ambiguity of 'Argives', which can mean 'Greeks' generally; but that does not apply to the present passage.

113.2 ἄλλοι τε ἔπεσον πολλοὶ καὶ δὴ καὶ Ὀνήσιλος: note the characteristic reluctance to give details about the manner of his death, especially given what we are about to be told about his severed head (114–15 below). See Boedeker 2003: 20. The historians copied Homer in many ways, but none of them before Procopius went in for gory Homeric descriptions of battle-wounds, unless we count Plutarch as a historian (gory deaths of Caesar and the younger Cato). **καὶ ὁ Σολίων βασιλεὺς Ἀριστόκυπρος ὁ Φιλοκύπρου**: the names are interesting indicators of pride in whole-island (as opp. individual *polis*) status, a type of pride well discussed by Constantakopoulou 2005; compare the similarly formed names Stasikypros (above), also Onasikypros and Onesikypra (**104**.1n.). A possible alternative or simultaneous explanation is that they are theophoric names formed from Κύπρις i.e. Cyprus-born Aphrodite (see already Hom. *Il.* 5.330); but the difference is not great because that *epiklesis* is itself patriotically Cypriot. **Φιλοκύπρου δὲ τούτου τὸν Σόλων...αἴνεσε τυράννων μάλιστα**: in view of Solon's well-advertised negative views about tyranny (fr. 33, cf. 9 West), it is surprising to find him bestowing praise of this sort, but μάλιστα may merely imply he said that this man was best of a bad lot; and anyway, tyrant may be Hdt.'s word for 'ruler' and not have featured in Solon's poem. For this elegiac poem see fr. 19 West, giving the further details provided by Plut. *Sol.* 26.2–4 (including six lines of the poem itself), and by an ancient life of the Hellenistic poet Aratos.

For Hdt. and the lyric poets, see **95**.1n. on Alkaios. Some have thought that Solon could not have legislated at Athens as early as the 590s (the traditional date) if he was a friend of the father of a man killed as late as 498/7. But Solon travelled after his reforms, and there is no actual impossibility.

Plut. (as above) says that Solon was responsible for the synoikism of Soloi, moving it from a hill to a plain. This is improbable, and is an illicit extrapolation from, and extension of, what the poem itself says about the place. But the present passage of Hdt. (not cited by the over-sceptical Lefkowitz 1981: 44–5) is the earliest and best evidence for a genuine connection between Solon and Philokypros of Soloi. It is true that later writers sought to explain the city's name as derived from Solon's, but Hdt. shows no sign of having thought in this way. The chime is a coincidence and the etymology wrong: Soloi is already called 'Sillua' in Assyrian lists of Esarhaddon and Ashurbanipal in the 7th cent. (*IACP*: p. 1230; cf. Stadter 1998: 398).

114.1 κρεμαμένης δὲ τῆς κεφαλῆς... ταῦτα ἄμεινον συνοίσεσθαι: as presented by Hdt., this is a classic example of heroising an enemy so as to neutralise his hostility (or hers: it was done with heroines too). The decapitation was evidently felt by Hdt. to be excessive or barbarian (cf. 6.30.1, Histiaios decapitated by Artaphrenes). It is however possible (Petit 2004) that the Amathousians were really carrying out a ritual in two stages, (1) head hung high up and ritually cleansed and (2) dead man given hero-cult. On this view the decapitation is itself part of the heroisation. There were practical considerations too: in the Middle Ages, decapitation and display was the only way to prevent denial of death.

See Parker 2011: 117 for this and other heroisations of enemies. Onesilos has something in common with a well-attested category of disgruntled Olympic and other athletes who turn nasty after death – their statues fall on people, etc. – and so need to be appeased by hero-cult. (See Boedeker 1987: 190, drawing on Fontenrose 1968.) There is something in this, but it works better for Philippos of Kroton, **47**n., than for Onesilos, who is not known to have been an athlete.

114.1 (cont.) ἐσμὸς μελισσέων ἐσδὺς ἐς αὐτὴν κηρίων μιν ἐνέπλησε: bees are usually positive and benign (see e.g. Theok. 7.78–9, where they feed the rustic hero Komatas), so this was a sign of divine blessing leading to the cult (AHG). With these spontaneously appearing bees cf. Plut. *Kleom.* ch. 39 (that is, the late 3rd-cent. Hellenistic Kleomenes III of Sparta, not Hdt.'s Kleomenes I). A snake coiled itself round the crucified body of Kleomenes III and kept off the carrion birds. This was seen as a portent and he started getting hero-cult. But this stopped when a rationalising explanation was offered by learned citizens, who adduced examples of similar phenomena including bees 'produced' by putrefying cattle. (Scott: 373 thinks Onesilos' bees were 'probably blowflies'.) Cf. Fraser 1972: 1.779 and 2.1087–8 nn. 444–7.

The oracle was clearly Greek. Didyma is one possibility, but there was an oracle of Ares in Pisidia, which is closer to Cyprus (below 7.76 with Gonzalez 2005); or there might have been a local Cypriot oracle in an Amathousian sanctuary (Petit 2004: 15).

115.1 Ἀμαθούσιοι μέν νυν ἐποίευν ταῦτα καὶ τὸ μέχρι ἐμεῦ: see 86.3n. and the other passages there cited.   **ταύτην δὲ Γόργωι τῶι προτέρωι**

βασιλεῖ... παραδόντας: see 104.3n. on Gorgos' reinstatement. He will still be in power in 480 (7.98).

116 Ionians pursued and defeated on land

The narrative pace here and in the next ch. (the Hellespont) is very fast and lacking in detail, compared to the Cypriot and Karian narratives which enclose it. Jacoby 1956: 125 [= *R.-E. Suppl.* ii col. 441] explained the difference in terms of Hdt.'s oral informants: people in Ionia and the metropolis i.e. Athens did not want to remember these dismal events. That is not entirely satisfactory – Hdt. does not exactly rush the Lade narrative in bk. 6 – but it is not easy to think of a better reason. Perhaps it is precisely because Lade is going to be so full, and Hdt. wants to reserve Ionian fullness of narration until then.

116.1 Δαυρίσης δὲ ἔχων Δαρείου θυγατέρα, καὶ 'Υμαίης τε καὶ 'Οτάνης... θυγατέρας: for the name Daurises (from dahyu, 'land'), see Schmitt 1976: 30. For Otanes (son of Sisimnes), see above, **25–6** with **25.1n.** Daurises will be killed in battle at **121** and Hymaies will die of illness at **122.2**. It is astonishing, when you consider the size of the Persian empire and the other military demands the many satrapies must have made on the central administration all the time, that no fewer than three of Dareios' sons-in-law should have commanded on this one campaign. **ἐσαράξαντες:** from the transitive verb ἐσαράσσω, 'drive-pell mell into' (Powell).

117–121 Hellespontine and Karian narrative

The involvement of these areas in the Miletos-centred 'Ionian revolt' is not surprising if we recall that many Hellespontine city foundations were of Milesian origin (see **117n.**), and that Miletos itself, though counting as an Athenian colony (**97.2n.** with cross-refs.), had a Karian element from the start (1.146.2) and was considered in antiquity to belong to Karia geographically. Hdt. calls it the southernmost city of Ionia (1.142.3), but other ancient authorities assigned it to Karia: *LGPN* va: xiii. But see 6.20 for the political implications of the award of Milesian territory to Karians from Pidasa; and note that Hdt. records no common councils and mutually supportive rhetorical exchanges between Ionians on the one hand and either Hellespontines or Karians on the other, of the sort he records for Cyprus at **109**. Hdt. did not record everything that happened in these years (see **55n.** on ἤιε ἐς τὰς Ἀθήνας), and a Milesian appeal to the Hellespontines in terms of 'kinship diplomacy', i.e. mother-city to daughter-cities, would be natural and may have taken place. The reduction of the Hellespont is not complete, even after these Persian reconquests. The story will resume at 6.33.1, naval operations to complement the present land operations, which are there explicitly back-referred to.

117 τὰς ἐν Ἑλλησπόντωι πόλις: for these, see *IACP*: nos. 774 (Dardanos), 765 (Abydos), 788 (Perkote) all S. Mitchell; 748 (Lampsakos), 755 (Paisos), 756 (Parion), all A. Avram. It is relevant (cf. above) to a Miletos-led revolt that several of these were Milesian colonies: Abydos and Paisos were, and Milesians laid a claim to Parion. Dardanos and Perkote are of unknown origin. Lampsakos, though Phokaian, is said to be Milesian by Strabo (13.1.9) and though *IACP*: p. 987 (Avram) dismisses this as erroneous, it may indicate a Milesian element in the population (so *CT* III: 936, discussing Th. 8.62.1). For Kios (also Milesian), see **122.1n.** From bk. 6, add three more Milesian colonies in the Propontis which had evidently joined the revolt: for Prokonnesos (*IACP* no. 759), Artake (736), and Kyzikos (747) see 6.33.2. For Byzantion see **103.**2n. (possible Milesian element alongside the Megarian).   **ταύτας μίαν ἐπ᾽ ἡμέρηι ἑκάστηι** 'each in a single day', adopting the easy emendation μίαν for μέν (Powell 1938a: 216).

118–121 The Karian narrative: a smashing defeat for the Karians, who then stage a successful ambush

Hdt.'s own Karian (Halikarnassian) background should be borne in mind throughout, though if we were told he was from Cyprus, we should no doubt be able to 'detect' signs of childhood and youthful familiarity in the Cypriot narrative too. Nevertheless, the description of e.g. Labraunda (**119.**2) manages, despite its brevity, to be detailed, accurate and vivid.

For Karia see Bean 1971; *Mausolus*: ch. 1; Debord 1999: 130–46, particularly strong on the evidence of the coins; *IACP*: 1108–37 and nos. 870–941 for the *poleis* (P. Flensted-Jensen); and esp. now van Bremen and Carbon 2010. For the Karian language, now deciphered (1980s and 1990s), see Adiego 2010. For Karian personal names, see Zgusta 1964, Masson 1990b, and many writings of L. Robert (but Robert 1963 warns against hasty categorisation of Greek names as Anatolian).

118.1 συνελέγοντο ἐπὶ Λευκάς τε Στήλας καλεομένας καὶ ποταμὸν Μαρσύην: these 'White Pillars' have not been certainly identified, nor is it likely that they ever will be. They are tentatively identified with Gerga and marked at *Barr.* map 51 G2 (for another suggestion see Sahin 1976: 11–12, cf. *Mausolus* 55: n. 25; see also Cohen 1995: 273). For this Karian Marsyas river, a tributary of the Maeander, see *Barr.* map 61 F2 and 65 A1. The more famous Marsyas which (like the Maeander) rises at Phrygian Kelainai is called Katarrhektes by Hdt. (7.26.3). For this river see Thonemann 2011: 57–67.

The Karian league, perhaps with its own hereditary cultic 'king' or βασιλεύς, was the oldest of many such Karian κοινά, always with the proviso that κοινόν can be a less than technical expression, as we have seen (see **109**.3 on the Ionian version). See *Mausolus*: 55–62. There were many other Karian *koina*, of which the best attested is the Chrysaoric league, for which see Strabo 14.2.25 and Gabrielsen 2011.

If, as suggested in *Mausolus*, the Hekatomnids were hereditary 'kings of Karia', and if Pixodaros of Kindye (**118**.2 n.) was their ancestor, it is possible that his advice was given in that prestigious, though not authoritative, capacity (Hdt. makes clear that his proposal was only one of a democratic many).

118.1 (cont.) ἐκ τῆς Ἰδριάδος χώρης: the Idrias or Hidrias region of Karia was on the upper Marsyas (*Barr.* map 61 G3). The 'Edrieis' were assessed for tribute to the Athenians in the great reassessment of 425 BC: ML: no. 69 line 143 at p. 201; see *IACP*: no. 892, 'Idrias', and p. 1109 for the Chrysaoris region, with which Idrias was identified in antiquity.

118.2 ἐγίνοντο βουλαὶ ἄλλαι τε πολλαὶ καὶ ἀρίστη γε δοκέουσα εἶναι ἐμοὶ Πιξωδάρου: the Karian Pixodaros, the good but unsuccessful adviser, plays the Ionian roles of Bias and Thales (1.170) or of Hekataios at **36** (though Hdt. is not so obviously approving of the latter's advice). Other examples of right-but-ignored military warners: Alkibiades before Aigospotamoi (Xen. *Hell.* 2.1.25) and Phanokritos of Parion in Tod: 116 (386 BC). And there are Homeric precursors.   **Πιξωδάρου τοῦ Μαυσώλου ... θυγατέρα:** the names Pixodaros and Mausolos will be borne by two satrapal 4th-cent. brothers, sons of Hekatomnos (himself son of Hyssaldomos, see below) and brothers of Artemisia (not to be confused with Hdt.'s Artemisia, prominent in bks. 7 and 8 below), Idrieus, and Ada (Arr. *Anab.* 1.23.7–8 etc., and Heckel 2006: 3). For the Hekatomnid family tree see *Mausolus*: fig. 1, opp. p. 1. Pixodaros was the youngest brother; see Heckel 2006: 223 and R/O: no. 78. The family was associated with either Mylasa or Halikarnassos (**37**.1n.), and Kindye was roughly equidistant between those two cities (*IACP*: no. 902 and *Barr.* map 61 F3. Kindye later merged with Bargylia, *IACP*: no. 879). A family relationship between the 5th- and 4th-cent. men called Pixodaros is likely, perhaps even direct ancestry and descent. If so, see previous n., and compare Pigres, son of Hysseldomos (*sic*), at 7.98 below. As we saw above, Hysseldomos was the grandfather of Mausolos the satrap, and he and Pixodaros are 'likely forebears' of the Hekatomnid satraps (R/O: p. 263).

The link with the royal family of Kilikia may be Hdt.'s way of emphasising the high status of this Pixodaros; he does not name the daughter.

Syennesis' family resembles the Hekatomnid dynasts and satraps of Karia, over a century later than the events here described by Hdt.: local families which ruled large hellenised enclaves on a hereditary basis within the Achaemenid system; see Salmeri 2004: 191–2, part of a study of Kilikian 'hellenism on the periphery'. (The nurse Kilissa, 'the Kilikian woman', in Aesch. *Cho.* attests 5th-cent. slave trade with Athens.) Compare also the Cypriot rulers discussed above, notably Evagoras in *c.* 400. For these similarities, and the possibility of mutual influence, see Hornblower 2011.

For Achaemenid Kilikia see Casabonne 2004 and Salmeri 2004. Another Syennesis features in Hdt.; he antedates the Achaemenid takeover (1.74.3). The Kilikian ruler mentioned at 7.98 could be identical with Pixodaros' father-in-law. The family continues into the 4th cent. (Xen. *An.* 1.2; Diod. 14.20, and a fragmentary honorary decree attests a Syennesis at late 5th-cent. Karian Iasos, see *SEG* 57.1040). Syennesis is not a mere title; see below for an attempt at a family tree, which assumes that rulers called Syennesis alternated with other males whose names are lost to us (taken from Hornblower 2011: 360).

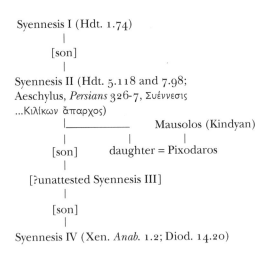

Syennesis I (Hdt. 1.74)
|
[son]
|
Syennesis II (Hdt. 5.118 and 7.98;
Aeschylus, *Persians* 326-7, Συέννεσις
...Κιλίκων ἄπαρχος)
|_____   Mausolos (Kindyan)
| | |
[son]   daughter = Pixodaros
|
[?unattested Syennesis III]
|
[son]
|
Syennesis IV (Xen. *Anab.* 1.2; Diod. 14.20)

118.2 (cont.) ἔτι ἀμείνονες τῆς φύσιος 'even better than their natural inclinations'.

118.3 οὐκ ἐνίκα ἡ γνώμη: as at **36**.4, the advice of Hekataios. See n. there (the exact expression is used there and here only in Hdt.). The argument ('backs to the river' or not?) recalls the choice of Kroisos at 1.206–7, and anticipates in some respects Alexander's problem at the Granikos.

119.1 Καρῶν δὲ ἐς μυρίους: this is much exaggerated. The total 'about ten thousand' Karian casualties is fantastic, and the vaguer hyperbolical sense (cf. English 'myriad'), is not used by Hdt. for numbers of troops. Karia was mountainous country with sparse population and limited urbanisation before the 4th cent. Also, on common-sense grounds, it is hard to see how, after a human catastrophe on that scale, there could have been enough Karians left to inflict the heavy defeat on the Pidasa road at **122** below, even though it was an ambush.

119.2 κατειλήθησαν ἐς Λάβραυνδα...πλατανιστῶν: 'they were trapped' at the sanctuary of Labraunda; the verb is from κατειλέομαι, found only in this passive form (see also below, κατειληθέντες). ἅγιος means '*hallowed*, appl. to foreign temples of special sanctity' (Powell); see also Lightfoot 2003: 349. This good description of Labraunda and its sacred grove of plane trees does not prove autopsy – virtually nothing ever does – but suggests it. Most of the evidence for Labraunda – epigraphic and architectural – is 4th-cent. (the Hekatomnid period) and Hellenistic; for the two important dossiers of inscriptions (1969, 1972) see *I. Labraunda*. Conditions in Hdt.'s time, and in the even earlier period of the Ionian-Karian revolt, have to be read back cautiously from this later evidence; see below.

The sanctuary is remote and high up, 13 km. N. of Mylasa (see *Barr.* map 61 F3 for both places, and for Mylasa cf. **37.**1n. above). It was not itself a *polis* (not in *IACP*), but was connected by a Sacred Way to Mylasa (Strabo 14.2.23), with which it was closely if acrimoniously involved: *IACP*: pp. 1128–9. For the relationship between Mylasa and the priests of Zeus at Labraunda, see Debord 2001: 26 and esp. Dignas 2002: 59–69, 95–106, 204–17 (and cf. *OCD*[4], 'Labraunda'; Hellström 2007; Reger 2010: 51–3, 'Labraunda'; Karlsson and Carlsson 2011). It is likely that the cultic relationship between Mylasa and Labraunda is at least as old as the events Hdt. here narrates, and that Persians ordinarily interfered little in the life of these inaccessible communities; but in the absence of inscriptions like those we have for the later periods, we cannot say more.

119.2 (cont.) μοῦνοι δὲ τῶν ἡμεῖς ἴδμεν Κᾶρές εἰσι οἳ Διὶ Στρατίωι θυσίας ἀνάγουσι: Zeus Stratios is Zeus of armies, and there is no reason to doubt the epithet. Debord 2001: 19 and 30 claims that Hdt. is in error here because there is no certain epigraphic evidence from Labraunda of Zeus Stratios, as opp. Labraundos, whereas Zeus Stratios is attested at Mylasa. But this is too confident, because the inscriptions do not begin until the 4th cent., and the position could have changed in between. On the unique cult of Zeus Stratios (i.e. unique to this part of Karia), see Pirenne-Delforge 2005: 279 n. 32. It is possible that this Zeus is related to Zeus Alalaxios, 'Zeus of the War-cry', of Kall. fr. 75.60–1 (the immediate context is Karian); see

Harder 2012: 2.641. The description here recalls that at 1.171.6 about Mylasa and its temple of Zeus Karios.

For the favourite formula τῶν ἡμεῖς ἴδμεν, Shimron 1973 (above **49**.5n.).

119.2 (cont.) ἢ ἐκλιπόντες τὸ παράπαν τὴν Ἀσίην: like the Phokaians in bk. 1 164ff. or the Samians at 6.22ff., or the various suggestions about Sardinia, discussed above, **106**.6n. Cf. also 8.62.2 (Themistokles on Italian Siris).

120 παραγίνονται βοηθέοντες Μιλήσιοί τε καὶ οἱ τούτων σύμμαχοι: the expression 'Milesians and their allies' indicates Milesian pre-eminence, but does not necessarily mean that Miletos was in formal command of the Ionian league; see Gorman 2001: 139.   τὰ μὲν πρότερον οἱ **Κᾶρες** ἐβουλεύοντο μετῆκαν 'the Karians abandoned their previous deliberations'.   ἐσσώθησαν: unfortunately Hdt. gives no indication where in Karia this even greater defeat happened. The answer would help with the problem of the Pidasa road, see **121** below. It would be natural to suppose that the battle, like that at **119**.1, took place in the region of the river Marsyas, north of Labraunda where the deliberations took place.

121 μετὰ δὲ τοῦτο τὸ τρῶμα ἀνέλαβόν τε καὶ ἀνεμαχέσαντο οἱ **Κᾶρες** 'after this defeat the Karians recovered and renewed the struggle'. Hdt. does not say how long it took the Karians to regroup.   πυθόμενοι γὰρ ὡς στρατεύεσθαι ὁρμέαται οἱ **Πέρσαι** ἐπὶ τὰς **πόλις** σφέων: ὁρμέαται is 3rd person plural of the Ionic perfect of ὁρμῶ. πόλις is one of several forms of the accusative plural of πόλις found in the MSS of Hdt. For ἐπὶ τὰς πόλις σφέων see next n. ἐλόχησαν τὴν ἐν **Πιδάσωι** ὁδόν: the road to the place in question is that leading to Pidasa (not Pedasa as in Hude's OCT) in Milesian territory on Mt Grion, for which see Cook 1961: 90–6, Ehrhardt 1983: 21 and *IACP*: no. 925 (*Barr.* map 61 F3). It makes good military sense here. This Pidasa is not to be confused with *IACP* no. 923 (*Barr.* map 61 E3), 'Pedasa', a long way south of the military theatre in which Hdt.'s fighting took place, and located certainly above Halikarnassos (at mod. Gökceler). The spelling Pidasa for the more northerly city is guaranteed by inscriptions, e.g. Rehm 1914: no. 149, *sympoliteia* (shared citizenship agreement) between Miletos and Pidasa, or *SEG* 47.1563, early Hellenistic *sympoliteia* between Pidasa and Latmos. If Hdt. meant Pedasa here – and despite Bean and Cook (below) it would have made poor military sense – he would surely have said 'the road to Halikarnassos', a much better known city nearby, and one never mentioned by Hdt. in the present narrative. Nevertheless some commentators have accepted that interpretation. Bean and Cook 1955: 150 (cf. Bean in *PECS*: 682) carefully distinguished the two places, but then argued that the ambush took place on the road to the Pedasa-by-Halikarnassos. They had two main reasons: (a) Pedasa-by-Halikarnassos had given Harpagos more trouble than any other Karian place (1.174); and (b) Herodotus says the Karians were worried that Persians were aiming 'at their cities', ἐπὶ τὰς πόλις σφέων, which Bean and Cook thought should mean the cities of the Halikarnassos peninsula. But both (a) and (b) are weak. Halikarnassos and Pedasa were far away to the SW, and there were many Karian cities in between the Marsyas (if that is where the Persians set out from, see above) and the Halikarnassos region: Iasos and Mylasa, for instance. The ambush on the 'Pidasa road', assuming Pidasa to be the Milesian Pidasa on Mt Grion, could have happened in the wild and difficult terrain in which Amyzon and Alinda were situated (the lower part of the square represented by *Barr.* map 61 F2): perfect for an ambush.

There is some confusion in the ancient sources. A Pedasa 'in the territory of the Stratonikeians' is mentioned by Strabo 13.1.59, where he distinguishes it from the Pedasa near Halikarnassos. Ruge, *R.-E.* XIX: col. 27 believed in the existence of this third place, located it between Labraunda and the later Stratonikeia, and suggested that it was the site of Hdt.'s. But Bean and Cook 1955 called this city 'shadowy', cf. von Aulock 1975: 124–5.

There are no MS variants for the bks. 1 and 8 passages, i.e. Hdt. was careful to distinguish them. Note that the suggestion in Rosén's app. crit. ἐπὶ Πηδασοῖσι was anticipated by Bean and Cook 1955: 150 n. 272. *ATL* I: 537 adopted a conjecture of Wesseling, and read ἐπὶ Μυλάσοισι ὁδόν i.e. Mylasa.

The priestess of Athena at Pedasa (*sic*) above Halikarnassos grew a beard when trouble threatened the neighbours: 1.175 and 8.104. Did she do so now? The ambush was a success, so no need for the beard; but the neighbours were in general trouble all right.

'Karians from Pedasa' will be given Milesian land at 6.20. The usual view is that these people were from Pedasa-by-Halikarnassos, but again the more northerly Pidasa may be meant, and that assumption would again make better geographical sense. Cook's conjecture, followed by Radt 1974/5: 169, that the Halikarnassian Pedasans, rewarded by the Persians *after* the revolt (but for what?) founded a new city in Milesian territory and called it by the slightly different name Pidasa, fails if the above argument is right, i.e. if the present passage is good evidence for the existence of the Milesian Pidasa near the *beginning* of the revolt.

121 (cont.) καὶ Ἀμόργης: mentioned only here. For the name, cf. the bastard son of Pissouthnes who is prominent in 413–411 BC (Th. 8.5.5 etc.). See Thonemann 2009: 174–82, with 187 n. 57 for the present passage of Hdt., citing Debord 1999: 80, who thinks the two men called Amorges (Hdt.'s and Th.'s) may have been related.   καὶ Σισιμάκης: this is the Zissamakka of the Persepolis Fortification Tablets; see *CAH* 4²: 469–70.

καὶ Μύρσος ὁ Γύγεω: Myrsos was a (blue-blooded) Lydian, to judge from his name (cf. 1.7.4, Kandaules son of Myrsos) and his patronym (for Gyges see 1.8.1 etc.); and in fact he is perhaps identical with, or at any rate related to, the man at 3.122.1, who is expressly said to be a Lydian. For the significance of this (a Lydian fighting on the Persian side against Karians and rebels) see **100**n. on αἱρέουσι Σάρδις.

121 (cont.) τοῦ δὲ λόχου τούτου ἡγεμὼν ἦν Ἡρακλείδης Ἰβανώλλιος ἀνὴρ Μυλασεύς: for the Karian patronym Ibanollis (father of Oliatos the Mylasan commander seized by Ietragores along with some identifiable tyrants), and for the ethnic Mylaseus, see on **37**.1. If Herakleides was son of the same Ibanollis, he and his brother Oliatos did not share each other's politics. Herakleides was written about by his fellow-Karian Skylax of Karyanda (4.44; cf. *FGrHist* 709 T 1, τὰ κατὰ Ἡρακλείδην τὸν Μυλασσῶν βασιλέα), in a work of which we have no actual fragments (quotations). See Momigliano 1971: 28–30 (S.'s work on H. perhaps the first biography); *Mausolus*: 21. For the name Skylax see **33** and n.

122.1 οὗτοι μέν νυν τῶν Περσῶν οὕτω διεφθάρησαν: this Karian success is the last we hear of military operations in Karia by the Persians in the present phase of narrative, and we might have taken away from it the idea that Karia was after all (i.e. despite the defeat of **119**.1) unsubdued. In fact, the eventual conquest of Karia will be reported in a mere sentence at the end of 6.25. But at 6.20, Milesian territory will be given to 'Karian Pedasans' (or rather Pidasans, see above on **121**), and this may suggest that Karian 'solidarity [with the Ionians] was not complete' (*Mausolus*: 21–2). That Miletos was itself considered part-Karian in antiquity (see introd. n. to **117–121**) is a complicating factor.

*122–123 Persian operations in NW Asia Minor (the Propontis and Aiolid).
Death of Hymaies*

122.1 (cont.) εἷλε Κίον τὴν Μυσίην: another Milesian colony (*IACP*: no. 745, Avram); cf. **117**n. for the significance of this.

122.2 ὅσοι τὴν Ἰλιάδα νέμονται: see **94**.2n. for the resonances of the 'Iliadic' territory.   Γέργιθας τοὺς ὑπολειφθέντας τῶν ἀρχαίων Τευκρῶν: the toponym and city-ethnic of Gergis are both variously given. For the 'Teukrian Gergithes' see also 7.43.2 and cf. Xen. *Hell.* 3.1.22–3 (Gergis and Skepsis were strongholds of the sub-satraps Zenis and of his wife and for a short time successor Mania) and *RC*: no. 10 line 6, where it is again bracketed with Skepsis, in a command letter of the Seleukid king Antiochos I (part of the 'Aristodikides dossier'). For Gergis, mod. Karincali, see *Barr.* map 56 D2 (not to be confused with Gergitha at E3); Cook 1973: 347–51 (the site was identified from the plentiful coins); *IACP*: no. 777.

Cf. also Parke 1988: 51 for the Gergithian sibyl who lived at nearby Marpessos. Cook 1973: 351 remarks that 'whether by deliberate policy or not, reduction by the Persians here resulted not only in a more settled way of life but in promotion to the ways of Greek civilisation'. For the Teukrian connection see **13**.2n.   αὐτός τε ['Υμαίης] αἱρέων ταῦτα τὰ ἔθνεα νούσωι τελευτᾶι ἐν τῆι Τρωιάδι: for the text see app. crit. (the redundant name Hymaies is probably a gloss). Hymaies dies in the same way as another high-ranking Persian on campaign in Asia Minor, Mazares at 1.161: μετὰ δὲ ταῦτα αὐτίκα νούσωι τελευτᾶι. The expression νούσωι τελευτᾶι is otherwise used only of the Spartan king Aristodemos at 6.52.2, but cf. also 7.117.1: Artachaies the Persian happened to fall ill and die at Akanthos, συνήνεικε ὑπὸ νούσου ἀποθανεῖν. Considering how often this must have happened in ancient Greek history, it is surprising that we do not hear of it more often. Cf. Th. 8.84.5, the Spartan Lichas at some year later than 411 BC dies of unspecified illness at Miletos. Unfamiliar diet may have been partly to blame, see *CT* I: 76 for epigraphic and literary evidence for diplomats dying on overseas missions, a common phenomenon; add now Habicht 2001. This might account for Mazares, Hymaies and Lichas. As with deaths in battle (**113**.2n.), the historians tend to give no details, unless to illustrate spectacular divine punishment, like the worms which ate Pheretime at Hdt. 4.205; and we eventually learn that Nikias' illness was kidney trouble, Th. 7.15.1.

The similarity between what is said about Mazares and about Hymaies is the last significant reminiscence of bk. 1 in bk. 5. To be sure, Hdt. did not invent these two men, or the fact that they both died of illness; but he did make the choice to present the fact in identical terms.

123 Ἰωνίης μέν νυν Κλαζομενὰς αἱρέουσι, Αἰολέων δὲ Κύμην: Klazomenai (1.142.3, *IACP*: 847) is at the northern end of Ionia. The city inflicted a surprise defeat on the Lydian king Alyattes (1.16.2), and was a participating polis at Egyptian Naukratis, 2.178.2.

Kyme is *IACP*: no. 817 (Rubinstein again), see **37**.1n. for its tyrant Aristagores (who is not the famous Milesian). Kyme was Aiolian, as Hdt. says; but here too (cf. **117**n. on the Hellespont), there was a Milesian connection: at 1.157–8 they sent messengers to consult the oracle at Branchidai.

124–126 The end of Aristagores

This is an 'escape section' such as often closes a *logos* (Immerwahr 1966: 91 n. 36; 116); compare 6.17 for Dionysios of Phokaia.

There is a parallel account of Aristagores' failure at Th. 4.102.2 (giving the background to the foundation of Amphipolis in 437, by describing

earlier attempts at settlement on the site, and the disaster of the 460s when
10,000 Athenian settlers were killed there, see below **126**.2n.; Th. himself
had mentioned this disaster more succinctly at 1.100.3, but with no ref.
there to Aristagores). It is not clear if Th.'s narrative is also aware of, and
seeks to correct or amplify, Hdt. In Th. (4.102.2), Aristagores is not said to
have been killed but pushed out or knocked out by the Edonians (the verb
is ἐξεκρούσθη) of the χωρίον he had attempted to colonise. But this is hardly
intended as correction: Th. in his brief account is not concerned to deny
that Aristagores was killed (presumably Hdt., is right and he *was* killed);
he is not interested in Aristagores biographically, but in the failure of his
attempted settlement. There is condensation of events, but no necessary
correction of Hdt. But there is another consideration (see *CT* II: 322): Th.
in 4.102 is talking about *Athenian* attempts to colonise the site; to this, the
actions of the *Milesian* Aristagores were strictly irrelevant, even allowing
for the colonial relationship between the two cities. Th. may have wished
to establish, what Hdt. had not, the geographical and thematic connection
between the failures of Aristagores the Milesian and of the Athenians in
the mid 460s. Hdt. will refer to that latter failure in a proleptic reference
– at 9.75, in the context of the death in battle of Sophanes of Dekeleia
'at the hands of the Edonians, during a battle for possession of the gold-
mines at Datus, when he was in joint command of the Athenian forces
along with Leagrus the son of Glaucon' (tr. Waterfield). That this defeat is
identical with the disaster described by Th. 1.100 and 4.102 is traditionally
and rightly assumed. (For Sophanes see further 6.92.3). But neither in the
present passage, nor in bk. 9, does Hdt. make any connection between
the two events in the Drabeskos/Daton region (Aristagores' failure and
the Athenian defeat), and Th. may have felt that this needed to be put
right.

The hearers or readers of both Hdt. and Th. will have been much interested in this area because of these later developments, not only Amphipolis
but the disaster of the Nine Ways in the 460s, see above and **126**.2n.

124.1 ψυχὴν οὐκ ἄκρος 'not conspicuous for his courage'; litotes for 'cow-
ard'.   **ὃς ταράξας τὴν Ἰωνίην καὶ ἐγκερασάμενος πρήγματα μεγάλα**: the verb
ἐγκεράννυμι is found only here in Hdt. (ἐγκεκρημένοι at 7.145.1 is a conjecture). The metaphor is from mixing wine, cf. *Il.* 8.189. But that is perhaps
too pleasant an idea. The idea is more like 'he stirred things up'.

The denunciation is authorial, ferocious, uncharacteristic, and so problematic. (Histiaios gets off more lightly, 6.29–30.) To attribute it to 'oral
sources hostile to the Ionian revolt' is no answer, because Hdt. has
accepted and internalised it. If it is a mere judgment on the man's personality we can only listen to it and leave it. But if it is a judgment on the revolt,

it is intemperate, in that Hdt.'s account itself contains clues that there was more to the revolt than one man's intrigues and trouble-making; so rightly How and Wells. See Introduction pp. 16–18.

124.1 (cont.) δρησμὸν ἐβουλεύε: the noun (and whole expression) is something of a favourite with Hdt (see esp. 8.97.1: Xerxes), and δ. ἐ. is used of contemplated large-scale flight from the Persians at e.g. 8.4.1. δρησμός (Attic δρασμός) is from διδράσκω, so perhaps 'he thought of doing a runner'. See Bowen 1992: 136.

124.2 συγκαλέσας τοὺς συστασιώτας: the exact noun, with the prefix, is otherwise used only at **70**.2 above (the Alkmaionids and their σ.), but the closer broad parallel is with Aristagores' kinsman Histiaios at **36**.1, ἐβουλεύετο ὧν μετὰ τῶν στασιωτέων. Histiaios is about to re-enter the narrative, and this echo subtly prepares us for it.   κρησφύγετον 'a refuge'. A popular etymology (*Etymologicum Magnum* 538.1) connected the word with Krete: 'κρησφύγετα, fortresses in which the islanders hid when fleeing from Minos…'. But the real etymology is unknown.   εἴτε δὴ ὧν ἐς Σαρδὼ ἐκ τοῦ τόπου τούτου ἄγοι ἐς ἀποικίην: see **106**.6n. It is curious that both Aristagores and Histiaios (as we are about to be reminded, 6.1.2) had their eye on Sardinia, surely without immediate co-ordination, though perhaps they had chatted about it on earlier and happier sympotic evenings in Miletos.   εἴτε ἐς Μύρκινον τὴν Ἠδωνῶν, τὴν Ἱστιαῖος ἐτείχεε παρὰ Δαρείου δωρεὴν λαβών: see **11**.2 and **23**.1 and nn.

125 Ἑκαταίου μέν νυν τοῦ Ἡγησάνδρου, ἀνδρὸς λογοποιοῦ: Hekataios has been mentioned or quoted many times before, but only now, and for no easily ascertainable reason, do we get told his patronym (again at 6.137.1). For Hekataios as a λογοποιός, and for his name, see **36**.2n. The patronym might have come better there, his first appearance as a political agent in the *Histories*, as opposed to 2.143 (his exchanges with the Egyptian priests). The patronym (Doric Ἀγήσανδρος) is not rare anywhere, but there are several Milesians, including an early attestation from Didyma (*Syll.³* no. 3a line 3 with *LSAG²*: 342 no. 22). Otherwise Richard Catling (pers. comm.) puts it well: 'it is a name par excellence (in its Doric form) of the Dodecanese, and Rhodes in particular.'

The introduction of Aristagores at this point has been seen as a mere compositional device: Hdt. knew that Aristagores died in Thrace and wished to present him as having ignored sound advice so that his death would 'achieve its proper narrative force'; so West 1991: 156–7, perhaps hypersceptically.

125 (cont.) ἐν Λέρωι δὲ τῆι νήσωι τεῖχος οἰκοδομησάμενον ἡσυχίην ἄγειν: Leros (between Patmos and Kalymnos) was a Milesian colony (cf. **117**n.), and has some of the best harbours in the Mediterranean. See *IACP*: no. 504 (and p. 1083 under Miletos, no. 854); also *CT* III: 824, discussing Th. 8.26.1.   **ἔπειτα δὲ ἐκ ταύτης ὁρμώμενον κατελεύσεσθαι ἐς τὴν Μίλητον** 'it would make a good base for him to return to Miletos at a later date'. That is, to Miletos, the mother-city of Leros. This tr. is, in effect, that of Waterfield. It is correct in its avoidance of any implication of a plan to attack Miletos (κατελεύσεσθαι is from κατέρχομαι, and merely means '*return*, esp. from exile': Powell). Aristagores still needed such a base: he could not rely on being welcomed back at Miletos. In de Selincourt's tr. 'it would make, he said, a useful future base for attacks on Miletus, which might procure his return', the idea 'attacks' is extracted from ὁρμώμενον. Cf. Powell ὁρμῶ II, passive (1): 'pres. partic. often implying a base'. So too Thonemann 2011: 284. But here the idea of offensive operations is not certainly present.

126.1 Πυθαγόρηι ἀνδρὶ τῶν ἀστῶν δοκίμωι: not identical with Pythagores son of Mnesarchos at 4.95.1–2 (more familiar to us as the famous Samian philosopher Pythagoras). For –agores names at Miletos, see **30.2n.** They are sometimes theophorically formed from Apollo or an Apolline cult epithet, or are otherwise Apolline in flavour, and this one is no exception, cf. *Pyth*ian Apollo: see Parker 2000: 58. The name Pythagores is fairly common everywhere: there are some in all published vols. of *LGPN*, including the famous Samian (above, and Pelling 2011: 5 n. 19). There are, however, no occurrences in the earliest two of the Milesian *stephanephoroi* lists (Rehm 1914: nos. 122–3, cf. 30.2n.). Unpublished *LGPN* files for Karia reveal another possible Milesian, at *IG* 11 (4) 526 (Delos); and there are several at Karian Tralles.

126.2 ἀπόλλυται ὑπὸ Θρηίκων αὐτός τε ὁ Ἀρισταγόρης καὶ ὁ στρατός αὐτοῦ: Th. 4.102.2 specifies that it was the Edonian Thracians who 'pushed out' Aristagores, and see Th. 1.100.3 with *CT* I: 155–6 for the disaster which befell the next attempt to colonise the area (which Th. calls the Nine Ways), by the Athenians in the 460s (also described by Th. at 4.102.3, giving the name of the commander, Hagnon son of Nikias); 10,000 settlers were killed.   **πόλιν περικατήμενος καὶ βουλομένων τῶν Θρηίκων ὑποσπόνδων ἐξιέναι...:** for the initial verb see **104.3n.** (προσκατήμενος). The last six words are difficult, and there may well be a lacuna after them (so Maas at Wilson 2011: 66, already reported by Maas' friend Enoch Powell at Powell tr. 2: 708). The best tr. of the text as transmitted is that of Waterfield: 'he was investing a town (even though the Thracians were perfectly prepared to leave it under a truce)'. This is the most straightforward way of taking the Greek, but even so we may feel that Hdt. has not told the whole story. This tr. is adopted by Baragwanath 2008: 185, calling Aristagores' death sordid and needless.

* * *

Bk. 5 ends with Aristagores' death, but the carry-over to bk. 6 (see 6.1.1, Ἀρισταγόρης μέν νυν...οὕτω τελευτᾶι) is as imperceptible as that between chs. **122** and **123** above, about Hymaies, οὗτος μὲν δὴ οὕτως ἐτελεύτησε...See above first n. on **1**.1, and Introduction p. 1, for the unreality of the book divisions, which are probably Alexandrian (i.e. Hellenistic) in date.

WORKS CITED

Journal abbreviations follow those in the *Oxford Classical Dictionary*, fourth edition.

Adiego, I. J. 2010: 'Recent developments in the decipherment of Carian', in van Bremen and Carbon 2010: 147–76

Ager, S. 1996: *Interstate arbitrations in the Greek world, 337–90 BC*, Berkeley, Los Angeles and London

Alter, R. 2011: *The art of biblical narrative*, revised and updated edn, New York

Amit, A. 1973: *Great and small poleis*, Brussels

Amyx, D. A. 1988: *Corinthian vase-painting of the archaic period*, vol. II: *Commentary: the study of Corinthian vases*, Berkeley, Los Angeles and London

Andrewes, A. 1936/7: 'Athens and Aegina, 510–480 BC', *BSA* 37: 1–7
1956: *The Greek tyrants*, London
1966: 'The government of classical Sparta', in Badian 1996: 1–20

Antonaccio, C. 1994: 'Contesting the past: hero-cult, tomb cult and epic in early Greece', *AJArch* 98: 389–410

Aravantinos, V. L. 2006: 'A new inscribed *kioniskos* from Thebes', *BSA* 101: 369–77

Archibald, Z. 1998: *The Odrysian kingdom of Thrace: Orpheus unmasked*, Oxford

Asheri, D. 1990: 'Herodotus on Thracian society and history' in Nenci and Reverdin 1990: 131–69

Aston, E. 2011: *Mixanthrôpoi: animal-human hybrid deities in Greek religion. Kernos Supplément 25*, Liège

Athanassaki, L. 2011: 'Song, politics and cultural memory: Pindar's *Pythian* 7 and the Alcmaeonid temple of Apollo', in Athanassaki and Bowie 2011: 235–68

Athanassaki, L. and E. L. Bowie (eds.) 2011: *Archaic and classical song: performance, politics and dissemination*, Berlin

Aulock, H. van 1975: 'Eine neue kleinasiatische Münzstätte: Pedasa', *Jahrbuch für Numismatik und Geldgeschichte* 25: 123–8

Aupert, P. 2001: 'Amathousiens et 'Etéochypriotes', in V. Fromentin and S. Gotteland (eds.), *Origines gentium*, Bordeaux: 161–8

Austin, M. M. 1990: 'Greek tyrants and the Persians, 546–479 BC', *CQ* 40: 289–306

Baatz, D. 1999: 'Wehrhaftes Wohnen: ein befestigter hellenistischer Adelssitz bei Ephyra (Nordgriechenland)', *Antike Welt* 30: 151–5

Badian, E. (ed.) 1966: *Ancient society and institutions: studies presented to V. Ehrenberg on his 75th birthday*, Oxford

1994: 'Herodotus on Alexander I of Macedon; a study in some subtle silences', in Hornblower 1994: 107–30

Badino, R. C. 2010: *Filostefano di Cirene: testimonianze e Frammenti*, Milan

Baragwanath, E. 2008: *Motivation and narrative in Herodotus*, Oxford

2012: 'The mythic plupast in Herodotus', in J. Grethlein and C. Krebs (eds.), *Time and narrative in ancient historiography*, Cambridge: 35–58

Baragwanath, E. and M. de Bakker (eds.) 2012: *Myth, truth and narrative in Herodotus*, Oxford

Barrett, C. K. 1955: *The gospel according to St John: an introduction with commentary and notes on the Greek text*, London

Battistoni, F. 2010: *Parenti dei Romani: mito troiano e diplomazia*, Bari

Bauer, A. 1878: *Die Entstehung des Herodotischen Geschichtswerkes. Eine kritische Untersuchung*, Vienna

Bauslaugh, R. A. 1979: 'The text of Thucydides iv 8. 6 and the south channel at Pylos', *JHS* 99: 1–6

1991: *The concept of neutrality in classical Greece*, Berkeley, Los Angeles and Oxford

Bean, G. E. 1971: *Turkey beyond the Meander*, London

Bean, G. E. and J. M. Cook 1955: 'The Halicarnassus peninsula', *BSA* 50: 85–169

Bechtel, F. 1917: *Die historischen Personennamen des Griechischen bis zur Kaiserzeit*, Halle

Belayche, N., P. Brulé et al. (eds.) 2005: *Nommer les dieux: théonymes, épithètes, épiclèses dans l'Antiquité*, Turnhout

Berman, J. C. 1999: 'Bad hair days in the Paleolithic: modern (re)constructions of the Cave Man', *American Anthropologist* 101: 288–304

Bernhardt, R. 1987: 'Die Entstehung der Legenden von der tyrannenfeindlichen Aussenpolitik Spartas im 6. und 5. Jhdt. v. Chr.', *Historia* 36: 257–89

Berranger, D. 1992: *Recherches sur l'histoire et la prosopographie de Paros à l'époque archaïque*, Clermont-Ferrand

Berve, H. 1926: *Das Alexanderreich auf prosopographischer Grundlage*, 2 vols., Munich

1937: *Miltiades: Studien zur Geschichte des Mannes und seiner Zeit, Hermes Einzelschrift* 2, Berlin

Bicknell, P. J. 1970: 'The exile of the Alkmaionidai during the Peisistratid tyranny', *Historia* 19: 129–131

1972: *Studies in Athenian politics and genealogy. Historia Einzelschrift* 19, Wiesbaden

1982: 'Herodotus 5.68 and the racial policy of Kleisthenes of Sikyon', *GRBS* 23: 193–201

Binder, G. 1964: *Die Aussetzung des Königskindes*, Meisenheim a. G.

Boardman, J. 1957: 'Early Euboian pottery and history', *BSA* 52: 1–29

   1982: 'Herakles, Theseus, and Amazons', in D. Kurtz and B. Sparkes (eds.) *The eye of Greece: studies in the art of Athens*, Cambridge: 1–28

Boedeker, D. 1987: 'The two faces of Demaratus', *Arethusa* 20: 185–201

   2003: 'Pedestrian fatalities: the prosaics of death in Herodotus', in Derow/Parker: 17–36

Boedeker, D. and D. Sider (eds.) 2001: *The New Simonides: contexts of praise and desire*, New York and Oxford

Bolin, T. M. 1999: 'The use of the past in the Hebrew Bible', in Kraus 1999: 113–40

Borza, E. N. 1990: *In the shadow of Olympus: the emergence of Macedon*, Princeton

Bowden, H. 2005: *Classical Athens and the Delphic oracle: divination and democracy*, Cambridge

Bowen, A. J. 1992: *Plutarch:* The malice of Herodotus, Warminster

Bowie, A. M. 1993: *Aristophanes: myth, ritual, and comedy*, Cambridge

   2003: 'Fate may harm me, I have dined today: near-eastern royal banquets and Greek symposia in Herodotus', *Pallas* 61: 99–109

   2007: *see* Abbreviations

Bowra, C. M. 1953: 'The daughters of Asopus', *Problems in Greek poetry*, Oxford: 52–65

Braccesi, L. 1999: *L'enigma Dorieo*, vol. 11 of *Hesperìa*

Bravo, B. 2008: 'Passi strani in Erodoto e Tucidide su cose della Grecia del VI secolo o più antiche. Autentico e non-autentico', *Palamedes* 3: 93–133

Bremen, R. van 2003: 'Family structures', in A. Erskine (ed.) *A companion to the Hellenistic world*, Oxford: 313–30

Bremen, R. van and J.-M. Carbon (eds.) 2010: *Hellenistic Karia*, Bordeaux

Briscoe, J. 2008: *A commentary on Livy books 38–40*, Oxford

Brock, R. 2000: 'Sickness in the body politic: medical language in the Greek polis', in V. M. Hope and E. Marshall (eds.), *Death and disease in the ancient city*, London: 24–34

   2003: 'Authorial voice and narrative management in Herodotus', in Derow/Parker: 3–16

   2004: 'Political imagery in Herodotus', in Karageorghis and Taifacos 2004: 169–77

Brosius, M. 2007: 'New out of old? Court and court ceremonies in Achaemenid Persia', in A. Spawforth (ed.), *Courts and court society in ancient monarchies*, Cambridge: 17–57

Bruck, E. F. 1926: *Totenteil und Seelgerät im griechischen Recht*, Munich

Brunt, P. A. 1966: 'Athenian settlements abroad in the fifth century BC', in Badian 1966: 71–92 [=Brunt 1993: 112–36, with 1991 postscript at 134–6]

1993: *Studies in Greek history and thought*, Oxford

Buck, R. J. 1979: *A history of Boiotia*, Edmonton

1981: 'Epidaurians, Aeginetans and Athenians', in G. S. Shrimpton and D. J. McCargar (eds.), *Classical contributions: studies in honour of M. F. McGregor*, Locust Valley, NY: 5–13

Bugh, G. R. 1988: *The horsemen of Athens*, Princeton

Buraselis, K. and K. Meidani (eds.) 2010: *Marathon: the battle and the deme*, Athens

Burkert, W. 1985: *Greek religion: archaic and classical*, Oxford

1990: comments on Nenci 1990a, in Nenci and Reverdin 1990: 319

1992: *The orientalizing revolution: near eastern influence on Greek culture in the early archaic age*, Cambridge, MA and London

1993: 'Concordia discors: the literary and archaeological evidence on the sanctuary of Samothrace', in N. Marinatos and R. Hägg (eds.), *Greek sanctuaries*, London, 1993: 178–91

2001a: *Savage energies*, Chicago and London

2001b: 'Demaratos, Astrabakos, and Herakles: kingship, myth, and politics at the time of the Persian wars (Herodotus 6. 67–69)', in Burkert 2001a: 97–110

Burn, A. R. 1962: *Persia and the Greeks. The defence of the west 546–478 BC*, London (reprinted 1984 with Postscript by D. M. Lewis at 587–609)

Burnett, A. P. 1988: 'Jocasta in the west: the Lille Stesichorus', *Cl. Ant.* 7: 107–54

2005: *Pindar's songs for young athletes of Aigina*, Oxford

Burnyeat, M. 2011: 'Episteme', in B. Morison and K. Ieradiakonou (eds.), *Episteme etc.: essays in honour of J. Barnes*, Oxford: 3–29

Bury, J. B. 1902: 'The epicene oracle concerning Argos and Miletus', *Klio* 2: 14–25

Busine, A. 2002: *Les Sept Sages de la Grèce antique. Transmission et utilisation d'un patrimoine légendaire d'Hérodote à Plutarque*. Paris

Buxton, R. 1994: *Imaginary Greece: the contexts of mythology*, Cambridge

(ed.) 2000: *Oxford readings in Greek religion*, Oxford

2009: *Forms of astonishment: metamorphosis in Greek myth*, Oxford

Cagnazzi, S. 1984: 'Decreti dell' assemblea popolare Ateniese in Erodoto e in Tucidide', *Miscellanea greca e romana* 9: 9–37

Cahill, N. D. (ed.) 2008a: *Love for Lydia: a Sardis anniversary volume presented to Crawford H. Greenewalt, Jr.*, Cambridge, MA

2008b: 'Mapping Sardis', in Cahill 2008a: 112–24

Calame, C. 1997: *Choruses of young women in ancient Greece: their morphology, religious role, and social functions*, Lanham, MD

Calder, W. M. 1925: 'The royal road in Herodotus', *CR* 39: 7–11

Cameron, A. 1995: *Callimachus and his critics*, Princeton
  2004: *Greek mythography in the Roman world*, Oxford
Carey, J. 1992: *The intellectuals and the masses: pride and prejudice among the literary intelligentsia, 1880–1939*, London and Boston
Cartledge, P. A. 1982: 'Sparta and Samos: a special relationship', *CQ* 32: 243–65
  1987: *Agesilaos and the crisis of Sparta*, London
Cartledge, P. and F. D. Harvey (eds.) 1985: *CRUX: Essays presented to G. E. M. de Ste Croix on his 75th birthday*, Exeter
Casabonne, O. 2004: *La Cilicie à l'époque achéménide*, Paris.
Catling, R. 2010: 'Sparta's friends at Ephesus. The onomastic evidence', in *Onomatologos*: 195–237
Cawkwell, G. L. 1978: *Philip of Macedon*, London
  1993: 'Cleomenes', *Mnemosyne* 46: 506–27 [= 2011: 74–94]
  2005: *The Greek wars: the failure of Persia*, Oxford
  2011: *Cyrene to Chaeronea: selected essays on ancient Greek history*, Oxford
Ceccarelli, P. 1996: 'De la Sardaigne à Naxos: le rôle des îles dans les Histoires d'Hérodote', in F. Létoublon (ed.), *Impressions d'îles*, Toulouse 1996: 41–54
Chadwick, J. 1956: 'The Greek dialects and Greek prehistory', *G&R* 3: 38–50; repr. in G. S. Kirk (ed.), *The language and background of Homer*, Cambridge, 1964: 106–18
Chamoux, F. 1980: 'Caucasa', in Στήλη εἰς μνήμην Ν. Μ. Κοντολέοντος, Athens: 216–21
Chaniotis, A. 1988: *Historie und Historiker in den griechischen Inschriften*, Wiesbaden
  1998: 'Willkommene Erdbeben' in E. Olshausen and H. Sonnabend (eds.), *Stuttgarter Colloquium zur historischen Geographie des Altertums 6, 1996, Naturkatastrophen in der antiken Welt*, Stuttgart: 404–16
  2005: *War in the Hellenistic world*, London
Chantraine, P. 1968–80: *Dictionnaire étymologique de la langue grecque*, 5 vols., Paris
Chiasson, C. C. 1983: 'An ominous word in Herodotus', *Hermes* 111: 115–18
Christesen, P. 2007: *Olympic victor lists and ancient Greek history*, Cambridge
Cohen, G. 1995: *The Hellenistic settlements in Europe, the islands, and Asia Minor*, Berkeley, Los Angeles and Oxford
Coldstream, J. N. 1976: 'Hero cults in the age of Homer', *JHS* 96: 8–17
Coleman, R. G. 1977: *Virgil, Eclogues*, Cambridge
Colvin, S. 2007: *A historical Greek reader: Mycenaean to the koiné*, Oxford
Connelly, J. B. 2007: *Portrait of a priestess: women and ritual in ancient Greece*, Princeton

Constantakopoulou, C. 2005: 'Proud to be an islander', *Mediterranean Historical Review* 20: 1–34

 2007: *The dance of the islands: insularity, networks, the Athenian empire, and the Aegean world*, Oxford

Cook, J. M. 1961: 'Some sites of the Milesian territory', *BSA* 56: 90–101

 1973: *The Troad: an archaeological and topographical study*, Oxford

Coste-Messelière, P. de la 1946: 'Les Alcméonides à Delphes', *BCH* 70: 271–87

Currie, B. 2005: *Pindar and the cult of heroes*, Oxford

Dakaris, S. 1993: Το νεκρομαντείο του Αχέροντα, Athens

Darbo-Peschanski, C. 1987: *Le discours du particulier: essai sur l'enquête hérodotéenne*, Paris

Davies, J. K. 1977: 'Athenian citizenship: the descent-group and the alternatives', *CJ* 63: 105–21 [= P. J. Rhodes (ed.), *Athenian democracy*, Edinburgh, 2004: 18–39]

 1994: 'The tradition about the First Sacred War', in Hornblower 1994: 193–212

Davison, J. M. 1992: 'Greeks in Sardinia: myth and reality', in R. H. Tykot and T. K. Andrews (eds.), *Sardinia in the Mediterranean: a footprint in the sea: Studies in Sardinian archaeology presented to M. S. Balmuth*, Sheffield, 1992: 382–93

Debord, P. 1999: *L'Asie mineure au IVe siècle (412–323 a. C)*, Bordeaux

 2001: 'Sur quelques Zeus Cariens', in B. Virgilio (ed.), *Studi ellenistici* 13, Pisa: 19–38

Demand, N. 1982: *Thebes in the fifth century BC: Heracles resurgent*, London

Denniston, J. D. 1954: *The Greek particles*, 2nd edn, Oxford

Develin, R. 1985: 'Herodotus and the Alkmaionids', in J. W. Eadie and J. Ober (eds.), *The craft of the ancient historian: essays in honor of C. G. Starr*, Lanham, MD: 125–139

 1989: *see* Abbreviations *under AO*

Dewald, C. 1987: 'Narrative surface and authorial voice in Herodotus' *Histories*', *Arethusa* 20: 147–170

 1998: end-notes to Waterfield (see Abbreviations)

 2003: 'Form and content: the question of tyranny in Herodotus', in K. Morgan (ed.), *Popular tyranny*, Austin, 25–58

 2011: 'Happiness in Herodotus', *Symbolae Osloenses* 85: 52–73

Dewald, C. and J. Marincola, 2006: *see* Abbreviations under *Cambridge companion*

Dickey, E. 1996: *Greek forms of address from Herodotus to Lucian*, Oxford

Dignas, B. 2002: *The economy of the sacred in Hellenistic and Roman Asia Minor*, Oxford

Dilke, O. A. W. 1985: *Greek and Roman maps*, London

Douglas, M. 2004: *Jacob's tears: the priestly work of reconciliation*, Oxford
  2007: *Thinking in circles: an essay on ring composition*, London
Dover, K. J. 1960: *Greek word order*, Cambridge
  1974: *Greek popular morality*, Oxford
Drachmann, A. B. 1910–1927: *Scholia vetera in Pindari carmina*, 3 vols., Leipzig
Driver, G. R. 1957: *Aramaic documents of the fifth century BC*, Oxford
Dubois, L. 1989: *Inscriptions grecques dialectales de Sicile*, vol. I, Geneva
Dueck, D. (with a chapter by K. Brodersen) 2012: *Geography in classical antiquity*, Cambridge
Dunbabin, T. J. 1936/7: ' ῍Εχθρη παλαιή', *BSA* 37: 83–91
Dunbar, N. 1995: *Aristophanes: Birds*, Oxford
Dusinberre, E. R. M. 2003: *Aspects of empire in Achaemenid Sardis*, Cambridge
Edwards, M. 1991: *The Iliad: a commentary* (general ed. G. S. Kirk), vol. V, *Books 17–20*, Cambridge
Edwards, R. B. 1979: *Kadmos the Phoenician: a study in Greek legends and the Mycenaean age*, Amsterdam
Egetmeyer, M. 2010: *Le dialecte grec ancien de Chypre*, 2 vols, pagination continuous, Berlin
Ehrhardt, N. 1983: *Milet und seine Kolonien: vergleichende Untersuchung der kultischen und politischen Einrichtungen*, Frankfurt am Main, Bern and New York
  1998: 'Didyma und Milet in archaischer Zeit', *Chiron* 28: 11–20
Eidinow, E. 2007: *Oracles, curses and risk among the ancient Greeks*, Oxford
  2011: *Luck, fate and fortune: antiquity and its legacy*, London and New York
Ekroth, G. 2007: 'Heroes and hero-cults', in Ogden 2007: 100–14
Erbse, H. 1992: *Studien zum Verständnis Herodots*, Berlin and New York
Errington, R. M. 1981: 'Alexander the Philhellene and Persia', in H. Dell (ed.), *Ancient Macedonian Studies in honor of C. F. Edson*, Thessaloniki: 139–43
Fantuzzi, M. and R. Hunter 2004: *Tradition and innovation in Hellenistic poetry*, Cambridge
Faraone, C. 1992: *Talismans and Trojan horses: guardian statues in ancient Greek myth and ritual*, New York
Farnell, L. R. 1921: *Greek hero cults and ideas of immortality*, Oxford
Faulkner, A. 2008: *The Homeric hymn to Aphrodite*, Oxford
Fearn, D. 2007a: *Bacchylides: politics, performance, poetic tradition*, Oxford
  2007b: 'Narrating ambiguity: murder and Macedonian allegiance (5.17–22)', in Irwin/Greenwood: 98–17
  (ed.) 2011: *Aegina: contexts for choral lyric poetry*, Oxford
Feeney, D. 1991: *The gods in epic*, Oxford
  2007: *Caesar's calendar: ancient time and the beginnings of history*, Princeton
Fehling, D. 1974: *Ethologische Überlegungen auf dem Gebiet der Altertumskunde*, Munich

1985: *Die Sieben Weisen und die frühgriechische Chronologie: eine traditions-geschichtliche Studie*, Bern and New York

1989: *Herodotus and his 'sources': citation, invention and narrative art*, Leeds. [Original German edn 1971]

Figueira, T. 1981: *Aegina*, New York

  1986: 'Xanthippus and the *Prutaneis* of the *Naukraroï*', *Historia* 35: 257–79

  1993: *Excursions in epichoric history*, Lanham, MD

  2010: 'Khalkis and Marathon', in Buraselis and Meidani 2010: 185–202

Flensted-Jensen, P., T. H. Nielsen and L. Rubinstein (eds.) 2000: *Polis and politics: studies in ancient Greek history presented to M. H. Hansen on his sixtieth birthday*, Copenhagen

Flower, M. 2008a: *The seer in ancient Greece*, Berkeley and Los Angeles

  2008b: 'The Iamidae' in B. Dignas and K. Trampadach (eds.), *Practitioners of the divine: Greek priests and religious officials from Homer to Heliodorus*, Cambridge, MA and London: 187–206

Flower, M. and J. Marincola 2002: *see* Abbreviations

Fontenrose, J. 1968: 'The hero as athlete', *Calif. Stud. Class. Ant.* 1: 73–104

  1988: *Didyma: Apollo's oracle, cult, and companions*, Berkeley, Los Angeles and London

Fornara, C. W. 1971: *Herodotus: an interpretative essay*, Oxford

Forrest, W. G. 1956: 'The first sacred war', *BCH* 80: 33–52

  1969a: 'The tradition of Hippias' expulsion from Athens', *GRBS* 10: 277–86

  1969b: 'Two chronographic notes', *CQ* 19: 95–110

  1979: 'Motivation in Herodotus: the case of the Ionian revolt', *International History Review* 1: 311–22

  1980: *A history of Sparta 950–192 BC*², London

  1981: 'A lost Peisistratid name', *JHS* 101: 134

  1984: 'Herodotus and Athens', *Phoenix* 38: 1–11

Forsdyke, S. 2002: 'Greek history c. 525–480 BC', in *Brill's companion*: 521–49

Fortin, M. 1980: 'Fondation de villes grecques à Chypre: légendes et découvertes archéologiques', in J.-B. Caron, M. Fortin and G. Maloney (eds.), *Mélanges d'études anciennes offerts à M. Lebel*, Quebec: 25–44

Fossey, J. M. 1988: *Topography and population of ancient Boiotia*, Chicago

Fowler, R. 1996: 'Herodotus and his contemporaries', *JHS* 106: 62–87

  2003a: 'Herodotus and Athens', in Derow/Parker: 305–18

  2003b: 'Who were the Pelasgians?', in E. Csapo and M. Miller (eds.), *Poetry, theory, praxis: the social life of myth, word and image in ancient Greece. Essays in honour of W. J. Slater*, Oxford: 2–18 (revised version in *EGM* 2, section 2.1)

Fragoulaki, M. forthcoming: *Kinship in Thucydides: intercommunal ties and historical narrative*, Oxford

Fraser, P. M. 1972: *Ptolemaic Alexandria*, 3 vols., Oxford
  2009: *Greek ethnic terminology*, Oxford
Frazer, J. G. 1898: *Pausanias' description of Greece*, 6 vols., London
French, D. H. 1998: 'Pre- and early-Roman roads of Asia Minor. The Persian Royal Road', *Iran* 36: 15–43
Gabrielsen, V. 2011: 'The Chrysaoreis of Caria', in Karlsson and Carlsson 2011: 331–53
Gantz, T. 1993: *Early Greek myth* (2 vols., pagination continuous), Baltimore
Garland, R. J. 1984: 'Religious authority in archaic and classical Athens', *BSA* 79: 75–123
Garvie, A. F. 1986: *Aeschylus*: Choephori, Oxford
Gauthier, P. 1972: *Symbola: les étrangers et la justice dans les cités grecques*, Paris
Geddes, A. D. 1987: 'Rags and riches', *CQ* 37: 307–31
Gernet, L. 1981 (tr. J. Hamilton and B. Nagy): *The anthropology of ancient Greece*, Baltimore and London
Giangiulio, M. 1989: *Ricerche su Crotone arcaica*, Pisa
  2005a: *Erodoto e il 'modello erodoteo'. Formazione e trasmissione delle tradizioni storiche in Grecia*, Torino
  2005b: 'Tradizione storica e strategie narrative nelle *Storie* di Erodoto: il caso del discorso di Socle Corinzio', in Giangiulio 2005a: 91–122
Goff, B. 2004: *Citizen Bacchae: women's ritual practice in ancient Greece*, Berkeley
Golden, M. 2008: *Greek sport and social status*, Austin
Gomme, A. W. 1933: *The population of Athens in the fifth and fourth centuries BC*, Oxford
Gonzales, M. 2005: 'The oracle and cult of Ares in Asia Minor', *GRBS* 45: 261–83
Gorman, V. B. 2001: *Miletos: the ornament of Ionia. A history of the city to 400 BC*, Ann Arbor
Gottesman, A. 2010: 'The beggar and the clod: the mythic notion of property in ancient Greece', *TAPA* 140: 287–322
Gould, J. 1989: *Herodotus*, London
  1994: 'Herodotus and religion', in Hornblower 1994: 91–106
Gow, A. S. F. 1950: *Theocritus*, 2 vols., Cambridge
Graf, D. 1994: 'The Persian royal road system', in H. Sancisi-Weerdenburg, A. Kuhrt and M. C. Root (eds.), *Achaemenid History VIII: continuity and change*, Leiden: 167–89
Graf, F. 1979: 'Apollo Delphinios', *MH* 36: 2–22
Gray, V. 1996: 'Herodotus and images of tyranny: the tyrants of Corinth', *AJP* 117: 361–89
  2007: 'Structure and significance (5. 55–69)', in Irwin/Greenwood: 202–25

2011: 'Thucydides' source citations: "it is said"', *CQ* 61: 75–90

2012: 'Herodotus and Melampus', in Baragwanath and Bakker 2012: 167–91

Graziosi, B. 2002: *Inventing Homer: the early reception of epic*, Cambridge

Graziosi, B. and J. Haubold 2010: *Homer, Iliad* VI, Cambridge

Greaves, A. M. 2002: *Miletos, a history*, London

Green, P. 1996: *The Greco-Persian Wars*, Berkeley, Los Angeles and London

Greenwood, E. 2007: 'Bridging the narrative (5. 23–7)', in Irwin/Greenwood: 128–145

Griffin, A. 1982: *Sikyon*, Oxford

Griffith, G. T. 1966: 'Isegoria in the Assembly at Athens', in Badian 1966: 115–38

Griffith-Williams, B. 2011: 'The succession to the Spartan kingship, 520–440 BC', *BICS* 54: 43–58

Griffiths, A. H. 1988: 'Earth and water', unpublished, but see material at Kuhrt 1988: 87 n. 2

1989: 'Was Kleomenes mad?', in Powell 1989: 51–78

2001: 'Behind the lines: the genesis of stories in Herodotus', in F. Budelmann and P. Michelakis (eds.), *Homer, tragedy and beyond: essays in honour of P. E. Easterling*, London: 75–88

2006: 'Stories and story-telling in Herodotus', in *Cambridge companion*: 130–44

Gruen, E. S. 1990: *Studies in Greek culture and Roman policy*, Leiden and New York

1993: *Culture and national identity in Republican Rome*, London

Habicht, C. 1957: 'Samische Volksbeschlüsse der hellenistischen Zeit', *AM* 72: 152–274

1985 [revised edn. 1998]: *Pausanias' guide to ancient Greece*, Berkeley, Los Angeles and London

2001: 'Tod auf der Gesandtschaftsreise', in B. Virgilio (ed.), *Studi ellenistici* 13: 9–17

Hadzisteliou-Price, T. 1973: 'Hero-cult and Homer', *Historia* 22: 129–44

Hainsworth, B. 1993: *The Iliad: a commentary* (general ed. G. S. Kirk), vol. III, *Books 9–12*, Cambridge

Hall, J. 2001: 'Contested ethnicities: perceptions of Macedonia within evolving definitions of Greek identity', in Malkin 2001: 159–86

Halliday, W. R. 1928: *The Greek Questions of Plutarch*, Oxford

Hammond, N. G. L. 1955: 'Studies in Greek chronology of the sixth and fifth centuries BC', *Historia* 4: 371–411

Hampe, R. and E. Simon 1981: *The birth of Greek art*, Oxford and New York

Hands, A. R. 1974: 'Postremo suo tantum ingenio utebatur', *CQ* 24: 313–17

Hanell, F. 1934: *Megarische Studien*, Lund

Hanfmann, G. (assisted by W. M. Mierse) 1983: *Sardis from prehistoric to Roman times: results of the archaeological exploration of Sardis 1958–1975*, Cambridge, MA

Hansen, M. H. 1987: *The Athenian assembly in the age of Demosthenes*, Oxford
1999: *The Athenian democracy in the age of Demosthenes*, 2nd edn, Oxford
2006: *Studies in the population of Aigina, Athens and Eretria*, Copenhagen

Hansen, M. H. and T. H. Nielsen 2004: *see* Abbreviations *under IACP*

Harder, A. 2012: *Callimachus: Aetia*, 2 vols., Oxford

Harman, R. 2008: 'Viewing, power and interpretation in Xenophon's *Cyropaedia*', in J. Pigón (ed.), *The children of Herodotus*, Newcastle: 69–91

Harper, P., K. Aruz and F. Tallon (eds.) 1992: *The royal city of Susa: ancient near eastern treasures in the Louvre*, New York

Harris. W. V. 2009: *Dreams and experience in classical antiquity*, Princeton

Harris-McKoy, D. E. 2012: *Artemidorus' Oneirocritica: text, translation, and commentary*, Oxford

Harrison, T. 2000: *Divinity and history: the religion of Herodotus*, Oxford
2002: 'The Persian invasions', in *Brill's companion*: 551–78

Hartog, F. 1988: *The mirror of Herodotus: the representation of the other in the writing of history*, Berkeley, Los Angeles and London

Harvey, F. D. 1985: '*Dona ferentes*: some aspects of bribery in Greek politics' in Cartledge and Harvey 1985: 76–117

Haubold, J. 2007: 'Athens and Aegina (5. 82–9)', in Irwin/Greenwood: 226–44

Head, B. V. 1911: *Historia numorum*, 2nd edn, Oxford

Heckel, W. 2006: *Who's who in the age of Alexander the Great*, Oxford

Hellström, P. 2007: *Labraunda: a guide to the Karian sanctuary of Zeus Labraundos*, Istanbul

Helly, B. 1995: *L'état Thessalien*, Paris

Henderson, J. 2007: '"The fourth Dorian invasion" and "The Ionian revolt" (5. 76–126)', in Irwin/Greenwood: 289–310

Herda, A. 2006: *Der Apollon-Delphinios-Kult in Milet und die Neujahrsprozession nach Didyma. Ein neuer Kommentar der sog. Molpoi-Satzung*, Mainz

Herman, G. 1987: *Ritualized friendship and the Greek city*, Cambridge

Heubeck, A., S. West and J. B. Hainsworth 1988: *A commentary on Homer's Odyssey*, Vol. 1: *Introduction and books i–viii*, Oxford

Higbie, C. 2003: *The Lindian chronicle and the Greek creation of their past*, Oxford
2010: 'Divide and edit: a brief history of book-divisions', *HSCP* 105: 1–31

Hignett, C. 1963: *Xerxes' invasion of Greece*, Oxford

Hill, G. F. 1940: *A history of Cyprus*, vol. 1, Cambridge

Hodkinson, S. 2009 (ed.): *Sparta: comparative approaches*, London

Hopkirk, P. 2006: *The great game: on secret service in High Asia*, London

Hordern, J. H. 2002: *The fragments of Timotheus of Miletus*, Oxford

Hornblower, J. 1981: *Hieronymus of Cardia*, Oxford

Hornblower, S. 1982: *see* Abbreviations *under Mausolus*

    (ed.) 1994: *Greek historiography*, Oxford

    2000: 'Personal names and the study of the ancient Greek historians', in Hornblower and Matthews 2000: 129–43

    2001: 'Epic and epiphanies: Herodotus and the "New Simonides"', in Boedeker and Sider 2001: 135–47

    2003: 'Panionios of Chios and Hermotimos of Pedasa (Hdt. 8. 104–6)', in Derow/Parker: 37–53

    2007a: 'The Dorieus episode and the Ionian revolt', in Irwin/Greenwood: 168–78

    2007b: 'Athletic victory-language in Homer, Pindar and inscriptions', in D. Maronitis (ed.), *Games and rewards in the Homeric epics, Proceedings of the 10th international symposium on the Odyssey held at Ithaki, Greece, September 2004*, Ithaca, Greece: 331–8

    2008: 'Greek identity in the archaic and classical periods', in K. Zacharia (ed.), *Hellenisms: culture, identity, and ethnicity from antiquity to modernity*, Aldershot and Burlington, VT: 37–58

    2010: 'Lykophron's *Alexandra* and the Cypriot name Praxandros', in *Onomatologos*: 84–90

    2011: 'How unusual were Mausolus and the Hekatomnids?', in Karlsson and Carlsson 2011: 355–62

    2012: 'What happened later to the families of Pindaric patrons – and to epinician poetry?', in P. Agocs, C. Carey and R. Rawles (eds.), *Reading the victory ode*, Cambridge: 93–107

Hornblower, S., forthcoming: 'Agariste's suitors: an Olympic note', in Moreno and Thomas forthcoming

Hornblower, S. and E. Matthews (eds.) 2000: *Greek personal names: their value as evidence*, Oxford

Hornblower, S. and C. Morgan (eds.) 2007: *Pindar's poetry, patrons and festivals, from archaic Greece to the Roman empire*, Oxford

Hrdy, S. B. 2009: *Mothers and others: the evolutionary origins of mutual understanding*, Harvard

Hunt, P. 2010: *War, peace and alliance in Demosthenes' Athens*, Cambridge

Huxley, G. L. 1962: *Early Sparta*, London

    1969: *Greek lyric poetry from Eumelos to Panyassis*, London

Immerwahr, H. R. 1966: *Form and thought in Herodotus*, Cleveland, OH

Indergaard, H. 2011: 'Thebes, Aegina, and the temple of Aphaia: a reading of Pindar's *Isthmian* 6', in Fearn 2011: 294–322

Instone, S. 2007: 'Origins of the Olympics', in Hornblower and Morgan 2007: 71–82

Irwin, E. 2007: ' "What's in a name?" and exploring the comparable ono-
    mastics, ethnography and *kratos* in Thrace (5. 1–2 and 3–10)', in
    Irwin/Greenwood: 41–87
    2011: 'Lest the things done by men become *exitela*: writing up Aegina in
    a late fifth-century context', in Fearn 2011: 426–57
Irwin, E. and E. Greenwood 2007: 'Introduction: reading Herodotus,
    reading Book 5', in Irwin/Greenwood 2007: 1–40
Isaac, B. 1986: *The Greek settlements in Thrace until the Macedonian conquest*,
    Leiden
Ismard, P. 2010: *La cité des réseaux: Athènes et ses associations VIe–Ier siècle av.
    J.-C.*, Paris
Jacobsthal, P. 1956: *Greek pins*, Oxford
Jacoby, F. 1902: *Apollodors Chronik: eine Sammlung der Fragmente*, Berlin
    1956: *Griechische Historiker*, Stuttgart [contains 'Herodotos' from *R.E.
    Suppl.* 2. This is cited both by 1956 p. nos. and *R.-E.* col. nos.]
    see also Abbreviations *under FGrHist*
Jameson, M. H., D. R. Jordan and R. D. Kotansky 1993: *A lex sacra from
    Selinous*, Durham, N.C.
Janko, R. 1992: *The Iliad: a commentary* (general ed. G. S. Kirk), vol. IV:
    Books 13–16, Cambridge
Jeffery, L. H. 1976: *Archaic Greece*, London
Johnson, D. M. 2001: 'Herodotus' story-telling speeches: Socles (5.92) and
    Leotychides (6.86)', *CJ* 97: 1–26
Johnston, S. I. 1999: *Restless dead: encounters between the living and the dead
    in ancient Greece*, Berkeley, Los Angeles and London
Jones, C. P. 1986: *Culture and society in Lucian*, Cambridge, MA
    1987: '*Stigma*: tattooing and branding in Graeco-Roman antiquity', *JRS*
    77: 139–55
    1988: 'A monument from Sinope', *JHS* 108: 193–4
    1999: *Kinship diplomacy in the ancient world*, Cambridge, MA
    2010: *New heroes in antiquity from Achilles to Antinoos*, Cambridge, MA
Jones, N. F. 1987: *Public organization in ancient Greece: a documentary study*,
    Philadelphia
Jong, I. de 1993: 'Studies in Homeric denomination', *Mnemosyne* 46:
    289–306
    2001: 'The anachronical structure of Herodotus' *Histories*', in S. Har-
    rison (ed.), *Texts, ideas, and the classics: scholarship, theory, and classical
    literature*, Oxford: 93–116
    2012: *Homer: Iliad Book XXII*, Cambridge
Jost, M. 2005: 'Quelques épiclèses divines en Arcadie: typologie et cas par-
    ticuliers', in Belayche, Brulé et al. 2005: 389–400
Kallet, L. 2001: *Money and the corrosion of power in Thucydides: the Sicilian
    Expedition and its aftermath*, Berkeley, Los Angeles and London

Kamptz, H. von 1982: *Homerische Personennamen: Sprachwissenschaftliche und historische Klassifikation*, Göttingen

Karageorghis, V. 2004: 'Herodotus and Cyprus', in Karageorghis and Taifacos 2004: 1–7

Karageorghis, V. and I. Taifacos 2004: *Herodotus and his world*, Nicosia

Karlsson, L. and S. Carlsson (eds.) 2011: *Labraunda and Karia: proceedings of the international symposium commemorating sixty years of Swedish archaeological work in Labraunda, Nov. 20–21, 2008*, Uppsala

Kearns, E. 1985: 'Change and continuity in religious structures after Cleisthenes', in Cartledge and Harvey 1985: 189–207

1989: *The heroes of Attica. BICS Suppl.* 57, London

Kertesz, I. 2005: 'When did Alexander I visit Olympia?', *Nikephoros* 18: 115–26

Kett, P. 1966: *Prosopographie der historischen griechischen Manteis bis auf die Zeit Alexanders des Grossen*, diss. Nuremberg

Kidd, D. 1997: *Aratus: Phaenomena*, Cambridge

Kinzl, K. H. 1975: 'Herodotus-Interpretations', *Rh. Mus.* 118: 193–204

Köhnken, A. 2006a: *Darstellungsziele und Erzählstrategien in antiken Texten*, ed. A. Bettenworth, Berlin 2006

2006b: 'Der listige Oibares. (Dareios' Aufstieg zum Grosskönig)', in Köhnken 2006a: 452–71 [originally *Rh. Mus.* 133 (1990): 115–37]

Kowalzig, B. 2007: *Singing for the gods: performances of myth and ritual in archaic and classical Greece*, Oxford

2011: 'Musical merchandise "on every vessel": religion and trade on Aegina', in Fearn 2011: 129–71

Kramer, N. 2004: 'Athen – keine Stadt des Grosskönigs', *Hermes* 132: 257–70

Kraus, C. S. (ed.) 1999: *The limits of historiography: genre and narrative in ancient historical texts*, Leiden

Kroll, J. 2000: review of Kurke: *CJ* 96: 85–90

Kron, U. 1976: *Die zehn attischen Phylenheroen, Athenische Mitteilungen*, Beiheft 5

Kühr, A. 2006: *Als Kadmos nach Boiotien kam: Polis und Ethnos im Spiegel thebanischer Gründungsmythen*, Stuttgart

Kuhrt, A. 1988: 'Earth and water' in H. Sancisi-Weerdenburg (ed.), *Achaemenid History* III, Leiden: 87–99

2007: *The Persian empire*, 2 vols., pagination continuous (pb. reprint in 1 vol., 2010), London

Kuper, A. 2009: *Incest and influence: the private life of bourgeois England*, Cambridge, MA and London

Kurke, L. 2009: '"Counterfeit oracles" and "legal tender": the politics of oracular consultation in Herodotus', *Classical World* 102: 417–38

Kurtz, D. and J. Boardman 1971: *Greek burial customs*, London

Lambert, S. D. 1986: 'Herodotus, the Cylonian conspiracy, and the ΠΡΥ-ΤΑΝΙΕΣ ΤѠΝ ΝΑΥΚΡΑΡΙѠΝ', *Historia* 35: 105–112

Lane Fox, R. (ed.) 2004: *The long march: Xenophon and the Ten Thousand*, New Haven and London

Lang, M. 1984: *Herodotean narrative and discourse*, Harvard
2011 (ed. J. S. Rusten and R. Hamilton): *Thucydidean narrative and discourse*, Ann Arbor

Larsen, J. A. O. 1968: *Greek federal states: their institutions and history*, Oxford

Larson, J. 1995: *Greek heroine cults*, Madison, WI

Larson, S. L. (2007), *Tales of epic ancestry. Boiotian collective identity in the late archaic and early classical periods*, Historia Einzelschrift 197, Stuttgart

Lateiner, D. 1980: 'A note on δίκας διδόναι in Herodotus', *CQ* 30: 30–2
1982: 'A note on the perils of prosperity in Herodotus', *Rh. Mus.* 125: 97–101
1987: 'Nonverbal communication in the *Histories* of Herodotus', *Arethusa* 20: 83–119

Lattimore, R. 1958: 'The composition of the *History* of Herodotus', *C Phil.* 53: 9–21

Lavelle, B. 1985: 'Kimon's Thessalian proxeny', *LCM* 10: 12–13

Lefèvre, F. 1998: *L'amphictionie pyléo-delphique: historie et institutions*, Paris
2011: 'Quoi de neuf sur l'amphictionie?' *Pallas* 87: 117–31

Lefkowitz, M. 1981: *The lives of the Greek poets*, London

Legrand, P. E. 1955: *Hérodote: introduction*, Paris

Leitao, D. D. 2003: 'Adolescent hair-growing and hair-cutting rituals in ancient Greece. A sociological approach', in D. B. Dodd and C. Faraone (eds.), *Initiation in ancient Greek rituals and narratives*, London: 109–29

Lendle, O. 1987: 'Herodot 5. 52/3 über die "persische Königstrasse"', *WJA* 13: 25–36

Lewis, D. M. 1963: 'Cleisthenes and Attica', *Historia* 12: 22–40 [= 1997: 77–98]
1977: *Sparta and Persia*, Leiden
1984: *see* Burn 1962
1985: 'Persians in Herodotus', in *The Greek historians: papers presented to A. E. Raubitschek* (no editor named), Saratoga CA: 101–17 [= 1997: 145–361]
1997 (ed. P. J. Rhodes): *Selected papers in Greek and near eastern history*, Cambridge

Liberman, G. 2011: 'Variations sur des thèmes Thucydidéens', *Rev. Ét. Anc.* 113: 609–31

Lightfoot, J. 1999: *Parthenius of Nicaea, extant works edited with introduction and commentary*, Oxford
2003: *Lucian on the Syrian goddess*, ed. with intro. and comm., Oxford

Lillo, A. 1991: 'Ionic κώς, ὄκως, ὄπως, Thessalian κις: a phonetic problem of analyzable compounds', *Glotta* 69:1–13

Lobel, E. 1927: 'Trivialities of Greek history', *CQ* 21: 50–1

Lolos, Y. A. 2011: *Land of Sikyon: archaeology and history of a Greek city-state. Hesperia Suppl.* 39

Londey, P. 1990: 'Greek colonists and Delphi' in J.-P. Descoeudres (ed.), *Greek colonists and native populations*, Oxford: 117–27

Loraux, N. 1993: 'Melissa, moglie e figlia di tiranni', in N. Loraux (ed.), *La Grecia femminile*, Rome: 3–37

Luraghi, N. 1994: *Tirannidi arcaiche in Sicilia e Magna Grecia da Panezio di Leontini alla caduta dei Dinomenidi*, Florence

(ed.) 2001: *The historian's craft in the age of Herodotus*, Oxford

Luther, A. 2004: *Könige und Ephoren: Untersuchungen zur spartanischen Verfassungsgeschichte*, Frankfurt am Main

Ma, J., N. Papazarkadas and R. Parker (eds.) 2009: *Interpreting the Athenian Empire*, London

MacDowell, D. M. 1986: *Spartan law*, Edinburgh

Macleod, C. W. 1982: *Homer: Iliad book XXIV*, Cambridge

Malkin, I. 1994: *Myth and territory in the Spartan Mediterranean*, Cambridge

1998a: *The returns of Odysseus: colonization and ethnicity*, Berkeley, Los Angeles and London

1998b: 'The middle ground: Philoktetes in Italy', *Kernos* 11: 131–41

2001 (ed.): *Ancient Greek perceptions of Greek ethnicity*, Cambridge, MA

2011: *A small Greek world: networks in the ancient Mediterranean*, New York

Malten, L. 1911: *Kyrene: sagengeschichtliche und historische Untersuchungen*, Berlin [= *Philologische Untersuchungen* 20]

Marek, C. 2006: *Die Inschriften von Kaunos. Vestigia* 55, Munich

Marg, W. (ed.) 1965: *Herodot: eine Auswahl aus der neueren Forschung*, Darmstadt

Mari, M. 2006: 'Tucidide e l'anfizionia di Delfi', *BCH* 130: 231–61

Martin, R. 1993: 'The Seven Sages as performers of wisdom', in C. Dougherty and L. Kurke (eds.), *Cultural poetics in archaic Greece: cult, performance, politics*, Cambridge: 108–28

Masson, O. 1990a: *Onomastica graeca selecta*, ed. C. Dobias and L. Dubois, Paris

1990b: 'Notes d'anthroponymie grecque et asianique IIIA: noms cariens et noms grecs à Halicarnasse', in Masson 1990a: 19–24

1990c: 'Variétés chypriotes', *Kadmos* 29: 144–56

Mavrojannis, T. 2007: 'Herodotus on the introduction of the Phoenician alphabet to the Greeks, the Gephyraeans, and the Proto-Geometric building at Toumba in Lefkandi', *Klio* 89: 291–310

McGlew, J. F. 1993: *Tyranny and popular culture in ancient Greece*, Ithaca and London

Mee, C. and A. Spawforth, 2001: *Greece (Oxford Archaeological Guides)*, Oxford

Meidani, K. 2010: 'Μιλτιάδεια: remarks on Miltiades' activities before and after Marathon', in Buraselis and Meidani 2010: 167–83

Meiggs, R. 1964: 'A note on the population of Attica', *CR* 14: 2–3
 1982: *Trees and timber in the ancient Mediterranean world*, Oxford

Miller, S. G. 2000: 'Naked democracy', in Flensted-Jensen et al. 2000: 277–96

Millinder, E. 2009: 'The Spartan dyarchy: new perspectives', in Hodkinson 2009: 1–67

Mitford, T. B. 1950: 'Kafizin and the Cypriot syllabary', *CQ* 50: 97–106

Moles, J. 2002: 'Herodotus and Athens', in *Brill's companion:* 33–52
 2007: '"Saving" Greece from the "ignominy" of tyranny? The "famous" and "wonderful" speech of Socles (5. 92)', in Irwin/Greenwood: 245–68

Momigliano, A. 1971: *The development of Greek biography*, Harvard
 1980: 'The historians of the classical world and their audiences', in *Sesto contributo alla storia degli studi classici e del mondo antico*, Rome, 1980: 361–76

Moreno, A. 2007: *Feeding the democracy: the Athenian grain supply in the fifth and fourth centuries BC*, Oxford
 2009: 'The Attic neighbour', in Ma, Papazarkadas and Parker 2009: 211–21

Moreno, A. and R. Thomas (eds.) forthcoming: *Patterns of the past: epitedeumata in the Greek tradition* (Festschrift for Oswyn Murray), Oxford

Moretti, L. 1957: *Olympionikai. I vincitori negli antichi agoni Olimpici*, Rome

Morris, S. P. 1984: *The black and white style: Athens and Aigina in the Orientalizing period:* Yale

Morrison, J. S., J. F. Coates and B. Rankov, 2000: *The Athenian trireme*, Cambridge

Most, G. W. 1993: 'A cock for Asclepius', *CQ* 43: 96–111

Mousavi, A. 1989: 'The discovery of an Achaemenid way-station at Deh-Bozan in the Asadabad valley', *AMI* 22: 135–8

Müller, 1987: *Topographische Bildkommentar zu den Historien Herodots. Griechenland*, Bonn

Müller, C. W. 2006: *Legende – Novelle – Roman. Dreizehn Kapitel zur erzählenden Prosaliteratur der Antike*, Göttingen

Munn, M. 2006: *The Mother of the Gods, Athens, and the tyranny of Asia. A study of sovereignty in ancient religion*, Berkeley, Los Angeles and London

Munson, R. V. 2001a: *Telling wonders: ethnographic and political discourse in the work of Herodotus*, Ann Arbor
 2001b: review of Harrison 2000, *Bryn Mawr Classical Review* 2001.06.22

2006: 'An alternate world: Herodotus and Italy', in *Cambridge companion*: 257–73

2007: 'The trouble with the Ionians: Herodotus and the beginnings of the Ionian Revolt (5. 27–38. 1)', in Irwin/Greenwood: 146–67

(ed.) 2013: *Oxford readings in Herodotus*, 2 vols. Oxford

Murray, O. 1967: 'review of Binder 1964', *CR* 17: 329–32

1988: 'The Ionian revolt', *CAH* 4²: 461–90

1990: 'Cities of reason', in Murray and Price 1990: 1–25

2001: 'Herodotus and oral history', in Luraghi 2001: 16–44

Murray, O. and S. Price (eds.) 1990: *The Greek city from Homer to Alexander*, Oxford

Myres, J. 1953: *Herodotus: father of history*, Oxford

Näf, B. 2004: *Traum und Traumdeutung im Altertum*, Darmstadt

Nafissi, M. 2008: 'Asteropos ed Epitadeus: storie di due efori spartani e di altri personaggi dai nomi parlanti', *Incidenza dell' antico* 6: 49–89

Nagy, G. 1990: *Pindar's Homer: the lyric possession of an epic past*, Baltimore and London

2011: 'Asopos and his multiple daughters: traces of pre-classical epic in the Aeginetan odes of Pindar', in Fearn 2011: 41–78

Naiden, F. S. 2006: *Ancient supplication*, Oxford and New York

Nenci, G. 1990a: 'L'occidente "barbarico"', in Nenci and Reverdin 1990: 301–18

1990b: reply to Burkert 1990, in Nenci and Reverdin 1990: 319

Nenci, G. and O. Reverdin (eds.) 1990: *Hérodote et les peuples non grecs. Fond. Hardt Entretiens* 35, Vandoeuvres

Nicolaou, I. 1971: *Cypriot inscribed stones*, Cyprus

Niese, B. 1907: 'Herodot-Studien, besonders zur spartanischen Geschichte', *Hermes* 42: 419–40

Nilsson, M. P. 1906: *Griechische Feste von religiöser Bedeutung mit Ausschluss der attischen*, Leipzig

1951a: *Opuscula selecta*, 3 vols., Lund

1951b: 'Der Ursprung der Tragödie', in Nilsson 1951a: 1. 61–145

1951c: *Cults, myths, oracles and politics in ancient Greece*, Lund

1967: *Geschichte der griechischen Religion* 1, 3rd edn, Munich

Nock. A. D. 1972: *Arthur Darby Nock: essays on religion and the ancient world*, Oxford

Nünlist, R. 2009: *The ancient critic at work: terms and concepts of literary criticism in Greek scholia*, Cambridge

Ogden, D. 1993: 'Cleisthenes of Sicyon, ΛΕΥΣΤΗΡ', *CQ* 43: 353–63

1997: *The crooked kings of ancient Greece*, London

2001: *Greek and Roman necromancy*, Princeton

(ed.) 2007: *A companion to Greek religion*, Oxford

Ogilvie, R. M. 1965: *A commentary on Livy, Books 1–5*, Oxford

Ohly, D. 1977: *Ägina. Tempel und Heiligtum*, Munich

Oost, S. 1972: 'Cypselus the Bacchiad', *C Phil.* 67: 10–30

Osborne, R. 2002: 'Archaic Greek history', in *Brill's companion*: 497–520
2007: 'The Paeonians (5. 11–16)' in Irwin/Greenwood: 88–97
2009: *Greece in the making, 1200–479 BC²*, London

Osborne, R. and S. Hornblower (eds.) 1994: *Ritual, finance, politics: Athenian democratic accounts presented to David Lewis*, Oxford

Ostwald, M. 1969: *Nomos and the beginnings of the Athenian democracy*, Oxford
2009a: *Language and history in ancient Greek culture*, Philadelphia
2009b: 'Isokratia as a political concept (Herodotus, 5. 92a. 1)', in Ostwald 2009a: 22–38

Padel, R. 1992: *In and out of the mind: Greek images of the tragic self*, Princeton

Page, D. L. 1955: *Sappho and Alcaeus*, Oxford

Papalexandrou, N. 2008: 'Boiotian tripods: the tenacity of a panhellenic symbol in a regional centre', *Hesperia* 77: 251–82

Pariente, A. 1992: 'Le monument argien des "Sept contre Thèbes"', in M. Piérart (ed.), *Polydipsion Argos*, Paris: 195–229

Parke, H. W. 1985a: *The oracles of Apollo in Asia Minor*, Oxford
1985b: 'The massacre of the Branchidae', *JHS* 105: 59–68
1988: *Sibyls and Sibylline prophecy in classical antiquity*, London

Parke, H. W. and D. Wormell 1956: *The Delphic oracle* vol. 2, Oxford

Parker, R. 1983: *Miasma: pollution and purification in early Greek religion*, Oxford
1985: 'Greek states and Greek oracles', in Cartledge and Harvey 1985: 298- 326 [reprinted in Buxton 2000: 76–108]
1987: 'Myths of early Athens', in J. Bremmer (ed.) *Interpretations of Greek mythology*, London: 187–214
1989: 'Spartan religion', in A. Powell 1989: 142–72 [pp. 152–163 reprinted as 'Religion in public life' in M. Whitby (ed.), *Sparta*, Edinburgh 2000: 161–73]
1996: *Athenian religion: a history*, Oxford
1998: *Cleomenes on the acropolis*, inaugural lecture, Oxford
2000: 'Theophoric names and Greek religion', in Hornblower and Matthews 2000: 53–79
2005: *Polytheism and society at Athens*, Oxford
2008: 'Molpoi' (review of Herda 2006), *CR* 58: 178–80
2010: 'Agesilaus and the bones of Alcmena', in H.-G. Nesselrath (ed.), *Plutarch*, On the daimonion of Socrates: *human liberation, divine guidance, and philosophy*, Tübingen: 129–37
2011: *On Greek religion*, Ithaca NY and London

Parker, V. 1997: *Untersuchungen zum Lelantischen Krieg und verwandten Problemen der frühgriechischen Geschichte. Historia Einzelschrift* 109

Parry, A. 1989: *The language of Achilles: and other papers*, Oxford

Pelling, C. 1996: 'The urine and the vine: Astyages' dreams at Herodotus 1. 107–8', *CQ* 46: 68–77

2002: 'Speech and action: Herodotus' debate on the constitutions', *PCPS* 48: 125–58

2006: 'Homer and Herodotus', in M. Clarke, B. G. F. Currie, and R. O. A. M. Lyne (eds.), *Epic interactions (J. Griffin Festschrift)*: 75–104

2007: 'Aristagoras (5. 49–55, 97)', in Irwin/Greenwood: 179–201

2008: 'Parallel narratives: the liberation of Thebes in *De genio Socratis* and in *Pelopidas*', in A. Nikolaidis (ed.), *The unity of Plutarch's work: Moralia Themes in the* Lives *and features of the* Lives *in the* Moralia, Berlin 2008: 539–56

2011: 'Herodotus and Samos', *BICS* 54: 1–18

2013: 'East is east and west is west – or are they? National stereotypes in Herodotus', in Munson 2013: 2. 360–79

Petit, T. 2004: 'Herodotus and Amathus', in Karageorghis and Taifakos 2004: 9–25

Petropoulou, A. 1986–7: 'The Thracian funerary rites (Hdt. 5. 8) and similar Greek practices', *Talanta* 18–19: 29–47

1988: 'The interment of Patroklos (*Iliad* 23. 252–57)', *AJPhil.* 109: 482–95

Pfeiffer, R. 1968: *History of classical scholarship from the beginnings to the end of the Hellenistic age*, Oxford

Philippe, A.-L. 2005: 'L'epithète Delphinios', in Belayche, Brulé et al. 2005: 255–61

Pickard-Cambridge, A. W. 1927: *Dithyramb, tragedy and comedy*, Oxford. [2nd edn, revised by T. B. L. Webster, 1962; see under Webster 1962]

Piérart, M. 2003: 'The common oracle of the Milesians and the Argives (Hdt. 6. 19 and 77)', in Derow/Parker 275–96

Pipili, M. 1987: *Lakonian iconography of the sixth century BC*, Oxford

Pirenne-Delforge, V. 2005: 'Des épiclèses exclusives dans la Grèce polythéiste? L'exemple d'Ourania', in Belayche 2005: 271–90

Pleket, H. 1969: 'The archaic tyrannis', *Talanta* 1: 19–61

Podlecki, A. J. 1976: 'Athens and Aegina', *Historia* 25: 396–413

Pohlenz, M. 1937: *Herodot. Der erste Geschichtsschreiber des Abendlandes*, Leipzig

Polignac, F. de (1995): *Cults, territory, and the origins of the Greek city-state*, Chicago

Poralla, P. 1913: *Prosopographie der Lakedaimonier bis auf der Zeit Alexanders des Grossen*, Breslau

Powell, A. (ed.) 1989: *Classical Sparta: techniques behind her success*, London

Powell, J. E. 1935: 'Notes on Herodotus – II', *CQ* 29: 150–63

1938a: 'Notes on Herodotus – III', *CQ* 32: 211–19

1938b: 'Scaliger on Herodotus', *CR* 52: 58–9

Price, S. R. F. 2008: 'Memory and ancient Greece', in A. H. and S. W. Rasmussen (eds.), *Religion and society: rituals, resources and identity in the ancient Greco-Roman world*, Rome: 167–78

Pulleyn, S. 2000: *Homer* Iliad *Book 1*, Oxford

Raaflaub, K. 1985: *Die Entdeckung der Freiheit: zur historischen Semantik und Gesellschaftsgeschichte eines politischen Grundbegriffs der Griechen*, Munich [Eng. tr. 2004]

   2009: 'Learning from the enemy: Athenian and Persian "instruments of power"', in Ma, Papazarkadas and Parker 2009: 89–124

Radt, S. L. 1958: *Pindars zweiter und sechster Paian*, Amsterdam

Radt, W. 1974/5: 'Pidasa bei Milet. Ergänzende Bemerkungen zu einer "karischen" Stadtanlage', *Ist. Mitt.* 23/24: 169–74

Reed, J. R. 1997: *Bion of Smyrna: the fragments and the* Adonis, Cambridge

Reger, G. 2010: 'Mylasa and its territory', in van Bremen and Carbon 2010: 43–57

Rehm, A. 1914: *Milet III: Das Delphinion*, Berlin

   1958: *Didyma* II, Berlin

Rhodes, P. J. 1972: *The Athenian Boule*, Oxford

   1976: 'Peisistratid chronology again', *Phoenix* 30: 219–33

   1981: *A commentary on the Aristotelian* Athenaion Politeia, Oxford

   2003: 'Herodotean chronology revisited', in Derow/Parker: 58–72

   2006: 'Milesian *stephanephoroi*: applying Cavaignac correctly', *ZPE* 157: 116

Richardson, N. J. 1974: *The Homeric Hymn to Demeter*, Oxford

   1993: *A commentary on the Iliad* (general ed. G. S. Kirk), vol. vi: *Books 21–24*, Cambridge

   2010: *Three Homeric hymns: to Apollo, Hermes and Aphrodite*, Cambridge

Richer, N. 1998: *Les éphores: études sur l'histoire et sur l'image de Sparte (VIII–III siècles avant J.-C.)*, Paris

Robert, L. 1963: *Noms indigènes dans l'Asie mineure gréco-romaine*, Paris

   1969–90: *Opera minora selecta*, Amsterdam

   1973: 'Les inscriptions', in P. Bernard (ed.), *Fouilles d'Ai Khanoum* vol. 1, Paris: 207–73

   1989: *Documents d'Asie mineure*, Paris

Robinson, B. A. 2011: *Histories of Peirene: a Corinthian fountain in three millennia*, Oxford

Robinson, E. W. 1997: *The first democracies: early popular government outside Athens*, Historia Einzelschrift 107, Stuttgart

Roettig, K. 2010: *Die Träume des Xerxes: zum Handeln der Götter bei Herodot. Studia classica et mediaevalia, Bd 2*, Nordhausen

Roller, L. 1999: *In search of god the mother: the cult of Anatolian Cybele*, Berkeley, Los Angeles and London

Rollinger, R. 2004: 'Herodotus, human violence and the ancient near east', in Karageorghis and Taifakos 2004: 121–43

2010: 'Extreme Gewalt und Strafgericht. Ktesias und Herodot als Zeugnisse für den Achaimenidenhof', in B. Jacobs and R. Rollinger (eds.), *Der Achaimenidische Hof/The Achaemenid court. Classica et Orientalia* 3, Wiesbaden: 559–666

Rollinger, R., B. Truschnigg and R. Bichler (eds.) 2011: *Herodot und das persiche Weltreich/Herodotus and the Persian Empire*, Wiesbaden

Rollinger, R. and J. Wiesehöfer 2012: 'Kaiser Valerian und Ilu-bi'di von Hamat. Über das Schicksal besiegter Feinde, persische Grausamkeit und die Persistenz altorientalischer Traditionen', in H. Baker, K. Kainuth and A. Otto (eds.), *Stories of long ago: Festschrift für Michael D. Roaf,* Münster: 497–515

Rood, T. 1998: *Thucydides: narrative and explanation*, Oxford
    1999: 'Thucydides' Persian wars', in Kraus 1999: 141–68
    2010: 'Xenophon's parasangs', *JHS* 130: 51–66
    2013: 'The Cylon conspiracy: Thucydides and the uses of the past', in M. Tamiolaki and A. Tsakmakis (eds.), *Thucydides' techniques: between historical research and literary representation*, Berlin: 119–38

Roos, P. 1985: 'Alexander I in Olympia', *Eranos* 83: 162–8

Rosén, H. 1962: *Eine Laut- und Formlehre der herodotischen Sprache*, Heidelberg

Roux, G. 1963: 'Kypselé: Où avait-on caché le petit Kypselos?', *Rev. Ét. Anc.* 65: 279–89

Runciman, W. G. 2005: 'Stone age sociology', *Journal of the Royal Anthropological Institute* 11: 129–42

Rutherford, I. 2001: *Pindar's paeans: a reading of the fragments with a survey of the genre*, Oxford

Sahin, S. 1976: *The political and religious structure in the territory of Stratonicea in Caria*, Ankara

Said, S. 2011a: *Homer and the Odyssey*, Oxford
    2011b: 'Reading Thucydides' *Archaeology* against the background of Herodotus' preface', in G. Rechenauer and V. Pothou (eds.), *Thucydides – a violent teacher? History and its representations*, Göttingen: 61–77

Sallares, J. R. 1991: *The ecology of the ancient Greek world*, London

Salmeri, G. 2004: 'Hellenism on the periphery: the case of Cilicia in Hellenistic Asia Minor', in S. Colvin (ed.), *The Greco-Roman east: politics, culture and society*, Cambridge, MA (= *YCS* 31): 181–206

Salmon, J. B. 1972: 'The Heraeum at Perachora and the early history of Corinth and Megara', *BSA* 67: 159–204
    1984: *Wealthy Corinth: a history of the city to 338 BC*, Oxford
    2003: 'Cleisthenes (of Athens) and Corinth', in Derow/Parker: 218–34

Salomon, N. 1997: *Le cleruchie di Atene: caratteri e funzione*, Pisa

Sánchez, P. 2001: *L'Amphictionie des Pyles et de Delphes. Recherches sur son rôle historique, des origines au IIe siècle de notre ère. Historia Einzelschrift* 148, Stuttgart

Sancisi-Weerdenburg, H. (ed.) 2000a: *Peisistratos and the tyranny: a reappraisal of the evidence*, Amsterdam

—— 2000b: 'Cultural politics and chronology', in Sancisi-Weerdenburg, H. 2000a: 79–106

Scaife, R. M., 1989: 'Alexander I in the *Histories* of Herodotus', *Hermes* 117: 129–37

Schachermeyr, F. 1973: 'Athen als Stadt des Grosskönigs', *Grazer Beiträge* 1: 211–20

Schachter, A. 1981–94: *Cults of Boiotia*, 4 vols., London

—— 1994: 'The politics of dedication: two Athenian dedications at the sanctuary of Apollo Ptoieus in Boiotia', in Osborne and Hornblower 1994: 291–306

Schaps, D. 1977: 'The woman least mentioned: etiquette and women's names', *CQ* 27: 323–30

Schmitt, R. 1976: 'The Medo-Persian names of Herodotus in the light of the new evidence from Persepolis', *Acta Ant. Hung.* 24: 25–35 [=J. Harmatta (ed.) 1979: *Studies in the sources on the history of pre-Islamic central Asia*, Budapest: 29–39]

—— 2000: *Selected onomastic writings*, Winona Lake, IN

Schneege, G. 1884: *De relatione historica quae intercedat inter Thucydidem et Herodotum*, diss. Breslau

Schubert, C. 2011: 'Der Traum des Hipparch: Fiktionalität und Ereignis bei Herodot', *MH* 68: 1–19

Schwabl, H. 1978: *Zeus*, Munich [= reprinted entries from various vols. of *R.-E.*, without new pagination. Column nos. 253–376, on *epikleses* of Zeus, are at the end of the book, preceded by cols. 993–1481]

Schwartz, E. 1959: *Griechische Geschichtsschreiber*, Leipzig

Schwartz, J. 1969: 'Hérodote et Périclès', *Historia* 18: 367–70

Scullion, S. 2006: 'Herodotus and Greek religion', in *Cambridge companion*: 192–208

Seaford, R. 1994: *Reciprocity and ritual: Homer and tragedy in the developing city-state*, Oxford

Segal, C. 1985: 'Messages to the underworld: an aspect of poetic immortalization in Pindar', *AJPhil* 106: 199–212

Serghidou, A. 2007: 'Cyprus and Onesilus: an interlude of freedom (5. 104, 108–16)', in Irwin/Greenwood: 269–88

Shapiro, H. A. 1993: *Personifications in Greek art: the representation of abstract concepts. 600–400 B.C.*, Zurich

Shimron, B. 1973: 'Πρῶτος τῶν ἡμεῖς ἴδμεν', *Eranos* 71: 45–51

Shipley, G. 1987: *A history of Samos 800–188 BC*, Oxford

2011: *Pseudo-Skylax's PERIPLOUS. The circumnavigation of the inhabited world*, Exeter

Siewert, P. 1982: *Die Trittyen Attikas und die Heeresreform des Kleisthenes*, Munich

Silk, M. 1974: *Interaction in poetic imagery*, Cambridge
    2000: *Aristophanes and the definition of Comedy*, Oxford

Sinn, U. 1993: 'Greek sanctuaries as places of refuge', in N. Marinatos and R. Hägg (eds.), *Greek sanctuaries: new approaches*, London: 88–109

Smarczyk, B. 1990: *Untersuchungen zur Religionspolitik und politischen Propaganda Athens im Delisch-Attischen Seebund*, Munich

Smith, R. R. R. 2007: 'Pindar, athletes and the early Greek statue habit', in Hornblower and Morgan 2007: 83–139

Smyth, H. W. 1894: *The sounds and inflections of the Greek dialects: Ionic*, Oxford

Sokolowski, F. 1955: *Lois sacrées de l'Asie mineure*, Paris
    1962: *Lois sacrées des cités grecques: Supplément*, Paris
    1969: *Lois sacrées des cités grecques*, Paris

Solmsen, L. 1943: 'Speeches in Herodotus' account of the Ionic revolt', *AJPhil* 64: 194–207

Sordi, M. 1958: *La lega tessala fino ad Alessandro Magno*, Rome

Stadter, P. A. 1989: *A commentary on Plutarch's Pericles*, Chapel Hill
    1998: notes to R. Waterfield (tr.) *Plutarch: Greek lives. A selection of nine lives*, Oxford
    2006: 'Herodotus and the cities of mainland Greece', in *Cambridge companion*: 242–56
    2012: 'Speaking to the deaf: Herodotus, his audience, and the Spartans at the beginning of the Peloponnesian war', *Histos* 6: 1–14

Stauffenberg, A. Schenk Graf von, 1960: 'Dorieus', *Historia* 9: 181–205

Ste. Croix, G. E. M. de 1972: *The origins of the Peloponnesian war*, London
    2004a: *Athenian democratic origins and other essays* eds. D. Harvey and R. Parker, Oxford
    2004b: 'Herodotus and King Cleomenes of Sparta', in De Ste Croix 2004a: 421–38
    2004c: 'But what about Aegina?', in De Ste Croix 2004a: 371–420

Stengel, P. 1920: *Die griechischen Kultusaltertümer*, Munich

Stewart, C. 1991: *Demons and the devil: moral imagination in modern Greek culture*, Princeton, NJ

Stickler, T. 2010: *Korinth und seine Kolonien: die Stadt am Isthmus im Mächtergefüge des klassichen Griechenland. Klio Beiträge* n. F. 15, Berlin

Strasburger, H. 1982: *Studien zur alten Geschichte*, vols. 1 and 2 (pagination continuous) eds. W. Schmitthenner and R. Zoepffel, Hildesheim and New York

Stroud, R. 1998: *The Athenian grain-tax law of 374/3 BC, Hesperia Suppl.* 29, Princeton

Stüber, K. 1996: *Zur dialektalen Einheit des Ostionischen*, Innsbruck

Syme, R. (ed. A. Birley) 1995: *Anatolica: studies in Strabo*, Oxford

Tamiolaki, M. 2010: *Liberté et esclavage chez les historiens grecs*, Paris

Tausend, K. 1992: *Amphiktyonie und Symmachie: Formen zwischenstaatlicher Beziehungen im archaischen Griechenland. Historia Einzelschrift* 73. Stuttgart

Taylor, L. R. 1960: *The voting districts of the Roman Republic*, Rome

Taylor, M. C. 1997: *Salamis and the Salaminioi: the history of an unofficial Athenian demos*, Amsterdam

Thomas, R. 1989: *Oral tradition and written record in classical Athens*, Cambridge

    2000: *Herodotus in context*, Cambridge

    2001: 'Ethnicity, genealogy and hellenism in Herodotus', in Malkin 2001: 213–33

    2007: 'Fame, memorial, and choral poetry: the origins of epinikian poetry – an historical study', in Hornblower and Morgan 2007: 141–66

Thonemann, P. 2006: 'Neilomandros. A contribution to the history of Greek personal names', *Chiron* 36: 11–42

    2009: 'Lycia, Athens and Amorges', in Ma, Papazarkadas and Parker 2009: 167–94

    2011: *The Maeander valley: a historical geography from antiquity to Byzantium*, Cambridge

Tod, M. N. 1913: *International arbitration amongst the Greeks*, Oxford

Toepffer, J. 1889: *Attische Genealogie*, Berlin

Tozzi, P. 1978: *La rivolta ionica*, Pisa

Traill, J. S. 1975: *The political organization of Attica: a study of the demes, trittyes, and phylai, and their representation in the Athenian council, Hesperia Suppl.* 14, Princeton

    1986: *Demos and trittys: epigraphical and topographical studies in the organization of Attica*, Toronto

Travlos, J. 1971: *Pictorial dictionary of ancient Athens*, New York

    1988: *Bildlexikon zur Topographie des antiken Attika*, Tübingen

Tuchelt, K. 1988: 'Die Perserzerstörung von Branchidai-Didyma und ihre Folgen – archäologisch betrachtet', *Arch. Anz:* 427–38

Untersteiner, M. 1949: *La lingua di Erodoto*, Bari

van: for names in van, see under second part of the surname

Vannicelli, P. 1993: *Erodoto e la storia dell'alto e medio arcaismo (Sparta-Tessaglia-Cirene)*, Rome

Vernant, J.-P. 1982: 'From Oedipus to Periander: lameness, tyranny, incest in legend and history', *Arethusa* 15: 19–37 [=Buxton 2000: 109–29]

Versnel, H. S. 2011: *Coping with the gods: wayward readings in Greek theology*, Leiden and Boston

Vlastos, G. 1953: '*Isonomia*', *AJPhil* 74: 337–66

1964: '*Isonomia politike*', in J. M and E. G. Schmidt (eds.), *Isonomia: Studien zur Gleichheitsvorstellung im griechischen Denken*, Berlin: 1–35

Vollgraff, J. C. 1895: 'Herodotea', *Mnemosyne* 23: 124–32

von: for names in von, see under second part of the surname

Wade-Gery, H. T. 1958: *Essays in Greek history*, Oxford

Wallinga, H. 1993: *Ships and sea power before the great Persian War*, Leiden

Walter, U. 1993: 'Herodot und die Ursachen des Ionischen Aufstandes', *Historia* 42: 257–78

Wankel, H. 1976: *Demosthenes Rede für Ktesiphon über den Kranz*, Heidelberg

Watkin, H. J. 1987: 'The Cypriote surrender to Persia', *JHS* 107: 154–63

Watson, J. 2011: 'Rethinking the sanctuary of Aphaia', in Fearn 2011: 79–113

Weber, L. 1937: 'Lectiones Herodoteae', *Phil. Wochenschr.* 57: 219–24

1940: 'Nugae Herodoteae II', *Riv. Fil.* 68: 272–6

Wecowski, M. 1996: 'Ironie et histoire. Le discours de Soclès (Hérodote V 92)'. *Anc. Soc.* 27: 205–58

Wees, H. van 2002: 'Herodotus and the past', in *Brill's companion*: 321–49

Wees, H. van 2013: *Ships, silver, taxes and tribute*, London and New York

Wehrli, F. 1969: *Die Schule des Aristoteles*, vol. VII² (Herakleides Pontikos), Basel and Stuttgart

Wells, J. 1923: *Studies in Herodotus*, Oxford

Wesselmann, K. 2011: *Mythische Erzählstrukturen in Herodots Historien*, Berlin and Boston

West, M. L. 1966: *Hesiod*, Theogony, *edited with prolegomena and commentary*, Oxford

1978: *Hesiod*, Works and Days, *edited with prolegomena and commentary*, Oxford

1985: *The Hesiodic catalogue of women*, Oxford

1997: *The east face of Helicon: west Asiatic elements in Greek poetry and myth*, Oxford

2007: *Indo-European poetry and myth*, Oxford

2011a: *The making of the* Iliad: *disquisition and analytical commentary*, Oxford

2011b: *Hellenica* vol. 1, Oxford

2013: *The epic cycle: a commentary on the lost Troy epics*, Oxford

West, S. 1985: 'Herodotus' epigraphical interests', *CQ* 35: 278–305

1988: *Commentary on the Odyssey, books i–iv* in Heubeck, West and Hainsworth 1988: 51–245

1991: 'Herodotus' portrait of Hecataeus', *JHS* 111: 144–160

2011: 'A diplomatic fiasco: the first Athenian embassy to Sardis (Hdt. 5. 73)', *Rh. Mus.* 154: 9–21

Westlake, H. D. 1977: 'λέγεται in Thucydides', *Mnemosyne* 30: 345–62

Whitehead, D. 1986: *The demes of Attica 508/7–ca. 250 BC: a political and social study*, Princeton

2008: 'Athenians in Sicily in the fourth century BC', in C. Cooper (ed.), *Epigraphy and the Greek historian*, Toronto: 57–67

Whitley, J. 1994: 'The monuments that stood before Marathon: tomb cult and hero cult in archaic Attica', *AJArch* 98: 213–30

Wiesehöfer, J. 2011: 'Herodot und Zypern', in Rollinger, Truschnegg and Bichler 2011: 717–734

Wilamowitz[-Moellendorff], U. von 1884: *Homerische Untersuchungen*, Berlin

1893: *Aristoteles und Athen*. 2 vols. Berlin

1902: *Griechisches Lesebuch* II.1, Berlin

1931–2: *Der Glaube der Hellenen*, 2 vols., Berlin

Will, E. 1967: 'Hérodote et la jeune Péonienne', *Rev. Ét. Grec.* 80: 176–81

Willi, A. 2005: 'Κάδμος ἀνέθηκε: Zur Vermittlung der Alphabetschrift nach Griechenland', *MH* 62: 162–71

Wilson, N. G. 2011: 'Maasiana on Herodotus', *ZPE* 179: 57–70

Wilson, P. 2000: *The Athenian institution of the Khoregia*, Cambridge

Worley, L. 1994: *The cavalry of ancient Greece*, Boulder, CO and Oxford

Zahrnt, M. 1984: 'Die Entwicklung des makedonischen Reiches bis zu den Perserkriegen', *Chiron* 14: 325–68

1989: 'Delphi, Sparta und die Rückführung der Alkmeoniden', *ZPE* 76: 297–307

2011: 'Herodot und die Makedonenkönige', in Rollinger, Truschnigg and Bichler 2011: 761–779

Zgusta, L. 1964: *Kleinasiatische Personennamen*, Prague

Ziskowski, A. 2012: 'Clubfeet and Kypselids: contextualising Corinthian padded dancers in the archaic period', *BSA* 107: 211–32

INDEXES

2 GREEK WORDS AND PHRASES

Refs. are to ch. and para. of Hdt. 5

Printed in Great Britain
by Amazon